By Accident of Geography

ALSO BY ERICH EIPERT

Nonfiction

The Secret She Carried: A Perilous Odyssey Through the Time of Hitler
(Companion volume to *By Accident of Geography*)

Fiction

Guy Going Under

Butterfly Powder

By Accident of Geography

The Unusual Saga of an Iowa Farmer Who Saved His Own Life as a Waffen SS Conscript on Hitler's Eastern Front

Erich Eipert

ErichEipert.com
ericheipert@gmail.com

Turnbuckle Press
Seattle, Washington

Copyright ©2025 by Erich Eipert
ISBN 978-0-9642349-7-0

Publisher's Cataloging-in-Publication Data

Eipert, Erich
    By Accident of Geography: The Unusual Saga of an Iowa Farmer Who Saved His Own Life as a Waffen SS Conscript on Hitler's Eastern Front / Erich Eipert
    Includes bibliographical references.
    ISBN 978-0-9642349-7-0

1. World War, 1939-1945—Campaigns—Eastern Front—Personal narratives, German. 2. World War, 1939-1945—Personal narratives, German 3. Danube Swabians—Biography. 4. Danube Swabians—20th century. 5. Waffen-SS. SS-Freiwilligen-Panzergrenadierregiment "Nordland"
I. Title

D757.85 E37
940.5421 EI36

                                            Library of Congress Control Number:
2025902096

Cover design: Susan Eipert

With the exception of brief quotations for book reviews, no portion of this book may be reproduced or used without the express written permission of the publisher. Although every effort has been made to ensure that the information in this book was correct at press time, the author and publisher disclaim all liability for any loss, damage, or disruption caused by errors or omissions, whether such errors or omissions result from negligence, accident, or any other cause.

Dedication

To my father, a man who refused to let rancor and bitterness take over his soul despite traumatic combat memories of war, exile from his loved ones, and the theft of his homeland farm.

Acknowledgments

This book would never have seen the light of day, or the electronic print of reading devices, without the selfless research assistance and truly tireless editing by my spouse, Susan Eipert. Credit for copyediting goes to my sister Mary Eipert. For sharing their stories and allowing me to make their life experiences a part of my book, I express my gratitude to Ingrid Slavik and four Magdalenas—my grandmother, aunt, cousin Leni, and great cousin Anni. Acknowledgement is also extended to many others who helped my information gathering. Among them are Esther Neeser, Brian Atwater, Lenz Reiter, Blackie Johnson, and various Eipert relatives. Thanks also go to El Al Airlines historian Marvin Goldman, Oranienburg city archivist Christian Becker, former Volkswagen archivists Manfred Grieger and Ulrike Gutzmann, and Shaw Historical Library librarian Anne Hiller Clark. And a belated special appreciation is extended to my old friend and infantry squad mate from the boonies of Vietnam, the late Michael Pruett, for the invaluable World War II technical information he provided. Let it be noted that any opinions expressed in this book are entirely my own and should in no way reflect on anyone mentioned here.

Contents

1 The Backstory 9
2 Parents, Johann and Magdalena 17
3 The Banat Revolving Door 23
4 The Swabian Migrations 27
5 A Grim Reaper 38
6 Orzydorf 42
7 The Geographic Merry-Go-Round 53
8 Childhood 58
9 Fidel the Farmer 65
10 Bad Luck Finds Hans 74
11 Romania and WW II 77
12 The Red Army 80
13 Fidel Gets a Notice 83
14 Rise of the SS 91
15 Wiligut and the Black Knights 101
16 Back Door to the Black Angels 105
17 The Disaster at Stalingrad 114
18 Waffen SS and NKVD Expansion 119
19 Fidel's New Insignia 124
20 Waffen SS "Volunteer" Anton Krämer 140
21 Winter on the Eastern Front 150
22 Horses and Corduroy Roads 158
23 The Oranienbaum Pocket 165
24 Awaiting Catastrophe at Leningrad 173
25 The Catastrophe Unfolds 176
26 Stalin's Penal Battalions 190
27 The Costly Withdrawal 197
28 A Bullet Buys a Ticket 205
29 Hospital Respite 214
30 Out of the Cauldron 221

31 The People's Car	227
32 Volkswagen Relief	236
33 Holzgas to the Rescue	246
34 Skorzeny and the Endgame	251
35 The Risky Mission	265
36 Alpine Redoubt	273
37 On to Bavaria	284
38 Out of Uniform	299
39 Magdalena and Josef	303
40 Josef's Diary	309
41 Josef's Fate	323
42 Slave Labor Roundup	331
43 Classmate Josef Adam	338
44 Berlin and Hans's Destiny	342
45 A Slave Labor Sentence	354
46 Magdalena's Return	364
47 Romania, Farewell	375
48 Orzydorf Via an Outsider's Eyes	380
49 Anni's Story	385
50 Fidel's Haven	390
51 Postwar Hell Primer	397
52 The New Family	405
53 Farewell, Alps	417
54 Troubled Journey	423
55 The Tule Lake Basin	434
56 Where the Tall Corn Grows	448
57 Their Passing	464
This series	467
Works of fiction by the author	467
About the author	468
Image Attributions	469

1 The Backstory

Here follows the story of an overalls-wearing, five-decade Iowa farmer, an ordinary man with a far-from-ordinary past. That he fought for the Germans as a young man in World War II certainly makes that past unusual, but what renders it extraordinary are the things he saw and experienced before, during, and after the war. In the telling, his story is also the chronicle of an extended family that navigated its way through the tragic war era on the losing side, a homeland that was made to disappear, and the controversial German military branch called the Waffen SS (Armed Schutzstaffel). The Waffen SS is pertinent because its uniform is what the Midwest farmer-to-be wore, and that reality played no small part in his tale. This revelation might understandably tempt the reader to promptly condemn the man, but let it be noted that like several hundred thousand fellow soldiers in that service, he was a nonideological conscript from beyond Germany's border. The harsh political reality in the corner of Eastern Europe that he called home made it so.

That homeland had changed hands often in the past, most recently just before the conscript's birth when World War I's victors pruned it from the defunct Austrian Empire and grafted it onto Romania. As happens so often, the forced allegiance change resulted in rancor and border disputes. But the soldier-to-be left such politics to others, for like his ancestors, he had agriculture coursing through his veins and wished for nothing more than the placid life of a farmer in his ethnic German village. It was a life he'd first tasted at age 15 when he began farming half his family's land because World War I had left him fatherless. That personal tragedy also left him wanting nothing to do with soldiering.

When Hitler and the Nazis rose to power in Germany and provoked new tensions throughout Europe, Romania's border disputes threatened to turn into fighting. Romania's leaders reacted by joining in the greater madness. Their alignment with Hitler dragged the Romanian populace into yet another world war and caused the young farmer to learn a hard lesson about fate and how it is not the least moved by gestures and wishes. As clever and determined as he imagined himself to be, he couldn't avoid conscription, first by the dangerously inept Romanian Army, then by the Germans. The latter happened by way of a 1943 Nazi political arrangement that stuffed tens of thousands of Romanian boys and men of German heritage into the field-gray uniform of the aforementioned Waffen SS. That service was still perceived as both elite and competent at this juncture and hadn't yet been irreparably tainted through association with its heinous SS political parent organization or by the war crimes the field force itself would later be charged with. Regarding the latter, let it be noted that not all 38 Waffen SS divisions participated in criminal activity. Some units were led by professional soldiers, and even the Jewish Virtual Library notes that "divisions like the Nordland [in which the young farmer served] ... have virtually spotless records."[1]

The young soldier, along with other inadequately-trained ethnic German conscripts, soon saw himself thrust onto the most massive battlefield the world has ever known—the Eastern Front, where the combat was particularly brutal because it was so tightly bound up in the ambitions and monstrous inhumanity of both Hitler and Stalin. There, he found himself trapped in a hopeless and deadly environment of harsh weather, rough terrain, and overwhelming numbers of Soviet Red Army infantrymen, tanks, aircraft, artillery guns, snipers, and sappers. The majority of Hitler's soldiers caught in this lethal milieu failed to return home. The young farmer was one of them, but fortunately not in the sense that his flesh rotted on that battlefield like that of well over a million fellow soldiers in German uniforms. In his case the vengeful politics of the Cold War peace that followed the fighting exiled him from his family for a generation, robbing him of his farm and the village life he held so dear. Through a risky and timely action, he extracted himself from the battleground and avoided near certain death. He never dreamed this would present him an entirely different view of the war—one seen by few others of his lowly rank. Or that it would eventually lead him to America.

The successful Iowa farmer that this soldier became was able to leave the momentous and painful events of that past behind to the extent that the neighbors and friends who paid him their last respects at the funeral home after his passing remembered only a quintessential local farmer who happened to have a German accent. They had no idea how unusual his past was. I only know his story, at least the parts not too painful or private for him to have revealed, because this man, Fidel Eipert, was my father.

Fidel (pronounced feedle in German) never expected anyone in his adopted country, the homeland of his former enemy, to have any interest in a chronicle about a soldier on the other side. Believing he was mistaken, I decided to tell his tale for him. But in the proper way, for in my view war stories and stories of war are vastly different. War stories build illusions of glory, heroism, and the expectation that good will eventually dominate over evil, while realistic stories of war trample such notions. Every battlefield develops its own nuances of mayhem, and no matter what rulebook evolves, combat is unforgiving. Few participants walk away from it whole.

That Fidel's story would be a book that practically writes itself was my hope in the beginning. Unfortunately, the pedantic and sedentary task of beating a heap of research and interview notes into coherence on the written page could never quite compete with the appeal of gathering ever more historical information, particularly when it came to sparsely-covered events that affected the losing side. An expression I'd jotted down at an archeological site aptly summed up why I'd been engaging in this prolonged information gathering: "Without context, it's just a bone."[2] With World War II's scale, depth, and complexity, that pursuit became intoxicating enough that decades of off-and-on information gathering and yes, procrastination, followed. Then one day an evocative anecdotal memory leapt from the scrapbook of childhood memories in my head to intervene and set some real writing in motion at last. The memory was a stark reminder that stories in need of telling are best not left unattended too long. Life events are only too ready to step in and thwart a story's preservation, as happened with my father's friend.

The stark contrast in fate and outlook that distinguished my father and his friend in this tale of two men, as I labeled it, made me think of Charles Dickens's novel, A Tale of Two Cities. In the era of my youth, every high school student read that story in English class and was familiar with its emotive opening lines. I'd never forgotten them, and Dickens's poetic contrasts applied as readily to the two men of my reminiscence as they did to the moving times in his novel. Those lines go,

> It was the best of times, it was the worst of times, . . . it was the
> season of Light, it was the season of Darkness, it was the
> spring of hope, it was the winter of despair, we had everything
> before us, we had nothing before us, we were all going direct to
> Heaven, we were all going direct the other way

Both men had seen enough bloodshed in World War II to leave a residue of trauma baked into their being. Although each appeared whole, only one could truly be called a survivor. The other, apparently unable to suitably process the war's toxic legacy, existed as a walking ghost who lived on borrowed time. Fortunately for me, that man wasn't my father. Although Fidel's combat experiences left him bluntly stoical and prone to emotional avoidance, he largely transcended the darkness that weighed on his soul.

My reminiscence took me back to the New Year's Eve midafternoon of 1957 as a boy of nearly 11 who saw his father getting ready to leave for town from our Iowa farm. Being a bit bored and cunningly aware that trips to town with his dad usually netted him a soda, ice cream, or candy bar, that boy grabbed his coat and hopped into the family Dodge sedan to tag along. Fidel was ostensibly picking up a few groceries for my mother, Maria, but she and I both knew his primary motivation for going had more to do with socializing than groceries. That socializing usually took the form of a euchre or penny-a-point rummy game in one of the taverns. My mother must have expected my presence to hasten his return.

Fidel's destination, the community of West Point, supported five watering holes despite being a mere 1,000-resident pinprick astride a secondary highway in the southeast corner of Iowa's road map. The town's surrounding farms made for a robust number of drinking establishments, for farming was a lonely occupation and farmers sought places to congregate. However, on that particular day Fidel didn't make it as far as one of the taverns, and I missed out on the treat I'd come along for because upon exiting the corner grocery, he spied a pair of acquaintances behind the plate-glass window of Archie's service station across the street. Before long I found myself seated near the cash-register counter in the cozy little office as the men—Fidel, Archie, and the town marshal—chatted, joked, and circulated a bottle of whiskey.

TV westerns were popular in that postwar era at the dawn of the television age, and like many other families, ours regularly watched a popular western called Gunsmoke. The show pitted a languid and likeable good guy, Dodge City marshal Matt Dillon, against lawbreakers and troublemakers. In my impressionable young mind, our own town's sole lawman cut a similar figure and even came with a fitting surname. In actuality, law enforcement was the lesser part of Marshal Good's job; his main responsibility was street and water-utility maintenance. I was acquainted with the marshal, the contrasting figure in my reminiscence, because Fidel worked as Good's part-time assistant to supplement the meager income from our yet-small farming operation.

I soon regretted coming along, for I could have been watching afternoon TV at home, hunting rabbits, or playing on the ice of our farm pond instead of sitting in the tight confines of the gas-station office. After what seemed an interminably long time, the short winter-afternoon daylight faded noticeably enough that Fidel begged off, citing farm chores. It was surely an alcohol-infused and comradely warm glow that then prompted Marshal Good to declare he'd help Fidel with those chores.

The marshal's pickup truck was right behind us as we arrived at the farm. The men, with faces aglow, exited the warm vehicles and jovially stepped out into the frosty winter air. But their cheer dissipated the moment my mother emerged from the rear door of the milking barn where she was about to begin milking, as she did every evening while Fidel handled the other chores. Her icy look conveyed what words didn't need to! Maria assumed Fidel's tardiness was again due to a card game. His passion for cards had always annoyed her. What she failed to understand was that being the astute player that Fidel was, to him card games were more than petty gambling. The mental acuity required in gauging probabilities and smart play was both an intellectual exercise and a stress reliever. That particular day, the reek of whiskey on his breath certainly didn't advance Maria's understanding of this.

My mother's frosty ambush threw the men off balance. When they'd recovered their poise, one of them—I don't recall which—offered to do the milking for her. The men interpreted the impassive look she returned as agreement and ducked into the building. She and I followed and watched as each man took a turn at the closest cow in the milking stanchions. In their wobbly state, coordinating the milking action while sustaining the right balance between the milking stool and the flank of the animal proved challenging. When Maria didn't find the same amusement in their efforts as I did, the marshal picked up on the bad vibes and to his credit made a tactical exit.

That occasion was the only time I ever saw my father tipsy, it occurred to me. But then a deeper perception eclipsed that thought. The assured farmer Fidel had become no longer bore any resemblance to the conscripted and conflicted Waffen SS infantryman I knew he'd been on the lethal Eastern Front. Or to the homeland-banished refugee who doggedly struggled to provide for his growing family in shattered postwar West Germany. Those Fidel iterations had already morphed into an archetypal seed-corn-cap-wearing, pickup-driving, corn- and hog-raising Iowa farmer able to mix comfortably with typical Americans like the marshal and Archie. At least outwardly, surprisingly little remained to distinguish him from the born-and-bred Midwest farmers and townspeople around him.

As for the marshal, he could have used a healthy dose of Fidel's adaptability and resilience because sadly, his departure from the milking shed is not where my tale of two men ends. The real ending came late one night the following summer with another departure by Good. This time a final one because a bullet through the brain from a .38 caliber Smith and Wesson service pistol is prone to delivering such an exit. According to a local newspaper account, around midnight Good retrieved the pistol from his truck parked on the street, held it to his head as he stood curbside, and uttered his last words, "It'll only take one shot."³

And so it did. I was shocked to learn of it the next day not long before Fidel and I left with our tractor, hay baler, and two wagons to bale at a distant farm. Good's suicide weighed heavily on me throughout the afternoon as I operated the tractor. At the time, my father's equanimity perplexed me almost as much as the seemingly senseless death itself. Fidel had worked closely with Good and liked him, yet didn't appear much troubled. It is possible he held back his emotions for my benefit, but I think the coping and hardening mechanism inflicted on him in the war by the sudden loss of friends in combat is a more likely explanation. Violent trauma is known to induce neurobiological changes in the brain to make tolerable that which would otherwise leave a person unable to carry on in a vulnerable situation. These brain alterations can later express themselves in benign situations in undesirable ways. Emotional repression of the type Fidel showed on that day is one. Today, these trauma-induced effects fall under the broad umbrella of post-traumatic stress disorder (PTSD).

Why a man who seemed as personable and self-assured as the marshal would kill himself baffled me enough after the tale-of-two-men memory brought Good to mind that I acquired a photo of his Veterans Administration-issued tombstone. The picture revealed that Good served in the US Army's 543rd Engineer Boat and Shore Regiment during World War II. Boat and Shore regiments saw heavy action in the Southwest Pacific where they carried out open landing-craft assaults against fortified islands held by the fierce, dug-in Japanese enemy, according to the commemorative excerpt below.

> The Army Amphibious Brigades or "Frogs" as they were affectionately called, were involved in all of the major amphibious landings of World War ll. These units were asked to perform the impossible—to establish a beachhead, support it with firepower, and fight as infantry . . . in the face of superior forces, established defensive positions, and overwhelming armament. The tasks had to be accomplished in rapid time and often with inadequate equipment . . . . Their techniques were the foundation of the successful Normandy landings on D-Day.⁴

Combat like this was a first-rate prescription for PTSD. The deputy sheriff who investigated the marshal's death attributed the shooting to a domestic squabble following an outing that involved drinking. This was probably true enough superficially but I would guess that PTSD, which was underdiagnosed in World War II veterans, contributed heavily. Things are so different today that nearly every contact a veteran has with a Veterans Affairs Medical Center begins with the question, "Do you have thoughts of harming yourself?" It is likely that the emotional confusion brought on by alcohol and a quarrel galvanized the haunting war-related demons that resided in Good's head and allowed his mental anguish to overwhelm his coping capacity.

The marshal certainly stopped his own pain by killing himself, but the stigma attached to suicide shifted some of the agony to the people around him and blurred his true character. In my mind, any veteran who risked life and limb for fellow countrymen and faced fears and terrors unimaginable to those far removed from the horrors of the battlefield deserved remembrance and recognition. Good had paid a great price for his service and deserved better than to be defined by one precipitous action, but his story died with him and left his community unable to extend the understanding he had due.

It struck me that although Fidel's death was natural, he departed life with even less of a remembrance for his military service and what it had cost him. Yes, he'd soldiered for the once-hated enemy, but his combat had been no less deadly or painful than that of his American counterparts. Telling his story and supplying an appropriate testimonial was up to me, and it wouldn't happen until I stopped pursuing ever more detail and sat down to pummel into text the mass of research and interview notes I'd collected in America and Europe over the years. Visiting people, archives, libraries, and sites with a bearing on Fidel's story in foreign environs like Prague, Munich, Moscow, Salzburg, Wolfsburg, Berlin, Vienna, Nuremberg, Budapest, Bucharest, Buchenwald, Dubrovnik, Transylvania, Sarajevo, Timișoara, Sachsenhausen, Berchtesgaden, and St. Petersburg would be hard to give up. But it was time to stop.

The cautionary tale of two men did provoke a burst of writing, but still failed to advance Fidel's story because of a second realization: my mother also had a dramatic and exceptional war era experience. And Maria was still alive and able to appreciate seeing her own life story in print. But sadly, nature once again imposed a deadline I couldn't meet, and *The Secret She Carried*[5] came along too late for her eyes and heart to take in. A draft of Fidel's book did follow, but a seemingly endless need for additions left the manuscript languishing.

The chance rediscovery of a note I'd written four decades earlier finally led to resolution. That annotation simply recorded a gesture and utterance from a character in Kurt Vonnegut's novel, *Slapstick*: "Tapping his forehead with his fingertips, 'It isn't the museum it should be.' "[6] That metaphorical nugget of clarity had me see my situation was not so different. The word museum of Fidel's narrative might not now, or ever, be all it should be, but would have to do. I can only hope its chapters passably exhibit the hazardous and challenging road traversed by Fidel, his extended family, and millions of others who by accident of geography found themselves on the wrong side of history during World War II and beyond. Here goes!

---

1. Jewish Virtual Library, "The SS (Schutzstaffel): The Waffen-SS," accessed January 15, 2024, https://www.jewishvirtuallibrary.org/waffen-ss.
2. Hovenweep National Monument, "Interpretive Site Display" (Dinosaur Excavation Visitor Center, Utah, 2021).
3 "Rule Death of Marshal as Suicide," *The Fort Madison Evening Democrat*, June 23, 1958.
4. Ralph Denlinger, "593rd Engineer Boat and Shore Regiment EBSR," August 22, 2019, http://ebsr.net/593rdEBSR.htm.
5. Erich Eipert, *The Secret She Carried: A Perilous Odyssey Through the Time of Hitler* (Turnbuckle Press, 2015).
6. Kurt Vonnegut, *Slapstick* (New York: Delacorte Press/S. Lawrence, 1976).

2 Parents, Johann and Magdalena

As the car quickly reversed, a thin stream of blood spurted from His Highness's mouth onto my right cheek. As I was pulling out my handkerchief to wipe the blood away from his mouth, the Duchess cried out to him, "In Heaven's name, what has happened to you?" At that she slid off the seat and lay on the floor of the car, with her face between his knees. I had no idea that she too was hit and thought she had simply fainted with fright. Then I heard His Imperial Highness say, "Sopherl, Sopherl, don't die. Stay alive for the children!" At that, I seized the Archduke by the collar of his uniform, to stop his head dropping forward and asked him if he was in great pain. He answered me quite distinctly, "It's nothing!" His face began to twist somewhat but he went on repeating, six or seven times, ever more faintly as he gradually lost consciousness, "It's nothing!" Then, after a short pause, there was a violent choking sound caused by the bleeding.[1]

The above excerpt is Count Franz von Harrach's description of what occurred on the Sunday morning of June 28, 1914, in Sarajevo, Bosnia, when a young Serbian nationalist who'd earlier failed to get off a shot at Archduke Franz Ferdinand received a second chance. Ferdinand, the presumptive heir to the crown of the Austro-Hungarian Empire, had just given a speech and was riding in an open-top car that was turning around at an intersection after making a wrong turn. Through this accident of geography, if you will—only the first of many that might be noted in this book by those readers inclined to see the heavy hand of fate in human affairs—the novice terrorist suddenly found himself mere feet from his target. He acted without hesitation. Stepping forward, he fired two hurried shots with the pistol he barely knew how to use. The first bullet hit the

Archduke's wife, Sophie, in the abdomen. The second passed through Ferdinand's uniform collar and severed a jugular vein. The killer was exceedingly lucky in his mission for both victims died a short time later. But to the world's misfortune, his act sparked the Great War, or World War I as we now call it.

Like several million other young men in the Austro-Hungarian Empire's reserve army, 28-year-old Johann Eipert, who would later father Fidel, received a mobilization notice within days of that shooting. That reporting date was subsequently put off until July 26 to allow Johann and other farmers time to bring in their grain harvest and secure the Empire's food supply. When the harvest was finished, Johann and the other farmers in the village of Orzydorf had no choice but to dust off their *kaiserlich und königliche (k.u.k.)* (Imperial [Austrian] and Royal [Hungarian]) army uniforms and report to their local regiment's staging area. Even then, he and the others still hoped Serbia's government would accede to Austria's harsh political demands and avert warfare. When the Serbians didn't, the freshly mobilized army was tasked with punishing the country. Like almost everyone else, Johann surely thought he'd be back home by Christmas because the large Austrian Empire was expected to easily overwhelm its small neighbor.

The great European powers were so entangled in trade disputes, alliances, treaties, and colonial aspirations that what should have been a small regional conflict soon ensnared most of the continent. What later became known as the Great War kept Johann away from his home for over four years without a single home leave. Unfortunately, the predominant European victors, France and England, had learned little from the punishing war by the time it ended because the severely flawed peace settlement they and others imposed on the war's losers led to a second Great War barely a generation later. The new war rendered the Great War name obsolete and necessitated designating the two conflicts as World Wars I and II. Although the second war would come along only two decades after Johann returned home, he would not live to see it.

During Johann's war, the companies, banks, offices, and individuals of his region plowed millions of kroners into the government war bonds that financed the war effort. The buyers viewed the bonds as a good investment. As described by Gertrude Adam and Anton Peter Petri in *Heimatbuch der deutschen Gemeinde Orczydorf im Banat*, a book detailing the history of Orzydorf (Orţişoara in Romanian), some farmers in the entirely ethnic German village of 2,000 even sold off a field or two in order to participate. With so many men off fighting, women and children took on the heavy work formerly done by men. But within months, a number of Russian POWs (prisoners of war) were sent there to ease the burden. Two of the Orzydorf men who went off to war were school teachers, so their now-empty classrooms and living quarters were converted into an auxiliary hospital, and by early December 1914, 34 of the 40 beds were already filled with wounded men. Throughout the war, local collections helped support war widows, orphans, and the needy. The village also housed a large group of malnourished children from Vienna for a time.[2]

Germany, Austria, and their allies were cut off from outside trade markets, making industrial goods and food scarce. Strict price controls for grain and groceries followed. Eventually the government requisitioned grain and produce from farmers and compensated them poorly. Because of profiteering by middlemen, farmers resorted to hiding their grain or feeding it to their swine. By the summer of 1918, both the villagers at home and their soldiers off fighting on either the Italian or Russian front were demoralized after realizing that their sacrifices had been in vain and their side could no longer win.[3]

Orzydorf, which lay in the agriculturally rich and productive plain known as the Banat, had been part of the Austrian Empire for 200 years. Its residents were justifiably proud of what generations of their German ancestors had accomplished in settling and taming what had been a marshy and wild region. Like my maternal grandfather from the Austrian province of Moravia (another Johann), Johann Eipert finally wended his way home from the war in November 1918. He'd have expected the lost war to lead to change, but couldn't have anticipated changes profound enough to place his village and fields in a different country. Johann had barely resumed working his soil in 1919 when the village learned their region had been awarded to Romania through the Treaty of Trianon—one of several treaties to emerge from the Versailles Peace Conference of 1919.

Primarily at the behest of France, which sought to permanently cripple its European rivals, the Peace Conference delegates dealt very harshly with both the German and Austrian Empires by cleaving off large swaths of territory. What had been Austria's Hungarian Kingdom lost most of the Banat to Hungary's neighbors. Johann and his fellow Orzydorf residents had no great affection for Hungary and its rulers, but joining Romania, a country their army had defeated and knocked out of the war in 1917, was not palatable. Smaller portions of the Banat went to the newly and haphazardly assembled states of Yugoslavia and Czechoslovakia, making Hungary a small and impotent rump state that retained just a tiny portion of the Banat in the north.

The Orzydorf villagers could not change the political reality, so they had to swallow their bitterness and pick up the threads of their lives. The families and businesses that had bought war bonds as an investment were left with worthless paper when the Austrian Empire dissolved. If there was any joy for Johann, it came a year after his return when my grandmother Magdalena gave birth to the couple's first child, a daughter. They named the baby in the traditional way after her mother, even though the name Magdalena was already more than adequately represented among the females of the village. A son followed the next year, and tradition prevailed again as the boy received his father's name. According to my father, the village had 11 Johann Eiperts when his older brother was born. As often happens with a German Johann, the boy soon became known as Hans.

When my father, the third and final child, came along in the summer of 1922, the couple named him Fidel. This too was a name already well represented both in the community and in the family ancestry. Sadly, the joy of this birth was short-lived because barely a week later, Johann Sr. died unexpectedly at the age of 36. The village doctor attributed his death to pericarditis, a painful inflammation of the lining around the heart, and an accompanying accumulation of fluid within this sac. Magdalena was still recovering from a difficult childbirth when she had to attend her husband's funeral.

Johann hadn't returned from the war a well man and never fully regained his vigor. He'd lived with a congenital heart condition from birth, and his family suspected that four years of harsh wartime field conditions had further impaired his heart and weakened his immune system to the point that he was unable to fully fight off the respiratory infection he contracted during his journey home in 1918. Then, three weeks before Fidel's birth in 1922 a downpour soaked and chilled Johann as he returned from the fields during the grain harvest. A severe cold set in, and the pneumonia complications that followed killed him. He'd fathered three children and was able to see Fidel, his latest, before dying. The guns had been silent for three-and-a-half years by then, but the war still reached out to claim lives. His family at least had the comfort of knowing Johann's remains were buried in the church cemetery rather than in the cold earth of some remote battlefield. The family was only too well acquainted with grief, for next to him and his parents lay three of Johann's sisters in a row. They'd all died young. Magdalena expected that someday she'd lie next to Johann, but fate had something entirely different in store for her.[4]

Unfortunately, by the time my interest in the family history developed, all knowledge of where Johann had fought in the war had been lost. A book about the village's history stated that the first Orzydorf reservists called up were rushed to the nearby Serbian front. These men, along with new conscripts, subsequently saw action on both the Russian and Italian fronts.[5] Based on Johann's recruiting district location, his unit was likely the k.u.k 61st Infantry Regiment. A website dedicated to the memory of this regiment notes the following about World War I participation:

I.R. [Infantry Regiment] 61 was a virtual microcosm of Austria-Hungary in the First World War. With its recruiting area in the Banat region, centered around the city of Temesvár (now Timișoara, Romania), the 61st drew roughly equal numbers of ethnic Germans, Magyars, and Romanians, as well as an assortment of Poles, Ruthenes, Serbs and Croats.

The unit served on every major front in Europe at one point or another during the war, including the Balkans, Eastern Front, Italian Front, and even the Western Front during the final months of the war.[6]

The dissolution of the Austrian Empire at the end of the war proved detrimental in preserving records which might have provided more information. A response from my query to the Österreichischen Staatsarchivs (Austrian State Archives) stated that the personnel records I sought did not make it into the Vienna War Archives after the collapse of the Habsburg monarchy in 1918 because the peace provisions of Saint-Germain in 1919 dictated the records belonged to the successor states "where they were largely destroyed." The reply went on to state, "For your self-study in the research room of the Austrian State Archives, you will be provided with the following boxes from the inventory of phonetic cadastre for war losses 1914–1918: Johann EIPERT: Boxes 'E' No. 7 and 8."[7]

Fidel's parents, Magdalena and Johann Eipert, at undetermined ages. The photo of Johann is the only image the author has of his grandfather.

In Vienna, my wife, Susan, and I failed to turn up anything pertinent in these boxes. Nor did other military materials at the archive yield so much as a mention of Johann. Facts about my grandfather's civilian life were just as scarce because he'd died so long ago. The only photo I have of him reveals a dapper, handsome young man with dark hair and a roundish, fine-featured face that sported a broad handlebar mustache of the type in vogue early in the 20th century—a likeness that resembled a scholar more than a farmer.

Johann's death left Magdalena to cope with a sizeable farm and a trio of children under the age of three. Fortunately, once the main cereal-grain crops were harvested and threshed with the help of relatives and hired labor, sale of some of the grain allowed Magdalena to keep food on the table through the fallow season. In that rural environment, women like Magdalena had long been working alongside men and standing in for them when they were fulfilling their military training obligation or fighting wars. She knew something about farming, but was unable to take care of her babies and operate the farm too. So she chose to cut expenses by selling all horses and livestock not essential to her immediate needs and renting out her fields until her sons were old enough to work them.

Magdalena was slight in stature and build, but not in energy and resourcefulness. As a war widow in all but name and pension, she needed to find strength and perseverance for the sake of her children. Like her ancestors who'd settled the once largely empty and challenging land, her situation called for the same industry and adaptability. What she failed to anticipate was that this period would not be the last to require such strength.

In 1974, fifty-two years after her husband's death, Magdalena's vigor and industry was still evident. The occasion was my second visit to impoverished communist Romania. Several family members and I arrived at her house at 5:30 a.m. after a long drive from Germany, but even at that early hour, we were too late to catch her at home. A neighbor informed us that Magdalena routinely left for the local market at 4 a.m. to sell vegetables from her garden.

---

1. Luigi Albertini, *The Origins of the War of 1914*. (London; New York, Oxford University Press, 1952), 37.
2. Gertrude Adam and Anton Peter Petri, *Heimatbuch der deutschen Gemeinde Orczydorf im Banat* (Marquartstein: Breit, 1983), 137.
3. Adam and Petri, *Heimatbuch der deutschen Gemeinde Orczydorf im Banat*, 138.
4. Ingrid Slavik, "Johann Eipert" (Email, 2009).
5. Adam and Petri, *Heimatbuch der deutschen Gemeinde Orczydorf im Banat*, 138.
6. Larry Dunn, "K.u.K. IR 61," accessed November 15, 2024, https://steamcommunity.com/groups/KuK61.
7. Tepperberg, Der Archivdirektor of Vienna War Archive, "Betrifft: Johann Eipert" (Email, April 26, 2010).

3 The Banat Revolving Door

The Banat is a topographically diverse region of East Central Europe that covers a substantial portion of the Pannonian Lowland Plain. Its historical bounds are the Danube River on the south, the Tisa River on the west, the Maros River on the north, and the Carpathian foothills on the east. The major portion of the Banat today makes up the eastern portion of Romania. Perhaps the most remarkable thing about the Banat is the instability that is its historical legacy.

The Austrian Empire prior to World War I. The more intense shading denotes the areas with the highest concentration of German speakers. The arrow marks the relative position of the Banat within the empire.

The earliest descriptions of the Banat come from Greek historians who reported the area as inhabited by Illyrians or Thracians. Celts assumed control during a great expansion across Europe. They were followed by Dacians, then Romans when the latter's army subjugated the region in 107 AD and made it the Roman province of Dacia. Rome abandoned Dacia in 270 AD due to frequent outside incursions. The Germanic Visigoths then absorbed the entire Danube region, including the Banat, until Attila the Hun ended the Goth dominance a century later and left the settlements and towns of the Banat in ruins. After a tribe known as the Gepids briefly took over, the succession became even messier. The Ostragoths regained power but were defeated by a combined force of Romans and pro-Roman Germans. Rule next passed fleetingly through the hands of Avars, Slavs, and Bulgars.

Not until the end of the ninth century when the Magyars (Hungarians) wrested control over the region and Christianized it, did any stability appear. That peace ended in 1552 when the Ottoman Turks overran the whole of southeastern Europe, subdivided the Banat into three districts, and placed a military governor known as a *ban*, meaning "master," in charge of each. It was from this title that the Banat name comes. The Ottoman Empire, during its 1552-to-1716 rule, spurned a benevolent approach to governance and allowed Turk raiders to repeatedly plunder or destroy villages, castles, monasteries, and cities, as well as murder and enslave inhabitants. Some 50 Banat cities and nine monasteries disappeared during this time.[1]

The Banat's population of four million at the beginning of the Ottoman rule had dwindled to one-and-a-half million by the time the Hungarians regained control. In this period the Romanian, Serb, and Hungarian residents were mainly nomadic herdsmen who accompanied their grazing animals on large, landed estates. Greek and Jewish minorities dominated the merchant trades, and the Roma specialized in the gold and silver trade. Agriculture was regarded as commercially unimportant except as a means for families to feed themselves. The Turk domination undid centuries of land transformation and ruined the land to the extent that much of it reverted back to marsh.[2]

Shortly after Prince Eugene of Savoy captured the region with his Austrian Habsburg army in 1718, the process of city reconstruction and land reclamation resumed. Bricklayers, masons, carpenters, and other craftsmen recruited from Austrian and German lands began the arduous process of rebuilding the destroyed city of Temeswar.[3] In 1779 the Habsburgs shifted administration of the Banat from Vienna to their Hungarian Kingdom's capital of Budapest—an arrangement that lasted until the end of World War I when the 1919 postwar peace conference at

Versailles, through the Treaty of Trianon, dismantled the Habsburg Empire and turned Hungary into a small state. For short-sighted political reasons the delegates ignored ethnic, economic, and humanitarian boundaries and assembled new, discordant countries from the ethnic jumble.

Strikingly obvious from this history is the fact that because the Banat served as an incursion highway to and from the rest of Europe, it was seldom a safe or peaceful place to live. The Habsburgs understood that to leave their reconquered land empty when they reconquered it in 1718, was to provide the Ottoman Empire an invitation to return, so they devised a plan of settlement and appointed a governor to implement it. This effort had three goals: fortify the land against invasion, make the land productive by settling it with industrious farmers, and promote the Roman Catholic religion so that religious struggles would not be a source of revolt.

Although the Habsburg Court had the foresight to appoint a competent first governor in the person of their great field general, Count Claudius Mercy, the Banat couldn't be transformed overnight. In 1720, Mercy sent out recruiters to offer free land, construction materials, livestock, and temporary tax exemptions to Catholics from Habsburg domains as well as large swatches of the Holy Roman Empire in Western, Central and Southern Europe.

The prospect of a better life free of servitude, onerous military obligations, and stifling taxes that supported high-living and greedy noble landowners was a siren song to many a longsuffering peasant in the westerly German domains. Immigrants were promised farmland of their own and preassigned dwellings in master-planned villages. The Habsburgs also offered settlers a 10-year tax holiday, a travel allowance, and a loan for the seed, implements, and tools necessary for farming. However, both the eager settlers and the Habsburgs were surprised to learn that taming the new land was costly and difficult. Although many homesteaders eventually prevailed, lasting regional stability proved elusive because the development of ever more modern mobile weapons allowed outsiders to keep invading.

Currently the bulk of the Banat remains split between Romania and Serbia. Perhaps the territorial wheel of fortune has finally stopped spinning and the word *currently* is now unnecessary. But the lengthy and tempestuous regional history, with over 20 changes of sovereignty or possession in as many centuries, argues that *permanent* might still be a relative term in that part of the world.

1. Nikolaus Engelmann and John M. Michels, *The Banat Germans: Die Banater Schwaben* (Bismarck, ND: University of Mary Press, 1987), 7.
2. Lothar Renard, "The Colonization of the Banat Following Its Turkish Occupation, (Die Kolonisation Des Banats Nach Der Türkenzeit, 2006)," Donauschwaben Villages Helping Hands, October 26, 2007, http://www.dvhh.org/history/1700s/banat-colonization-after-turks.htm.
3. Engelmann and Michels, *The Banat Germans*, 8.

4 The Swabian Migrations

The two principalities that in modern times became the German state of Baden-Württemberg contributed over 600,000 emigrants to America in the 19th and early 20th centuries. However, before America became the destination of choice, the people of this region had mainly migrated in the opposite direction. Near the end of the Middle Ages (1500–1600), many residents of what would become southwestern Germany were desperate to leave. They and their ancestors were left demoralized and impoverished because they were beset with calamity after calamity. Their status as serfs, which left them bound to serve on the lands and in the armies of nobles, would have been devastating enough for them even without the frequent occurrence of invasion, pillaging, drought, famine, and epidemic disease.

Johann's ancestors originated from the southwest corner of what was then the Holy Roman Empire. The villages they left behind were largely within 100 miles of each other, but located in various territories and possessions. Ancestors with the Eipert name came from the village of Wurmlingen near Rottenburg am Neckar, which was then in the Duchy of Württemberg and is today in the Tübingen district of Baden-Württemberg, Germany. Other ancestors emigrated to Orzydorf from villages in the Palatinate and Rhenish Hessen districts. Today these villages are in the German state of Rheinland-Pfalz. Still other ancestors emigrated from the cultural and historical region of Lorraine, now in the department of Moselle in the northeast of France. This corner of France has a long history of turmoil and shifting borders. Although some of emigrants from this area had French-sounding names, they'd become Germanized long before settling in the Banat.

Wurmlingen, the Eipert ancestral home, is now a largely middle-class community, but even the briefest history of this region from the Middle Ages onward explains why so many of its people migrated. In the 16th century they suffered greatly from the Black Death, which caused the population to drop precipitously. Several decades of recovery and prosperity followed. Then in 1618, two years before the Pilgrims set out

Regional map of modern Germany and a segment of France. The dots denote the location of villages that Fidel's ancestors left when they resettled in the Banat during the late 1700s. Those locations today lie within the modern German states of Baden-Württemberg, Rheinland-Pfalz and the proximal area of Moselle in France.

for America, the Thirty Years War ruined the region's fortunes once more. Midway through the war, villages like Wurmlingen lost many of its men in disastrous battles. Further impoverishment followed when in 1634 foreign troops surged through, stole much of the livestock, and killed many residents. Without livestock to eat or farm with, terrible starvation ensued. In 1635 the food situation eased, but only because the plague returned and wiped out much of the population that had survived the earlier catastrophes. Near the end of the war, Swedish and Bavarian troops plundered and burned villages as they swept through the region and finished the task of fully impoverishing the countryside. These calamitous events halved the local population and left a legacy of lawlessness and scarcity that ensured that suffering would persist for decades. Near the end of the 18th century, just before Napoleon's French troops wreaked further havoc and misery as they passed through on their conquest adventures, my ancestors escaped to the Banat.

A perusal of Wurmlingen's parish register quickly dispels any doubts about the dreadful conditions during this period. The number of infants surviving their first year, let alone reaching adulthood, was abysmal. Things didn't get much better for those that did reach maturity. Childbearing-aged women had a noticeably higher mortality rate than men of equivalent age in times of peace, but those times of peace seldom lasted long because German nobles conscripted their serfs for military service and frequently started wars or participated in the wars of other nobles. When the serf soldiers were not engaged in these wars, they were commonly rented out as foreign mercenaries in order to support their noble's extravagant lifestyle.

The burden of taxes and servitude was so great that many families became hopelessly indebted to the landowning gentry. Not surprisingly, when Austrian Emperor Josef the Second dangled the offer of free land without servitude or conscription, many an oppressed family jumped at the chance. Johann and Magdalena's ancestors were among the 60 thousand would-be settlers who responded to the call during the 1782-to-1787 wave of colonization, the third of three waves, that came to be called the Josefinische Ansiedlung (the Josef colonization).

The Banat resettlement had begun 50 years earlier, just prior to the American Revolution. In those days, the Banat was a European frontier much like the storied American West that lay beyond the Appalachian Mountains. Settlers in both locales soon discovered that homesteading was not an instant ticket to prosperity. Perhaps surprisingly, the Banat frontier was the more perilous of the two. The newly arrived immigrants did find the land uncrowded as promised, but the overly bright picture painted by the Banat promoters—a land of milk and honey—was highly exaggerated.

Border wars and raiders were just two of the perils. The chief difficulty was that large swatches of the terrain were soggy marshland that harbored serious illnesses. The new settlers also found that they were not as free of bureaucracy as they'd been led to believe. Austrian homesteading was not the same independent, hands-off experience that their counterparts in the American West enjoyed, where settlers were largely left alone after they chose their acreage and fulfilled a term of residency. In the Austrian Empire things were done in a more orderly fashion via central planning in Vienna.

Taming the wilderness was a long and difficult process. Between 1722 and 1787 the Austrian crown recruited three waves of immigrants to achieve this goal. Once they reached Vienna, all three received tariff-free passage down the Donau (Danube) River and the provisions necessary to help start new farms and businesses. Skilled workers were particularly valuable and highly recruited, but most settlers were simple serfs or peasants who'd been stifled by lowly prospects or insufferable obligations to the upper classes.

Before a young single man could hope to obtain his paperwork for escaping his circumstances, he needed a bride. Fortunately, young single women also wanted to leave, so last-minute marriages were common. The Wengen Catholic Church in Ulm, one of the main exit ports, was known to have done a particularly brisk business conducting such marriage ceremonies. Despite the marriage requirement, on the Banat frontier itself men still greatly outnumbered women because defense-force soldiers stationed there commonly enlisted as settlers upon discharge. To restore balance, single women had to be found for them. Their transit down the river was called a *Frauenzug*, or women's transport.[1]

The first two migrations were restricted to Roman Catholics. The third Schwabenzug included Protestants because after the death of Empress Maria Theresa, her son Josef the Second established freedom of religion throughout the empire in 1781.[2] Because many of the first settlers were Germans from Swabia, a cultural, historic, and linguistic region of southwest Germany, the settlers as a whole acquired the name Donauschwaben (Danube Swabians), whether they came from the historic regions of Baden, Württemberg, Alsace, Lorraine, Rhineland, Westphalia, or Bavaria. It even applied to the sprinkling of French, Italian, and Spanish immigrants who arrived.

A few settlers migrated the entire distance to the Banat by road, but most crowded aboard log rafts that came in several versions. Settlers made their way by foot or wagon to one of the Danube River's major upstream ports, like Ulm, and there applied for travel documents. The designs that departed from Ulm were known as Schwabenplätten (Swabian rafts),

Ulmer Plätten, or Ulmer Zillen (barges). The Kehlheimer Plätten, boats of another design, departed farther downstream from the cities of Regensburg and Kehlheim.

All these vessels were smaller versions of the large cargo-carrying boats that plied the Rhine River. The smaller rafts of the Danube carried 20, 80, or sometimes 150 passengers. Most were little more than untarred logs lashed together, with a shack on the deck. The largest sported a cabin of two rooms. Humans, animals, supplies, and equipment were crammed or stacked all over the deck for the six- to nine-day journey to Vienna, the first leg of the trip.

For the settlers, this relocation was not a trivial undertaking. They understood that they might never see their families and friends again and that many hardships lay ahead on the long journey. Those who opted to go packed a minimal load of life-sustaining possessions, paid their portion of the steep transport fee to Vienna, then camped as they awaited Austrian entry papers and space on a boat. In Vienna, fresh rafts awaited to take the emigrants onward once they'd secured a full load of colonists. Although the wait necessitated additional shore camping for the settlers, most had come prepared with enough food. On the boat decks, people and cargo were packed so tightly that the trip was anything but pleasant. The boats were unable to travel at night, so even more camping in the open was called for. To make the camping bearable, many settlers brought straw mattresses along.

At Regensburg, not far upstream from where the Danube entered Austrian Crown State territory, the competition for boat space was fierce due to a bottleneck caused by rapids, sandbanks, unpredictable water

Modern map of the Danube River, the waterway that brought German settlers to the Banat. Arrows denote Ulm, the boarding point for Fidel's ancestors, and Vienna, where they changed boats. The shaded area marks Banat, where they disembarked and continued on to their assigned villages.

levels, and dangerous rocks in the navigation channel. These hazards kept out large deep-draught vessels. Only small rafts steered by oars were practical here. At a stopover in Passau, the passengers received a partial travel allowance. A second installment would follow in Vienna. At Engelhartzell near the Bavarian border with Austria, all boats stopped for a day to allow Austrian customs agents to collect duty on cargo and rigorously inspect the emigrants and their belongings. Prior to the third Schwabenzug, these agents confiscated and burned Lutheran Bibles.

May or June departures were favored for the mild temperatures, but adverse weather conditions still often made the departure miserable. After time was spent waiting to leave, the week-long passage to Vienna could easily stretch into two weeks because of rain and fog. Men who assisted with the oars traveled free; everyone else was charged by distance traveled. Not only was the ride uncomfortable, it also had appreciable risk. Dangerous rapids and shifting sandbars exacted a toll, and sudden storms and heavy rains made the river even more treacherous.[3]

The risk was greatest on the upper Danube where cliffs, rapids, and sandbanks could quickly destroy the flimsy rafts. High water presented the most danger because it masked the rocky obstructions below the surface.

The Danube River flowing through a strategically important narrow as depicted by Georg Matthäus Vischer in a 1674 copper engraving called Der Strudel an der Donau (The Eddy on the Danube). The bend was guarded by a castle, Schloss Werfenstein. The Werfenstein (vortex stone) in the middle of the river created a dangerous whirlpool much feared by river travelers. This castle was one of three Austrian Empire toll or security structures along the Danube in Upper Austria. Fidel's ancestors would have passed through these frightening narrows.

Vessels could flip or break apart in the rapids and drown many passengers. The most dangerous part of the upper Danube was along the cliffs of Düppstein, between Engelhartzell and Vienna. Vicious vortices created by a large rock in the middle of the river terrorized passengers and sailors alike. "The oars were pulled in and the sailors asked the passengers to pray an 'Our Father' each in their own language. Then the raft was left to the floods, as no steering was possible."[4] Vienna lay just ahead the following day. There, the rafts entered the Donaukanal and moored in a suburb of Vienna. Most colonists camped near the river while being processed for their next departure. In spells of bad weather, more than a few emigrants became sick and died here or farther downstream.

The first phase of the journey ended in the Donaukanal (Danube Canal) in Vienna, where everyone disembarked. There, after acquiring their documents from the authorities, the emigrants awaited openings on the barges that would carry them onward. They'd paid some of their own expenses to reach Vienna, but the Austrian government covered their costs the rest of the way. Reaching their new homes would take about a month due to nightly camping stops, burials, acquisition of provisions, paperwork checks, and final overland travel.

Meanwhile, the original boat crews had finished their job and returned upriver to their starting ports. Bringing the rafts back against the current was impractical for them. In earlier centuries, boats were small enough that they could be pulled by humans, but by the 15th century technology and commerce had advanced to the point where the boats were so large that they required towing by draft animals walking along riverbank towpaths. Although towing was doable for more valuable cargo-carrying vessels, the job required up to 60 horses, which did not make economic sense for log rafts. Only a few of the rafts were suitable to continue on downriver, so the majority were relegated to a bevy of Vienna raft dismantlers who negotiated for purchase of the logs, which they then turned into firewood or lumber. Hence, the crewmen were left to make their way home by land, which was particularly dangerous for the boat captain or owner's agent who carried the money collected for passage and commercial cargo.

To obtain their Banat documents in Vienna, the emigrants presented themselves at the Imperial Chamber where officials grilled them about their place of origin, occupation, and religion. Satisfactory answers were required. Those falsely claiming to be farmers to obtain free land were whipped and sent packing. Until the third Schwabenzug, applicants suspected of being Protestants were either beaten and turned away or given religious instruction by a priest if they agreed to convert. The second travel allowance installment was not paid until an official had confirmed the registered emigrant or family was actually aboard a raft at departure time.

This payment had to sustain the travelers until they reached their Banat settlement villages.

The rafts dropped their passengers at a Danube River port in the Banat. From there most emigrants completed the journey by road. A few were accommodated on small rafts that floated all the way to Temeswar via the Bega Canal, a waterway primarily constructed between 1728 and 1733 to drain some of the extensive swamplands. Before locks were built on the canal in 1748, small rafts towed by humans transported the settlers up the canal. Convicts were sentenced to this agonizing job when paid laborers couldn't be found. As for the barges that delivered the settlers to their new lives, they also found a new existence here. As in Vienna, most of them were broken up. The reclaimed lumber was used in the construction of the 46 German villages rebuilt on the ruins of earlier settlements.[5]

Most settlers arrived at their destination with unrealistic expectations regarding what they'd been promised by the government and what it took to tame a wilderness. Throughout the migration period, many of the newly-arrived found progress on the marsh-drainage canals and related infrastructure necessary to control the flood-prone rivers near their land incomplete due to incompetence of administrators or unavailability of soldiers to protect the government's workers from Turk raiders. As a result, malaria and other fevers raged. Turk marauders also exacted a toll when they crossed the Danube in force and killed or dragged off settlers for a lifetime of slavery. The raiders exacted a particularly heavy toll upon first-wave settlers in 1738. Even a high birth rate was unable to compensate for the loss of life throughout much of the settlement period.

The Banat settlers were unprepared for how precarious life might be where the Austrian Empire rubbed against its antagonistic Ottoman neighbor. The Ottoman (Turkish) Empire, which had reached its apex in the 16th century, stretched from Hungary and the Balkans in the west to the Persian Gulf in the east, and from Egypt in the south to the Caucasus in the north. Sited squarely between East and West, it was in a position to plague its neighbors throughout its 600-year history, but by the 17th century, costly wars against Persia, Russia, and Austria-Hungary had sapped the empire's might. Internal reforms managed to hold the Ottoman Empire together, but it never regained its former dominance. After the Ottoman Empire joined Germany and Austro-Hungary in World War I, only to suffer defeat at the hands of the Allied Powers, it lost its last outlying territories. The modern state of Turkey was founded in 1923 from the remnants of the old empire.

In its heyday the Ottoman Empire fielded one of the most advanced military forces in the world, but corruption and incompetent government in the 17th century caused the Ottoman military structure to devolve into a complex fief system that prevented the formation of a modern fighting force. The light cavalry that made up the core of the fief army, like the Mongol raiders of an earlier time, fought with short swords and bows. Such Turk marauder forces were mobile enough to repeatedly raid the Banat after the Habsburgs gained control of the territory in 1716, but lacked the might to retake their former lands.

The security deficiencies allowed neighboring Serbs, Romanians, and Bulgarians to form raiding gangs of their own and plunder what hadn't already been looted or destroyed by the Turks. This havoc and violence particularly affected the southern Banat and left much of it in ruins. Only half of the 20,000 Germans in the 55 settled southern Banat villages survived the intrusions. Twenty-eight villages were abandoned entirely and never rebuilt. Adding to the misery, in 1738 a battalion of soldiers dispatched to reinforce the fortress of Temeswar carried plague into the region, causing an epidemic that took many more lives. These catastrophes led to an exodus of colonists that undid most of what had been accomplished in the first Schwabenzug. For much of the next decade, the unending Turk incursions kept the southern Banat uninhabitable.

In 1740, 23-year-old Maria Theresa inherited the Austrian crown. Although she was keen to restart the resettlement program, for the next two decades the Banat frontier was unable to attract new settlers. Adding to the empress's woes was the cost of two wars whose debts forced her to mortgage the Banat to a large Vienna bank that was unwilling to invest further in the region. So until such time as another large resettlement could take place, she chose to build up a military frontier along the Danube to stop the Turk invasions. Toward this end, in 1747 she recruited a core group of soldiers and former soldiers to homestead the troubled frontier border area.

By 1763 the success of the security program and the resolution of the financial obstacles allowed the empress to once again advertise free land in the region. Maria Theresa's promotion campaign produced a second wave of migrants who responded to the promise of free land, a 10-year tax exemption, loans, and resettlement assistance. Through hard work these newcomers reclaimed some of the abandoned and destroyed settlements. The new campaign progressed well enough that Vienna laid out plans for ever more villages in marsh areas drained by a decades-long canal project along parts of the Bega River. However, the remaining marshland still allowed malaria, cholera, and other fevers to claim many lives. Only the high birth rate and a continuing stream of new settlers kept the population steady.[6]

Unfortunately for the new arrivals, much of the already tillable agricultural land in the Banat had been leased to large livestock-trading companies with huge herds of animals. Settling on the grazing land was often delayed because the commercial interests had ties to the land administrators in Temeswar. The tardy termination of leases slowed settlement or caused settlers to be assigned swampland or thorny ground. Despite this corruption, within three years the state's revenue from the grain produced in the Banat surpassed the fees collected for grazing and gave cultivation a new impetus.

In much of the Banat, particularly around Temeswar, farming couldn't begin until the marshes harboring endemic swamp fever, cholera, and malaria were drained. Marshes did more than jeopardize health; they also made farming risky because of the flood potential. A substantial proportion of the settlers continued to lose their lives taming the wilderness, yet the survivors persisted. Their progress so impressed the nobility that Hungarian and Austrian land-holding families elsewhere in the region actively recruited their own German settlers to repeat the miracle on their holdings. The growing prosperity of the villages in the area recharged the old Roman stronghold city of Temeswar to such a degree that the city became known as the Pearl of the Banat.

The third and final Schwabenzug began in 1782. The United States was only six years into its independence and Lewis and Clark would not explore the American West for another two decades. Maria Theresa's successor, Emperor Joseph II, opened the third round of Swabian immigration by again promising each farming family a comfortable house, a garden, fields, farming tools, and breeding stock. Tradesmen and craftsmen received a house, a smaller plot of land, and an extra allowance to buy the merchandise or tools necessary for their trade. By then a proclamation of freedom of religion and conscience allowed Protestants to participate without converting to the Catholic faith.

Recruiters were well received by Lothringia and Luxemburg serfs because they'd come under the harsh rule of France and were now heavily taxed and exploited. Nearly every village saw an exodus for the promise of better conditions in the fertile Banat. The local authorities commonly refused to grant exit permission, but the lure of acquiring a house, land, and personal freedom spurred many an oppressed family to pack up and disappear into the night. The new emigrants, like their predecessors, underestimated the difficulty and danger of what lay ahead in both the journey down the Danube and in the Banat itself.

---

1. Hans Kopp, "Migration Voyage, The Danube & The Ulmer Schachteln," Donauschwaben Villages Helping Hands, 2020, http://www.dvhh.org/history/1700s/1723-ulmer-schachteln.htm#Womens-Migration-Transport.

2. Lothar Renard, "The Colonization of the Banat Following Its Turkish Occupation, (Die Kolonisation Des Banats Nach Der Türkenzeit, 2006)," Donauschwaben Villages Helping Hands, October 26, 2007, http://www.dvhh.org/history/1700s/banat-colonization-after-turks.htm.
3. Nikolaus Engelmann and John M. Michels, *The Banat Germans: Die Banater Schwaben* (Bismarck, ND: University of Mary Press, 1987), 8.
4. Renard, "The Colonization of the Banat Following Its Turkish Occupation."
5. Renard, "The Colonization of the Banat Following Its Turkish Occupation."
6. Renard, "The Colonization of the Banat Following Its Turkish Occupation."

5 A Grim Reaper

In the summers much of the shallow standing water of the extensive Banat swamplands dried up. The rotting vegetation this cycle produced not only created an appalling stench, it provided an ideal breeding ground for the *Anopheles* mosquito, the carrier of the parasite that causes malaria. The term *malaria* comes from the Italian *mala aria* (bad air), which was once common in Italy as well as in most of Europe and North America. The illness is also known as ague or marsh fever for its association with swamps and marshland.

Clouds of mosquitoes swarmed through Banat villages in the evening and spread malaria, which the colonists called Hungarian sickness. The disease had no treatment and victims experienced headaches, stomach pains, diarrhea, delirium, thirst, and rashes. In the febrile stage sufferers became dull, unresponsive, and sometimes lost consciousness. In some circles the Banat became known as the grave of the Germans.[1]

As if malaria weren't enough, during the second migration in the summer of 1770 typhus arrived and killed thousands. In May of that year resources were already strained to the breaking point and the authorities were short of housing for 900 recently arrived families. By fall 2,300 more families had faced the tribulations of the Danube only to find there were no houses ready for them, so the authorities crammed them together in unhygienic conditions and provided too little food. The new immigrants became so weak that malaria, dysentery, typhus, and especially typhoid (known locally as *Petetschenfieber*) killed them in droves. The starving and crowding were largely the fault of the incompetent and insulated aristocratic administrators in Temeswar (Landesadministration des Temeswarer Banates) who'd allowed construction in the new settlement villages to fall far behind schedule.

The tiny village of Mercydorf mirrored what happened in various locales. Jammed with newly arrived colonists, the village suffered 220 deaths in the summer epidemics. Then a winter food shortage made the survivors vulnerable to other diseases, and many more died. Fearing an investigation, the land administrators covered up the extent of the fatalities by vastly underreporting the deaths to Vienna. However, the magnitude of the 1770 disaster leaked out, and the shock of so many deaths wrecked the colonization effort. The crown suspended its second wave recruitment efforts in November 1770 and decreed that colonists already in the Banat were released from their settlement agreement and could leave.

Few had the resources to return to their homes, but some did receive assistance to settle on land under the domain of Hungarian aristocrats. In 1771 the villagers who'd stayed pleaded for more houses, but once again the shortage was not adequately addressed. Weakened by lack of food, and having never fully recovered from the rigors of the long journey, settlers continued to die. Older people were especially vulnerable. Despite the end of state recruitment for new settlers, emigrants continued to arrive because conditions back home were just as deplorable. In 1778 Vienna finally abolished the Landesadministration des Temeswarer Banates and turned the administration over to Hungarian officials. Eventually, housing and sanitary conditions improved but settlers continued to die of swamp diseases. In some areas conditions were so grim that the majority of inhabitants died over the course of just four or five years.

Empress Maria Theresa died shortly after the scandal ended the second wave of settlement. Josef II, Maria Theresa's son and the brother of Marie Antoinette, ascended to the throne and within two years initiated the third Schwabenzug. In 1784, six years after the Banat housing scandal, Johann and Magdalena's ancestors left their villages in the southwest German state of Baden-Württemberg and braved the Danube journey to become Banat farmers. This third settlement campaign spanned the years from 1782 to 1787 and established 14 new villages. Several were in the vicinity of Temeswar on previously uncultivated land. Some 3,000 families were to be accommodated, but construction again fell behind schedule and many newcomers were jammed into other villages until their houses were ready. The program ended abruptly when Turk raiders again ravaged the southern Banat. In 1788 alone, they devastated 134 villages. This time both Joseph

II and Catherine II of Russia declared war on the Ottoman Empire. Government-sponsored colonization ceased when the Banat became a battlefield. It never resumed, but an influx of settlers arrived anyway. Some paid their own way. Others received subsidies from land-owning nobles who wished to see their lands cultivated. Most highly recruited throughout the settlement period were families with at least 200 gulden in savings—a considerable sum of money. For purposes of comparison, a good horse was worth 18 gulden and a house, as much as 160 gulden.[2]

Relatively few immigrants had such wealth. The majority were the penniless serfs who were legally obligated to buy themselves out of bondage or obtain a declaration of freedom from their nobles. Since many couldn't pay, they fled in the dead of night. They could afford to emigrate only because of the subsidies offered by the nobles in the frontier lands. In 1829 the Banat barrier to entry rose considerably when Austria drastically altered the rules to allow in only new immigrants with a purse of at least 500 gulden. This all but ended immigration.

Temeswar, the regional fortress city contested violently many times through the centuries, lay in the middle of a broad band of particularly marshy land. Some of the marshes had been drained into the Bega and Temes Rivers and turned into productive farm land in earlier times. But the drastic population decline brought about by neglect, war, and pestilence during Ottoman rule had resulted in the abandonment of much of this land. As one historian wrote, "The Bega and Temes rivers degenerated into an incoherent mess of marshland and watercourse." Reclamation posed such a formidable challenge that the drainage projects continued well into the 20th century.[3]

As the settlement effort proceeded, newly laid out communities reached ever deeper into the lower-lying marshes and exposed the new residents to epidemics and natural catastrophes. The most common disaster was flooding because most of the Banat was so flat and low. The rivers ran slow because they dropped little as they meandered to the Danube, which itself coursed through a low basin. Heavy rains further upstream inundated the Danube and caused water to back up into the draining rivers and canals of the Banat, flooding huge areas. Such flooding recharged marshes and caused havoc. Banat floods remained a serious problem for decades after Johann's ancestors arrived, as the following excerpt from an academic paper reports,

> In 1854, the Bega overflowed its banks and inundated all the fields. 1863, in contrast, brought a drought. 1869 brought a renewed inundation and in that year the villagers harvested from canoes and rafts! To make up for this, however, fish

could be caught 'by the basketful'. Inundation and drought have 'often recurred to the present day'. In some cases settlements proved untenable, and had to be abandoned or relocated on higher ground . . . . A series of devastating floods, beginning in 1867 and recurring almost every year for a decade, practically destroyed this last officially backed colonisation of the Habsburg period.[4]

---

1. Lothar Renard, "The Colonization of the Banat Following Its Turkish Occupation, (Die Kolonisation Des Banats Nach Der Türkenzeit, 2006)," Donauschwaben Villages Helping Hands, October 26, 2007, http://www.dvhh.org/history/1700s/banat-colonization-after-turks.htm.
2. Hans Kopp, "Migration Voyage, The Danube & The Ulmer Schachteln," Donauschwaben Villages Helping Hands, 2020, http://www.dvhh.org/history/1700s/1723-ulmer-schachteln.htm#Womens-Migration-Transport.
3. Bruce Mitchell and Saša Kicošev, "Geographical and Economic Influences on the Colonisation of the Banat," in *Geographica Pannonica*, vol. 2, 1998, 20–25, http://www.dgt.uns.ac.rs/pannonica/papers/volume2_04.pdf.
4. Mitchell and Kicošev, "Geographical and Economic Influences on the Colonisation of the Banat."

6 Orzydorf

Die Ersten fanden den Tod,
Die Zweiten litten Not,
Erst die Dritten hatten Brot!

These evocative lines—The first found death, The second suffered hardship, The third were the first to have bread!—appear often in accounts of the Banat Donauschwaben because they encapsulate the fate of the three migration waves. Fortunately, the ancestors of Johann, Magdalena, and my father arrived in the third wave when conditions had turned more favorable. Those ancestors were assigned to a village 25 kilometers north of the city of Temeswar, a site on solid ground that didn't border existing marshland. Upon their arrival, the community was still so raw that it had no name. Vienna didn't permit the settlers to choose their own names as in America. Instead, government administrators did the naming, and the names almost invariably honored noblemen or important officials. In 1785 the turn of Ladislaus Baron Orczy came around. He was the land settlement administrator in Temeswar. The Orczydorf name used during Austrian rule changed to Orczyfalva when the region became part of the Hungarian Kingdom and then Orțișoara after World War I when the region became part of Romania. But its former German residents still know it by its original German name and spell it Orzydorf.

Auroch horns and mastodon bone fragments have been recovered in the vicinity of Orzydorf, but the site has no record of prehistoric human habitation. The earliest known human activity comes from a medieval record dated 1318 when two side-by-side Slav settlements, Kakat and Toet Kakat, occupied the site. That township became a feudal landholding and subsequently passed through the hands of a number of families. When the Turks besieged and captured Temeswar in 1552, the entire region fell under Ottoman control. The Turks tolerated the Christian inhabitants for a time, but eventually taxed them dry. So the land essentially became uninhabited once again.[1]

Fidel's forebears arrived in 1784, 68 years after a six-week siege by Austrian Habsburg forces overran the Ottoman Temeswar fortress in 1716 and reclaimed the Banat. In the early 1780s when Orzydorf was surveyed and laid out, only a post office and horse change station occupied the site. As the new settlers began to trickle in during the fall of 1784, 65 houses were under construction or already built, but none of the buildings were yet habitable.[2]

As in all such settlements, the church and school were high on the priority list, but paramount was a *Wirtshaus* (inn). This establishment was necessary to house and feed construction workers, administrators, and newly arrived colonists whose houses were still unfinished. Although some parish records still exist, none note Orzydorf's earliest buildings or whether the original settler was a craftsman or farmer. Many records were lost in the course of two events—a village office move and an 1883 fire. Only one personal record of an original Orzydorf settler survived into the modern era, and it pertains to the immigration of a Fidel ancestor named Scheible. Below is the translated text of his passport/character reference issued by the local parish office in the village of Wurmlingen in Württemberg:

> Emigration from Wurmlingen Passport and Testament for Johannes Schäuble
>
> Johannes Schaible, a known commoner and former resident of Wurmlingen, which is located in the Niederhohenbergischen Amtsflecken, wishes to travel to Hungary. He intends to settle there permanently for an improved life and income to better care for his wife Maria Juhrerin and nine children, 7 girls and 2 boys. Although he was a good craftsman and field laborer, he could not earn enough money where he lived.
>
> In truth, we have to admire him. He was always a hard and peaceful worker and we have been very satisfied with him.
>
> For these reasons we can do nothing but recommend him wherever he decides to settle.
>
> Thank God we are breathing healthy air here and have no sign of any infectious sickness. Therefore, we can allow Johann Schaible and his family to leave and have asked only a standing fee. We kindly request Johann Schaible and his family be allowed to pass safely and unhindered at all locations and settle wherever they wish.
>
> So testified in Wurmlingen, August 23, 1784

Anton Bierlinger Schultheis
Peter Bißinger Deputat
Fidele Miller Deputat[3]

The Orzydorf settlement site and the surrounding terrain had not lain fallow during the preceding decades of Austrian rule, but had been leased by a large trading company as grazing land. The agrarian development plan called for 203 houses, 100 homestead allotments of approximately 20 hectares, or 50 acres), and 100 half-sized allotments, which were to be meted out according to how much land a settler family could reasonably farm. To the consternation of the newly arrived settlers, they found every aspect of their resettlement behind schedule due to the incompetence and disinterest exhibited by the local administrators. With the houses not yet habitable, the new arrivals were temporarily crowded into shared lodging in other villages.

Although 65 of the houses were erected by the end of November of 1874, the adobe in the thick walls dried slowly during the winter and remained too soft and moist to allow habitation. Several families defied the authorities and moved in anyway. Another problem was a scarcity of potable water. The local surface water was neither palatable nor safe, and wells couldn't be dug because the necessary rock for lining the wells hadn't been delivered. Neither rock nor timber was available locally because the low-lying Banat was a sedimentary plain that had few trees and virtually no exposed rock. Yet a third impediment to settlement was the cozy political influence the grazing lease holder had with the land administrators. Orzydorf's farm-ground survey hadn't been completed, so the allotting of land to families needed to be put off until well into the 1785 growing season. Political corruption also delayed the settlement of many other areas with standing grazing leases.

The newly arrived colonists were desperate to rebuild their lives and support themselves, so when the delays dragged on and it became evident to them that farming couldn't begin for nearly two years after their arrival, they became angry. While they waited, they were at the mercy of an imperious district treasurer for food, firewood, and other necessities. The discontent drove Orzydorf's newly elected mayor and a group of his supporters to militancy. Their complaints about the land distribution delay and the inadequate supplies of food and firewood incensed the corrupt bureaucrats. The officials subsequently arrested the strident mayor and sentenced him to a whipping. The mayor and his livid supporters responded by forming a committee that took their grievances directly to the emperor's court in Vienna.

Not surprisingly, the commission that Vienna dispatched to look into the grievances sided with the administrators and ruled that most of the settler complaints had no merit. Yet it did find defects in the construction of many of the houses and ordered repairs. Meanwhile, confrontations between the unhappy group of settlers and officials continued. When the mayor was arrested a second time, a crowd of 70 men armed with clubs and farm implements directly confronted the authorities. This led to more arrests. Settler anger became so great that the investigators needed the protection of 50 mounted guards to enter the village. In the end, the mayor was expelled from the county and two of his accomplices were punished in lesser ways.[4]

Needless to say, like the colonists that had preceded them, the third-wave colonists did not find the paradise that was promised. Still, most settlers felt liberated to some degree and remained optimistic about their future prospects despite the problems. Their optimism was later transmitted back to their former homes. Predictably, the nobles that lost serfs, tenants, tradesmen, and potential soldiers to the new frontier lands were keen to prevent such advertising because it tempted even more serfs and subjects to seek a better life elsewhere.

The most effective advertisements were letters sent back home—letters extolling the opportunities in the new lands—so mail became a target of censorship. Several Orzydorf men learned this the hard way. When they returned to visit relatives in their old home of Lothringen (French: Lorraine), they were prosecuted for conveying letters from other Orzydorf residents lauding the opportunities to be found in the Banat.[5] However, not all letters were positive because swamp fevers and cholera still took a frightful toll. Twenty kilometers west of Orzydorf in the village of Biled, "734 of 908 settlers died of these illnesses within a period of 6 years. Had it not been for the high birth rate and the steady influx of new settlers, many villages would have soon been depopulated."[6]

The Orzydorf parish records reveal that one-third of its settlers died in the first four years of the village's existence. Many of the dead were young people in their prime. As a result, new family names soon replaced many of the original names in the local records. Names disappeared when a husband died and the wife remarried, the family died off entirely, or the family moved elsewhere because of misfortune. Other settlers left when they realized they were not earning enough to pay back the seed money they'd been advanced or were unable to pay their taxes at the end of the 10-year tax-free period. New arrivals often found vacant land and picked up where the previous farmer had left off.[7]

In addition to epidemics, natural catastrophes, and the usual crop failures endemic to farming, the last wave of settlers still faced the same external danger that had plagued their predecessors. Just four years after the first Orzydorf settlers arrived, Turk raiders penetrated to within a half day's ride of Orzydorf. In the middle of the 19th century a new menace emerged in the form of a social revolution that swept Europe. A Hungarian peasant uprising embroiled the Banat and put pressure on the Germans to choose sides. But by then most of the German settlers were content with life in their ethnic villages and stayed out of the fray. The rebellion was suppressed, but problems arose anyway when the Banat was incorporated into the newly formed Hungarian Kingdom within the Austrian Empire. Settlers were subjected to a homogenization program designed to form a completely Hungarian nation out of a population containing large minorities. The Magyarization threatened to wipe out the language, schools, and culture of the Donauschwaben settlers.[8]

Many family names were rendered into Hungarian during this process. Common names such as Schmidt, Mueller, and Wagner became Kovacs, Molnar, and Bogner. Names that didn't readily translate were arbitrarily changed to conform to Hungarian. Forty German communities sought to gain exemption from this internal onslaught by petitioning the Austrian Emperor to place them under the patronage of an Austrian noble, but the petition was denied. Orzydorf and the other ethnic villages were forced to use Hungarian in official dealings and to teach Hungarian alongside German in their self-funded school. The Temeswar district escaped the worst of the Magyarization, and Orzydorf's German residents kept their names and continued to speak their dialect.[9]

The new Donauschwaben settlements were laid out in orderly checkerboard patterns with streets up to 40 meters wide. The broad streets were pleasing to the eye and provided privacy for the settlers, but a more serious purpose lay behind this layout. Distance between buildings prevented the spread of fire—a constant threat in the old, closely packed villages of Western Europe.

In Orzydorf and the other Banat settlements, farmer's dwellings consisted of a one-acre (0.4-hectare) farmyard called a *Bauernhof*, or *Hof*. These hofs were separated from neighboring units by high walls and fences. A city block usually contained five hofs. The long and narrow single-story houses within were sited along one lot edge or corner of the lot and served as part of the hof's surrounding wall. Utility buildings such as the outhouse, barn, stalls, and granary extended from the back of the house, with one long roof covering the entire structure. A typical lot had gardens with flowers, vegetables, and fruit trees near the house. To allow access for farm machinery into the rear farmyard area, each hof had a large gate opening onto the street.

The original houses were of simple design with walls of compacted adobe bricks. The ceilings consisted of stringers and boards covered with adobe. A stucco exterior kept the moisture out. The roof of the house had long overreaching eaves to protect the thick clay walls. Locally abundant canes and reeds provided the roofing material. Most houses were only one room wide, with rooms connecting to adjoining rooms through side doors. The inward-facing side of the house supported an open veranda that spanned the entire length of the house and faced the garden. Not uncommonly, hofs contained a small second house across the garden for the farmers who retired when one of their sons married and began farming on his own. Daughters who married typically set up housekeeping in the groom's hof.

In the American frontier, homesteaders staked one contiguous plot of farmland and lived on it, but in the Banat, farmers lived in villages. Field allotments were small manageable plots spread about in the various terrains outside the village, with each settler family being assigned fields of varying soil conditions and soil quality. This made the overall land distribution more equitable and improved a family's survival chances by reducing the risk of total crop loss due to localized hail, drought, or flood. Most families maintained at least a small vegetable plot within their residential compound, but the serious gardening took place in a family field not far from the village. Orzydorf, like neighboring villages, also maintained a discrete area dedicated to fruit orchards and vineyards. Because the majority of farmers fermented wine, growing grapes was vital.

Midway through the 19th century larger houses began to replace the original houses. In some villages fired-clay bricks and tiles were the new building materials, but in Orzydorf most replacement houses were still constructed with thick adobe bricks held together with a binder of chaff or straw. The replacement houses included more rooms and exterior styling. Gables became more decorative and sometimes the family name was even integrated into the facade. Many courtyards acquired a summer-kitchen outbuilding to keep cooking stoves from heating the main house during the warm months. These larger houses often also incorporated a room or two for the retired parents or grandparents. After corn was found to grow well locally, most farmers added a corn drying and storage shed to their hof. In Fidel's region, such a building was called an *ambar*, a word that descended from the Turkish era and meant "storehouse."[10]

Orzydorf successfully held on to its culture during the Hungarian Magyarization push because its population, which consisted almost entirely of ethnic German Catholics, provided its own school and teachers. This remained so until the end of World War II. Fidel recalled that only a handful of Romanian families lived in the village. The residents were also almost uniformly Catholic in religion and Fidel was unaware of any Jews, although the census records report several. The village also had a small number of Protestants.

Orzydorf sat astride the roadway that connected the two largest regional cities, Arad and Timişoara (Temeswar officially became Timişoara after World War I), so it was natural for a business district to develop along this throughfare. In the automobile age, this road became a major highway. Because Orzydorf also had a major railway line passing through, the district capital of Timişoara was just a short hop by train. That city too retained a largely German population until after World War II, and many Orzydorf residents had relatives there.

In my father's youth, the ethnic German villagers paid both a national and city tax, but the community largely operated as a cooperative. Farmers were required to put in two days of street work annually and to provide a team of horses for gravel hauling and street maintenance. Because the streets were extra wide, they demanded considerable maintenance. Being an industrious and progressive community, Orzydorf worked to continuously improve all other aspects of its infrastructure as well. By Fidel's day, trees lined the sidewalks, the two main streets were paved, and drainage gutters separated the streets and sidewalks. All street surfaces were raised and rounded over the middle to facilitate rain runoff. All of these improvements were achieved by cooperation.

Near the end of the 19th century, Orzydorf residents became early adopters of electric lighting. The power was generated locally at first. Several years later the community purchased power from another municipality, only to see local generation return when a large mill that ground flour for export found itself with an excess of power as it generated electricity to run its machinery. Most houses were wired for lights by this time. Fidel remembered the spectacular fire that destroyed that mill when he was a young boy.

Although Orzydorf was advanced in electrification, it lagged in the field of communication because Romania was not progressive in that matter. Fidel said that telephones were rare in Orzydorf before World War II; he knew of only two. Still, because all the farmers lived in town, life without a telephone did not result in the same isolation as farmers living out on their land in America. Mail service was reasonably reliable and arrived from Timişoara each morning by train. A German newspaper came daily on the 5 p.m. train. As for automobiles, Fidel said there'd been several in Orzydorf during the 1920s, but by the following decade the rough Romanian roads had pounded them to death and spare parts were unavailable.

At harvest time farmers created separate piles of oats, wheat, and barley straw as the grain was threshed in the hof. A pile of corn shucks and cobs also grew through the winter as the shucking and shelling of stored ear corn progressed. The shelling was done by hand, often as part of an evening family social activity. Corncobs served as stove fuel. As for the straw, it had various uses, but the prime one was livestock bedding.

Most households kept a cow or two for milk. This made for a sizeable village herd, considering the community had about four hundred households. During the grazing season, each animal needed to go from the hof to a pasture every day. Farmers couldn't sacrifice part of their morning to this chore, so like most Banat villages, Orzydorf developed a cooperative solution. Every morning at a given time, someone in each hof opened the gate and turned their cow(s) out onto the street. This sounds like a prescription for chaos, but was actually quite orderly. All four- to five-hundred cows were trained to make their way to the large community pasture. Five men, each walking a separate route, trailed the animals along the street until they merged into one large herd. Two men tended them in the pasture throughout the day, then released them late in the afternoon.

Within the village, the herd split up as cows dropped out of the procession to move down the street leading to their part of town. The handler for each route trailed behind his cows. Each cow then stopped and waited outside its hof until someone opened the gate. The handler knew each cow and came to the house if he had any new information for the farmer—information such as when their cow had been bred by one of the 10 to 12 community bulls. These men were paid by the community, but farmers also tipped them with a slab of bacon or a measure of grain for the information.

Orzydorf and the surrounding communities had once also used swine herders for sows. The practice lingered on longer in the Hungarian Banat than in the Romanian Banat. Orzydorf had formerly also employed community sheep herders. If a lamb died, or when the lambs were weaned at two months, these herders could be hired to milk the ewes within the farmer's stall. This milk was used to made *Brenze* (a sheep cheese) in four-kilogram balls. Brenze was a staple for Fidel. He took sheep-cheese sandwiches, made with half-inch-thick bread slices, out to the fields with him for lunch all summer long.

All farmers tended their own horses. After Johann died, Magdalena kept only one horse for riding and light vineyard work during the growing season. She sold it each fall because boarding it through the winter made for both extra work and expense. When Fidel's older brother Hans was 14 and old enough to begin farming in 1934, his mother bought two work horses. By 1935, the family again owned six horses, and then eight. Two were light riding horses.

Riding was never a problem in town. The well-maintained and rounded streets remained firm in any weather, but beyond town it was a different story. Those roads were heavily traveled regardless of the weather and became very rutted once they dried out after heavy rains. Access to fields was by small dirt lanes, but to keep these lanes in good condition, farmers never went out to their fields when conditions were muddy

Over the course of two centuries, the German villages of the Banat had developed a fine-tuned barter system that made them self-sufficient. Nearly every need and occupational niche was filled locally. In the fall, apple sellers in covered wagons came around to trade apples for wheat. The locally abundant plum crop was turned into jam and schnapps. Everyone made wine from their own vineyard grapes. Barbers made the rounds twice a week to each house, offering shaves and haircuts. They kept a running tab, settled in wheat after the fall harvest. Wheat was the principal local crop and the currency for labor and services of all sorts. Even the grain-threshing crew received its wages in grain, which the crew leader doled out in wheat, barley, or oats at threshing time.

Orzydorf also had a volunteer fire department that fortunately found little to do. Aside from the previously mentioned mill fire, Fidel recalled only two other fires during his childhood. One was a house fire. The other, a smoky, straw-pile fire that several boys had accidentally started. The damage was minimal, but the conflagration resulted in considerable peripheral heat, principally on the bottoms of the boys involved.

In that era and culture, families prepared their own dead for burial. Following a death, family and friends gathered in the deceased's home on the evening of the death—men in one room and women in another. The visitors stayed to comfort the family until midnight, or beyond if necessary. The following day the body, laid out in a wood coffin, was driven to the church in a horse-drawn hearse housed in a special carriage house at the cemetery. The horses pulling this vehicle were draped in black fabric. After the funeral mass, the deceased took their final earthly journey as the hearse led a procession of mourners to the cemetery on the outskirts of the village. Often, a band played as it accompanied the procession. In this time of grief and need, the stricken family incurred no costs because the community kept a special funeral account book. Several times each year someone came around and collected each household's fair share of what was necessary to maintain the fund. It was in effect an insurance policy, a custom that prevailed throughout the Banat.

According to Fidel, the main Orzydorf businesses consisted of 11 small groceries, a number of taverns, several tinsmiths who repaired pots and fashioned house gutters and other products from sheet metal, several blacksmiths who shoed horses and made wagon and machinery parts, and about a dozen cabinet makers who built furniture. A creamery bought surplus milk from farmers each morning and evening. After the creamery centrifugally separated out the cream, the farmer reclaimed the skim milk to mix with grain or other feed for hog slop.

Two woodcutters supplied the local firewood. Because this part of the Banat was a broad plain without any forests, firewood was imported by rail in the form of meter-long logs. Several businesses in the village burned this length, but for home heating the woodcutters sawed this stock into three chunks with a large, steam-engine-driven circular saw. One business that used a large quantity of wood was the rebuilt flour mill, which burned wood to produce the steam powering the mill machinery.

The local *Gasthaus* establishments were the most interesting businesses, at least to a young man of a certain age. Orzydorf had three large inns along the main street, and later yet another near the train station. Two of the main-street inns had a dance floor, something essential to young people since much of their socializing took place at the weekly Sunday afternoon dances. The inns were also venues for wedding festivities and other celebrations. Fidel recalled spending considerable time in them with his friends as an adolescent and young adult.

In Orzydorf, as in most small German communities, the gasthaus bars were a haven for interesting characters. Fidel particularly remembered a neighbor who lived on the opposite corner of his block. This farmer regularly stopped at his favorite tavern with his wagon and team of horses. After he'd passed out from drinking, the innkeepers or patrons carried him outside, placed him in the bed of his wagon, and sent the horses on their way. Like the local cows, the horses knew their way home.

Farmers and workers who'd been compensated in grain for their labor regularly brought sacks of grain to the mill to be ground into flour. If this household chore happened to fall to an enterprising young man, he could easily sell 5 kilograms of the 75 kilograms without his mother being any the wiser. This earned the lad enough cash to buy a bottle or two of beer at his favorite tavern every day for a week. Fidel seemed to know a little about this practice.

The local grain mill, at the terminus of a two-block-long access road paved by the owner, was widely known beyond the environs of Orzydorf as the finest mill in the Banat. Fidel called the owner *Onkle* in the customary way children addressed various older male relatives. In this case, the Onkle was an older cousin. As a teen, Fidel earned spending money by delivering firewood to the mill once a week with one of the family's farm wagons and a pair of horses. The freight-yard pickup point for the wood had always been a place of great interest for Fidel. As a child, he'd been captivated by the trains passing through. The main-line track carried all the export oil that went to Germany from Romania's prolific oil field. Two outbound trains of tank cars passed through almost every day. The same tracks also carried much of the grain exported to Germany. Fidel couldn't have guessed then that only a few years later these tracks would carry a very different export east to Germany and west to Russia—one that would drastically alter his own life and destiny as well as his sister's and his brother's.

---

1. Gertrude Adam and Anton Peter Petri, *Heimatbuch der deutschen Gemeinde Orczydorf im Banat* (Marquartstein: Breit, 1983), 17-18.
2. Adam and Petri, *Heimatbuch der deutschen Gemeinde Orczydorf im Banat*, 25.
3. Adam and Petri, *Heimatbuch der deutschen Gemeinde Orczydorf im Banat*, 40.
4. Adam and Petri, *Heimatbuch der deutschen Gemeinde Orczydorf im Banat*, 67–76.
5. Adam and Petri, *Heimatbuch der deutschen Gemeinde Orczydorf im Banat*, 41.
6. Engelmann, Nikolaus, and John M. Michels. *The Banat Germans: Die Banater Schwaben*. Bismarck, ND: University of Mary Press, 1987, 16.
7. Orzidorf community council and church council (Orzidorf Gemeinderat und Kirchenrat), *Geschichte Der Gemeinde Orzidorf 1785*-1935 (History of the Community of Orzidorf 1785-1935), 1935, 55.
8. Engelmann and Michels, *The Banat Germans*, 17–18.
9. Engelmann and Michels, *The Banat Germans*, 17–18.
10. Nick Tullius, "A Short History of The Danube Swabian," Donauschwaben Villages Helping Hands, 2013, http://www.dvhh.org/history/1700s/DS-history~tullius.htm.

7 The Geographic Merry-Go-Round

In the latter part of the 19th century, the Banat death rate dropped dramatically, and the population of Orzydorf shot up, creating a land shortage for many of the young people in the community. The resulting underemployment and lack of opportunity forced them to emigrate. From 1899 to 1913, over 90,000 Banat Swabians left. Most chose to seek their fortune in America. According to Fidel, some of the Banat expats who'd done particularly well in America returned to their villages in the 1920s and 1930s. The investment money they brought back helped their old communities weather the Great Depression. As a child in Iowa, I met a distant relative who'd emigrated during this period. Fidel had re-established contact with him not long after our family arrived in the United States. Later, as an adult, I found, and communicated with, yet another branch of the family that had come to America in the early 1900s.

World War I was devastating for the young men of Orzydorf. Seventy-five village men (out of a population of 2,000) lost their lives in an Austro-Hungarian uniform between 1914 and 1918. As already noted, the postwar Treaty of Versailles compounded the suffering. Forged maps, figures, and outright lies misrepresented regional ethnic majorities as minorities in order to justify awarding key pieces of the Austrian Empire's territory to the allies of the major victors and to allow new ethnic jigsaw-puzzle countries to be created out of most of the rest. The extremely harsh and punitive settlement terms sowed the seeds of discord that ultimately blossomed into World War II. In Germany, the crippling economic burden, loss of territory, and political chaos that ensued provided an ideal milieu for the rise of Hitler.

When France and Britain redistributed sizeable portions of the Austro-Hungarian Empire's territory after World War I in order to destroy their rival power, a major beneficiary of the largess was Hungary's neighbor to the east, Romania. Romania had abandoned its neutrality half way through World War I and aligned itself with Britain, France, and Russia against the Central Powers of Germany and Austro-Hungary. When the Bolshevik Revolution led to the Russian Empire's withdrawal from the war, and Romania found itself nearly surrounded by its Central Powers enemies, it capitulated and signed an unfavorable treaty with them. One day before Germany surrendered on the Western Front to end World War I, Romania re-entered the war on the Allied side and was rewarded for its tokenism with the lion's share of Hungary's Banat. Smaller portions went to Yugoslavia and Czechoslovakia. The giveaway reduced Hungary to a small and impotent state.

That transfer of territory put the village of Orzydorf well inside Romania. For the villagers, it meant learning Romanian and discarding the Hungarian they'd previously used in government dealings and taught in their school. The new government, like the last, was just as suspicious of them as a minority, for their work ethic and cultural identity had long paid dividends in the form of better schools, farms, infrastructure, and local government than the non-German villages around them. The Romanian government saw this as a threat and largely ignored the rights the ethnic German minority had been guaranteed by the Versailles Treaty. It put politics ahead of economics in an attempt to crush its most industrious minority. The ethnic Germans were too established to expel or scatter outright, so the government employed tactics of phony land reform, language restrictions, under-representation in government, and denial of administrative and civil service jobs to bring them down. Because Orzydorf was entirely German, the village wasn't as severely affected by the restrictive Romanian policies as tinier ethnic German communities when the Romanian government sought more "equality" for Romanians.

Despite the government's efforts, the community's industriousness allowed it to weather the Great Depression of the early 1930s and even prosper enough that a considerable number of villagers could afford to travel to Germany for the 1936 Berlin Olympics. The economic disparity continued to rankle the government, but Hitler's ascendence in Germany and his engineered takeover of Austria with the Anschluss of 1938 rattled the Romanian government enough that ethnic German communities were suddenly allowed to reopen their closed schools, use their own language in public gatherings, and receive mail addressed in German.

While the rise of Germany was keenly felt in the village, the residents were conservative by nature and took little part in outside politics—unlike some of their city cousins. But when the rapid economic re-emergence of Germany brought prosperity to the village through the grain that Germany imported in the 1930s, the population began to look favorably upon Germany and its Nazi government.

About the only visible change the new German influence brought, as far as Fidel could recall, was the establishment of a chapter of Turnverein, an organization founded by Friedrich Ludwig Jahn early in the 19th century when Germany was occupied by Napoleon. In German, *turnen* refers to gymnastics, and *Verein* to an association. The Orzydorf organizers managed to interest some children in gymnastics but found stiff competition from football (soccer). Because the latter was well established as the dominant youth sport, Turnverein didn't gain the type of acceptance it did in ethnic German areas of other countries such as the Sudetenland of my mother's youth. There, the sport was so popular that every village had a chapter and Turnverein Festivals drew large audiences. Many of the residents of my mother's village, and possibly even her parents, were attending such a festival the day World War I was triggered by the assassination of Archduke Franz Ferdinand.

Turnverein arrived in America long before it came to Orzydorf. German immigrants brought the movement to America around the middle of the 19th century. There, the organization gained considerable popularity in the Midwest where many Germans had settled. In its new locale, not all Turner club members joined for the gymnastics. The German-American gymnastic unions were often politically active and sternly opposed slavery because it reminded them too much of the serfdom many of them had left their homes to escape. Turners played no small part in helping to elect Abraham Lincoln as president and served as bodyguards at his inauguration and burial. During the Civil War many Turners joined German militia regiments and fought for the Union Army. The names of two such veterans, Anheuser and Busch, are still well known today for the brewing empire that arose from the brewery they founded after the war. In the decades after the Civil War, the clubs and their members became active in organizing labor and the education system.[1] [2]

Although Turnverein gymnastics failed to catch on in Orzydorf in the 1930s, German influence did penetrate the community in other ways. The strong export market that brought prosperity to the village allowed many residents to replace their small radios with the more powerful imported German sets prominently marked with German stations on their tuners. Residents sometimes listened to Romanian stations but preferred broadcasts in their everyday language. Of course, the German language broadcasts largely came from Germany, along with German propaganda.

Fidel was in his teens at the time and too busy socializing and farming to pay much attention. Still, he and his friends understood that at a time when much of the world was in a depression, their own locale enjoyed success because Germany paid well for the Banat's agricultural and natural resource surplus. Fidel said young people like himself picked up cues from the adults around them, but they learned little about the Nazi party and what was truly happening in Germany until several years later.

Soviet communism was another thing Fidel learned little about, even though he knew several communists in town. One, a cousin with the family name of Rabong, was the son of an uncle in the grain threshing business that Fidel worked closely with during the harvest season each year. Another communist Fidel knew was a close neighbor named Kierer. This likeable man, better known as Kierer Schneider (Tailor Kierer), sewed some of the family's clothes. Fidel also knew a communist tavern keeper, but suspected it was the man's wife that really held the political convictions.

Fidel recalled no Nazi recruiting efforts until 1939 when several young Germans came to Orzydorf to establish a local party chapter. Nothing much came of the effort because by that time many residents were unhappy about Hitler's pact with Stalin to split Poland between them. Fidel clearly remembered that his girlfriend's father, who always listened to the news on Sunday evenings, predicted that Hitler wouldn't stop with Poland and that Germany would eventually pay a price for Hitler's actions.

Over the next two years Germany conquered most of Western Europe and planned even further expansion. Eventually, Hitler quietly placed a large German force in Romania, Hungary, and Bulgaria in order to take Yugoslavia, Romania's southern neighbor. The German 12th Army, the designated invasion force in Romania, was partially assembled near Timișoara. The Germans subsequently crushed Yugoslavia in just two weeks. After this, despite whatever political opinions Orzydorfers held, they had a high regard for German military professionalism.

One advance element of the invasion force bivouacked just outside of town for a night, then pulled through Orzydorf the next morning. These soldiers didn't learn that Orzydorf was an ethnic German village until the pullout. They said they could have had a good time, had they known. This group moved by road, while the main body and their equipment passed through later on trains. The transit of so many military trains was a memorable sight, and a sobering one too.

A second force assigned to take Greece passed through Orzydorf a short time later. It included the select 1st SS Panzer Division Leibstandarte SS Adolf Hitler (1. SS-Panzerdivision Leibstandarte SS Adolf Hitler). Serving in Leibstandarte was an Austrian sergeant who'd just recently been appointed a junior officer. This man was devoid of scruples, had a penchant for getting into trouble, and was destined to become a Hitler favorite and Nazi propaganda star. Late in the war, at a time when he was referred to by some as the most dangerous man in Europe, Fidel would receive orders sending him to this officer's battalion. The man's name was Otto Skorzeny.³

---

1. Scott Williams, "Hungarians in Civil War Missouri," March 3, 2012,
   https://web.archive.org/web/20120303013738/http://www.mcwm.org/history_germans.html
2. Robert Knight Barney, "Forty-Eighters and the Rise of the Turnverein Movement in America," in *Ethnicity and Sport in North American History and Culture*, ed. David Kenneth Wiggins and George Eisen (Westport, CT: Praeger, 1995), 19–42,
   https://www.google.com/books/edition/Ethnicity_and_Sport_in_North_American_Hi/fmSj2rzCcvoC?hl=en&gbpv=1&pg=PA28&printsec=frontcover.
3. Glenn B. Infield, *Skorzeny, Hitler's Commando* (New York: St. Martin's Press, 1981), 23, https://archive.org/details/skorzenyhitlersc00infi.

8 Childhood

The family came close to losing Fidel when he was several months old. The occasion was a 50-kilometer Walfahrt (pilgrimage). Magdalena had set out with her three small children and other family members to visit a shrine in the village of Radna, where the Franciscan religious order held pilgrimages on various religious feast days throughout the year. Radna was just across the Mures River from the town of Lipova, where she would stay with relatives.

The shrine at Radna, dedicated to the Blessed Virgin Mary, is today still one of the most famous church sites in southeast Europe. It had fallen into disrepair under Ottoman rule in the 16th century when churches and chapels were plundered and priests persecuted. When the Ottomans permitted Bosnian merchants to return to the region several decades later, a number of Catholic priests accompanied them, but they were restricted in the religious services they could conduct and in the church renovations they could undertake. In 1642 the state of his church spurred one determined Franciscan priest from Radna to walk all the way to Constantinople to implore the Sultan to allow restoration of the Radna chapel. The large bribe the priest carried with him helped persuade the sultan.

Unfortunately, the restoration didn't keep the Turks from ransacking the building again. That desecration led a benefactor to donate an Italian woodcut impression of the Madonna to the chapel. Legend has it that this Blessed Virgin Mary woodcut survived a subsequent raid when soldiers heaped it and all the chapel's holy pictures on the floor and set them on fire. The congregation considered the woodcut's survival a miracle, and thereafter the unburned icon became the symbol of Roman Catholicism on the border between Islam and the Orthodox Christianity."[1] A second legend asserts that a soldier was prevented from riding up the hill to attack the church when his horse's hoof sank into a stone. Pilgrimages to the church began early in the 18th century when the Black Death ravaged the nearby city of Arad. The inhabitants promised to hold a pilgrimage to Radna "for the termination and salvation from this terrible plague."[2]

Large fluffy pillows served as infant car seats in that era, so when Magdalena set out, she bundled Fidel in such a pillow and entrusted him to the care of relatives in a horse buggy driven by an uncle. She and her other two children rode in a second buggy. When the travelers stopped along the way and momentarily left Fidel's buggy unattended, the horse

Portrait of Fidel and his siblings as young children. Hans, the oldest, is on the left, with Magdalena in the center and Fidel on the right.

bolted and ran away with the baby. Magdalena thought the buggy was sure to overturn and kill her baby in the process, but other travelers down the road stopped the horse before anything happened. Little Fidel was unharmed and learned of his adventure only later in life.

Fidel could have been lost to the family even earlier had Magdalena given in to a childless relative named Margaretha, who beseeched her for the baby. Margaretha couldn't conceive so tried to convince Magdalena to allow her and her husband, another Fidel, to adopt the infant. She argued that this would relieve Magdalena of the burden of raising three children, and as their only child, Fidel would receive their entire inheritance. But Magdalena couldn't think of doing such a thing. Sadly, Margaretha died young and unfulfilled, but her husband went on to father two children after he remarried.

Fidel began school at age five as did all children in the community. The village *Kindergarten*, supported by the local Catholic Parish of St. Hubertus, was taught by an international order of nuns, the School Sisters of Notre Dame. The seven-hour school day was interrupted by an hour-long break for lunch at noon. Children attended the kindergarten for two years. In 1927 when Fidel started there, four nuns taught 143 children. Fidel's class and the preceding one marked the school's highest enrollment ever.[3]

The primary school included grades one through seven. It opened and closed with a prayer even though it was not church-affiliated or taught by nuns. The school week ran from Monday through Saturday. Students began their day at seven-thirty each morning with Mass in the nearby church. After mass, the children hurried to the school building where classes started at eight. Thursday afternoons were free, and a few Saturday afternoons were as well, although most were reserved for handicraft instruction to foster the agricultural and household skills the students needed as adults. A summer break freed the children for two months.

Very occasionally a boy's help was needed at home in order to butcher a hog or to harvest grapes. To excuse his absence on his return, the boy customarily brought his teacher a sausage or other small offering. At the beginning of the fourth grade, each boy received a fruit-tree seedling to plant in a school-reserved plot adjacent to the cemetery. Through the next four years the boy learned how to nurture his tree and tend the more-mature trees in the orchard. After graduation, each boy took his tree home to replant in the family's orchard.

The school often combined two grades of both boys and girls into one class. During Fidel's school days, only the first and fourth grades had their own classrooms. Orzydorf was prosperous enough to support its own school, which allowed the community to teach classes in German, as had been the tradition for 150 years. However, the Romanian language was a required part of the curriculum from third grade on. The teachers largely came from places other than Orzydorf. Fidel was taught by a female teacher in the first and fourth grade, but Herr Wittmann was his teacher the other five years. Wittmann was partially deaf so the boys in the class

Family photograph showing Fidel as a boy (on the right) posing with his mother, Magdalena Sr., and older siblings, Magdalena and Hans. By local Catholic tradition, families presented a watch to their children upon church confirmation. The tab of Fidel's watch hangs from his pocket. In that era, the Eipert family's dress clothes were made by a local tailor.

got by with a lot of mischief and had a grand time. Education for most children ended at age 14 because the village had no secondary school.

Like nearly every local schoolboy, Fidel played football (soccer) during his school days. School teams were formed by combining boys from two classes. The majority of boys wanted to keep playing after graduation, so they joined a league team. On summer Sunday afternoons the various teams competed with neighboring villages, often a considerable distance away. The older boys and young men always played first, then left the field to the school teams. Two exceptional players for the league team were Sepp Rabong, a Fidel cousin, and Josef Eipert, Fidel's future brother-in-law. Their team outplayed everyone throughout the district for years.

The formal education of most students was marked by a graduation ceremony at which a city official spoke and presented each student with a small monetary gift. The most capable children were able to attend secondary schools located in larger towns if their family could afford it. After the fifth grade, Fidel's sister Magdalena attended a Catholic girl's school taught by nuns in the town of Perjamosch, some 30 kilometers away. Then Fidel's brother Hans left for a year of agricultural study in the city of Arad. When Fidel's turn came, he told his mother that if he went away to school, she'd need to provide him a cow so he'd get enough milk. And he warned her that he wouldn't be coming home very often. He said it in jest, but it conveyed to his mother that he had no interest in further education or in leaving Orzydorf. He loved his life there and his ambition was to become one of the most successful farmers in town.

Fidel developed a passion for cards in his youth and became quite skilled. Card playing apparently ran in the family. It was said that Fidel's maternal grandfather liked to play at a local gasthaus and seldom lost money. However, he also never drank alcohol while playing. As a teen, Fidel spent considerable time playing during the farming slack season. Like all good players, he developed a keen ability to gauge odds. Applying this skill to farming also allowed him to succeed in that endeavor. In the next chapter of his life, his practical awareness of probabilities would prove even more valuable because on the battlefield soldiers risked much more than pride or money. However, one memorable day late in his teen years, Fidel learned that probabilities could not help with every problem. Following an evening session of cards and beer with a friend in an inn, Fidel left a short time after his friend did, walked home, and went to bed. Around 11 p.m., barely an hour after he'd fallen asleep, the village police pounded on his door and rousted him out of bed. Orzydorf's police force consisted of a chief and three subordinates. The village was 99 percent ethnic German, yet the Romanian government required the village to hire a Romanian police force. All four of the men were crude thugs despised by the locals.

"Why did you do it?" were the first words Fidel heard when he answered the door. Fidel had no idea what they were talking about and insisted he hadn't done anything as the questioning went on. At length the men hauled him to the police station where the interrogation became rougher. Eventually his questioners revealed what he was accused of. Earlier in the evening near the tavern door, the police chief was mugged by someone hiding in the shadows. The perpetrator whacked the chief on the head, then disappeared. When the chief revived, he discovered the assailant had taken his pistol. Since this occurred near the tavern, the chief sent his underlings into the establishment to learn who'd left around the time of the incident. Fidel's name had come up.

The interrogation continued and Fidel kept insisting that he knew nothing. After a couple hours it became apparent that the police weren't going to give up. Fidel, fearing the chief needed someone to blame, realized

Left: Fidel in the family hof. The main entrance of his house is behind him. *Right:* Fidel posing in his Sunday best on the porch of his home.

he had to clear himself before this could happen. So he asked the police to check with his friend, who'd left about the same time. He might have seen something that could help identify the perpetrator. Fidel hoped that was enough to get him released, but instead, the police locked him inside a holding room. Everything remained quiet until about 4 a.m., when he heard his friend being questioned. The friend also denied seeing or hearing anything, but was eventually also tossed into the holding room. As soon as the two were alone, the friend confessed that he'd hidden in a doorway half a block from the tavern upon spotting the obnoxious drunk police chief stumbling down the street. To embarrass the hated cop, he'd jumped from the shadows on impulse, grabbed the chief's flashlight, and whacked him with it. After the policeman dropped to the ground, the friend grabbed the man's gun and rushed home.

About 6:30 in the morning, the chief, who had by then slept off the worst of his intoxication, came in and questioned the boys himself. They both stuck to their story and denied any involvement. The man now realized that he had more to lose than gain if the embarrassing story went any further, so he released both suspects with a stern warning that they'd better forget what happened or else!

By 1942, Fidel had less time for card games and carousing with friends. He was 20 years old, had taken on a considerable amount of farmland, and had acquired a serious girlfriend. Much of his free time was spent with that young woman, and they'd begun to discuss marriage. All in all, it was a good life and Fidel couldn't imagine living anywhere else. He had no regrets about passing up further schooling, for he had farming in his blood and it was the only thing he wanted to do. At times that occupation required long hours and heavy labor, but in compensation the work was largely seasonal and left plenty of time to enjoy the many three-day local festivals, celebrations, and holidays.

---

1. Erika Vass, "Radna: The Holy Shrine of the Multinational Banat Region," *Journal of Global Catholicism* 4, no. 2 (2020), https://crossworks.holycross.edu/jgc/vol4/iss2/5/.
2. "History: Maria Radna, the Most Significant Place of Pilgrimage in South-Eastern Europe," Basilica Maria Radna, 2017, https://www.mariaradna.com/en/history.
3. Gertrude Adam and Anton Peter Petri, *Heimatbuch der deutschen Gemeinde Orczydorf im Banat* (Marquartstein: Breit, 1983), 188.

9 Fidel the Farmer

The traditional unit of land measurement in the German-speaking parts of the Austrian Empire was the *Joch*, about 0.6 hectares (1.4 acres). *Joch*, which comes from the German word for yoke, was a practically derived measurement representing the area that could be plowed by a yoke of oxen in one day. At the time of Orzydorf's settlement, farmers received either a 36-*Joch* whole *Ansässigkeit* (settler allocation) or a half *Ansässigkeit*. Locally, the terms were more commonly known as *Ganzegrund* (whole ground) and *Halbgrund* (half ground). The Austrian government had used these standardized land allotments for settlers since the first Banat settlement wave of 1722. The government deemed these allotments adequate for a family's self-sufficiency and included several categories of land, as listed below. Farmers were typically assigned a *Ganzegrund*, while shopkeepers and tradesmen were allotted a *Halbgrund*. The amount of land in the latter's package was proportionately greater than half because everyone's allotment needed to include a vineyard, a garden plot, and livestock pastureland. Need was also a factor in determining the size of an allotment. Understandably, large families required more land than small families or single men.

Ansässigkeit or Ganzegrund (settler allocation)	Joch
Ackerfeld (cropland)	24
Wiesen (grassland)	6
Hutweide (community pasture)	3
Haus und Garten (house and garden)	1
Zusammen (total)	34 (19.6 hectares or 48.4 acres)

Land allotted to famers.

Halbe Ansässigkeit or Halbgrund (half-sized settler allocation)	Joch
Ackerfeld (cropland)	12
Wiesen (grassland)	4
Hutweide (community pasture)	2
Haus und Garten (house and garden)	1
Zusammen (total)	19 (10.9 hectares or 26.9 acres)

Land allotted to tradesmen and merchants.[1]

Disbursement of fields among various locales helped equalize soil quality and decrease the chance that localized hail or floodwater could wipe out a settler's entire crop. Proximity of fields to the village was luck of the draw. Distant fields were less desirable because farmers with these fields had to rise earlier to finish their morning chores and reach their land by daybreak, the usual start time for field work. The two standard land packages the Austrian government allotted to settlers in the Banat region are listed above as described in the Adam and Petri book *Heimatbuch der deutschen Gemeinde Orczydorf im Banat*. The *Hutweide* allotment was considered part of the common meadowland laid aside for grazing the community's livestock.

Few of the new settlers had owned land or tilled enough ground to prosper where they'd come from, and they understood that if their farms were to remain viable for succeeding generations, they had to contain an adequate amount of land. As a result, many of the Donauschwaben communities adopted an inheritance system known as *Anerberech* (entitlement) whereby the landholding was maintained through the firstborn male. This preserved the size of the farm, but forced younger boys to either enter other professions or become landless laborers. Orzydorf adopted a more equitable inheritance system that divvied the land up among all siblings, even daughters. This allowed women to bring an important asset to a marriage. Each child received their portion when they married, which provided new families a means of support from the start.

Fidel said parents retired as early as age 45 or 50, when their last child married. This practice benefitted not only the offspring, but the parents too, since the latter were usually still healthy enough to enjoy retirement. If there was not already a second house in the hof for the parents, one was usually built on the opposite side of the compound. For their support, the retired couple received an annual agreed-upon allotment of the land's production from their children. Parents commonly retained the vineyard plot and the garden next to the house. Their grain allotment might be a ton of wheat and enough corn for fattening a hog to 500 or 600 lbs. The retired farmer pitched in occasionally when extra labor was needed, but still had time to socialize, play cards, and smoke a pipe. Whether the wife, who cooked all the meals and took care of the house, enjoyed retirement to the same degree is not known.

Fortunately, toward the close of the 19th century when the local population grew to the extent that the offspring of some families were no longer able to make a living from ever-smaller plots divided among heirs, America's industries were booming. The appetite for industrial workers was so ravenous that labor recruiters ranged far and wide. These agents were particularly drawn to places with a strong work ethic—places such as the Banat. So a considerable number of Germans left for America.

Fidel's family possessed enough land to allow all three siblings to remain. A Ganzegrund had come into the marriage from Johann and a Halbgrund from Magdalena. Fidel and his brother split the Ganzegrund, which was sited in two different locations. When their sister married, she inherited the Halbgrund that came from her mother. It was situated in three different places. Fidel's Halbgrund was all in one contiguous parcel, but because it was over five kilometers from his family farmstead, it took considerable time to reach. Until the war interceded, he planned to acquire land closer to Orzydorf. Farmers readily sold or swapped plots when inherited or marriage ground was too fragmented, widely separated, or distant to be economically farmed.

Farmers who owned considerable grazing land sometimes built a hut for a worker in a pasture, Fidel said. At the time Fidel began farming, these workers were largely Romanians or Hungarians, as were most day laborers. Germans had done this work until the depression era when cheaper labor moved in and priced them out. The richer farmers, who might own several farm-sized grazing properties, needed herders because fields were unfenced. One of Fidel's cousins owned four such farms.

Because the Banat, with its rich soil, had become a breadbasket for the rest of Europe, the Great Depression that began in 1929 affected the Banat for just a short time. By 1931 Germany's industrial production had increased sufficiently that it could offer a ready market for the Banat's surplus. The market for Banat grain continued to improve after Hitler came to power. Wheat was the principal grain crop because it grew particularly well in the lowland soil. However, farmers also grew barley, oats, and corn. The grain moved to Vienna by rail, then on to Germany. Some farmers used a portion of their grain to fatten hogs, which found a ready market in

Vienna. Beginning in 1933, some of the more progressive farmers discovered that new crops like lentils and soybeans could also be very profitable.

When Fidel's father died in 1922, the family's land was rented to other farmers through 1934. The limited income from this sustained Magdalena and the children until Fidel's older brother Hans began farming in 1935. He was 15 then and had just returned from a year of agricultural school. The family had begun to prepare for this the previous year by buying farm machinery. Hans had no farming experience, so he partnered with the husband of his father's sister for a year. Fidel, then 13, worked as his brother's assistant. In the local parlance, Hans became known as the *big farmer* and Fidel the *little farmer*. These terms had a specific meaning that reflected their roles. The big farmer was the boss, and the little farmer the helper. The latter role was normally filled by a hired man, but sometimes by a wife or daughter. When plowing, the helper drove the horses while the big farmer guided the plow. Fidel and Hans had occasional arguments, as teenagers do, but for the most part got along well.

After finishing elementary school at age 14, Fidel worked full time with his brother, but he was still the little farmer. Being older, Hans was always in charge. The situation changed in 1938 when Hans opted to leave home and get his military obligation out of the way. Fidel put the *little farmer* tag behind him, worked hard, and made the most of the opportunity. With some experience under his belt the following season, he rented an additional 53 hectares (128 acres) and become one of the larger crop farmers in Orzydorf. This was too much land for a farmer to cultivate by himself using horses, so he hired a 15-year-old Romanian boy as his little farmer. Fidel recalled paying this boy a salary of 4,000 lei per year. The two of them were the same age and got along well. Since the helper was illiterate, Fidel had to maintain the boy's account book.

To make such a large parcel manageable, Fidel sowed wheat on most of it but also raised some hay and corn. When the latter was about a foot high, Fidel and his helper each drove a horse-drawn cultivator along the rows to plow out weeds. To keep the fields weed free, he also hired day laborers to hoe out the weeds between the plants.

In the fall Fidel and his helper spent a couple of hours picking corn each morning. They threw the ears into piles and later hauled them to the hof storage crib. As was the local practice, every part of the plant was used. The dried stalks were cut down and fed to the cows. Once the cows chewed the leaves off, the bare stalks were burned in stoves as fuel along with the cobs that became available during the winter as the family shelled the ears on the floor of a large outbuilding room.

Out in the field after the harvest, it was the practice to hire Orzydorf's poor to pull up the root stumps and knock the dirt off them. The workers then gathered the stumps for stove fuel because wood was expensive in the largely unforested Banat. They collected dry cow pies for fuel at the same time. These practices benefitted both the needy and the farmers.

During the growing season Fidel and his helper reached the fields about 5 a.m. and spent the entire day there. After a couple hours of work, they dug into the basket of food they'd brought along. Breakfast normally consisted of ham and bread. Lunch was bread, cheese, and vegetables. Often, the basket also contained a bottle of homemade slivovitz for sipping throughout the afternoon. Such Damson plum brandy was popular throughout Central and Eastern Europe.

Fidel hired day laborers with scythes to mow hay during his first two years of farming. These men were mainly tobacco farmers with tiny plots of land. The mowing was usually finished before 9 a.m., and everyone was back home before the day's heat set in. The men returned the following day and turned the hay over with rakes to allow it to dry better. On day three the same men helped fork the fragrant hay onto wagons and haul it to the hof. In 1939 Fidel bought a horse-drawn sickle mower to make the mowing more efficient.

The summer grain harvest was the dirtiest and most labor-intensive operation. Today, a combine can make short work of many acres in a day because the machine cuts and threshes the grain in one pass. But in the early part of the 20th century the process was quite different. First, the grain had to be cut. Fidel's new horse-drawn mower sped up that process by eliminating hand-cutting with scythes. The cut stalks were then gathered with large rakes, tied into sheaves, and piled high onto large wagons to be hauled to the farmer's village hof for threshing. There, the sheaves were fed into the large stationary threshing machine to beat the grain from the plant stalks and remove the chaff.

Farmsteads were the most practical and efficient place to separate the grain because that was where the labor necessary to operate the large threshing machines was most readily available—and where the grain, straw, and chaff needed to end up. The harvesting occurred in July, but since most farmers couldn't afford their own thresher, they often had to wait weeks until a machine became available. The 11 threshing machines that operated in Orzydorf at that time were busy for six to eight weeks during the harvest season, providing the machine owners most of their annual income.

Depending on the thresher model, the work crew consisted of either 20 or 24 men and four women. In Orzydorf the tobacco farmers, whose own farming demands were slack at this time of year, made up the bulk of the crews. Crews were divided into two teams who in alternating short, but strenuous, shifts kept the machines running. One team rested while the other worked.

The four women likewise worked in two teams. Wives commonly helped their husband in various farm tasks requiring two people. In threshing, one of their jobs was to collect the chaff. This chaff, along with a little water, was added to grain as it was run through a grinder to make livestock feed. Sometimes beets or squash were added as supplement. The grinder was powered by a horse turning a wheel as it walked in a circle.

Threshing-crew wages were paid in grain. The job site had a scale available to weigh out the crew's share of wheat, oats, and barley, which was sacked and set aside after each job. These allotments went into storage until the end of the harvest season, at which time each member of the crew received their percentage. As with corn, every part of the plant was used. Most straw went for livestock bedding, but some was used as a binder to strengthen adobe bricks, the main construction material in the village. These bricks needed to be durable because buildings here employed heavy, thick walls to provide good insulation.

Fidel explained that corn, generally known as maize in the Banat, grew throughout the summer and was harvested in the fall. The main growing months of July and August were typically dry, but the plants still produced large ears because the soil held moisture well. However, the limited rainfall did prevent farmers from planting the crop as densely as in the American Midwest. On rented land, a farmer typically plowed the ground and planted the corn himself, then hired laborers to weed it with horse-drawn cultivators and large manual hoes. Hired labor also often picked the corn when ripe. At harvest time the crop was divvied into thirds and split between the land owner, the farmer, and the field crew. Farmers with their own land typically had a similar arrangement with laborers, but kept two-thirds of the crop. This practice provided a living for some of the landless and poor members of the community and at the same time made the lives of farmers easier.

In 1939 Fidel learned that his uncle with the threshing business and communist son planned to buy a tractor to replace the steam engine powering his thresher. Fidel, now 17 and farming a great deal of land, saw that the future of farming lay in mechanization and desired a tractor. He couldn't afford one himself but convinced his uncle that splitting the cost and sharing the machine made economic sense. The uncle used it for only two months during the threshing season, which left it available to Fidel the rest of the year. Since Fidel's machinery was all designed to be drawn by horses, the tractor initially proved practical only for his biggest and toughest job, plowing, once he bought a new plow.

The partners bought a new 55-horsepower German-made Lanz Bulldog tractor from a large Timișoara implement dealer who sold German farm equipment. The horizontal one-cylinder hot-bulb engine was crude but easily maintained and burned low-grade fuels like diesel.[2] Fidel said to start this tractor the operator first heated the engine head with a blowtorch that attached to the bulb-shaped cylinder head protruding from the front of the tractor. Then the driver removed the detachable steering wheel, connected it to the flywheel shaft at the side of the tractor, and spun it in a quick motion until the engine caught. Diesel fuel was unavailable in Orzydorf, so Fidel periodically drove to Timișoara with a horse-drawn wagon and brought back four 55-gallon drums at a time.

Orzydorf had just two other tractors at that time, both of which were used only to power threshing machines. This made 17-year-old Fidel the

Left: Fidel posing next to a straw pile produced by his uncle's threshing machine during the summer wheat harvest. *Right:* The Lanz Bulldog tractor Fidel co-owned with his uncle. The drive belt on the large flywheel powered the threshing machine, which is just beyond the right edge of the photo.

first local farmer to use a heavy tractor for field work. The stock tractor came with spiked steel wheels for maximum traction, but since such wheels tore up roads, the co-owners had special rims built so they could drive the machine in town. With his tractor, Fidel could plow 25 to 30 acres per day by himself—much more than was possible for two men working a team of horses. And he came home much less tired than when he'd manhandled a plow all day. I can only guess that neighboring farmers were impressed, if not downright envious.

In the early 1920s a couple of farmers had bought small Fordson tractors manufactured by Ford Motor Company in England, but these machines were no longer used in the 1930s. They hadn't held up well and replacement parts were unavailable. It was the same for autos. There'd been several in town in the 1920s—mainly Fords and Chevrolets, Fidel thought—but they were no longer running either.

Fidel recalled that 1939 and 1940 were profitable years for Banat farmers because the crops were good and grain prices high. Fidel's uncle invested in a second threshing machine and Fidel earned extra money hauling the grain to the railroad terminal. Orzydorf's farmers now produced enough grain to support three grain buyers. The prosperity allowed Banat farmers to buy better machinery. Much of the improvement in quality and availability was the result of a trade deal Romania struck with Hitler's Germany. Consumption in industrial Germany was up and the resulting grain demand led to bartering grain for farm machinery. Machinery such as horse-drawn mowers and binders proved great labor savers and made farmers much more efficient.

At the time, Fidel wished this efficiency extended to hauling manure out of livestock stalls. Removal by pitchfork was hard, tedious work, particularly when snow covered the ground and heavy sleighs were needed to haul it away. Forking out the packed manure, taking it out to a field, and

Left: A teenaged Fidel (on the right), with two friends. The trio was probably about to head to the weekly Sunday afternoon dance at a local gasthaus. *Right:* Winter celebration at the home of one of Fidel's female classmates. By village tradition, groups of older boys and young men took to horse and sleigh after the first snowfall and visited the homes of all the girls and young women they knew. To the accompaniment of accordions, they serenaded their female acquaintances at each stop and were rewarded with hot spiced wine. The photo does not show Fidel because he was the photographer. Fidel sadly noted that many of these boys died in the war.

unloading it into piles required three such sleighs and consumed three or four days. The whole process had to be repeated at the end of winter. Then, before the other field work could begin in the spring, the manure piles needed to be spread about in the field.

Sleighs were much better used for socializing during winter holidays. When the first snow fell, Fidel and his friends hitched horses to light passenger sleighs and spent the day visiting the homes of all the girls they knew. Each sleigh carried an accordion player to accompany the boys' singing. Their endeavors were aided by the hot spiced wine that was served at each girl's house. Needless to say, by the end of the day the boys were stewed. A white Christmas was not a given, but when one came, the magical setting put everyone in a celebratory mood. Snow or no snow, the holiday celebrating lasted three days and only work that was absolutely necessary got done. Certainly, no manure hauling.

---

1. Gertrude Adam and Anton Peter Petri, *Heimatbuch der deutschen Gemeinde Orczydorf im Banat* (Marquartstein: Breit, 1983).
2. Sam Moore, "Remembering the Lanz Bulldog Tractor," Farm Collector: Dedicated to the Preservation of Vintage Farm Equipment, 2016, https://www.farmcollector.com/tractors/lanz-bulldog-zmlz16sepzhur/.

10 Bad Luck Finds Hans

In the spring of 1938, 18-year-old Hans enlisted in the Romanian Army. He wasn't obligated to serve until age 21, but Hans and his sweetheart were eager to begin a future together, and in Orzydorf it was customary for men to put off marriage until their military duty was behind them. The tradition was grounded in history and recent experience. World War I and the brief Hungarian-Romanian War that followed in 1919 lay only two decades in the past. Memories of the 75 men who hadn't returned from those conflicts were still fresh. Hans decided it was a good time to get his service obligation behind him because he didn't see a war on the horizon. The marriage would allow him to farm on his own, since it would combine his land inheritance with his bride's, and the couple would receive a house from her family.

Hans arranged to complete Romania's nine-month military active service obligation in two installments. His basic training would take place over three months in the spring, then after a summer leave to help with the harvest, he'd complete his obligation with six months of field training and maneuvers. His fiancée was a distantly related 17-year-old girl named Magdalena. Fidel knew his future sister-in-law well for she'd been his classmate throughout their school days. As would be the case with Fidel's sister, she was another Leni who wouldn't have to adopt a new surname when she married because hers too was already Eipert.

Fidel recalled that Hans bought a fine riding horse before he reported for duty because horses still played a large role in the Romanian Army. Bringing his own mount was meant to make his life easier and keep him out of the dreaded infantry. Like most other men who could afford to do so, he also purchased a better-quality uniform more comfortable than the scratchy, standard army-issue version. Michael Pruett, a friend from my infantry days in Vietnam and the author of *Field Uniforms of German Army*

Panzer Forces in WW II and other books, examined a photo of Hans in dress uniform. From Hans' cavalry saber, the special cavalryman buttons affixed to his shoulder straps and boots, and his helmet—an Adrian Model 1915 surplus helmet that Romania purchased in quantity from France—he determined Hans had served in an elite unit of cavalry.[1]

Serving in the Romanian Army was not a pleasant experience for men in the lower ranks. In the 1930s and through World War II, the antiquated

Hans Eipert, Fidel's older brother, attired in his Romanian Army cavalryman's uniform.

service still maintained a class system that provided officers special privileges, better food, and military servants. So it should not be surprising that the Romanian military also still depended heavily on horses. But in all fairness, horses were also indispensable in nearly every other national military of the day, including the mobile Germany army. The Romanian Army consisted of 18 field divisions and several frontier and guard divisions. Two of the field units were cavalry divisions. Aside from them, the regular infantry divisions also maintained their own cavalry companies. Hans might have served in either type division.

Hans had the misfortune to don the brown Romanian uniform just before a border dispute with Hungary flared up. This quarrel first erupted in 1919 and never completely went away. The new tension followed on the heels of Adolf Hitler remilitarizing the Rhineland along the French border and annexing Austria. Both events occurred in early March 1938 when Hitler used the inequity imposed by the Treaty of Versailles to justify his actions. Hungary's government saw this as an opportunity to harness the growing fear of Hitler to redress its own perceived territorial inequities that had stripped it of the Banat and Transylvania in the Treaty of Trianon at Versailles. Hungary's sudden alliance with Germany aroused fears in Romania's government that Hungary would once again try to move the border eastward by force, as it tried to do after the close of World War I.

Those developments turned Hans's three-month obligation into an indeterminate term of service. Instead of being home to help with the harvest, he was manning a station on the Hungarian border some 30 kilometers from Orzydorf. Fidel visited Hans at his post "a time or two" via bicycle and filled his brother in on what was happening at home and in Hans's fields. Hans was still in uniform the following year on September 1, 1939, when Germany tested out its new blitzkrieg (lightning war) tactics on Poland and sparked World War II. Hans feared that he'd be in uniform for a long time after Romania was drawn into Hitler's orbit and hatched its own expansion plan to regain territory the Soviets had recently taken from Romania. So Hans decided to marry Leni as soon as he got a leave, breaking with the tradition of waiting until his military service was finished. That opportunity didn't come until he'd completed five years of service in 1943.

---

1. Michael Pruett, "Romanian Cavalry" (Email, June 6, 2016).

11 Romania and WW II

After World War I, when the victors stripped Hungary of two-thirds of its territory, millions of ethnic Hungarians (Magyars) and their property were consigned to other countries. Hungary refused to forget the injustice and its huge economic loss. Miklos Horthy, Hungary's dictatorial

Romanian territorial losses of 1940. Romania ceded territory in its northeast (upper right white area) to the USSR after Stalin imposed a 24-hour ultimatum. Romania suffered two further losses after aligning itself with Germany for defensive purposes. To settle a longstanding border dispute between his allies, Hitler ordered Romania to give up most of Transylvania (speckled area) to Hungary and to relinquish Dobruja (white area at bottom of map) to Bulgaria. Romania regained much of Transylvania from Hungary after World War II, but the other losses were permanent.

leader, recognized the rising fear of Hitler and Mussolini by the rest of Europe and contrived to regain the lost territory by aligning himself with the two feared fascist governments.[1]

With Germany and Italy acting as intermediaries, Horthy forced Romania to cede northern Transylvania back to Hungary but allowed Romania to keep southern Transylvania, the region in which Orzydorf lay. The term Transylvania sometimes includes the Romanian part of Banat. Around the same time the tyrannical leader of the Soviet Union, Joseph Stalin, stripped Bessarabia and northern Bukovina from northeastern Romania through a coercive treaty. More bad news for Romania followed. Under German pressure, Romania had to cede back to Bulgaria the southern Dobruja border region, which was largely populated by Romanians and had been taken militarily in a 1913 border war. The Romanian government's popularity plummeted because of the losses. Following a short period of political intrigue and fascist infighting, army general Ion Antonescu subdued his rivals and assumed power in January 1941.

By the time Hitler launched Operation Barbarossa and invaded the Soviet Union on June 22, 1941, Antonescu had allied his country with Germany to curry Hitler's favor and for help in retaking Bessarabia and northern Bukovina militarily. However, joining the German coalition came with the obligation for Romania to fight alongside Germany in Russia. Because of the new alliance with Hitler, the Hungarian border dispute disappeared and freed up Hans's cavalry unit in time to join the invasion of the Soviet Union. Each German ally was assigned a section of the attack front and logically enough, the Romanian Army was tasked with attacking eastward along the southernmost section of the front. In short order, Hans found himself in combat against Romania's huge neighbor to the east.

Hans wrote to his family about once a month and kept everyone abreast of his location and how the fighting was going. Sharing this information was possible because unlike most other militaries, Romania's was lax in censoring the mail of its soldiers. Hans even mentioned the towns that had been captured or lost and how far Romanian forces had advanced or retreated. Unfortunately, Fidel couldn't recall any specifics from the letters.

Like the Germans, the Romanians advanced rapidly at first, but unlike the more mechanized and mobile German military, the poorly equipped and trained Romanian Army moved largely on foot, horseback, and farm wagons as it crossed Ukraine and Bessarabia. Romania's front-line assault utilized 13 infantry divisions, one armored division, and two cavalry divisions. These units comprised their 3rd and 4th Armies. Romania also deployed six divisions south to the Caucasus and two to Crimea. After several months of fighting, followed by an eight-week siege, Romanian units and a large force of Germans captured the Black Sea port city of Odesa, to the west of the Crimean Peninsula. The Romanian Army had absorbed 130,000 casualties by then. This great loss, along with a lack of competent officers to replace those killed, hobbled the Romanian Army for the rest of the war.

During the severe winter of 1941–1942, when temperatures fell far below freezing along much of the front, the inadequately equipped Romanians were desperate for reinforcements to hold their lines. The relief troops were pulled from the 26 divisions assigned to occupation and security duties in the captured territories. Not only were these divisions more poorly staffed than the front-line divisions, they were also less well-equipped and trained.[2] In July 1942, Romanian formations, assisting the German 11th Army, helped capture Russia's major Black Sea naval port of Sevastopol. The final dramatic moment came when the Russians blew up a large ammo dump and mercilessly killed thousands of their own wounded soldiers assembled there. The Romanians were subsequently ordered to advance eastward to the Don River region.[3]

---

1. Denis Sinor, *History of Hungary* (N.Y.: Praeger, 1976), 289.
2. Kretaner, "Romanian Armed Forces 1942," WW3-Weapons.com: the World Wars, accessed May 27, 2016, http://ww2-weapons.com/romanian-armed-forces-1942/.
3. Gottlob Herbert Bidermann, Derek S. Zumbro, and Dennis E. Showalter, *In Deadly Combat: A German Soldier's Memoir of the Eastern Front* (Lawrence, KS: University Press of Kansas, 2000), 141.

12 The Red Army

The Romanians were spared even worse casualties because the Soviet Union's Red Army was also in a deplorable state when Germany invaded Russia. The Soviet generals, and Stalin in particular, were largely to blame for their army's enormous casualties, retreats, and mass desertions during this invasion. Their inept leadership and poor decision making had thoroughly demoralized ordinary soldiers and officers alike in the years prior to the war. The greatest Soviet liability was its lack of a competent and cohesive officer corps despite two decades of effort spent trying to address the deficiency. The army was so beset with problems that Hitler's Barbarossa invasion in 1941 severely reduced its numbers. By concentrating his poorly led army along the USSR's western border, Stalin placed great numbers of soldiers and equipment within reach of the efficient and mobile German Wehrmacht—the Heer (army), Luftwaffe (air force) and Kriegsmarine (navy). The Wehrmacht subsequently killed or captured enormous numbers of Russian soldiers.

One common misconception is that the leadership vacuum stemmed from the massive and paranoic bloody purge of both real and imagined Stalin rivals in the 1930s by the NKVD (People's Commissariat for Internal Affairs). At least in the military, this enemies-of-the-people house-cleaning operation was much smaller than commonly believed. The real driver behind the officer problem was the rapid expansion of the officer corps. Stalin and his henchmen wanted youthful officers that came from the working poor and peasant classes, but these candidates had little education and lacked military experience. The officer schools too often couldn't properly train these soldiers because the instructors themselves had little experience in the jobs they were teaching. Officer candidates were also routinely given menial work assignments that took them away from the classroom.[1] [2]

In 1932 the Revolution Military Council responded to the famine resulting from Stalin's collectivization program by ordering all divisions to establish supplementary farms to feed themselves. The standard for each division was 400 cows, 3,200 hogs, 20,000 rabbits and 1,000 hectares (2471 acres) of crop land on which to grow wheat, rye, and fruit. Operating these farms interfered with the proper training of new officers.[3]

By 1939 the army was in such a critical state that Stalin signed a nonaggression treaty (Molotov-Ribbentrop Pact) with Hitler to give himself time to fix and rebuild his forces. He embarked on a rapid expansion and massively increased the army's armor force to make it more mobile. This expansion aggravated the situation because the noncommissioned officer (NCO) schools were also of poor quality, and the training was often minimal. The situation put young men into command positions they were not ready for. Fresh NCOs and officers were expected to lead companies when they lacked experience at the platoon level. Officers were promoted to lead battalions, regiments, and divisions when they had little or no experience in company level tactics and leadership, leaving companies and battalions unable to work together effectively. The Red Army also had no idea of how to best use its new armor units. The many new divisions formed at this time were commonly at half strength. Low pay, poor housing, substandard medical care, and mistreatment of men by officers compounded the problems.[4]

Nevertheless, the army's sheer immensity, with its huge number of artillery guns, tanks, troop carriers, and aircraft, made it look formidable. After Stalin signed the nonaggression pact, he positioned over 150 divisions on Russia's western border, the bulk of them opposite Germany and Romania. These troops and vast quantities of arms and supplies were in place by the beginning of 1941. Meanwhile, Stalin also worked furiously to build 251 new air bases, four-fifths of them proximal to his northwestern border and in alignment with the German homeland to the west.

Stalin had reason to be concerned about Hitler, for by May 1941 the Nazis were bombing England and had taken control of nearly all of Europe, either through conquest or by alliance. Hitler's control extended from the North Sea to the Mediterranean Sea and from the Atlantic to the very borders of the Soviet Union. Aside from Germany's declared enemy, Britain, only the neutral countries of Switzerland, Sweden, Spain, Portugal, Ireland, and Turkey remained outside of Hitler's sphere.

Since the war's end, the prevailing historical view in Europe and America has been that on June 22, 1941, Hitler treacherously broke his pact with Stalin and launched his unprovoked Barbarossa surprise attack against an unprepared Soviet Union. However, in recent years, this view has come to be challenged. The change is not about bestowing any righteousness on Hitler. Rather, it is about new evidence indicating the real driver of the Eastern Front conflict was Stalin, a man no more trustworthy than Hitler. Both Hitler and his top commanders had insisted that they invaded Russia in 1941 to preempt the Red Army's own mobilization against Western Europe. The new evidence comes from Russian sources and suggests that a Russian attack on Western Europe was only weeks or months away. The details of the controversy are far too involved to discuss here, but make compelling reading.[5] [6]

The German attack proved devastating. Stalin responded to his opening losses by conscripting an additional two million men. When the staggering losses continued in the opening months of the German campaign, Stalin called for up to five million replacements by the end of 1941. This incredible number of new recruits was one-and-a-half times the size of the entire Soviet military when the war began. To meet such a target, the Red Army encouraged women to enlist, and over 800,000 served over the course of the war. Many were used as nurses and orderlies, but women also fought as riflemen in infantry companies. Some became the fiercest of Soviet snipers, who like their male counterparts kept a kill tally to earn rewards.[7] A sons-of-the-regiment practice also boosted the army's numbers. This despicable custom allowed field companies to adopt orphan boys. Companies sometimes adopted girls or women too. The adoptees shared the danger, the poor conditions, and the fighting.[8]

---

1. Roger R. Reese, *Stalin's Reluctant Soldiers: A Social History of the Red Army, 1925-1941* (Lawrence: University Press of Kansas, 1996), 25, 132.
2. Roger R. Reese, *Soviet Military Experience: A History of the Soviet Army, 1917-1991* (New York: Routledge, London, 2000), 77.
3. Reese, *Stalin's Reluctant Soldiers*, 49.
4. Reese, *Soviet Military Experience*, 77, 93.
5. Daniel Michaels, "New Evidence on the 1941 'Barbarossa' Attack: Why Hitler Attacked Soviet Russia When He Did (Review)," *The Journal of Historical Review* 18, no. 3 (1999), http://www.ihr.org/jhr/v18/v18n3p40_Michaels.html.
6. Laurent Guyénot, "Barbarossa: Suvorov's Revisionism Goes Mainstream," The Unz Review, May 8, 2021, https://www.unz.com/article/barbarossa-suvorovs-revisionism-goes-mainstream/.
7. Reese, *Soviet Military Experience*, 108.
8. Reese, *Soviet Military Experience*, 110.

13 Fidel Gets a Notice

When Fidel turned 17 in 1939, he received official notification of his obligation to attend Romanian military instruction on Saturdays throughout most of the year and on Sundays during the summer. All young men were now required to complete three years of preliminary training before they began their actual military service at age 21. Fidel, having already seen what happened to Hans and others, wanted nothing to do with the military and ignored the notices. He said, "I never went. Not once!"

Four years later the war was at its apex, and the Romanian Army had been all but destroyed by disasters on the Eastern Front while fighting alongside the German Army. The greatest loss had occurred at Stalingrad where the overstretched Romanian 3rd and 4th Armies were assigned the critical fronts north and south of the city as the Germans concentrated on taking the city itself. By late fall the German generals foresaw defeat, yet Hitler ignored their advice to allow the German 6th Army to break out. The end result was the bloodiest battle in human history. The Germans called their hopeless static position *der Kessel* (the cauldron) and the style of fighting there, *Rattenkrieg* (rat war).[1]

The Soviets employed a dual flanking maneuver to trap the Germans. This November 1942 counter-offensive by vastly superior Soviet groups shredded the Romanian forces north and south of Stalingrad. By the time the surviving German forces in the city surrendered at the end of January 1943, the Romanian Army had lost nearly half of its active field force. The Romanian command realized that the country could no longer afford an induction age of 21, so on April 1, 1943—three months before Fidel turned 21—he and thousands of other young men received a call-up notice. The situation for the Romanian Army was so dire that even 2,000 convicts serving sentences for murder, rape, and looting were formed into a unit. Since so many of these criminals ran at the first contact with the enemy, the unit had to be disbanded.

Military sign in German, pointing the way to Kommandantur Stalingrad Mitte (Stalingrad Command Central). Fidel's cousin Hans Rabong, a Romanian soldier, is standing next to the sign on the far right

Relations between the soldiers of Romania and Germany were never good, and brawls were frequent. Still, the common German soldier had empathy for Romania's enlisted men. Whenever German units came in contact with the Romanian Army, the Germans were shocked to see Romanian officers treat their men like serfs and show little interest in their welfare. One German soldier noted that the Romanian field cooks supplied three different meals, one for officers, one for NCOs, and one for enlisted men. The latter's portions were puny and inadequate.[2]

The Soviets logged the recovery of 250,000 German and Romanian corpses in and around Stalingrad. Estimates of total Axis (German coalition) casualties in that theater—German, Italian, Romanian, and Hungarian—came to over 800,000. The victorious Red Army sustained about 1,100,000 casualties at Stalingrad, not including approximately 40,000 dead civilians.[3] The Romanian Army never recovered from the Stalingrad mauling, and from then on could only engage in defensive battles as the Soviets pushed them back to the Romanian border. Of the 91,000 Germans still alive to surrender to the Russians, only 5,000–6,000 ever returned home. The rest all died in Soviet labor camps where they were starved and worked to death. The Germans didn't work their Soviet POWs to death; they merely starved them.

Fidel's induction notice was not a surprise for he'd learned it was coming the previous autumn. Skipping the mandated three years of training sessions automatically condemned him to three years of infantry duty, which was double the normal service period of 18 months. By this time Fidel and his girlfriend were considering marriage, so a longer service period wasn't welcome news. However, the required duty period was probably meaningless because by then all soldiers were in uniform for the duration of the war, and it looked far from over. Hans had already served five years and in all that time had barely gotten to know his wife because he'd had only a few scant weeks of home leave. Given the uncertainty, Fidel wasn't ready to inflict the same on his intended, so he put all thoughts of marriage on hold. Because Fidel knew from friends and relatives already in the army that the military experience wouldn't be pleasant, he took steps to try to make it more comfortable and survivable.

A Romanian inductee named Sandu Aurel described the shoddy training that conscripts could expect, through his own two months of "soldier about left, soldier about right" drill instruction. Night training and other inconvenient exercises were skipped altogether because his platoon commander, a lieutenant, was related to two high-ranking staff officers and could get away with anything. Aurel said that after the war he heard American recruits didn't train for parades. For them it was, "Private John, here's your rifle, now shoot until you hit your target 2–3000 meters away. When you do, you're off to war." For Romanians, it was different.

> Because of the poor quality of the uniform, our superiors weren't allowed to give the order "down" directly, but we still had to do it when they yelled "enemy airplanes." Because of this our uniforms ended up very ugly and torn. Perhaps we should have trained in our underpants. The drill instruction was followed by weapon familiarization and target practice . . . once a week, 5 cartridges per soldier!! The Germans were shooting 100 cartridges daily while we had 5 a week. And some still wondered why a German soldier was 10 times more competent than any of us.
>
> Food was the same throughout the training period – a cup of coffee substitute with a quarter of a bread; lunch and dinner consisted of peeled barley with prunes and beans . . . .
>
> In the barracks we didn't stay too long. From the first night I realized they were full of bed bugs. On 29 July 1943 we took all the beds outside to have them cleaned. You should have seen the ground, it was red because of them. We were saved thanks to an inspection of general Dascalescu, who seeing the atrocious living conditions and the boils on our bodies had us all relocated to a small forest nearby, where we lived in tents until we left for the front.[4]

Few Orzydorf men joined the Romanian Army voluntarily. Four or five men, including Fidel's best friend, Fidel Bischof, wanted no part of the inept Romanian military, so they enlisted in the German Army in the belief that the German Army was more survivable. To sign up, they had to cross into nearby German-occupied Serbia because German enlistment was forbidden within Romania. Happily, Bischof survived the German Army, and Fidel visited him in Germany a time or two decades later. From Bischof's survivors I learned that he was captured by the Americans in North Africa and sent to Utah as a POW. There, he worked as an orchard laborer and fruit picker. Bischof wanted to remain in Utah when the war ended, but America shipped all POWs back home. He retained a hope of returning someday, but life got in the way.

Hitler's invasion of the Soviet Union hadn't ever been popular in Orzydorf, and by 1943 it lost what little support it had had. By then, most of its World War I veterans understood that Germany could no longer win. They knew from experience that things always went terribly wrong in the vast distances of the east.

From Hans and others, Fidel had learned that service was usually more tolerable and survivable as a specialist of some sort than as an infantryman. On the whole, because ethnic Germans were better educated and skilled than most Romanians, many qualified for such jobs—at least in the enlisted ranks. The Romanian-dominated officer corps kept most Germans out. The few Germans who managed to reach officer rank seldom earned promotions beyond a junior rank.

In the autumn of 1942 when Fidel had first learned he'd be inducted, he heard there might still be a way to avoid assignment to the infantry. So he went to his aunt's Romanian husband and asked him to talk to a Romanian Army officer familiar with the ins and outs of the system to see

Left: Fidel's serious expression and the manner in which he holds the broom suggests this photo was taken shortly before he was to report for Romanian Army training. *Right:* Fidel (rear, second from right) poses with fellow students at the Scoala Reg. De Soffeur driving school in Timişoara. He hoped the chauffeur's license he earned there would keep him from infantry duty.

what he could learn. The officer hinted that although men of Fidel's designation were automatically assigned to the infantry, a young man who happened to have a chauffeur's license might land himself a different assignment. So for the next three or four months Fidel commuted to Timișoara twice weekly for driving instruction.

In April, when the new conscripts were asked if anyone had such a license, Fidel raised his hand. He and several others with the qualification were taken aside while everyone else went on to infantry training. Fidel and his small group were assigned to a base at Târgoviște in the eastern part of the country. In the hope of training near his home rather than hours away by train, he talked to a cousin who knew an officer in a position to get those orders changed. Fidel authorized the cousin to offer the officer an Easter lamb and 100 eggs if he arranged for training near Orzydorf.

The gambit worked and Fidel reported to a small training base at Lipova, the pilgrimage town his mother had taken him to as a baby when he'd been bundled up in the runaway horse carriage. Fidel became one of a group of 15 German field-telephone line-maintenance trainees. His biggest headache was the Romanian language, with which he had only a classroom familiarity. However, he picked it up rapidly from those around him. His training regiment consisted of seven infantry companies of 60 men each. Fidel saw little of the base's officers and noted only a small German representation. All of the officers were middle- or upper-class career soldiers.

Fidel's first six weeks at the base were devoted to basic training. Like Romanian inductee Aurel, he was surprised that with a war going on, and going badly at that, the training was largely drill instruction. Very little time was devoted to combat skills. The old World War I rifle issued to him was so rusty that he had to tackle it with sandpaper. When even that didn't make it functional, he asked his sergeant for a better weapon. The specialty training began with week seven and consisted almost entirely of stringing about a kilometer of telephone wire onto poles, testing the line, then tearing it down again. The exercise was repeated over and over. In the German Army such a specialist was referred to as a *Strippenzieher*. Fidel apparently didn't realize at the time that there was hardly a more dangerous job on the battlefield. Artillery explosions, bombs, grenades, armor, and other forms of mayhem routinely severed communication wires, so reestablishing connections required repairmen to scramble out to exposed positions to splice in new wire. During the training period, someone in authority wanted a broken steam engine fixed. Fidel heard about it and was so bored by the wire stringing that he volunteered to fix the machine because he knew a little about steam engines from having worked with them on the farm. His tinkering was successful, and it killed a week of otherwise tedious training.

Fidel encountered a bit of luck by getting a platoon sergeant who came from a village near Orzydorf and also happened to be well disposed toward ethnic Germans. It quickly became obvious that this sergeant was on good terms with a number of Germans on the base, so Fidel and several other Orzydorf trainees began to build their own rapport with him. Soon, they were able to get themselves excused from weekend duties, but of course this involved a bit of glad-handing. The trainees already knew that the guard at the rear gate of the base could be bribed for a couple packs of cigarettes, so they only needed one further arrangement at an inn to get home on weekends. From the rear gate, the trainees made a beeline across the street to the inn where they donned the civilian clothes they'd previously stashed in a basement room. Then they hitchhiked to Orzydorf. Eight to ten of them left nearly every weekend. When the group returned on Sunday night around 11 p.m., they donned their uniforms, slipped the guard a couple more packs of cigarettes, and delivered a ham or hunk of bacon to the sergeant. Fidel never had weekend duties during his entire time at the base, from April to July.

The permanent cadre at this base consisted mainly of specialists who staffed workshops—wood workers, bricklayers, electricians, and mechanics. Fidel, with his knack for making friends, soon came to know some of them and was invited to drop by one of the workshops in the evening. He slipped out of his barracks and arrived to find relaxed men drinking beer and playing cards. To Fidel's surprise, his training sergeant tolerated this absence too. The setup suited Fidel and he became a regular at the gathering. As for his military training, it was mind-numbing but bearable. He knew this easy duty wouldn't last, but couldn't have anticipated what followed due to fast-moving political events and high-level diplomatic machinations.

During his training, Fidel had little exposure to actual field conditions but did come in contact with veterans who'd had their fill of them. After hearing the stories of men who'd been at the front, he came to dread what was to come—rampant corruption, bad leadership, terrible food, and ill treatment. All ethnic Germans knew enlistment in the German military was possible but required fleeing Romania. Few were willing to take this step because it invited punishment upon return.

The German military was equally aware of this problem and understood that many disaffected ethnic Germans could be theirs simply by removing the existing legal barrier to recruitment. Hence, Nazi diplomats and the political wing of the SS decided to test the waters in mid-1940 by asking Romanian leader Ion Antonescu to grant permission for a thousand ethnic

Germans to enlist in the German military. Antonescu acquiesced and arrangements were made to quietly shuffle the new recruits out of Romania by posing them as agricultural workers.[5] Whether these men knew that they were being shunted into the Waffen SS rather than the Wehrmacht is doubtful.

Toward the end of 1940, the SS began to push harder. Its emissaries pressured Antonescu to allow formation of the German Ethnic Group (*Grupul Etnic German [GEG]*), a Nazi-led organization that would represent all Germans in Romania. But the GEG was little more than a vehicle to advance SS recruitment of ethnic Germans. The plan was to have the GEG's early Waffen SS recruits acquire combat experience, then make them the backbone of an active recruiting corps which would draw in ever more young men.[6] [7]

However, Hitler faced a dilemma in implementing this plan. He couldn't afford to upset the Romanian generals by brazenly hijacking men from their own recruiting pool at the very time he needed their cooperation in covering his southern flank when he launched his invasion of the Soviet Union. Hence, he ordered the GEG recruiting drive be temporarily scaled back to a shadow operation. Yet, Germany's success in the quick and successful takeover of Yugoslavia and Greece in the spring of 1941 convinced another thousand Romanian ethnic Germans that it was better to join the winning Germans than wait to be inducted into the Romanian military. These men were again either steered, or drawn, into the Waffen SS.

German military prowess appeared far less impressive by the spring of 1943. By then, Hitler had become desperate enough to demand Romania transfer the bulk of its ethnic German fighting men to his own military. General Antonescu recognized the futility of resisting Hitler and quietly acceded. The general needed his German ally to win the war if Romania was to regain the Romanian territory the Soviet Union had seized before the war began. By supplying the Germans enough men to form two or three more German divisions, he hoped Germany could regain the upper hand against the Soviets. At this point it would cost him little to give up these men since the Romanian Army had already been left nearly impotent.

On its face, the negotiated agreement allowed German males over the age of 17 to voluntarily enlist in the German armed forces instead of the Romanian services. As for men already in a Romanian uniform, they could also voluntarily transfer. Active-duty officers, NCOs, soldiers engaged in combat at the front, and essential military specialists were exempted. Despite the wording, German national service had now become all but mandatory because the agreement permitted the GEG to physically examine all young ethnic German males not yet in uniform and allow those who passed to "volunteer" for the Waffen SS. In actuality, most of these boys had no choice because of the GEG's forceful methods. The SS recruitment chief boasted that "in the Rumanian part of the Banat, 'strong-armed-squads' of the Ethnic Group had 'knocked down the houses' of those who hesitated'." The coercion made it unnecessary to formally order men to join the SS.[8]

The arrangements for this agreement concluded while Fidel was training at the Lipova base. Upon full implementation, the deal would deliver 54,000 ethnic Germans—soldiers from the Romanian Army and new civilian recruits as young as 17—to the Waffen SS. News of the agreement took Fidel and the other German trainees by surprise. The soldiers knew little about the Waffen SS, other than it purportedly being the most elite German service. And they knew even less about its parent SS organization. Only after the war did they, along with the rest of the world, learn how despicable its leaders were.

---

1. David L. Robbins, *War of the Rats* (New York: Bantam Books, 2000), 1.
2. Antony Beevor, *Stalingrad: The Fateful Siege: 1942-1943* (New York: Viking, 1998), 184.
3. Raymond Limbach, "Battle of Stalingrad: World War II," Encyclopedia Britannica, October 2022, http://www.britannica.com/event/Battle-of-Stalingrad.
4. Gabriel Szekely, "Sergeant Sandu Aurel - War Memories," WorldWar2.ro: Romanian Armed Forces in the Second World War, 2, accessed September 6, 2020, http://www.worldwar2.ro/memorii/?article=107.
5. Theodor Schieder, ed., "The Fate of the Germans in Rumania: A Selection and Translation from Dokumentation Der Vertreibung Der Deutschen Aus Ost-Mitteleuropa," in *Documents on the Expulsion of the Germans from Eastern-Central-Europe*, vol. III (Bonn: Federal Ministry for Expellees, Refugees and War Victims, 1961), 55.
6. Schieder, "The Fate of the Germans in Rumania," 130.
7. Florin Abraham, *Romania since the Second World War: A Political, Social and Economic History* (Bloomsbury Publishing, 2016), 88.
8. Schieder, "The Fate of the Germans in Rumania," 58.

14 Rise of the SS

The SS (Schutzstaffel) is undoubtedly the most famous and at the same time, the most infamous Nazi organization. Ironically, it is also one of the least understood. Movie, television, and media portrayals of the SS are usually stereotypical and present a corps of goose-stepping goons or black-uniformed thugs. The reality is something far more complicated. The organization began simply enough as a protection squadron, as the translation of its *Schutzstaffel* name implies. Until after the 1920s, it remained a small paramilitary group that protected Hitler, Nazi speakers, organizers, and events. Thereafter, it grew into a complex organization with vast influence in Germany's political, police, and military spheres. In effect it became a protection squadron for the entire Nazi movement. The entry in the US military's wartime Handbook on German Military Forces states that the SS has:

> extended its influence and power into every conceivable aspect of German national life and has finally acquired a large measure of control over the Army itself. It is more than a state within a state; it is superior to both the Party and the government . . . high-ranking officers . . . occupy controlling positions in most of the central departments of the government, in regional and local administration, in heavy industry, finance, and commerce, and in cultural and charitable activities. Directly or indirectly the SS controls the training of youth in the Hitler Youth organization, the storm troops (SA), and most of the other Party organizations and activities.[1]

Organizationally the SS nearly defies description because it changed continuously. It could be loosely dissected into three functional areas with different but wide-ranging responsibilities. Its administrators sometimes directed more than one department, which blurred the lines among the branches.

The Allgemeine (General) SS comprised the organization's headquarters and directed all SS functions. The various Nazi security services eventually all gravitated to Allgemeine SS under the umbrella of the Reich Main Security Office (RSHS) and included the Sicherheitsdienst (SD) intelligence wing, the Gestapo (secret police), and the Kripo (criminal police). The security services included subdepartments like the paramilitary Einsatzgruppen (Special Mission Groups) that followed the German invasion forces in the East to eradicate Jews, intellectuals, and other "undesirables." The Allgemeine SS also controlled the part-time regional civilian SS formations that mustered monthly.

The Totenkopfverbände (Death's Head Formations) branch of the SS managed the numerous Nazi concentration camps and the camp guard corps. As the camp system expanded, this wing became heavily involved in commercial enterprises that exploited camp labor to manufacture war material and develop weapons. Totenkopf also contracted out camp and POW slave labor to alleviate the severe labor shortage that resulted when the majority of working age men in Germany were mobilized to fight the war.[2]

The Waffen SS (Armed SS) was the third SS branch and the easiest to understand. Some Germans regarded it as Hitler's black angels. In Christianity, angels were supposed to serve as God's messengers to mankind, but Lucifer-led black angels chose good over evil and tempted humans into wrongdoing. That black angel image had been most appropriate during the prewar period when Waffen SS men were all volunteers and wore black uniforms. The nature of the force evolved as Heinrich Himmler turned the once-small Hitler protection detail into a large combat force that fought alongside the regular military services. The SS leadership certainly remained evil incarnate, but all Waffen SS soldiers could no longer be condemned along with them. Many, if not most, were just ordinary soldiers.

After the war, the Allgemeine SS, Totenkopfverbände, and a variety of their departments were charged with war crimes and crimes against humanity. Particularly deserving of these charges were the Einsatzgruppen, the Reich security service, and the Gestapo secret police. The Waffen SS was largely condemned along with them, even though many divisions were never accused of wrongdoing. But it cannot be denied that it had its share of overzealous SS commanders who directed the soldiers under their command to commit war crimes. Particularly deserving condemnation are those divisions formed late in the war from indoctrinated Hitler Youth boys, camp guards, and headquarters staffers who lost their frontline exemptions. Unfortunately, ordinary reservists, police officer candidates, and men from the other service branches were placed in the same units with these ideologues.

Fighting as an ordinary soldier in the Waffen SS cannot be equated with serving the Nazi leadership in the Allgemeine SS, acting as a camp guard, or engaging in mass killing with the Einsatzgruppen. Most Waffen SS men, like soldiers in other services and armies, had a moral compass and acted by it. The International Military Tribunal acknowledged this to some extent during the Nuremberg Trials when it branded the Waffen SS, along with the other SS branches, a criminal organization but exempted the many ethnic Germans who were conscripted or pressured into joining. This cleared about 350,000 of the approximately half-million men from outside Germany who served in the 38 Waffen SS divisions during the war.

Many of the remaining 150,000 unexonerated foreign soldiers acted out of political feelings unrelated to National Socialism. Herbert Maeger was one—an idealistic young Belgian volunteer who joined the SS out of a desire to help contain communism. Maeger eventually came to feel betrayed on the Eastern Front by the leaders in Berlin who used soldiers as if "nothing were more inexhaustible and cheap than human material." Many men like Maeger were originally drawn into the war because they believed battling the Bolsheviks was a just cause and would help save Europe from the Soviet terror regime that had already murdered millions of its own people. Maeger wrote in a memoir that these volunteers, who had to swear loyalty and to fight to the death for Hitler, learned too late that the burden didn't extend the other way.

> The Führer, the Government and the upper echelons of the military failed to reciprocate with the most primitive duty of care towards the fighting troops: thereby they broke faith and committed an unparalleled act of treachery against their soldiers.[3]

The Waffen SS might be thought of as the fourth branch of the German Wehrmacht alongside the Heer, Luftwaffe, and Kriegsmarine, but was unique in that ultimate strategic control always remained in the hands of Hitler and SS Reichsführer Himmler rather than Wehrmacht commanders. The force was a highly skilled combat entity with a number of elite units that distinguished themselves repeatedly in World War II because of the very high physical standards originally set for its recruits, the unique training of its officers and men, and the anticommunist idealism of many of its soldiers. Its elements were often superior to regular German Army units until combat losses claimed too many of its most highly trained and motivated men. Waffen SS performance deteriorated once the ranks began to fill with new, less-fit, and less-dedicated replacements midway through the war.

The SS can't be truly understood without some knowledge of its architect's background. This man's rise is almost as improbable as Hitler's. The 1945 US War Department's *Handbook on German Military Forces* had this to say about Heinrich Himmler:

> The development of SS power is intimately linked to the career of Heinrich Himmler. This seemingly unassuming and quiet-mannered man has obtained one important post after another until today more power is concentrated in his person than in any other man except Hitler. Indeed, his power is much more absolute than that of Hitler, since the latter's actions and decisions are necessarily influenced by various pressure groups within the Party, by consideration of public opinion, and by other outside forces.[4]

When Hitler turned over the leadership of his 280-man palace guard to Himmler in 1929, no one could have predicted how powerful the Schutzstaffel and its head would become. Himmler steadily maneuvered and manipulated himself into command of ever more of the most powerful Nazi agencies, departments, and operations. Himmler was reasonably honest in money matters and unlike most other Hitler sycophants, was also hardworking, administratively competent, and content to work in the background. Unfortunately for the world and millions of his victims, he unquestioningly believed in the Nazi ideology that held "violence, severity, and ruthlessness" to be "lofty virtues in all aspects of life."[5]

During his teen years Himmler had acquired a fascination with runes (ancient pre-Christian alphabets) and immersed himself in the mysticism that became popular throughout Germany after World War I. Guido von List, a man who added the *von* to his name to make himself appear more aristocratic, was the preeminent mystic of the era and developed a strong cult following. A List admirer named Adolf Joseph Lanz soon imitated List and formed his own cult after becoming Jörg Lanz von Liebenfels. He and a few other prominent mystics added the idea of Aryan superiority to the ideology. Lanz published a magazine called *Ostara* with a subtitle meaning *Newsletter of the Blonde and Masculist*. Young Adolf Hitler was a subscriber. The term *Aryan* originally encompassed hundreds of ethnicities that used an Indo-European language, but List, Lanz and others distilled that down to the concept of *Ariosophy* to convey the superiority of the Nordic master race.[6]

These cultist influencers and their publications led young Himmler to see himself as the reincarnation of Heinrich I the Fowler through the transmigration of souls. He believed he conversed with the king in his sleep.[7] Heinrich I was an important father figure in German national identity because he'd assembled the first medieval confederation of German states. The dynasty he founded went on to rule the Holy Roman Empire.

Himmler, as a teen watching World War I from the sidelines, dreamed of leading men in combat. Through a family connection to Bavaria's royal family, young Himmler eventually gained admittance to an officer candidate school and then secured a position in a reserve battalion, but the war ended before he could see any fighting. Still, he later claimed he'd led men in combat.[8] The post-war 1919 Versailles Treaty and its severe limitation of German military strength ended his dream of becoming an officer, so he pursued a university agronomy education. But in the postwar period the rampant chaos and violence in a now shrunken and impoverished Germany continued to fuel Himmler's occultist beliefs. When the racist groups he admired blended the mystical master race idea into their own beliefs, Himmler did too. Before long the anti-Semitism that had long festered below the surface in Germany and throughout Europe melded with the new fascist philosophy.

That fascist philosophy rose to the surface because Corporal Hitler, instead of spying on upstart political parties as he had been assigned to do by the army, joined one (the Nationalsozialistische Deutsche Arbeiterpartei, or NSDAP) and went on to lead it. Hitler's fascist rantings attracted Himmler, who grew his own version of the Hitler brush mustache after joining the NSDAP in 1923. Himmler's party supervisor found Himmler doubly useful, stating, "He's got a motor-bike and he's full of frustrated ambition to be a soldier."[9]

Himmler gained Hitler's attention and soon worked himself into local leadership roles. In 1925 he joined the fledgling SS Hitler protection detail and two years later became second in command after supplying Hitler with a vision of the SS as an elite and racially pure paramilitary body. A short time later, Hitler flew into a rage when he "somehow" learned that Himmler's boss had used a Jewish tailor to alter his SS uniform. Himmler, in turn, acquired the grand title of *SS Reichsführer*.[10]

After Himmler took charge, the nature of the organization changed. It became an elitist political police and central bureaucracy for dispensing terrorism and put Himmler in a position of power second only to Hitler."[11] Hitler soon learned that he'd badly underestimated Himmler and feared that the SS would become a paramilitary powerful enough to lead a coup, so he ordered Himmler to keep the unit small and establish cells of no more than 20 men throughout the major German cities. These small units were to be a loyal and elite force able to not only protect Hitler and the party but also to intimidate and neutralize the opposition. The latter function was to be stealthy because brutish tactics had already provoked a public backlash.

The SS recruiters chose strong physical specimens and screened them for racial ancestry and Nordic looks. Himmler's legion, wearing the black uniforms he introduced, handled its job so effectively that the communists and other rival groups stopped disrupting Nazi party functions. The black uniforms were no accident. Himmler said, "I know that there are many people in Germany who feel sick when they see this black tunic; we can understand that and do not expect to be loved by over many people."[12]

Himmler was a psychopath—a man totally devoid of empathy and conscience. In the many letters to the wife and daughter he spent very little time with, he closed with some variation of "many affectionate greetings and kisses." He could write those words one minute and dispatch an order to liquidate thousands of *Untermensch* (subhumans) in the next without an afterthought.[13] Himmler surrounded himself with men just as morally vacuous, ruthless, and ideology-bound as himself, which allowed him to force thousands under his command to set aside their moral standards and engage in state-sanctioned persecution and murder.

One officer who'd joined the SS to help create a new type of military organization with high standards, had this to say:

> After Hitler founded a government of sorts, which really consisted of himself manipulating his friends who had helped him to win, the power of Himmler grew enormously, for with Hitler's connivance he took over the Gestapo and police forces and turned the SS into something neither I nor my closest friends had ever envisaged—a political force of repression. It is a fact that the SS and the political power associated with it were split down the middle—the political and the military, and it was difficult to reconcile the two.[14]

At first, Himmler's title of SS Reichsführer sounded extremely grandiose for someone in charge of a small force of bodyguards. But the frustrated wannabe combat officer was clever enough to skirt around Hitler's size-limit orders and rapidly expand the SS. Between 1929 and 1932 he grew the organization from under 300 members to 52,000 and stationed Politisches Bereitschaften (Political Readiness Detachments) in German cities and towns throughout the country in case the Communists ever came to power. After Hitler gained control of the German government in 1934, Himmler changed the name of his force to SS Verfügungstruppen (Special Use Troops). The SS-V's primary training now became military rather than political, justifying a change in the law to qualify SS-V service as meeting a man's military obligation.

Himmler had long admired the Teutonic Knights because they demonstrated the value of a secret society with tough rules, secret rites, and a strong hierarchy to bind members together. Yet the actual structure for his organization came from the Jesuit religious order. Himmler had assembled an enormous personal library about the Jesuits and studied the order intensively.

Ignatius de Loyola was one of the order's 16th century founders and its first vicar general. As an ex-soldier, he was familiar with military discipline and called for loyalty to the pope, but even more forcefully, demanded obedience to himself as the "Supreme Vicar of Christ." The Jesuit charter required subordinates to, without excuse, proceed to any part of the world as directed. The charter stipulated that each member "should permit themselves to be moved and directed under divine Providence by their Superiors just as if they were a corpse, which allows itself to be moved and handled in any way."[15] Himmler saw his "Black Guards as an elite cadre of ... medieval knights protecting their lord, Adolf Hitler" in ways he himself personally directed.[16]

From the Jesuits, Himmler also borrowed the idea that rigorous preparation and testing must occur before officers could become full members of his SS. And he insisted that investiture only occur on November 9 at 10 p.m. each year at a Nazi shrine in Munich where a special mystical ceremony bound new acolytes to the führer.[17]

The SS-V gradually took on a more formal military regimental structure. To develop a training protocol, Himmler recruited two exceptional World War I officers, Paul Hausser and Felix Steiner. Based on their experience on the Eastern Front, they incorporated their advanced ideas about warfare and training into two new progressive SS officer candidate schools. Quite uniquely, they didn't require a gymnasium (high school) level degree, but mandated only that candidates first serve in the enlisted ranks if they had no prior military experience. By contrast, the regular army accepted the well-educated into officer candidate schools immediately without any prior experience.

Both new SS schools relegated political education to the background. Hausser's curriculum focused on tactical training and leadership. Steiner replaced most parade-ground drill with arduous physical exercise, encouraged enterprise over blind obedience, and advocated infiltration instead of direct attack whenever possible. There were claims that at lesser SS officer candidate schools the training emphasis went in other directions and conditioned men to respond unemotionally and pitilessly to the tasks that lay ahead. One exercise was said to require warding off a vicious dog attack for 12 minutes while bare-chested. Men who broke and ran during this exercise were supposedly shot.[18]

Steiner insisted that officers and enlisted men train together in order to build trust and break down the social barriers that existed between the two groups. This and other innovations created closer bonds between officers and soldiers and readied men to step into their superior's shoes if the need arose in combat. Fidel appreciated this relaxed relationship with officers after dealing with the class system of the Romanian Army.

Steiner's curriculum also advanced the modern small-unit shock troops concept that the Germans exploited relentlessly early in World War II.[19] The emphasis on speed, speed, speed suffused the entire Germany military by the time Hitler plunged the nation into war, but the Waffen SS led the pack in this tactic.

Although Himmler was progressive in the sense of removing education and class barriers, he insisted the SS-V remain highly selective in other ways. Recruits had to: be physically strong and healthy, be at least five feet nine inches tall and 17 to 22 years of age, lack a criminal record, and prove their pure Aryan descent dating back to 1800 for enlisted men and 1750 for officers. The minimum service period was four years for enlisted men, 12 years for noncommissioned officers (NCOs), and a whopping 25 years for officers. Only one out of seven applicants was accepted. In the early days of the organization, Himmler himself personally studied each officer candidate's photograph for Aryan looks and to gain intuition into the man's makeup. To him, these warriors were the first step on the road to a superhuman mutation.[20]

The new, more egalitarian force that offered young working-class men and boys the chance to rise rapidly in the ranks and even become officers attracted many recruits from modest backgrounds. Due to the high level of unemployment plaguing the nation in the early years, Himmler had the luxury of choosing from a super fit cohort of candidates for his SS-V and selecting only the cream for his SS officer candidate schools. The schools further culled candidates by passing only 60 percent of them. Advancement in the SS-V was primarily based on merit; usually only the best officers received promotions. Some of the "best of the best" were those officers who began as enlisted men.[21]

At that time Himmler could boast that his SS did not accept a candidate with even one filled tooth and that just 15 percent of applicants met his rigorous standards. He was not troubled by the fact that he himself couldn't come remotely close to meeting these requirements, for he wore thick glasses, did not look particularly Aryan, and was dogged by a gastric ailment. Later, Himmler could draw on a new crop of even healthier German males because as one historian noted:

The youth of Germany grew fitter as never before under the marching and sport activity of the Hitler Youth, Labour Corps, and various organized fitness tests that appealed to young males. The latter ranged from the common military sports award badge of the SA to shooting proficiency badges in the Hitler Youth. The country didn't suspect that Hitler's regime was gearing itself for war by raising large numbers of 'super-fit, athletic young men' who 'put to shame' the specimens abroad.[22]

Some Waffen SS divisions truly became elite because of the forward thinking of men like Hausser and Steiner, but combat took an enormous toll on its best and most motivated. Midway through the war, green replacements degraded even the best divisions. Nevertheless, most Waffen SS units continued to perform professionally and shouldered many of the toughest combat operations. As a result, towards the end of the war Hitler assigned the SS his extremely difficult or impossible missions. Often it was the job of the Waffen SS to remain behind as a rearguard during withdrawals

Herbert Maeger, the previously mentioned Belgian Waffen SS veteran of the Eastern Front, wrote that despite the common perception, the Waffen SS was not a conscienceless army, but an organization "full of contradictions. It was not unequivocally heroic with stainless shield but neither is it right to say that it showed ruthless harshness towards prisoners of war or brutality against the civilian populations in occupied territories, contrary to what has been said of it repeatedly ever since." Despite the psychopathic leaders in Berlin and the individual soldier's "limited moral latitude" when it came to carrying out orders, he argued that as in all armies, the Waffen SS soldier's dealings with those he encountered was "determined by his disposition, talents and upbringing" as well as the traumatic experiences from confrontations with death.[23]

As for the blind and unwavering loyalty to Hitler that the Waffen SS is often accused of, Maeger maintained that not all commanders were automatons. When his Leibstandarte division was encircled by the Reds in Hungary and under orders from Hitler to fight to the last man, the division's commander, Sepp Dietrich, ignored the foolish order. He "broke out of an encirclement and so saved the 6th SS Panzer Army, and with it the Leibstandarte." For disobeying the order, Hitler directed the entire division to remove the silver embroidered LSSAH ADOLF HITLER cuff title from all uniforms. Maeger said that the rumor circulating through the division had Dietrich and his staff officers throwing their cuff insignias and the rest of their military decorations into a fire to show their disgust with Hitler. Maeger concluded by saying, "These foregoing events prove that the representation of the Waffen SS as a force blindly and unconditionally devoted to Hitler is not correct. As early as 1943 amongst the Leibstandarte it was being said quite frankly: 'If we want to win this war, we have to first have a thorough clear-out at home of the Party bigwigs and 'gold pheasants.' "[24] In Nazi Germany, *gold pheasant* was a derogatory term applied to the Nazi bigwigs.

---

1. U.S. War Department, *Handbook on German Military Forces. Chapter III: Other Military and Auxiliary Organizations*, War Department Technical Manual, TM-E 30-451, 1945, https://www.ibiblio.org/hyperwar/Germany/HB/.
2. Charles B. MacDonald, *The Last Offensive*, United States Army in World War II: European Theater of Operations (Office of the Chief of Military History, U.S. Department of the Army, 1973), chap. III p. 2, http://www.ibiblio.org/hyperwar/USA/USA-E-Last/.
3. Herbert Maeger, Geoffrey Brooks, and Charles Messenger, *Lost Honour, Betrayed Loyalty: The Memoir of a Waffen-SS Soldier on the Eastern Front* (South Yorkshire: Frontline Books, 2015), 27.
4. U.S. War Department, *Handbook on German Military Forces. Chapter III."*
5. Heinrich Himmler, *The Private Heinrich Himmler: Letters of a Mass Murderer*, ed. Katrin Himmler and Michael Wildt, trans. Thomas S. Hansen and Abby J. Hansen (New York: St. Martin's Press, 2016), 12.
6. Bill Yenne, *Hitler's Master of the Dark Arts: Himmler's Black Knights and the Occult Origins of the SS* (Minneapolis, MN: Zenith Press, 2010), 35, 37.
7. Dusty Sklar, *The Nazis and the Occult* (New York: Dorset Press, 1989), 85.
8. Yenne, *Hitler's Master of the Dark Arts*, 9.
9. Joseph Howard Tyson, *The Surreal Reich* (Bloomington: iUniverse Inc., 2010), 377.
10. Yenne, *Hitler's Master of the Dark Arts*, 58.
11. Sklar, *The Nazis and the Occult*, 85.
12. Sklar, *The Nazis and the Occult*, 85.
13. Maeger, Brooks, and Messenger, *Lost Honour, Betrayed Loyalty*, 27
14. Edmund L Blandford, *Hitler's Second Army: The Waffen SS* (Osceola, WI: Motorbooks, 1995), 17.
15. Ignatius, *The Constitutions of the Society of Jesus*, ed. George E. Ganss (St. Louis: Institute of Jesuit Sources, 1970), 55.
16. Sklar, *The Nazis and the Occult*, 85.
17. Sklar, *The Nazis and the Occult*, 97.
18. Sklar, *The Nazis and the Occult*, 100.
19. Marc J. Rikmenspoel, *Waffen SS: The Encyclopedia* (Garden City, N.Y.: Military Book Club, 2002), 74.
20. Sklar, *The Nazis and the Occult*, 96.
21. Rikmenspoel, *Waffen SS: The Encyclopedia*, 73.
22. Blandford, *Hitler's Second Army*, 33.
23. Maeger, Brooks, and Messenger, *Lost Honour, Betrayed Loyalty*, 27.
24. Maeger, Brooks, and Messenger, *Lost Honour, Betrayed Loyalty*, 127.

15 Wiligut and the Black Knights

Himmler's peculiarities and proclivities allowed him make exceptions to promotion only by merit. One beneficiary was Karl Maria Wiligut, a harmless looking older man who reinforced Himmler's dark and irrational beliefs. Wiligut was noted in this book's companion volume, *The Secret She Carried*, because he also tied into the fabric of my mother's story. Like her father, Wiligut served in Austria's 99th Infantry Regiment, which was garrisoned in her Austrian district's seat. Wiligut as a professional military officer came to believe he was a direct descendent of Germanic gods and kings and could commune with spirits. Much of the information about him is detailed in a book by Hans-Jürgen Lange.[1]

When Wiligut's ravings became intolerable to those around him, the authorities committed him to a Salzburg insane asylum for schizophrenia treatment. Upon his eventual release, he reinvented himself and expanded his "spiritual insights" into the pagan past. Unfortunately, his new visions were taken seriously by some. A year before Hitler took over Germany, Wiligut moved to Munich and changed his name to Weisthor (Thor knows).[2] Under this new persona, Weisthor boasted of his direct descendance from a long line of Germanic mystics that conveniently reached back many hundreds of thousands of years. He claimed special occult powers as well as the ability to recall precepts, beliefs, and traditions from his race's Nordic past by way of genetic memories from his ancestors. Those ancestors practiced something called Irminism and worshiped a Germanic god named Krist, which Christians later made into their Christ. Weisthor also implied the original language of the Bible was German.

Weisthor claimed lineage passed through the lost continent of Atlantis and other great civilizations and allowed him to see back to a time when the earth was the dwelling place of mythical inhabitants and had three suns. During his three-year asylum confinement, Weisthor had convinced himself that he was being persecuted by the Catholics, Jews, and Freemasons, the same entities behind Austria and Germany's loss in World War I. Because these beliefs were in tune with those of the raving former German corporal experiencing a meteoric rise to power in Germany, some sort of alignment was inevitable.

In the tumultuous and catastrophic period following World War I, so many Germans had lost faith in the government, the church, and traditional institutions that they became vulnerable to the wild and irrational beliefs that allowed occultism to flourish. Weisthor, as a Germanic prophet, tapped into this market and invented prehistory as fast as his occult magazine readers could swallow it.

Weisthor's channeled mystic revelations attracted Himmler's notice. There were claims that Hitler's Reichsführer never wearied listening to his new friend expound on the history of Atlantis, the Holy Grail, and his mythical ancestors. Himmler hoped to replace Christianity in Germany with an Aryan paganism, and Weisthor, who some began to think of as Himmler's Rasputin, seemed just the man to provide the scripture for this new religion. As Himmler's top occult advisor, Weisthor committed his ancestral memory to paper for Himmler. Within a year of Weisthor joining the SS, Himmler promoted him to the rank of brigadier general (*SS-Brigadenführer*).

In Weisthor, Himmler saw a foundation for his new state religion. And in Himmler, Weisthor found a golden opportunity to immortalize himself and legitimize Irminism through his "genetic memories." Weisthor also helped Himmler find an SS Valhalla. During a visit to a decrepit old castle called Schloss Wewelsburg in central Germany, Weisthor grasped that the gruesome old legends attached to the castle fit Himmler's dark needs, so he gave the place his blessing. The castle had a cellar dungeon within which thousands of witches were racked and executed, according to local folklore. More importantly, rituals associated with a Holy Grail and Knights of the Round Table-like tale were said to have been conducted there. Additionally, the location had symbolic meaning because the Germans had defeated the legions of Caesar Augustus in the nearby Teutoburg Forest. Himmler acquired the castle and over the next several years lavished money on its restoration and repurposing.[3]

The centerpiece of Wewelsburg was the 1350-square-meter (14,500-square-foot) dining hall that Himmler used as a meeting room. The room was bedecked with swastikas, SS lightning bolt runes, and other Nazi symbols appropriate to the secret pagan celebrations and rituals he staged there.[4] It was said that in these ceremonies, 12 senior SS Black Knights assembled around a large oak round table in high-backed pig-leather chairs. Every man's name was engraved in silver plate on the back of a chair.

Himmler's apartment in the castle, occupied for just a few days annually, was furnished as if still occupied by medieval king Heinrich I. Each knight's room was supposedly also styled for a particular German hero and also only used a few days per year while the occupants participated in rituals and spiritual visualizations.[5] Deep beneath the castle, Himmler built a large circular crypt with an elaborate swastika inset in the ceiling high above a ceremonial fire pit. This room was dedicated to the adoration of SS martyrs and used for storing cremation urns of Himmler's closest SS associates.[6]

Weisthor, as high priest, conducted SS wedding and baptism ceremonies in the castle and likely participated in darker goings-on as well. These ceremonies became a goldmine of occultist speculation, wild rumor, and stories of gruesome human sacrifice, both at Wewelsburg and elsewhere. One story held that in a secret séance-like ceremony an SS man was beheaded and his head used to divine enemy intelligence. Another version had blood being drunk from the severed head.[7][8] But today, with the participants all long since dead, truth can no longer be separated from fiction.

In addition to inventing SS rituals as needed, Weisthor designed the runic symbols immortalized on SS uniforms and flags. He also devised one of the most coveted items of Nazi memorabilia—the sinister *Totenkopfring* (death's head ring) that Himmler bestowed on favored SS officers. The ring's runes and mystical symbols were important in establishing an aura of mystique and building a mantle of obscurity around Himmler's near-medieval SS brotherhood. Himmler presented these rings with the stipulation that they would be forfeited if the wearer violated the SS discipline code.

Comrades of fallen SS men were required to make every effort to retrieve and return the rings to permit a mystical union of the dead and to keep the rings out of the hands of the enemy. As an indication of how perilous it was to be a Waffen SS officer, by January 1945 nearly two-thirds of the 14,500 issued rings had come back to Wewelsburg, and another 10 percent were irretrievable on the battlefield. In the final days of the war Himmler purportedly ordered the returned rings hidden in a cave within the Niederhagen Forest, after which the cave was blasted shut.[9]

Weisthor's world crashed in 1939 when his alcoholism became problematic and Himmler learned of the mystic's previous asylum confinement in Salzburg. To avoid the embarrassment that would arise if the public learned he'd been duped, Himmler quietly ordered Weisthor to return his Totenkopfring and retire for reasons of ill health. Himmler thereafter kept his former high priest under the watchful eye of a staff member. Yet, he continued to consult the disgraced mystic now and then.[10]

1. Hans-Jürgen Lange and Karl Maria Wiligut, *Weisthor: Karl-Maria Wiligut : Himmlers Rasputin und seine Erben* (Engerda: Arun, 1998).
2. Bill Yenne, *Hitler's Master of the Dark Arts: Himmler's Black Knights and the Occult Origins of the SS* (Minneapolis, MN: Zenith Press, 2010), 105.
3. Yenne, *Hitler's Master of the Dark Arts*, 110.
4. Yenne, *Hitler's Master of the Dark Arts*, 113.
5. Dusty Sklar, *The Nazis and the Occult* (New York: Dorset Press, 1989), 99.
6. Yenne, *Hitler's Master of the Dark Arts*, 296.
7. Yenne, *Hitler's Master of the Dark Arts*, 115.
8. Sklar, *The Nazis and the Occult*.
9. Chris McNab, ed., *Hitler's Elite: The SS 1939-45* (Oxford: Osprey Publishing, 2015), 100.
10. Lange and Wiligut, *Weisthor: Karl-Maria Wiligut*, 72.

16 Back Door to the Black Angels

Ordinary Waffen SS soldiers knew nothing of Wiligut or Himmler's wild spiritual beliefs and practices. For most, the combat was frequent, serious, and deadly enough that their focus was on staying alive. Until midway through the war, SS soldiers had mainly themselves to blame for their circumstances because they'd enlisted willingly. The disaster at Stalingrad changed that. From then on, most replacements were non-Germans or ethnic Germans inducted from outside the Reich—men who came to the Waffen SS with varying degrees of willingness and experience. The majority of the ethnic Germans from Romania were combat veterans transferred from the Romanian Army. Their experience gave them a higher level of competence than almost any other group of East-Central European conscripts. In July and August 1943, these men, along with young Romanian ethnic German inductees not yet exposed to combat, fleshed out III (Germanic) SS Panzer Corps (III. [germanisches] SS-Panzerkorps), a new corps in which Himmler concentrated the majority of his surviving non-German Aryan (Germanic) volunteers from West European and Nordic countries.

Many of the Banat ethnic Germans were assigned to two elements within that corps, 11th SS Volunteer Panzergrenadier Division Nordland and SS Volunteer Panzergrenadier Brigade Nederland. The term *Panzergrenadier* designates a Waffen SS mechanized (combat-vehicle equipped) infantry division. A lesser number of Banat men helped fill out another new division primarily composed of Balkan conscripts, SS Prinz Eugen. All three of these units were built around a cadre of experienced German or Nordic nationals from the early-war SS formations.

Unlike the thousands of men from the Western and Northern European countries that joined the Waffen SS willingly, the ethnic Germans had no real choice. It is true that Fidel and many of his compatriots were not unhappy to forgo service in the sorry Romanian Army, but given a say, they'd have preferred to serve in the regular German Army rather than in the elite but riskier Waffen SS. Nevertheless, they believed that because of its professionalism and leadership, the Waffen SS offered them a better chance of survival than did the Romanian Army. That belief would eventually be shaken by the reckless way in which Hitler continued to sacrifice SS soldiers.

A few ethnic German men were already well aware that Hitler had little empathy for his soldiers. They were the victims of a previous forced transfer of Romanian ethnic German soldiers to the Waffen SS dating back to 1939, not long after the start of the war when Hitler and Stalin negotiated the fateful Molotov–Ribbentrop Pact that split Poland between them. The two dictators had at that time agreed to a secret annex that allowed the region called Bessarabia, which Romania claimed and occupied after the end of World War I, to be reclaimed by Russia. In the summer of 1940, the Soviets threatened war if the Romanian Army didn't evacuate the territory within days. The Romanians capitulated and agreed to pull out in the allotted time, but Stalin underhandedly attacked the Romanian Army anyway as it left, inflicting tens of thousands of casualties on the Romanians.

Hitler subsequently negotiated a second agreement with Stalin. This one allowed Bessarabian ethnic Germans to leave for settlements in his recently annexed Polish territory. A Bessarabian named Emil Stickel described what happened to the ethnic German Bessarabian soldiers in the Romanian Army, as well as Himmler's formerly demanding SS selection process.

> While stationed in Temeshvar, in one single move we were not only dismissed from the Romanian army, but also deprived of Romanian citizenship, thus making us stateless persons, and then all Bessarabian soldiers were to be transported back to their homeland. Herbert [Stickel's brother] and I were standing outside the gate to the barracks, having been forced to give up all of our army equipment and clothing, and next to us stood a bunch of still incredulous comrades without boots and wearing nothing but their underwear. Fortunately, the two of us had entered the Romanian cavalry and brought along our own personal uniforms.[1]

The cashiered Bessarabian soldiers learned that they would not be returning to civilian life and their families. Since the entire resettlement process was in the hands of SS-controlled ethnic German lackeys, the men were subjected to a medical screening to allow the SS first crack at the men who could meet the demanding Waffen SS standards. Most failed and were sent on to Germany for other service. At this time the SS still had an enviable military reputation. Those men who passed the screening were proud to have made the cut into such an elite service after their experience in the shoddy Romanian Army. Stickel said, "Presentations given to us about this particular corps filled us with great enthusiasm. It was trumpeted as being the spearhead for Hitler, and only the very best could ever hope to fulfill its high demands." The impressionable young Bessarabians quickly volunteered.[2]

After these new SS recruits helped resettle the Bessarabian civilians in Poland, they went by train to Berlin for further screening. The focus of the Race and Settlement Commission that conducted this screening centered around racial purity and background. Everyone had to fill out a detailed form listing their ancestry. Regarding the physical exam, Stickel said, "The doctors of the commission used compasses to examine the proportionality of limbs, entered the resulting measurements in tables, checked the head, the nose and the way the ear was formed, checked the eyes and compared hair color with specific parts on a table of hues." The examiners also analyzed the body as a whole.

> In no case must an SS-man lack a proportionally formed body on which, for example, the lower legs are in the wrong proportion relative to the upper legs. Whenever the lower legs and upper legs are entirely disproportional with the upper body, the desired proportional form does not exist, unless the candidates can prove that, despite unsatisfactory physique, the way they carry themselves demonstrates that they are Nordic human beings. Equally important is that the candidate does not comport himself like a servile being, but that his gait, his hands—in short, everything truly corresponds to what we consider as ideal." These examinations consumed an entire day, with the results to be announced the following day.[3]

As the war dragged on, the need for cannon fodder superseded the strict standards. Practically anyone was suitable to die in an SS uniform by the winter of 1943. In the Balkans, Himmler snatched up every man he could lay his hands on—including those that had already been rejected for military service by their own region's army. Even Muslims were Aryan enough for the Waffen SS by then. In raiding Romania for its ethnic Germans in 1943 through the agreement between Hitler and Antonescu, the SS gained strong farmers and tradesmen—physical specimens who still met most of the earlier SS standards. Men like Fidel. Not only were they hard working, many already had Eastern Front combat experience.

The men at Fidel's Lipova base knew nothing of this agreement until early July 1943 when the ethnic German infantry and artillery trainees were told they'd go to the Waffen SS within the month. Following a leave, they were to board military trains for induction and training in the Reich. Fidel and five other ethnic German specialist trainees were exempted. Specialists were harder to replace than combat soldiers, so the Romanian command wished to keep them. The departure of the other men surely brought Fidel an awareness that his own comfortable existence at the base would soon end too. Instead of heading west for training with the majority of his friends, he could expect to join the Romanian Army on the dreaded Russian front.

Given Fidel's growing awareness of how dysfunctional this army was, facing the numerically superior Red Army in a Romanian uniform must have looked akin to suicide. Nine Orzydorf men had died in the vicinity of Stalingrad in just the previous months, to make a total of 23 locals lost since the war began.[4] Fidel would have known most of them. But then, just days after the other men had left with home leaves, the base commander released Fidel and the other specialists to the Germans as well.

The parish war-dead records suggest that few of Orzydorf's soldiers still remained in the Romanian Army after the transfer since only one more man, Josef Eipert, died in a Romanian uniform. Fidel knew Josef well because he was married to Fidel's sister. Josef was a quartermaster for a medical company at the time of the SS transfer and apparently concluded his odds of survival were better by choosing to remain at the front as a specialist in a noncombat post than to risk being made a German front-line soldier. His eventful story appears in later chapters.

Although Josef was not in Orzydorf for Fidel to talk to during his home leave, Fidel's brother Hans was. The German transfer agreement had a tight timeline and was to be complete by the end of July, which meant the leaves of the recently called-up conscripts and the veterans from the front overlapped. As they rubbed shoulders, the new soldiers learned that morale was so bad at the front that thousands of Romanians had deserted and were hiding from the authorities.

This contact with the seasoned veterans eased some of Fidel's anxiety about what lay ahead with the Germans. Despite their recent major defeats at Stalingrad and in North Africa, the German military was still perceived as capable, if no longer invincible. The Orzydorf veterans had fought alongside German divisions at the front and had seen how much more professional that military was. There were multiple reasons why the average German soldier was more competent than his Romanian counterpart. Besides being ill-equipped in transport, weaponry, and training, the Romanian soldier was poorly motivated because of mistreatment by his superiors. These factors hindered Romanian units at every level when they tried to achieve the objectives assigned to them by the Germans. The outdated Romanian Army was also unsuited for a mechanized war on the difficult terrain and infrastructure-poor vastness of the Russian steppe. The Red Army wasn't particularly well trained or effective either, but made up

Fidel in his new Romanian Army uniform. The fit indicates this was a tailormade uniform rather than one issued by the army. Conscripts and recruits who could afford to have a uniform sewn did so because the standard issue uniform was of poor quality and uncomfortable.

for its deficiencies with better equipment, an unmatchable manpower pool, and a willingness to sacrifice as many soldiers as it took to press ahead.

For the ethnic German transferees, German service promised more benefits than just superior field leadership and modern weapons. Better pay and medical care were two, but the most anticipated was a greater regard for the lives of soldiers by commanders. I expect that Fidel didn't wish to increase the hazards he might face by letting his new service know that he'd been training for the dangerous specialty of Strippenzieher.

On his two-week leave, Fidel was determined to enjoy the time he had left before shipping out. His stay overlapped his brother's by a week, but Fidel didn't see much of him. Hans had his own house and was busy making up for lost time with the wife he'd been with for a scant few weeks since their marriage three years earlier. The foolish optimism of youth had Fidel believing there'd be plenty of opportunity for time with his brother in the future. With the war about to become very real, he was too busy enjoying his own last days of freedom. And like all soldiers about to face combat, he would have tried to avoid thinking about what lay ahead. When he wasn't playing cards with friends also on leave, he was in the company of the girlfriend who'd now become his fiancée. Fidel never saw Hans again and for the remainder of his life regretted not making more of an effort to spend time with him.

Although Fidel was almost certainly relieved to escape the clutches of the Romanian Army, the thought of leaving his fiancée, family, and farm to go wherever the Germans sent him was still frightening. His brother's experience prepared him for the possibility of being away for a long time, but he couldn't have imagined he'd never call Romania his home again and would not return at all for more than 20 years. This reality imposed itself because of one aspect of the transfer agreement between Hitler and Antonescu that did not become meaningful until after the war. It had to do with citizenship. The original deal stipulated that the men serving in the German military would keep their Romanian citizenship, but just weeks after the signing, Hitler bestowed blanket German citizenship on all foreign ethnic Germans serving in his armed forces. The postwar puppet communist governments of Eastern Europe twisted this technicality around and declared that the transferred ethnic Germans had relinquished their native citizenship. Hence, as traitors they were banned from returning home.[5]

A week after Hans left for Austria on a train with other veterans, it was Fidel's turn to say goodbye to his family, neighbors, and sweetheart. On the day of each train's departure to Hitler's Reich, the ethnic German parishes and communities gave their men a festive sendoff. Conflicting emotions must have reigned behind whatever brave faces the men's families and friends tried to put on. On the one hand, they expected that their men would fare better in the more professional German military than in the second-rate Romanian Army. Yet, they also understood that this might be the last time they'd ever see their young men. Dry eyes were surely a rarity as the men boarded the primitive freight cars that had been decorated with flowers and chalked inscriptions. Fidel, like Hans had a week before, posed for photos in the open door of his boxcar before he exchanged private goodbyes with his tearful family members.

The soldiers had been instructed to leave their Romanian uniforms behind to avoid attracting undue notice from the Romanian public. German uniforms would be issued after the men reached their unit's replacement battalion base and took their new military oath. Meanwhile, the boxcar trains offered no real accommodations for their passengers, who were to be largely self-sufficient. Besides a personal food supply sufficient for several days, the men had been instructed to bring a change of underwear.

Trains from the southern Banat traveled north through the city of Arad, picking up young men at villages like Orzydorf along the way. The trains

Fidel, seated between two friends in the doorway of the boxcar that would deliver him from Orzidorf, Romania, to Vienna, Austria, for induction into the freshly formed Nordland division of the Waffen SS in 1943. Standing behind Fidel are an unhappy mother and wife/girlfriend/sister of the conscripted soldier whose shadowed face is visible between them. His hands rest on their shoulders.

then crossed the border and clipped through rural Hungary in a northwesterly direction toward Budapest. As the young inductees passed through that city, the largest most of them had ever seen, they marveled at the ornate buildings from which the Hungarian Kingdom had ruled their part of the Banat not long before. From Budapest the trains continued northwest across the Austrian border until reaching Vienna, an even more spectacular city that had once ruled a vast empire.

After the initial SS processing in Vienna, Fidel's group boarded another train that took them south to the Austrian city of Graz. From the station there, they proceeded to a base that housed the replacement battalion of the 11th SS Volunteer Panzergrenadier Division Nordland one of the several new units making up the III (Germanic) SS Panzer Corps. For Fidel, a farm boy traveling outside of Romania for the first time, the journey was filled with new sights. He saw trains and stations full of soldiers, but little sign of an all-out war to the south and east.

Some 41,500 men had left Romania and boarded trains to Germany by the end of July 1943. Not everyone in that group was the most desirable of recruits. The Romanian government had taken full advantage of the arrangement with the Germans by emptying its jails of military-aged ethnic German men. Their civilian or military prison sentences were deferred until the war was over.[6] In Vienna, the primary destination of the trains, the transferees were routed to various reserve and replacement units. Some went to actual training bases. Others received their training through live fire. Nearly all would spend the remainder of the war on the Eastern Front as that zone moved ever westward. They would see no respite from the fighting.

For many of the new ethnic German recruits, the honeymoon with the Germans ended quite soon. Some became disillusioned when they were treated as lesser Germans in their training units. Others soured after learning from letters that their families and communities back home were experiencing severe economic difficulties because they were not receiving the pay packets they were due. But there was nothing to be done about it at this point, except for men in the Prinz Eugen division. When that unit was positioned in Serbia just south of Romania, some of the disenchanted ethnic Germans in the division were close enough to their families to desert and walk back home.[7]

---

1. Klaus Stickel, *Im Sturm der Geschichte* (Münster, Westfalen: Buding & Tebbert, 2005).
2. Stickel, *Im Sturm der Geschichte*.
3. Stickel, *Im Sturm der Geschichte*.

4. Gertrude Adam and Anton Peter Petri, *Heimatbuch der deutschen Gemeinde Orczydorf im Banat* (Marquartstein: Breit, 1983), 148.
5. Theodor Schieder, ed., "The Fate of the Germans in Rumania: A Selection and Translation from Dokumentation Der Vertreibung Der Deutschen Aus Ost-Mitteleuropa," in *Documents on the Expulsion of the Germans from Eastern-Central-Europe*, vol. III (Bonn: Federal Ministry for Expellees, Refugees and War Victims, 1961), 59.
6. Schieder, "The Fate of the Germans in Rumania," 60.
7. Schieder, "The Fate of the Germans in Rumania," 61.

17 The Disaster at Stalingrad

Hitler's incompetent meddling in military decisions was a major reason the Germans and their allies faced a critical shortage of replacements at this juncture of the war. That was never more evident than during the German effort to capture Stalingrad. Not only was that struggle the largest battle of the war, with nearly four million combatants, it was also a decisive turning point for both the German and Romanian military. In his pride, Hitler had forbidden the German 6th Army—once 200,000 men—to break out of the city's core. Later, it became impossible because most of the 6th Army transport horses were in rehabilitation camps to the west and well outside of reach. "Without those horses, the Sixth Army would not have been able to move its heavy weapons or ammunition during a breakout attempt."[1]

By the time of its surrender, the once-substantial army was down to 91,000 starving and half-frozen men. Without food or ammunition, it was impossible to fight to the last man as Hitler demanded. Hitler's stupidity simultaneously destroyed Romania's 3rd and 4th Armies, which held the flanks north and south of the city. This cost Romania two-thirds of its field force and left the surviving units in tatters.

The Russians counted about a quarter million German and Romanian corpses in the Stalingrad vicinity. The total Axis dead, wounded, missing, or captured added up to more than 800,000. Of the men who surrendered, less than one out of 15 survived the Soviet prison and labor camps. On the Soviet side, military historians estimate that the Red Army suffered 1,100,000 dead, wounded, missing, or captured. About 40,000 Soviet civilians died as well. A prominent factor in the civilian deaths was Stalin's insistence that civilians remain in the city to give his forces more motivation to fight.[2]

Romania was left with few battle-worthy divisions. Remnants of the shattered forces hobbled back to Romania. There, more than a few men deserted. Fidel's first cousin Hans Rabong was one of them. Like Fidel's brother Hans who had supplied his own horse to secure better duty in the army, cousin Hans provided a motorcycle to earn himself a special posting as a messenger. The motorcycle also brought him back home from Stalingrad. Decades later when I asked Hans about his experience, he didn't

Hans Rabong, Fidel's first cousin, in his Romanian Army uniform.

want to talk about it but did reveal that he'd deserted on his return home. Having had his fill of the Romanian Army, he hid until he could manipulate his way westward through Austria to Germany in the chaos of the war's close.

Hans Rabong and fellow soldiers on the Eastern Front in World War II. Hans is in the center of the group, astride the civilian motorcycle he brought with him to the Romanian Army in order to secure a more comfortable and survivable military occupation than infantryman.

Not all Romanian ethnic German soldiers were lucky enough to make their way back to Romania after the Stalingrad disaster. When the Soviet Army wiped out whole Romanian divisions, some 10,000 ethnic German soldiers who'd been among the footloose Romanian troops cut off from their units were taken in by the Wehrmacht and SS units in the vicinity. Hitler subsequently prohibited their return to the Romanian Army.[3]

At this time in early 1943, the Romanian Army remained Germany's second largest allied force despite the severe casualties it had suffered. Quite surprisingly, this army's anachronistic cavalry made up for some of its other failings. The horse units showed great discipline and cohesiveness, and provided mobility under the difficult field conditions of the Soviet Union. Fidel recalled that his brother Hans Eipert had taken part in Hitler's 1941 invasion of the Soviet Union with his cavalry unit. Fidel thought it had advanced east of Crimea as far as Rostov in the Caucasus before being called back to Stalingrad in support of the trapped German 6th Army in 1942. This would have placed him on or near the dangerous lines on the flanks of Stalingrad when he learned he was to become a German soldier. He probably wasn't unhappy to be leaving an army where men on horseback fought against tanks and fighter planes.

Confirmation that Fidel's brother Hans had indeed been at Stalingrad with the mauled Romanian Army came some years ago via one of those rare coincidences that occurs now and then. At the time, I'd been collaborating with a distant American relative, the late Frank Jansen, on the genealogy of common Orzydorf ancestors. Through a bureaucratic stroke of the pen, Frank's Eipert branch of the family had become *Eibert* after arrival in America from Orzydorf around the beginning of the 20th century. I happened to mention to him that Fidel thought his brother had been recalled from Stalingrad at the time of the Waffen SS transfer.

Frank emailed back, "A neighbor of mine, originally from Salzburg, has a Donauschwaben wife. The neighbor's brother-in-law served at Stalingrad and Leningrad with a Johann Eibert from Orzydorf. The unit was the 11th Flak Abteilung (11. SS-Flak Abteilung in German nomenclature) of the W-SS Nordland Division. In talking to relatives at family weddings etc. when everyone gets loosened up, I gather that most ethnic German young men were 'recruited' directly or 'transferred' from Romanian units into usually the Nordland (11th Waffen SS) or the Prinz Eugen (7th Waffen SS) divisions."[4]

It is extremely unlikely that this Johann Eibert could be anyone but my uncle. I already knew that Hans (short for Johann) served with the 11th SS Flak Abteilung, an antiaircraft battalion of about two hundred men. Eipert (there were no Eiberts in Orzydorf) was a name largely confined to the village of Orzydorf, so it is hard to conceive there could have been a second Banat soldier named Johann Eibert/Eipert who fought at Stalingrad in the Romanian Army and then ended up in the 11th SS Flak Abteilung near Leningrad. Unfortunately, when I tried to follow up on this information several years later, it was too late. Frank and the man who'd served with Hans had both died, and the neighbor's wife knew nothing more.

My uncle Hans had originally enlisted in the Romanian Army for a term of nine months so he could get his military obligation out of the way and get on with being a farmer. By the time of his home leave prior to climbing aboard the boxcar that would take him to Vienna and his new Waffen SS unit in the German Reich, he'd already put in five years of service. As had his horse, for Hans returned home with the same mount. Both Hans and his horse had survived two years on the deadly Eastern Front.

Hans and the other Orzydorf soldiers who boarded the freight train to Vienna likely also went on to Wetzelsdorf, Austria, the replacement battalion headquarters for the newly forming 11th SS Volunteer Panzergrenadier Division Nordland. As a seasoned soldier with two years of combat experience on the Eastern Front and some high school education, he would have entered the new service at a rank and pay grade higher than most of his cohorts—probably as a private first class (*SS-Oberschütze*). And he likely considered himself lucky to end up in the 11th Flak Abteilung, a new unit filled almost entirely with fellow Banat Germans. It promised to be an assignment that relieved him of the hardships and discomfort of infantry duty. And for a time, it did.

---

1. William G. Dennis, "U.S. and German Field Artillery in World War II: A Comparison," The Army Historical Foundation, January 26, 2017, https://armyhistory.org/u-s-and-german-field-artillery-in-world-war-ii-a-comparison/.
2. Raymond Limbach, "Battle of Stalingrad: World War II," Encyclopedia Britannica, October 2022, http://www.britannica.com/event/Battle-of-Stalingrad.
3. Theodor Schieder, ed., "The Fate of the Germans in Rumania: A Selection and Translation from Dokumentation Der Vertreibung Der Deutschen Aus Ost-Mitteleuropa," in *Documents on the Expulsion of the Germans from Eastern-Central-Europe*, vol. III (Bonn: Federal Ministry for Expellees, Refugees and War Victims, 1961), 58.
4. Frank Janson, "Hans Eipert" (Email, 1996).

18 Waffen SS and NKVD Expansion

After Germany's Stalingrad and North Africa defeats, anxiety set in among the Nazi leaders in Berlin. To regain the initiative on the Eastern Front, they had to fully mobilize the population. Unfortunately for Himmler, the SS didn't benefit greatly from the mobilization because Hitler's original recruiting restrictions for the SS in Germany were still in effect. By limiting recruiting within Germany, Hitler hoped to protect himself from an SS coup. Himmler had already drained the supply of replacements in the countries to the west and north of Germany by then, so he had nowhere to go for manpower but east.

Himmler's original idealistic dreams of destroying the Bolsheviks, spreading a new religion, and creating a race of super warriors needed to be put on hold because the war of conquest had turned into a struggle for survival. Before the war and during its early stage, Himmler skirted Hitler's limits with administrative tricks like over-enlisting men into less restricted SS branches such as the Totenkopf camp guards, police, and political SS, then clandestinely transferring the surplus to the Waffen SS. He'd also cozied up to the Nazi Hitler Youth organization to lure boys to the SS before they became available for regular military service.

Originally, it was possible to pitch the Waffen SS to potential recruits as a multinational force intended to defend Europe against the Bolsheviks. After an enticing SS recruitment poster depicting a soldier shouting "To arms for Europe's civilization" enjoyed success in German-occupied Holland, a whole collection of attractive recruitment posters designed to appeal to adventure-seeking young men followed.[1] In Germany itself, a book called *Der Ruft die SS* (*The Call of the SS*) saw some success, so Himmler had the book translated into multiple languages to attract "Germanic" Europeans from the conquered West European countries of the

Netherlands, Norway, Belgium, Denmark, Sweden and Finland. These nationalities had all suddenly turned Aryan enough to fit the Nazi ideal.

Holland alone produced 25,000 recruits. Some men from Switzerland, Italy, and Spain answered the call as well when Germany still appeared invincible and easily rolled through Poland, Western Europe, and the Balkans. As these sources dried up, Himmler began to foster ties with ethnic German groups in the eastern parts of Europe. He acquired a considerable number of men from the Soviet-oppressed Baltic countries to volunteer after Hitler invaded the Soviet Union.

The earliest eastern recruits went to the Das Reich SS division that Fidel had watched pass through Orzydorf on its way to Yugoslavia in 1941. On the division's return to Germany, it brought along those new recruits on its military trains. After the Germans installed a sympathetic government in Yugoslavia, Serbia became the first place in Eastern Europe where the Waffen SS could directly recruit ethnic Germans. Most other suitable Yugoslav ethnic minorities such as Croatian ethnic Germans, were still required to serve in their own regional military. Although the Romanian generals objected to Romanians going to another country's military and threatened to charge those leaving with treason, they couldn't follow through without incurring Hitler's wrath.

After the myth of German invincibility was shattered, Himmler resorted to shadier methods of conscripting SS "volunteers" in Romania, Hungary, and the Balkan states. By then the criteria for deciding who was good enough to bleed for the German cause were greatly relaxed and, out of necessity, Himmler no longer made a distinction between the battlefield blood shed by Aryans and that shed by non-Aryans. At this time he also dropped any pretense of Aryan ideals so he could form non-Germanic divisions. Foreigners only needed to take a loyalty pledge to Hitler in place of the normal SS oath and to wear a different SS insignia patch on their uniforms. For access to such recruits, Himmler played opposing ethnic groups against each other and used trickery such as staged sports events to snare volunteers. Sometimes his recruiters resorted to press gangs. The enlistment period of these non-Germanic recruits was two years, but in reality they had little choice but to serve for the duration of the war.

By the end of the war some 60 SS foreign-unit names had been created. The Indische (Indian) Freiwilligen Legion, 29th Waffen Grenadier Division of the SS (1st Italian), Waffen Grenadier Regiment of the SS (1st and 2nd Romanian), 25th Waffen Grenadier Division of the SS Hunyadi (1st Hungarian), and 33rd Waffen Grenadier Division of the SS Charlemagne (1st French) are just a few. Some units existed for only a short time. Beginning in 1944 the Waffen SS even facilitated transfers from foreign auxiliary units into new or existing SS divisions. Many of these soldiers couldn't come close to meeting the already-low SS racial and military fitness standards. As the Reich was falling apart in 1945 and the government combined army and SS recruiting centers, the only real remaining physical SS standard was an ability to walk and to fire a gun.

To carry out the demanding missions Hitler assigned to the Waffen SS, field commanders resorted to supplementing their ranks with Russian *Hilfswilliger* (voluntary helpers), or *Hiwis* for short. The regular army used them also. Although Hitler had no use for such *Untermenschen*, the German field generals of both the Waffen SS and Heer did. They used these "volunteers" as ammunition bearers, messengers, cooks, litter bearers, and laborers. Many Hiwis also became an integral part of the German military machine as combatants.

The situation at Stalingrad was illuminating. It is unknown how many Hiwis were attached to the German 6th Army's accessory units, but some estimates place it at over 70,000. One historian wrote, "Sixth Army had over 50,000 Russian auxiliaries attached to its front-line divisions, representing over a quarter of their strength. The 71st and the 76th Infantry Divisions had over 8,000 Hiwis each. By mid-November [1942] this was roughly equal to their total German strength."[2] The overriding reason such great numbers of the enemy's soldiers worked for the Germans was the grave conditions in German POW camps. The Nazis already had their hands full feeding their own population and troops and weren't about to further reduce their supplies by adequately feeding a couple million Russian prisoners. Volunteering to assist the Germans offered a reprieve from starvation.

Hitler would have had to feed those POWs better out of reciprocity if he'd gotten Stalin to agree to abide by the Geneva Conventions late in the war. His efforts weren't out of any feeling for the starving Russian POWs. Rather, the war had begun going so badly for the Germans that Hitler wanted to improve the morale of his forces by securing humanitarian treatment for German POWs held by Stalin. Then, they'd have been allowed German Red Cross packages and communication with their families.

Stalin barbarically refused to have anything to do with the Geneva Conventions and rebuffed Hitler's overture because he depended on brutal tactics and fear to keep his Red Army fighting hard. German medical personnel, ambulances, trains, and ships, normally identified by a red cross on a white background, were supposed to be exempt from attacks, but Stalin made them priority targets for his army. To protect themselves and their patients, German medical companies removed their Red Cross armbands and repainted their ambulance vehicles in camouflage patterns.[3]

Back when it still looked like the German war machine would prevail in Russia, many people living under Moscow's control welcomed liberation from the oppressive Bolsheviks. Stalin's relentless purges, his uprooting of ethnic minorities from their homelands, as well as his deliberate starvation of millions of peasants in the drive to collectivize agriculture had alienated a large swath of the population. Because fear and terror were the glue that held Stalin's empire together, some civilians and POWs willingly served the Germans in the hope they were helping rid Russia of the Bolsheviks. However, instead of harnessing this desire for liberation, Hitler antagonized the occupied population with his own brand of terror when he treated their people as subhuman and exterminated Jews and other so-called undesirables. The Hiwis and others who'd thrown their lot in with the Germans eventually found themselves trapped in their new servitude much like the ethnic German soldiers of Eastern Europe did.

When the Red Army had all but collapsed in the opening weeks of the German Barbarossa invasion, Stalin hid in panic for days. Upon re-emergence, his fear of defection by whole divisions led him to use drastic measures to force his soldiers to stand up to the enemy. Since the cost in lives was immaterial to him, he issued a secret military directive ordering soldiers to kill themselves rather than surrender. Stalin's directive also reclassified all Red Army soldiers in German hands as traitors and promised them harsh punishment when recaptured.[4][5]

Stalin simultaneously ordered the NKVD to annihilate any Red Army units that had been retaken from the Germans or allowed themselves to be cut off from their own forces. Even troops that had broken out of an enemy encirclement were to be killed. NKVD soldiers largely complied with these harsh directives because their family members were essentially hostages whose well-being depended on good behavior by their soldier. Their families faced a loss of livelihood and food rations at best, and torture, a Gulag sentence, or execution at worst.[6] Because the NKVD was also noted for its terror tactics and its network of snitches in the both civilian and military ranks, soldiers and their families had further reason to remain cooperative.[7]

During the initial stages of Barbarossa when the Germans were advancing rapidly, Stalin decided that he couldn't afford to let the large number of political prisoners and slave laborers he held in the threatened regions fall into German hands, lest they work with the Germans. Consequently, he ordered them evacuated eastward to holding facilities— or executed if they couldn't be moved in time. The rapidly expanding NKVD was given the highest authority to implement this task.

This work could be trusted to the NKVD because its personnel were handpicked. Stalin bought their loyalty with pay up to 25 times that of regular soldiers. They also received better food, weapons, and equipment than regular soldiers. The organization was already proficient in torture, infliction of pain, and prolonged suffering, but at the war's onset inherited a vastly expanded playground.[8] When the Germans reached Minsk, Smolensk, Kiev, Kharkov, and other major cities, they found nearly all Soviet prison inmates slaughtered.[9] The entire city of Lvov reeked from the massacre of 3,500 people, many of whom had died after brutal and slow torture.[10]

At the very time that supply-starved Red Army units along the front were ordered to hold off the German invaders in 1941, Stalin's NKVD troops monopolized the rail system. The swift German advance had so frightened the local NKVD brass that many fled with their families and possessions. The bulk of rail capacity was tied up transporting residents with clout, and political prisoners, eastward. Red Army units that had escaped the German onslaught were transported to the Gulag by the NKVD rather than sent back into the fight. To handle all this additional workload, the NKVD was drastically expanded.[11] As this hideous madness was going on, the Russian government was begging Britain to send 25 to 30 fighting divisions to assist them on the Russian front.[12]

---

1. Edmund L Blandford, *Hitler's Second Army: The Waffen SS* (Osceola, WI: Motorbooks, 1995), 82.
2. Beevor, Antony. *Stalingrad: The Fateful Siege: 1942-1943*. New York: Viking, 1998, 185.
3. Herbert Maeger, Geoffrey Brooks, and Charles Messenger, *Lost honour, betrayed loyalty: the memoir of a Waffen-SS soldier on the Eastern Front* (South Yorkshire: Frontline Books, 2015), 57.
4. Nikolai Tolstoy, *Stalin's Secret War* (New York, N.Y.: Holt, Rinehart, and Winston, 1982), 240, 282.
5. Svetlana Allilujeva and Paul Chavchavadze, *Only One Year* (New York: Harper & Row, 1969), 353.
6. Tolstoy, *Stalin's Secret War*, 240.
7. Allilujeva and Chavchavadze, *Only One Year*, 353.
8. Tolstoy, *Stalin's Secret War*, 65, 245.
9. Tolstoy, *Stalin's Secret War*, 243.
10. Tolstoy, *Stalin's Secret War*, 245, 246, 247.
11. Tolstoy, *Stalin's Secret War*, 250.
12. Tolstoy, *Stalin's Secret War*, 248.

19 Fidel's New Insignia

The anxieties and fears of Fidel and his group surely eased upon arrival at a modern SS *Kaserne* (barracks) compound in Wetzelsdorf, a suburb of Austria's second largest city, Graz. The facility, just two years old, had been designed by a Berlin architect to blend into the alpine setting. It was originally meant to serve as the base for SS regiment Der Führer, but the start of the war saw the facility repurposed. The planned officers' mess, swimming pool, and ballroom were never built because the funds were needed for the war effort.[1] Throughout most of the war, SS Kaserne Wetzelsdorf, known today as Belgier-Kaserne, housed several Waffen SS replacement battalions. Unbeknownst to the transiting replacements, the Kaserne was also an execution site for persons convicted of serious crimes in military and police courts.

The new men were to find the SS quite different from the anachronistic Romanian Army they'd just left. The absence of a strict class separation between officers and enlisted men surely surprised them. SS officers were addressed by their rank, never by Herr and weren't normally saluted. On those occasions when a salute was called for, a slack version of the Heil Hitler salute (right arm rotated up at the elbow) sufficed.

The oath taking and the issuance of uniforms, gear, and the *Soldbuch* booklet that contained a German soldier's most important pay and identification records would all have occurred in Wetzeldorf. By 1943, the basic Waffen SS uniform being issued to new soldiers like Fidel was nearly indistinguishable from that of the regular army. The blending came about after the SS-V, the forerunner of the Waffen SS, transitioned into a real military force in both structure and training. The black uniforms the SS-V wore originally did intimidate and project authority as intended, but proved too impractical for field service. So in the mid-1930s the SS-V switched to the same utilitarian *feldgrau* (field gray) color worn by the Heer (army). Only panzer (tank) crews continued to wear black because black hid grease and oil stains. Just prior to World War II the force adopted a closed-collar feldgrau uniform for combat wear. This uniform differed from the army's only in having a wider collar and angled slash-type lower pockets. It doubled as a dress uniform when worn with a necktie and a buttoned-down collar. By the middle of the war, fresh recruits could have been issued an SS uniform or simply a regular army uniform since the uniform suppliers couldn't always keep up with the SS demand.

Recycling uniforms became increasingly common by 1943 because of Germany's material and labor shortages, so it is possible Fidel received a recycled uniform. At that time, Waffen SS troops in the same company commonly found themselves outfitted in a variety of uniform styles. The chaotic combat environment of the front, where steady supply lines were the exception rather than the rule, forced soldiers to utilize whatever uniform parts they could find. Some soldiers even wore enemy clothing items. Uniforms and insignia became more mixed as stragglers and soldiers from depleted units were absorbed into whichever unit they came across.

Late in the war the SS introduced camouflage clothing, further breaking down standardization. Both Germans and Russians were known to outfit themselves with whatever was useful from battlefields when the need arose, for the chancy supply lines often left soldiers little choice but to scrounge.[2] The Red Army reportedly collected the boots of dead soldiers to reissue. The Russian soldier, who expected to get by on little from the start, had to be adaptable. One example is the practice of wearing boots several sizes too large so they could be stuffed with paper or straw for insulation in the winter. Russian soldiers also carried their heavy winter greatcoats all year long to serve as blankets.

Fidel's stay at Wetzeldorf proved short, and he and his companions were soon aboard another train. If they expected the next destination to be a training facility, they were disappointed, for formal Waffen SS training at this critical juncture of the war was not assured. Those men with a higher level of education or a valuable skill had the best chance of being sent to one for training as an artillery or panzer (tank) specialist. Fidel's group, designated to fight as infantry, was routed to a rural area for something they thought they'd left behind—farm labor!

Some of those who did go on to training facilities were lucky enough to land under the command of officers such as the one who wrote, "Recruits arrived, including many ethnic Germans from Romania. All of them were healthy, strong young men with a naturalness and openness that made it a joy to be in a unit with them."[3]

Fidel's group was assigned to a division within III (Germanic) SS Panzer Corps, specifically the 11th SS Volunteer Panzergrenadier Division

Nordland (11. SS-Freiwilligen Panzergrenadier Division Nordland). Hitler had approved Nordland's formation only months earlier in February of 1943. Until fleshed out by the ethnic Germans from the Banat, the unit was understrength and consisted primarily of the remnants of various depleted and disbanded Danish, Norwegian, and German companies. The bulk of the division's officer and NCOs were Scandinavians and Germans drawn from the 5th SS Panzer Division Wiking (5. SS-Panzerdivision Wiking). At the time Hitler approved Nordland, he also authorized two other new SS divisions, SS Prinz Eugen and SS Handschar. Both were to be filled with men from the Balkans. Prinz Eugen was allocated some Banat men, but Handschar received only Bosnian Muslims and Croatian Catholics.

The Nazis were not slouches when it came to symbolism. Himmler was particularly adept at appropriating symbolic and propagandistic names for his Waffen SS units. The Nordland division had two regiments—SS Panzergrenadier Regiment 23 Norge and SS Panzergrenadier Regiment 24 Danmark. Their names reflected the two countries from which the core of its men originated, Norway and Denmark. Since there were no longer enough Nordic Europeans to form a complete division, Himmler used the newly conscripted ethnic Germans from Romania, Hungary, and Serbia to fill out the rolls. This made Nordland 40 percent Scandinavian, 25 percent German, and 35 percent Banat ethnic German. The unit also had a tiny smattering of Swedish, Dutch, Estonian, French, Finnish, Swiss, and British volunteers, which gave it the distinction of having the greatest variety of nationalities of any German military division.[4][5]

The *Freiwilligen* in Nordland's official name implied that its soldiers were all volunteers, but as already noted, the Nazis were not known for truth in labeling. Only its Scandinavians, West Europeans, and German nationals were truly volunteers. Despite the overall diversity, Fidel said the nationalities were concentrated by unit, and he experienced little mixing or contact with other nationalities. The Swedes, Norwegians, Danes, and Finns largely had their own companies or platoons and usually their own ethnic officers.

The alphanumeric designations that apply to small units are easily forgotten. Some 40 years after the war, Fidel could no longer recall the designation number of his Nordland battalion or his company. The sort of specifics he did retain were more practical or personal. He recalled that in his battalion most of the Orzydorf men he'd arrived with were clustered in two companies and that his company of just over 100 soldiers had 30 to 40 Banaters. Of these, eight hailed from Orzydorf. Correspondence to or from Fidel would have revealed a unit designation through his five-digit *Feldpost* (field postal address), but none survived. Out of fear that a Waffen

SS association might pose an administrative problem for our family when we immigrated to America, my mother burned all mementos and records that bore any reference to the Waffen SS. I expect she worried that not all US officials might be aware that conscripted non-German Waffen SS soldiers had been officially exonerated.[6] Fidel's mother and sister had no old letters from him either. The restrictive luggage-weight allowance when they left Romania hadn't permitted the luxury of bringing along keepsakes such as bundles of old letters.

Inquiries to the families of other Orzydorf soldiers who might have served with Fidel were also fruitless, as were queries to the appropriate German government archives. These inquiries came back with replies like "In response to your request... I can tell you that the staff papers [Wehstammbuch (identification) and Soldbuch (pay book)] of your father Fidel Eipert, born 1922 in Orzydorf are not available. They were probably lost in the war," and "Here the other existing records of the former German Wehrmacht had no findings."

The few surviving photos of Fidel in uniform were of no help because they were taken later in the war after he had been reassigned. A proper 1943 Waffen SS uniform would have displayed both rank and unit type on the shoulder boards, but by then, concern about such details had passed and not uncommonly the shoulder boards carried little or no decoration beyond branch of service, which was indicated by the color of the wool underlay (backing) color. The Waffen SS service was designated by light gray. A man's specialty, unit, or assignment was indicated by letters, numbers, or ciphers attached to the shoulder board. The right collar tab of the Waffen SS uniform displayed an SS runic patch (stylized double S), and the left collar tab showed rank. On a complete uniform, the cuff band on the lower sleeve designated unit assignment. The left sleeve might also indicate a specialty.[7] The three 1944 photographs of my father in uniform that survived my mother's housecleaning showed only a minimum of decorations. Aside from a black patch on the left collar tab, which indicated a rank of *SS-Schütze* (private), Fidel's uniform sported a wound badge pinned to his left pocket and Nordland's variant of the SS rune on his lower-left sleeve.

It seemed that the only hope of identifying Fidel's Nordland regiment, battalion, and company lay in correlating his recollection of eventful dates with the positions of Nordland's subunits as reported in division and regiment histories. Then, late in the completion of this book, several valuable clues surfaced to provide reasonably definitive answers.

The key to determining the latter was Fidel's mention of that second assignment's commander—Otto Skorzeny—a man well known by Hitler and the German public alike. His name led me to several declassified US

Army postwar interrogation documents. Certain facts in those documents aligned with Fidel's movements and allowed me to identify his company as well as uncover the hidden purpose behind his final assignment.

As for Fidel's original Nordland assignment, unit histories state that basic training was conducted at the Grafenwöhr training area in Germany from June until August 1943. There, a battle-tested cadre group from the Wiking division had been assembling since April to conduct the training. When Fidel's train left Wetzelsdorf in June of 1943, he may have expected this to be his next stop. After all, the Waffen SS was touted as an elite force, and if its recruits were to fight effectively and have a decent chance of surviving in the process, they needed appropriate training.

That Grafenwöhr base, which covers 65,000 acres, is today the US Army's largest training area in Europe but it carries an unhappy history. The base was initially constructed as a moderately sized artillery training facility for the Royal Bavarian Army in 1907 near the town of Grafenwöhr. That effort required razing some 58 small villages. In 1938 Hitler expanded the facility to its current size by expelling 3,500 more residents. The Waffen SS recruits who received basic infantry instruction there then went on to train in panzers either at the Panther tank training center in Erlangen, the tank factory in Nuremberg, the armor school in Wündsdorf, or the tank gunnery school in Putlos.[8] [9]

However, Fidel's group of Romanian Army transferees never set foot in Grafenwöhr or any other training base. When the train dropped the men off at Regensburg, Germany, they were dispatched to the countryside for farm harvest duty. Ironically, Regensburg was the port city on the Danube that had served as the exit point for some of their ancestors when they'd escaped the vassalage and mandatory military service of German nobles in the late 1700s. And now they were once again tied to a similar form of German servitude. The labor duty gave Fidel reason to question just how elite the Waffen SS remained. It was easy to understand that because of the battlefield manpower shortage, not every new recruit could get lengthy training, but it was also possible that poorer combat preparation for the Banaters was acceptable because foreigners were more expendable than Reich Germans.

It didn't take Fidel and the others long to learn that because so much of the German labor force was in uniform, the country no longer had enough working-age farmers to bring in the harvest. So the Banat men who should have been harvesting their own fields in Romania were harvesting Germany's fields. In the fields, Fidel worked alongside Russian POWs from a nearby POW camp. Most of the POWs were male, but there were a few women among them. These prisoners had picked up enough German to allow Fidel to talk to them. He identified with them and saw them less as enemy combatants than simple rural people who'd been thrown into the brown Soviet uniform. Fidel particularly remembered one man for the question he asked. The war was raging fiercely and death lurked everywhere, but this man's greatest concern seemed to be, "Does the farmer water down your beer too?" Fidel laughed when he recalled replying, "I get the same beer you do."

The POWs had come to know all the local farmers and told Fidel who was good to work for and who was stingy. After the two groups of laborers became more familiar with each other, the POWs confided that they'd never willingly go back to the Soviet Union because even prisoner life was better in Germany than back home under the communists. When the harvesting was done, Fidel and his companions were released to rejoin the rest of the division.

Gertrude Adam, the primary author of *Orczydorf*, the book about the history of my father's village, was able to provide valuable additional information about both the impressment of the Banat men into the Waffen SS and the harvest labor stint, since both her father, Josef Adam, and Josef's brother Hansi (Johann) were swept into the Waffen SS at this time. Her father was a year older than Fidel, but the two had become friends in their early school years. Unlike Fidel, Josef had academic ambitions and pursued higher education in Timişoara after his primary education ended.

From 1939 to 1943, the period during which Fidel had been skipping the weekly Romanian military training demanded of young men of his age, Josef was already serving in the Romanian Army. The mandatory enlistment demanded by his school saw to it that he was repeatedly called up for two to three months at a time, leaving him soldiering for nearly half the year. In a letter to his daughter Gertrude, Josef described what happened next.

> Already in April, May [1943] it was made known in Orczydorf: everyone from 15 to 35 years of age, everyone volunteers [for the Waffen SS]. Except for a few, whose windows were then smashed . . . . But I wasn't included, I was a one-year volunteer with the Romanians as part of my agricultural studies; we did military service there [academic year 1942/43]. That means we went for a walk in the hunting forest once a week in a nettle suit with a rifle, like the Romanian non-commissioned officers [of the 2nd Heavy Artillery Regiment].

Gertrude said that when her father started his studies in Timişoara, his diligent younger brother Hansi stepped in to help keep the farm going. In the spring of 1943 when Hansi returned from a neighboring village after an examination taken by a group of freshly drafted men and boys, Hansi called out happily to his parents in front of his house, "Atollery! Atollery!" He'd been assigned to the artillery, to the great relief of his parents, because the artillery was considered to be safer than the infantry. That evening, the parents of another friend, Nikolaus Leichnam, confronted Hansi's parents and demanded to know what strings they'd pulled to get Hansi assigned to artillery, for their own son was made an infantryman. They wanted to know why they hadn't been told how to get the same for their boy. Gertrude explained that her Adam grandparents wouldn't have dreamed of intervening in something that affected the lives of others, for they believed in the saying "Man thinks and God directs." Ironically, Nikolaus survived his infantry assignment, while the artillery assignment didn't allow the same for Hansi.

Gertrude, because she'd recorded an interview with her father about the war years, was able to pass along her father's exact words about the Waffen SS transfer. The following is a translation of a portion of that interview:

> What happened to us [he and his fellow students serving part time in the Romanian Army]? No, we didn't go with the Orzydorf group [younger draftees], but went separately by way of Hermannstadt, since high school students, graduates, as future officers were to go to a separate unit. Whatever happened, . . . then we came to the Grafenwoehr military training ground—Grafenwoehr in the Upper Palatinate of Germany.
>
> There we experienced a heavy air raid on the Schweinfurt ball bearing factory during the night. They put us in a former horse stable, where no one took care of us (17. August 1943).
>
> So who did we find there? It's all the young people from Orczydorf, including my brother, who are pictured [reference to an old photo]. They're all there, all disappointed, all sad and ready to desert. They had Danish non-commissioned officers [NCOs] who treated them as Balkans [lowly outsiders rather than fellow Germans]. They were—my brother told me and the other peasant boys—sent to harvest in the Upper Palatinate, where they stacked heavy sheaves of rye in the barns. These boys came from using binding mowers [modern machinery at home], from wheat fields, and then found—yes, that in Germany they are far behind! Very sad. Then, after two weeks or more, we were suddenly loaded up again, but didn't know where we were going. In Passau there was another train, and that's where I ran into my brother for the last time. They went to the Danmark Regiment in Ragusa, Dubrovnik. He wrote

home from there, and also to me. From there they went to Narwa [Estonia]. There, 80% of the boys fell in one year. They didn't have any training, they all fell, one after the other. Of my brother's class, three survived out of 20.

Gertrude reiterated that her uncle Hansi Adam and the other boys who'd been coerced into joining the Waffen SS and then sent to Grafenwöhr on July 15, 1943, were brought to tears by their treatment from the great "motherland" and the abuse doled out by their NCOs. They had expected much better and lamented that they'd been taken from the advanced farms of the Banat and sent as base laborers to primitive farms where mechanization didn't exist and cows were still used as draft animals. The torment there ended at the close of August 1943 when Germany's Italian ally was rapidly losing control to the guerrilla partisans. The company was then rushed to Croatia as part of the newly formed Nordland division and thrown into the fight against the partisans.

Panzergrenadier Division Nordland was nominally a mobile mechanized-infantry division. The core of a such a Waffen SS unit typically included a panzer battalion and two or three regiments of infantry with motorized transportation in the form of halftracks or trucks. However, by this point in the war all military units were short of vehicles. Newly formed units like Nordland were particularly affected.

On August 28, 1943, III SS Panzer Corps, which consisted mainly of Nordland and its sister unit, SS Volunteer Panzergrenadier Brigade Nederland, received orders to deploy to Croatia. Obergruppenführer Felix Steiner, the corps commander, had requested that the unit not be sent to the Western Front because many of his West European men had enlisted with the stipulation that they would not fight in their own countries. Further "training" was the official reason cited for the transfer, but this training turned out to consist of large-scale sweeps to engage the communist partisans in combat. The division still lacked vehicles, artillery, and heavy weapons, so the trainees maneuvered mainly on foot and had to rely only on small arms.[10]

Croatia had been occupied by both German and Italian soldiers until Hitler invaded the Soviet Union in 1941. At this point Hitler ceded Croatia to the Italian Army in order to free up the German force there. However, when the Italian Army failed to control the partisan guerillas, the German military needed to return. Throughout the war German soldiers mocked the Italian military for its tendency to call for help whenever something went wrong. One joke went, "In Italy there's a new dance craze. It's called the Retreat and it goes like this: You take one step forward, then two steps back, spin around your axis, and hide behind your partner." Other jokes included: "the shortest book ever written—Italian War Heroes"; "the Italian battle flag—a white cross on a white background"; and "Italy, the country whose soldiers had the most sunburnt armpits in the war."[11]

III SS Panzer Corps set up its headquarters in Croatia's capital, Zagreb (Agram to the Germans), on September 1, 1943. Only days later the training regimen unexpectedly expanded beyond antipartisan operations when Hitler learned the Kingdom of Italy had secretly negotiated a surrender to the Allies through a contingent of politicians and generals who'd lost their stomach for war.

The capitulation caught both Mussolini and Hitler by surprise. They'd been unaware that highly placed Italians had carried on negotiations with the Allies. In response, various German divisions were hastily scrambled to disarm the Italian Army units before the partisans could acquire their weapons. The Germans were to also protect sympathetic Italian officers from their own soldiers. The Italian retreat gained some tanks for Nordland, but for the most part they were inferior Italian tanks without radios. Communication and coordination between them were difficult as they required the use of flags, signal disks, and a line of sight.[12]

Croatia was a state within Yugoslavia, the jigsaw-puzzle country haphazardly assembled by the Allied victors of World War I. The assemblage, because it contained ethnic groups that hated each other, devolved into one of the most vicious theaters of World War II. Several conflicts raged simultaneously as a dizzying number of factions battled each other. Aside from the main conflict between the Axis powers and the Allies, three other political factions were at war—communist partisans, Chetniks (Serbian royalists), and Ustaše (fascists). It has been said that the latter's militiamen were terrorists that made the Nazis look like boy scouts.

The Chetnik forces were split. Some were friendly to the Germans, some not. Other partisan groups were nominally friendly to the Germans or Ustaše but could turn on either without notice. To complicate matters, additional age-old ethnic conflicts existed between the resident Croat, Serb, Bosnian Muslim, and ethnic German populations. If that wasn't confusing enough, territorial disputes between Italy, Hungary, and Romania over claims for Yugoslavian territory were also in play. In the simplest terms, after Italy surrendered, Germany and the Croat Ustaše comprised one side and Chetniks the other. The various communist partisan factions had by then united under an antifascist resistance movement known as the People's Liberation Movement and made up a third side. All three sides fought against each other as circumstances warranted.

The 380,000 men of Italy's Army Group East were already in the process of pulling back in Croatia when Italian government officials secretly signed an armistice that aligned Italy with the Allied nations. The talks between the Allies and the new Italian government had been conducted in such secrecy that the sudden capitulation surprised the Italian commanders just as much as it did Mussolini and Hitler. As soon as the Germans learned what was happening, they launched Operation Konstantin to seize control of the Italian-held areas and to disarm the Italian units that refused to keep fighting, which was most of them. The Germans knew the partisans wouldn't waste the opportunity to seize Italian weapons and equipment, so a race ensued. The partisans called on the various Italian garrisons to surrender, but most of the Italian units awaited the Germans before capitulating because once disarmed they were defenseless against guerilla vengeance. Large and small German detachments scrambled to secure territory and supplies.[13]

Fidel's *Zug* (platoon), upon arrival in Croatia, received orders to proceed to southern Croatia to retrieve Italian munitions. So Fidel and his party boarded two rail coach cars and were soon on the way to Dubrovnik, some 600 kilometers distant. The Zug's job was to secure the munitions and weapons being collected at a supply depot, load them onto boxcars, then guard the train against partisan attack on its return north.

To soldiers who'd yet to receive any training in German maneuvers and equipment, the assignment must have looked risky. Dubrovnik lay several days away, and the rail line ran through daunting mountainous terrain that left the tracks vulnerable to sabotage from the 160,000 communist guerillas active in Yugoslavia. At this time the guerrillas roamed everywhere and controlled almost all territory outside the towns and villages the Germans were garrisoned in. The men reached Sarajevo, a large rail hub in the south, without incident, but there encountered a complication. Continuing on required a different train because from here on the track to Dubrovnik was a 760-millimeter narrow-gauge spur line known as *vlak* Ćiro (train Ćiro). Up to this point the tracks had been standard gauge. The soldiers were successful in garnering a train and pressed on, but the new train was small, light, and just a few cars long.

According to a period rail map, vlak Ćiro passed through historic Mostar, a city which was destined to suffer great damage during heavy fighting in a civil war four decades later. When I passed through that city in 2003 not long after that conflict ended, the bullet holes and destruction attested to the level of fighting. The warring factions had battled across the river that divided the city and pounded each other with artillery and machine guns until the city was all but destroyed.

Fidel would have been surprised to learn that a section of the track he traveled in 1943 had a link to his own locale in Romania, described in the following excerpt from an article about Croatia's trains:

The introduction of the narrow-gauge network in Bosnia and Herzegovina came about randomly. The first track from Brod to Žepče had originally been standard gauge and built for transporting war material. It was later modified to narrow gauge so that left-over material from the construction of the Timișoara–Oršava narrow-gauge railway could be used up.[14]

Vlak Ćiro passed through what today are the two countries of Bosnia and Herzegovina, and Montenegro. The segment that connected Capljina and Dubrovnik was abandoned in 1976 and is no longer on the regional rail map, so only a portion of the line still remains.

Fidel was surely relieved when he reached Dubrovnik and found the city peaceful. Probably almost as comforting was finding that he wouldn't be sleeping in a tent and pulling nighttime guard watches. The city quickly grew on him once he was situated and his platoon leader announced that they "might as well get in some relaxation while there." The men took the lieutenant's suggestion to heart. Collecting and loading arms and ammunition onto rail cars was still work, but when spread out among a couple of squads, the job took just a few hours each day and didn't tire anyone unduly. Eventually the soldiers filled all five of their small boxcars.

The soldiers lodged in a closed hotel near a beach—two to a room. The beds had all disappeared but sleeping on a floor with a roof overhead wasn't a terrible hardship for field soldiers. Fidel grinned when he said their main concern each day was nothing weightier than deciding from which market or restaurant to buy their next meal. The daily routine was to arise at 8 a.m., eat breakfast, and walk to the beach for a dip in the warm Adriatic Sea. Only then did they begin the work of sorting and loading the Italian supplies. At lunchtime the process was repeated. Fidel was amazed at how exceptionally clear the Adriatic's water was. The air was not always as clear, but from a certain height it was sometimes possible to catch a glimpse of distant Italian mountains across the water. The platoon managed to stretch their mission out for an entire month. Fidel's only regret was that he didn't have a chance to connect with more locals. The few he got to know were friendly and not unlike the villagers back home.

As for what Hansi Adam experienced in Croatia, Gertrude Adam said her knowledge is limited to what he wrote in the last letter his parents received from him. It is the only surviving letter addressed to the family and is dated October 24, 1943—Hansi's 20th birthday. According to the boy's mother, he wrote from the Dubrovnik area. The text of the letter follows, but according to Gertrude, the name of the place became "blurred and illegible due to traces of tears." Hansi's grandmother kept this letter in her prayer book for the rest of her life.

Dear Parents!

24.X.43 [24 October 1943]

First of all, I am happy to tell you that I am still healthy, and I hope the same from you, dear parents! It's Sunday today. Just before noon. You might be in church or somewhere else, you might still have a lot of work to do, and I just got off the post. I quickly shaved and washed and now I'm sitting here, on a rock next to the sea, the water splashes from time to time when a big wave comes, even biting my feet and, as so often before, I've taken the pen in my hand and send Dear parents, a message from me, your faithful son, from far, far away. I'm sure you think the same way I do about today. Because today is my birthday. Today I am twenty years old. Twenty years since I saw the light of day. If you look into the future like that, how long is twenty years. But when I think back, how quickly the twenty years have passed and I still feel so young. We sing a song here every day, life is a game of dice, yes, that's how it is. I am happy and I thank our Lord God that he has given me so healthy and strong, my old age, and I especially owe a thousand thanks to you, dear mother, because you gave me life. And finally, I am grateful to both of you, dear parents, for raising me and raising me to be an honest, hard-working person. I want to remain grateful and faithful to our Lord God and to you, dear parents, in the hope of living as healthy and obediently as I have been up to now.

We are still here on [illegible]. Yesterday we had to go to another guard house, a wooden barracks abandoned by the Italians. Was only awake for an hour last night and put to sleep in the barracks. But there's no sign of sleeping because I've never seen bugs like this in my life. They attacked you and bit you so badly that your eyes close and you can't sleep. I don't know, they don't go to everyone. Zornek [Zornig] is even now inside and asleep, he also feels something but not so strongly. [These tiny bugs were apparently sand flies, insects that feed most ferociously at night and are well known near area beaches.]

I have another watch from twelve to two and then I'm free until six in the evening. Then I'll lie down somewhere in the open, because nothing is done without sleep. If only the order to leave came immediately, because as much as we liked it here on the blue Adriatic Sea at first, we are fed up with it now. During the day a heat like here in August, cool at night, and then a plague of flies that you can hardly move. I haven't been as fed up with life here as I am. It's not just like that for me, but for everyone. Those who aren't sick yet don't have a good appetite either, and I don't either. Tomorrow it will be a month since I got the last post. Hopefully it doesn't take as long as it used to. What else is new at home, everything is still fine. Cattle. The work goes halfway. I hope for the best. I close my letter. Since I have to go back to the post immediately with the hope that we won't stay here much longer and that the journey will be successful. Greet grandparents and relatives too. Many warm greetings and a happy reunion at home sends you from far away your son Hans!!!

This letter was central in pinning down Fidel's regiment with a high degree of confidence. Because Hansi Adam mentioned being mistreated by Danish NCOs, it became clear that he and the other boys from his train had been assigned to Regiment Danmark rather than Nordland's other regiment, Regiment Norge, where the boys would have encountered Norwegian NCOs. Identifying Hansi Adam's placement allowed me to place Fidel in Danmark too because he'd told me practically all the Orzydorf men who left Romania within days of his own departure landed in two sister companies of one battalion. That reduced Fidel's assignment possibilities to either Hansi's company or a sister company within the same Danmark battalion. Even though Fidel's group of former Romanian soldiers and Hansi's group of new recruits arrived in Germany separately, the fact that they shared the same farm labor experience at Regensburg during the relatively short wheat-harvest period was further indication that their unit assignments overlapped very closely.

Hansi's birthday letter placed him in the vicinity of Dubrovnik when Fidel was there. Apparently only a small contingent of soldiers was sent on this mission—likely just one platoon, to judge by the small size of the commandeered train they rode. An additional clue strongly suggesting that the two men were in the same platoon came in Hansi's mention of another Orzidorf soldier, Zornek (Zornig). Since Zornig was an uncommon surname in Orzidorf, use of just the last name told me there was only one Zornig among the new recruits. I already knew Fidel and Zornig were in the same platoon because Fidel had told me that he and Zornig were in the same machine-gun team. Still more evidence that Hansi Adam and Fidel were in the same platoon came from a later letter Hansi wrote to the family of his best friend. The text of that letter will appear in context later.

On a visit to Dubrovnik in 2003, as I walked the beach, the city streets, and the historic Old Town, I tried to form a picture of the city that Fidel experienced on his mission there. The city had grown and modernized since the 1940s, passed through another war, and recovered yet again. Dubrovnik was no longer the place it had been under the fascists and then the communists—the worst ills of the 20th century had passed. I could still visualize some semblance of the old city that my father saw. A vibrant tourist industry was budding, but the place wasn't yet crowded with the hordes of cruise ship and bus passengers that now disgorge daily on the port city.

I could understand Fidel's reluctance to return to the north when departure could no longer be put off. His contingent of the platoon had been lucky enough to be in the city and away from the sand fleas that Hansi's group experienced in their outlying location, but I know Fidel's reluctance was about more than the easy duty, good food, and sunny beach. He knew he was returning to the real war and its hazards, which began right outside the city. Riding a train loaded with explosive ordinance in rebel territory was not the most enviable of tasks. The rugged terrain ahead allowed the partisans plenty of opportunity for ambush or sabotage. Upon reaching the first of several steep coastal mountain grades, the three small steam locomotives at the head of the train didn't have the power to pull the five heavy freight cars and two coaches up the slope in one pass. So two munition cars and one passenger coach were uncoupled and left on a siding while the locomotives and two of the platoon's four squads proceeded. Fidel was with the group that remained behind. Fortunately, nothing happened during the two days it took for the locomotives to return, and after a day's travel, the full train was reassembled. Upon arrival in Sarajevo, the city in which the 1914 assassination of Austrian Archduke Franz Ferdinand had triggered World War I, the men had no time to see the sights; they were too busy transferring the munitions to standard-gauge boxcars so they could be on their way.

Sarajevo was yet another destination during my trip through the Balkans. Visualizing the World War II look and feel of that city was easier than in Dubrovnik, for Sarajevo saw few tourists in 2003 and still carried the grimy, dilapidated, communist-era patina that was universal during the USSR's domination of Eastern Europe. Sarajevo was surrounded by mountains and had no easy port access or sunny beaches. The city hadn't yet begun to modernize because when the Iron Curtain lifted, it became a regional civil war hotspot that had only recently cooled. Buildings still showed damage from mortar and artillery shells that had rained down on the city from the heights of the surrounding mountains, and white United Nations armored vehicles patrolled the streets.

When the munitions transfer to the wide-gauge boxcars was complete and the journey resumed, the men confronted a new problem—hunger. The extra days in the mountains had cost them most of the food they'd packed, and attempts to scrounge food at whistle stops and in Sarajevo weren't very productive because the countryside was a war zone. Some of the towns and villages along the route had changed hands a time or two since their earlier passage, so foraging was risky. The town they'd started from turned out to be one of these, for there were no longer any German troops to be found there. They'd either abandoned the place or been driven out. The rail station lay deserted and ransacked. Some freshly butchered meat found there indicated that a group of guerillas had pulled out hastily when they heard the train coming. This spurred the platoon to hurry on as well. Not much later, the soldiers reconnected with their own forces, turned the munitions over to others, and rejoined their company.

On his return Fidel learned from other Banat men in the company that while he'd been off sunbathing in southern Croatia, they'd engaged in vicious live-fire "training" against the partisan enemy and had taken casualties. Companies had been assigned to outlying villages, some of which were isolated in the mountainous terrain. Fidel didn't talk about how much fighting he participated in during the weeks that followed, but it must have been a considerable amount. Several of Danmark's companies were mauled, and one was completely wiped out in Hrastovicka. The relief force sent to help the company reported that by the time of its arrival, the partisans had disappeared into the mountains. The soldiers "found their comrades . . . as mutilated corpses. Only a few escaped the massacre."[15]

For Fidel and his division, the combat in Croatia ended in early November when its commanders declared Nordland sufficiently trained and equipped to be upgraded to *ready* status. Despite the upgraded status, the unit was still inadequately trained and consisted of only two regiments, a sparse panzer battalion, and several attached small units. The two infantry regiments, Danmark and Norge, were supposed to be supported by reconnaissance, engineer, heavy weapons, and antiaircraft companies, but these ancillary units were still incomplete, or as in the case of the heavy weapons company, lacking entirely.

During the time Fidel was deployed in Croatia, his brother Hans was training with Nordland's 11th SS Flak (antiaircraft) Abteilung. Hans served in the flak unit's 1st battery, which could be determined from the feldpost (address) on the back of a picture postcard that showed Hans in dress uniform.[16] Flak training in East Prussia consumed five months. A translation of the pertinent 1943 history for that detachment reads, "While from August to December the Division moved to Croatia, the antiaircraft section remained at the military training area of Arys-Nord."[17]

Neither brother knew much about what the other was doing at this time. Fidel wasn't a letter writer, as I know from my childhood. Letter writing was all done by my mother. Correspondence was likely also difficult during the weeks Fidel spent in Dubrovnik. Anything he heard of Hans would have come via letters from his mother or his fiancée back in Orzydorf. I suspect Hans wasn't a prodigious letter writer either, except perhaps when it came to his new bride.

---

1. Moniroth You-Bell, "SS-Panzergrenadier Ausbildungs- u. Ersatz-Bataillone (SS Panzergrenadier Training and Replacement Battalions)," Axis History Forum, July 13, 2011, http://forum.axishistory.com/viewtopic.php?t=179930.
2. Gottlob Herbert Bidermann, Derek S. Zumbro, and Dennis E. Showalter, *In Deadly Combat: A German Soldier's Memoir of the Eastern Front* (Lawrence, KS: University Press of Kansas, 2000), 116.
3. Wilhelm Tieke, *Tragedy of the Faithful: A History of the III. (Germanisches) SS-Panzer-Korps* (Winnipeg, Manitoba: J.J. Fedorowicz Publishing, 2001), 5.
4. Tieke, *Tragedy of the Faithful*, 5.
5. Jewish Virtual Library, "The SS (Schutzstaffel): 11th SS Volunteer Panzergrenadier Division Nordland," accessed August 2, 2016, https://www.jewishvirtuallibrary.org/11th-ss-volunteer-panzergrenadier-division-nordland.
6. "Judgment of the International Military Tribunal. The trial of German major war criminals: proceedings of the International Military Tribunal sitting at Nuremberg Germany," The Avalon Project: Yale Law School, Lillian Goldman Law Library (Government Printing Office, 1946), https://avalon.law.yale.edu/imt/judorg.asp.
7. GermanDaggers.com, "SchutzStaffel (SS) Collar Tab and Shoulder Board Identification Gallery," 2013, http://www.germandaggers.com/Gallery/CT3W.php.
8. Tieke, *Tragedy of the Faithful*, 5.
9. Martin Egnash, "Relics of Germany's Past Dot Army's Grafenwoehr Training Area," Stars and Stripes, September 6, 2017, https://www.stripes.com/migration/relics-of-germany-s-past-dot-army-s-grafenwoehr-training-area-1.486291.
10. Tieke, *Tragedy of the Faithful*, 6.
11. Rudolf Herzog, *Dead Funny: Humor in Hitler's Germany* (Brooklyn, N.Y.: Melville House, 2011), 140.
12. Tieke, *Tragedy of the Faithful*, 7.
13. "11th SS Volunteer Panzergrenadier Division *Nordland*," in *Wikipedia, the Free Encyclopedia*, June 3, 2016, 29, https://en.wikipedia.org/w/index.php?title=11th_SS_Volunteer_Panzergrenadier_Division_Nordland&oldid=723544088.
14. Marija Benić Penava, "Traffic Connectivity in Croatia in the Past: The Dubrovnik Region Case" 1, no. 3 (2015): 197.
15. Tieke, *Tragedy of the Faithful*, 10.
16. "Can Anyone Identify These W-SS Decorations?," *Axis History Forum*, 2009, https://forum.axishistory.com/viewtopic.php?f=9&t=151441.
17. Robert Balsam, "Die SS-Flak-Abteilung 11," Balsi, accessed November 15, 2024, https://balsi.de/Weltkrieg/Einheiten/SS/Waffen-SS/SS-Artillerie-Einheiten/SS-Flak/Abteilungen/11-SS-Flak-Abt.htm.

20 Waffen SS "Volunteer" Anton Krämer

In a memoir, Anton Krämer, yet another Banater from Fidel's locale who was affected by the fateful agreement between Hitler and Antonescu, presented more information about how the transfer process worked. He'd been a 17-year-old boy when on May 12, 1943, the politicians formalized what was already a tacit agreement to induct ethnic Germans into the Waffen SS. His story filled in some of what I never thought to ask Fidel about before he died. Krämer, a good student, had academic aspirations and wanted no part of farming. He'd just finished high school and was about to begin a four-year course of study at a teacher-training institute when Germany began conscripting Romania's young ethnic Germans. By then a few Banaters had already completed two years of German military service to avoid duty in the harsh and regressive Romanian Army.[1]

The pact stipulated that those males born before April 1, 1926, could "voluntarily" report for German Wehrmacht or Waffen SS duty. In actuality, the conscripted boys were allotted solely to the Waffen SS. The differentiation between the regular military and the SS force wasn't clearly imparted to the ethnic German communities, and the deceptive wording was meant to keep it that way. A Führererlass (führer decree) guaranteed that the men would retain their Romanian citizenship, but when the Romanian government capitulated to the Soviets and switched sides the following year, the new government refused to recognize the Romanian nationality of these soldiers. Romania claimed that the men were now German citizens because Hitler had also automatically granted them citizenship. Krämer wrote,

> In the eyes of the Romanians we were 'deserters,' and on top of that 'Nazis,' 'fascists' and 'Hitlerists.' The German authorities of the three western zones of occupation (and probably the Soviets, also) did not recognize Hitler's decree because they did

not regard it as a 'naturalization.' Thus we were not only homeless but also stateless.²

In typical Nazi fashion, the "voluntary" part of reporting for induction was anything but voluntary thanks to other parts of the agreement that made service mandatory. Ethnic German students protested, but to no avail. Some, like the younger brother of Krämer's best friend, were arrested. The boy was tortured so severely that he died during his incarceration. Classmates born before April 1, 1926, had already shipped out when Krämer and the remainder of his class were told to report to Timișoara at the end of July 1943. Most of the fathers rode there on the train with their boys. When Romanian officials alerted the group that only those boys born before April 1, 1926, were obligated to go, most fathers pulled their boys off the train. This left just Krämer and another boy from his class to proceed beyond Timișoara with boys from other locales. At the Hungarian border,

> Romanian officers took Mathias Becker and me off the train and tried to prevent us from continuing our journey. They cited a clause according to which high school students are exempted from conscription to the German Wehrmacht if they so request. That was true, but we had not applied because we did not want to be drafted into the Romanian Army for anything in the world. Nobody could have guessed at the time that those of our year, who had returned to Ulm [in Romania] with their fathers, were deported to forced labor in the Soviet Union in January 1945.³

The interior of the freight cars was so hot and unbearable as the train moved slowly across the plain that many men climbed up onto the roof of the cars. In Hungary the train stopped to delouse the passengers in preparation for Reich entry, as if the new recruits had come from primitive, filthy hovels. The boys tasted their first military meal there as well, which consisted mainly of "rough commissary bread." These young men, accustomed to good food and enough of it, had trouble stomaching the poor offering and found the food didn't improve in quantity or quality in the days ahead. In Budapest, the next stop, the recruits mixed with local residents at the station and received offers to help them escape their military commitment. Rumors that one or more boys planned to desert spread through the train, but the journey resumed without anything having come of it.⁴

The recruits were marched from the Ostbahnhof (East Train Station) to the arsenal upon arrival in Vienna. This building today houses the Austrian Army Museum, a place well worth visiting by anyone interested in the world wars. I spent most of a day exploring it while researching material for this book and *The Secret She Carried*. One display that still particularly stands out in my mind was Archduke Franz Ferdinand's blood-stained uniform and the car in which he rode in Sarajevo the day he was assassinated in the terrorist act that touched off World War I.

Krämer and the other new recruits, still in civilian clothes and carrying rucksacks, were dogged by a "greedy pack" of Viennese begging for bacon and cigarettes. Krämer was stunned to find that the morally upright Austrian who the people back home so admired, could act so despicably and think only of their stomachs. The unruly crowd not only begged, it also jeered and harassed the young men and called them *Kriegsverlängerer* (war perpetuators). This was a propaganda term the Nazis applied to Jews when blaming them for prolonging the war. This caused the young men to ask themselves why they were there, if these were the sort of people they were fighting for.

What followed dismayed Krämer and the other boys even more. To everyone's surprise, they learned they didn't have the option to join the German Army, Navy, or Air Force, but went directly to the Waffen SS. Krämer wrote,

> Today we know that the Waffen SS as elite troops had serious casualties and we were nothing but bitter cannon fodder. We were 'expendable' because they [the Nazis] did not have to account to the German people for the 'Volksdeutsche' from abroad. Some cohorts of our compatriots, such as those born in 1924, suffered so heavily that few survived the war; some families lost two, even three of their sons![5]

Krämer also stated that Reich families were protected from the loss of all their male offspring. Surviving sons, particularly farm boys, were dismissed from military service to assure succession of the male line and the productivity of farms. The same did not apply to Volksdeutsche—people whose language and culture were German in origin but lived beyond Germany's borders and did not hold German citizenship.

And some of the Volksdeutsche entities were treated more poorly than others. In one example, Krämer cited how differently he and his fellow Banat Swabians were received than the recruits of the Transylvania Saxons—a second Romanian Volksdeutsche group. Following the issuance of uniforms, the formation of marching column, several more days of awful food, and the usual training harshness new recruits everywhere faced, Krämer's group was told to assemble for a speech by a high-ranking officer. At the assembly area they found many officers and a Ministry of Propaganda film crew waiting. Krämer believed that this spectacle had been arranged to show the war-weary German populace how eager the new soldiers were to get to the front.

When the speechmaking ended, a young soldier jumped up, assumed a stiff military posture, and shouted, "Siebenbürgers step forward." The Transylvania Saxons (Siebenbürgers) had obviously rehearsed this maneuver, for as soon as they formed up, the speaker recited the history of the Transylvanian Saxon Germans and repeatedly praised them for preserving their Germanness. No one saw fit to mention the Banat Germans. This charade to curry favor with the Nazis had been set up by the Saxon-German politicians in Transylvania out of self-interest. Yet back in Romania, these same leaders were espousing only the greatest kinship with their Banat "brethren."

Within days the young soldiers were back aboard freight cars heading northwest to the Upper Palatinate, one of the administrative districts of the state of Bavaria in Germany. The train passed through the city of Regensburg and continued on to the huge Grafenwöhr military training base where boys with any high school education were assigned to panzer armor training with the 5th SS Panzer Division Wiking (5. SS-Panzerdivision Wiking). Krämer described the Grafenwöhr base as a place like most training areas, "scenic, but climatically rough." The cool and rainy weather didn't agree with the Banaters. Most were still boys, and the merciless course brought many of them to tears. They were shunted about and shouted at from early morning until late at night. In their exhaustion they cursed the day they'd let themselves be brought to Germany. Throwing the various ethnicities together in this close confinement produced still more friction and inflamed everyone. The quarrels and loud curses directed at Germany in various dialects and languages never stopped.

Krämer and the others found that minorities like the Banaters were held to be beneath even the "Germanic" volunteers—the Danes, Dutch, Flemings, Swedes, and Norwegians. Men from these countries could get a discharge from the service and return home after two years of service. "But we, the so-called 'booty men,' were sent to the front after a very short training period and had to remain there until the end of the war, unless a hospital stay intervened. Of the Romanian Germans in our company, not a single one had even been granted home leave for one day."[6]

Hardest on the boys was the attitude of the training cadre—men from the countries of Western Europe who conducted themselves as if they were ethnically superior and more Germanic than the new trainees. They called the new men *Beutegermanen*, or booty Germans, which destroyed all rapport. The recruits couldn't fight back and took it as long as they could, but eventually complained to the company commander. The Romanian Army veterans who'd already fought bloody battles in support of the Germans around Stalingrad were the most furious at being treated like filth by young, arrogant trainers.

The captain listened to the trainees without speaking a word. When he dismissed the men, they feared for what would happen next. To everyone's surprise, the next morning he unleashed a furious tirade on the trainers in front of the whole company. When finished, he explained to these men who the recruits were, where they'd come from, and reminded them that everyone there was on the same side. This didn't lead to any gentler treatment, but it did stop the ethnic insults. Then at the next political assembly the captain told the entire company his own life story. His grandparents had emigrated to Brazil, and he'd only come to the newly awakened Reich in 1937. The Wehrmacht didn't accept him because he was a Brazilian citizen, so he joined the Waffen SS. His revelation further eased the tension and now most trainers accepted the men as equally worthy Germans. But not all. The loudest screamers were those who'd come from a lowly position in civilian life and hadn't yet been to the front. There were many such men on the regimental staff.

During the training period a number of wounded Wiking veterans just released from hospitals came to the unit. Krämer called them splendid companions for they were open and didn't stand behind their rank or decorations. Some of these men had been infantrymen who'd moved to panzers. They knew every move and survival trick in those smaller, earlier model tanks, but because their habits were so ingrained, retraining on the new models was in some ways harder for them. What these soldiers invaluably instilled in the untested men was the idea that training offered the best chance of surviving the mess on the front. They'd endured and survived a calamitous retreat from the Caucasus in the Soviet Union when their Wiking Division was all but destroyed. It had been sacrificed in several rearguard blocking actions that allowed other units to escape rearward in a last ditch, but futile, attempt to help save the 6th Army at Stalingrad. The panzer regiment these men served in once had over 200 panzers. Just five were left by the time it recrossed the Don River at Rostov.

The training became a blur for Krämer's reconnaissance platoon as it rushed around in panzers, not all of which had real mounted guns. Three radio operators trained simultaneously in each vehicle, and Krämer wrote he felt caught in a bad dream. The trainees were constantly tossed about and dizzy, like they were riding some crazy merry-go-round. Suddenly, right in the middle of training in mid-September, the division was rushed to Croatia because the Italians had suddenly switched sides. German forces were needed to keep the enemy partisans at bay and to seize the Italian weapons and munitions before they were captured or sold to the partisans.

After disembarking from the freight car transport, the battalion resumed some semblance of training. In Croatia Krämer had a chance to interact with some of the locals and reported that he felt more comfortable with these people than with the Germans, for like him, they'd once been part of the Austrian Empire.

The trainees hadn't tasted fruit since leaving home so when they discovered the local market, they spent their entire pay filling their stomachs. They hadn't ever been satiated on their meager rations, and everyone looked and felt undernourished. The Germans could no longer adequately feed their soldiers, which was particularly hard on still-growing boys. Everyone called the monotonous German chow *Saufraß* (hog slop). The Romanian Army was noted for serving beans and the German Army for potatoes. Breakfast and lunch at Grafenwöhr were cold, always the same, and served in a soldier's extended field cap.

The trainees were only about halfway through the instruction course in late 1943 when the division received orders to return to the Eastern Front. The men were granted a Christmas leave first, but Krämer and his fellow Banaters were only allowed to take this leave within the Reich. To use it, the trainees had to know someone to stay with. Krämer was one of the few who could take advantage of the offer because his family had acquaintants he could call on. He divided his time between Berlin, which by then had already amassed considerable bomb damage, and Silesia in the Czech Protectorate. But all too soon, the lucky personnel who'd had Christmas leave—soldiers, Red Cross nurses, and military-associated civilian workers—crammed aboard the passenger trains heading east to rejoin "the real war."

As Krämer's journey to the southern sector of the front dragged on and on through the vast east, the soldiers killed time with card games or endless chatter. Krämer found that even hundreds of kilometers from the front, the train stations were surrounded by protective barricades with firing position openings. Just as in Croatia, the defenses marked active partisan activity. Here and there the wrecks of locomotives and cars lined the sides of the tracks. In such areas, two flatbed cars were attached to the front of their locomotive to detonate mines and spare the valuable engines from destruction. Krämer speculated that nothing happened to his train because the weather was very cold and the guerillas were holed up somewhere warm. His journey ended at the Dnieper River in Ukraine, where Wiking was caught up in another disaster-in-the-making. He and the other men arrived just in time to celebrate the New Year and to fall into a Russian trap that would snap shut shortly.

Upon arrival, Krämer found Wiking's food situation was much better than in Germany. By then some Banaters had worked their way into the mess tent, and their cooking made the food more palatable to their compatriots. But the main reason for the improvement was a better supply of food. Like some of the other divisions, in 1941 after the Barbarossa invasion, Wiking had taken over a large Soviet collective farm in Ukraine and paid the workers to continue operating the farm. That collective supplied the division with an abundance of grain, vegetables, and meat. The situation came about because in some ways, the German command had prepared and "printed a German-Russian phrasebook that allowed the Germans to communicate with the Russian workers. The booklet contained questions such as, 'Where is the collective farm chairman' and 'Are you a Communist?' " The interrogated knew it was inadvisable to answer the latter question in the affirmative.[7]

Unfortunately, winter on the front introduced an entirely new meal problem—hot evening meals could not always be delivered safely to tank crews. The meal might start out hot, but arrive frozen. Crews warmed it up by running their tank engines, which consumed scarce fuel.

To Krämer's misfortune, the Russian general staff had promised Stalin they would deliver a second Stalingrad after Hitler ordered his generals to hold a largely encircled bulge of land known as the Cherkassy Pocket on the Dnieper River. The Russians employed the Stalingrad strategy again and deeply outflanked the six German half-strength divisions within the pocket along both sides to create a trap, then built up their forces. When they closed the trap on January 24, all supplies and fuel had to be airlifted in. As the most mobile force within the entrapment, Wiking's panzers carried the heaviest defensive load as they waited for permission from Hitler to break out. By mid-February the pocket had shrunk to just five kilometers in diameter, which left the Germans little maneuvering room and few options. Group South's commander finally defied Hitler and ordered a breakout. The chosen escape corridor turned into what the survivors called Hell's Gate. The Russian generals understood what was happening and unleashed furious artillery and rocket bombardments, interspersed with aerial bombing and strafing, on the vulnerable, escaping troops.

The German rearguard blocking element was under such heavy pressure that it had to abandon nearly 1,500 wounded men and medical personnel upon withdrawal. Although German combat units destroyed the Russian ground forces blocking the escape corridor along three different paths westward, the original evacuation plan fell apart when III SS Panzer Corps, the relief force sent to link up with the evacuating divisions, ran out of fuel before it could capture a critical piece of high ground called Hill 239. The fuel shortage occurred because earlier, Hitler had interfered in the group's planning by ordering the force to surround and outflank the encircling Russians—something III SS Panzer Corps clearly did not have the strength and supplies to do. The mission soon had to be abandoned, but by then the panzer element assigned to capture Hill 239 ran out of fuel before it reached the objective. When the unit's commander then failed to communicate to his superior that his unit failed to take the hill, the pullout was set in motion. As a result, the withdrawing German units in the valley below had to run a gauntlet of Russian tanks raining fire down on them from the hill.

Various other Red units were able to maneuver and position themselves because they were well equipped with US lend-lease four-wheel and six-wheel drive trucks. The German panzers and two-wheel drive vehicles down in the valley lacked the traction to negotiate the mud and melting snow on the hillsides and escape from the low ground. Hence, they were destroyed or abandoned in great numbers.[8] [9]

The long German columns of support troops, stragglers, and medical staff ferrying wounded and sick men in Red Cross vehicles were caught in a maelstrom and ripped apart. In a follow-up to the shell fire, the Russians dispensed some of the most despicable mayhem imaginable. Their tanks went straight for the columns and repeatedly drove up and down them to crush as many Germans as they could with their tracks. Germans who tried to flee up the hillsides were massacred by pursuing Cossack cavalry troops who hunted them down and hacked them to death with their sabers. Soldiers who tried to surrender by raising their hands were chased down and had their arms hacked off. This human hunt went on for hours.[10]

General Erhard Raus, in post-war comments, said he saw many similar instances of German troops and POWs killed and mutilated throughout the war. He commented that the Russians "sought to impress the German troops and lower their morale by committing numerous atrocities upon them. The great number of such crimes, committed on all sectors of the fronts, tends to support that presumption."[11]

The massacre created a blockage at the column's head and pushed the main body of trailing Germans further south than they intended to go, putting an additional barrier between them and the relief force. That barrier was the small but snowmelt-swollen Gniloy Tikich River. Nearly every soldier was on foot by this point, and Krämer noted that when the Wiking survivors reached the Gniloy, not one panzer or assault gun had made it through.

In this escape, Krämer was a medical evacuee rather than a combatant. On his arrival in the pocket, he'd been assigned to a reserve company on the Dnieper River along with other new arrivals, survivors from other units, and men returning from hospital recuperation. He hadn't been issued winter clothing, causing his joints to ache in the brutal cold. In the first week of February, Krämer was taken to a field hospital for frostbite and badly inflamed joints. He was still there when the breakout began several days later, but his condition had worsened to the point that he'd been moved to a school building where patients in serious condition awaited evacuation on flat horse-drawn sleighs. The nightmare of the escape that followed haunted Krämer for years because the entire route was lined with shot-up vehicles full of bodies, crushed sleds, dead and dying horses, and men squashed to pulp by Russian tank treads.

At the Gniloy Tikich River, further horror awaited. Fearing the Soviets would catch up from behind and massacre everyone on the river bank, the bunched men believed their only chance lay in plunging across the swift, icy river. They were unaware that relief-force engineers had constructed temporary bridges not far upstream. The raging river swept away soldiers, horses, and vehicles alike. Hundreds of men drowned in the panicky chaos because they either couldn't swim or succumbed to exhaustion or hypothermia in the icy water. And on the far shore, hypothermia continued to claim men who did make it across.

A young Russian woman who'd worked for Krämer's unit as a kitchen helper "swam the river three times with a non-swimmer on her back." She was later honored for this and remained with the unit until just before the war's end. Unconscionably, when the Wiking division pushed westward to the American lines to avoid being taken by the Russians at the close of the war, she was left behind. Later, to the men's anger and disgust, they learned the German Feldgendarmerie, a military police formation, coldly shot this brave woman. Krämer knew this group by a term that translates as "the soldiers' claw," but it was also commonly known by the pejorative term *Kettenhunde* (chained dogs) for its brutal policing tactics and the large identifying gorget (ornamental collar) its members wore over their uniform on a chain around the neck. Their tactics and viciousness also earned them the name *Heldenklauer* (hero snatchers) for the ruthless way they hanged or shot the deserters they pursued among refugee columns and hospital transports. For no good reason, the Feldgendarmerie executed this girl who risked her life to save soldiers and had faithfully served the Division for three years.

Krämer, soaking wet after crossing the river, mentioned the tortuous walk in stiffly frozen clothes that followed when he and the other survivors were guided to a waiting train. Upon reaching it, the men were crowded into freight cars where they waited "endlessly" for the train to start moving west. Once underway, the train stopped at every station so the bodies of soldiers who'd died since the last stop could be removed. The journey was long and the men's only sustenance was hot broth twice, but never any food. Experienced soldiers kept telling Krämer not to fall asleep or he'd freeze to death. He doesn't know how he survived because his joints and fingers were so stiff and painful that he could barely move. At one station he heard Romanian spoken outside and got someone to call over a Romanian Army officer. The officer promised to notify Krämer's parents that he was on the way to a hospital in Germany, but the family never received the message.

The trip terminated in Krakow, Poland, days later because apparently the German public was not supposed to glimpse soldiers so medically neglected and in such poor condition. From the train station, Krämer endured a couple more transports before being delivered to a hospital. There, a nurse stripped him and placed him in a warm bath without realizing his hands were too stiff to keep a grip on the sides of the tub. He sank under the water, but fortunately the nurse noticed in time and lifted his head before he drowned.

---

1. Anton Krämer, *Vom Banat an den Rhein: Wege und Stationen zwischen Heimatverlust und Heimatfindung* (Erding: Banat Verlag, 2008).
2. Krämer, *Vom Banat an den Rhein*, 125.
3. Krämer, *Vom Banat an den Rhein*, 130.
4. Krämer, *Vom Banat an den Rhein*, 131.
5. Krämer, *Vom Banat an den Rhein*, 131.
6. Krämer, *Vom Banat an den Rhein*, 131.
7. History News Network, "Andrew Roberts: Frozen to Death by the Fuhrer," *Columbian College of Arts & Sciences, The George Washington University*, July 25, 2009, https://historynewsnetwork.org/article/106314.
8. Douglas E. Nash, *Hell's Gate: The Battle of the Cherkassy Pocket, January-February 1944* (Stamford, CT: RZM Imports, 2009), 162.
9. Nash, *Hell's Gate*, 162.
10. John Erickson, *The Road to Berlin* (London: Cassell, 2008), 178.
11. Erhard Raus, *Panzer Operations: The Eastern Front Memoir of General Raus, 1941-1945*, ed. Steven H. Newton (Cambridge, MA: Da Capo Press, 2005), 38, 136, 203.

21 Winter on the Eastern Front

On November 12, 1943, after weeks of battling partisans, orders arrived instructing Nordland's parent unit, III SS Panzer Corps, to prepare for a new mission—Unternehmen (Operation) Lützow. Fidel was unaware of where he'd be going—only the staff officers knew. Nordland's battalions systematically disengaged from combat and pulled back to their bases in preparation, but some elements remained engaged in heavy fighting as late as the day before the transfers began on November 25. Over the next four weeks the various units, including Fidel's, boarded northbound trains.

Earlier in the war every German division still relied on horses to some extent, but horses complicated relocations. Himmler became determined to remove all dependence on horses, so the newest divisions like Nordland were to be fully motorized. In Croatia, Nordland had yet to be issued most of the armor, heavy weapons, and vehicles that would bring this about, but had nevertheless remained free of horses. The inferior armament and other Italian equipment the division had picked up was to be left behind for use by the unenthusiastic Cossack troops [both the Germans and Soviets had Cossack units] who were to take over Nordland's task, so the trains primarily carried soldiers and light weapons. Fidel recalled when he and his battalion embarked, they climbed aboard aged passenger cars with hard wooden bench seats. Each train carried about 400 soldiers and their gear.

The planning, logistics, and infrastructure involved for any division-sized move was considerable, and transferring an entire Panzergrenadier division required many trains. A description compiled after the war by German Generaloberst (US Army four-star general equivalent) Erhard Raus depicts the magnitude. My mother likely met Raus a time or two before the war because his parents and grandparents were close neighbors in the Sudetenland village in Moravia where she lived during the prewar and wartime years. Raus's story is told in *The Secret She Carried: A Perilous Odyssey Through the Time of Hitler*.[1]

Raus commanded the 6th Panzer Division early in the war and knew firsthand what it took to move divisions. His tank division was all but destroyed in the German withdrawal from Moscow during the severe winter of 1941–1942. After being rebuilt in France, it was sent to Stalingrad for what was supposed to be a relief operation to help free the trapped German 6th Army. That move required an incredible 87 trains of about 50 cars each.[2]

Nordland's exact destination was still a secret when Fidel's train exited Croatia in early December. The issuance of warm winter clothing didn't sit well with the men and incited many rumors. Fidel estimated that the trip consumed about 10 days. The journey took so long because the train made many stops and even halted for a day or two in the Czech Protectorate. Beyond that stop, when they turned to the northeast through Poland, the soldiers' worst fears were confirmed—they were destined for the cold northern portion of the dreaded Eastern Front.

The idea of fighting in Russia was unsettling for Fidel because as a child he'd heard too much about how things always went wrong for invading armies in that vast empire. The immensity and harsh conditions had destroyed invaders for centuries, and the same appeared to be happening again. More than a few Orzydorf World War I veterans returned with a bad experience in Russia after World War I. Hans's father-in-law had spent years there as a POW. This time around, the outlook was much worse, for neither Hitler nor Stalin treated POWs humanely. And the Red Army showed a particular hate for Waffen SS soldiers.

The fear in the passengers surely deepened as the train traversed the small Baltic states of Lithuania, Latvia, and Estonia. The train crossed the Russian border just beyond Estonia's easternmost city of Narva when it passed over the railway bridge spanning the Narva River. The Nordland soldiers would get to know this city and the river banks all too intimately several months later. The train continued into Russia for another 90 kilometers before it reached the northern terminus of the long Eastern Front and disgorged its weary passengers. By then the train was less than a half-hour's ride from Leningrad.

During the time of the Czars, Leningrad was known as St. Petersburg and had been Russia's imperial city. At the start of World War I, the city's name was changed to Petrograd so it would sound less German. Seven years after the 1917 Bolshevik Revolution, the city was renamed Leningrad to honor Vladimir Lenin. The name reverted back to St. Petersburg only after the Soviet Union's breakup in 1991.

By September 1941, Erhard Raus was a *Generalmajor* (major general, two-star US Army equivalent) in charge of a battle group making its way through difficult Baltic forests and swamps to capture Leningrad. His forces overcame extreme difficulties along the way and eventually pressed through Leningrad's dangerous 10-kilometer-deep defenses. As the general prepared for a final assault on the city, he had to delay his plans because Hitler suspended Army Group Center's push to take Moscow and redirected a large part of its armor force to assist in Leningrad's capture. Just as control of the city and its Baltic Sea port lay within grasp, Hitler changed his mind again and called off the drive. Raus's group and other panzer forces were now directed to resume the capture of Moscow. Hitler had decided to starve Leningrad into submission by siege, instead. That strategy ultimately failed because Stalin would not allow the city to surrender, no matter the cost in lives. Later, after the Germans lost the initiative in Russia, they had to tie up extra divisions to maintain the blockade and keep Leningrad from becoming a staging area for a large Russian counteroffensive.

At the time of Nordland's arrival, the city had been under German siege for two-and-a-half years and had suffered immensely. When Fidel's train finally disgorged its butt-sore Regiment Danmark passengers from their wooden-bench confinement on a spur line at a village called Kolty, the men didn't know just where they were. I suspect that Fidel had conflicting feelings when he stepped into the cold, wintry Russian air. The farmer in him probably appreciated the pastoral setting, while the infantry soldier in him feared it. The flat countryside, dappled with open grazing land and boggy woods, allowed Russian infantry troops too much freedom of movement.[3]

Like other Soviet villages the train had passed through, most buildings lay in ruins. Some destruction occurred when the German Army surged through two years earlier in pursuit of the fleeing Russian forces, but most of the damage was inflicted by Stalin's Red Army, which had been under orders to destroy any infrastructure useful to the Germans. General Raus wrote that the Russian army destroyed everything in its wake and left only "ashes and ruins." It also executed thousands of Russian "undesirables" and abducted many others.[4]

Nordland was not adequately equipped to engage in heavy fighting, but was judged capable of strengthening the key defensive line that faced a nub of boggy land held by the Russians. This bump, known to the Germans as the Oranienbaum Pocket, jutted 50 kilometers into the Gulf of Finland. The name came from the coastal town of Oranienbaum, which is today known as Lomonosov. In 1941 the German invaders bypassed the pocket out of expediency in the initial rush to take Leningrad. Instead of securing this difficult terrain containing some Soviet elements, the Germans walled it off. As the Red Army subsequently reinforced the position by sea, it became an ever-greater threat to the west flank of the German line that encircled Leningrad. The German line walling off the pocket stretched for 75 kilometers and presented "a formidable front-line sector for the undermanned German-European volunteer side to defend."[5]

When the first Nordland company commanders and platoon leaders arrived in the area on December 10, 1943, they scouted the terrain, then led their men to the new defensive positions under cover of darkness the following night. The last Nordland soldiers arrived from Croatia on December 22. The new troops relieved soldiers of the 9th and 10th Luftwaffe Field Divisions. According to Fidel, these divisions had a poor reputation among Heer and Waffen SS soldiers. The Luftwaffe soldiers weren't any less physically fit than other soldiers; they simply weren't well trained and equipped for infantry tasks. It was the same for their commissioned and noncommissioned officers. They lacked ground fighting experience and training in the maintenance of weapons or horses. The Heer was so overextended that it couldn't afford to draw down its own weapons stocks and cadre of experienced officers and noncoms to upgrade the Luftwaffe units. As a result, Luftwaffe soldiers suffered high casualties in combat.

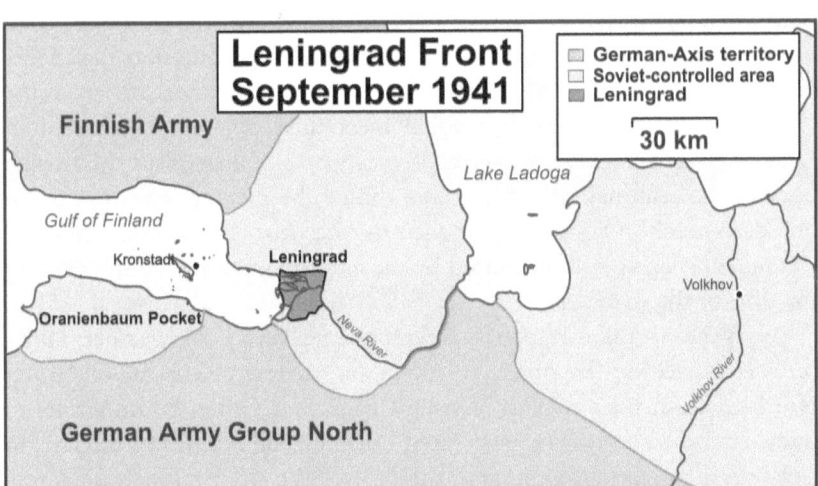

The relative position of Leningrad and the Oranienbaum Pocket on the Leningrad sector of the Eastern Front on September 21, 1941. Keeping the Red Army elements bottled up within the pocket was crucial for the Germans because a breakout by the Red Army would allow Soviet forces to outflank the many German divisions further east. The Finnish Army and German Army Group North labels designate territory held by the Germans or its ally Finland. Russian-held territory includes the Oranienbaum Pocket, the Leningrad area, and territory east of Leningrad.

Hitler had authorized the formation of the Luftwaffe field forces late in 1942 when Germany ran short of replacements for the Eastern Front. The original idea was to transfer excess men from other services to the army, but Luftwaffe chief Herman Göring wanted to preserve his fiefdom, so he devised a plan to build his own Luftwaffe infantry force. Before his men could be sent to the army, Göring convinced Hitler that using his soldiers in defensive roles in quiet areas allowed better-trained soldiers to be freed up. Hence, Göring's empire was preserved, and Luftwaffe soldiers were deployed to static sections of the Eastern Front. Göring's ground soldiers, identifiable by their field-blue uniforms, numbered over 200,000 at one time.

Hitler allowed Göring jurisdictional control over his force but required him to reorganize it into combat divisions and cede tactical control to the army. This command structure proved awkward, so the army lobbied hard for direct control. Fearing a total loss of momentum on the Eastern Front if he didn't give in, Hitler granted the request and ordered all Luftwaffe field divisions to be fully absorbed into the army.[6] This occurred just before Fidel arrived in Russia in 1943.

To grasp Fidel's situation, it is necessary to understand what had been happening in Leningrad since the Germans invaded the Soviet Union two-and-a-half years earlier. Initially, Hitler had put the German military in a bind when he delayed the start of Barbarossa, the invasion of Russia, for a month in order to first seize Serbia. It was due to this late start that Army Group North's advance elements had to wall off the Soviet troops in the Oranienbaum Pocket so they could meet their objectives and capture Leningrad. Thereafter, the Germans could do nothing about the pocket because the seasonal rains of autumn turned the marshy area's few roads into deep muck and incapacitated their mobile army. The Russians referred to the recurring condition caused by the autumn rains and spring thaw as the time of the *rasputitsa*.

With the northern Barbarossa offensive stalled by the weather, Hitler ordered a hold on the objectives there and diverted elements of Group North to assist the struggling Group Center and Group South armies in pursuing more strategic targets. Pared-down Group North was directed to isolate and lay siege to Leningrad and destroy the city after it surrendered. However, a particularly fierce winter set in and completely shut down German mobility. This, in turn, created a logistical nightmare of insufficient replacements, equipment, and fuel along the entire front. The German troops that were supposed to have already conquered Russia had neither adequate food nor winter clothing. Many a German soldier froze to death or suffered ghastly cold-related injuries during that winter. Thereafter, the Germans never regained their former momentum.

The Russians trapped inside the besieged city of Leningrad were in dire straits as well when their food and fuel ran low in the winter. The Red Army set up a crude water and ice road across Lake Lagoda to reach the city, but their relief efforts proved inadequate until later in the siege. The 2.5 million inhabitants and 200,000 soldiers trapped in the city burned floor boards and furniture for fuel and resorted to eating horses, cats, dogs, rats, and crows. Some residents became desperate enough to eat sawdust or commit murder to acquire an extra ration card. Others resorted to eating human flesh. Those apprehended for cannibalism by the secret police were cited either with corpse-eating or person-eating. Corpse-eaters were prosecuted for banditry, person-eaters for murder.

Although many residents managed to flee Leningrad over the 872-day siege, up to a million people died of starvation and disease in the city. Only 40 percent of the original population remained when the siege ended. Reminders of the enormous human toll are still to be found in the city now known as St. Petersburg. There is little about World War II that was not exploited for propaganda purposes by the Soviets to foster national unity and international sympathy, but the Piskariovskoye Memorial Cemetery at the eastern edge of St. Petersburg needed little help in telling its ghastly tale as I walked its grounds during a visit. Behind the extensive masonry of the raised entrance with its somber, twin, museum pavilions and eternal flame, the immensity of the calamity is eerily visible. Nearly half a million civilians and soldiers lie buried in 186 flat-topped earthen mounds that flank a long walkway. Each rectangular mound is marked with a plaque bearing the year it was filled. At the end of the long walkway stands a huge statue of a grieving woman who represents the Motherland.

The city leaders who guided the population through the siege were not admired by all after the siege ended. Stalin saw them as a threat to his own standing. Rather than treating them as heroes, he manufactured accusations of embezzlement to eliminate them. Before his campaign ended, he'd purged the entire city administration—some 2,000 people. Stalin executed the most prominent of them and sent the rest to Siberia. Thereafter, he declared the local defense of Leningrad a myth created by anti-Soviet traitors determined to diminish his own greatness and ordered the destruction of the large Museum of Leningrad Defense that the city had assembled.[7]

The possession of Leningrad had more symbolic than actual military importance for both sides. With combat troops more sorely needed elsewhere, the lattice of German trenches and shell craters surrounding Leningrad soon became a backwater manned by the minimum number of soldiers required to maintain the status quo. It remained so for two-and-a-half years until Hitler, in desperation, ordered Group North commander

Georg von Küchler to send four more of his combat divisions to Group Center. This stretched Küchler's Leningrad lines to the breaking point. Subsequently, Küchler had to dispatch even more defenders south to halt a Russian breakout, leaving the entire Oranienbaum Pocket containment in the hands of a few noncombat units and the weak 9th and 10th Luftwaffe field divisions. The situation grew even more worrisome when the Germans learned the Russians were ferrying massive numbers of men and weapons into the Oranienbaum Pocket. A breakout there would cut the main German supply line and outflank the German divisions encircling Leningrad.

America was by this time sending the Soviets an enormous supply of vehicles, weapons, ammunition, and airplanes. The latter posed an additional threat to the German soldiers on the defensive lines, for each month the Russians "received more new airplanes from the United States than the German Luftwaffe had available for the entire Eastern Front.... The Soviets were able to carry out constant air raids ... for every plane downed, the Russians had two or three replacements and they cared nothing about their losses."[8] This was the situation Fidel found himself in upon his arrival at the Eastern Front.

The worried German high command in Berlin knew the Luftwaffe infantry was powerless to stop a determined Russian offensive, so it sent Küchler two new Waffen SS divisions and a small contingent of Spanish Legionnaires largely sympathetic to the communist side. One of the SS divisions was nearly useless because it had only recently been formed from poorly fit Balkan conscripts. The other was Nordland, which Küchler knew to be robust but lacking in heavy weapons and the type of combat experience necessary to stop a major Russian breakout. Küchler assigned Nordland to the static, but crucial, Oranienbaum defensive line and sent the other unit to a less critical area.

The Leningrad front was already familiar to some of Nordland's Dutch, Norwegian, and Swedish volunteers, for they were the survivors of units that had previously fought in the area. The entire III SS Panzer Corps, of which Nordland comprised the major part, was proclaimed combat fit on December 13 despite Nordland's panzer battalion being unready and unable to leave Croatia for weeks yet. Its men were still training in the new Panther tanks they'd finally received.

The new arrivals in Russia had few trucks, making it necessary to commandeer vehicles from the Luftwaffe divisions just to carry on basic functions like the distribution of supplies and evacuation of the wounded. As scarce as trucks were on the marshy front, roads were even scarcer. In the grip of winter, the bare surface roads that did exist consisted of frozen, but somewhat passable, ruts. In the spring when the rasputitsa mud season returned, these roads would regress back to quagmires.

As Fidel's company assumed its assigned position, the Luftwaffe defenders they were replacing told Fidel and his companions that Russian snipers had shot at them occasionally, but the conditions weren't too bad "if you kept your head down." The Luftwaffe divisions were sent to new positions along the eastern part of the line because Küchler wanted the western portion in the hands of the stronger Nordland force, for a breach there would imperil his entire Leningrad Army and cut off its westward escape.

---

1. Erich Eipert, *The Secret She Carried: A Perilous Odyssey Through the Time of Hitler* (Turnbuckle Press, 2015), 126.
2. Erhard Raus, *Panzer Operations: The Eastern Front Memoir of General Raus, 1941-1945*, ed. Steven H. Newton (Cambridge, MA: Da Capo Press, 2005), 137.
3. Wilhelm Tieke, *Tragedy of the Faithful: A History of the III. (Germanisches) SS-Panzer-Korps* (Winnipeg, Manitoba: J.J. Fedorowicz Publishing, 2001), 24.
4. Raus, *Panzer Operations*, 137.
5. Richard Landwehr and Holger Thor Nielsen, *Nordic Warriors: SS-Panzergrenadier-Regiment 24 Danmark, Eastern Front, 1943-45*, Armed Forces of the Third Reich - Unit Histories Series (Halifax, West Yorkshire: Shelf Books, 1999), 63.
6. Ken Weiler, "Manpower Squandered: The German Luftwaffe Field Divisions," Ostfront Publications, April 29, 2013, https://weilerpublications.com/2013/04/29/manpower-squandered-the-german-luftwaffe-field-divisions/.
7. "Museum of the Defense and Siege of Leningrad, St. Petersburg Russia," accessed May 16, 2020, http://www.saint-petersburg.com/museums/museum-of-the-defense-and-siege-of-leningrad/.
8. Richard Landwehr, *Narva 1944: The Waffen-SS and the Battle for Europe* (Silver Spring, MD: Bibliophile Legion Books, 1981), 22.

22 Horses and Corduroy Roads

The Oranienbaum Pocket defenders were totally dependent on two all-weather roads. Both had to be hurriedly built at the start of Barbarossa by German military engineers in 1941 in order to make a timely capture of Leningrad possible. These roads contained kilometers-long stretches of logs laid down in two or more crossed layers to form a solid surface through boggy ground. Fidel recalled that the logs on top were about the size of a man's arm, but the supporting logs beneath them were larger. He marveled that the engineers had been able to find enough trees for such a project because they didn't grow in sufficient quantity locally. These corduroy roads made for a bone jarring ride, but did keep vehicles from sinking into the mud.

The Germans launched Barbarossa with surprisingly little idea of the difficulties their troops would encounter. The fierce winter cold would strike them later, but the lack of roads in the difficult terrain of northern Russia was an immediate problem. The log-surfaced corduroy road was one of the main solutions. The difficulty of operating in that environment is still not fully appreciated by many war history buffs. General Raus explained the situation.

> War could never have been waged in the vast swamp regions of Russia had they not been made accessible by improvised corduroy roads. These were the most important static improvisation of the entire Russian campaign and many operations . . . were feasible only because of the construction of such roads. The first corduroy road was built soon after the Germans crossed into European Russia; the last one during the westward retreat across the German border. In the intervening period hundreds of miles of corduroy road had to be built or repaired during the muddy seasons in order to move up

supplies and heavy equipment . . . to get hundreds of bogged-down vehicles back on the move . . . .

In constructing these roads it was important to select logs about ten inches in diameter and place them in several layers. As in the superstructure of a bridge, stringers, double layers of crossed logs, and siderail lashings had to be used. The guard rails had to be wired because nails could not be used. The cross logs had to be topped with a layer of sand—not dirt—or, when no sand was available, with cinders or rubble. Time and personnel permitting, the top layer of logs was to be levelled off. Only such thoroughly constructed corduroy roads could stand the strain of constant traffic.[1]

In the vicinity of Leningrad two types of construction were commonly used: a heavy-duty corduroy road built atop a foundation of five lengthwise log stringers and a light-duty road that was laid directly on the ground. The two layers of logs resting across the stringers to form the heavy-duty roadway consisted of logs about five inches in diameter that were secured on both ends by guard rails anchored to the ground with drift pins and wire loops. The road was just wide enough for one truck because longer logs were unavailable. Turnouts were built at 1,000-meter intervals and special traffic-regulating detachments directed all movement along these roads.[2]

However, it wasn't just the poor roads that crippled the mobility advantage of the German war machine in the USSR. Their problems began during the 1941 invasion when huge numbers of trucks, many captured from West European countries, broke down under the harsh winter conditions of the east. In the push to take Moscow, the German Army lost nearly 6,000 trucks in November of 1941 alone, a figure more than double what German factories could replace. To ease the shortage, the high command sent 1,900 trucks and 6,000 other vehicles to Army Group Center along with 500 buses full of soldiers. Soldiers collected vehicles throughout Germany and as far away as Paris, then drove them to the front even though it was anticipated that most would need repairs by the time they got as far as Warsaw.[3]

Hitler planned to have Russia under control by winter's onset in 1941, but instead found himself with troops stuck, starving, and freezing. To regain momentum, he drafted another half-million men for the front, and in the process greatly exacerbated the civilian labor shortage. Paradoxically, the men he drafted were no longer available to produce the weaponry they needed to arm themselves or to restock the soldiers already at the front.[4]

The military responded to the problem of Russia's difficult environment in the only way it could. Reluctantly, it returned to the beast it tried to banish after World War I. Horses had been on the way out because of their serious limitations, but the new reality in Russia turned back the clock. Scarce fuel, vehicle shortages, and difficult terrain suddenly created a demand for horses again. Even highly mechanized panzer and artillery units couldn't operate in Russia without them. It took 10 horses to tow just one large artillery piece, and that was on pavement. But the Germans were far from alone in horse dependence, as the following table makes clear.

	Germany	Romania	Soviet Union	United States
National stock of horses			21 million (1940)	14 million (1940)
Horses used by the military	2.75 million	90,000	3.5 million	52,000
Maximum number cavalry units deployed	6 divisions (February 1945)	6 divisions (1942)	80 light cavalry divisions (December 1940)	13 regiments (1939)
Main role of horse elements	field logistics	mobile troops	mobile troops, logistics	logistics in the Pacific Theater

Horses used in World War II militaries.[5]

After turning back to the horse, the Germans learned another lesson: when everything turned to mud in the fall and spring, and snow blanketed the frozen ruts of roads in the brutal winter, their heavy West European horses didn't hold up any better than their trucks. During the disastrous winter of 1941–1942, the horses suffered tremendously from the cold right alongside the men. The misery was in large part due to Hitler's hubris.

Hitler had little use for weather prediction and ignored the advice of meteorologists about winter preparation. The führer liked to boast about his own cold hardiness and believed his soldiers would be able to bear up in one of the coldest countries in the world with improvisation and the clothing they arrived in. Some scholars believe that Hitler purposely hadn't ramped up mass production of winter clothing so as not to tip off Stalin to the invasion. Whatever the reason, thousands of soldiers needlessly died or were maimed.[6] As soon as the German field generals recognized how damaging the extreme weather and subzero temperatures in Russia were to their soldiers and plans, they tried to act, but were thwarted.

> All across Germany, under propaganda Minister Joseph Goebbels' sponsorship, Nazi party offices were collecting furs and woolen garments. Goebbels was about to open a drive to requisition restaurant tablecloths to use in making camouflage snow pants and jackets. However, the OKH [Oberkommando des Heeres or military high command], saw a public relations threat, so insisted that the fighting troops had adequate clothing and consigned the collected goods to storage until they could be quietly issued to replacements going out later in the winter.[7]

German horses struggling through the deep mud of the Russian rasputitsa (season of mud) that accompanied the spring thaw.

The fierce cold inflicted permanent injuries on many a soldier. Below is one historian's gruesome description:

> The Italian journalist Curzio Malaparte recalled in his novel, *Kaputt*, how he had watched the German troops returning from the Eastern Front, and was in the Europeiski Café in Warsaw when 'suddenly I was struck with horror and realised that they had no eyelids. I had already seen soldiers with lidless eyes, on the platform of the Minsk station a few days previously on my way from Smolensk. The ghastly cold of that winter had the strangest consequences. Thousands and thousands of soldiers had lost their limbs; thousands and thousands had their ears, their noses, their fingers and their sexual organs ripped off by

the frost. Many had lost their hair . . . . Many had lost their eyelids. Singed by the cold, the eyelid drops off like a piece of dead skin . . . . Their future was only lunacy.[8]

At the dawn of New Year's Day, 1942, the temperature across central Russia was around −32 degrees Celsius (−25 Fahrenheit) and the snow waist deep. The few roads open had to be shoveled by hand and in spots quickly drifted shut again. Machine guns jammed and tank turrets wouldn't turn. Engines refused to start at such temperatures, so some of the war machines had to be kept running continuously, using up precious fuel. Even though retreats were hard on soldiers and equipment, the brutal conditions had field commanders requesting permission to pull back to save their men. Hitler, of course, refused to allow such a thing.[9] The conditions were so severe that everyone who served on the front during the winter campaign received the Ostmedaille (East Medal), which soldiers commonly referred to as the Frost Medal or the Frozen Meat Medal. The horses received no medals, although the winter was every bit as hard on them.[10]

Writing for the US Army after the war, General Raus described how vital the horse became when the army had to adapt to the lack of roads in the north.

> When the German armored and motorized units swept across the dusty plains of Russia during the summer of 1941, nobody paid much attention to the insignificant little peasant horses of the Russian steppe. The tankers and truck drivers could not fail to notice the industrious little animals pulling heavily loaded peasant wagons cross-country whenever they were pushed off the road by the modern mechanical giants . . . what was their performance compared to that of the steel colossi and munition carriers . . . . Many a man dismissed them with a disdainful gesture and the words: 'A hundred years behind the times.' Even next to the heavy cold-blooded draft horses and the tall mounts of the infantry divisions their dwarfish cousins seemed slightly ridiculous and insignificant.

> A few months later the Panje horse was judged quite differently. It came into sudden demand during the muddy season when no motor vehicle could operate and any number of cold-blooded horses could not move the heavy guns and ammunition. How were the advance elements to be supplied when they were stranded without provisions? By Panje columns. Who brought the urgently needed ammunition to the front when the organic divisional supply columns were stuck in the mud as far as fifty miles to the rear of the advance

elements? Again the Panje column. Who was capable of moving gasoline from the railheads to the mechanical colossi even through the deepest mud? The Panje horse. By what means of transportation were the badly wounded to be transported when the most modern ambulances could no longer advance in the mud? The answer was always the Panje horse and wagon. From then on they became faithful, indispensable companions of the field forces. In winter the Panje horse proved even more essential. The Panje sleigh became the universal means of transportation when motor vehicles were incapacitated and roads were snowbound or nonexistent. During the first months of 1942 some panzer divisions had as many as 2,000 Panje horses but hardly a single serviceable motor vehicle. For that reason they received the nickname "Panje divisions." This unexpected turn of events made the veterinarian the busiest man in any panzer division.[11]

During that ferocious winter of 1941–1942, Group Center lost about 1,000 heavy horses per day to the cold. Many more became sick and unfit for use. The resulting horse shortage hobbled German artillery support and supply operations. Like their poorly clothed German masters, the horses also suffered from frostbite and pneumonia. The Wehrmacht transported so many horses to the Eastern Front that each of its armies needed to set up and staff several horse hospitals. These facilities were designed to accommodate around 500 horses each, but in the extreme weather were deluged with two to three thousand horses at a time. The German 7th Army maintained 130,000 horses and the mobile 1st Panzer Army, which hadn't even a single veterinarian at the beginning of the invasion, found itself burdened with more horses than vehicles—60,000 versus 45,000. The mammoth feed requirements of these horses consumed a massive amount of valuable space on the already strained supply trains from the west. Incredibly, by October 1941 the Germans employed 24,000 veterinary troops on the Eastern Front—the equivalent of one-and-a-half infantry divisions.[12] When the Germans learned that only the small Russian panje horses were suited to this environment, they also learned these small horses weren't able to pull the same loads as the large horses. Even the German sleds were too much for the light horses, so the Wehrmacht turned to small Russian panje sleds drawn by a single horse.[13]

---

1. U.S. Army European Command Historical Division, "Chapter 5: Indispensable Expedients," in *Military Improvisations during the Russian Campaign*, DA Pam 20-201 (Washington: Department of the Army, 1951), 51–55, https://history.army.mil/books/wwii/milimprov/fm.htm.
2. U.S. Army European Command Historical Division, "Chapter 5: Indispensable Expedients."
3. Earl F. Ziemke and Magna E. Bauer, *Moscow to Stalingrad: Decision in the East*, Army Historical Series.

CMH Pub 30-12 (Washington, D.C.: Center of Military History, U.S. Army, 1987), 120, https://www.history.army.mil/html/books/030/30-12-1/index.html.
4. Earl F. Ziemke, *Stalingrad to Berlin: The German Defeat in the East*, Army Historical Series. CMH Pub 30-5-1 (Washington, D.C.: Center of Military History, U.S. Army, 1968), 120, https://www.history.army.mil/html/books/030/30-5-1/index.html.
5. "Horses in World War II," in Wikipedia, accessed December 18, 2023, https://en.wikipedia.org/w/index.php?title=Horses_in_World_War_II.
6. History News Network, "Andrew Roberts: Frozen to Death by the Fuhrer," *Columbian College of Arts & Sciences, The George Washington University*, July 25, 2009, https://historynewsnetwork.org/article/106314.
7. Ziemke, *Stalingrad to Berlin*, 120.
8. Andrew Roberts, *The Storm of War: A New History of the Second World War* (New York: Harper, 2011), 214.
9. Ziemke and Bauer, *Moscow to Stalingrad*, 118.
10. Antony Beevor. *The Second World War*. New York: Little, Brown and Co., 2012, 327.
11. U.S. Army European Command Historical Division, "Chapter 5: Indispensable Expedients."
12. R. L DiNardo, *Mechanized Juggernaut or Military Anachronism?: Horses and the German Army of World War II* (New York: Greenwood Press, 1991).
13. DiNardo, *Mechanized Juggernaut or Military Anachronism?*, 50.

23 The Oranienbaum Pocket

By ordering the 18th Army's best divisions south to aid Group Center in late 1943, Hitler strained his force at the Leningrad Front to the breaking point. Not only did his action leave the lines too thinly manned, it placed some sections in the hands of poorly trained and underequipped divisions. The German force holding the Reds within the Oranienbaum Pocket was particularly affected. Rapid reinforcement there became critical because a Russian breakout from the pocket would endanger the entire German line that encircled Leningrad farther east and cut the 18th Army's supply route. This in turn could lead to the collapse of the entire northern portion of the Eastern Front.

Even with Nordland's added presence, the line was uncomfortably short of defenders. To further bulk it up, Group North reassigned district military police, coastal artillery troops, Estonian police, veterinary troops, and convalescent companies to this infantry duty. Even a chemical decontamination company got the call. This mix of noncombatants took up station along the westernmost 15 kilometers of the pocket's containment line. Meanwhile, Nordland assumed charge of the critical middle 24 kilometers, which allowed the very thinly stretched 9th and 10th Luftwaffe divisions to concentrate along a shorter 38-kilometer stretch at the eastern end of the line.

Regiment Danmark shouldered the western half of Nordland's middle section and set up a 20-bunker regimental command post south of the line. Just behind the command post lay the main corduroy supply road and a swamp. Regiment Norge took over the eastern half of Nordland's defensive line and linked up with the 10th Luftwaffe positions to the east. Norge's 1st Battalion and Danmark's 2nd Battalion served as the division's ready-reserve forces in the rear. Because Fidel was assigned to a bunker on the defensive line, he could not have belonged to Regiment Danmark's reserve battalion, the 2nd.[1] [2]

Upon reexamining a book about Regiment Danmark, *Nordic Warriors*, late in the preparation of this manuscript, I noticed that the volume contained individual photos of companies 1–7 on parade during their training at Grafenwöhr. Armed with the information gathered from Hansi Adam's letter that tied Fidel to Regiment Danmark, the significance of the photos struck me. These seven companies had already been formed and filled out with Danish and German volunteers in April and May of 1943, two months before the Orzydorf recruits arrived in Germany. The Waffen SS Panzergrenadier Order of Battle (hierarchical organization and command structure) dictates that companies 1–4 make up the 1st Battalion of each division, 5–8 form the 2nd, and 9–12 comprise the 3rd. This meant the Orzidorf men and other ethnic Germans mainly filled out the 3rd Battalion.[3]

The Oranienbaum line was little more than a string of ground-level log bunkers when Nordland arrived, so Fidel and his companions worked relentlessly to fortify their position. Despite the sniper danger, digging protective trenches between the guard positions was paramount. Where trenching was not possible, log barriers were erected to shield the defenders and provide firing positions. The Reds had largely refrained from shooting at the Luftwaffe troops, perhaps because they hadn't considered the blue-clad soldiers much of a threat, but it is more likely they wished to avoid drawing German attention to their own buildup. However, sniper activity picked up as soon as the Waffen SS arrived, Fidel said. Early in the war, the ferocity with which the idealistic volunteer Waffen SS force had fought and the excessively harsh tactics some commanders had used provoked a bitter hatred in the Red Army. Nordland now paid the price of those sins. Fidel said the situation was bearable only because in the dead of winter the days were so short that the snipers had limited working hours.

The fear induced by skilled snipers is not appreciated by those who've never faced the threat. I found the terror succinctly described in a novel when the protagonist said, "The infantry puts up with a world of shit. They live in holes in the ground, cold, wet, muddy, hungry, with incoming mortars and artillery and rockets, and bombs . . . and they have nothing ahead of them except barbed wire and machine-gun nests, but you know what they hate most of all?" The answer: snipers! They are "random death, out of nowhere, anytime, anyplace, no notice, no warning. Every minute of every day. No relief. The stress becomes unbearable. It sends some of them mad, literally."[4] That and the unending routine of guard duty ground down the Germans holding the pocket.

Not a great deal of snow fell during December, but Fidel recalled that the snow that did fall blew around incessantly and formed large drifts. The weather was not as cold as in 1941 when men and horses alike died in great numbers, but the temperature remained low enough to make life uncomfortable. Perhaps even worse than the cold was living with lice, the universal complaint of the Eastern Front soldier. The creatures congregated on the warmest parts of the body under clothing. Some men picked them off their body or clothes and crushed them with their fingernails whenever an opportunity presented itself. The effort was satisfying but futile. The bites of these tiny pests itched persistently and resulted in rashes from scratching. Even leaving infested clothes out in the freezing cold for days didn't kill the beasties.

The shorthanded defenders, condemned to broken sleep by ever-repeating watch shifts throughout the long nights, were unable to catch up on sleep during the short days because they had to work relentlessly to improve their fortifications. The result was a state of exhaustion. Morale was further wrecked by meager, poor-quality food that failed to provide sufficient calories for the cold conditions. All too often the fare was moldy bread and lentil soup. So it is not hard to imagine that out in the dark, lonely listening posts—where persistent hunger made stomachs growl and the freezing temperatures caused extremities to ache—the men's thoughts turned to their loved ones, the family dinner table, and the warm bed they used to sleep in. The approach of the Christmas holidays only amplified their discontent at having to endure these hardships and fight for Hitler's cause when they wanted to be at home with their families.

The Banat soldiers had good reason to question their presence there. They'd had nothing to do with Hitler's rise to power and hadn't cheered on his military adventurism. Lurking in their minds was the fear that he'd doom them here just as he'd doomed the 6th Army in Stalingrad earlier that year when he refused to allow a breakout while one was still possible. The Banaters all knew men who'd died there, and some of them had even fought there as Romanian soldiers. Had Fidel and the other men known the extent of the unimpeded Soviet buildup just a few kilometers to the north, they'd have been even more alarmed.

Fidel's living quarters consisted of a crude log bunker four- to six-feet high. To the right and left, similar bunkers were laid out at 75- to 100-meter intervals in a staggered pattern with one forward and the next back. After the improvements made by Nordland were complete, an irregular log barrier with slots for observation and firing extended out from both sides of every bunker. Each bunker housed four men and provided some protection from the elements, but cold air and snow blew through the cracks between the logs relentlessly.

Left: Exhibit of a field oven of the type Fidel used in his bunker. The display background shows how this design allowed tight and efficient stacking for transport to the front. A translation of the sign reads "100000 front ovens were manufactured in the period from December 11, 1941, to January 24, 1942, after a preparation period of three weeks at the instigation of Reich Minister Dr. Todt. This was only possible through the complete commitment of everyone involved. —Workmates." *Right:* Workers assembling Organization Todt (OT) designed military field ovens at the Wolfsburg Volkswagen factory in Germany. Soviet POWs and East European forced laborers had not yet become a ready labor source, hence the assemblers appear to be soldiers, OT members, and civilians. The M38 overseas cap worn by some of the men is very similar to the American military's garrison caps and was utilized by the OT as well as all German military branches. The Deutsche Wehrmacht armband seen on one man was worn by nonuniformed personnel working for the Armed Forces.

Each bunker contained a small wood stove known as an OT oven. The stove warmed food but was far too small to heat the living space. These units were designed by Organisation Todt (OT), a Nazi engineering conglomerate that planned and constructed civil and military projects. The organization was named after its founder, Dr. Fritz Todt, a man Hitler ultimately fell out with because of the message the man delivered.

> On 17 March 1940, he was appointed Reichsminister für Bewaffnung und Munition ("Reich Minister for Armaments and Munitions") and . . . after the invasion of the Soviet Union in June 1941, he was appointed to manage the restoration of the infrastructure there . . . he became increasingly distant from the commanders of the Wehrmacht and from Reichsmarschall Hermann Göring . . . in particular. He did remain close to Hitler at this time; yet, after an inspection tour of the Eastern Front, he complained to Hitler that, without better equipment and supplies for the armed forces, it would be better to end the war with the USSR. Inevitably, Hitler rejected such an assessment of the situation . . . . On 8 February 1942, while flying away from the conclusion of a meeting with Hitler at the

Wolfsschanze ("Wolf's Lair") at Rastenburg, his aircraft exploded and crashed.... It was ... suggested that Todt was the victim of an assassination plot, but this has never been confirmed.[5]

When the Germans were caught unprepared for the harsh Russian winter, this OT-designed stove was rushed into production for Germany's Eastern Front troops on an emergency basis at the Volkswagen factory—a facility that Fidel would come to know well, later. The factory could take this on because it wasn't allowed to build civilian vehicles during the war and its capacity for military vehicles was never fully utilized. Eventually 221,505 of these Organization Todt (OT) field ovens were turned out for the ill-equipped and freezing German troops. Side contracts utilizing some of VW's excess plant capacity were necessary to stay in business.

Along Fidel's section of the line, every bunker team was responsible for manning two outdoor listening posts throughout the night, one on each side of their bunker. Usually, each post was staffed by a single soldier while the remaining two team members rested or slept. But sometimes it was prudent to keep three men out on watch. Fidel recalled that one of his posts was about 10 meters away; the other about halfway to the next bunker.

One night in particular, "10 or 12 days" into January 1944, was burned into Fidel's memory, never to be forgotten. When he came off his watch at dusk, he alerted the two men heading out that conditions had turned hellish and a blizzard was setting in. Because the howling wind and fiercely blowing snow made it all but impossible to hear or see anything, the team decided to post three guards instead of two. Had the men known how powerful a force the Reds had amassed within the pocket, all four of them would probably have gone out.

A comrade from a neighboring bunker joined Fidel in his bunker after his shift. As the pair heated up some food in the largely blacked-out shelter, the other man mentioned that toward the end of his watch he thought he'd seen something suspicious and shot at it. Fidel was stirring the food a short time later when the bunker door crashed inward from a violent kick. What followed happened so quickly that Fidel was never sure if there'd been more than one Russian in the doorway. Both Fidel and his friend instinctively flung themselves under a bunk—a response that came of frequent threats posed by Russian aircraft, snipers, artillery guns, and reconnaissance probes.

A moment later, the bunker's interior was raked with a burst of submachine-gun fire. Luckily, the bullets missed both men. The need for haste and the near darkness inside the bunker were surely factors. Or the adrenaline-charged shooter, already considering his getaway, failed to compensate for the muzzle-lifting effect of firing on full automatic. As soon as the shooting stopped, Fidel heard the thud of a grenade and covered himself as best he could. He thought he'd breathed his last as he tried to melt into the floor. But somehow both he and the other soldier escaped with only abrasions and painful blast injuries, which are a complex of physical traumas that may include internal injuries to the lungs, brain, or other organs as well as extremity injuries such as burns, hearing loss, and eye damage. Due to the blizzard raging outside, the listening-post sentries neither saw nor heard anything. The sapper was likely from the 168th Rifle Division, a Soviet unit that had recently been positioned opposite Danmark to attack and probe the German defenses in order to convince the German generals that the coming offensive would hit the western portion of the pocket when the true target was the opposite end.

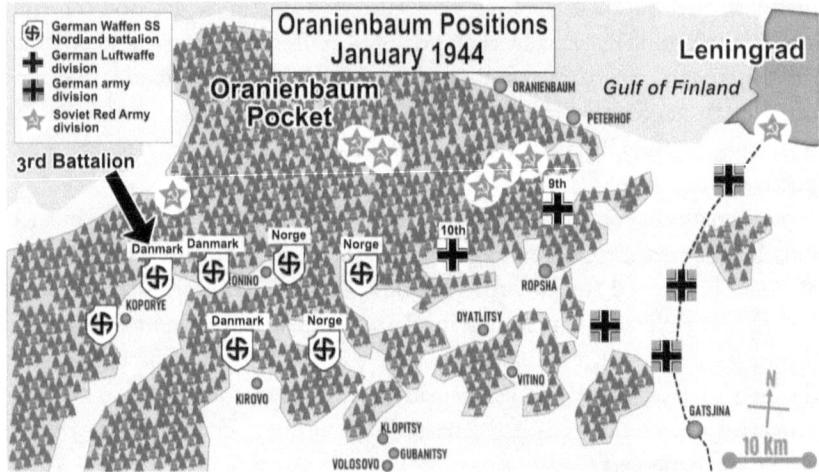

The situation at the Oranienbaum Pocket shortly before the Red Army breakout in mid-January 1944. The positions of Soviet divisions are marked by stars. The other symbols denote various German unit positions. Regiment Danmark's 3rd Battalion (marked by arrow), in which Fidel served, manned the westernmost section of the Nordland division's portion of the defensive line meant to keep the Soviets bottled up in the pocket. The Soviet Red Army's 168th Rifle Division, just north of Fidel's position, closed on Danmark's 3rd Battalion as a diversionary tactic shortly before the Soviets launched their actual breakout attack against the German defenders holding the eastern side of the pocket.

Concussive traumas can leave the victim with a variety of debilitating symptoms: headache, lethargy, fatigue, anxiety, poor concentration, insomnia, depression, and post-traumatic stress disorder (PTSD). Fidel considered himself lucky to escape with barely a scratch, but no one walks away from such an assault unscathed. As Fidel recalled the incident, his quavering voice told me he hadn't and still carried an invisible wound.

As a child I sometimes paged through the compact photo album with a faded, fabric-bound plaid cover that my father kept in a drawer. The black matte pages inside held miniature black-and-white photos with white margins and thin, scalloped edges whose corners were tucked into perforations in the album pages. The pictures showed family and friends from Fidel's home in Romania. At the time, I never attached any significance to the thin hole that pierced the cover and half of the pages. During a conversation late in his life, Fidel mentioned that he found the album near him on the floor after the bunker attack. Clearly, it still reminded him that things could have turned out far worse, for he explained the hole came from a wooden splinter that the explosion had driven deep into the album.

During the 11th hour of compiling this book, I received the text of a letter that Hansi Adam wrote to the family of his dearest friend, Stefan Scheible, after Stefan was wounded. Hansi and Stefan had grown up next door to each other in Orzydorf and been inseparable, according to Stefan's sister, who provided Hansi's niece Gertrude Adam a copy of this letter. Gertrude shared it with me for its mention of Fidel, and I was able to tie it to the sapper attack within his bunker. This, the second of Hansi's two letters to survive the war, was mentioned earlier as confirming Fidel's placement in the Danmark Regiment. Details in this letter, which was written shortly after the attack on Fidel's bunker, suggest that Hansi, Stefan, and Fidel were all in the same company, and possibly even in the same platoon. Had they been in different companies, Hansi probably couldn't have learned of Fidel's injury and condition so quickly.

Also of interest in the letter is Hansi's statement that Nordland's live-fire "training" experience in Croatia had been harsh. Fidel hadn't noted any combat there, but then he never talked about any fighting aside from one clash that particularly troubled him. My translation of Hansi's letter follows:

In the field, January 13, 1944 (*Im Felde den 13.1.1944*)

Dear neighbor!

You must be astonished to get a letter from me, but I can't find peace, because who knows when Stefan will have the opportunity to write himself. That is to say, he is wounded. It's now been two months since we left our fellow countrymen for another unit. We two shared joy and sorrow. It wasn't, this is mine or yours, everything was ours. We were like two brothers. Back in Croatia, we had hard days in the Partisan war, but we were always together. We also always said we wouldn't part unless fate separated us. And now it has come. Last night I stood watch from 8 to 10 and he relieved me, and was to watch until twelve. That's when he caught it in the left leg under the knee. The bullet remained inside. I quickly packed up and gave him his most necessary items, that he could use. I could still speak with him for about ten minutes until the sleigh came and took him away. He was in pain, I could see, but he didn't whimper. Might not be so bad, maybe this is lucky for him, for who knows what lies ahead of me. It is war and the enemy doesn't shoot with sand grains. Two letters also came for him today. One from his brother-in-law and one from Lissi [his sister]. 16. XII. [December 16] appears on the envelope. Eipert F. is supposedly lying not far to the rear too, with him it is not so bad. Should soon be mended. Perhaps he and Stefan will cross paths. I have thus made you aware of how things stand, so that you won't be concerned. Many cordial greetings and goodbye to you in our beautiful homeland from your neighbor Hans![6]

When Stefan's sister sent Gertrude Adam a copy of this letter, she also communicated that the family later learned Stefan's injury was serious enough to have warranted recuperation at home instead of in the Vienna hospital to which he was confined. I would speculate that the German command purposely disallowed home recuperation for injuries sustained by ethnic Germans because it would result in many desertions. To Stefan's misfortune, he was still in the hospital when, as Gertrude wrote in a subsequent note in 2018, "the last contingent for the 'final victory' was being marshalled together, at least those who could still move." Stefan appeared "fit" enough to return to the front, this time to France. He was killed there in 1945. Hansi Adam had by then already perished on another Eastern Front battlefield Nordland came to know, Narva.

---

1. Wilhelm Tieke, *Tragedy of the Faithful: A History of the III. (Germanisches) SS-Panzer-Korps* (Winnipeg, Manitoba: J.J. Fedorowicz Publishing, 2001), 9, 27.
2. Richard Landwehr and Holger Thor Nielsen, *Nordic Warriors: SS-Panzergrenadier-Regiment 24 Danmark, Eastern Front, 1943-45*, Armed Forces of the Third Reich - Unit Histories Series (Halifax, West Yorkshire: Shelf Books, 1999), 65.
3. Landwehr and Nielsen, *Nordic Warriors*, 24, 11, 13.
4. Lee Child, *Personal: A Jack Reacher Novel* (New York: Delacorte Press, 2014), 30.
5. "Fritz Todt," in *Wikipedia*, December 7, 2022, https://en.wikipedia.org/w/index.php?title=Fritz_Todt&oldid=1126177593.
6. Gertrude Adam, "About My Uncle Johann Adam: Letters and Background" (Email, April 1, 2018).

24 Awaiting Catastrophe at Leningrad

When the German blitzkrieg invasion of the USSR stalled near the end of 1941, the Germans lost the advantage that their military doctrine was based on: mobility. Most of the blame for this failure can be laid on Hitler. Instead of invading Russia on May 15, 1941, as the professional military planners laid out, Hitler delayed the offensive until June 22 so that he could seize Yugoslavia. The six-week delay subsequently cost the Germans dearly because when the heavy autumn rains and an early, fierce winter set in, the mobile German war machine hadn't yet reached its prime destinations—Leningrad and Moscow. Caught short of their objectives, they became trapped in a war of attrition that forced them to assume a permanent defensive posture. Their extremely long supply lines only compounded their troubles.

By mid-1943, when Fidel was just getting used to his new Waffen SS uniform, the German forces on the Eastern Front were in such a shaky state that the war planners had to devise a fallback position. This new defensive line, the Panther–Wotan Line, stretched from the Gulf of Finland all the way to the Black Sea. Construction of the northern portion began in September of 1943, the month Nordland arrived in Croatia. The Panther leg spanned from the Baltic Sea to Smolensk, while the Wotan section covered the remaining distance to the Black Sea. Panther was able to incorporate natural river and lake barriers in the north, but the remainder of the line lacked the advantage of natural geographical barriers and inconveniently needed to bend eastward to retain two vital rail and road supply hubs.

The new fortified line was devised to straighten Group North's old line and reduce the length of the front by one quarter. Hitler counted on this shortening to free up divisions to help fend off the growing Allied threat in Western Europe. Along the northern stretch, a labor force of 50,000 began construction of the proposed 6,000 wood, earth, and concrete bunkers the line required. The laborers dug trenches, lay coiled barbed wire, excavated tank traps, and strung communication lines rearward to German command centers. During November and December, the feverish construction pace required importing building material at the rate of 100 carloads per day. However, the project was so enormous and its lead time so short that relatively little of the infrastructure was ever completed. Additionally, the Soviets were already dangerously close to much of it.[1] [2]

In concert with the construction, the planners prepared a pullback plan for Group North and called it Operation Blue. Arranging such a fallback was complicated because Hitler believed he couldn't afford to leave any support structure behind for the Red Army. The military's transport experts estimated that it would require 4,000 train loads to move all supplies, livestock, grain, and equipment from the area they were abandoning. What Hitler least wanted to leave behind was the population from which the Red Army formed replacement units by rounding up all able-bodied men and women. By conscripting even women into the Red Army in recaptured zones, Stalin netted several hundred thousand extra soldiers who served in various capacities, including front line combatant, pilot, and sniper.

The relocation of these Russian inhabitants was to take place prior to the withdrawal of equipment and troops, but got off to a rocky start in October 1943 when the German military tried to march large groups of Russian civilians westward. The forced marches created so much hostility, disarray, and misery that the Germans had to resort to the use of trains. The exercise dumped a quarter million people in Latvia and Lithuania and tied up a large proportion of the military's valuable train capacity, only to end when the local authorities ran out of housing.

As the Panther Line construction proceeded, the front-line troops readied their large fixed guns and equipment for withdrawal. The logical time to begin withdrawing was mid-January, before the spring thaw made roads impassable. But Hitler became convinced the existing line could hold, making the fallback unnecessary, because the Reds had lost too many soldiers in the preceding months to allow them to mount a substantial offensive. In truth, the Russians had been prepared to attack from both Leningrad and the Oranienbaum Pocket since November. German military intelligence noticed heavy boat traffic between the two areas but wrongly assumed the Reds were limited to conscripts from the starving population of Leningrad. Thus, they concluded that the inevitable Russian offensive would be a weak one which could be repulsed like three earlier offensives. The reality was, entirely new Russian armies were moving in.

At the time of Fidel's arrival at Oranienbaum in December 1943, Küchler understood that Hitler was ready to issue the Operation Blue order for withdrawal to the Panther Line, but while conferring with Hitler he foolishly let slip that his ambitious 18th Army commander had boasted of being able to hold his lines. In reality, that general didn't even have enough soldiers to man every post.[3] Despite Küchler's pleas, Hitler denied the request to launch the fallback, saying, "I am against all withdrawals." Hitler wanted the Soviet force to bleed by incurring massive casualties before it descended on the Panther Line. Von Küchler argued that if the move was delayed, his army group might no longer have the troops to man the new line when finally allowed to retreat.[4]

Küchler's blunder reinforced what the increasingly delusional führer wanted to believe—that whatever his forces lacked in strength could be compensated for with extra effort. With Hitler in full denial, Küchler returned to his headquarters only too aware that just one decisive Soviet penetration of his lines could spell disaster for his entire army group. Not only was Hitler in denial over the folly of invading Russia, he was also totally blind to how greatly the misadventure had sapped his entire military. By delaying Operation Blue, Fidel and the thousands of others who manned the short-staffed defensive lines at Oranienbaum and Leningrad were put at great risk.

---

1. Earl F. Ziemke, Stalingrad to Berlin: The German Defeat in the East, Army Historical Series. CMH Pub 30-5-1 (Washington, D.C.: Center of Military History, U.S. Army, 1968), 249, https://www.history.army.mil/html/books/030/30-5-1/index.html.
2. Pat McTaggart, "Race to the Panther Line: Final Liberation of Leningrad," *WWII Quarterly* 14, no. 3 (April 2015), https://warfarehistorynetwork.com/2019/01/20/race-to-the-panther-line-final-liberation-of-leningrad/.
3. McTaggart, "Race to the Panther Line."
4. Ziemke, *Stalingrad to Berlin*, 250.

25 The Catastrophe Unfolds

Fidel and his companion were badly shaken following the sapper attack inside the bunker. The men were no longer thinking about food or about warming themselves near the little field stove. Medical evaluation was their chief concern now. Both the Wehrmacht and Waffen SS had competent medical care and the men were soon on their way to the nearest dressing station. There, a medical corpsman determined them unfit to resume their listening post rotations and sent them on their way to a division treatment station for evaluation by a doctor. German infantry divisions normally set up two such stations several kilometers behind the front line. The doctor who saw to the men determined that they needed a day of bed rest to settle their nerves and to recover from the worst of their blast injuries.

Fidel was sent to a different bunker when he reported back to his company. Such reassignment was probably a standard practice on this front to lessen the anxiety of injured soldiers when they returned to the defensive line. But for Fidel, more trauma awaited. On January 14, 1944, the morning after his return, all hell broke loose on a scale new to the Leningrad area when the Red Army launched a massive offensive. Just before dawn, shelling, air attacks, and ground assaults struck the German forces all along the defensive line, but luckily for Fidel, the spear of the attack was directed further east.

After the fall of Stalingrad in the winter of 1942–1943, the Germans were confronted with the serious and ever-growing problem of how to replace their huge losses of Wehrmacht and Waffen SS men, given their limited population. They tried to cope by shuffling exhausted divisions from one crisis spot to another but lost ground steadily. Neither could they adequately make up for their equipment losses because of their labor shortage, bombed-out factories, and limited access to raw materials. By contrast, the Soviets had a much greater population from which merciless conscription roundups could extract ever more cannon fodder. And when it came to equipment and supplies, the Reds had factories far from the reach of German bombers, adequate labor, and abundant raw materials. They also received massive amounts of equipment and supplies from America. Thus, the Red generals could throw ever more soldiers and armament into offensives. At Leningrad and the Oranienbaum Pocket, they amassed an attack force that outnumbered the Germans four to one.[1]

To break the siege of Leningrad and lay the groundwork for a broader westward offensive, a large-scale Russian amphibious attack along the 20 kilometers of coastline between the German Oranienbaum Pocket's right flank at the Gulf of Finland and the German line encircling Leningrad was not feasible. So the Red Army's strategists opted to punch through the Oranienbaum line. That southward-moving force would then link up with a second westerly moving Soviet force cutting through the German line just south of Leningrad. Each force needed to penetrate just 15 kilometers to converge and secure a bridgehead position for a second offensive that would block the escape route of the German divisions encircling Leningrad and others further south. The sapper probes that wounded Stefan Scheible in his listening post and nearly killed Fidel in his bunker were almost certainly a part of the Red Army's last-minute preparations for this offensive. When the main thrusts were launched, their scope took the German forces by surprise. One historian summarized it as follows:

> Under cover of darkness, Soviet units moved into their well-camouflaged jump-off points on January 12 and 13. Massive piles of shells lay beside the artillery battalions of all three Fronts as the gunners zeroed in on preplotted enemy positions. Heavy snow began to fall as the clock ticked down to midnight, further concealing Russian assault units' movements.
>
> The snow added a surreal picture to the landscape as German soldiers in outposts strained to see into the area before them. Visibility was almost zero, and it was eerily quiet. Suddenly, the stillness was broken by the hum of motors overhead . . . the Soviets had pinpointed the weakest points in the German line . . . more than 100 Soviet night bombers approached. Even though the snow prevented visibly identifying targets, the Russians dropped their loads with credible accuracy. The German positions erupted in flames and explosions . . . . For the rest of the night the troops of the two divisions frantically worked on rebuilding their shattered defenses and gathered their dead and wounded while worrying what would come after the raid . . . on the 14th they found out. As the snow abated,

the sky in the distance turned yellow and red as the Leningrad Front unleashed hell on the two divisions and other units of Steiner's corps. In a 65-minute bombardment the Soviet artillery, assisted by guns of the Red Navy, fired almost 105,000 shells, obliterating the enemy defenses.[2]

The massive wall of fire came from a huge number of artillery batteries, the heavy naval batteries on an island fortress, and three naval vessels. Most shells targeted "the positions of the 9. and 10. Luftwaffen-Feld-Divisionen."[3] But Nordland didn't escape entirely. Some of the fire was also directed "onto the positions of the III SS Panzer Corps ... shells of all calibers fell onto the trenches and bunkers of the SS and Luftwaffe soldiers."[4]

Combat soldiers who have experienced intensive shelling or carpet-bombing attest that it is impossible to adequately describe the sphincter-loosening terror, disorientation, and panic that results from the massive force of the incredibly destructive explosions. Cinema simulations can never come close to depicting the real thing. The intensity is both maddening and deafening. No other sounds penetrate the din. Explosions heave the earth so violently that sprawled humans, both dead and alive, levitate off the ground, as does everything else not rooted in the soil. Buildings and trees sway impossibly or simply shatter and disappear. The air is laden with dust and smoke so thick that it even hides nearby burning equipment and structures. All the while, the sky rains dirt, masonry, wood, metal, and flesh. The natural instinct is to curl up tightly in any depression. Standing is impossible. When the panic-seized do try to run, for the short time they remain on their feet they face flying metal, wood, and other shrapnel. If the ground is rocky or frozen, sharp flying shards compound the hazards. Shells from large-bore guns intensify the ferocity and violence.

As soon as the earth quit heaving at Oranienbaum, the survivors emerged, numb with shock. They had difficulty absorbing the scope of human carnage before them. Bodies and body parts littered the ground. The landscape they'd known had transformed completely. One witness wrote, "The front-line positions and the wood line presented a gruesome picture. Bunkers had been shot to pieces by the naval guns and the earth plowed up. The woods had been cut down to a height of two meters. Dead and wounded were everywhere."[5] At the intersection of the 9th and 10th Luftwaffe positions, the sudden quiet proved illusory for it signaled that the enemy infantry was already in motion. The witness to the action went on to say,

> As the last shells and bombs were still falling, the 2nd Shock Army attacked.... For many soldiers, the first great baptism

of fire was too much for their nerves .... By the time those who were left had been briefed, the first Russians, in white winter clothing had already reached the edge of the wood and infiltrated into the wooded area. One after another, the last weapons of the Luftwaffe soldiers fell silent.[6]

Soviet shock armies were formed to overcome difficult defenses. When the 2nd Shock Army struck the eastern portion of the Oranienbaum line that morning, it quickly punched through the German line, then turned southeast to link up with a second Soviet force striking westward from Leningrad. A third Russian group thrust westward and attacked an 18th Army position about 200 kilometers south of Leningrad with the aim of collapsing another section of the front and tying up the sparse German reserves to prevent them from moving north to aid the Leningrad defenders. The terrain at all three points of attack favored the numerical superiority of the Red Army and denied the Germans maneuvering room for their mobile units. The only success the German defenders had on the day of the attacks came immediately south of Leningrad where the 18th Army was able to disperse the initial ground assault with artillery.

At Oranienbaum, the numerous and well-equipped Soviet fighters opened a gap several kilometers wide in what remained of the German line, then rapidly penetrated five kilometers. Much of the 9th Luftwaffe Division was wiped out or encircled, as was a considerable portion of the 10th Luftwaffe Division. Low-level aircraft bombed and strafed any targets that remained, then targeted German headquarter positions in the villages further to the rear.

The ferocity of the shelling and subsequent air and ground attack obliterated the German defensive posts so thoroughly that when a Nordland Waffen SS engineer company building new defensive positions nearby rushed to the scene, it found the forest in front of the Luftwaffe defenders splintered into sticks. All nearby ground was incredibly cratered, and the German defenses were completely shattered. Dead and wounded littered the ground. Those soldiers still ambulatory were either immobilized by shock or fleeing rearward in a dazed panic. The engineers returned some order to a short section of line by calming the remaining soldiers and organizing the evacuation of the wounded on boat-like *akjas* sleds. However, the white-clad Russian troops had obliterated the resistance of the Luftwaffe troops on both sides of the engineer company, leaving their position an island in the middle of a huge gap.[7] [8]

The German engineers, lightly armed with just grenades and machine pistols because they'd been carrying tools instead of heavier weapons, had to fight their way back out and rally further to the rear where their first sergeant was able to deliver their weapons. After the now severely depleted company was joined by a sister engineer company, the small group launched a counterattack into the forest. The assault quickly devolved to hand-to-hand fighting that accomplished little and forced the men to fight their way back out of yet another encirclement.

The engineers found, then hurriedly fortified, an existing defensive position. The Soviets tried to dislodge them with artillery, Stalin Organ rockets, aircraft, and infantry. After the Germans beat back two infantry battalions and endured another fierce artillery barrage, the Russians sent in three T-34 tanks. Two engineers sprinted out in the snow and destroyed two of the tanks by clapping magnetic mines on them. An antitank gun stopped the third. Two days later, the few men still alive were able to make an escape.[9]

Regiment Norge's 1st Battalion, the division's ready-reserve component, was dispatched forward in support of the Luftwaffe divisions as soon as the Corps commander could confirm that the area of attack was confined to the Luftwaffe's positions. The reserve battalion almost immediately encountered hard fighting against vastly superior numbers of Russians. The adjoining Nordland positions also came under fire, but the westernmost portion of the line escaped the full Russian onslaught. Fidel never talked about the fighting along his section of the line on the day of the attack, but Stefan Scheible's wound indicates that some action took place there also.

On the second day of the offensive, the Russian 42nd Army, whose westward attack from Leningrad had been dispersed by German artillery the previous day, renewed its assault against the German containment force with an extremely heavy shell bombardment from multiple sources, including the naval guns and hundreds of artillery batteries. "The preliminary artillery barrage was even more fierce than the one the day before. About 2,300 guns, mortars, and rocket launchers hit a 17-kilometer section of the German line from Uritsk to Pushkin with more than 220,000 shells."[10] A historian noted the firing was so intense that

> mortar and artillery impacts could not be distinguished from the explosions of the bombs, the noise of the Stalin Organs and the guns from the ships at Kronstadt. At 0820 hours, the fire jumped into the rear, and the Russian companies and battalions marched through the trenches, which were flattened by the fire ... the few combat capable soldiers remaining in the main combat line did their best," but were doomed.[11]

The Soviet 42nd Army partially encircled two German divisions, linked up with the 2nd Shock Army, then set about consolidating the bridgehead that would allow them to launch additional attacks westward and capture the vital supply-line rail facilities the Germans depended on.[12] In desperation, the Wehrmacht commanders marshalled every rear soldier they could lay their hands on and threw them into the battles raging all around. Soldiers returning from home leaves were pressed into service the moment they stepped off the train. The Waffen SS men fought hard because capture meant execution or worse. The division staff lost communication with many of its units in the chaos. Commanders outside of the main attack front launched frantic assaults against the Russians in attempts to rescue what remained of their encircled forces. In the process they retook some of the lost ground but were so heavily outnumbered that they were beaten back with heavy losses. Only a few remnants of the encircled units managed to escape.

Norge's 1st Battalion confronted the Soviets at the head of the penetration near Ropscha. There, its companies and platoons were parceled out among the units already engaged in the desperate fighting. Whenever the Germans retook ground in the bloody exchanges, they soon lost it again because they were so heavily outnumbered and outgunned. A prime German objective was to hold on to the forward rail terminal at Witino to allow supplies to reach the fighters trying to evacuate the precious heavy guns and combat vehicles of the retreating 18th Army. As the high command bickered with Hitler, the German line of defenders nearest Leningrad had to swing southward like a closing door to hold back the Red Army long enough to allow units still further east to fight their way westward.

On January 25, the German defensive positions cracked and tremendous bottlenecks subsequently developed along the main corduroy road. In the ensuing scramble to pull back, exhausted fighting units had to remain engaged with the Russians to buy precious time for the jams to clear and allow the surviving Leningrad units to make their way through. Most of the fleeing soldiers were on foot because trucks were scarce and the few roads that existed were jammed. Fidel's 3rd Battalion still held its original line, but the adjoining 1st Battalion had given ground and pivoted southeastward. Lacking static defenses, the 1st was then "hit by an overwhelming enemy attack ... the whole sector was subsequently ripped apart and the Red Army poured through from 3 directions." With three of the unit's top commanders killed and the battalion virtually surrounded, the new commander ordered an immediate breakout. Only after a "long, difficult retreat that came perilously close to disaster," was the 1st able to link up with another Nordland unit.[13] [14]

As usual, Hitler was in denial about the unfolding disaster, as the following book excerpt reveals:

As the German lines continued to deteriorate, Hitler ordered von Küchler to attend a National Socialist leadership conference in Königsberg on the 27th [of January] At the meeting, von Küchler once again confronted Hitler. He told the Führer that the Eighteenth Army had already lost 40,000 men and that retreat was the only way to save it. Hitler gave him little time to continue. He said that he expected the Eighteenth Army and Army Group North to continue to hold . . .

Unbeknownst to von Küchler, his chief of staff, Maj. Gen. Eberhard Kinzel, had already started the ball rolling. While von Küchler was gone, Kinzel informed Colonel Friedrich Foertsch, chief of staff of the Eighteenth Army, that the army must retreat no matter what. Knowing that Berlin would never approve, Kinzel issued the order verbally rather than in writing.

The plan was put into action even as von Küchler was arguing with Hitler . . . . Hitler was furious when informed of the withdrawal. Von Küchler was relieved, and General (soon to be Field Marshal) Walther Model was sent to take his place. Model was a favorite of Hitler's and was known as "The Führer's Fireman."

Even before taking off for his new assignment, Model issued his first order to Army Group North. "Not a single step backward will be taken without my express permission," he telegraphed to his army group headquarters . . . . Things were going from bad to worse for the Germans, and not even Model could stop the Soviets.[15]

The Leningrad disaster was a loss of face for Hitler, just as Stalingrad had been. His soldiers were once again hardly a consideration. The scope of Hitler's latest military fiasco couldn't be publicly acknowledged, so Berlin's propagandists tried to pass it off as a strategic move by calling the repositioning after the defeat a *Rückmarsch* (rearward march) instead of a *Rückzug* (retreat). The German public wasn't fooled.

Fidel and everyone else still defending a position anxiously awaited their own order to withdraw. The code word that set the retreat in motion finally arrived on January 26. When the withdrawal began early the next day, the entire fighting front swung further southwestward. An engineer company held off the Russians as best it could while everyone else mined roads and destroyed unmovable equipment and facilities.[16]

When Nordland's heavy weapon and grenadier companies reached the main supply route, they found the corduroy roads already jammed with vehicles of all kinds. Contributing to the gridlock was a never-ending stream of freshly wounded soldiers aboard trucks and ambulances. To give straggling unit remnants more time to catch up, the German field commanders hastily improvised an interim defensive line at the next geographically favorable position to the west—the Luga River. Most Nordland companies battled the advancing Russians at some point in the withdrawal. Some fought almost continuously and lost up to two-thirds of their men as the Soviets doggedly pursued them. The second day of the retreat proved particularly harrowing and one report states, "On January 28, 1944, Soviet armored units were able to catch up with the flanks and quickly enclose parts of Nordland . . . some 45 km east of Narva."[17]

The rampaging Russians were determined to kill as many of the reeling Germans as they could. Details about Nordland's continuing engagements during the flight are sparse. The histories simply note that the corps withdrew to the Luga River to take up positions near the Russian city of Jamburg (also known as Yamburg, now Kingisepp). Getting there proved perilous because Nordland was a mechanized infantry division in name only and lacked the mobility that the Panzergrenadier title implied. Nordland had been short of transport vehicles when it arrived at Oranienbaum in December, and little had changed by the time of the Red Army breakout in January. The battalions hadn't yet been in place long enough to acquire adequate numbers of the sought-after Russian panje horses and sleds that would have allowed its companies and platoons to retreat faster and haul more food and ammunition. Most of the supplies the soldiers assembled or scrounged before they fled—weapons, ammunition, and food—they needed to carry on their backs or drag along on sleds across the terrain because the roads were choked with German military vehicles and armor fleeing the Leningrad area.

Even before the mass exodus began, the few roads in the region were in terrible shape, according to General Raus.

> The crossing of the many small swamps found along almost any Russian road caused many special difficulties . . . . As a result, serious traffic disruptions lasting many hours and sometimes even several days occurred quite frequently. Over and over again the convoy commanders made the same mistake of failing to wait until the roadbed was repaired by the construction of corduroy roads. Instead, they believed that they could force their way through. The flat swampy stretches, which could have been repaired within a relatively short time before they were completely torn up, were soon in such a condition that their restoration became extremely difficult. The road had to be closed to all traffic . . . . Frequently repair work

could not be undertaken in time because the road construction engineers had no motor transportation and therefore arrived too late at crucial points . . .

Corduroy roads . . . slowed down traffic. The average march performance of foot troops dropped to two miles an hour whereas motor vehicles could cover about five miles an hour. Traveling along a corduroy road . . . was very strenuous, and . . . complicated and slowed urgent movements of reserves in critical situations.[18]

In the Leningrad area there was not a single serviceable hard-surface road leading east toward the German front. In this sector the local army commander was wholly dependent upon two long corduroy roads that covered a total distance of 130 km (80 miles). Since they were the only arteries for troop movements and supply traffic, they were used by day and night; hence, their maintenance presented many problems.[19]

All vehicles in the withdrawal needed to funnel onto the two main roads, which were declared off limits to foot traffic in order to allow the stream of trucks, tanks, halftracks, motorcycles, ambulances, and staff cars to keep moving. The infantry was left to trudge through the countryside in the snow—something it considered not entirely unwelcome because the roads proved rich targets for enemy planes and artillery. Upon attack, there was little that drivers and passengers on the roads could do but fling themselves onto the snowy ground and endure what was thrown at them.

When the orders to prepare for Nordland's retreat came on January 26, the division was much smaller than when it had arrived. At least seven Orzydorf soldiers were lost in this stage of the fighting. The number is imprecise because in Orzydorf's list of war dead, as compiled by the church and community, the date and place of death for some men was never learned.[20]

Fidel said that early on the morning of January 27 at the coordinated withdrawal time each position set fire to their bunker and destroyed everything that couldn't be brought along—weapons, equipment, ammunition, and wooden fortifications. Toting rations, gear, and ammunition on their backs or on hand-towed sleds, the men left the protection of the trenches and log walls. The pullout made them vulnerable to Russian snipers, artillery, and aircraft, so the men had reason to move briskly. Fidel said that the Russians seemed to know about the pullout as soon as the Germans did and stayed right behind, making the retreat a high-tension cat and mouse game. A number of Russian patrols slipped ahead of the Germans in the chaos and forced some elements to fight their way out of ambushes in running skirmishes. Activated partisan units in place behind the Germans also killed many a soldier and caused the loss of a great deal of German equipment when they derailed trains and blew up small bridges. Soviet ski patrols attacked the fleeing Germans in wilder terrain and tanks pursued them where the ground was suitable. The entire German 18th Army, which was suddenly thrown into full retreat from around Leningrad, faced the same.[21]

The perils units like Fidel's faced as they exited were not trivial, as the following excerpt from a unit history makes clear:

> The enemy repeatedly attempted an encircling pursuit, advancing through the porous front. Again and again the German formations had to fight to clear the route of their retreat. The way was one of combat, torturous exertion and marches through snowbound woods and marshland with wounded and equipment loaded onto Akjas.[22]

Throughout the sector, the Germans were under severe pressure from the advancing Russians and didn't have time to organize a coordinated pullback. Specific details regarding the pullout of Danmark's 3rd Battalion are sparse, but the available information suggests much of the unit retreated as a group. One account states that the 3rd Battalion "left its positions and marched over 30 kms on foot to Kyerstovo."[23]

When it came time for Fidel and the other soldiers on the bunker line to leave, they couldn't do so by way of roads, which were prioritized for vehicles and already jammed with traffic created by the 18th Army's flight from Leningrad, further east. Most soldiers fleeing on foot also avoided paralleling the roads and rail lines because such routes were susceptible to Russian artillery, bomber, and fighter plane attack. So most infantry units scrambled cross-country. The circumstances and the need for haste effectively limited the size of the retreating groups.

Fidel's account of his experience suggests that he moved with a small assemblage. Whether this consisted of just his shorthanded platoon, a couple platoons, or the entire company, I don't know. His group, like others, soon found that security gained by avoiding the roads came at the cost of having to break trail and slog across snow-covered fields, deep drifts, marshes, and forests while bearing heavy rucksacks or towing sleds loaded with supplies, and possibly wounded men. This strength-sapping work afforded little time for rest or sleep.

If Fidel's group spent the first night of the pullback at the village of Kerstova with other 3rd Battalion elements, it is likely he saw action the next morning because the soldiers there came up against a strong Soviet advance element. Danmark's commander "then realized that his battalion had only one direction left open to it: south. It was not where he wanted to go, but given the desperate situation any detour was welcome!" Despite the change in direction, the rest of the way became a "fighting retreat."[24]

Nordland's withdrawing units had instructions to head to Jamburg (Kingisepp) on the Luga River. From Fidel's departure point, this was some 70 kilometers as the crow flies—a hard two- or three-day tramp on foot, given the conditions and difficult terrain. It is quite possible that Fidel's group abandoned the westward course it intended to take on the morning of the second day and instead turned south due to Soviet advance units in its path, as did the main 3rd Battalion elements. But it eventually ran into a large mass of Russians anyway, just "a couple of hours" from the new German position along the Luga River. The encounter could only have been accidental, for the unit's path was too unpredictable to have been targeted by a Soviet intersecting force. The Red formation was most likely meant to hit the shaky line of German defenders hastily forming along the Luga River.

The confrontation could have occurred on either January 28 or 29, the second and third day of the trek. If the latter, the Nordland unit history information available makes clear that everywhere along the front the situation was dire: "Beleaguered troops . . . had been cut off . . . withdrawal routes had been cut at several points . . . sharp enemy attacks . . . strong enemy formations began closing in on the retreating SS troops . . . fighting soon became very intense and ugly."[25]

Fidel's exhausted unit, burdened down with weapons, ammunition, and supplies, apparently saw it had little hope of distancing itself from the Russians or of finding favorable nearby high ground, so it made a stand on the far bank of a nearby small, frozen river. The few small, scattered trees there did not offer cover, but the bank itself, being slightly higher than the one opposite it, gave the defenders a slight advantage. Fidel had no idea of the stream's name, but a perusal of maps and a satellite image showed that the Kaskolovka River was a possibility.

Fidel said he was the assistant gunner of a machine gun team at the time. As the number-two man, his primary job would have been to load ammunition belts into the weapon's breech and to keep them coming. The gunner was Sepp (Josef) Zornig, the Orzydorf boy mentioned earlier in Hansi Adam's letter from Dubrovnik. Sepp, three years younger than Fidel, was one of the boys conscripted directly into Waffen SS along with Hansi Adam and Stefan Scheible.

The predominant German machine gun in 1944 was the MG 42. That weapon was light, reliable, cheaper to manufacture than its MG 34 predecessor, and highly feared by enemy infantrymen. The fear stemmed from the gun's appalling rate of fire. At 1,200 rounds per minute, the output was twice that of Allied infantry machine guns. Some MG 42s were even configured to fire as many as 1,800 rounds per minute. The gun fired so rapidly that to the human ear the sound it made resembled the tearing of cloth and was known by various names: Russians called it the linoleum ripper, Brits dubbed it the Spandau, and Americans knew it as either Hitler's zipper or the buzz saw for the way it cut down attackers. The Germans themselves called it Hitler's saw or the bone saw. Facing this weapon was psychologically daunting for the enemy because small numbers of German soldiers could suppress a large number of enemy infantrymen with it. The American army's attempt to copy it in 1943 failed because they tried to adapt it to their .30-06 cartridge.

At this stage in the war the Germans utilized their machine guns in a very different way than their opponents. The Red Army and the other Allied forces supported riflemen with their machine guns. The superiority of the MG 42 allowed the Germans to turn this philosophy on its head and use riflemen to support its machine gunners. Consequently, German units fielded many more machine guns than the forces they opposed. The MG 42 was typically deployed to rake the enemy and at the same time provide crossfire for neighboring MGs. The gun's crew commonly moved the weapon between several prepared positions while riflemen covered them with fire. As soon as the gun was set up in the field, the team's riflemen dug foxholes for the machine-gun crew while the gunners covered them. When the MG 42 was firing, designated riflemen carried ammunition to the gun.

The gun's main strength—its rate of fire—was also its main weakness. The weapon's appetite was so voracious that if gunners didn't fire only in short bursts, they'd quickly run out of ammunition. The heavy rate of fire also heated the barrel and eroded it rapidly, so to preserve the life of barrels the weapon was designed to allow changeouts in seconds. However, swapping a barrel required that a spare be available, and Fidel's team was without one.

The gunner usually toted the weapon, which came equipped with a light fold-down bipod for quick deployment. But the gun worked better when mounted on a larger accessory tripod that the number two lugged on his back via two sling straps and pads mounted on one of the tripod legs. To preserve mobility, light machine gun crews on the move usually didn't pack a tripod because it weighed more than the gun itself. Forgoing a tripod allowed for a smaller team, but gave up considerable stability and long-range accuracy.[26]

Such was the case for Fidel's crew. Each rifleman in the team was essentially an ammunition mule—in German military parlance, a *Schütze Arsch* (protection ass). These men each packed up to four heavy boxes of belted ammunition. Standard Panzergrenadier platoons like Fidel's, when fully staffed, had three 12-man squads, each of which was typically armed with two light machine guns. Ammo bearers carried various rifles; squad leaders, a submachine gun; gunners and loaders, a side arm. The standard MG ammunition came in 50-round flexible metal belts, although the gun could also operate with 75-round snail drum magazines. Gun crews usually linked several belts together because a 50-round belt fed the gun for only two-and-a-half seconds. The belts came in metal ammunition cans that contained five 50-round belts and weighed 10 kilograms each (22 pounds). A heavy-machine-gun platoon consisted of four such squads, and late in the war sometimes even six, giving such platoons incredible fire power against infantry troops.

The purported "bowel-loosening fear that grips a man and robs him of his senses"[27] on being shot at was greatly amplified when the weapon was one as fearsome as the German MG 42 machine gun. Those who survived that gun's bullet storms certainly never forgot their encounter. And soldiers behind the MG 42's trigger didn't forget engagements either, especially when they were bloody. Wholesale slaughter has a way of eating at the soul and leaving soldiers haunted by the killing they'd been forced to engage in. Few writers have done better in depicting just how vulnerable soldiers are to the trauma of mass battlefield killing than Erich Maria Remarque in his 1928 World War I novel, *All Quiet on the Western Front*. The sentiments expressed in his book clashed forcefully enough with Nazi militaristic propaganda that Hitler banned the book in Germany. Reminding the public about the unforgiving brutality of modern warfare and its psychologically damaging consequences was not conducive to Hitler's plans.

The defensive carnage Fidel helped dole out on the Russian riverbank remained with him the rest of his life. If the sentiment in his voice hadn't given this away when he told me what happened, I'd have realized it anyway. This particular experience apparently transcended all the other fighting he'd seen because it was the only combat that he ever talked about. I can only guess he told me about it to unburden himself. Perhaps he expected that because I'd been an infantryman myself, I might understand. Had Fidel been a book reader, I'd have given him a copy of Remarque's book to help him understand he was not alone in dealing with such powerful feelings.

After Fidel relayed what happened on the riverbank I brimmed with questions, for his telling was spare in detail. Yet, I couldn't bring myself to invade a fellow veteran's privacy and pry deeper. I always hoped that someday he'd tell me more about the encounter, but it didn't happen. A couple of years later when I brought up the subject again, Fidel didn't add anything new. Fortunately, later research provided me enough context to offer a reasonable guess as to who the attackers were and why they were there.

---

1. Earl F. Ziemke, *Stalingrad to Berlin: The German Defeat in the East*, Army Historical Series. CMH Pub 30-5-1 (Washington, D.C.: Center of Military History, U.S. Army, 1968), 251, https://www.history.army.mil/html/books/030/30-5-1/index.html.
2. Pat McTaggart, "Race to the Panther Line: Final Liberation of Leningrad," *WWII Quarterly* 14, no. 3 (April 2015), https://warfarehistorynetwork.com/2019/01/20/race-to-the-panther-line-final-liberation-of-leningrad/.
3. Wilhelm Tieke, *Tragedy of the Faithful: A History of the III. (Germanisches) SS-Panzer-Korps* (Winnipeg, Manitoba: J.J. Fedorowicz Publishing, 2001), 30.
4. Werner Haupt and Joseph G. Welsh, *Army Group North: The Wehrmacht in Russia 1941-1945* (Atglen, PA: Schiffer Publishing Ltd., 1997), 199.
5. Tieke, *Tragedy of the Faithful*, 31.
6. Tieke, *Tragedy of the Faithful*, 31.
7. Lars T. Larsson and Steve Waites, *Hitler's Swedes: A History of the Swedish Volunteers in the Waffen-SS* (Solihull: Helion & Co., 2015), 148.
8. Tieke, *Tragedy of the Faithful*, 31.
9. Tieke, *Tragedy of the Faithful*, 31.
10. McTaggart, "Race to the Panther Line."
11. Haupt and Welsh, *Army Group North*, 201.
12. Tieke, *Tragedy of the Faithful*, 30.
13. Richard Landwehr and Holger Thor Nielsen, *Nordic Warriors: SS-Panzergrenadier-Regiment 24 Danmark, Eastern Front, 1943-45*, Armed Forces of the Third Reich - Unit Histories Series (Halifax, West Yorkshire: Shelf Books, 1999), 68.
14. Tieke, *Tragedy of the Faithful*, 40.
15. McTaggart, "Race to the Panther Line."
16. Tieke, *Tragedy of the Faithful*, 28.
17. Rolf Michaelis, *The 11th SS-Freiwilligen-Grenadier-Division "Nordland"* (Atglen, PA: Schiffer Military History, 2008), 47.
18. U.S. Army European Command Historical Division, "Chapter 5: Indispensable Expedients," in *Military Improvisations during the Russian Campaign*, DA Pam 20-201 (Washington: Department of the Army, 1951), 51–55, https://www.history.army.mil/html/books/104/104-1-1/index.html.
19. U.S. Army European Command Historical Division, "Map 5: Corduroy Roads in the Leningrad Area," in *Military Improvisations during the Russian Campaign*, DA Pam 20-201 (Washington: Department of the Army, 1951), 109, https://www.history.army.mil/html/books/104/104-1-1/index.html.
20. Gertrude Adam and Anton Peter Petri, *Heimatbuch der deutschen Gemeinde Orczydorf im Banat* (Marquartstein: Breit, 1983), 148.
21. Haupt and Welsh, *Army Group North*, 205.
22. Tieke, *Tragedy of the Faithful*, 43.
23. Landwehr and Nielsen, *Nordic Warriors*, 69.
24. Landwehr and Nielsen, *Nordic Warriors*, 36.
25. Landwehr, *Narva 1944*, 44.
26. Paul Richard Huard, "The MG-42, AKA 'Hitler's Buzz Saw,' Is Still An Impressive Weapon," The National Interest (The Center for the National Interest, September 25, 2021), https://nationalinterest.org/blog/reboot/mg-42-aka-hitlers-buzz-saw-still-impressive-weapon-194312.
27. Time-Life Books, ed., *The Soldiers*, The Old West (New York: Time-Life Books, 1973), 122.

26 Stalin's Penal Battalions

Standard procedure for a mobile German MG team coming under fire dictated that two or more riflemen hurriedly dig a pit for the gunner and his assistant. However, because the frozen ground beneath the snow cover prevented this and the need to begin firing was urgent, the riflemen could probably do little but drop flat in the snow and lay down suppressive fire while Fidel and Sepp positioned the machine gun. On both occasions that Fidel talked about the assault he mentioned his puzzlement as where the frighteningly large number of onrushing attackers had come from and who they might be. They certainly weren't regular soldiers; neither were they partisans, who operated in small groups and shunned such open tactics. Not even the most ideologically driven of them banded together into suicidal mobs to frontally assault disciplined infantry troops. Some of the assailants, women among them, were dressed in civilian clothing. Not everyone was armed, either. But what the mob lacked in firepower, it compensated for in sheer numbers. If the attackers weren't stopped before they reached the far riverbank, the German soldiers were doomed.

Had the person relating what happened there been someone other than my father, I'd probably have dismissed the story. But Fidel didn't tell war stories or possess an ego that needed inflation. Not once in my childhood had I ever heard him mention the war to anyone. And in our conversations, he never brought it up on his own. People well acquainted with him knew him to be bluntly truthful, even if the truth was unflattering. I never doubted that the river encounter was factual, but did wonder whether the horror of the encounter had magnified the scale in his mind.

Such thoughts vanished after I learned about Stalin's punishment policies and penal battalions. The soldiers and civilians he wanted to punish were used in the cruelest ways imaginable, such as in forced shoulder-to-shoulder marches across minefields and frontal assaults on strong German positions. Prisoners who balked were shot from behind, for penal battalion prisoners were meant to die. The attackers Fidel's group encountered were likely a mix of Soviet army deserters, Soviet soldiers who had been recaptured after joining the German Army to avoid starvation in the German POW camps (Hiwis), and civilians accused of collaborating with the Germans.

Stalin harbored no sympathy for the residents of Soviet areas liberated from German occupation and considered all repatriated people tainted and untrustworthy. Even communist party members who'd failed to engage in resistance were traitors. The leader of the Soviet people's paradise believed that to reassert control, nothing worked better than brute force and terror.[1]

"Collaborators" were arrested as soon as the Red Army regained Soviet territory. Not uncommonly, locals then denounced others to curry favor and spare themselves or their family members. The burden of proof for accusations was low, and there was no due process. Some of the arrested were tortured or executed outright. The rest were assigned to penal battalions or deported to the infamous Gulag system to be starved and worked to death. The individuals in penal battalions didn't dare resist because the safety of their family members was at stake. Everyone knew what the NKVD could inflict on their loved ones. The brutality wasn't just reserved for Russians; the same was inflicted on any Soviet Republic territory liberated from the Germans. Ukrainians well remember the Soviet vengeance that began immediately after their World War II "liberation" and spoke out after gaining independence from Russia. A 2013 article titled "The Revenge of the Liberators" in *Ukrainian Week* describes the cruelty. Needless to say, like Stalin's other crimes, this one didn't make it into Soviet history texts.

> The return of the Red Army was accompanied by "purges of collaborationists" and an overall mobilization of the local population, which Soviet generals used as veritable "cannon fodder." . . . For a large part of the Ukrainian population, Stalin's 'liberation from the Germans' was a mirror image of Hitler's "liberation of Ukraine from the Bolsheviks"—providing freedom without liberation.[2]

The story goes on to say that not just those who actively helped the Germans by serving in the German police or Wehrmacht were targeted. Stalin also punished many innocent people who'd lived under German occupation. They include hundreds of thousands of army deserters, local village heads, women who had had sexual contact with Germans, Communist Party members who hadn't joined partisan groups, and Crimean Tatars in general. In fact, anyone who hadn't actively fought against the Germans could be viewed as guilty. In the two years that

Ukraine was occupied by the Germans, most individuals would have had to cooperate in some way because they worked in factories or agriculture, paid taxes, and served in German administrative institutions. In essence, Stalin's authorities considered the entire population guilty of having "connections" with the enemy, so it needed to pay.

> Individual evidence remains that the total male population of some villages . . . was sent to penal battalions. "When the soviets returned in the autumn of 1943, almost immediately, they grabbed virtually all conscript-aged men in the village of Bulayivka," Valeriy Semyvolos tells the Ukrayinska Pravda (Ukrainian Truth) website . . . . "They would take all the men, be they weak, sick or crippled. Of them, only one finally returned . . . . As people under German occupation, they . . . were sent to a penal battalion . . . . The only weapons they were given . . . were one rifle per ten people. The officers allowed the soldiers a shot of vodka and sent them to their deaths, with stop-the-way detachments comprised of Uzbeks and other Central Asian soldiers following them with machineguns."[3]

As insensitive as Hitler was to his fighting men, German soldiers on the Eastern Front came to see that Stalin cared even less about his soldiers. Stalin fought a war of attrition and was willing to accept the death of five or ten of his soldiers for each German killed because he had a much greater population to draw on and countless "enemies of the people" to sacrifice. The army's poor performance in 1941 had caused Stalin to issue Order 270. It forbade commanders from surrendering, required soldiers to "fight to the last," and imposed severe penalties for desertion and dereliction of duty. Order 227 in July 1942 allowed summary execution of men accused of what Stalin defined as cowardice.

The order also established penal battalions for this and other offenses and noted how Hitler, to keep discipline among his troops, instituted *Strafbattalions* (penal battalions)—infantry units made up of incarcerated soldiers and various felons. Stalin's penal units were assigned the most lethal of missions. A first-time offender could look forward to redemption, should he survive the war. But the main hope of the poorly fed and ill-equipped prisoner was redemption by blood, whereby a battle wound earned him a transfer back to his regular unit. This preserved hope, even though wounded men could not always count on medical attention in the field. Beyond this, a sympathetic penal-battalion commander also occasionally found the courage to release his charges after a period of service. Not surprisingly, Russian troops latched onto Hitler's term and called their own penal battalions *shtrafbats*.

Stalin, whose name was originally Josef Vissarionovich Dzhugashvili, grew up in an area of the Caucasus that spoke a Russian dialect. His early talent for scheming and patience in exacting revenge on his enemies served him well in politics. During his rise he changed his name to Stalin, a word that means "steel." In actuality, Stalin was anything but a man of steel. He was terrified of many things, including flying, swimming, and even his own bodyguard troops. That he should impose a death sentence for cowardice on others is the ultimate irony because after Stalin's death some who knew him well denounced him as a great coward. One was Stalin's successor, Nikita Khrushchev, who wrote in his memoirs that in 1941 "Stalin . . . was paralyzed by his fear of Hitler, like a rabbit in front of a boa constrictor." Khrushchev also said that out of fear of leaving any evidence that might later implicate him in a crime, Stalin avoided signing documents.[4]

One accuser claimed that when the Germans first launched their attack against Russia, Stalin ordered his military not to fire on them for fear of provoking Hitler. As for his "not one step back" policy—it applied only to his troops, not to himself because when the German Army neared Moscow in 1941, Stalin reportedly hid out for days when leadership action was critical. That cowardice resurfaced during a subsequent German air raid on Moscow.[5][6]

When the fight-to-the-last-man dictate (Order 227) made crimes of cowardice and unauthorized withdrawal, it became routine to station heavily armed political commissars and blocking forces behind attack lines. The barrier troops were usually NKVD soldiers. As enforcers, they had cause to fear for their own lives should they fail in their mission, so readily fired on the combat soldiers who ran or retreated without orders. The practice was costly in lives, but it did have the desired effect of forcing soldiers to stand up to the enemy.

The NKVD's ever-increasing responsibilities allowed it to grow into a massive organization with enormous enforcement power. Himmler's Waffen SS reached 38 divisions at its peak strength, but just one arm of the Soviet NKVD fielded an army with more than 50 armed military divisions. These were noncombat units that were assigned to every major Soviet combat force to brutally put down mutinies and keeping soldiers from falling back. Combat soldiers feared the NKVD troops to their rear as much as the enemy to their front. The NKVD also disposed of whoever the leadership wished to get rid of. It killed hundreds of thousands of soldiers and citizens, as well as an unknown number of American and British POWs liberated by the Red Army. NKVD destruction battalions—troops specially trained to inflict large-scale devastation—did much of this killing. The mass graves of their victims are still being uncovered today.

During the war, some 422,000 Soviet soldiers were declared cowards or traitors of the homeland and sentenced to penal battalions. Because penal battalions were meant to be expended, relatively few shtrafbats survived their sentence. Shtrafbats were commonly marched against points of German strength in groups large and small, either to engage and wear down the enemy or to simply learn its strength. Shtrafbat units were also sacrificed as suicidal blocking forces to allow regular Russian forces to escape. They might also only carry mock wooden rifles and be sent out as decoys in readily visible clothing to draw enemy fire. The Ukrainian Week story cited earlier also describes a particularly appalling example of the Stalin's barbarity during one of the largest operations of the war as the Red Army attacked the Germans along a 1,400-kilometer (870-mile) front across the Dnieper River.[7]

> German soldiers were shocked by the insanity of penal soldiers. 'Crowds of people walked the minefields in a tight formation, side by side,' a German soldier wrote in a letter to his family. 'People in civilian clothes and penal battalion soldiers moved forward like robots. Only the mines that injured or killed people, cleared their rows. These people looked as if they felt no fear or had no hesitation. We noticed that the injured who fell, were shot by a small group of commissars or officers that followed the advancing line . . .
>
> Towards the end of September 1943, the soviet army reached the Dnipro. The penal battalion came first . . . without proper armor or preparation. This was their penance for being under occupation.
>
> People swam to the right bank of the river holding on to logs, pieces of wood and raincoats filled with hay under a hail of bullets. They [the German defenders] . . . were pouring bullets over the bank, the island and the river, which was swarming with human bodies. The old and the young, the passionate and the indifferent, volunteers and conscripts, penal and regular soldiers, Russians and non-Russians, were all screaming one and the same thing; "Oh Mother!", "Oh, God!", "Help us" and "Save us" . . . . The injured and those who escaped the bullets grabbed at one another and drowned in packs. The river was bubbling, quivering from human convulsions and covered in red foam." . . . . Stop-the-way detachments were waiting there in the rear, with their machineguns ready.
>
> Of the 25,000 soldiers who entered the water on the Dnipro's left bank, only 5–6,000 reached the right bank, Mr. Astafiev

recalls. Overall, Joseph Stalin's whim to take over Kyiv by the 26th anniversary of the October Revolution on 7 November 1943 cost 417,000 lives.[8]

When the Soviet commanders leading the Dnipro crossing discussed the weapons and uniforms needed by 300,000 new conscripts prior to the operation, Chief Commander Georgy Zhukov reportedly said, "They will fight in what they wear now! Why are we wasting our time here, my friends? Why should we dress and arm these khokhols? They are all traitors. The more of them we drown in the Dnipro, the fewer we'll have to send to Siberia after the war."[9]

As frightful as the ordinary shtrafbat's lot was, his station was still not the lowest to which a penal soldier could descend. For men meriting further punishment, a demotion to trampler meant almost certain death. Tramplers carried out the most suicidal missions of all, such as shoulder-to-shoulder tramps across enemy minefields to clear paths for the regular infantry or for vehicles. Vehicles were considered of more value.[10] Wounded tramplers were left to die where they fell or were shot in place by the NKVD troops after the danger had passed. One report claimed that when the Russian army was offered mine detectors by the British, the head of the Soviet military mission in Britain declined, saying that in Russia "we used people."[11]

Another report of the incredible sacrifice of human life comes from a German veteran of the fighting at Cherson (Kherson) in Crimea. He wrote, "Thick masses, with arms linked to prevent shirkers from breaking ranks and holding back waves of survivors, attacked against our lines. Many of these suicidal charges were women and girls of the Communist Youth Organization." Needless to say, these people were poorly trained and armed, so casualties were high. The Soviet leadership was willing to sacrifice anyone but themselves.[12]

Various German veterans said that on the battlefield the Russians didn't make the same effort as their side to care for and recover the wounded. When the Russians retrieved their wounded, particularly early in the war, the quality of medical care was poor. Later, it came to vary greatly by unit. The problems were multiple—poor coordination, lack of transport, shortages of personnel, and substandard medical training. Often, lightly wounded men gave up waiting for transport to a field hospital and walked there. It was not unusual for wounded Soviet soldiers to be left to their fate where they lay. Sometimes no attempt was even made to collect them via a temporary white flag truce. Wehrmacht soldiers recalled that when possible, their own medics treated wounded Russians and brought them to the rear. However, the Germans were on the run through much of the war on the Eastern Front, leaving them chronically short of food and medical supplies and often barely capable of handling their own injured.[13]

1. Vladyslav Hrynevych, "Freedom without Liberation," *The Ukrainian Week*, February 8, 2013, https://ukrainianweek.com/History/71837.
2. Hrynevych, "Freedom without Liberation."
3. Yaroslav Faizulin, "A Death Row Army," *The Ukrainian Week*, October 27, 2011, https://ukrainianweek.com/History/33990.
4. Nikita Sergeevich Khrushchev, *Khrushchev Remembers*, ed. Edward Crankshaw and Strobe Talbott (Boston: Little, Brown and Co., 1970), 180.
5. Khrushchev, *Khrushchev Remembers*, 180.
6. Nikolai Tolstoy, *Stalin's Secret War* (New York, N.Y.: Holt, Rinehart, and Winston, 1982), 57.
7. Grigori F. Krivosheev, *Soviet Casualties and Combat Losses in the Twentieth Century* (London: Greenhill Books, 1997), 92.
8. Faizulin, "A Death Row Army."
9. Faizulin, "A Death Row Army."
10. Tolstoy, *Stalin's Secret War*, 240.
11. Tolstoy, *Stalin's Secret War*, 282.
12. Gottlob Herbert Bidermann, Derek S. Zumbro, and Dennis E. Showalter, *In Deadly Combat: A German Soldier's Memoir of the Eastern Front* (Lawrence, KS: University Press of Kansas, 2000), 141
13. Roger R. Reese, *Soviet Military Experience: A History of the Soviet Army, 1917-1991* (New York: Routledge, London, 2000), 118.

27 The Costly Withdrawal

With the Russian attackers closing rapidly on Fidel's small unit at the riverbank during the helter-skelter retreat from Oranienburg, Fidel and Sepp were under pressure to get their machine gun firing quickly. Ordinarily, this was straightforward. But here, Sepp couldn't sight the weapon on the attackers because the gun's bipod legs sank down into the snow of the riverbank. What he sorely needed was the height-adjustable tripod made specifically for the weapon, but to save weight and allow faster flight, neither that nor a spare gun barrel had been brought along.

German machine gunners sometimes encountered situations where it was expedient to place the gun's barrel on the shoulder of a standing soldier or across the back of a man on hands and knees. But here, such a stance was probably too unstable for effective shooting and left the both the gunner and his assistant too exposed to enemy bullets. Because the terrain offered no protruding rocks or logs on which to rest the bipod's short legs, improvisation was called for. Fidel said he dropped onto his back in the snow, hoisted the bipod onto his shoulders, and gripped the bipod legs to allow Sepp to shoot.

Machine gunners were trained to shoot in short bursts, but the weapon still chewed through belts of ammunition rapidly. Since Fidel was stuck beneath the bipod on his back, he was unable to feed in fresh belts as the assistant gunner normally did. Fidel didn't say whether one of the ammunition-bearing riflemen filled in, but I suspect the riflemen were fully engaged in laying down fire to protect the gunners or assembling and delivering longer belts of ammunition for them. Hence, the gunner was likely feeding the gun himself and steadying the belt with his left hand as he fired. Fidel said, "I was shooting and then he [Sepp] was shooting while I was laying on my back holding up the gun. You could shoot and shoot and still more came." I would guess that Fidel and Sepp rotated as gunner because the job was both physically and mentally draining. Effective shooting demanded sharpness and a degree of restraint. Firing too furiously here was life-threatening for it could cause the ammo to run out or the gun barrel to be ruined if allowed to overheat.

When I picture the frantic scene, I see Fidel sprawled on his back in the snow, trying not to flinch when hot shell casings and ammo-belt bits spurting from the weapon pelt him. He is enveloped in the stench of battle: hot gun oil, expended powder, and the acrid sweat of fear. His prone position leaves him blind to the attackers, but he tries to put that out of his mind as he steadies the gun and stays attuned to any communication from Sepp. Then he and Sepp scramble to exchange places, and it is Fidel's turn to slap in fresh ammo belts and guide them to avoid jams. Out to the front, his bullets cut into the screaming enemy. Shouts or hand signals help coordinate his fire with the shooters around him to keep from duplicating effort and make the ammunition supply last longer. Piercing the cacophonous combat sounds around him—Mauser rifles popping, bullets ripping the air, and German stick-grenades exploding—are the cries of terror and despair from the attackers still on their feet and the agonizing shrieks of anguish and pain from the wounded flailing about in the snow that blanketed the river ice and the bank beyond.

Combatants caught in the midst of preserving their own skin have little time to ponder the troubling aspects of morality that spring from having to kill fellow humans. Such thoughts arise only after the mayhem subsides, the adrenaline feed stalls, and the brain's circuitry has time to try to make sense of what transpired. Such questioning still haunted many a World War II soldier years later. Fidel was one. As he relayed what happened at the riverbank, it was obvious that he wasn't at ease with what he'd had to do. I suspect the killing was particularly troubling because of the familiarity he'd developed with the unpretentious Russian POW laborers he'd gotten to know during the harvest near Regensburg months earlier. They, like himself, were simply people who had fallen into harm's way by accident of geography. The victims of his bullets here wouldn't have been much different.

After Fidel finished relaying the story, I empathized with his emotional struggle and couldn't bring myself to further peel back the scab of his inner wound by asking the many questions that popped into my head. So I asked only an innocuous question—one that a fellow infantryman might ask, "Did you burn out your gun barrel?" He replied that they had, but it no longer mattered by then because they'd also shot up all their ammunition.

Fidel didn't mention how long he and the others stayed on the riverbank, but it would have been foolish to linger after the attack had been broken. Their shortage of ammunition and the threat of regular Soviet troops, tanks, or fighter planes appearing were strong motivators for resuming the dash toward the German lines. The hellish sounds of the dying and wounded enemy and the disconcerting sight of heaps of enemy bodies lying in blood-stained snow could only have helped drive them onward.

Given their much-lightened load after expenditure of their ammunition and the pull of relative safety behind their own line, the pace to the Luga River would have been a rapid one. But once in sight of their goal, they'd have paused, for here they faced one last hazard—hyper-alert German sentries, scouts, and artillery spotters. Those soldiers would themselves have recently run the gauntlet. They knew the Ivans (German soldier slang for Russian soldier) were in hot pursuit and racing to cross the river ice themselves in the hope of outflanking the main German concentrations. Fleeing Germans were forced to approach the river cautiously so as not to trigger a mortar, artillery, or machine-gun reception from their compatriots already in place. Since it is unlikely that Fidel's group carried a radio, their commanding officer would have needed to send out a runner or two to alert the German guards of friendlies approaching.

Most retreating German motorized units exited Russia by road and crossed the river via the bridge at Jamburg, but groups like Fidel's simply walked across the ice wherever they reached the river. Once behind the forward defenders, they'd have sought out and rejoined the other remnants of their battalion. Fidel must have felt relief in being able to draw fresh rations and replace the machine gun barrel and ammunition, but he was not pleased about the poor defensive posts there. The new line was nothing more than a temporary fallback position that took advantage of a geographic feature, the Luga River, to slow down the Russians and give withdrawing German units and stragglers a chance to catch up. The defense that Hitler really counted on was the line along the Estonian border 40 kilometers to the west. At the Luga, Nordland encountered only more chaos and dangerous assignments.

Group North's new commander, Generaloberst Model, ordered Nordland's Regiment Norge to hold a bridgehead at the town of Jamburg in the belief that most of the remaining Group North units still trying to escape westward would need to cross the Luga River on either the rail or road bridge. Felix Steiner, the commander of Nordland's parent corps, considered the order foolhardy because it was sure to seriously degrade or destroy Nordland, by then already dangerously weak after having lost a great many soldiers, panzers, and combat vehicles. Keeping the bridges accessible would be difficult since Jamburg lay east of the river and would require building a defensive line around the entire city. Steiner understood that it was far too late to construct this position, so he tried to convince

Model to blow up the bridges instead. Keeping these approaches open unnecessarily was asking too much. Steiner argued that the river was frozen solid and could be crossed almost at will by the last German units still to the east, including most of their light combat vehicles. Once the German units were across the frozen river, explosives could break up the river ice at key crossing points to keep heavy Russian vehicles from following. Model dismissed Steiner's plea and ordered him to get on with fortifying the bridgehead.[1]

Left no choice, Steiner positioned Regiment Norge's infantry and artillery companies around Jamburg in the open countryside where they had to blast fighting positions out of frozen ground. Not only was this slow and difficult work, it was also very dangerous because many Red Army elements with formidable air and artillery resources had already consolidated around the Nordland position.

Fidel likely crossed the river on January 29 and was fortunate to do so because the Reds were engaged in an all-out effort to trap or outflank any retreating Germans and had already pinched off most escape routes. No organized German unit escaped by road after that date. Already by the evening of the 28th, "there'd been no 'front lines' *per se*, as Soviet forces probed and penetrated at will between the various Waffen SS elements." As ever more Germans piled into Jamburg, the city's residents fled in the knowledge that heavy fighting was sure to follow.[2]

Had Fidel mentioned the fierce fighting around Jamburg, or that which occurred during the next withdrawal to Nordland's new defensive positions along the Narva, I'd have asked the many questions that arose when I focused on this later. The unit histories that reported on Nordland were short on detail regarding Regiment Danmark at the Luga River, but did reveal that the companies of Fidel's 3rd Battalion were assigned to secure a section of the Luga River's west bank north of Jamburg near the town of Pagoda.[3]

The Soviet forces that quickly came to outnumber the defenders all along the river prioritized the capture of the bridges to facilitate the transfer of their own heavy equipment across the river. Consequently, the Norge bridgehead defenders came under repeated ground and air attack. When the Soviet generals failed to dislodge Norge from the east side of the river, they decided to trap the regiment by destroying the bridges themselves and break up the river ice with artillery fire to prevent escape across the river. However, Steiner employed a countermeasure and obscured the bridges from Russian planes and artillery spotters with enormous smoke screens.

As "other parts of the division [Nordland], along with what remained of the 10th Field Division (Luftwaffe), fought vigorously on both sides of Yamburg," the remaining German guns returned fire and did their best to keep the enemy at bay.⁴ Because the outgunned Wehrmacht and Waffen SS units lacked functional reserve elements to relieve front-line defenders, the smoke, ceaseless explosions, and endless nighttime watches rapidly wore down the soldiers. Men who stood guard much of the night and then repaired defenses or repelled attacks during the day were unable to catch up on sleep and quickly became exhausted, confused, and less than fully alert. Many of them had already been in this condition when they arrived at the Luga.

On January 31, the Red Army launched a fierce attack on Norge's bridgehead position and other points along the river. The bridgehead soldiers managed to hold their position, but other divisions did not. The Red Army broke through the German lines both north and south of Jamburg, which allowed a huge number of Soviet soldiers to pour across the frozen river. That presence on the west bank of the river left the remaining German bridgehead position on the east side indefensible, so Model finally allowed those defenders to pull back.⁵ Norge's rearguard engineers fought fiercely there and held up the Russians until all other German units in the city were on the west bank or already moving on to the Panther Line. The bridgehead position was nearly encircled by then, but the engineers somehow managed to fight their way out and blow up the two bridges behind them. Meanwhile, elsewhere along the west shore of the river, the fighting was so bloody and ferocious that even clerks and cooks needed to take up weapons and fight as infantry.⁶

Regiment Danmark's defensive position in the Pagoda area north of Jamburg had no actual river bridge to secure. But because the spot was well suited as a major ice-crossing point for the enemy, it needed to be defended like another bridgehead position. The fighting there cost many lives, but Danmark's sacrifice was in vain because the Soviets had already broken through the German defenses in multiple other spots. One was in difficult terrain north of Pagoda before the regiment had even fully deployed. According to one source, there the Reds "infiltrated like ants, in small groups that later joined together and were soon on the banks of the Narwa River." That river was part of the so-called Panther Line west of the Luga River where Hitler hoped to hold the Russians until his forces had a chance to regroup.⁷

Soviet pressure all along the Luga was so intense that the German command issued the following retreat order late in the day on January 31: "The Russians have broken through the Luga position. The Narwa River main line of resistance is to be occupied immediately." But before Danmark's 3rd Battalion could pull back, the Russians hurled a strong attack force against its flank after crossing the river to the west bank. In this action, they badly mauled two of 3rd Battalion's four companies.⁸ It appears likely that Fidel's company was one of them because the Orzydorf death records indicate that one local man died on January 30 and another two on February 1. A fourth would die on February 7, and still more in the weeks that followed. Fidel would have known them all.

On February 1, Norge and Danmark alternated as rearguard elements for each other as they retreated in leapfrog fashion. Their battalions remained locked in heavy combat with the Reds throughout the 40-kilometer withdrawal to the Panther Line at the Narva River. The terrain they had to navigate—a chokepoint of waterways, soupy swamps, and dense forests—was ill suited for rapid movement. The chaotic fighting and intense running battles continued to inflict heavy casualties on Nordland and cost the division even more of its precious remaining equipment. Upon arrival at the Narva, which was also the Estonian border, Nordland was once again assigned the same dangerous mission it had just left—securing the main river bridges that allowed the withdrawing German vehicles and heavy equipment so desperately needed along the Panther Line to cross the river.[9]

The new bridgehead area to be defended was larger than the previous one. Its defenses, which the Germans called the Tannenberg Line, were based on three east-west strategic hills considerably east of Narva. Staffing this line absorbed the battalions of several understrength and morale-drained Waffen SS divisions. Regiment Danmark's 3rd Battalion had the bad luck to draw what was arguably the most exposed section of the new bridgehead line. This placement, 30 kilometers west of Jamburg and 16 km east of Narva, crossed flat, open terrain near the main east-west regional highway and straddled the railway bridge approach that the Reds needed to transport their heavy equipment across the river. The combination of these circumstances made the battalion's position one of the most inviting attack points. A Danmark regimental history characterized it as "the softest target for the enemy on the eastern sector on the Tannenberg front."[10] As with the earlier fighting at Pagoda, this dangerous assignment was a situation that Fidel failed to mention.

The German side had lost a huge amount of equipment since the start of the Leningrad offensive. The Soviets reported capturing "275 armored vehicles, 1,926 large bore guns, 3,642 machine guns, 4,276 trucks, and 42,000 rifles."[11] Needless to say, Nordland's soldiers arrived at their new assignment exhausted and demoralized. With the Red Army right on their heels, the last thing the soldiers wanted to find was that defenses at the touted Panther Line barely existed. Fidel said that back at the Oranienbaum Pocket his team had been assured that concrete bunkers awaited them at the Narva and that they'd hold the Russians there. But there were no defensive structures to be found.[12]

Not even the German commanders had hardened structures within which to set up their headquarters, according to a panzer lieutenant who recalled looking for Nordland's headquarters in Narva on arriving in the city. He learned it was set up in two city buses. When he located them, he found himself talking directly to the division's commander, General Fritz von Scholz. The general, who was affectionately known by his men as Old Fritz, said to him, "Look, in reality, the position only exists on paper. I have laid out a proper bridgehead line and your mission is to help my men construct and fortify that line."[13]

Under the threat of constant attack by Soviet aircraft and artillery, the battalion's lower ranks once again contended with frozen ground as they blasted out trenches, strung barbed wire, constructed gun emplacements, and built barriers. The troops closest to the bridges often worked amidst the dense oil smoke their side put up to hide their positions. With the Narva River kilometers to the rear, a massive Red Army force building to the front, and snipers, artillery, and attack planes always lurking, this was not a comfortable place to be.[14]

By February 2, 1944, elements of the Russian 47th Army already occupied numerous positions along the Narva River and around the eastward Tannenberg Line bulge that formed the newly established bridgehead defenses for the city of Narva. The new German positions were almost immediately imperiled when a Russian unit fought its way across the Narva River between the Baltic Sea Coast and the city of Narva to establish a bridgehead. Only the efforts of a tiny Waffen SS reserve force that pushed the Reds back across the river kept the German defensive line from being outflanked. The Red buildup on the east bank of the Narva soon became so dense that just a few small groups of German stragglers managed to sneak through to reach their own line. These soldiers somehow evaded the Reds after the disaster at Leningrad, survived subsequent running battles during the retreats, and sneaked through. One panzer unit remnant breached the Russian presence by fighting its way along the coast. After losing all their panzers, the men fought on foot and dragged along a flak gun they employed as an artillery piece. Another escape occurred on February 3 when 30 ravenous survivors of a Norge infantry company nearly annihilated in the Soviet breakout at Oranienbaum made it to the river. They'd carefully threaded their way west through enemy forces for two full weeks and had subsisted largely on a sack of flour scrounged along the way. On February 12, three more soldiers reached safety. A German machine gun fired on them as they crawled over the river ice, but the men shouted out their identify in time to save themselves. One platoon mate hadn't been so lucky four days earlier. He was shot and killed by German sentries while trying to do the same.[15]

1. Wilhelm Tieke, *Tragedy of the Faithful: A History of the III. (Germanisches) SS-Panzer-Korps* (Winnipeg, Manitoba: J.J. Fedorowicz Publishing, 2001), 49.
2. Tieke, *Tragedy of the Faithful*, 52.
3. Tieke, *Tragedy of the Faithful*, 39, 47, 71.
4. Rolf Michaelis, *The 11th SS-Freiwilligen-Grenadier-Division "Nordland"* (Atglen, PA: Schiffer Military History, 2008), 47.
5. Richard Landwehr, *Narva 1944: The Waffen-SS and the Battle for Europe* (Silver Spring, MD: Bibliophile Legion Books, 1981), 45.
6. Tieke, *Tragedy of the Faithful*, 52.
7. Tieke, *Tragedy of the Faithful*, 49.
8. Tieke, *Tragedy of the Faithful*, 52.
9. Landwehr, *Narva 1944*, 48.
10. Richard Landwehr and Holger Thor Nielsen, *Nordic Warriors: SS-Panzergrenadier-Regiment 24 Danmark, Eastern Front, 1943-45*, Armed Forces of the Third Reich - Unit Histories Series (Halifax, West Yorkshire: Shelf Books, 1999), 105.
11. Werner Haupt and Joseph G. Welsh, *Army Group North: The Wehrmacht in Russia 1941-1945* (Atglen, PA: Schiffer Publishing Ltd., 1997), 209.
12. Tieke, *Tragedy of the Faithful*, 52.
13. Tieke, *Tragedy of the Faithful*, 54.
14. Tieke, *Tragedy of the Faithful*, 74, 77.
15. Tieke, *Tragedy of the Faithful*, 55.

28 A Bullet Buys a Ticket

As Soviet planes and artillery pounded the Nordland defenders at Narva, Hitler's foolish overreach in attacking the vast Soviet Union was on full display. Few, if any, of the besieged soldiers frantically digging in and building defenses could still believe they would hold the Reds back for long, given their side's huge losses in men, weapons, and transport. The limited supplies that the battered and under-strength companies found at Narva did not boost the men's low spirits. Neither did the lack of meaningful Luftwaffe air support and their division's severe shortage of combat vehicles and panzers. Without the mobility provided by tanks and other vehicles, the division could no longer function as designed. And the men had surely heard rumors, if not actually seen evidence, that the Russians they faced were tapping an inexhaustible supply of American artillery shells, trucks, weapons, boots, and canned food.

Perhaps most demoralizing to the German field soldiers was the knowledge that their commanders couldn't protect them from Hitler's sudden impulses. Had these men known that German defenses in some areas were down to just "one soldier for every 50 meters of front,"[1] they'd have despaired even more, for a major Soviet breakthrough anywhere imperiled the entire front that tenuously stretched from the Baltic Sea to the Black Sea. The weakness of the German defensive line rendered it a series of catastrophes waiting to happen.

Many a combatant had become cynical by then, making jokes such as: "Hitler visits the front and asks a soldier, 'When under artillery fire here, what do you wish for?' The soldier replies, 'That you, my führer, are standing right next to me!'" The low morale prompted Hitler's propagandists in Berlin to alter their emphasis in an attempt to wring extra resolve out of the dispirited combatants. With victory no longer in the picture, the message changed from conquest to patriotism. The propaganda now conveyed to soldiers that the survival of the fatherland and German culture itself was at stake and that only the German military stood in the path of the Russian barbarian horde.

That message may have resonated with some of the Reich German and West European volunteers, but it meant nothing to the conscripted men of other nationalities. Preventing the Soviet Army from reaching Germany didn't help their own homelands or speed up a return to their families. Fidel certainly hadn't forgotten what his fiancée's father said the previous year about the war being lost already because of Hitler's overextended position. Among the now seasoned Banat men at Narva, the belief that the professionalism of the German military would see them through the war had vanished. The string of recent military disasters and Hitler's continuing reckless disregard for the lives of his soldiers had eroded their confidence in German competence. Although Fidel couldn't have known precisely how many of his fellow villagers had made Nordland's casualty list, he undoubtedly had a reasonable approximation in his head and grasped how deadly his situation was. As best as can be determined, of the approximately 110 Orzydorfers who'd donned German Waffen SS uniforms the previous summer, nearly 50 had become casualties in the previous month. Some 20 were dead, with the rest missing or wounded. Every man left standing had friends and relatives who'd paid in blood for Hitler's folly.

War stories and accounts of battle exploits make it all too easy to forget that soldiers are not robotic action figures that can operate fearlessly and fight indefinitely without suffering consequences. Trauma wrought by intense or frequent combat quickly affects normal functioning and breaks soldiers down. His close call in the bunker attack at Oranienbaum, the calamitous German collapse that followed in the Soviet offensive, the slaughter during the disastrous retreat to the Luga River, and the heavy fighting from Pagoda to Narva surely shook Fidel. The lack of defenses he found at the Panther Line could only have added to his despair. Building fortifications during the day and manning listening posts at night, all the while under threat of sniper bullets, shelling, sapper probes, and air attack, was asking far too much of him and his fellow soldiers. He, like everyone else, must have been wondering why he should continue to risk disablement or death for the likes of Hitler.

Despite whatever exhaustion, fear, and depression plagued Fidel at Narva, the probability calculator in his head that made him such an exceptional card player had to have been screaming "get out or you'll never see your home again!" That would certainly explain the decisive action he took one night about 10 days after reaching the Panther Line.

By 1944, the enlisted man's disillusionment with Hitler over the hopeless military situation he'd left them in had spread to the officer corps. Nevertheless, field commanders continued to lead and fight hard because self-preservation and a lack of alternatives demanded it. The discontent affected not only Wehrmacht officers, but Waffen SS officers as well. Hitler's incompetence and incessant meddling in military matters had even disillusioned some staff officers. One career man, Siegfried Knappe, described the particular disgust he and General Weidling—the general in charge of Berlin's final defense—felt for Hitler in the last days of the war. Knappe, who served as Weidling's adjutant, wrote that he and the general dodged from doorway to doorway through ruins daily, braving artillery, tank, and machine-gun fire to brief Hitler and his aides, who were safely ensconced in the Führerbunker. Knappe stated that all hope of stopping the Russians east of Berlin was long since lost, yet Hitler refused to surrender and spare Berlin's civilians and soldiers. Hitler's insistence on defending the city to the last instead of allowing military units to break out while such a thing was still feasible needlessly doomed thousands of soldiers. Knappe described General Weidling's reaction to the refusal in the following terms:

> This man [Weidling] whom I had seen remain calm under even the most adverse circumstances was so furious that his voice quivered. "He [Hitler] listened to my proposal, and then he said, 'No, Weidling, I do not want to risk dying in the streets like a dog.' Our soldiers have been dying in the streets of Europe for the past six years—at his command! For him to imply now that such a death is somehow dishonorable is loathsome." . . . . For Hitler to be so disrespectful toward the men who were sacrificing their own lives every day just to keep him alive one more day filled me with anger also . . . As soldiers, we had accepted death . . . as a price we had to pay for a cause we had thought just, at least in the beginning. We were perhaps only now . . . beginning to see clearly what kind of man we had been following.[2]

Knappe was wounded four times in the war. Writing as a man who'd chosen to be a professional soldier, he described what it took for someone like him to function.

> I tried to be as small a target as possible—but I knew that I was going to be killed or badly wounded sooner or later . . . and I accepted my eventual death or maiming as part of my fate. Once I had forced myself to accept that, I could put it out of

my mind and go on about my duties; I would not have been able to function had I not done so.³

Fidel eschewed such acceptance. He'd chosen to be a farmer, not a soldier. The same practicality and common sense I saw in him during my childhood had apparently asserted itself in Russia also. He'd seen too many friends go down and experienced too many close calls to be unaware that his odds of surviving the front were poor. And he owed Germany and Hitler nothing, so abandoning the cause probably didn't produce any pangs of guilt.

His exit choices were limited. Simply melting into the countryside was not possible on the Eastern Front, but defection to the enemy was. German soldiers were aware of this option because Russian psychological warfare units air-dropped leaflets promising food, alcohol, and sex to deserters. The Reds sometimes employed loudspeakers to blast out comforting defection promises to the accompaniment of nostalgia-inducing German music. However, few German soldiers took up the offer because they didn't trust the communists to honor their word. And almost no one wished to spend the rest of his life in the Soviet Union. So outside of suicide the only remaining means of escape was medical evacuation through a self-inflicted wound.

Fidel said he was alone in his bunker between watches when he carried out his action. Shooting yourself obviously violated the Waffen SS loyalty oath to Hitler that all conscripts were forced to recite. However, for Fidel and other ethnic Germans, the overriding loyalty they felt was to family and community, and many considered themselves no more bound to the Hitler oath than Hitler did to the oaths and treaties he routinely broke as soon as it served his purpose. Atop it all, it is unlikely that Fidel had ever forgotten that fighting for a similar lost cause had ruined his father's health, ultimately leading to his death.

Yet, shooting himself posed risks that weren't trivial. Death by hanging or manual strangulation was the dictated SS punishment, although sympathetic commanding officers didn't always follow through. The shooter also had to come to terms with permanent damage because anything less than a debilitating wound bought a man only a temporary reprieve. Then, when that soldier returned to the battlefield he had to cope with a disability. Many a young, able-bodied man found it difficult to contemplate a wound serious enough to permanently keep him away from the battlefield, for that might also leave him incapable of supporting himself or a family later. So while many a soldier contemplated wounding himself, not all summoned up the determination to follow through.

At some point in my childhood, I became aware that my father's crooked right forearm came from a war wound, but since he didn't ever talk about the war, the subject was never at the front of my mind. I didn't begin to ask Fidel about his childhood, World War II, and life in postwar Germany until shortly after returning from my own war. In time, the story pieced together from our conversations struck me as quite worthy of a book. Then, in the course of one of our chats Fidel said that he'd shot himself and the crooked forearm was the result of this self-inflicted wound. In a few spare sentences he described how he'd gone about it. His admission was simple, straightforward, and unaccompanied by any excuse or other explanation, other than to say he wasn't the only man who'd shot himself. He knew more than one soldier who'd put his foot under a loaf of hard bread or some other object (to absorb telltale powder burns) then shot off some toes.

I took the mention of foot mutilation to mean he realized this wound was overused and prone to arouse suspicion upon arrival at an aid station. Hence, he opted for a more serious and convincing wound. When the opportunity presented itself, he said he sat down and rested his rifle across his legs, pressed his arm against the bunker wall, and then propped a small board against the inside of his forearm to keep powder burns from his uniform sleeve and skin. After lining up the rifle muzzle against the board, he pulled the trigger and sent the bullet tearing through his ulna not far below the elbow.

When my initial shock over Fidel's bombshell revelation passed, my first thought was that his admission came of guilt because I'd come home from my war with a combat wound and he didn't want me to think his wound was also genuine. Shooting yourself struck me as blatantly dishonorable and left me so disappointed with him that I didn't want to hear anything more about it. And I feared that with further questioning, my voice would betray that disappointment. The story I'd hope to write suddenly appeared very dead, for I couldn't see how someone who shot himself could retain the reader's respect. At the time, the flip side of his disclosure—that a person who didn't value their honor wouldn't have admitted that a wound was self-inflicted in the first place—completely escaped me.

Such a reaction was perhaps predictable in someone who'd grown up in a victorious post-World War II America that abounded in book, movie, magazine, and television stories bursting with idealized heroism and patriotism. The sentiment expressed in those tales left no room for battlefield desertion. A soldier's honor bound him to suck it up and go down stoically, if not heroically. Only later, after the picture behind my father's action became clearer and I'd reached a better understanding of just how bleak the future looked for the wretched German soldiers who'd reached Narva, did I see how misguided my condemnation had been.

The grinding fear and exhaustion that now weighed heavily on Eastern Front German soldiers did not foster "Heil Hitler" enthusiasm. Understandably, conscripted foreign nationals like Fidel had good reason to seek an exit. The recitation of an oath to an unfeeling dictator and his lost cause wasn't enough to override the instinct of self-preservation. As for Fidel in particular, I would guess that revulsion and guilt over the machine-gun killing at the riverbank also weighed on him.

I never asked my father whether his bunker mates knew that he'd shot himself, but the answer seems obvious. The powder stench and blood spatter where the bullet entered the wall surely told the story. Most of his squad mates had probably contemplated doing the same at some point and accepted his action without resentment. They all knew how grim their situation was and that they could make the same choice if willing to accept the consequences.

Once I arrived at a better understanding of what Fidel had struggled with at Narva, I realized that my own war experience hadn't qualified me to pass judgment. My service in Vietnam was not nearly equivalent. It too had ultimately proven pointless and not worth risking life and limb for. But during my 13 months *in country*, as we called it back then, I'd never come anywhere close to Fidel's level of peril and desperation. I was glad then that I hadn't responded to his revelation by telling him no reader would want to pick up a story about a soldier who'd shot himself. At the time, all I said was that with his admission I'd no longer be able to tell his story because of the negative impression a self-inflicted wound would leave on the reader. He replied, "What do I care what people think after I'm dead!"

By the time I'd arrived at a better understanding of Fidel's situation and resumed work on the story, I'd also learned more about how combat alters the brain and affects behavior. And how common these effects are. PTSD was not yet fully recognized during World War II but was no less present than it is today. The German military categorized soldiers with combat fatigue symptoms as *Kriegsneurotiker* (war neurotics). Commanders often dealt harshly with them in the field. The luckier men, those whose symptoms were recognized by sympathetic leaders, were sent to a hospital. In time, these men either received orders to return to the front or won a combat reprieve with a Kriegsneurotiker reclassification. One historian who noted the scale of the problem wrote:

> Records show suicides and self-mutilations increase both prior to, and after, large engagements. Only a few months into the invasion of the USSR, when the German ranks had had to kill

enormous numbers of the enemy, then confronted the unusually severe winter without adequate clothing and supplies, German military suicides surpassed the number for the entirety of World War I. Three years later, at a time when German military hospitals already struggled with huge numbers of wounded, they were overwhelmed with men suffering from combat related psychological issues. One postwar report stated that after major battles, there came "a spike in suicides and self-mutilation, a key example being the aftermath of Stalingrad where there was a huge spike. By 1944 the Army reported that it was treating over 20,000 'Kriegsneurotiker' and military hospitals were clogged with soldiers suffering mental issues because of the harsh warfare on the Eastern front."[4]

Even earlier, in 1943 when the military situation turned dire for the Germans during the largest and deadliest battle in human history—Stalingrad—many German soldiers intentionally shot themselves in order to be evacuated. For most, their action came too late. They ended up in decrepit field hospitals where they shared space with wounded soldiers who'd actually been injured while fighting for the führer who had little empathy for them. And there both types died the same way, in droves when the Russians arrived. According to the German author of the following anecdotal account excerpted from an online history forum, it was a hellish death. The entry is no longer to be found in the referenced forum, but is included because it is so poignant.

> I don´t have to tell you that at least from middle december all those low rank deserters [referring to soldiers who shot themselves] were doomed to die amongst the endless at the field hospital in Stalingrad-Mitte, which was a high multi-floor building. During the last days the doctors operated on helpless cases under soviet artillery fire. One of them had literally both of his hands cut off by splinters while operating, he was instantly pushed onto the corridor and left to die . . . . Some exterior walls of the hospital were being bombed away in late december. They carried the older and most serious cases on the corridors constantly nearer to the abyss and before they were being pushed onto the streets, they had been already frozen brick hard. In the hospital itself a strange situation emerged, stragglers were living in some floors hiding from military police while the latter one combed other floors to mount their famous alarm units . . . that´s not fairytales or myths, I have myself spoken to 3 survivors, one of my own family. My great uncle was one of the last to pass by the hospital, he saw the Russians lit it on fire and burn to the ground with his own eyes—with at

least a thousand or many more immobilized soldiers inside. He was a child of a cattle farmer and said it sounded like a mixture of a barn fire and animals groaning. Though he had no hard feelings, as he said that any help from the soviets would have been impossible.[5]

Although the topic of soldiers shooting themselves was rarely addressed by Hollywood or the popular press, the American army was no less plagued with the problem than the Germans. The takeaway from the following excerpt is that soldiers have a breaking point that no amount of training or experience can overcome.

> In ... the fierce and sustained fighting on the beaches and in the hedgerows of Normandy, fully 98 percent of those who were still alive after 60 days of fighting became psychiatric casualties. In less sustained fighting, the breaking point is typically reached between 200 and 240 days on the line ... so many men wounded themselves that Army hospitals had to set up special wards to house those soldiers designated as SIWs (self-inflicted wounds). When they recovered, most were tried and convicted of "carelessness with weapons" and given six-month sentences in the stockade.[6]

As for the combat fatigue that led to most self-inflicted wounds, few people comprehend how enormous the incidence was in World War II. Combat exhaustion begins to set in after just two to three weeks of intense exposure. The American statistics speak for themselves. "More than 504,000 troops were lost due to 'psychiatric collapse,' an early term for reaching the breaking point." This number was the equivalent of about 50 infantry divisions. Quite surprisingly, "Some 40 percent of all the medical discharges in World War II were for psychiatric reasons, the so-called 'Section 8s.' .... Overall, 1,393,000 soldiers, sailors, and airmen were treated for combat fatigue in World War II"[7]

Fidel's odds of survival would have been vanishingly small had he remained with his division. He'd almost surely have been killed, severely injured, or captured and sent off to one of the many Soviet POW camps that few men returned from. The numbers tell the story. Of Fidel's 12,000 fellow Nordland soldiers deposited in Russia in December 1943, less than half remained one year later. Sepp Zornig, Fidel's machine-gun team partner, died at Narva in June 1944, three months after Fidel's medical evacuation. Many other Orzydorf men perished at Narva as well. Even with replacements and the suborning of another depleted division, just several hundred of Nordland's original 12,000 men remained when the last large battle of the war commenced in central Berlin in late April 1945. By the time Hitler committed suicide and the Russians took the city, that number was even lower. And on May 1, "the few survivors of the Nordland who surrendered to the Russians were sent east, most never to be seen again. Of the few survivors who reached the Allied lines, most were handed over to their respective countries and tried as traitors."[8]

---

1. Pat McTaggart, "Race to the Panther Line: Final Liberation of Leningrad," *WWII Quarterly* 14, no. 3 (April 2015), https://warfarehistorynetwork.com/2019/01/20/race-to-the-panther-line-final-liberation-of-leningrad/.
2. Siegfried Knappe and Ted Brusaw, *Soldat: Reflections of a German Soldier, 1936-1949* (New York: Dell, 1993), 45.
3. Knappe and Brusaw, *Soldat,* 192.
4. "PTSD and the Nazi SS and Gestapo?," reddit r/AskHistorians, April 15, 2014, https://www.reddit.com/r/AskHistorians/comments/233szt/ptsd_and_the_nazi_ss_and_gestapo/.
5. "Did German Soldiers Intentionally Shoot Themselves to Be Sent out of Stalingrad for Medical Treatment and Army Discharge?," Quora, n.d., https://www.quora.com/Did-German-soldiers-intentionally-shoot-themselves-to-be-sent-out-of-Stalingrad-for-medical-treatment-and-army-discharge.
6. Duane Schultz, "Combat Fatigue: How Stress in Battle Was Felt (and Treated) in WWII," Warfare History Network, September 30, 2016, https://warfarehistorynetwork.com/combat-fatigue-how-stress-in-battle-was-felt-and-treated-in-wwii/.
7. Schultz, "Combat Fatigue."
8. Jewish Virtual Library. "The SS (Schutzstaffel): 11th SS Volunteer Panzergrenadier Division Nordland." Accessed August 2, 2016. https://www.jewishvirtuallibrary.org/11th-ss-volunteer-panzergrenadier-division-nordland.

29 Hospital Respite

As soon as the initial shock of his injury passed, Fidel tossed his rifle and the board outside in the snow. Grasping his wounded arm, he made his way to an aid station. There, a medic administered a dose of morphine, cleaned and dressed the wound, and bound Fidel's arm in a sling. The aid station transferred him to a collection point near the regiment's staff headquarters where Fidel waited a considerable time. Eventually, a truck already carrying other injured men picked him up and delivered the casualties to an improvised field hospital. It was in such a station, where doctors examined and treated wounds more thoroughly, that Fidel needed to worry about detection. Fortunately, his doctor was all business. The physician rewrapped the arm and told Fidel that his ulna, the forearm bone that runs from the pinkie-finger side of the wrist to the elbow, was badly shattered near the elbow. The badly shattered part couldn't have been what Fidel wanted to hear, but relief surely replaced anxiety upon learning he would be evacuated to a regular military hospital. Fidel figured that at worst he'd bought himself two or three months of recuperation time before having to return.

Late in the afternoon of the next day, a truck arrived to pick up the medical cases requiring specialized treatment and evacuation. The driver helped load the seriously wounded, then began the long, slow drive west toward the port of Tallinn on the Gulf of Finland. The truck reached the city that evening and dropped off the patients at a large aid station for further medical attention. Before dawn the next morning, the medical evacuees were loaded aboard what Fidel described as a large passenger ship. The vessel carried no refugees, only crew members, medical staff, and injured soldiers. By the time the ship sailed at 7 a.m., its passenger spaces were crammed with patients in bunks stacked four beds high.

Hospital Respite 215

Fidel couldn't recall the name of the ship, but the possibilities are limited. If his ship was a midsize vessel, it would have been Lazarettschiffe (hospital ship) Rügen, Lazarettschiffe Alexander Von Humboldt, or Lazarettschiffe Glückauf. My best guess is he was instead aboard Grosse Lazarettschiffe (large hospital ship) SS Berlin, which regularly plied the northern waters at this time.[1]

SS Berlin was one of the eight cruise vessels built or acquired in the 1930s by the Nazi leisure organization, Kraft durch Freude (KdF) (Strength through Joy) to make sea cruises affordable for working class Germans.[2] The most famous of these repurposed KdF vessels was the Wilhelm Gustloff, which left Gotenhafen (now Gdynia, Poland) on January 30, 1945, crammed with 8,000 passengers, most of whom were desperate refugees. At 1:30 a.m. in an icy and stormy Baltic Sea, the boozy captain of a Soviet submarine torpedoed and sank the Gustloff, drowning over 9,000 people. That sinking remains the greatest naval disaster in history.

The Grosse Lazarettschiffe Berlin began life in 1925 as the SS Berlin of the North German Lloyd shipping line in Bremen, Germany. Until 1939, she carried passengers between Bremerhaven and New York. The vessel cruised for KdF only a few weeks, presumably in the Baltic, before her conversion to a hospital ship. In January 1945, the ship was evacuating refugees from the Eastern territories when she struck mines twice in the same day and was towed to shallow water and allowed to settle on the bottom. She was salvaged by the USSR in 1948 and restored as a cruise ship. Twenty years later she sank again after a collision in the Black Sea, this time due to the negligence of both her skipper and the captain of the freighter that plowed into her side.[3]

Evacuations such as Fidel's became risky in 1944 due to the presence of Soviet submarines and aircraft. The latter could operate more openly in the Gulf of Finland and the Baltic then because the Germans didn't have enough warships and planes left to patrol there. Fortunately, Fidel's vessel encountered only stormy seas. He recalled that the tossing and rolling of the vessel in the wintery weather was rough on some of the wounded, but most men were so relieved to escape the despair of the Eastern Front that they gladly accepted the discomfort. Not surprisingly, Fidel spent most of his waking hours during the two-day trip playing cards from his bunk with the men around him. I would venture that he won his share of hands even playing one-handed. The ship made one stop along the way to cram in even more wounded men. Fidel thought this was the Latvian port of Riga, but couldn't recall for sure. The voyage ended in Danzig, West Prussia, where the wounded were loaded onto ambulances and trucks at the dock for distribution to the many military hospitals in the area.

Fidel's transport took him a considerable distance southwest of Danzig to a large hospital in the city of Marienburg. This city of 30,000 had its origin in the 13th century when the medieval Knights of the Teutonic Order chose a hill near the Nogat River on which to construct a fortress. The Order called the castle and the town that sprang up around it Marienburg to honor their patron saint, the Virgin Mary. The fortified brick castle expanded during the next 230 years to become Europe's largest Gothic stronghold. In the 15th century the castle and town were incorporated into Poland and renamed Malbork. The castle then become one of the Polish royal residences. In the 18th century the town (Marienburg again) became part of German Prussia, and in the late 19th century, the German Empire. The name Marienburg reverted back to Malbork when Germany was forced to cede its eastern territory to Poland after World War II.

Eating regular meals and sleeping in a real bed for the entire night without the interruption of cold outdoor watch shifts must have felt blissful. As did living indoors with heat. Each hospital room had a stove in which a detail of four American POW airmen built a coal fire every morning. These men, who looked well dressed and fed, served the whole hospital. Their German was limited, but Fidel described them as nice fellows and he always exchanged a few words with them. The detail returned twice more daily at six-hour intervals to restoke the fire.

Theirs was the sort of work the Third Geneva Convention of 1929 dictated could be done by enlisted rank prisoners. They could also work in industry and agriculture, but not in war production. The Germans called a POW camp for work-eligible prisoners a *Stalag*. Officers and soldiers with the rank of sergeant and above lived in a separate camp called an *Oflag*. They could not be used in labor. The same held for the German Kriegsmarine (navy), which operated separate *Marlag* and *Milag* camps for naval and merchant marine captives. Air-wing officers and noncommissioned officers went to *Luft* camps run by the Luftwaffe. The Germans subdivided their camps with fencing to segregate different nationalities, but did not bother to separate American and British soldiers.[4]

The local camp, Stalag XXB (20B), expanded greatly as the war progressed and POW numbers grew. Like many other camps, XXB established satellite camps to position POWs closer to their work place. XXB internees worked not only in factories, sawmills, and warehouses but also on farms. During the winter, some sawed ice on the river for ice-house storage. The first POWs at Marienburg were Poles and Serbs. After Dunkirk in 1940, captured Brits joined them. The original camp consisted of huts and tents inside a double fence interspersed with watchtowers.

POW labor subsequently built an administration block and a prison hospital at the main site.

The enlisted rank American airmen who maintained Fidel's stove and filled other hospital jobs were likely housed in a compound within Malbork Castle, since the main XXB camp was some distance south of the city. It is possible that several of the airmen at the hospital were captured the previous year when two bombers were shot down during a mission by 96 United States Army Air Force B-17s to bomb the Focke-Wulf assembly plant at Marienburg. This plant turned out half of all Germany's Fw-190 one-engine fighter planes, the most effective fighter the Germans had at this time. The Allied bombing campaign to the west had forced Berlin to disperse such vital factories east of Germany proper. Since the Fw-190 plant was crucial to the war effort, the Germans sited it there in the belief that Marienburg was beyond the range of Allied bombers. But in the early afternoon of October 9, 1943, five waves of B17s blanketed the facility with over 200 tons of bombs. On April 9, 1944, not long after Fidel left Marienburg, the Americans bombed the plant a second time.

Fidel shared a room with three other patients in the four to five weeks he spent at the hospital in February and March. One of the men had a serious leg wound and had been there much longer than the other patients. The doctors told Fidel his wound was healing nicely but that the reconstructed bone had mended crookedly; hence, his arm would never regain its full strength. That was the price of his ticket from the front. Fidel expected he'd have to return to the fighting eventually, but hoped Hitler would have negotiated an end to the war before his arm was again fit.

Life in the hospital was good and came with none of the inspections and formations found in military rear areas. Once the surgeon had reset the bone sections and the wound had healed enough to immobilize in a cast, Fidel was allowed on his feet again. Ambulatory patients were restricted to the hospital grounds, but on Sundays when it was easy to blend in with the many other soldiers out and about, Fidel sneaked out, hopped aboard a streetcar, and ventured around the city. I would be surprised if Malbork Castle, the most prominent landmark in the city, wasn't one of his destinations. But without a doubt, he'd have stopped at a tavern, had a couple of beers, and played cards.

Fidel regretted that during his hospital stay he'd failed to learn about his brother Hans's confinement in another military hospital in the same city. A letter from home stated that Hans was not wounded, but merely sick. Like most of his company, he'd contracted an illness in the field and was being treated for it.

The most infectious diseases in the war, contracted by thousands of soldiers on the Eastern Front, were tularemia and typhus. Some historians believe the Soviets engaged in biological warfare—that they unleashed tularemia on the German forces in Stalingrad and the disease spread from there. The epidemic could also have sprung up on its own, then been transmitted via the explosive increase in the rodent population that fed on the considerable unharvested grain left in fields due to the labor shortage. Typhus might have been employed as a weapon against the Germans by Polish partisans.[5] [6] [7]

However, the illness explanation for Hans's hospitalization was almost surely a cover story for a military train crash that Berlin wished to hide. Otherwise, it is too great a coincidence that 11th Flak Abteilung's entire complement of men should fall ill at the very time that the battalion was the victim of an incident noted in two separate unit reports, one of which is quoted below:

> At the end of February 1944, SS-Flak Abteilung 11 left East Prussia by rail to join the rest of the 'Nordland' Division at Narva, Estonia. While enroute the troop train derailed due to what was probably partisan sabotage, causing great damage and injury. Practically all of the Flak detachment's weaponry and equipment were lost in the incident and most of the officers were injured as well. Several weeks would pass before the unit would be considered fit for duty again. In the meantime it was shipped by rail back to the Ayrs Camp 'South' for refitting.[8]

Hans Eipert with wife, Magdalena, during home leave—the only one he received during his Waffen SS service. Hans was reportedly proud enough of his military professionalism to wear his uniform for this portrait. His sleeve patch denotes the rank of SS squad leader (SS-*Rottenführer*), a rank equivalent to corporal in the American Army. Magdalena would never see him again after this leave.

The men were most probably given the cover story and warned not to tell their families that their train was sabotaged. The Nazis hid defeats, retreats, and acts of resistance and excelled at spinning negative events into something else. Containment of such stories was possible because like most other World War II militaries, the German services censored mail. Sometime after his hospital discharge in 1944, Hans received a home leave. Whether he told anyone at home about what really happened to the train is unknown.

The 11th Flak refit and recovery process took until mid-April. Its five batteries then embarked for Narva where their guns were desperately needed on the Panther Line because the depleted German forces there had come under severe pressure from the enormous offensive force the Soviets had amassed. With that force, the Russians intended to plow through the German defenders and advance to the German homeland itself. Upon arrival, 11th Flak's antiaircraft guns were most often deployed as artillery support. These missions were a demanding task and came at great cost because the firing exposed their positions and opened them up to ferocious return fire. The flak unit's main responsibility was to support the Nordland infantrymen holding the bridgehead between the Hermannsburg and Ivangorod Fortresses on each side of the Narva River.[9]

Meanwhile, back in Marienburg, Fidel's wound healed sufficiently for discharge from the hospital. His orders sent him back to Nordland's replacement battalion at Wetzelsdorf, Austria, by train to finish his recuperation. He carried with him, as was customary for a recovering soldier, military hospital release papers that detailed his injury and placed him in one of the following three classifications.

> AF: severe wound such as a missing arm or leg; eventual discharge
> KF: light wound; still able to serve in combat
> BKF: partly disabled; still able to perform certain duties such as standing guard, etc.[10]

At Wetzelsdorf, Fidel got "three or four weeks" of leave, but it was a restricted leave that seldom allowed him off base. He didn't lack for company because to his surprise he found quite a number of other Banat soldiers from his locale already there. Six men alone were from Orzydorf— all recuperating from wounds received at Oranienbaum or during the subsequent fallback to Narva. It would not surprise me to learn some of those men had come by their wounds the same way Fidel had. Undoubtedly, Fidel passed much of his time there playing cards.

Considering the severe shortage of German combat replacements and the ever lower physical standards for conscription, Fidel was surely given the KF classification, but both KFs and BKFs were typically dispatched to their division's *genesenden Kompanie* (convalescent company)—a component of each Waffen SS division's Training and Replacement Battalion. The luckier men received home leaves upon arrival. The rest performed light duty as they convalesced.

Wetzelsdorf gave Fidel a better idea of just how dire the Eastern Front situation had become. With less than half of Nordland's original complement still on the active roll, field commanders became so desperate for replacements that the Banat men in the replacement battalion were offered a future home leave in exchange for volunteering to return to Narva immediately rather than when they'd fully mended. The SS was playing to the intense desire of the men to see their wives and families again. Fidel rebuffed the offer and said that "never for a minute" did he believe the pledge would be kept. But many men did sign. Some were so desperate that they convinced themselves the deal would be honored. Others figured that they'd just get sent back to the front anyway, so why not take a chance and perhaps get a home leave out of it?

---

1. "Lazarettschiffe of the Kriegsmarine," Feldgrau: German Armed Forces Research 1918-1945, accessed October 1, 2018, https://www.feldgrau.com/WW2-German-Kriegsmarine-Hospitalships.
2. "Lazarettschiffe of the Kriegsmarine."
3. "Lazarettschiff A (Berlin)," Feldgrau: German Armed Forces Research 1918-1945, accessed October 1, 2018, https://www.feldgrau.com/WW2-Germany-Berlin-Lazarettschiff.
4. "Stalag," in *Wikipedia*, 2022, https://en.wikipedia.org/w/index.php?title=Stalag&oldid=746153739.
5. Ken Alibek, *Biohazard: The Chilling True Story of the Largest Covert Biological Weapons Program in the World, Told from the inside by the Man Who Ran It* (New York: Random House, 1999), https://www.nlm.nih.gov/nichsr/esmallpox/biohazard_alibek.pdf.
6. Amy E. Krafft, "Tularemia," in *Weapons of Mass Destruction: An Encyclopedia of Worldwide Policy, Technology, and History*, vol. I: Chemical and Biological Weapons (Santa Barbara, Denver, Oxford: ABC Clio, 2005), 288–91.
7. Alibek, Biohazard, p. 29.
8. Jewish Virtual Library. "The SS (Schutzstaffel): 11th SS Volunteer Panzergrenadier Division Nordland." Accessed August 2, 2016. https://www.jewishvirtuallibrary.org/11th-ss-volunteer-panzergrenadier-division-nordland."
9. Stiftelsen norsk Okkupasjonshistorie (Norwegian Occupation History Foundation), "The 'Nordland' SS Division Flak Units," 114764, accessed August 8, 2016, http://sno.no/files/documents/114764.pdf.
10. Michael Roman Hrycyszyn, *God Save Me from My Friends, and from My Enemies, I'll Save Myself Alone: A Ukrainian Memoir* (Cambridge: Vanguard, 2011), 185.

30 Out of the Cauldron

At a company formation in Wetzelsdorf near the end of March 1944, an officer asked men with tractor experience to step forward. Fidel's farming certainly qualified him, but like every soldier he was reluctant to volunteer for anything because it could turn out to be dangerous or have unintended consequences. He certainly didn't wish to end up driving a panzer or recovering disabled combat vehicles under fire. But after weighing this possibility against the certainty that he'd be sent back to the front sooner or later anyway, he took a chance and stepped out.

This turned out to be Fidel's lucky day, for far from earning a quick ticket back to the front, he'd stumbled into a training program that would send him to Vienna to the Stabs-und Ostblockgebäude (staff and eastern block buildings) at the Wien-Schönbrunn SS Kaserne (Vienna-Schönbrunn SS barracks). He and a small number of others who'd stepped forward would receive automotive training through a program known as Kraftfahrtechnischen Lehranstalt der SS (KTL), or Automotive Engineering School of the SS. The program was established in 1941 to train *Schirrmeister* specialists. Most literally, schirrmeister means "harness master" and relates to a time when horses and wagons were the motor pools of the day. In the World War II era, a German schirrmeister worked in company-sized or larger military motor pools and field-equipment repair shops. KTL was now looking for men with mechanical experience to train in various aspects of maintenance in order to keep its vehicles operating on the front lines.

At the time of Fidel's selection, Hans Jüttner (SS-Obergruppenführer and General), as head of the SS Leadership Main Office (SS-Führungshauptamt), had just instituted this new automotive program. It was open only to men with front-line experience, and would turn out specialists in three areas: 1) technical guide production, 2) schirrmeister, and 3) schirrmeister foreman. The new training program and the trainees would billet within the Schönbrunn Palace complex. Surely the best news for Fidel concerned the three months his course would consume.

The Waffen SS trainees comprised a mix of enlisted men, NCOs, and officers. It was possible to group them into one training class because the Waffen SS had reduced the great divide between officers and enlisted men. Fortunately for Fidel, the officers in his group turned out to be easygoing men. With Fidel's knack for getting along with nearly everyone, he could joke with the officers as easily as with his enlisted peers even though he was still a private who wanted to maintain his lowly rank as long as possible. Mixing with officers could have been difficult had these men been ideologues.

The training began at the Opel factory in Vienna. The Nazis had seized Opel, a subsidiary of America's General Motors, at the outbreak of the war and converted the Opel auto-production lines to military hardware. The Vienna plant manufactured a mainstay military transport vehicle, the Blitz truck, as well as half of the Luftwaffe's Junker 88 bomber engines.

A military truck picked up the 12 trainees every morning except Sundays at their barracks and dropped them off at Opel, outside the city. Like Austria itself, the plant had so far escaped destruction from the huge waves of Allied bombers striking Germany daily. The factory was a sprawling affair operated largely with forced labor. Fidel and the other men trained just outside of the main facility in a small repair garage. Knowing Fidel, he'd have liked nothing better than to wander about and explore the plant, but the men were restricted to their limited work area.

The training class was broken down into teams of four, each of which was assigned the task of tearing down an old Opel automobile to its components then reassembling it. With the war going so badly, and both the Waffen SS and the Wehrmacht coveting every man they could get their hands on, no one in the group tried to break any speed records. All three teams managed to string out this relatively simple assignment for over a month. The program was a testament to bureaucratic nearsightedness—or misplaced optimism—for by this juncture of the war total defeat loomed large on the horizon. It seems absurd that a program useful only in the long term would still be initiated. Someone back in Berlin was either convinced the war would continue indefinitely or was trying to hold on to his own safe job.

For the six weeks Fidel spent in Vienna during the initial phase of the program, his billet remained the grounds of the historic Schloss Schönbrunn, most of which is now a UNESCO World Heritage Site. The Habsburg palace itself was an enormous edifice whose construction began in 1696. Over the years the various Austrian emperors had added to or rebuilt the place multiple times. Its 1,440 rooms and gardens were intended to rival Versailles. Empress Maria Theresa had completely rebuilt the palace and gardens in a Rococo style, but the ruler most closely associated with Schönbrunn was Franz Josef I. He spent nearly his entire 68 years within its confines and died in his palace bedroom in 1916 at the time Fidel's father, my mother's father, and Corporal Hitler were fighting on various fronts of World War I. Franz Josef, during his tenure, turned Schönbrunn into a *Gesamtkunstwerk* (total work of art).

Upon dissolution of the Austrian Empire at the close of World War I, portions of the palace, including the imperial apartments, became a museum. When World War II began in 1939, outbuildings such as the stables were commandeered for grain and ammunition storage by the Nazis. In 1943 when the labor shortage forced closure of the museum, the priceless contents of the imperial apartments were removed to preserve them. Precious works of art traveled to salt mines for protection from the ravages of the war. Although the palace museum closed during the war, other activities in the palace continued. Balls and receptions took place in the Great Gallery. Films such as *Tanz mit dem Kaiser* and *Wiener Mädeln* were shot there. Schönbrunn concerts sponsored by Kraft durch Freude (KdF) were held in the main courtyard and south gardens. Tours of the grounds continued, and the Schönbrunn Tiergarten, the world's oldest public zoo, remained open. The zoo was still popular during the war, but suffered greatly when the short-staffed workers were unable to adequately feed the animals.

Fidel's quarters were in what is now the Maria Theresien Kaserne. The construction of the barracks, which were designed to be compatible with the other historic architecture of the Schönbrunn Palace grounds, began in 1937. The buildings, which were only completed after Austria became part of the Reich, were subsequently assigned to the Waffen SS.

Living within palace grounds in a city like Vienna was hard for a field soldier to top. Fidel would have been satisfied for much more modest accommodations than a room shared with just three other men. He said that store items and military clothing were readily available and the mess hall even served decent food. This was as soft as life got for a Waffen SS private, since the trainees were also exempt from formations, inspections, and other duties.

Fidel and the other enlisted men received a pass each Sunday but weren't allowed to leave the palace grounds. Officers could come and go from the base freely. However, seeing the city by hopping onto a streetcar was again too inviting for Fidel to pass up. From conversations with civilians during these outings, he learned that Vienna had so far avoided the massive bombings of Germany because the city was still too far from the Allied bomber bases. Food like meat and sugar were strictly rationed with stamps just as in Germany but were still available.

Many targets around Vienna were bombed repeatedly later in 1944, but not until nine months after Fidel left Vienna did two raids in February 1945 shatter the quiet of the palace grounds and end all public activities. The bombers deliberately targeted the historic palace and caused major destruction. The second raid damaged many of the remaining historic outbuildings and left behind multiple bomb craters. Sadly, many bombs from this raid rained down on the zoo and killed most of the animals.

Fidel left Vienna when phase two of the schirrmeister training program required trainees to obtain a military driver's license. He wasn't about to mention that he'd previously completed a driver training course and already had a driver's license. The orders sent the men to a Waffen SS Driver Training and Replacement Unit located in Germany at an SS complex that would become a household word after the war—Buchenwald—because it was the first Nazi concentration camp liberated by the Western Allies. This liberation gave the world its initial confirmation of the enormous atrocities committed by the regime.[1]

Buchenwald means "beech forest," but is today synonymous with concentration camp. In the Nazi scheme of things, the four concentration camps sited within Germany were by and large labor camps. Extermination camps were built outside of Germany, away from the eyes of the German public. Of course, many people also died in labor camps. Some of these deaths resulted from execution, but most stemmed from disease, starvation, unsafe working conditions, and mistreatment.

Buchenwald, situated on Ettersberg Hill outside of Weimar, Germany, ended up in the postwar Russian occupation zone and ultimately in the Soviet puppet state called the German Democratic Republic. The camp was opened in July 1937 to incarcerate professional criminals and political prisoners—particularly communists. During the war years, Jews, homosexuals, and other prisoners joined the mix. Buchenwald continued to expand and soon evolved into a huge industrial enterprise covering two-and-a-half square kilometers. As it grew, the SS participated in additional industrial enterprises outside the complex, and in the process constructed about 90 subcamps throughout the area.

The industrial portion of the Buchenwald camp was operated by Deutsche Wirtschaftsbetriebe (DWB) (German Economic Enterprises), a holding company devised by the political wing of the SS to profit from forced labor. With its hand in some 25 industries, the DWB controlled well over 100 factories, storage depots, mines, and workshops throughout Germany. In 1942 the SS leased out a large plot of land to the Wilhelm Gustloff Stiftung (Foundation), a state-owned corporation assembled from nationalized Jewish industrial holdings the Nazis had seized between 1933 and 1936. The new enterprise added 11 large factory buildings and one secret underground facility to the periphery of the camp.

Buchenwald and its subcamps has been likened to a Silicon Valley for weapons development and manufacturing, so it required a huge guard force. By the end of the war this amounted to 46 companies of 150 Waffen SS men each. The concentration of factories, secret projects, and large-scale weapons projects necessarily drew in many ancillary soldiers and spawned military specialty schools such as the one that conducted Fidel's driver training.

The large facility was sited in the midst of a forest about 10 kilometers outside of Weimar, the city of German Classicism that was home to Goethe and Schiller. A railroad and a road cutting through the forest connected the camp to the outside. The main camp entrance on the northeast edge of the site was protected by large guarded gates and fortified pill boxes. Not far inside the gates was the Wilhelm Gustloff manufacturing compound and the extensive motor pool and training area where the driving course was taught. The camp administrative offices and SS guard barracks were considerably southwest of the motor pool. The secured prisoner barracks were in a separate compound that extended even farther westward.

At the peak of its shameful existence, the camp housed 48,000 prisoners. Conditions were such that several hundred prisoners died in the camp each month during the later war years. The work camp and the Gustloff factory complex were independently ringed by tall electrified barbed wire fences that together incorporated 35 watchtowers.[2][3] The various segregated prisoner work brigades in the labor camp toiled in a quarry, cleared forests, and operated a brick mill. Up to 6,000 camp inmates labored in the Gustloff factory to turn out rifles, carbines, optical devices, pistols, gun mounts, and various mechanical V-1 and V-2 rocket parts in the underground section of the factory.[4]

The double gate at the prisoner barracks entrance just beyond the Gestapo district office and camp administration buildings was inscribed JEDEM DAS SEINE (To each his own)—words seemingly at odds with the Nazi one-size-fits-all brand of fascism. If Fidel ever saw this gate, he didn't tell me of it. Buchenwald had many guards and fences, and Fidel had little free time in the two weeks he was there. Transient Waffen SS soldiers also surely knew better than to show too much curiosity about what went on beyond their own portion of the camp. Although Fidel hadn't been inside the prisoner barracks part of the camp and couldn't tell anything about what went on there, he did say he once saw a detail of 60 or 70 prisoners being marched under guard. He'd heard that the bulk of the work in the

Gustloff factories was done by slave laborers, at least some of whom were housed in subcamps segregated by nationality within the complex. Historians say that people from 35 different nationalities had been interned in the camp.[5]

After completing the driving course and earning military driving certificates in May 1944, the 12 men awaited their next orders. Always looming over them was the dread that their training program would be scrapped and they'd be returned to Nordland, or whatever other division they'd come from, and end up back on the front. However, fortune continued to smile upon them because when their new orders arrived, they learned they were heading to the town of Fallersleben in central Germany. The next phase of training was to take place in the sprawling Volkswagenwerk manufacturing plant there. Fidel now dared to hope this posting would see him through the end of the war.

---

1. Holocaust Historical Society, "Buchenwald," November 9, 2021, https://www.holocausthistoricalsociety.org.uk/contents/concentrationcamps/buchenwald.html.
2. Loewe1869, "Gustloff-Werke Weimar," *The Military Rifle Journal*, December 17, 2014, https://militaryriflejournal.wordpress.com/2014/12/17/gustloff-werke-weimar/.
3. Joseph F. Moser and Gerald R. Baron, *A Fighter Pilot in Buchenwald: Joe Moser's Journey from Farm Boy to Fighter Pilot to near Starvation in a Nazi Concentration Camp* (Bellingham, Wash.: All Clear Pub. in partnership with EdensVeil, 2010).
4. Holocaust Historical Society, "Buchenwald."
5. Holocaust Historical Society, "Buchenwald."

31 The People's Car

The Volkswagen factory was one of Hitler's more practical ideas. The facility, completed just five years earlier in 1939, was state of the art. Unlike some of Hitler's other grand schemes, this one would have enjoyed great success had not a grander scheme, the conquest of the rest of Europe, gotten in the way. Before he came to power, Hitler recognized that Germany had far fewer cars and car owners than other industrial countries. Germany's disastrous financial meltdown and the poverty of its citizens after the Great War was one reason. Perhaps a greater one was that the German public transport system was one of the best in the world. Germans had little need to own a car. To increase auto ownership, Hitler set out to change this by building superior roads, specifically, autobahns. The original idea wasn't his. Portions of the system had been planned in the 1920s and the first segment was already open in 1932, a year before Hitler came to power.

Hitler wasted no time high-jacking the highway program and expanding its scope and vision. New construction began the same year he took power. By the time war needs halted the project at the end of 1941, 3,860 kilometers were complete and another 2,400 were under construction. The main impediment Hitler faced was the enormous cost, which had to be underwritten long before there would be enough cars to justify the roads. As things stood, only the wealthy could afford a car in a depressed Germany after the loss of World War I. Cars in Germany were too pricy for working people, yet Hitler needed to put lots of cars on his road to justify the expensive road system. His remedy was to offer the working class an inexpensive *people's car*.

Hitler first pounced on the idea of a car for the masses while in prison back in the 1920s. After reading Henry Ford's biography, he became convinced that development of a people's car would offer enormous voter appeal in an election. When he became Reichskanzler of Germany, he got his chance to turn the idea into reality. Ironically, he'd managed to eliminate national elections so quickly that he no longer needed the plan to win votes. Yet, he implemented a modified version of the idea anyway because he expected it would prove useful in other ways.

A German car designer and technical innovator named Ferdinand Porsche had already tinkered with plans for a people's car for years. Porsche first tried to sell his idea to his employer, carmaker Daimler, but because such an auto could not yield the same profits as the expensive cars Daimler produced, the company rejected the idea. So Porsche left Daimler, formed his own design company, and subsequently worked with two motorcycle manufactures to turn his ideas into prototypes. Although these collaborative efforts failed to produce a viable car, each redesign furthered the concept. When Hitler learned Porsche shared his vision, he set up a meeting.

Hitler became enthused with Porsche's ideas but laid down some tough technical requirements if the government were to get behind the project. "The car would have a one-liter displacement air-cooled motor, produce approximately 25-brake horsepower at 3,500 RPM, weigh less than 1,500 pounds, have a four-wheel independent suspension, and attain a speed of 100 kilometers per hour." Hitler also required that the car seat four persons and be able to drive 100 kilometers on seven liters of gasoline. Porsche wanted a price around 1,550 marks, which was $620 at the 1934 exchange rate. Hitler restricted the price to 900 marks and allowed Porsche only 10 months to complete a prototype.[1]

Some historians believe that a sixth requirement—the ability to carry three battle-equipped soldiers and a machine gun—was kept from the public. Beyond all that, the car would also have to compete with the top-selling American-owned General Motors and Ford models being built and sold in Germany. Porsche was troubled by only one of the requirements, the cost, but signed on anyway.

The consortium of German auto manufacturers tapped to build the prototypes feared that the affordable small-car idea might actually reach the production stage. To sabotage Porsche and void the contract, they stalled on their parts of the development in an effort to kill the idea by making the 10-month design deadline unreachable. When Hitler learned of the gambit, he ordered government supervision of the project.

The small and inefficient German car manufacturers (27 at this time) were to share the burden of production. They didn't see enough profit in it; hence, they demanded a government subsidy of 200 marks per car. The government was already financially strapped by Hitler's many other plans, particularly rearmament, and couldn't afford this. Since the plan was to produce over a million cars per year, Hitler decided the state could do better by funding its own factory through the Deutsche Arbeitsfront (German Labor Front), the Nazi organization that replaced the German labor unions. The Labor Front's money came largely from a compulsory 1.5 percent wage contribution garnered from each German worker.

With the design of the car well along in 1937, the parties involved formed a production company tightly bound to the German Labor Front, calling it the Gesellschaft zur Vorbereitung des Deutschen Volkswagen (Group to Plan the German People's Car). The name changed to Volkswagenwerk GmbH the following year. The Labor Front's leisure division, Kraft durch Freude, became the car's merchandiser. At Hitler's insistence the car was to be called the *KdF-wagen*.

Since every worker belonged to the Labor Front, and every member of the Labor Front was also a member of the KdF, the potential reach of the organization was enormous. The Nazi leadership understood it was vital to keep workers content. They reasoned that of the 8,760 hours in a year, 2,100 were spent working and 2,920 in sleep, which left 3,740 hours of free time. If KdF helped workers relax and enjoy that free time, not only would they be more productive on the job, they'd also be pliable and more accepting of National Socialism.

To its credit, the KdF was largely beneficial to workers and never developed a paramilitary wing like some of the other Nazi organizations. It gave laborers the right to an annual vacation and paid holidays, something workers in no other country enjoyed at the time. As a result, KdF was very popular before the war. Not only did it help rebuild the German tourism industry, it placed affordable leisure activities in the hands of the working population and in the process made KdF the world's largest tour operator. Every factory of 20 or more employees had a representative able to offer workers inexpensive leisure activities including plays, sports, concerts, day trips, cultural events, and vacation packages. The war put an end to vacationing, but by then millions of Germans had already taken a KdF trip by train or ship and experienced a real vacation. At the height of its popularity the program operated a fleet of nine cruise ships, including the already mentioned SS Berlin. Later, these ships were repurposed for the war effort.

What the KdF accomplished selling vacations, it was also expected to do by putting automobiles into the hands of ordinary people. To fill the newly built 3,819.7 km (2,373.5 mi) of autobahn with cars, Hitler launched a publicity campaign to encourage workers to buy five-mark savings stamps weekly, which they pasted into a booklet. After accumulating 997 marks worth of stamps in four or five years, the holder could redeem the stamps for a car. Nearly 340,000 Germans bought the stamps.[2]

In 1937, 30 final prototypes were extensively road tested by an assigned group of Waffen SS soldiers. After each car had accumulated at least 80,000 kilometers over a broad variety of terrain, the design was finalized. At this point the term Volkswagen was still a class of automobile rather than a brand name. Porsche's son, Ferry Porsche, also a car designer and talented engineer, supervised the testing program. Ferry assumed that the SS soldiers would be mindless automatons, but found most to be attentive, amenable to suggestions, and even able to offer ideas for improvements.[3] The testing earned the car considerable praise. This was not good news for the established German automakers because an inexpensive mass-produced auto would cut into their profits.

The soldier evaluation program earned the VW people's car venture a valuable new ally, for the Waffen SS relationship sped up the development of a military off-road version of the car—the Kübelwagen. This sold the Waffen SS generals on the advantages of taking part in a military vehicle's design and gave them an edge over the Wehrmacht, too. Fidel's training assignment at the Volkswagen plant was made possible by this Waffen SS connection.

Ferdinand Porsche derived the original beetle body style from a 1931 prototype. Although this prototype never entered production, Porsche liked the car enough to drive it as his personal vehicle. Its styling resembled the look Hitler had in mind for his Volkswagen—one he'd sketched on a table napkin during a restaurant lunch when he supposedly said, "It should look like a beetle; you have to look to nature to find out what streamlining is."[4] Because the German populace quickly saw the same resemblance, Hitler's awkward *KdF-wagen* name didn't stick, and the public soon nicknamed it the *Kaefer* (beetle).

Hitler broke ground for the Fallersleben plant in May 1938. A common misconception is that the plant was based on Henry Ford's River Rouge plant near Detroit, then one of the most modern auto plants in the world. Although the Porsches did copy some of the assembly techniques they saw in Detroit, Ford had already constructed a newer and more efficiently laid-out factory at Dagenham, England, so Dagenham became the model for the VW factory.

The factory was to be capable of pushing iron ore into one end and cars out the other, so Hitler laid out the following requirements for its siting. The plant needed to be on a convenient waterway in an open area of central Germany as well as close to both an autobahn and a rail line. As with Ford's new British plant, the workers would live in a new town near the plant, and the plant would have its own large power station capable of serving the town. From the candidates, Hitler chose a site about 60 kilometers east of Hannover, near the village of Fallersleben on the banks of the Mittelland

Canal. The new town was named KdF-Stadt to correspond with the name Hitler chose for the car. But this name didn't stick any better than did KdF-wagen as the car's name. To remove the Nazi stink of the place after the war, KdF-Stadt was hastily renamed Wolfsburg, after a nearby castle the government had seized by eminent domain at the beginning of the project.

Upon completion in 1939, the factory boasted not only the latest and best American equipment and machine tools, but also a core complement of skilled American-trained German workers who'd been persuaded to return to Germany from America. Production goals were ambitious— 150,000 vehicles the first year and up to 10 times that number within two years. Despite the enormous potential, the factory delivered very little for Hitler in the end. Only 30 cars had been assembled when Hitler plunged the country into war two months after the startup. Demand for civilian cars all but died, so the plant converted to wartime production needs. It eked out only 600 more cars before car production ceased altogether.

The car, like everything else in the Nazi era, made it into German dark humor. One of these jokes targeted the Nazi collections for its Winter Relief Fund, a charity started in the depression era to help those struggling. Commoners and high-ranking Nazis alike took to city sidewalks with special donation cannisters to solicit for the charity. Posters urged citizens to give to the fund rather than to beggars directly. Even Joseph Goebbels, the Nazi head of the Reich Ministry of Public Enlightenment and Propaganda (Reichsministerium für Volksaufklärung und Propaganda, or Propagandaministerium), which controlled all radio, press, publishing, cinema, and other arts in the regime, participated for the sake of appearance. The drive did good work, but at the same time was recognized as a propaganda tool. The sidewalk collectors were notorious for their persistence, so the joke went that the lights on the People's Car should have been made from Winter Relief Cannisters because people were always quick to get out of their way.[5]

Most of the finished cars the VW plant produced before it stopped production were claimed by Nazi officials, but some became demonstration vehicles or served other propaganda needs. The German workers who'd bought the five-mark savings stamps were out of luck. Their money was spent on armaments. However, in 1946 when VW was denazified and once again became a private enterprise, the company did redeem the stamps.[6]

When civilian car production ceased near the war's onset, one section of the plant was converted to military vehicle production. The vehicles from that line were all derivatives of the original 1936 KdF prototype. That design morphed into an astonishing number of different variations during the war—58 by one count. All became working prototypes, but few made it to the production stage. The derivative models included 4X4s, pickups, delivery vans, command cars, tracked vehicles, reconnaissance cars, and even mock tanks. The latter found use as panzer training vehicles, props, and decoys to dupe Allied reconnaissance.

At one point the military asked for a vehicle that could operate in the snow. When a front ski design didn't pan out, the designers fitted a prototype with tank-like tracks. Another prototype was equipped with grooved tires and axles wide enough to fit standard-gauge railroad tracks. One of the most elaborate designs consisted of a six-wheeled, cross-country combat vehicle with two engines and controls in front and back to allow the car to be driven in either direction. Turbocharger, supercharger, automatic transmission, fuel injection, diesel engine, power take-off shaft for starting large equipment, and coal- or wood-power capability were features of other prototype models.[7]

The first military production line built a jeep-like vehicle. Unlike the Waffen SS, the army's commanders did not take to this Kübelwagen. Only after considerable lobbying by Ferry Porsche and a glowing record in difficult conditions in Russia could the plant finally start low-volume production. On the Russian Front this car maneuvered through mud that stopped all other vehicles. It was also more stable and versatile than a motorcycle with a sidecar, so the Kübelwagen became popular with the troops—first with the Waffen SS and later with the Wehrmacht. But the fortunes of war turned against Germany before the company could benefit from large orders. With the German military in retreat in Russia and fuel scarce, the Germans had too many other pressing manufacturing needs. Fidel's Nordland division, like most other Waffen SS divisions, used both the Kübelwagen and a second derivative produced by VW. However, in the chaos of the retreat the average life span of these vehicles was just three weeks, which made replacement logistically impossible.

A Kübelwagen with balloon tires and a few modifications to protect vulnerable components against dust performed so well in the deserts of North Africa that it was sought after there also. The brilliant and ambitious German commander of the Afrika Korps (Deutsches Afrikakorps), Erwin Rommel, had used it earlier in the conquest of France and stated that it could follow anywhere that a camel could go. He requisitioned hundreds more Kübelwagen early in the Saharan Desert campaign, but his order was never approved. Some war historians speculate he'd have captured the Suez Canal if he'd gotten them. Rommel is credited with saying, "The battle is fought and decided by the quartermasters before the shooting begins." This saying might have been more applicable in North Africa if Rommel hadn't also been saddled with an ally so undependable that a telling German joke making the rounds was "What has six reverse gears and one forward gear?" The answer: "An Italian tank! The forward gear is needed in case they get attacked from behind."

When some of Rommel's desert Kübelwagen vehicles arrived with the wrong tires, his men scrounged aircraft tires for them. Among American and British troops in the Sahara, it was said that one Kübelwagen was valued at two American jeeps. The Germans eventually had to abandon most of their cars due to lack of fuel. After the war, these cars found their way into the hands of locals and were driven for many years. The American jeep was superior in a number of ways, or in every way according to America's military propagandists, but the Kübelwagen and its Schwimmwagen sister derivative were much lighter and performed surprisingly well in Allied testing facilities when several captured vehicles were evaluated.[8]

The second military derivative of the People's Car, the Schwimmwagen, joined the VW production line in 1942. This vehicle was a four-wheel-drive amphibious car capable of moving nine kilometers per hour in the water by means of a retractable propeller in the rear. The car, which carried an anchor and a paddle for emergencies, outclassed competing vehicles from other factories. When tested in America in 1945, it was noted for the smoothness of its ride as it hugged the road, the ease with which it entered and left the water, and the way it floated. It easily bested the amphibious jeep. As a lark after the war, British officers liked to prove the Schwimmwagen was waterproof by driving it off the Mittelland Canal wharf at 40 miles per hour. "The car would belly flop into the water, bob about on the surface and cruise back to the jetty."[9]

Fidel's Nordland division used a few of these vehicles in the marshy areas they operated in, but could never get enough of them because most of the VW plant's output was devoted to products other than vehicles. Usually only one vehicle assembly line operated. A large proportion of the factory was devoted to making various parts for the Luftwaffe's Junkers 88 bombers. During one period, the plant turned out 1.5 million simple stoves for soldiers on the Eastern Front. It was on one of these stoves that Fidel was warming his food at the time of the grenade attack in his bunker in Russia.

The world's most modern car plant, even during its construction phase, could never find enough German workers, so the German Labor Front contracted to import several thousand Italian workers. After the government drafted most of the factory's remaining German production workers into the military, or into the Reich Labour Service (Reichsarbeitsdienst, or RAD) to build military fortifications, the factory faced a crisis. Recruitment in neighboring countries to the west did not come close to filling the labor needs, so in the mid-1940s the plant made its first foray into involuntary labor via a contract with the German government to import 300 Polish women. Forced labor soon became the go-to solution. By 1943, over 12,000 such laborers worked at VW—students, POWs, concentration camp internees, German soldiers from penal units, and people rounded up in Eastern Europe.

According to VW's historians, when the area under German control expanded, the workforce inevitably turned multi-ethnic. Civilian workers were either enlisted, "recruited" under duress, or conscripted right off the street. Soviet and French POWs, and even Italian military internees, became part of VW's forced labor program in October 1943. These people worked in maintenance, production, and aircraft repair. Some even worked on assembling the V-1 flying bomb in the last year of the war when the factory grew to be the main V-1 manufacturer.[10]

The SS became the dominant forced-labor supplier for factories and other enterprises throughout the Reich after German men were mobilized and put into uniforms. Companies either had to compete for Himmler's forced laborers or shut down. VW was no exception. Additional pressure to use forced labor arose when the Waffen SS stepped in and assumed much of VW's security needs because of the plant's size and the sensitive military nature of its production. At that point there was no question of shutting it down.

In 1999 the long-since private company was still trying to shake off the lingering resentment of its World War II practices. Hoping to show the slave laborers of that era and their survivors that it accepted some moral responsibility for what occurred, VW assembled a permanent exhibit in the basement of one of the original factory buildings and named it the Place of Remembrance.[11] The little-known exhibit exists largely for the visits of former forced laborers and their descendants. Appropriately enough, it is laid out inside a repurposed bunker-like bomb shelter. My wife and I were its only visitors on the day of a prearranged visit with VW's archivists. During the tour our archivist host related the following story, which appears both in the exhibit's printed and digital guides.

When the war-era Volkswagen company planned to open V-1 production in 1944, the project lead engineer, a Nazi party member who subscribed to Hitler's ideas on the racial inferiority of Jews, needed 300 specialized metalworkers. To fill his needs, he traveled to Auschwitz and screened recently arrived Hungarian Jews to fill the open jobs. His "recruits" did core V-1 production work at VW and trained other laborers as well. Because the engineer treated these new workers respectfully in the factory, the new situation "almost seemed like salvation" after the conditions at Auschwitz. "On their arrival . . . they had their own beds and sheets as well as shower facilities in rooms close to the Hall 1 air-raid shelters." Unfortunately, the laborers were later transferred from the VW factory to a bombproof underground plant where conditions were harsher and some of the laborers died. Following the war, the plant engineer's daughter commented that although her father had been a Nazi, he was not really an evil person. Nevertheless, she was surprised to learn that one of the Jews he'd brought to the factory expressed his gratitude, saying he'd even been addressed as "Mein Herr." The daughter hadn't been aware of the practical side of her father that allowed him to put aside his prejudices for the sake of efficiency.[12] [13]

---

1. Albert Mroz, "The Volkswagen Beetle," Warfare History Network, June 8, 2016, https://warfarehistorynetwork.com/the-volkswagen-beetle/.
2. Jean Denis G.G. Lepage, *German Military Vehicles of World War II: An Illustrated Guide to Cars, Trucks, Half-Tracks, Motorcycles, Amphibious Vehicles and Others* (McFarland, 2007), 57.
3. Karl Ludvigsen, *Battle for the Beetle: The Untold Story of the Post-War Battle for Adolf Hitler's Giant Volkswagen Factory and the Porsche-Designed Car That Became an Icon for Generations around the Globe* (Cambridge, MA: Bentley Publishers, 2000), 55.
4. Ludvigsen, *Battle for the Beetle*.
5. Rudolf Herzog, *Dead Funny: Humor in Hitlers Germany* (Brooklyn, N.Y.: Melville House, 2011), 132.
6. Lepage, *German Military Vehicles of World War II*, 57.
7. Ludvigsen, *Battle for the Beetle*, 70.
8. Ludvigsen, *Battle for the Beetle*, 177, 180.
9. Ludvigsen, *Battle for the Beetle*, 179.
10. Manfred Grieger and Ulrike Gutzmann, "VW in the Nazi era," interview by Erich Eipert, April 16, 2010, Volkswagen Aktiengesellschaft Corporate Archives, Wolfsburg, Germany.
11. Volkswagen AG Corporate History Department, *A Catalogue on the Exhibition "Place of Remembrance of Forced Labor in the Volkswagen Factory"* (Wolfsburg, Germany: Volkswagen AG Corporate History Department, 2001), https://www.volkswagen-group.com/en/publications/more/place-of-remembrance-of-forced-labor-in-the-volkswagen-factory-1721.
12. Volkswagen AG Corporate History Department, *A Catalogue on the Exhibition*, 88.
13. Manfred Grieger and Ulrike Gutzmann, "VW in the Nazi era."

32 Volkswagen Relief

When Fidel and his Buchenwald driver-training group of 20 arrived at the Volkswagen plant in mid-May 1944, they were assigned to the factory SS administrative command, SS Sondersturm Volkswagenwerk. This security unit now had a smaller presence than earlier because of the critical shortage of Waffen SS replacements on the fighting fronts. The factory was forced to assume some of the security duties, but the SS remained in overall charge of this and the foreign worker camps.[1] Fidel and his companions found themselves part of a larger group of 200 Waffen SS trainees subdivided among three training companies. The army also had a few trainees at VW, but because it was less technically advanced and mechanized than the Waffen SS, as well as having a shorter history of working with VW, its presence was small.

Fidel and the other trainees bunked in standard wooden military barracks buildings about two kilometers from the plant, most likely in an area known as Camp Hohenstein, from which they were trucked to the plant and back each day. The training program was intended to give the soldiers an intimate knowledge of both the Kübelwagen and the Schwimmwagen by rotating them through the various jobs on the production line alongside the regular workers. Each week every man shifted to a new job. This rotation exposed him to all the steps along the vehicle and parts assembly lines, including the testing of engines and finished vehicles. During Fidel's assignment to the plant, which lasted from May until October of 1944, the production line switched between Schwimmwagen and the Kübelwagen production every three months.

During a 2010 day-long visit with VW's Corporate History Department head and his associate, I learned something that my father hadn't told me. Soldiers like Fidel, whose training at VW lasted several months, were being groomed to train others or to supervise technical repair and maintenance at the battalion level or higher. Soldiers destined to work in motor pools at a company level trained for only six weeks.

The VW plant was larger than the Opel factory Fidel had just come from and larger than I expected, as well. On being driven around the enormous factory grounds toward the end of my day there, I had a chance to view the spot along the reservoir where Fidel tested a Schwimmwagen amphibious car by driving it into the water. He must have had faith in these cars during the testing because I know he couldn't swim.

Fidel testing a Schwimmwagen, one of the two vehicle types produced at VW during the war, by driving into the reservoir adjacent to the factory complex in Wolfsburg, Germany.

Of the nearly 18,000 workers employed at the plant when Fidel arrived, fewer than 4,000 were Germans. The involuntary workers were housed by nationality in barracks along the Mittelland Kanal, the waterway on which raw materials arrived. Fidel said that the huge complex had 11 different housing areas, all sited on the other side of the canal. Each had its own kitchen and mess hall. In the plant itself the eating areas were also usually segregated by nationality and sometimes even by department. The trainees ate in the cafeteria for German civilians. Fidel found the food surprisingly good given the wartime shortages and the rationing in effect throughout the country.

Not everyone ate equally well. The quality and quantity of the food depended on status and nationality. The factory operated on a hierarchy that stratified the laborers. Germans were at the top of the heap. Just below them were the other western nationalities, then came the East Europeans. Russian POWs ranked lowest. The same system prevailed in housing, with German civilians living in masonry buildings. Fidel and the other soldiers bunked in wooden barracks somewhat better than those of the foreign laborers. After the first Allied bombing raid, a shortage of barracks space disturbed this separation. Segregation was also supposed to extend to the air raid shelters under the plant, but such a thing was difficult to enforce during a rush to safety.

At Opel the trainees had been confined to their own small workshop and had no outside contact, but at VW Fidel interacted with an international menagerie of people daily. He talked to them all—Poles, Russians, Ukrainians, Serbs, etc.—and observed no obvious friction among the nationalities, or between them and Germans. Politics were never discussed. His impression was that despite the difficult circumstances, most workers seemed content with their jobs. The work was monotonous, but far less demanding and uncomfortable than working outdoors all year round—the situation many of the workers had come from. And for the trainees and civilian male workers alike, factory work was much preferred over the battlefield.

Although many of the workers came from countries occupied by Germany—countries with governments-in-exile actively waging war against Germany—Fidel said there was surprisingly little barbed wire strung about and only a light security guard presence. Despite the low security, he never heard of any sabotage during his months there. I suspect that Fidel would have liked to explore the huge multi-building facility, but his job confined him to the auto-production sections of the plant. He did

Left: Fidel and companion posing in front of barracks near the Volkswagen (VW) factory in 1944. *Right:* Fidel at VW, no longer looking like the fresh-faced inductee that he was the year before.

hear rumors that V-1 rockets were being assembled somewhere in the facility; however, he remained unaware of any of the other armament manufacturing taking place there, or even of aircraft repair work.

On Sundays, Fidel's only free day, he and a couple of his friends were sometimes invited to the home of an engineer he'd met in the plant. Fidel had struck up a conversation with this man and discovered they had something in common. The engineer was a Banat German who'd grown up in Bruckenau, a village just 20 kilometers from Fidel's home. After working in the auto industry at Ford in Detroit for over 10 years, he was induced to come to the VW plant in Germany when it opened in 1938. Ferdinand Porsche had recruited him and a contingent of other German engineers and skilled workers while researching auto plants in America. Once Fidel came to know the family better, he and his pals sometimes showed up at the house without an invitation. It was an opportunity to taste normal life and eat a home-cooked meal, but the main incentive had more to do with the engineer's two pretty daughters.

During Fidel's 1944 tenure at VW, an important July event showed the extent to which the military leadership was dissatisfied with Hitler's incompetence and meddling in military affairs. A group of them plotted to kill Hitler with a bomb and take over the government. The organizer of the assassination and coup plot was Claus von Stauffenberg. Unfortunately, Hitler survived the briefcase bomb Stauffenberg himself bravely placed under the conference table at a meeting in Hitler's field headquarters. The large-scale purge and executions Hitler carried out afterward only increased the resentment.

The factory's outer perimeter, which was ringed with a series of stations manned by Russian POWs, was one place that Fidel could visit. The men there were responsible for putting up a smoke screen whenever the threat of an Allied air raid materialized. Fidel liked to talk to the prisoners and got on well with them. For the most part they were older Russians, 40 to 50 years of age. They'd been POWs for two or three years already, and Fidel learned that they weren't unhappy to be there. Despite their poor circumstances, their lot was better than that of their countrymen still fighting for Stalin. They said they liked it in Germany and didn't want to return to Russia after the war.

Sirens howled whenever enemy planes were detected in the vicinity. Fidel recollected the dense smoke screens these men sent up to obscure the plant from the air. In his first months the bombers just passed by on their way to targets elsewhere, but no one ever knew if the plant was the day's target, so the smoke always went up. At the sound of the sirens the POWs opened valves on pipes to feed oil into the bottom of smoke generators, then ignited the fuel. These devices were little more than open-top oil drums.

One commonly held belief is that the auto plant was spared from any major bombing attack until the final year of the war because it was too new to appear on most Allied maps. However, the VW archivists and other historians say this is little more than a legend. In reality, the plant didn't have a high enough priority to warrant an attack. What finally drew the attention of the Allied target selectors was the output of a profitable new weapons contract VW procured.

The new product was the V-1 rocket, a forerunner of the modern cruise missile. The V-1 made use of a recent German invention—the pulse jet engine. Most simply, the technology was a stovepipe with an intake flap. When the flap closed, fuel discharged into the chamber. A spark then detonated the fuel air mixture, and each pulse provided a rearward thrust. This cycle repeated rapidly—44 times per second. The design engineers mounted this new engine in a small midwing airplane able to carry a ton of high explosives. The result was an unmanned vengeance weapon that the British knew as a buzz bomb because of its distinctive throbbing or buzzing sound.

The V-1 was crude at best because it had a range of only 240 km and little accuracy. Fewer than half even made it across the English Channel. Hitler intended to launch the flying bomb in numbers so great that their massive destruction would force Britain to quit the war. The Allies feared the V-1 because it flew faster than most fighter aircraft of the day and was hard to shoot down. Had the Germans perfected this weapon's guidance and reliability, it would have posed an enormous defensive challenge for the Allies.

A German effort to start up V-1 production in a Peugeot auto plant in France is what ultimately led to the large-scale bombing of the VW factory. French spies gleaned enough intelligence information at Peugeot to allow the Allies to conclude that the primary source of the weapon was the VW factory, earning it a spot on the priority bombing target list. VW had previously been hit by a few bombs in two small raids in 1940, but in 1944 the US Eighth Air Force attacked in a more determined way. The German Luftwaffe had relatively few planes still flying so antiaircraft guns were the principal deterrent. On April 8th, bombers dropped 146 tons of bombs and blew the roofs off three of the large halls and damaged the rail line. Then on April 29, a disabled British Lancaster bomber by sheer chance crashed through the roof of the tool-and-die hall. The plane's full bomb load exploded inside the plant and caused a great deal of damage. The crew bailed out before the crash and was picked up by the plant's antiaircraft gunners. Fidel arrived some weeks after this event.[2]

The largest bombing raid occurred on June 20, several weeks after Fidel's arrival. By his recollection, four daylight waves of about 50 US planes each, appeared at half-hour intervals to drop their loads. It was truly frightening for the workers. The pressure wave of one detonation flung Fidel 20 feet across the floor, but he escaped serious injury. Fidel had overestimated the number of bombers involved, but not by much. The released figures indicate 137 American B-17s dropped 130 one-ton bombs, along with numerous smaller bombs, on the factory. As usual, not all of the bombs detonated. One was uncovered and defused during an expansion as late as 2016.[3]

The attacks continued, and only nine days later a British nighttime firebombing mission inflicted yet more damage. On August 5, 85 American B-24s raided the plant for a third time to make sure the factory was out of the V-1 production business. This raid convinced Allied intelligence analysts that on-site V-1 production was no longer possible and whatever production capacity did remain would have been dispersed to less vulnerable sites. But the analysts were wrong. In November the plant re-established enough V-1 fuselage production to account for 35 percent of this component's output once again. And V-1 improvements were still being implemented.

To keep their own design business operating and generating income, the Porsche development team contracted to improve the V-1's performance. The missile needed more speed to outfly the improving Allied airplanes and a greater range because the D-day invasion of France had pushed the launch sites farther from England. So the team developed a small jet engine. Developing the engine was relatively easy; the difficult part was figuring out how to make it affordable enough to put on a disposable bomb. Porsche's group was by this time competing with the V-2, a more sophisticated missile being developed by a competing team headed by rocket scientist Werner von Braun. The Porsches did complete the new V-1 engine design after the bombings, but the war front overran the plant before it could be built or tested.[4]

When the vehicle assembly line ceased production after the August 5 raid, just 630 Beetle sedans and 13 cabriolet coupes had ever been built. And the entire military Kübelwagen and Schwimmwagen production run had amounted to only about 50,000 and 14,000 vehicles respectively. By comparison, American assembly plants built at least 10 times this many jeeps. With only a fraction of the VW factory floor space devoted to vehicles through the war, it could never hope to produce the number of vehicles it was designed for.

The August raid left a large portion of the plant's buildings in ruins. Much of the floor space was now unusable, and huge sections of the roof had collapsed. Fidel recalled that the plant managers estimated 75 percent of the factory was destroyed. According to the company's historians, the correct figure was later determined to be 60 percent. The factory was no longer capable of producing anything in quantity, but management resisted closing the facility. What Allied intelligence didn't know was that 80 percent of the production machinery survived the bombing and the crucial electrical power generation plant remained operational.

That so much of the plant equipment survived was the result of advance planning rather than luck. Workers had been directed to move much of the machinery. Some went to the plant's spacious basements that were largely protected from bomb damage by the thick concrete floors above them. Other machines were stashed for kilometers around the plant in commandeered barns. In some cases, the machines were even operated there. The heavier pieces of equipment rode there on improvised sheet metal sleds towed by farm tractors. Equipment that couldn't be removed from the main factory floor, machines such as the tall sheet-metal stamp presses, were walled in with protective heavy masonry. These measures allowed parts production to continue after the raids, but in a dispersed fashion and on a smaller scale than before. The skilled labor force, parts stockpiles, and functioning machine shops also allowed some assembly and vehicle repair to continue.

August was truly a cruel month for the Volkswagen plant. And it was just as punishing for Fidel personally. The Red Army pushed through Romania that month and seized control of the government. With Stalin's stooges in charge, Romania switched sides and cut mail service to the Reich, giving Fidel cause to worry for the safety of his family. The new government also disenfranchised him and all the other ethnic German boys and men the previous government had sent off to fight in Hitler's Waffen SS. Fidel was now locked into his German military identity. which would prevent him from returning to Romania when the war ended. And with an end to VW's vehicle production, Fidel now also had reason to worry about being sent back into battle, since the fronts were fast closing on Germany and sucking up nearly every man who could pull a trigger.

After vehicle production ended, the factory buildings were deliberately left in ruins to discourage further bombing. Fidel and the other trainees expected to quickly receive orders that returned them to one of the fronts, but weeks later they were still lodged at Wolfsburg, nursing a hope that the higher ups had forgotten about them. However, in late October new orders directing Fidel and about 15 other Nordland men to various locations closer to the front did arrive. The men were told they'd receive home leave first, but Fidel had heard that spiel before and "knew it wouldn't happen," given the dire situation on the Eastern Front and the critical replacement needs of his shot-up division. Even had he gotten papers for such a leave, he couldn't have traveled home because Romania was now firmly in Stalin's maw.

With low expectations, Fidel and several other trainees submitted requests for further training. Fidel applied for *Holzgas* (wood gas) operator schooling. Holzgas refers to the technology and equipment that gasifies organic substances to power internal combustion engines. This relatively simple but crucial technology had allowed Germany to prosecute the war as long as it had despite its perpetual shortage of petroleum. To grasp why holzgas became so important, it is necessary to understand a little about Germany's petroleum supply.

When Hitler came to power in 1933, he knew how badly Germany was constrained by limited petroleum resources within its borders and immediately invested in oil exploration. Although this effort tripled domestic output in six years, that success would have fallen far short of meeting the needs of an industrial country the size of Germany even if Hitler hadn't also been rearming at a furious pace. Given that Germany had abundant coal resources, the government also invested heavily in the production of synthetic oil from coal, a process that soon became a much more important source of fuel than Germany's oil wells. Yet, despite the mandatory austerity imposed on civilian consumption and the purchase of outside oil, the fuel supply continued to fall short of what Hitler needed to fulfill his expansionist dreams. No matter how much his Wehrmacht craved the total mechanization of its army, its dream could not come to fruition as long as two-thirds of its distribution channel supplies still used horse transport at one leg or another.

During the prewar rearmament period, German military planners realized how seriously their fuel supplies hampered the mobility of the highly mechanized force they were building. A panzer division burned a thousand gallons of fuel for each mile it moved. The supplies on hand simply couldn't sustain the long drive east that Hitler envisioned, so the war planners changed strategies and developed the blitzkrieg concept. In essence, the new doctrine was a mad scramble to defeat the enemy quickly before the attacking force's fuel supply ran out. Oil stocks and oil fields would be captured before they could be sabotaged. For the specific purpose of rapidly securing the new fuel supplies, the Wehrmacht formed an oil commando unit of engineers and technical specialists to occupy and repair newly acquired petroleum facilities. Unfortunately for the Germans, when the Molotov-Ribbentrop nonaggression pact divvied up Poland between the Soviet Union and Nazi Germany in 1939, the Soviets beat the Germans to the punch and seized the bulk of Poland's oil. Germany then had to purchase this supply from Stalin until Hitler launched his 1941 invasion of the Soviet Union.

During Fidel's teen years in Romania, he'd seen firsthand how dependent Germany was on the westward bound tank-car trains that passed through Orzydorf daily. When the Soviet Union, then also a net oil importer, pressured Romania to surrender a large chunk of its northeastern territory in 1940, Stalin's new toehold placed the Red Army dangerously close to the Romanian Ploieşti oil fields and refineries that supplied Germany with much of its fuel. This threatening situation almost certainly played a role in Hitler's decision to invade the Soviet Union the following year, but is often overlooked as a contributing factor.

Germany's oil deficit actually worsened after it conquered its western neighbors because the occupied countries were also net importers of oil. Enlisting Italy as an ally proved particularly costly because Italy imported nearly all of its supply. So when Hitler decided to save this inept and faltering ally in North Africa, his German commander there, Erwin Rommel, had to share his own meager oil supply with the Italian forces. Rommel's mechanized military capability was already constrained by fuel more so than by tactics and equipment. Sometimes his fuel trucks consumed half the fuel they carried just in delivering their loads. Delivery trucks were then stranded without enough fuel to return.[5]

In May 1944, about the time that Fidel arrived at the VW plant, the US Army Air Force sent 935 bombers to attack Germany's five major oil plants. The mission's success delivered a paralyzing blow to Germany's ability to continue waging mechanized war. Elsewhere, another part of the Allied bombing campaign targeted and crippled the refineries at Romania's Ploieşti oil fields and dried up Germany's last large outside supply. Germany's stocks dwindled to a crippling level in short order. Hitler's dispersed factories could still turn out a large number of military vehicles but could no longer put oil in their crankcases or fuel in their gas tanks. Horses and oxen were commonly seen towing airplanes to the flight line and pulling military trucks to their destination.[6]

---

1. Volkswagen AG Corporate History Department, *A Catalogue on the Exhibition "Place of Remembrance of Forced Labor in the Volkswagen Factory"* (Wolfsburg, Germany: Volkswagen AG Corporate History Department, 2001), https://www.volkswagen-group.com/en/publications/more/place-of-remembrance-of-forced-labor-in-the-volkswagen-factory-1721.
2. Karl Ludvigsen, *Battle for the Beetle: The Untold Story of the Post-War Battle for Adolf Hitler's Giant Volkswagen Factory and the Porsche-Designed Car That Became an Icon for Generations around the Globe* (Cambridge, MA: Bentley Publishers, 2000), 47.
3. Jason Torchinsky, "Volkswagen Finds An American WWII Bomb In Their Factory," Jalopnik, July 12, 2016, https://jalopnik.com/volkswagen-finds-an-american-wwii-bomb-in-their-factory-1783482104.

4. Ludvigsen, *Battle for the Beetle*, 50.
5. Michael Antonucci, "Blood for Oil: The Quest for Fuel in WWII," Military History & Espionage, February 1993, https://ww2f.com/threads/the-quest-for-fuel-in-world-war-ii.14638/.
6. Holocaust Historical Society, "Buchenwald," November 9, 2021, https://www.holocausthistoricalsociety.org.uk/contents/concentrationcamps/buchenwald.html.

33 Holzgas to the Rescue

A vehicle fitted with a holzgas system is known as a *Holzbrenner* (wood burner). During the war its usual fuel stock was dry wood chunks, but coal, sawdust, charcoal, rubber, or other carbon compounds could be burned. The conversion process occurs in a firebox fitted with a blower to keep the combustion going. Once the fire becomes hot enough, the burn chamber is largely closed off. Since the fuel can no longer burn with a flame due to oxygen restriction, it decomposes in a way that releases a high level of carbon monoxide and other gases. The gaseous fuel produced in the process is piped through a precipitator or filter, cooled, and fed into a regular gasoline engine through a special carburetor. The result is akin to burning methane. Combustion of these gases comes with serious shortcomings. The most notable is a 20 percent reduction in engine performance because the fuel is less energy rich than gasoline. Burning this fuel also drastically shortens engine life due to carbon buildup.

At the same time that Hitler was trying to put many new cars onto his autobahns, his officials were trying to wean the country off imported oil. Companies were contracted to develop ways to substitute the fuels Germany had in abundance—wood and coal. Liquid fuel derived from coal was one answer. The development of the holzgas generator was another and gave the program a big boost. The government was so hopeful that it drew up plans to build 3,000 wood-fueling stations around the country. Throughout the war, the Allies were aware of Germany's critical petroleum shortage, so they bombed refineries, storage depots, transport links, and the electrical stations that supplied the power to operate fuel-processing plants. Had holzgas not filled some of the gap, Germany couldn't have sustained itself during the war.

By the middle of 1942, nearly the entire German oil supply was needed to keep the frontline troops supplied and the war planes flying. Even Nazi officials and the police force had to scramble to find enough petrol and lubricants to operate their vehicles. At the front, wood-burning technology was impractical for many reasons. The most limiting was that vehicles could not be instantly started and driven. Firing up a holzbrenner also took considerable labor and skill, which necessitated the assignment of trained operators, even in military rear areas.

In 1943 Albert Speer, who Hitler appointed to direct Germany's wartime economy, ordered all civilian vehicles adapted to holzgas. Wood-fuel technology did reduce the need for oil, but the civilian economy thereafter suffered from the shortage of fossil fuel for vehicles. Fueling stations were set up to sell holzbrenner wood fuel to the public, but because the conversion plan was never fully implemented, the fuel outlets were limited in number. In an online German automotive forum, one participant who was interested in buying an antique holzgas vehicle wrote,

> My father-in-law in Germany is supposed to be scouting the ads for a nice unit for sale, but he operated one during the war and he thinks I'm completely insane. The first time I talked to him about these he shook his head and said, "When the holzgas cars appeared that's when we all realized we had lost the war. They set up special 'Holzgas Fueling Stations' in Germany where they sold pre-cut wood chips (matchstick sized), and they told drivers on the Autobahn to take every exit and then get back on since the exits back then were paved with cobblestones and the vibration of the cobblestones would stir the ashes and keep the fire burning."[1]

Speer's plan to equip all German domestic vehicles with retrofit kits fell far short of its goal. Several hundred thousand gas generators had been manufactured by war's end, but most ended up installed on military vehicles in rear areas for use by replacement and training units. The military even fitted some training Panzers with gas generators. With so many holzbrenners in use, the Waffen SS needed to establish holzgas training programs such as the one Fidel applied for in order to keep their vehicles running.

Fifteen Nordland men from Fidel's group at the VW factory in Wolfsburg applied for holzgas training, but only Fidel and one other man were selected. Whether this was sheer luck or based on an evaluation, Fidel didn't know. The rest of the Nordland men in the group proceeded to the replacement battalion at Graz for reassignment and ended up back on the Eastern Front, which by this time was not very far away. None of these soldiers received the leave they were supposed to get. After the war, Fidel learned through the soldier network that few of these soldiers, men he'd worked with and come to know as friends, survived their return to the front.

Fidel's holzgas training took place in the same Buchenwald complex where he'd acquired his military driver's license prior to the start of his auto-plant training. The camp was now a very different place because like the VW complex, it too had been bombed. The prisoner-housing portion of the camp suffered only light damage, but the rest of the compound was largely destroyed on August 24, 1944, when a flight of 132 B-17 bombers from the US Army Air Force 401st Bomb Group targeted the Wilhelm Gustloff Works and SS facilities.

The bomb group tapped its best pilots and bombardiers for this mission to minimize the chance of hitting the prisoner camp. The mission, one of the most precise of the war, destroyed the entire factory complex and killed over a hundred SS men and civilians. Unfortunately, the raid also took the lives of nearly 400 workers in the factory area. This strike delivered a serious blow to the German V-2 rocket program by nearly drying up the manufacture of gyroscopes and other critical parts. The motor pool, adjacent to the factories, was also hit. By the time Fidel arrived in October, the motor pool had been restored enough to allow training to resume.

When I visited the camp in 2015, a display caption in the museum helped me identify the unit that conducted the training—SS Motor Vehicle Training and Reserve Regiment (SS-Kraftfahrzeug Ausbildungs und Ersatzregiment). I subsequently learned at the camp's archive office that a vehicle service building near the camp fence and administration buildings survived the bombing and was still in use. A helpful archivist took me to the building, which was identified by a sign in four languages. The English inscription read, "Garages and filling station of the SS military command headquarters."

We both soon realized that for a large factory complex with a garrison of 4,500 soldiers, this compact space didn't allow room for trucks and couldn't have served as a training area. A second pass through the museum exhibits turned up a photo with a caption that read, "The troop garages of the Waffen SS (armed SS) are part of the SS garrison." This pointed me to the much roomier motor pool area where both of Fidel's training courses at Buchenwald would have taken place. That space was located near the camp's main entrance higher on Ettersberg Hill, about a kilometer west of the work camp and prisoner barracks. Nothing remained of it or the adjacent armaments factories, but period photos show a tall command tower within the motor pool's confines that was prominent enough to be seen 10 kilometers away in the city of Weimar.

Fidel said his training consumed all daylight hours of the short autumn days, which would have left him little chance to explore the camp.

Wandering about and exhibiting curiosity might also have been a bit risky at a time when any infraction could get a man packed off to the front. However, Fidel did recall once passing a wire-enclosed compound holding about a hundred men. Upon hearing Romanian spoken, he walked over to the fence and talked to the men, but he could no longer remember any specifics about who they were or what was said. I would guess that because the Soviets had already occupied Romania for two months by then and Romania's army was now allied with the Red Army, these prisoners were Romanian soldiers who'd been in Germany at the time of Romania's takeover. Technically, this would have made them enemy combatants.

Fidel couldn't have known it, but until shortly before he arrived, the work camp also held 167 American, British, and French military POWs. They were all airmen who, contrary to rules of the Geneva Conventions, were incarcerated there instead of in POW camps. At Buchenwald these men were starved, beaten, and mistreated just like other inmates. Twenty-one of them were executed in mid-October and then, just days before a second group was scheduled to be executed, the fliers were transferred to another camp through the intervention of Luftwaffe officers. One of the prisoners due to be shot was Joe Moser, a fighter pilot shot down in France on his 44th combat mission. Had I heard of Moser just a bit sooner, I surely could have collected more information about the camp, for he lived just two hours north of me. He died not long after I visited Buchenwald, but I did learn a good deal about conditions in the camp from a book about Moser and his war experiences.[2][3]

In Germany toward the end of the war, the Wehrmacht had to rely on draft animals when fuel and lubricants ran short. Fidel said the SS was better prepared and its support facilities were still motorized despite the petroleum shortage. Holzbrenners were in wide use at Buchenwald, and he didn't recall any draft animals there. Besides, the camp no longer had any stables. They'd long since been converted to prisoner barracks.

Fidel and the other trainees became disenchanted with the troublesome holzbrenner technology as soon as they learned what many in Germany already knew by then: holzgas systems were labor intensive, finnicky, and produced considerably less power than petroleum fuels. The gas generator units were notoriously balky and required the operator to properly set a number of valves in response to readings from various system gauges. Hence, keeping vehicles running required a considerable investment in training operators and mechanics to troubleshoot and repair the fuel generation unit.

The system's greatest practical constraint was the length of time it took to get an engine running. Another serious limitation was the frequency with which the fire boxes needed tending and refueling. A five-ton truck burned about 100 kilograms (220 pounds) of hardwood or 42 kilograms (96 pounds) of coal for every 100 kilometers (62 miles) traveled. The smaller trucks that Fidel trained on could cover just 40 kilometers before they needed restoking, so keeping these vehicles going demanded access to a lot of wood. Germany had this fuel in abundance, but it did need some processing. Fidel recalled that the camp's vehicles primarily used fist-sized chunks. Holzbrenners had two further shortcomings that made them unloved and used only when absolutely necessary. Keeping them running was dirty and also potentially hazardous because the main fuel component generated—carbon monoxide—was a noxious but odorless gas.

Fidel's group trained largely on converted two-ton military trucks with cargo beds "three or four meters long." A few of the trucks would start with holzgas alone, but most required a start with gasoline before the engine could be switched over to the CO-rich gas. Prior to the switchover, the fire in the cylindrical fireboxes had to burn a considerable time before generating gas efficiently, which meant the wood in the fireboxes had to be lit well in advance. What Fidel remembered most about this school was having to work outside in the cold each morning to light those fires early.

The trainees finished their training course at the end of November and were put to other duties while nervously awaiting reassignment. The war couldn't end soon enough to suit them, yet it dragged on. Everyone thought that a surrender had to come soon because despite the propaganda about a secret weapon that would allow Germany to win the war, the military situation had deteriorated too much. The soldiers had good reason to be concerned because both fronts were getting close to the German heartland. Front-line replacements were in such high demand that the Nazis had begun inducting practically every German male able to rise from a chair. With the Luftwaffe short of fuel for its remaining planes, thousands of pilots had been made infantrymen. As were many panzer crews after they lost their tanks. So the new holzgas specialists had cause to fear that they'd soon be out there with the pilots and panzer crews.

---

1. "Holzbrenner - Tell Me about These and What It Might Be Worth," TheSamba.com, June 20, 2007, https://www.thesamba.com/vw/forum/archive/index.php/o-t--t-238539--.html.
2. Joseph F. Moser and Gerald R. Baron, *A Fighter Pilot in Buchenwald: Joe Moser's Journey from Farm Boy to Fighter Pilot to near Starvation in a Nazi Concentration Camp* (Bellingham, Wash.: All Clear Pub. in partnership with EdensVeil, 2010).
3. "Local WWII Hero Joe Moser Passes Away," *Whatcom News*, December 3, 2015, https://whatcom-news.com/local-wwii-hero-joe-moser-passes-away_13286/.

34 Skorzeny and the Endgame

Fidel's worst fears finally seemed to materialize in mid-December when a Waffen SS officer informed the 16 holzgas trainees that they'd been called to the Berlin area for duty. The fronts were still some distance away, but everyone knew that because Berlin was the Nazi capital it would become the scene of a tremendous battle. This transfer cut Fidel's ties to Nordland, for the new assignment attached him to an independent Waffen SS commando battalion, SS Jagdverband Mitte (SS Hunter Force Central). That unit was led by Otto Skorzeny, a household name in Germany. Skorzeny was extremely ambitious, but unprincipled. Three years earlier as a private in an unremarkable division, he'd gotten himself transferred to the prestigious SS Das Reich division as a sergeant. Then, through the political influence of an acquaintance, he manipulated his way into the officer ranks just before his new division invaded Yugoslavia.

When in 1943 the SS Security Service (SD) became convinced that it needed a commando element to carry out secret operations, Skorzeny snared the leadership post. By then, he'd studied the tactics of Britain's special commando units and already begun training operatives to carry out secret missions behind enemy lines. Skorzeny chose to base his new organization, Sonderverband z.b.V. Friedenthal, on the grounds of Schloss (Castle) Friedenthal near the small city of Oranienburg, some kilometers north of Berlin. The main structure, more of a mansion than an actual castle, was not immediately relinquished by its owner, but confinement in a concentration camp caused the man to change his mind. Skorzeny's commando compound soon expanded to include barracks, a hangar, a mess hall, an athletic hall, and training facilities. His unit's administrative offices and command center were on the ground floor of the castle as were the offices of the district's Gestapo and SD (Sicherheitsdienst, or Security Service). Skorzeny's living quarters were on an upper floor.

The Friedenthal location was ideal for Skorzeny because the resources of a large SS facility and the Sachsenhausen concentration camp were close by. The SS complex, comparable to the one at Buchenwald, contained factories, various SS command headquarters, as well as the work camp, which held inmates with specials skills that would prove useful to Skorzeny. The area's SS presence was so substantial that SS officers and their families had a formidable presence in the local social scene and phone directory.[1]

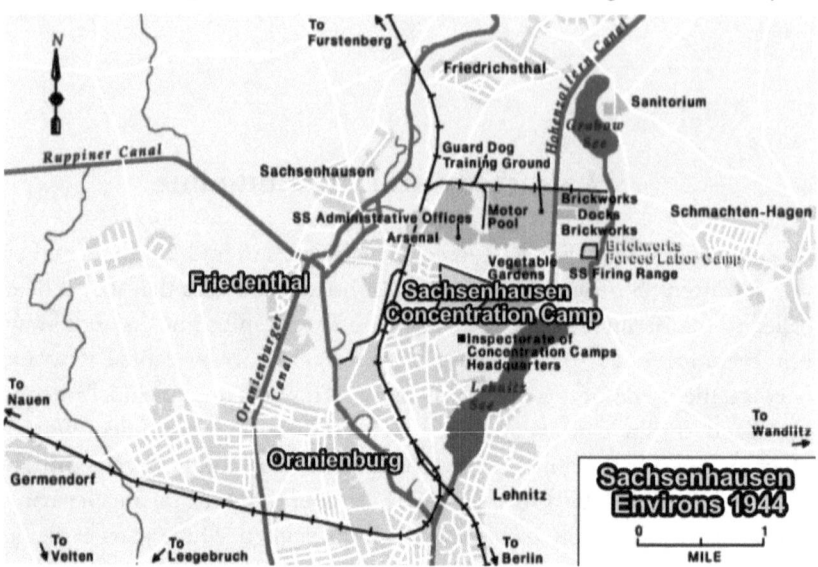

Skorzeny's Schloss Friedenthal headquarters and training base location. That facility lay north of Berlin near the city of Oranienburg and the Sachsenhausen concentration camp.

Skorzeny mounted a number of dangerous Waffen SS covert operations. These exploits led to promotions and even allowed him to become personally acquainted with Hitler.[2] Being in the public eye appealed to Skorzeny, and with considerable help from Goebbels's Propagandaministerium, his achievements became legendary throughout Germany. Fidel said that among soldiers, Skorzeny's commandos had the reputation of being "the toughest and meanest" in the business. One of Skorzeny's biographers says Skorzeny became "the Hitler-link to the present-day terrorism rampant around the globe" after discovering that "an act of terrorism committed by a minimum of people is often more effective than a large-scale, complex military operation."[3]

Skorzeny's six-foot-four (193-centimeter) height cut an imposing figure, and the long dueling scar across his cheek from his university days in Vienna lent him a menacing look. To say he was an unconventional soldier is an understatement. Skorzeny met Hitler for the first time in 1943 after the führer lost faith in his Abwehr (Intelligence Service). Hitler saw

Skorzeny as a faithful Nazi who would not let principles get in the way of an assignment, and thereafter called on him to execute ever more difficult and dangerous political and military operations. Two of his most notable successes, ones he led personally, were sold to the German public as near miracles.

The most famous of Skorzeny's exploits was the liberation of Benito Mussolini from captivity on a mountaintop ski-resort hotel at Gran Sasso, Italy. The Italian dictator was secretly being held prisoner there after the Italian public, the government, and the military leadership soured against the war in the summer of 1943. In late July, the government installed King Victor Emmanuel III as the country's leader and gave him control of the Italian military. The king acted immediately to imprison Mussolini but for the present kept Italian forces fighting alongside the Germans. However, sensing imminent defeat, the new government began secret negotiations with the Allies to switch sides. By then, Allied troops had already invaded southern Italy and were organizing Italian troops into what they termed a co-belligerent force.

To halt this advance, Hitler needed to control northern Italy. By freeing Mussolini, he'd again have a willing leader as the state's head, so he ordered Skorzeny to find out where the Italian was held and free him. Skorzeny located Mussolini through a combination of skullduggery and diligent detective work. He later wrote, "Thanks to a letter written by a love-sick carabinieri to his fiancée, we learned that the Duce was being held captive on the island of Ponza, where the ardent Italian soldier was in garrison." Skorzeny lost track of his quarry when the police guarding the Duce became suspicious and moved him to the mountains. An American team, also trying to capture Mussolini, sent a snatch team to Ponza, but arrived three days too late. Skorzeny was able to track the Duce down a second time.[4]

With Mussolini in his sights, Skorzeny devised a rescue plan he called Operation Eiche (Oak), but lost overall command of the operation when it became so complex that it required the cooperation of other military teams. Even so, he did lead the assault team that crash-landed in 10 small gliders on a mountain meadow near the hotel. To suppress any resistance, Skorzeny kidnapped an Italian general who valued his own life enough to order Mussolini's 200 military guards to stand down.

The exit plan called for Mussolini to be flown out in a two-seat Fieseler Storch spotter plane. Skorzeny had no intention of losing custody of Mussolini and allowing others to claim credit for the rescue, so he squeezed his large bulk into the second seat of the tiny plane and crammed Mussolini onto his lap. The plane was so grossly overloaded that the whole mission was endangered, but Skorzeny ordered the reluctant pilot to take off anyway. The plane failed to gain enough lift to take off by the time it reached the steep edge of the mountain, so it plunged downward. Not until the little plane was just short of crashing on the valley floor did it catch the lift needed to pull up.[5] [6]

Gaining Mussolini's release without a shot fired made Skorzeny's feat sound even more miraculous. After Hitler milked the rescue for all it was worth, he sent Mussolini to set up the new fascist state of Repubblica Sociale Italiana in northern Italy, which the Germans occupied by then.

Skorzeny carried out a second notable snatch the following year when Hitler sent him to stop Hungary from defecting to the Soviets. This time he kidnapped the playboy son of Hungary's dictator, Admiral Horthy. On his father's behalf, Miklós Horthy was negotiating Hungary's surrender to the Russians. While Skorzeny and his men engaged in a street shootout in Budapest with the young Horthy's Hungarian military guards, some of the Germans rushed into Horthy's residence, rolled the playboy up in a carpet, carried their bundle from the building, and hustled the captive out of the country. The next morning, in a bold action using minimal force and a great deal of bluff and bluster, Skorzeny succeeded in seizing Admiral Horthy's refuge—a huge fortification known as Berberg Castle. Admiral Horthy, fearing for his son's life, handed power over to a Nazi stooge.

Hitler's special missions kept Skorzeny away from his base so much that he lost touch with his men. Even so, his exploits proved that he was resourceful and could get things done with a small force, which won him special assignments and direct access to Hitler. Sometimes Hitler even granted Skorzeny plenipotentiary powers far beyond his rank of major, later colonel. This favoritism left Skorzeny a lone wolf who was scorned by most regular officers.[7]

Skorzeny had created the most recognized of Germany's World War II special forces units after gaining command in 1943 of a company-sized Waffen SS unit, Sonderlehrgang z.b.V. Friedenthal. The unit drew Waffen SS men as well as soldiers from the Wehrmacht's three branches. For the most part it was a mix of German, Hungarian ethnic German, Dutch, and Flemish soldiers, and even boasted a couple of Irishmen.[8]

Nearby Sachsenhausen concentration camp, within which tens of thousands of prisoners died during its nine-year existence, held both political and nonpolitical prisoners. Camp conditions were difficult and abuse abounded. Forced labor at the proximal SS armament industry workshops and a brick factory were the main work focus of the camp, but prisoners were put to other uses as well. One was the exhaustive testing of military footwear on a test track. Another was the testing of endurance-enhancing drugs for possible use by German soldiers. Prisoner executions were not uncommon, and the camp pioneered some of the mass execution methods used in other concentration camps during the war. The headquarters for the entire camp system was based here, as was a training school for SS camp administrators. Sadly, the liberation of the camp at the end of the war did not mark the end of the abuse there. Stalin's NKVD found the facilities just as useful as the Nazis had and soon filled it to capacity once again.[9]

Another office within Schloss Friedenthal directed Operation Bernhard—the infamous Nazi plan to ruin the British economy by flooding Britain with millions of forged bank notes. Quite practically, the schemers used some of their own counterfeit notes to finance their intelligence operations abroad. The *Fälscherwerkstatt* (counterfeiting workshop) engravers who made the currency printing plates worked right inside Schloss Friedenthal. The man in charge of the project, SS Major Bernhard Krüger, scoured concentration camps to find Jews skilled in engraving, drafting, printing, and banking to bring them to Sachsenhausen.[10] A 2007 movie, *The Counterfeiters*, is based on this operation.

The forging operation was a labor-intensive one that employed around 150 prisoners at its peak. The process began with printing the notes in sheets of four and cropping them with a steel ruler. To make the bills look more real, the edges were roughened to look used. The notes were passed hand to hand along rows of prisoners to accrue grime, wear, and tear. Other prisoners carefully wrote on the bills or marred them in ways that suggested they'd been counted and marked up by British bank tellers. In the final step, they were graded and sorted by quality. Bribing or hiring high-level people required the most perfect notes. Lower-level, less sophisticated help could be paid off with bills of lower quality.[11] [12]

After finalization of the British-pound-note product, the forgers set out to duplicate the American dollar. This project never advanced to the same stage because the dollar required more complex artwork, paper, and printing. The ultimate roadblock was the algorithm to produce the serial numbers for the bills, and the war ended before it was derived. However, another strong deterrent to completion was the realization by the prisoners that if they finished their work they would no longer be needed, and the Nazis would eliminate them. So the prisoners slowed down their work. There is also suspicion that Major Krüger himself was less than enthusiastic about finishing the job and receiving a posting to the front where officers' lives were short.[13]

When the fighting front approached Oranienburg, the counterfeiting operation was moved to more remote camps. Schloss Friedenthal eventually succumbed to Allied bombs. The parts of the facility that Allied bombing raids spared were turned to rubble by SS explosives to destroy any remaining evidence of criminal activity.[14] However, the castle did survive in a sense. In 2019, the City of Oranienburg's archivist notified me that a newly found post-war inventory control document noted that local residents near Schloss Friedenthal used "the remains as a quarry to extract building materials for . . . damaged houses."[15] This repurposing explained why there was no longer any sign of the place when I searched for it on a visit to Oranienburg.

Although the Germans were never able to adequately forge the US dollar, Stalin, who America supported throughout most of the war at the cost of many US sailors' lives and sunken ships via the North Atlantic convoys that delivered $11.3 billion ($180 billion in 2022 dollars) in military aid, did succeed grandly at printing American currency. This became public knowledge during a 1953 congressional hearing when Elizabeth Bentley, a wartime Communist spy-ring courier, testified that a group of Communists working within the US government helped the Soviets get printing plates in order to produce the new US-backed postwar German occupation currency with which the US government paid its soldiers. Stalin subsequently financed a considerable part of his occupation costs with currency printed from those plates. Bentley named two former Treasury Department officials who had helped provide the Soviets samples of the currency as well as the actual plates.[16]

The Chairman of the Permanent Subcommittee on Investigations of the Senate Government Operations Committee, Senator Karl E. Mundt, determined that there was a pattern of espionage in helping the Russians get the plates. Many of the Soviet occupation soldiers hadn't been paid in three years, so the unauthorized occupation currency fixed the problem and helped ensure that the Nazi tyranny in Eastern Europe was replaced with a new brand of tyranny. Mundt said the testimony showed that the Russians surrounded the US treasury secretary and other top assistants with disloyal people they'd recruited as spies and agents. The report concluded that the assistance helped Russia print at least $255 million in American currency for its own use.[17] [18]

The secret espionage operations Skorzeny was known for surely concerned Fidel less than the name of his new unit, SS Jagdverband Mitte, or SS Hunter Force Central. The *Hunter* part implied a return to active combat just when Germany looked close to defeat. The name was but the latest in a merry-go-round of monikers Skorzeny had bestowed on his organization. The newest name replaced one only several months old—SS Jäger Bataillon 502. That name had been adopted after completing sabotage operations in Denmark and Romania. Prior to then, Skorzeny called the unit Sonderlehrgang z.b.V Friedenthal, a name that had superseded the original Sonderlehrgang z.b.V Oranienburg moniker just weeks after the unit's founding.[19]

By inserting *Mitte* (Central) into the latest name, Skorzeny could call this Friedenthal-based component of his unit a headquarters group, which later allowed him to create sister formations for other geographic regions of Germany's remaining territory. However, these sister formations—SS-Jagdverband Nordwest, SS-Jagdverband Ost, SS-Jagdverband Südost, and SS-Jagdverband Südwest—never became fully-staffed detachments.

In its earlier designations, the unit's commando recruits received intense instruction in the use of rifles, pistols, grenades, artillery, sabotage, and secret weapons, along with the operation of cars, motorcycles, motorboats, and locomotives. But near the end of the war Skorzeny and his core cadre were seldom at the headquarters, so training was no longer possible. But when Skorzeny was present, visitors to his office might easily find themselves intimidated. Not only did Skorzeny's Herculean size discomfit them, so did his frightening desk—a copy of the one he saw in the office of Walter Schellenberg, the head of the Nazi intelligence service. Schellenberg's specially adapted desk was "an office fortress, fitted with recording equipment, alarms and concealed machine guns, all operated at the push of a button.... Skorzeny was greatly impressed by the office, though rather less so by Schellenberg himself."[20]

Fidel said he and the other holzgas men found the Friedenthal base nearly deserted after they traveled by train from Weimar to Berlin and then Oranienburg in early December. The barracks had been empty for some time already, as noted by an Irishman who'd arrived a couple of weeks earlier in late November and found just "5 or 6" men of his company there. The rest of the unit was training for a special mission at Grafenwöhr.[21]

Fidel almost certainly never saw Jagdverband Mitte's commander nor the man's armed desk in the castle. Several weeks before Fidel's arrival, Skorzeny had again been summoned by the führer and assigned to lead a daring secret operation to penetrate the American lines and create havoc during a German winter offensive in the Ardennes Forest. The Germans called this surprise offensive Unternehmen Wacht am Rhein (Operation Watch on the Rhine). The Allies called it the Ardennes Counteroffensive, but it is today almost universally known as the Battle of the Bulge because of the bulge the German attack created along the line of the Allied Front. The new Friedenthal men were fortunate to arrive too late to participate in the operation.

Skorzeny's part in the offensive was called Operation Greif. The name might easily be mistaken for the English word *grief* because the mission did cause the Allies considerable grief. But the name referred to Gryphon, a mythological creature with the head and wings of an eagle and the body of a lion. The bulk of Skorzeny's brigade-size Greif force, called Panzerbrigade 150, was to disguise itself as an American tank group. When the Germans couldn't round up enough operational American combat vehicles, the plan had to be scaled back. Fifteen trucks, thirty jeeps, and four American scout cars were insufficient, so the planners painted German vehicles to resemble US Army vehicles. Several Panther panzers were even fitted up with sheet metal to resemble M10 tank destroyers.

The specially selected Waffen SS soldiers in the group were supposed to have some English language fluency, but as with the vehicles, Skorzeny came far short in finding enough English speakers. Of the 2,500 men assigned to Panzerbrigade 150, only 400 knew some English. Half had merely a rudimentary knowledge of the tongue. The rest spoke good to excellent English, but only 10 knew any American slang. After donning American uniforms scrounged from prisoners in Germany's POW camps, the disguised "brigade" had little time for training before setting out in its motley collection of vehicles. In a separate operation, Skorzeny also sent nine small commando teams in American uniforms to create confusion and havoc in the American rear.

The primary German objective of the Ardennes offensive was to punch a hole through a weak section of the Allied front and recapture Antwerp, the primary Allied coastal supply port. Hitler believed this would split the Allied advancing forces and stop them for months. A lull in the fighting here was supposed to free up enough German divisions to bolster the depleted forces fighting the massive Soviet Army in the east.

Several hours after the main Wehrmacht force attacked the Americans, Skorzeny's disguised Panzerbrigade 150 was to take advantage of the confusion and slip through the American line to capture two vital bridges. But the Trojan Horse plan couldn't be implemented because the Wehrmacht failed to achieve its objective. The narrow Ardennes Forest roads Hitler's soldiers traversed in the attack became choke points that caused one of the worst German military traffic jams of the entire war and prevented the full deployment of German forces. Since the Panzerbrigade deception mission couldn't proceed as planned, Skorzeny was given permission to use his soldiers as a conventional force that wore the regular German uniform.

Skorzeny's commando teams enjoyed greater success in their mission than did his Panzerbrigade. The commandos penetrated the American lines and cut telephone wires, blew up an ammunition dump, passed along false orders, and altered road signs to snarl local Allied road traffic. Aided by wild rumors of infiltration that spread rapidly among the Allied troops, the tiny force had a disproportionate effect sowing fear and confusion. The penetration forced the American army to set up numerous checkpoints, which slowed the movement of men and supplies.

At these checkpoints the MP (military police) guards asked trivia questions that English-speaking Germans wouldn't know the answers to. At one post America's top Field Commander, General Omar Bradley, correctly replied that the capital of Illinois was Springfield but was detained because the MPs thought the answer was Chicago. Another general, Bruce Clarke, ran into trouble when he incorrectly replied that the Chicago Cubs baseball team was in the American League instead of the National League.

The Americans captured several Greif commandos. Under questioning these operatives spouted out every crazy rumor they'd heard while training for the operation. They were subsequently shot as spies, but their rumors had an effect. One rumor asserted that Skorzeny had sent agents to capture Allied Commander General Eisenhower at Allied headquarters in Paris. Consequently, Allied security restricted Eisenhower's movements during Christmas week as they sent a look-alike imposter around the city to draw out the commandos.

Another rumor asserted that Skorzeny had sent out a commando imposter resembling British Field Marshal Montgomery, who in the opinion of most American commanders had an ego that far outstripped his field command abilities. Eisenhower was said to be highly amused by Montgomery's experience at an American checkpoint. The General showed his identification, then ordered his driver to proceed because he believed himself too important for further questions. The irate guards responded by shooting out his tires and locking him in a barn for several hours.

Despite minor successes, the overall failure of the German Ardennes Offensive greatly worsened the Wehrmacht's situation. Many soldiers and much equipment were lost. The effort also consumed a substantial portion of Germany's remaining fuel and lubricant stocks, making the Wehrmacht even more dependent on holzgas and horses.

While Skorzeny and his men were away for their mischievous Greif assignment, the newcomers at Friedenthal found themselves with few duties and much time to fret about imminent combat. With the war obviously in its late stages, only the most diehard Nazis were still inclined to takes risks for Hitler and his lost cause. The newly arrived men certainly weren't in that category. The Soviets were already massing at the Vistula River and fast approaching the Oder River. Once across the Oder, there was little between them and the main Nazi hive in Berlin. Toward that end, American and British planes softened up the city with near-daily bombing raids. Some raids involved nearly a thousand bombers.

By the end of the war, Berlin had been the target of 363 bombing missions. The vast amount of housing this destroyed, and the danger the frequent raids posed, led to over a million residents abandoning the urban area. For a city whose prewar population had been 3.4 million, this was a substantial reduction. Yet surprisingly, civilian morale never broke. City workers continued to perform miracles daily clearing rubble and performing repairs on rail lines, airfield runways, and vital streets. Many attacks had already taken place when Fidel passed through the city on his way to Oranienburg. I'd guess when he saw the destruction, he was thankful that his destination was 15 kilometers farther north. He wouldn't be out of harm's way, but would be distant enough to escape the frequent raids on Berlin.

Fidel and his pals had few duties for several weeks after their arrival in December 1944, so they distracted themselves from what lay ahead by going out on the town nearly every night. With passes in hand, they walked some 12 to 15 blocks to what Fidel recalled as the Hotel Lichtenhof in central Oranienburg. This popular spot had a nightclub with a band and a dance floor. And right next door was a restaurant.

The howling wail of air raid sirens was a common sound in Oranienburg because of the many bombers flying to, or returning from, nearby Berlin. Fidel never talked about any raids, but ducking into bomb shelters must have been routine for him, given all the planes passing overhead and the number of times the small city was itself targeted. Today, Oranienburg looks placid, safe, and far removed from the troubles of World War II, but danger from the war still lurks below the surface throughout the city, as a Der Spiegel news magazine reporter made clear when he wrote about Oranienburg in 2016:

> Horst Reinhardt, chief of the Brandenburg state KMBD [Kampfmittelbeseitigungsdienst—police bomb-disposal technicians and firefighters], told me that when he started in bomb disposal in 1986, he never believed he would still be at it almost 30 years later. Yet his men discover more than 500 tons of unexploded munitions every year and defuse an aerial bomb every two weeks or so.[22]

The article goes on to say that between 1940 and 1945 the allied air forces dropped some 2.7 million tons of bombs on Europe, half on Germany. About one in ten bombs failed to explode, and as of 2016, seven decades later, more than 2,000 tons of unexploded munitions were still being uncovered in Germany annually. According to Reinhardt, Oranienburg was the most dangerous city in Germany.[23]

Nazi Germany was at the forefront of nuclear research prior to the war. Nuclear fission was discovered in Berlin in 1938, and during the war period German scientists were known to be experimenting with nuclear reactors to split atoms and release enormous amounts of energy for use as a fearsome new weapon. The fear that they'd succeed in their efforts spurred America to institute the Manhattan Project and build its own nuclear bomb. So when American intelligence assets learned that a chemical company had begun processing enriched uranium in Oranienburg, the head of America's bomb program, General Leslie Groves, became "determined to keep Nazi nuclear research out of the hands of rapidly advancing Russian troops." It is conceivable that the primary reason for the heavy bombing there was to prevent the Russians from acquiring Germany's nuclear bomb research. Of the 13 Allied air attacks launched against the city during the war, the raid of March 15, 1945, a month after Fidel's departure, was by far the biggest, when "In the 45 minutes between 2:51 and 3:36 a total of 4,977 explosive bombs and 713 incendiary bombs rained down from the sky".[24] The following Spiegel excerpt clarifies the motivation for this raid:

> Oranienburg ranked among the top targets of the American bomber fleet. The railway station was a point of departure for soldiers headed for the Eastern Front. At the nearby Auer Werke, uranium was processed for the Nazi's top-secret nuclear research program. A few hundred meters from there stood the Heinkel Aircraft Works and the main vehicle depot of the SS.[25]

Not only was the March 15 raid the largest to target Oranienburg, it also left the greatest legacy of unexploded bombs because of the type of fuse used. These bombs were

> armed not with percussion fuses, which explode on impact, but with time-delay fuses, which both sides used throughout the war in order to extend the terror and chaos caused by aerial attacks. The sophisticated, chemical-based fuses . . . were intended to be used sparingly; US Army Air Force guidelines recommended fitting them in no more than ten percent of bombs in any given attack. But for reasons that have never become clear, almost every bomb dropped during the March 15 raid on Oranienburg was armed with one.[26]

That fuse may have been sophisticated in its day, but today the mechanism's description reads like an invitation for failure.

The fuse contained a small glass capsule of corrosive acetone mounted above a stack of paper-thin celluloid disks less than half an inch in diameter. The disks held back a spring-loaded firing pin, cocked behind a detonator. As the bomb fell, it tilted nose-down, and a windmill in the tail stabilizer began spinning in the slipstream, turning a crank that broke the glass capsule.[27]

The reason so many of the bombs failed to detonate had to do with the local geology. Hundreds struck the sandy soil at an angle and came to rest nose-up, leaving their chemical fuses disabled. The mechanism only worked correctly with the bomb in a nose-down orientation. That allowed the acetone to drip downward onto the disks below, eat through them, and release a spring-loaded firing pin. The bomb detonated when the pin struck the priming charge, but the process could take from minutes to days.[28]

The abundance of unexploded bombs and the expensive disruptions they cause proved a firsthand learning experience for me during a visit to Friedenthal, Oranienburg, and Sachsenhausen in April of 2016. On that trip to Germany, I'd left a one-day window to see these places and to meet with Oranienburg's archivist, Christian Becker. Had my appointment been the following day, the opportunity would have been lost because train travel between Oranienburg and Berlin was halted the entire day after the discovery of yet another dangerous bomb. I wouldn't have missed much with regard to Schloss Friedenthal, where nothing remained of Skorzeny's headquarters. However, the archived information was enlightening, as was

1930s photo showing a business district along linden-tree-lined Breite Straße in Oranienburg. The building that housed the Hotel Lindenhof, where Fidel enjoyed evenings of cards, beer, and dancing during his Friedenthal posting, is in the center of the photo

a tour of the Sachsenhausen camp and Oranienburg itself. Becker was also able to direct me to the street, hotel, and restaurant buildings my father had described. What Fidel had recalled as the Hotel Lichtenhof was on Breite Straße, but he'd misremembered, for it was actually known as the Hotel Lindenhof.[29]

Fidel ventured into Berlin several times by securing a pass. He found the city awash with soldiers and not yet completely in ruins, but admitted he didn't see much of the central city where the damage was concentrated. On one occasion he ventured to the famous Brandenburg Gate. As in Dubrovnik, he'd have liked more contact with civilians there, but perhaps understandably, the locals were shy of SS soldiers. The few he did talk to made it clear that they never thought things would get so bad. As for soldiers stationed in the city, they didn't yet have the feeling of desperation that would set in some weeks later when many checkpoints went up and the public hanging and shooting of deserters began in earnest.

Fidel and most other ordinary soldiers still thought that Hitler would see reason and capitulate rather than see Germany completely destroyed. They believed such a surrender would allow everyone to finally go home. Of course, nearly all Germans hoped that the Americans would arrive in Berlin before the Soviets. They were unaware that President Roosevelt had already ceded Berlin to Stalin. They also didn't realize how unbalanced and ill Hitler had become since the July 20 assassination attempt by military officers. From that time on, Hitler felt betrayed by Germany and no longer cared about preserving any of it.

Skorzeny, however, remained a loyal Nazi. On Christmas Day 1944, his ad hoc Panzerbrigade 150 assemblage disengaged from the Ardennes mission and returned to the Grafenwöhr training grounds to disband. The withdrawal had barely finished when Hitler summoned him to a December 31 meeting. A conversation of several hours convinced Skorzeny that the days of special missions were over, so he granted a month's leave to those of his men whose homes were not yet occupied by the enemy. The majority couldn't go home, so were assigned temporary light garrison duty at the base. As for Skorzeny himself, once he knew Germany could no longer be saved, he set about preparing for the endgame.

---

1. Christian Becker, "Oranienburg in the Third Reich Era," interview by Erich Eipert, April 14, 2010, Oranienburg City Archive. Oranienburg, Germany.
2. Glenn B. Infield, *Skorzeny, Hitler's Commando* (New York: St. Martin's Press, 1981), 23, https://archive.org/details/skorzenyhitlersc00infi.
3. Infield, *Skorzeny, Hitler's Commando*, 1.
4. Otto Skorzeny, *My Commando Operations: The Memoirs of Hitler's Most Daring Commando* (Atglen, PA: Schiffer, 1995), 244.
5. Infield, *Skorzeny, Hitler's Commando*, 46.

6. Skorzeny, *My Commando Operations*, 228.
7. Infield, *Skorzeny, Hitler's Commando*, 74.
8. Terence O'Reilly, *Hitler's Irishmen* (Cork: Mercier Press, 2008).
9. "1936-1945 Sachsenhausen Concentration Camp," Stiftung Brandenburgische Gedenkstätten: Gedenkstätte und Museum Sachsenhausen, accessed May 30, 2023, https://www.sachsenhausen-sbg.de/en/history/1936-1945-sachsenhausen-concentration-camp/.
10. Lawrence Malkin, *Krueger's Men: The Secret Nazi Counterfeit Plot and the Prisoners of Block 19* (Little, Brown, 2008), 25.
11. Malkin, *Krueger's Men*, 104.
12. Adolf Burger, *The Devil's Workshop: A Memoir of the Nazi Counterfeiting Operation* (Barnsley, South Yorkshire: Frontline Books, 2009), 104.
13. Malkin, *Krueger's Men*, 150.
14. Christian Becker, Oranienburg city archivist, "Oranienburg" (Email, April 12, 2010).
15. Christian Becker, Oranienburg city archivist, "Schloss Friedenthal" (Email, November 18, 2019).
16. "World War II Allies: U.S. Lend-Lease to the Soviet Union, 1941-1945," U.S. Embassy and Consulates in Russia, May 10, 2020, https://ru.usembassy.gov/world-war-ii-allies-u-s-lend-lease-to-the-soviet-union-1941-1945/.
17. Kevin Conley Ruffner, "The Black Market in Postwar Berlin: Colonel Miller and an Army Scandal," *Prologue* (National Archives and Records Administration), Fall 2002, Vol. 34, No. 3, https://www.archives.gov/publications/prologue/2002/fall/berlin-black-market-1.html.
18. U.S. Senate committee on governmental operations, "Transfer of Occupation Currency Plates--Espionage Phase," Executive Sessions of the Senate Permanent Subcommittee on Investigations of the Committee on Government Operations (Vol. 4), 3403-3443, 1953, https://www.senate.gov/about/resources/pdf/mccarthy-hearings-volume4.pdf.
19. "502nd SS Jäger Battalion," Military Wiki, October 1, 2015, https://military-history.fandom.com/wiki/502nd_SS_J%C3%A4ger_Battalion.
20. Stuart Smith, *Otto Skorzeny: The Devil's Disciple* (Oxford: Bloomsbury Publishing, 2018), 48.
21. O'Reilly, *Hitler's Irishmen*.
22. Adam Higginbotham, "There Are Still Thousands of Tons of Unexploded Bombs in Germany, Left Over From World War II," *Smithsonian Magazine*, January 2016, https://www.smithsonianmag.com/history/seventy-years-world-war-two-thousands-tons-unexploded-bombs-germany-180957680/.
23. Higginbotham, "There Are Still Thousands of Tons of Unexploded Bombs in Germany, Left Over From World War II."
24. Higginbotham, "There Are Still Thousands of Tons of Unexploded Bombs in Germany, Left Over From World War II."
25. Carsten Holm, "Germany's WWII Duds Get Deadlier," *Spiegel International*, October 3, 2012, https://www.spiegel.de/international/germany/unexploded-wwii-bombs-pose-growing-threat-in-germany-a-859201.html.
26. Higginbotham, "There Are Still Thousands of Tons of Unexploded Bombs in Germany, Left Over From World War II."
27. Higginbotham, "There Are Still Thousands of Tons of Unexploded Bombs in Germany, Left Over From World War II."
28. Higginbotham, "There Are Still Thousands of Tons of Unexploded Bombs in Germany, Left Over From World War II."
29. Christian Becker, Oranienburg city archivist, "Oranienburg," (Email, April 12, 2010).

35 The Risky Mission

With the certainty of defeat looming over Hitler's Berlin military headquarters in January of 1945, a cancer of defeatism set in. The high command's goal had largely devolved to keeping the Russians out of Berlin as long as possible. Jagdverband Mitte couldn't yet play a part in this because Skorzeny was still away from the city, as were most of his veteran soldiers, who'd been given a leave following Operation Greif. Many of Mitte's officers recognized that their unit's glory days were over during this leave and trickled away to serve with active front line units for want of action or out of a sense of duty. SS Jagdverband Mitte continued to exist on paper but was fast becoming a ghost unit.[1] [2]

Skorzeny too saw the handwriting on the wall and set about implementing survival plans, both for himself and others. He'd always been careful to avoid the use of written orders for reasons of operational secrecy as well as deniability for his crimes and self-serving schemes. He hoped that this would be enough to keep him out of an American or Russian prison when the war ended. Then, an insurance policy of sorts fell into his lap when General Reinhard Gehlen approached him and sought help with his own postwar plans. Gehlen led the Army High Command's intelligence unit, Foreign Armies East (Fremde Heere Ost), which coordinated all espionage activities directed against the Soviets. Hence, he possessed many valuable files that the Allies would want to get their hands on after the war. He was a professional soldier who'd become disillusioned enough with Hitler to cooperate with the Wehrmacht's July 1944 assassination plotters. Having played only a minor role, he escaped detection during the subsequent house cleaning in which Hitler exacted deadly revenge on the plotters and their families.

In January of 1945 Gehlen grew even more disenchanted with Hitler for ignoring the general command staff's urgent request to send the 6th SS

Panzer Army to help contain the Soviet Army at the Vistula River. Gehlen warned Hitler that if Reds weren't held at the river, they'd be unstoppable and could reach Berlin at any time. When Hitler ignored the recommendation, Gehlen could no longer be sure his staff would have enough time to destroy all secret intelligence files and still escape. Consequently, he ordered three microfilm copies of all Soviet espionage paper records be prepared and the paper records destroyed. But what he was unable to do on his own was secure the microfilms. Because Gehlen had worked with Skorzeny on several infiltration missions in the east, he trusted the man enough to ask his help in burying a copy of the films in each of three separate mountain locations in the German state of Bavaria. The films, 50 cases of them, were enclosed in waterproof, boobytrapped drums set to explode if opened without the proper procedure.[3]

Gehlen told Skorzeny, "I know the Americans have not even considered building an espionage network in Soviet Russia. After the war ends, they will soon discover they will need such a network. . . . It will be good for us all, Skorzeny."[4]

Skorzeny had no problem taking this on. He was already carrying out similar secret missions for other top Nazis, so he had the drums conveyed to the mountains south of Berchtesgaden in Bavaria for burial. Gehlen's statement about the espionage files was prescient, for the mission later did benefit both men, and the Western Allies too. Despite his disdain for Hitler, Gehlen continued to brief the führer with accurate field intelligence. His information was at odds with Hitler's out-of-touch perceptions and the placating information fed him by some of the rear-echelon generals. Hitler, who could only see the truth as defeatism by then, sacked Gehlen. By ignoring the advice of Gehlen and other professional army commanders about hitting the Soviets hard at the Vistula, Hitler allowed Stalin's attack force to muster a five-to-one numerical advantage at favorable attack points. The Reds then easily rolled through the German defenses. That victory permitted the Reds to proceed rapidly to the Oder River.

Toward the end of January 1945, just weeks after the Ardennes disaster, Hitler foolishly placed Himmler in charge of Army Group Vistula and ordered him to contain the Russians at the Oder east of Berlin. Himmler knew he was unqualified as a battlefield commander so in a panic phoned Skorzeny on the evening of January 30. Over the phone, he promoted Skorzeny to the rank of acting general and ordered him to help by immediately dispatching all of his available forces to Schwedt, on the Oder River north of Berlin. Neither he nor command headquarters had any idea of what was happening there. They knew only that the Russians were moving in that direction, but had no idea how far they'd advanced. Skorzeny immediately cancelled all Friedenthal leaves and drew up plans to send the soldiers who remained at the base to the Oder. By 3 a.m. he'd dispatched two reconnaissance patrols to Schwedt to learn whether the Russians had already taken the city. The rest of his men, Fidel among them, followed two hours later in darkness and driving snow.[5]

As soon as the forward reconnaissance teams learned that Schwedt was still in German hands, Skorzeny informed Himmler. Himmler responded by ordering Skorzeny to secure and hold a bridgehead on the east side of the Odor as a gateway for a German offensive. In compliance, Skorzeny sent a small advance force across the river to set up three defensive rings. The furthest was seven kilometers out.[6]

In the following days, small units from elsewhere arrived to bolster the defending force. Among them were Cossack horse cavalrymen and a regiment of Romanian ethnic Germans. Skorzeny boosted the defenders under his command by corralling the fleeing and retreating survivors of units crushed by the advancing Soviet 5th Shock Army and Soviet 2nd Guards Tank Army. Interestingly, at this point Skorzeny's group became attached to the 3rd Panzer Army under the command of Generaloberst Erhard Raus, who came from my mother's village.[7]

Fidel's anxiety level must have been sky-high when he and his fellow holzgas trainees caught up to the small Jagdverband Mitte commando force dispatched to Schwedt ahead of them the night of Himmler's January 30 call to Skorzeny. He and the other new men were not commandos by any stretch of the imagination and did not relish encountering the Russian forces massing for an assault on Berlin. Fidel found good reason for concern when not long after arrival he and 15 other men were tapped for a frightening mission—scouting behind Soviet lines. After being issued Russian uniforms, cigarettes, and money, the men were informed they'd be trucked across the river to a forward position. Awaiting them there were two captured Russian T-34 tanks and two bulldozers. Each tank was to carry seven men; the remaining two men would operate the bulldozers. Both tanks would have a Russian speaker or two along.

The T-34's interior was a tight fit for its four-man operating crew—so tight that Russian crews called the machine the *pirozhok* (stuffed bun). At least three of the German soldiers would have been required to ride on the deck of the tank. Space wasn't the T-34's only problem. It also had a drive train that failed frequently, a stiff suspension that made for a rough ride, and a transmission that demanded considerable effort to shift gears. A further limitation was poor visibility for the driver and gunner. The latter was particularly troublesome at night, so the Russians commonly put men on the deck to act as guides. I don't know whether or not Fidel knew that the limited visibility actually provided his mission a cover for having soldiers atop the tanks.[8]

The team was told they'd leave the German lines late that night and reconnoiter the Russian positions. The accompanying bulldozers were to clear their road of blocking debris and fill in defensive tank traps so they could pass. Fidel had never done anything like this before, much less ever been in or on a tank. The men were warned not to dismount the panzer until it was back in a safe area. Although the inexperienced men were assured that such reconnaissance had been done before, Fidel wasn't remotely reassured and wanted nothing to do with this mission. It is unlikely that he caught any sleep that night before the mission was to get underway.

Such scouting parties had indeed been sent out in that area earlier. Skorzeny had little reason to lie about this when he wrote after the war, "In the beginning [upon arrival at Schwedt] I sent several detachments as far as possible to the east each day. These strong patrols drove as much as 50 to 60 kilometers behind the enemy lines and caused unrest among the enemy units."[9]

The how and why of Fidel's participation in this scouting mission is something I came to comprehend only after I gained more knowledge of Skorzeny's unit and its structure. That understanding began when I stumbled across the following in a declassified post-war report referring to Skorzeny: "Service Co: ... I-b. Total Personnel appr 80 men." In the Waffen SS table of organization, I-b (or Ib) refers to a supply company.[10]

Fidel was not a highly trained fighter suitable for one of Skorzeny's special commando teams, but his mechanic and driver training did make for a good fit in a service and supply company. The initial information led to other declassified reports, one of which provided a chart of Jagdverband Mitte's order of battle (hierarchical organization and command structure). Other postwar declassified interrogation reports gave a clearer picture summarizing the structure and organization of the supply company and how it blended into the battalion's command structure. One report showed me that the circumstances and timeline of Fidel's movements coincided closely with the movements of supply company elements, specifically the motor section of Mitte's headquarters service and supply company.[11] [12]

With this new understanding of Fidel's supply company role, reasons for assigning him to a risky scouting mission were not difficult to fathom. Like nearly every other German unit at this time, Jagdverband Mitte was sorely short of experienced fighters. As already noted, many of Skorzeny's commandos were on leave or had transferred to other units. The remainder were committed to holding the forward Schwedt bridgehead position. Because Skorzeny surely wished to maintain Mitte's fighting strength, rather than risk more of his valued fighters than necessary in the scouting operation he substituted several rear service personnel, such as Fidel. They were more expendable.

At 1 a.m. Fidel's group was told to be ready to set out at 3 a.m. But that hour came and went without any orders to mount the trucks. Fidel and the others were left to fret and sweat until around 5 a.m., when the mission was scrubbed. I'm sure Fidel hadn't been so relieved since he'd boarded the evacuation ship in the Gulf of Finland and left the Eastern Front the previous year. One explanation for the cancellation of this and other patrols at Schwedt was a recognition by German field intelligence that with the huge Soviet force already in place, such probes were no longer useful or feasible. Skorzeny himself wrote, "From February 5 our reconnaissance

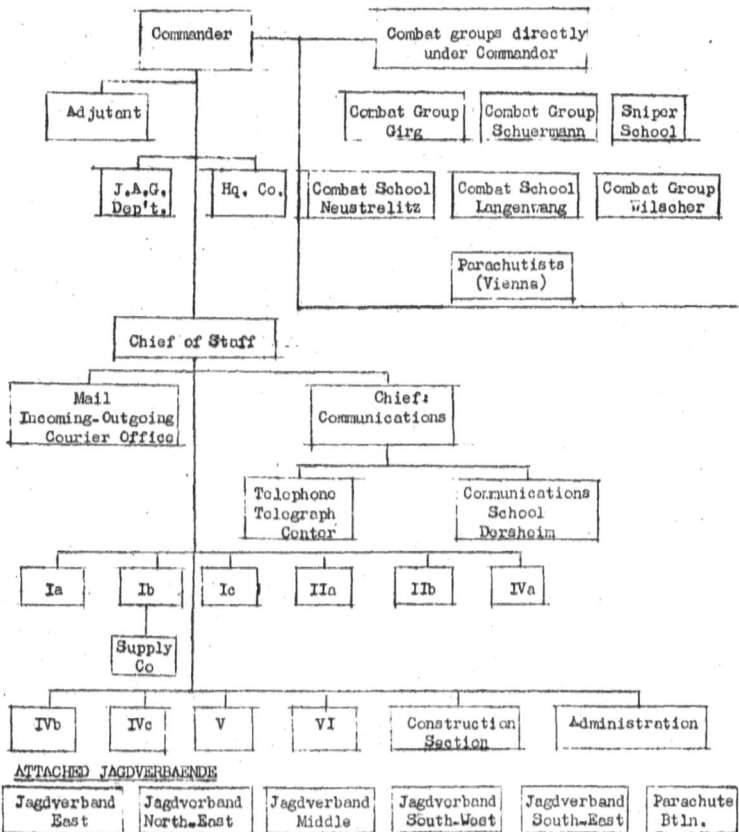

The Order of Battle (organization chart) of Otto Skorzeny's Jagdverbände, as reconstructed by US interrogators after the war. Fidel's movements near the end of the war, because they coincided closely with the I-b supply company's positions and movement, confirmed that he served in its driver and mechanic section. [1]

probes deep into the rear were no longer possible; they encountered a ring of Soviets which was growing ever thicker."[13] It is also likely that like most Nazis in some position of command, Skorzeny could see that the Allies were closing the two fronts at an alarming speed and that it was time to get on with personal survival plans. Toward this end, the supply company took on new value. What happened only hours after the reprieve adds credence to this idea, when without explanation, the entire service company was ordered to pack up and proceed south from Schwedt to Bavaria. Leaving Berlin far behind came as more good news to Fidel.

Skorzeny soon left the front as well to attend to other unknown business. The previously cited US Army declassified report describing the Jagdverbände's order of battle document makes it clear that Skorzeny set about moving his headquarters out of Friedenthal quite suddenly. He later insisted that the orders to transfer his command south came via a Himmler subordinate when Himmler saw the end fast approaching. But other officers reported that Skorzeny issued the orders on his own initiative.[14] [15]

Several sources testified that with the future so uncertain, Skorzeny chose to preserve his combat capability. Friedenthal was too close to Berlin to remain viable as a headquarters.[16] So he chose to relocate his headquarters to what was then the safest remaining German territory—Bavaria. The service company's contingent of drivers, mechanics, and quartermasters that had been of dubious value as infantry soldiers at the Oder bridgehead suddenly became essential for making Jagdverband functional in a new location.

At this time, the German high command still believed that Soviet armor and the re-formed Polish Army were massing at Schwedt for the final push to Berlin. The actual attack point would turn out to be farther north, but Schwedt was still a very dangerous place from which Fidel's luck had again removed him. He'd been in the Berlin area only two months, and at the Oder only days, but that was long enough for him. Shortly after his company passed through Berlin on its way south, the American and British air forces drastically upped their bombing campaign there. Truly massive raids commenced to make new rubble and to bounce that which already existed. Some of these raids pounded the smaller German communities along the Oder and targeted the military defenders stationed there.

Although Fidel didn't know what awaited in the more rural south, Bavaria lay in the path of the American army rather than the much-feared, barbarous Red Army, and combat seemed less likely there than near a hotspot like Berlin The commando component of Jagdverband Mitte didn't have the same luck and remained stuck in place east of the Oder at Schwedt. There, the fighters fortified their positions and awaited promised reinforcements and the launch of a panzer counteroffensive against the

Russians. To prevent Russian tanks from crossing the frozen river and outflanking the bridgehead defenders, German engineer teams kept the river ice broken up with explosives. The Germans were so short of supplies and artillery by then that field commanders fired their barge and truck-mounted antiaircraft guns from constantly changing positions to fool the Soviets into thinking they faced substantial artillery defenses.

Neither Skorzeny nor his superiors knew that the enemy was running its own deception during the time that Skorzeny's small force held the Schwedt bridgehead (February 1 until March 3). The Soviets continued to amass soldiers and equipment for the final assault into Germany, but they'd decided to bypass Schwedt and shift the 2nd Guards Tank Army to a weaker German point farther north even as they quietly sent the 5th Shock Army infantry troops south to Schwedt. Given the dense concentration of infantry troops around Skorzeny's bridgehead position, Fidel's scouting mission likely wouldn't have advanced far before encountering a tragic end.

By early March, Fidel's company had established itself in the vicinity of the Alps in southern Germany, where the scenery was much more agreeable than the panorama of ruined buildings, burned-out vehicles, and shell holes along the Oder in the north. When the German high command finally realized that it lacked the men and supplies to mount a counteroffensive at Schwedt and that the Russians were not going to attack there anyway, Jagdverband Mitte and its attached elements were sent several kilometers south to reinforce another bridgehead at Zehden. There, after a month of heavy combat that added to the battle group's already high losses, Jagdverband Mitte's surviving combat soldiers were pulled back to the Friedenthal base. From there, they too were dispatched south to what Berlin was now calling the Alpenfestung (Alpine fortress) in Bavaria.[17]

Skorzeny's battered battalion was replaced at Zehden by none other than survivors of badly battered Panzergrenadier Division Nordland. Fidel would no longer have recognized his old unit. Nordland had seen so much hard fighting that it was just a shadow of its former self. In retreat, its men had battled the Red Army most of the way from Leningrad. At one stop on that journey—the Courland Peninsula on the Latvian Baltic Coast—it had endured unimaginably ferocious artillery bombardments and frontal assaults time and time again under brutal winter weather conditions. The division had just recently been evacuated from that bloodied German holdout position, only to see itself inserted into another hellacious spot. From there, its men would soon find themselves pushed back all the way to central Berlin and locked in combat, fighting street by street and house by house against an overwhelming number of Red soldiers. One of the few Nordland veterans who made it that far was Fidel's brother Hans. The farmer who'd enlisted as an 18-year-old in 1938 to get his military service out of the way in a matter of months was now 25 years old and had worn a uniform for seven years. And much of that time, he'd been in combat.

---

1. Terence O'Reilly, *Hitler's Irishmen*. (Cork: Mercier Press, 2008), 223.
2. Glenn B. Infield, *Skorzeny, Hitler's Commando* (New York: St. Martin's Press, 1981), 95, https://archive.org/details/skorzenyhitlersc00infi.
3. Christopher Simpson, *Blowback: America's Recruitment of Nazis and Its Effects on the Cold War* (New York, N.Y.: Collier Books, 1989), 41.
4. Infield, *Skorzeny, Hitler's Commando*, 97.
5. O'Reilly, *Hitler's Irishmen*, 229.
6. O'Reilly, *Hitler's Irishmen*, 230.
7. O'Reilly, *Hitler's Irishmen*, 232.
8. T. Christos, "WWII Myths - T-34 Best Tank of the War," Christos military and intelligence corner, July 19, 2012, http://chris-intel-corner.blogspot.com/2012/07/wwii-myths-t-34-best-tank-of-war.html
9. Otto Skorzeny, *My Commando Operations: The Memoirs of Hitler's Most Daring Commando* (Atglen, PA: Schiffer, 1995), 417.
10. Headquarters US Forces European Theater Interrogation Center, "Annex No I - Organization of the SS Jagd Verbaende: Consolidated Interrogation Report (CIR) No 4, p. 21," July 23, 1945, https://www.cia.gov/readingroom/document/519bdeda993294098d515871.
11. Headquarters Intelligence Center, 6825 HQ & HQS Company, Military Intelligence Service in Austria, "First Detailed Interrogation Report: Bolz, Karl Ernst," January 11, 1946, 16, 25, https://www.cia.gov/readingroom/docs/GERMAN%20INTELLIGENCE%20SERVICE%20%28WWII%29%2C%20%20VOL.%202_0003.pdf.
12. Headquarters 12th Army Group Interrogation Center, "Intermediate Interrogation Report: Stubaf Karl Radl," June 4, 1945, 5, https://www.cia.gov/readingroom/docs/RUDL%2C%20KARL_0006.pdf#:~:text=CO%200/Stuf%20Karl%20FUCKER%20came%20in%20Nov%201944.%20Went%20with.
13. David M Glantz, *Soviet Military Deception in the Second World War* (London: Cass, 2006), 527.
14. Infield, *Skorzeny, Hitler's Commando*.
15. Perry Biddiscombe, *The SS Hunter Battalions: The Hidden History of the Nazi Resistance Movement 1944-45* (New York: The History Press, 2006), 351.
16. O'Reilly, *Hitler's Irishmen*, 239.
17. Biddiscombe, *The SS Hunter Battalions*, 351.

36 Alpine Redoubt

In March and April 1945, the final two months of the war, many of the ranking Nazis spent more time attending to their own future than to the soldiers still fighting and dying for them. Skorzeny was no exception. By then he'd made several trips to, and become familiar with, the Alps around Berchtesgaden in the German state of Bavaria and in the adjoining Obersalzberg area in Austria. During his visits, he or his men buried Gehlen's booby-trapped drums containing the microfilmed Soviet espionage records in separate locations. He also used these trips to hide large quantities of Nazi loot for the powerful in Berlin. By then, Berchtesgaden and the surrounding mountains had become central to the plans of Hitler's Nazi lieutenants, for that was where they expected Hitler to make his last stand. Inner-circle functionaries such as Martin Bormann, Herman Göring, and Albert Speer even sent their families to this fallback in preparation for what was to come.

Bormann, Hitler's private secretary, had gained vast wealth and power by controlling access to Hitler. He engaged Skorzeny to move the most transportable part of his fortune—gold bars and other valuables—to the Alps. The bulk of his gold came from tooth fillings extracted from murdered Jews. The fillings had been melted down and molded into bars by an arm of Degussa, a large chemical company.[1] In 2003 that company was embarrassingly caught in the spotlight when a news story noted the incongruity of winning a contract to provide a graffiti-proofing chemical to protect a new Jewish Holocaust memorial in Berlin when during the war a subsidiary of that company had produced a chemical to kill some of the very Jews being memorialized. That chemical, Zyklon B, was used in Nazi gas chambers.[2]

Another powerful Nazi, the devious chief of the Security Police and the Gestapo, Ernst Kaltenbrunner, hired Skorzeny to help hide 50 kilograms of gold bars, 50 cases of gold coins and artifacts, two million Swiss francs, two million US dollars, a valuable stamp collection, and five cases of precious stones. Adolf Eichmann, the notorious Kaltenbrunner underling heavily involved in the logistics of the Jewish final solution, hid a further 22 metal crates filled with Nazi records and gold for Kaltenbrunner. In the process of hiding Kaltenbrunner's booty, Eichmann didn't forget to conceal his own loot and set up several Swiss bank accounts for himself.[3]

Although Skorzeny helped Eichmann move his booty, Eichmann apparently didn't share the final location of his hiding places with Skorzeny. Following Eichmann's capture and abduction from Argentina by Israeli agents 15 years later, reports like this one appeared:

> According to Paris Presse, Eichmann, entrusted in 1944 with the task of hiding various Jewish treasures, also took charge of many valuables buried in a forest near the Austrian village of Maria Enzeldorf. Those treasures were reportedly buried by Russian prisoners of war, commanded by a high Nazi, who ordered the Russians killed to hide their secret. Later, it is alleged, Eichmann had those treasures reburied, and he is now supposedly the only man alive who knows where the valuables are. These valuables, the Paris Presse said, included a large ransom given to the Nazis by the Rothschild family in payment for the lives of some members of the Rothschild family.[4]

In addition to burying treasure, Skorzeny offered another service—escape preparation for rich industrialists and Nazi criminals like Eichmann. A part of that service involved shifting large quantities of liquid assets and valuables to neutral countries in defiance of Hitler's orders that such assets only be used to help pay for the war. No one knows how much of the stolen wealth that couldn't be exported was hidden around mountainous Berchtesgaden. The Alpine lakes in the area were suspected to be the prime hiding spots. At least many treasure hunters thought so because in later years several drowned in them while trying to find the caches. Only bits of the booty were ever recovered: a farmer dug up a hoard of over 10,000 gold coins while plowing, and a fisherman supposedly snagged a box of counterfeit dollar-printing plates from the Töplitzee (Lake Toplitz).[5] If true, the latter were likely the plates that had been under development in Friedenthal because a substantial amount of British currency was also recovered from the lake.[6]

When the wealth concealment was in full swing, Skorzeny became concerned that all the arriving trucks and the strange burials were arousing too much local curiosity, so he proposed opening several small SS hospitals in the area. Ambulances marked with a red cross could then be used to cover the transport of the gold, gems, and money. The Eichmann treasure is believed to have reached Obersalzberg in this way, prior to it being hidden by Eichmann.[7]

Stories of hidden loot abounded. One in particular has long been the object of treasure hunters. In the dying days of the Third Reich, Heinrich Himmler supposedly ordered his brutal deputy, Ernst Kaltenbrunner, to loot the Berlin Reichsbank of valuables and send them south on an armored train to the Alps. In one version of the story, allied air attacks and advancing Russians disrupted the plan, so the treasure had to be loaded onto wagons and buried in a secret location by subsequently executed prisoners. Yet other stories have the train reaching its intended destination. One version even had the train being driven into a mountain tunnel or a salt mine that was subsequently blasted shut.[8]

Some of the treasure stashing occurred because the hardcore Nazis pictured financing a postwar resistance in the Alps with this loot. Kaltenbrunner was executed without ever revealing the supposed treasure train's location or the burial sites of his personal stash. Like many other important Nazis, in the closing days of the war he fled Berlin by plane and left ordinary soldiers to die fighting the Russians. He got as far as his Austrian homeland, where a US military patrol arrested him on May 12, 1945. "In the garden of his villa, buried among the beetroot, was found 76 kilograms of gold in six bars—a small portion of the train's cargo."[9]

The largest loot recovery demonstrates the scale of Nazi theft. Near the war's end General Patton's Third Army discovered a cache within the Merkers Mine in Germany, 200 miles southwest of Berlin. An entire army battalion was assigned to guard the five entrances to the mine and secure the surrounding area. "Thirty-two ten-ton trucks from the 3628th and 4263d Quartermaster Truck Companies were made available" to hastily transport the recovered booty to a place of safekeeping because "under the Big Three arrangements at Yalta, the Merkers part of Germany would be taken over by the Russians after the war and they certainly needed to get the treasure out of the area before the Russians got there."[10]

The Americans had good reason to make such a fuss about this find. The Merkers treasure included much of the precious artwork the Nazis had looted throughout Europe, as well as a substantial portion of the Reichbank's gold reserves. Much of the latter had been plundered from other countries. A hasty inventory of one sealed room indicated that the vault contained much more than bales of paper currency from various countries. The following is just a partial list:

> 8,198 bars of gold bullion; 55 boxes of crated gold bullion; hundreds of bags of gold items; over 1,300 bags of gold

Reichsmarks, British gold pounds, and French gold francs; 711 bags of American twenty-dollar gold pieces; hundreds of bags of gold and silver coins; hundreds of bags of foreign currency... and 110 bags from various countries.[11]

Skorzeny is suspected of being behind a large shipment of gold, secret blueprints, machine tools, and other valuables sent to Argentina from the coast of Spain by U-boat for the support of escaped Nazis following the war. Whether true or not, Argentina did become a Nazi safe house because its government was controlled by Nazi sympathizers Juan and Evita Peron.[12]

When in early 1945 the Nazi inner circle began contemplating how to flee Berlin without inciting Hitler's wrath, they concluded that leaving was too dangerous until Hitler led the way. They reasoned that at some point Hitler would go to ground at Berchtesgaden but wouldn't take that step without having in place a strong Alpenfestung (Alpine fortress). This so-called "fortress" would likely consist of defendable mountainous terrain controlled by protective troops and cached supplies. Some of the Nazis even deluded themselves into believing that America would welcome the German military strength preserved in the Alpine fortress because the Soviet Union would shortly fight the Americans in an attempt to seize all of Germany. However, Berchtesgaden's appeal as a retreat died when Hitler announced he'd remain in Berlin until the end. At this point his henchmen could only hope that there was actually something behind the German propaganda machine's hype about a secret weapon that would still turn the tide of the war.

The redoubt, or fortification, idea first emerged in late 1943 when Germany's military fortunes had eroded enough to make the idea of an imminent collapse of the Reich no longer unthinkable. Himmler devised a fallback plan that included a retreat to southern Bavaria and Austria with units of his Waffen SS waging a guerrilla war from fortified underground strongholds sheltering Nazi leaders. The strongholds would contain factories, hospitals, and warehouses stocked with huge supplies of munitions and food. Himmler thought the war could be carried on from there for years if necessary. Hitler considered such a plan unnecessary because he still believed Germany would win the war. The idea also smacked of defeatism, so Alpenfestung planning proceeded only to an elementary stage.

The German populace was never fully convinced that an Alpenfestung existed because of all the other Nazi propaganda lies throughout the war, but toward the war's conclusion it was the US military command and its intelligence branch that the Nazis most wanted to deceive about the holdout preparations. Author and historian William Manchester wrote that the American military was obsessed "with the myth of the Alpenfestung, . . . the National Redoubt in the south to which the Fuehrer would withdraw for a last stand. No one knew exactly where the fortress was supposed to be, but SHAEF (Supreme Headquarters Allied Expeditionary Force) had tentatively circled Berghof, Hitler's celebrated retreat at Berchtesgaden. Berchtesgaden was within a few miles of Salzburg."[13]

An American news correspondent, Wes Gallagher, may have been the first to spread the fortress story when he wrote in late 1944 that Himmler had "started laying the plans for underground warfare in the last two months of 1943." Gallagher wrote that Nazi leaders were planning to flee to the Alps once the military was beaten in the rest of Germany and from there would continue to wage war on Hitler's enemies through a sabotage and guerrilla campaign.[14]

Historian William Manchester explained how the idea spread among America's generals and intelligence heads.

> In 1944 rumors of a formidable defense system in the Austrian Alps reached Allen Dulles, who sent Washington a warning from Switzerland. Somebody on Massachusetts Avenue talked out of turn at a cocktail party in a neutral embassy, a coded dispatch was relayed to Berlin, and Goebbels elatedly exploited the fable. By Christmas every American commander, including General George Marshall, believed it. "After the Ruhr was taken," Eisenhower's chief of staff General Walter Bedell Smith wrote the year after the war, "we were convinced that there would be no surrender at all so long as Hitler lived. Our feeling then was that we should be forced to destroy the remnants of the German army piece by piece, with the final possibility of a prolonged campaign in the rugged Alpine area of western Austria and southern Bavaria known as the National Redoubt."[15]

When Nazi propaganda chief Joseph Goebbels learned the Americans were buying into the idea, he directed his disinformation machine to reinforce the impression. Only then did the concept gain sufficient traction within the Nazi hierarchy to update the concept and actually initiate construction. The new plan envisioned a scattering of underground headquarters, housing, and factories with production lines for arms, munitions, and the world's first jet fighter. This plane, the Messerschmitt ME-262, was already being assembled in limited quantity in underground facilities not far away. But the situational reality was, it was far too late to begin building a mountain fortress.

Only beneath Hitler's retreat facility at Berchtesgaden was fortress construction being taken more seriously. The fortification preparations there had been underway since late 1943 when Allied bombing raids began to worry Hitler and his underlings. And the construction was still going on in 1945. Two portions of the vast, elaborate tunnels and bunker system under this Alpine town can be experienced firsthand by visiting the Dokumentation Obersalzberg Museum. For me, nothing brought out the reality of that era more than a walk through those tunnels and shelters.

Goebbels cared less about convincing the German populace than the enemy that a strong redoubt existed. To misdirect Eisenhower, he even formed a special department to spread rumors. But by March 1945 the Allies were advancing so rapidly against the collapsing German forces that field commanders realized the Germans no longer had the means to dispatch a significant military force to the mountains. The mountains certainly presented a natural fortress for a last stand, but to whatever extent the Alpenfestung existed then, it lacked the agriculture and industry to sustain a self-contained bastion. Nevertheless, Goebbels's efforts and those of the SS intelligence service kept belief in the fortress alive by printing phony blueprints, construction reports, and records that indicated a large military buildup and a substantial amount of supply and armament production. So Eisenhower kept Patton's Third Army heading toward the mountainous area.[16]

Eventually, even Hitler began to believe that some form of the redoubt actually existed because in late April, about a week before his suicide, he ordered the German government to evacuate to the Alpenfestung. By then it was far too late to carry out such orders because Berlin's ruins were already surrounded by masses of Russians. Hitler's directive also ordered the man in charge of Germany's POWs, SS Obergruppenführer (lieutenant general) Gottlob Christian Berger, to move 35,000 Allied POWs to the redoubt to serve as hostages against attack and as a bargaining chip in negotiations. That transfer was no longer realistic, either. Much earlier during the war, Berger had served as the SS recruiting chief and played a large role in delivering Fidel and his fellow ethnic Germans to the Waffen SS.

Nearly every powerful Nazi made self-serving statements after capture, but there was likely a kernel of truth in Berger's testimony that Hitler intended to execute the 35,000 hostages if a deal with the Allies couldn't be struck. Berger maintained that with the aid of Hitler's mistress, Eva Braun, he took a great risk to prevent a POW massacre. He claimed Braun arranged for Berger to meet with Hitler so he himself could get the typed copy of the execution order signed by Hitler and thereby keep it out of the hands of those willing to carry it out.[17]

Berger further contended that Hitler assigned him the task of intercepting a group of *prominente* (celebrity) hostages who were being taken to the redoubt as bargaining chips. Among them were relatives of Winston Churchill and King George VI. Berger stated that he'd been ordered to shoot them all, but instead, he escaped Berlin, located the prisoners, and ferried them from camp to camp until they could be delivered to the American military.[18]

The redoubt plan may not have amounted to much, but it had a disproportionately large impact on the war and the Cold War that followed. Despite the doubts of several American intelligence officials that a plan to defend the Alpine region actually existed, the American military hierarchy took the threat seriously. For them, the evacuation of a few high-ranking German officials and their offices from Berlin to southern Germany seemed to presage the enemy's plans to continue the struggle. Hence, in one of his most controversial actions of the war, General Eisenhower decided not to assault Berlin, the Nazi capital, and instead "ordered American and British forces to clear the northern and southern flanks. The role that Allied intelligence played in changing the course of the war in these last months still intrigues military and intelligence historians."[19]

Had Eisenhower's forces pushed north, as British Prime Minister Churchill and the British command begged him to do, Berlin and parts of eastern Germany could have surrendered to, or been taken by, American troops instead of the Red Army. This would have reduced Stalin's postwar influence in Western Europe. Instead, the territory was left to Stalin as had been agreed to in early February 1945 when the three chief Allied leaders—Franklin Roosevelt, Winston Churchill, and Joseph Stalin—met in Crimea to plan the final stage of the war at what is known as the Yalta Conference. There, these leaders agreed to the division of postwar Germany and Berlin into occupied zones administered by US, British, French, and Soviet forces, putting Stalin in control of a substantial part of Germany. The administration of the occupied areas was under the principle that the German people were owed nothing beyond a minimum subsistence.

Weeks later, as Eisenhower directed the American Third Army south to the Alps and the illusory Festung instead of north to Berlin, the general had enough cause to break the Allied agreement reached at Yalta, for Stalin had by then already broken nearly every pledge he'd made to Roosevelt and Churchill. By sticking to the letter of the agreement instead of listening to sensible British pleas to head for Berlin, Eisenhower cost the Western Allies an enormous amount of postwar influence, grief, and taxpayer dollars.

Map of the Nazi Alpine fortress (Alpenfestung) position in southeast Germany. The largely illusory fortress, or redoubt, was primarily a propaganda operation meant to mislead Allied intelligence units into concluding that an actual armed resistance had been organized. Points relevant to Fidel's postings are marked on the map. The inset shows the map's position relative to neighboring countries. Background map: Google Earth, Image Landsat / Copernicus

Skorzeny became involved with the redoubt when the idea of a zone of resistance captured the attention of the Nazi inner circle. Although it quickly became obvious to him that on a large scale the idea was just another pipe dream, he sensed opportunity and a path to self-preservation. Only a few preparations, like the underground factories that produced the V2 rocket, had begun. Skorzeny wrote, "We—Radl [Skorzeny's adjutant] and I—found the mountains, the glaciers, the forests, the wild streams all in 'their place,' but not a trace of military preparation or of fortification."[20]

The commando leader hadn't advanced from sergeant to acting general in four years through timidity. With military structure and oversight crumbling in Berlin, opportunities for enterprise and independent action abounded. A limited resistance operation looked supportable to Skorzeny, given the abundance of treasure floating around to support it. Such an undertaking merely needed a man to lead it. With events moving rapidly at this juncture, he had no time to waste. Even while his soldiers were still engaged in bloody fighting on the Oder, he prepared for a presence in the Alps and hoped to field several thousand fighters. So early in February, around the same time that Fidel and the service company were sent to

Bavaria, Skorzeny ordered a copper mine at Mitterberghütten, Austria, be stocked with tons of weapons and explosives.[21]

In a self-serving argument after the war, Skorzeny claimed that he was ordered to transfer his headquarters to an area west of Salzburg in the south to assist in establishing the Alpenfestung in the Austrian Alps. At least one Skorzeny biographer says that the evidence argues otherwise: "Although Skorzeny later suggested that he was 'ordered' into the Alps, there is no record of any senior echelon either devising or controlling such a shift of forces, and Radl later claimed that Skorzeny simply decided on his own initiative to leave Friedenthal . . . escaping the enemy advance."[22]

Another biographer provided further details about the headquarters move and later withdrawal of the surviving Jagdverband Mitte commandos from the Oder front.

> The Jagdverband headquarters staff (with the exceptions of Radl and Gerhard, who remained in Friedenthal) had been forced to move from its temporary location at Hof in Bavaria to Achthal near Teisendorf, west of Salzburg. By mid-April Skorzeny had won his tussle with OKW [German High Command] over Karl Fucker [a Jagdverband field officer]; and the 250 surviving members of Mitte were dispatched to Friedenthal, which was days away from capture by the Red Army, Radl shut up shop and accompanied them southwards on their march to Achthal, where they arrived around 20 April.[23]

The ultimate rationale behind Skorzeny's actions appeared to be based on the same hope as that of other important Nazis: following the breakup of the American and Soviet alliance, the resulting war between the two powers would make the SS and the Nazis a welcome American ally. Following the withdrawal of his Jagdverband Mitte commandos from the Oder to Friedenthal in early April, Skorzeny directed that battalion and two other depleted SS Jagdverband battalions to Linz, Austria. There, he merged these 400 to 500 fighters into a new unit he called the Alpine Guard Corps (Schutzkorp Alpenland, or SKA). From a hidden area location, he ordered seven platoon-sized units to establish positions in various out-of-the-way Alpine locations. One of these teams, commanded by an officer named Wilscher, was sent to the Mitterberghütten copper mine near the Austrian town of Bischofshofen.[24][25] That general location, along with the service company's headquarters in Achtal near the Bavarian town of Teisendorf, were to become central to my father's story both at the war's conclusion and afterward.

These actions and events all support the notion that Fidel's company owed its sudden extraction from the Oder front at Schwedt to Skorzeny's ambition and self-preservation scheming. Establishing a new headquarters in Bavaria was necessary to give him an Alpine fallback position once Berlin and the rest of Germany was occupied by the Allies. The rural, mountainous terrain allowed Skorzeny the necessary operating room and secrecy to use his force to further his own interests, whether that involved hiding, escaping, or setting up some form of resistance.[26]

In the Reich's final days near the end of April and the beginning of May 1945, the German military command structure disintegrated. Soldiers not engaged in fighting for their lives in rearguard actions against the advancing Russians were not waiting around to be captured by the Reds. Those still able to ride, walk, or crawl were rushing west as fast as possible to surrender to the American or British Army. When the Russians approached Linz, Skorzeny too slipped westward into the mountain redoubt zone to set up a temporary command post in the village of Annaberg, Austria. But instead of leading any guerrilla activity from there, he contented himself with hiding.

---

1. Glenn B. Infield, *Skorzeny, Hitler's Commando* (New York: St. Martin's Press, 1981), 97, https://archive.org/details/skorzenyhitlersc00infi.
2. "Nazi Row Hits Holocaust Memorial," *BBC News*, October 27, 2003, http://news.bbc.co.uk/2/hi/europe/3219199.stm.
3. Infield, *Skorzeny, Hitler's Commando*, 98.
4. "Eichmann Reported Knowing the Location of $750,000,000 Hidden by Nazis," Jewish Telegraphic Agency, April 10, 1961, https://www.jta.org/1961/04/10/archive/eichmann-reported-knowing-the-location-of-750000000-hidden-by-nazis.
5. Infield, *Skorzeny, Hitler's Commando*, 99.
6. Steve MacGregor, "The Mystery of Lake Toplitz: Reputed to Be The Dump For Nazi Gold, Platinum Bullion & Jewelry," War History Online, January 13, 2019, https://www.warhistoryonline.com/instant-articles/mystery-of-lake-toplitz.html.
7. Infield, *Skorzeny, Hitler's Commando*, 98.
8. Allan Hall, "Treasure Hunter Discovers £500million Nazi Loot in Forest but Landowner Blocks Dig," Express.co.uk, July 31, 2017, https://www.express.co.uk/news/world/834735/nazi-treasure-forest-germany-excavation-permission-landowner.
9. Hall, "Treasure Hunter Discovers £500million Nazi Loot in Forest but Landowner Blocks Dig."
10. Greg Bradsher, "Nazi Gold: The Merkers Mine Treasure," *Prologue Magazine*, National Archives and Records Administration, 31, no. 1 (Spring 1999), https://www.archives.gov/publications/prologue/1999/spring/nazi-gold-merkers-mine-treasure.html.
11. Bradsher, "Nazi Gold."
12. Infield, *Skorzeny, Hitler's Commando*, 192.
13. William Manchester, *The Arms of Krupp, 1587-1968* (Boston: Little, Brown, 2003), 613.
14. Nick Ottens, "The German National Redoubt That Wasn't," Never Was, August 21, 2012, https://neverwasmag.com/2012/08/hitlers-last-stand-in-the-alps/.
15. Manchester, *The Arms of Krupp, 1587-1968*.
16. Charles B. MacDonald, *The Last Offensive*, United States Army in World War II: European Theater of Operations (Office of the Chief of Military History, U.S. Department of the Army, 1973), chap. XVIII p. 407, http://www.ibiblio.org/hyperwar/USA/USA-E-Last/, chap. XVIII p. 407.

17. John Nichol and Tony Rennell, *The Last Escape: The Untold Story of Allied Prisoners of War in Europe, 1944-45* (New York: Viking, 2003).
18. Nichol and Rennell, 366.
19. Kevin Conley Ruffner, *Eagle and Swastika: CIA and Nazi War Criminals and Collaborators, Draft Working Paper* (Washington, D.C.: History Staff, Central Intelligence Agency, 2003), chap. 4, p. 6, https://archive.org/details/EagleAndSwastika/mode/2up.
20. Otto Skorzeny, *My Commando Operations: The Memoirs of Hitler's Most Daring Commando* (Atglen, PA: Schiffer, 1995), 428.
21. Perry Biddiscombe, *The SS Hunter Battalions: The Hidden History of the Nazi Resistance Movement 1944-45* (New York: The History Press, 2006), 352.
22. Biddiscombe, *The SS Hunter Battalions*, 351.
23. Stuart Smith, *Otto Skorzeny: The Devil's Disciple* (Oxford: Bloomsbury Publishing, 2018), 227.
24. Headquarters US Forces European Theater Interrogation Center, "Annex No II - Final Disposition of the Jagd Verbaende: Consolidated Interrogation Report (CIR) No 4, p. 27," July 23, 1945, https://www.cia.gov/readingroom/document/519bdeda993294098d515871.
25. Biddiscombe, *The SS Hunter Battalions*, 353.
26. Terence O'Reilly, *Hitler's Irishmen*. (Cork: Mercier Press, 2008), 245.

37 On to Bavaria

Fidel said that when the early February 1945 reconnaissance mission in Russian tanks at the Oder River was called off in the wee hours of the morning, his company of about 100 pulled back to the Berlin area. The company would have needed to collect personal belongings, supplies, rations, gear, and travel orders in Friedenthal. This preparation for the 550-kilometer rail passage to Bavaria commenced about a week into February, as Fidel recalled. The journey itself took some 10 days and was agonizingly slow for several reasons. Locomotives were in short supply due to intensive bombing and strafing of the transport system by Allied planes. When one was available, it and the train often needed to wait to avoid ongoing air raids down the line. Emergency repair work on damaged tracks and bombed-out rail yards also caused many a delay. Sometimes the train had to stop because the tracks needed to be held open for higher priority military trains. These difficulties made the journey a series of short daylight hops, with an occasional night leg thrown in.

The urban damage to the cities the train passed through was massive, but the countryside still looked surprisingly normal to Fidel through the coach windows. And the stations weren't yet packed with the hordes of refugees from the east that would soon clog them. At a long stop in the state of Thüringen, Fidel became separated from the rest of his company and ended up sleeping in a house for three days while he searched for his unit. Whether this separation resulted from playing cards, foraging for food, or just sightseeing, I regret not asking. Fidel said that luckily, he found the company again just before the train pulled out. Eventually one morning, his group disembarked in the picturesque Bavarian town of Teisendorf. That community was a mere 20 kilometers from the German-Austrian border, and even closer to Hitler's Berchtesgaden villa.

Fidel never learned why his company was dispatched to the Teisendorf vicinity in southern Germany, or just why the company's headquarters office was set up in tiny Achthal (sometimes spelled Achtal), a cluster of several houses, instead of in the more populous Teisendorf or Oberteisendorf where Fidel and the rest of the supply company were staying. But even without specific knowledge of what Skorzeny was up too, Fidel probably recognized that the two towns were large enough to billet the men without attracting too much curiosity, but not small enough to hide secret activities the way Achtal was.

The company, on foot, had barely left Teisendorf's train station when it encountered several army soldiers trying to revive a dead military holzgas truck. The vehicle had stalled, and the men couldn't restart it. The stranded soldiers asked the new arrivals if anyone knew how to get the vehicle going again. Fidel wasn't the only holzgas operator in the company, but he was the only one who offered to work on the truck. So the company commander left him to the job while the rest of the men moved on. My father could never have guessed how much this effort would later reward him and affect the course of his life.

Fidel went to work building a fire in the firebox as he'd done each morning during his weeks of training. He was aware that this truck model was normally started on gasoline, but because there was none available, kept working on the machine. Eventually, he deduced that the wood fuel was of such poor quality that it didn't burn hot enough to get the system operating. As the afternoon slipped away, the soldiers with the truck realized that it would be not going anywhere that day and drifted off.

Hunger overtook Fidel around four that afternoon. After rummaging through the truck but finding nothing to eat, he realized that feeding himself in his current situation demanded resourcefulness. Although he hadn't found any food in the truck, he did turn up a pair of civilian trousers and a shirt. He knew that clothing was in short supply throughout Germany, so he took the clothes to a nearby farmhouse to barter for food. The young woman who answered the door took an immediate liking to Fidel and fed him bread and bacon in exchange for the items. Then, as he was leaving, she shoved the clothes back into his hands and told him to return later that evening after her father was home. "He'll probably pay for the clothes all over again," she said. And sure enough, the farmer fed him again.

Fidel slept in the truck that night and again the following night after a long and futile search for a bit of gasoline, which was what was really needed to start the engine. Still, his situation wasn't something that caused him despair, since he was on his own and no one bothered him. By the time the soldiers returned on the third day to check on their vehicle, Fidel had made some arrangements. After the fire was stoked and burning, he fetched a truck and a chain from a nearby mill where he'd arranged for a worker to help him. Fidel then chained the running truck to the dead truck and instructed the mill's driver to start towing. When the balky holzgas truck had gathered enough speed, Fidel popped the clutch with the transmission engaged and the engine sputtered to life.

The repair adventure caused Fidel to lose track of his unit again. Although this separation in that rural setting seemingly offered a chance to slip away altogether, desertion was still too risky. Even at that late juncture of the war, it was hard for a healthy young man without proper identification papers to remain invisible. The Gestapo (state police) and the vicious Feldgendarmarie (Wehrmacht military police) actively hunted for deserters to hang. Fidel's current duty was about as good as it got, and in Bavaria the Russians were farther away than the Americans. It probably even seemed possible to him that the war would end without any real fighting here in southern Bavaria.

By questioning locals, Fidel learned his company was bivouacked a few kilometers away in the town of Oberteisendorf. He walked there and located his companions without trouble. The unit spent the remainder of February and half of March in the vicinity of Teisendorf and Oberteisendorf. Fidel said the locale was the most beautiful he'd ever seen. Both towns were within a valley and surrounded by gentle hills that were covered with small, verdant fields. To the south the valley was rimmed by the majestic Bavarian and Austrian Alps.

The assignment puzzled the men because they had no real duties. The district was very rural and lacked any obvious war production facilities or military installations. The nearest military base was in Berchtesgaden where a Waffen SS protection detail guarded the vacation homes of Hitler and other top Nazis. The Allied bombers and fighters that occasionally filled the sky as they passed overhead would have made short work of any worthwhile targets.

These bombers mainly pummeled Vienna and other targets to the east in support of the Russian advance. The German Luftwaffe was all but nonexistent by then and had little fuel for the planes that remained. Most of the Luftwaffe airmen that once flew and maintained aircraft had been reassigned to the infantry. A standing joke went, "When silver airplanes fly overhead, it's the Americans; when the planes are green, it's the British; when no planes fly, it's the Luftwaffe."

The service company men realized how extremely lucky they were to be in their station and eating well. Almost everywhere else, soldiers were hungry, for supply lines had largely ceased to exist. Around Teisendorf, Fidel worked on vehicles when the need arose, but, like the other soldiers, spent most of his time playing cards, drinking watery wartime beer, exchanging rumors, and flirting with the local girls. He and his companions were well aware that the longer they were here, the less likely that new orders would find them, given the chaotic situation in Berlin. The 314 bombing raids inflicted on the city by the end of March had turned 16 square kilometers of its center into rubble and greatly degraded the military's ability to command. Effective communication and coordination were all but gone.

Because Hitler refused to surrender and was determined to bring Germany down with him, remnants of divisions, regiments, and battalions continued to be sacrificed in rearguard actions meant to hold back the Reds so that other soldiers could escape and surrender to the Americans or Brits.

The combatants that Skorzeny brought south after withdrawing them from the mauling they'd received at the Oder River were said to be equipped with 70-watt wireless transmitters that allowed Skorzeny and his headquarters staff to coordinate movements and dispense orders. It was probably such a radio that delivered new orders to Fidel's company in early April. Undoubtedly, the men feared that the new orders would put them in harm's way. However, they were merely directed to proceed to a storage area in the vicinity of Salzburg to collect a number of trucks. Fidel recalled a short stay at a place he thought was called Neukirch before crossing into Austria and spending three or four days in Salzburg.

The 10 trucks the soldiers found were gasoline-burning, nonmilitary vehicles with TELEFUNKEN lettered on their sides. Telefunken was a large German telecommunications equipment maker. Fidel said that these trucks had cargo beds that measured about 2.5 by 3.5 meters and carried a number of full fuel drums. Some of the trucks looked almost factory new. He didn't mention the make, but they were probably the civilian version of the Wehrmacht's versatile work horse, the three-ton Opel Blitz—the most ubiquitous German truck in the war. The model had been in production since 1937, but none had been allocated for civilian use in some time. Late in the war when Opel could no longer build enough of these trucks to replace those lost or destroyed, Daimler Benz began to assemble them as well.

The soldiers were surprised to find such trucks sitting unused during an acute transport shortage. That the vehicles came with precious drums of fuel was even more startling because many a German military vehicle sat abandoned for lack of gasoline. It was obvious that whoever was behind the new orders was well connected.

In light of all the Nazi loot-burying, the presence of these trucks might best be explained by Skorzeny's efforts to help the Nazi elite preserve their wealth. If these were indeed trucks that been used to ferry Nazi loot to

Bavaria, the most likely point of origin was Berlin, the seat of Nazi power, which also happened to be the location of Telefunken's main facilities. With the Russians poised to encircle the city, another round-trip run would no longer have been feasible, which left the trucks available for some other purpose. Fidel and the other men would neither have known nor cared about Skorzeny's side activities. Their sole concern now was not being among the last soldiers to die for Hitler. From the collection point, half the company was ordered back to the Teisendorf locale with five of the trucks. Fidel and the rest were directed to drive the newest trucks into the Austrian Alps.

Any new fears this order raised in Fidel were surely miniscule in comparison to those the scouting mission along the Oder River had provoked, for here the front was far away and no Russian tanks and uniforms were involved—only German civilian trucks. And Fidel was quite happy to keep his current attire, as were the other eight or ten holzgas mechanics in the company. These men still wore the comfortable black leather jackets and matching leather trousers issued at the holzgas school upon completion of their training. The leather was warm and comfortable, but what Fidel liked best about the outfit was that it wasn't readily identifiable as a Waffen SS uniform, or even as a uniform at all, because it carried no insignia. He anticipated that this would be helpful after the war ended.

The leather uniforms had an interesting history. Early in the war the German Navy received orders to deliver a large supply of them to the Italian Navy. In 1943 after the Italians switched sides, the 1st SS Panzer Division Leibstandarte SS Adolf Hitler was ordered to Italy to help disarm Italian forces. It captured a large supply of these uniforms and subsequently issued them to 5th SS Panzer Division Wiking's panzer crews because the leather offered a degree of protection against fire—a hazard in tank battle. The rest apparently ended up back in Germany and made their way to other Waffen SS supply rooms. Buchenwald issued them to holzgas school graduates as protective clothing. The Hitlerjugend SS division (12. SS-Panzerdivision Hitlerjugend) panzer crews were also known to wear them. Hitlerjugend was formed in 1943 of 17-year-old Hitler Youth boys led by officers and NCOs from Leibstandarte SS Adolf Hitler.[1] [2]

Fidel's group headed up into the Austrian Alps south of Salzburg in the newly acquired trucks, as instructed. The 75-kilometer drive to their destination was scenic and remained uneventful because the small convoy didn't pass anywhere near targets worthy of an Allied air attack. The road passed small farms, cut through forests, and skirted mountains, but encountered no signs of war. No further orders awaited them at Bischofshofen, their destination. And once again, they were assigned no specific duties. Fidel mentioned that there was no other military presence in the town, but the place did have a Volksturm contingent made up of men way too old to serve as active-duty soldiers and also a few young boys.

Creating a last-ditch defense force was an idea that had floated around Germany for years. Implementation came about only in the final months of the war when the necessity of reassigning rear-area soldiers to the battle fronts left no one else to defend the homeland. Just as in my mother's village in the Sudetenland, unwilling old men and indoctrinated young boys were conscripted into the makeshift Volksturm force throughout the Reich and issued whatever odd assortment of weapons were available. Because the ersatz soldiers received no real military training, they stood no chance against seasoned combat soldiers.

Fidel noted that in Bischofshofen this militia consisted primarily of men in their sixties or beyond. Germany's resource shortage precluded a real uniform for the Volksturm, so its members normally received only an identifying armband. But surplus or obsolete uniforms from other services were sometimes issued if available. In Bischofshofen, the local Volksturm contingent was outfitted with the distinctive tan uniform of Organisation Todt—the previously mentioned Nazi-era civil engineering and construction consortium that built the German autobahn and designed the field stove used by German soldiers like Fidel in Russia. During the war the OT had been heavily involved in building fortifications to fend off Allied offensives. The most notable of these was the extensive *Atlantic Wall* defenses that ran from Norway to the Bay of Biscay. Somehow, a supply of OT uniforms had found their way to the Alps.

To learn more about why Skorzeny had dispatched Fidel's company to Teisendorf, Achtal, and Bischofshofen, I renewed my search for my father's military records from pertinent German archives. When none turned up, I resorted to an in-person search of the indexes to the 70,000 rolls of captured German microfilm at The US National Archives in Bethesda, Maryland. When nothing was found there either, I could only conclude that the records pertaining to foreign Waffen SS recruits like Fidel were lost or destroyed when events moved swiftly and division bases were overrun by the Red Army in Central and Eastern Europe. As for field records, by then commanders frequently improvised on the fly and soldier clerks were either in retreat or poised behind rifles instead of typewriters. Toward the end, with the war lost and organization falling apart, many units no longer even had a base to which records could be sent.

As I learned more about Skorzeny, it appeared increasingly probable that Fidel's company was a part of the Alpenfestung scheme. When I described the circumstances of Fidel's Bavarian assignment to Franz W. Seidler, a German historian who'd studied and written about the phantom

Alpenfestung, he agreed that an association of the service company with the redoubt scheme seemed likely. His translated message reads,

> Without my being able to document it, I think the observations about the last assignment of your father in Bischofshofen is probable. During the last weeks of war, several units of Wehrmacht and Waffen SS were ordered to southern Germany . . . without being told what to do there. The preparations for the Alpine fortress remained fragmentary. A scientific detailed analysis suffers from the fact that there are no files for the final phase of the war, especially no war records. The historians are limited to the assertions of the time.[3]

Not until an advanced draft of this book came together did I finally come across actual corroborating evidence that Fidel's unit was a part of the Alpine redoubt effort that Skorzeny slapped together. The following excerpt from a book about the Hunter Battalions states that Skorzeny established a headquarters at Achtal.

> According to a declassified US Army intelligence report, "Radio intercepts suggest that his [Skorzeny's] headquarters . . . by 24 April . . . was based at Achtal, where one observer described the organization as consisting of twenty officers and 170 men, many of them bearers of the Blutorden [Nazi Blood Order decoration] and the Golden Combat Badge and all bristling with armament."[4]

This paragraph from a declassified report specifically notes a I-b supply department in Achtal:

> Ia denotes the first staff officer, Ib the supply officer, and V the engineer officer. When source came to Station 2 in Achtal in April 1945 WALTER immediately ordered new transfers to Station 3 in Eben and Mitterberghuetten. He himself and his staff (with the exception of Ib and Section V) transferred to Eben. In Achtal, Station 2, he prepared Combat Groups GIRG, SCHUERMANN, and WILSCHER . . . . In Station 2 he had his headquarters in a villa outside of town [Achtal], where Section Ia was also located.[5]

Yet another declassified American interrogation report details Skorzeny's establishment of a I-b section in Bischofshofen, which was next to the mine referred to above as Mitterberghuette.

SKORZENY
RADL
H/Stuf BESEKOW
H/Staf SCHMIEL
O/Stubaf WALTER
O/Stuf SCHROETTER
O/Stuf Dr GRAF
Frl KOPFHEISER
The sisters KRUEGER
signal personnel and guards.

An I-b department was established in BISCHOFSHOFEN. The Service Co and maintenance section under Stubafs BLUMENTHAL and UEBERSCHER joined 6Pz [6th Panzer] Army.[6]

The following paragraph extracted from the findings of an Austrian researcher describes Skorzeny's Alpine redoubt activities, which underpin the basis of Fidel's postings to Skorzeny's activities at Achtal, Bischofshofen, and Mitterberghütten:

> At the end of February, 1945, after heavy fighting at Schwedt on the Oder, Skorzeny was ordered to Berlin, and afterwards in early March came to Bad Aussee in the Salzkammergut region. In the heart of the so-called "alpine fortress", which became the vanishing point of the Nazi elite, Skorzeny assembled between 250 and 300 men from various SS special forces. Around April 28, 1945, he named the force Schutzkorps Alpenland (Alpine protection force). Although as he himself admitted, the SKA "as a corps of the army, possessed nothing more than the name."[7]

A large weapons, ammunition and explosives depot was created in a copper mine in Mitterberghütten. Additionally, ten tons of supplies, enough for a small guerrilla army, were transported to Achtal. At the end of April 1945, the SKA built defenses and laid in supply depots and related sites. Then the group of commandos was broken up into small units of malleable strength that were dispersed to higher Alpine pastures. They remained in contact with each other via radio through the central station, "Carrier pigeon." A leadership group of 10 men was located in Annaberg, while the other detachments were placed around Bischofshofen.[8] To sum up, Skorzeny initiated his vision of final resistance in the Alps by establishing a base headquarters, transferring enough support personnel there to reconnoiter and staff the support facilities, and concealing the necessary military supplies and arms. Billeting Fidel's company in proximity to these supply dumps and securing trucks and fuel was a part of that operation. With the dispatch of half the supply unit and trucks to Bischofshofen, Skorzeny would be in a position to distribute the supplies and arms to his dedicated combat soldiers.

The hiding of munitions at Achtal and Mitterberghütten clearly dovetails with the supply company's dispatch to the Alps and the timeline of their movements thereafter. Fidel never learned exactly what their mission was in 1945 because Skorzeny and his lieutenants obviously hoped to protect themselves and the operation by keeping their scheme from the lower ranks until there was a need to know. Had I been able to put all this together 20 years earlier, Fidel could have had his curiosity about the nature of his Achtal/Teisendorf and Bischofshofen postings satisfied. And with that understanding, he would have seen how lucky it was that Skorzeny hadn't escalated matters by ordering the delivery of the secret munitions and supplies to his dispersed commando groups.

The rapid advance of the American army was almost certainly the reason the resistance plan fizzled out, as was noted in the interrogation of another Skorzeny associate, Karl Ernst Bolz.

> A year later on 1 November 1944 he was assigned to the SS Jagdverbaende with the rank of Obersturmfuehrer. This was a special assignment and sabotage unit, which even then was preparing to continue resistance after Germany's defeat. He was again charged with supply, quarters, and rations. The American advance, however, became too quick for the Jagdverbaende to set up the planned nest of resistance in the so-called Southern Redoubt. In April 1945 the unit began to disintegrate, and BOLZ left the organization.[9]

Prior to my discovery of the interrogation documents, the simplest explanation for the truck acquisition was that they'd been discovered accidentally. But after the US Army reports clarified Skorzeny's machinations at the war's close, it became obvious that the trucks and fuel were not in the locale by coincidence. Military caches, trucks, mechanics, quartermasters, and drivers all went hand in hand, and their convergence in the Alps had been arranged.

With no real duties in Bischofshofen, Fidel and his companions passed the time just as they had in the Teisendorf area. The war intruded only when waves of Allied bombers passed overhead. These planes never attacked nearby, but a wave of fear undoubtedly swept over Fidel each time this happened for no one who's been on the receiving end of an aerial bombing raid forgets the terror those planes unleash. Bombers had already hit the historic city of Salzburg several times before Fidel arrived at Bischofshofen, but before the war ended a month later, the tally had risen to 15 and left nearly half the buildings in the historic and militarily insignificant little city in ruins.[10]

Fidel's worst fright probably came on the morning of April 25 when 359 bombers from three British bomber groups, along with hundreds of fighter escorts, stacked up in the vicinity. The primary target that day, Berchtesgaden, was controversial for it was a place with only symbolic importance. Some of the bombers targeted secondary targets in the region, but the British bombing planners were determined to make a statement by thoroughly obliterating Hitler's Berghof chalet and the vacation homes of the other top Nazis. The high mountains made it difficult for the lead aircraft to mark the main targets, forcing the rest of the raiders to circle overhead. The final results were less than stellar because smoke soon filled the valley and obscured the targets, which were small enough to make them difficult to hit even under optimal conditions.

However, the sheer number of bombs assured that the SS guard barracks, administration buildings, and homes of Hitler's associates were all heavily damaged. Hitler's Berghof chalet was only moderately damaged by the two bombs that hit it, but the fire started by the matches the SS struck inside the building under Hitler's orders finished the job. After viewing the chalet's site, I could better understand the compound's sad but interesting history, which I described in my earlier book about my mother's wartime experiences.

> In the construction of the complex that grew around Hitler's house, workers demolished over fifty buildings, including houses, hotels, and a sanitarium for handicapped children.... The finished structure, Schloss Berghof, comprised 60 rooms filled with expensive furniture, rugs, and art. The enormous cost befitted the führer's ego. The complex eventually swelled to 80 buildings and included SS barracks, administrative offices, a hotel for important visitors, and a large greenhouse to satisfy Hitler's vegetarian diet all year round.[11]

Hitler's Eagle's Nest retreat atop nearby Kehlstein Mountain escaped damage entirely. Some claim that the complex wasn't targeted earlier in order to avoid accidentally killing Hitler, who the Allies considered their most valuable inside man due to his disastrous military leadership. Anyone who has visited the Eagle's Nest on Kehlstein Mountain via the shuttle bus or the foot trail that was once the steep road Hitler's car negotiated, would understand why the bombs missed the structure. The compact building perched atop the peak's tiptop appeared as a mere pinhead to the planes.

Hitler's Kehlsteinhaus, or Eagle's Nest, was the capstone of the complex. The little mountaintop chalet boasted a stunning view 3,000 feet above the main compound. Hitler's private secretary, Martin Borman, commissioned its construction to commemorate Hitler's 50th birthday. The project cost several hundred million inflation-adjusted dollars and the lives of 12 of the 3,000 construction workers who toiled around the clock for 13 months. The access road, an engineering marvel itself, terminated on a small plateau 400 feet below the chalet. From there a tunnel led to an elegant elevator finished in polished brass. Tourists today can either hike 2,600 feet up the trail to the chalet or board a bus from a parking lot where an SS barracks once stood. At the Kehlsteinhaus sightseers can enjoy a meal and a beer while taking in the panoramic view. I preferred the strenuous hike, but the ride also offers breathtaking views from the dedicated buses equipped with special brakes. Ironically, the expense and effort of the construction was wasted, for Hitler felt claustrophobic in the tunnel and feared the heights at the top. The few times he visited, he stayed only a few minutes.

When American and French troops arrived at the main Berchtesgaden complex nine days after the bombing, they found Hitler's Berghof chalet extensively damaged by the bombs and fire and already ransacked by locals. After they'd finished scouring it for souvenirs, they blew up the remains. To keep the site from becoming a Hitler memorial, the military declared it off limits to Germans until 1952, when the US Office of Military Government returned Obersalzberg to German control under the condition that all remaining Nazi ruins be removed. However, the American military was aware of the stunning setting that attracted Hitler and adapted a portion of the locale for use as a recreation area for its occupation troops.[12]

Hitler was already holed up in his Führerbunker under the Reich Chancellery building in Berlin when Skorzeny began his machinations in the Alps. Only in late April, with the Red Army on the outskirts of Berlin and the Nazi regime in shambles, did Hitler, in the throes of a nervous breakdown, finally acknowledge that Germany was defeated. Despite his delusional and paranoid state, no one dared oust him from power because of the Nazi fanatics who still stood by him. Hitler's paranoia was so great by then that he even questioned whether the cyanide capsules he'd obtained for his own suicide were genuine, so he had someone test one on his dog Blondi. At 1 a.m. on April 29, Hitler married Eva Braun. Later that same day Hitler learned that Italian partisans had killed Mussolini and strung him up by his heels. Just 40 hours after the marriage, Hitler and

Braun committed suicide. The Russians were by then barely half a kilometer away. To avoid an ignoble fate like Mussolini's, Hitler left instructions for both bodies to be carried outside and incinerated with gasoline in a pit.

Even before the news of Hitler's suicide reached Bischofshofen, Fidel and the other men knew that the end was very close. They were now too isolated to be ordered into battle, and further military action no longer

"Hitler Dead" headline from the May 2, 1945, edition of Stars and Stripes, the official US Army newspaper.

served much purpose, anyway. It was common knowledge that the Russians had advanced into Austria on March 30 and captured Vienna two weeks later. This rapid advance was surely frightening because if the Reds secured the Austrian side of the border with Germany, Fidel and the others would no longer be able to surrender to the Americans in Bavaria. Still, for fear of being shot as deserters, they dared not leave. And according to Skorzeny's postwar testimony, there was good reason for that.

> Schutz Korps Alnenland. SKOIZENY stuck to the following account of the Schutzkorps. when he observed the conditions in Upper Austria, where desertions were out of hand and entire units were withdrawing without proper authority, he suggested the organization of a stragglers patrol to Gau Leiter EIGRUBER. For this purpose Schutz Korps Alpenland was formed. It consisted of... seven groups with a total strength of appr 250 men.[13]

Quite interestingly, according to postwar testimony, Radl implied that by late April Skorzeny saw the futility of resisting the American advance from the west and passed along new directives to his officers to assist the local inhabitants and help assure an orderly takeover by Patton's army. Hindering the Russians coming from the east was not barred. Whether Radl responded truthfully in the following postwar interrogation (with regard to his and Skorzeny's new benign attitude toward the rapidly advancing American Army and the end of resistance) or fabricated convenient lies to soften his punishment is unknown.

> 3. INTELLIGENCE ACTIVITIES: . . .
>
> At the threat of the Russian advance on Berlin, SKORZENY took his command (SS Jagdverband) to the Oder front where they remained until mid-April 45. In April SKORZENY withdrew his 400 to 500 SS men (without orders from higher headquarters) into Austria in order to escape the Russian advance and:
>
> (1) Preserve law and order, and prevent plundering.
>
> (2) Prevent communistic organization from functioning.
>
> (3) Uphold the southern front as much as possible.
>
> ...at the same time a six point order was written by Subject of approximately the following content"

(1) No further belligerent activities against the west front and strict obedience to occupation troops when they come.

(2) All weapons were to be immediately collected.

(3) Continue resistance against Russia if occasion rose and prevent the functioning of communist organizations.

(4) To protect the public from marauders and robbers.

(5) To help farmers in agriculture and reconstruction. and to place Other German soldiers in the vicinity as helpers to the farmers.

(6) To prevent the political and other refugees from preying on the local population for food, etc.

…This order was issued two days before the arrival of American troops and contacts were made with commanding officer immediately by a representative sent by SKORZENY. Arrangements were also made to contact SS Oberstgruppenfuehre HAUSER and to arrange the surrender of his 13th (or 4th) SS Korps.[14]

---

1. Georges Bernage and Hubert Meyer, *Album historique: 12. SS-Panzer-Division Hitlerjugend* (France: Editions Heimdal, 1991).
2. "SS Panzer Leathers," *Axis History Forum*, 2006, #6, https://forum.axishistory.com/viewtopic.php?t=113132.
3. Franz W. Seidler, "Alpenfestung" (Email, March 18, 2017).
4. Perry Biddiscombe, *The SS Hunter Battalions: The Hidden History of the Nazi Resistance Movement 1944-45* (New York: The History Press, 2006), 352.
5. Headquarters Intelligence Center, 6825 HQ & HQS Company, Military Intelligence Service in Austria, "First Detailed Interrogation Report: Bolz, Karl Ernst," January 11, 1946, 2, https://www.cia.gov/readingroom/docs/GERMAN%20INTELLIGENCE%20SERVICE%20%28WWII%29%2C%20%20VOL.%202_0003.pdf.
6. Headquarters US Forces European Theater Interrogation Center, "Annex No II - Final Disposition of the Jagd Verbaende: Consolidated Interrogation Report (CIR) No 4, p. 27," July 23, 1945, https://www.cia.gov/readingroom/document/519bdeda993294098d515871.
7 Thomas Riegler, "Otto Skorzeny Und Das „Schutzkorps Alpenland"," Geheimes Österreich (Secret Austria), May 3, 2015, http://oesterreichterrorismus.blogspot.com/2015/05/otto-skorzeny-und-das-schutzkorps.html.
8. Thomas Riegler, "Otto Skorzeny Und Das ‚Schutzkorps Alpenland'".
9. Headquarters Intelligence Center, U.S.D.I.C. , United States Forces in Austria, U.S. Army, "Preliminary Interrogation Report: Bolz, Karl Ernst," October 19, 1945, 2, https://www.cia.gov/readingroom/docs/GERMAN%20INTELLIGENCE%20SERVICE%20%28WWII%29%2C%20%20VOL.%202_0003.pdf .
10. "Salzburg's History: Coming a Long Way," Visit-Salzburg, accessed August 10, 2022, http://www.visit-salzburg.net/history.htm.
11. Erich Eipert, *The Secret She Carried: A Perilous Odyssey Through the Time of Hitler* (Turnbuckle Press, 2015), 301.
12. Eipert, 302.
13 Headquarters US Forces European Theater Interrogation Center. "Annex No II - Final

Disposition of the Jagd Verbaende: Consolidated Interrogation Report (CIR)" No 4, 28, July 23, 1945. https://www.cia.gov/readingroom/document/519bdeda993294098d515871.
14. 307th Counter Intelligent Corps, 7th Army, "Interrogation of Radl, Karl, German, SS Sturmbannfuehrer, Personal Adjutant to SS Obersturmbannfuehrer Skorzeny, Otto, Head of RSHA Amt VI S.," May 28, 1945, 3, https://www.cia.gov/readingroom/document/519bdeda993294098d515875.

38 Out of Uniform

On May 7, 1945, a month after Fidel arrived in Bischofshofen, word of Germany's capitulation spread rapidly through the village. The war was to officially end at 11:01 p.m. the next day. Despite an expectation of POW confinement, Fidel and the other men were enormously relieved to learn their military service was finally over. They'd survived when millions of others hadn't. And until they were confined by the Americans, they wouldn't be under anyone's command but their own for the first time in at least two years.

With the harsh consequences of desertion removed, the men's concern became exiting territory that might soon be occupied by the Russians. No one relished a Soviet bullet through the back of their head or a slow death in Siberia. Even though the war would not formally end until late that night, on the morning of May 8 the soldiers wasted no time in dumping their weapons, packing up their personal possessions, and hopping aboard their trucks. They left via the same road they'd come on and expected to pass through the American lines at the German border in a couple of hours.

Unexpectedly, the trucks carried them only eight or ten kilometers in the direction of Germany on the narrow mountain road. The men could drive no farther because several trees much too large for them to move had been felled across the road to stop all traffic. The soldiers may have feared the barrier was created by a Russian advance party, but in light of declassified testimony, the trees were almost surely dropped by one of Skorzeny's commando teams concealed in the area. This idea is also supported by a postwar memoir in which Skorzeny wrote that on May 1 he received his last military orders from Wehrmacht High Command South. Among them were instructions to "prevent the Anglo-American troops from entering Austria."[1]

The trucks were of no further use, so the soldiers pushed them off the edge of the road and sent them crashing down a steep slope to keep them out of the hands of the Russians, should they arrive before the Americans or end up in control of Austria. Along with the trucks went any remaining transport capability Skorzeny might have had at Bischofshofen. This demolition was the last action of the men as a unit. Once done, the group of 40 to 50 men said their goodbyes and set out on foot in small clusters. Separation lessened their chances of being apprehended all at once by the Russians, but I suspect it was just as much an assertion that they were now in control of their own lives.

Fidel said he relied on a cane and limped along at a slower pace than the other men because he'd injured his leg in Bischofshofen not long before. But a good friend named Richard, a fellow ethnic German from Romania, stuck with him. After many kilometers, the two men came to a small river bridge guarded by American GIs. *GI*, generally interpreted as *government issue* or *general issue,* was a term commonly used during World War II to refer to American soldiers. It appeared to Fidel and Richard that the guards were there simply to prevent some overzealous Nazi from blowing up the bridge. Fidel and Richard waved their Romanian passports at the guards, but they weren't interested in the papers of unarmed soldiers hurrying to surrender to the US military police. The soldiers simply pointed west and, on a map, indicated a surrender point further along the river.

Another two kilometers of walking brought the pair to a recently liberated Polish POW work camp. Richard, who wore a regular Waffen SS uniform, was ignored by the Poles, but Fidel's leather holzgas trousers and jacket caught their eye. The Polish prisoners knew they outnumbered the now powerless German soldiers and forced Fidel to strip off the uniform. They also stole nearly everything else the men carried, including personal items. Surrendering soldiers were forbidden to carry weapons by the terms of surrender, so when the Poles found two cartridges in a pocket of Fidel's stolen clothes, they grew even more belligerent and accused Fidel of hiding a pistol. Fidel defused the situation by calmly explaining that he'd never had a pistol and the bullets were for the rifle he'd tossed away in Bischofshofen. This reassured the Poles enough to let the pair move on.

Luckily, Fidel didn't need to proceed in his underwear because they let him keep a worn and faded OT (Organization Todt) uniform he'd packed along. An old man back in Bischofshofen had given him the outfit, since his Volksturm group had a large supply of them. Fidel intended to use it as a work outfit later because it looked more civilian than his regular Waffen SS uniform, but never expected to have to wear the dingy thing on the road.

A little farther down the road they spied another bridge—a busy one. Germany lay on the other side, and many German soldiers were crossing under the eyes of GI guards. The sun was setting and since the pair was in no hurry, they decided to spend a night of freedom in Austria. I would guess that when they realized the Americans weren't actually chasing down German soldiers, the two began to entertain the idea that perhaps they could avoid the unpleasantness of a POW camp altogether by finding a quiet bridge over which to sneak into Germany early the next morning. However, that bridge had to come along in short order because the river road would soon reach Salzburg, an urban area sure to be crawling with *Amis* (German slang for American soldiers).

The two men didn't wish to sleep on the ground that night, so they stopped at a nearby Austrian police station to ask where they might bunk indoors. A policeman directed them to a tiny hovel across the road. The accommodations were not very comfortable, but the place was close to the bridge they'd just avoided. After the police loaned them a couple of blankets to ward off the chill, the pair settled in for what they expected would be a good night's sleep. Unfortunately, that first night of freedom turned out to be anything but restful. The blankets were so flea infested that the men lay awake all night scratching bites.

With the help of the fleas, Fidel and Richard woke up early on May 9 and left the shack. When they found the street deserted, and no American guards in sight yet at the border bridge or the road into Germany, the pair scurried across the bridge as fast as Fidel's injured leg would allow. Their reentry into Germany proved far less problematic than they'd feared as they scratched and worried all night. They knew that no matter what happened now, they were already beyond the grasp of both the Reds and the Waffen SS, and with any luck, the American MPs as well. Bavaria was a large area to occupy, and the US Army couldn't have soldiers watching every little village. Having already spent two months around Teisendorf, Fidel believed his familiarity with the area could keep him out of a POW camp. He might have thought twice about this had he known at the time that the American army was setting up a large POW enclosure right outside of Teisendorf.

The thoughts of freedom vanished near Bad Reichenhall. The pair's luck seemed to run out when two GIs pulled alongside them in a jeep and motioned for Fidel and Richard to hop into the back of the vehicle. Dejectedly, the men complied. It looked as if they'd let their hopes get too far ahead of reality and they were about to join the large group of soldiers taken into custody the night before at the border. But the jeep had driven barely a kilometer when a second jeep pulled alongside. A soldier in the other vehicle passed on fresh orders to the men in their jeep, then zoomed off. When their captors shouted, "*Raus, raus*" as they motioned for Fidel and Richard to climb out, the two of them were only too happy to oblige. They could hardly believe their luck.

Both Fidel and Richard had seen enough barbed-wire enclosures during the war to know that sleeping out in the open on the ground with constant exposure to sun, rain, and mud was not something to relish. The unexpected release presented them a second chance and infused them with a new determination to avoid capture. Fidel learned later that if not for the lucky jeep encounter, he'd have been reunited with his entire Jagdverbände supply company comrades, for the half of his company that stayed behind in Bavaria ended up in the same enclosure as the Bischofshofen half.

Following their close call with the MPs, the men left the road and thereafter moved cautiously through fields and farm lanes toward Teisendorf, where they knew the lay of the land and a few residents who could help them in their quest to elude the American MPs. The closer Fidel and Richard got to Teisendorf, the more determined they became to avoid confinement. This heightened caution cost them most of the daylight hours.

As Fidel walked on, he undoubtedly pondered the future. His concerns wouldn't have had much to do with Germany, for he had no plans to stay. As soon as conditions normalized in Romania, he intended to head home to the family he hadn't heard from since the mail service cutoff eight months earlier. Had he known that not even a short visit would be possible for two decades, he'd have despaired. As it was, even learning the fate of relatives and friends would take months, and in some cases, years.

---

1. Otto Skorzeny, *My Commando Operations: The Memoirs of Hitler's Most Daring Commando* (Atglen, PA: Schiffer, 1995), 435.

39 Magdalena and Josef

Fidel's sister Magdalena thrice saw her world turn upside down. She was just three years old the first time. On that occasion she learned that joy or excitement could quickly turn to sorrow and grief. Her young mind had scarcely adjusted to the change in family dynamics that followed the birth of her brother Fidel when her father died only four days after the birth. Magdalena was still too young to hold on to a clear memory of Johann's presence, but his absence remained with her throughout her childhood.

Magdalena's extended family tried to relieve some of the sense of loss and abandonment the young girl felt on being left fatherless, but the void was hard to fill. Some portion of her childhood was subsequently lost as adult responsibilities fell upon her sooner than they would have otherwise. Yet, because she grew up in a community with a strong farming tradition, she became imbued with the security of knowing that even when tragedies strike, families with land do not starve. It was comforting to know she'd inherit her share of the family's farmland and thereby secure the same protection for her offspring when she married. Never in her wildest dreams could Magdalena have imagined that not long after her world turned upside down a second time—again through the tragic death of a loved one—that a third shock would upend the security that land ownership brought and bring about a nightmare of slave labor.

When young Magdalena finished the fifth grade in Orzydorf's school, her mother chose to send her to a private school with a more academic curriculum—a girl's boarding school run by nuns in Perjamosch (now Periamos). Magdalena felt homesick at first, but never lonely or isolated because a cousin and several other Orzydorf girls attended the same school. She was also looked after by relatives who lived there—particularly her father's aunt, the town postmaster.

After two years in Perjamosch, the Great Depression intervened and Magdalena Sr. could no longer afford the boarding school fees. Magdalena soon got over the disappointment because in this period of adolescence she quickly made new friends. In her middle age she described what followed as "the most carefree time of my life." At age 15 she became part of an inseparable circle of seven girls "who did everything together." One of their most anticipated activities was the weekly Sunday afternoon dance in a local gasthaus. After mass and their families' midday meals, the girls got together and made their way to the dance. In the spring of 1935 she met Josef Eipert, her future husband, at this weekly dance. Josef was already 25—an advanced age in that community for a farmer to still be single.

Magdalena said that the two of them fell in love without ever actually discussing marriage. Everyone else already knew they would wed, but the subject of matrimony didn't come up between them until two of Magdalena's friends married, one right after the other in July and August of 1935. Weddings were such a major festivity in Orzydorf that after the August wedding Josef half-jokingly said that it was their duty to provide the next celebration. Magdalena took it as a proposal and became a bride at age 16. Conveniently, her Josef came with the same surname as hers, so she didn't have to practice writing a new name.

The community guidelines and traditions that helped assure an economically viable future were sometimes problematic for young people wishing to marry, but for them things fell together smoothly. Their grandfathers had long since realized a union was coming and had already hashed out the business end of the marriage—the all-important details about which land parcel each family would settle on the couple.

Fidel said that Josef greatly enjoyed sports. Being one of the most talented soccer players in the area kept him playing for the top local team long after his peers had dropped out. Josef was also a good student—clever enough that he could go on to secondary schooling elsewhere and enter a profession. With Josef being the second son in the family, his parents had anticipated this course and had settled their entire Ganzegrund of land on his older brother when he married. But Josef wanted to farm too, so his parents had to buy more land. They found enough near the village of Vinga to allow Josef to match what his bride brought to the marriage—the Halbgrund Magdalena Sr. had inherited when she'd married.

The couple took up residence in the bauernhof of Josef's parents in a new house built across the courtyard from the original one. The hof was a bit smaller than the one Magdalena had grown up in, but it suited her well. The new residence was on the opposite side of town, but Orzydorf wasn't so large that it kept her from visiting her mother and brothers often. The new family prospered and brought a daughter, Leni, into the world in 1937. Fidel well remembered playing with his niece when she was a toddler. He particularly liked to tease the little girl. One of his favorite ways involved a nail in the side of a work table from which his mother hung the pail she used for making cottage cheese. Fidel would suspend Leni's doll from the nail to provoke a squeal.

The household bliss was shattered when the World War II hostilities began and Josef, who was in the active reserves, was called up for duty in the Romanian Army. Instead of sending him to the front, his orders took him to Mühlbach, a town in Transylvania where he joined the support staff of a medical company that operated ambulances. Whether this assignment came of luck, scholastic aptitude, or an officer bribe is unknown. He and his family could only hope this assignment would keep him closer to home and away from the harsh and dangerous front lines. When I sought information about his service half a century later, even Magdalena could recall little more than him receiving one home leave.

By the time Germany launched Operation Barbarossa, the 1941 German offensive against the USSR, Romania had become a German ally and was obligated to help support the German effort with troops. In doing so, the Romanian leadership expected to regain the territories of Bessarabia and northern Bukovina, which the country had recently been forced to cede to Stalin. Josef's division became one of many dispatched to the USSR. Josef's job as a medical company quartermaster kept him behind the front lines and allowed him to exchange letters with Magdalena nearly every week, even after things started going badly for Germany in Russia.

After Himmler and Hitler coerced the Romanian government into sending its ethnic German soldiers and conscripts to the Waffen SS in mid-1943, Josef was one of few Orzydorf men who remained in the Romanian Army. The Romanian generals tried to retain their military specialists when the agreement went into effect, but it was Fidel's experience that within days the Romanians caved in to German pressure and released many specialists as well. Josef, either by choice or exemption, was able to remain with his Romanian division. He likely concluded that his chances were better as a supply sergeant in the hapless Romanian Army than as a front-line combatant in the German Waffen SS.

The already desperate Romanian ground situation became truly nightmarish after the disastrous German capitulation at Stalingrad in February 1943. The defeat allowed the Russians to mount massive offensives and retake territory held by shorthanded German and Romanian forces. By autumn the Reds had recaptured most of the important industrial Donets Basin in Ukraine. Sadly, this was a region that Russia would fight to take over a second time 79 years later in 2022 when it was a part of independent Ukraine.

For Stalin, the wholesale conscription he implemented in recaptured areas netted him numerous replacement soldiers to throw against the reeling German and Romanian forces. One of the places he would send the fresh Donets conscripts to was Josef's last battlefront posting—Krim (Crimea). The following excerpt from an online World War II history website describes the Soviet conscription practice:

> As soon as a town or city was reoccupied, the civilian men were immediately given a uniform and a rifle and sent to the front where they were expected to quickly master the art of war or die. This method of conscription replaced tens of thousands of casualties sustained in the previous fighting. With that extra force, the Red Army was able to push the Germans west, across the Dnieper River.[1]

Two years before Stalingrad, the Germans had anticipated easily rolling through Crimea after all but annihilating the Soviet Army in Operation Barbarossa. Then extreme weather, the great distances within the Soviet Empire, and Hitler's disastrous interference in military operations bogged down the German war machine along much of the front and saved the Russian forces from total defeat. Only in the south could the German drive proceed. Crimea was critical to Hitler's plans. Should the Soviets hold onto it, they'd be able to launch crippling air attacks on the vital Romanian oil refineries and storage facilities that supplied 75 percent of Germany's oil imports. Hitler also needed the strategically important Crimean supply port and naval base at Sevastopol as a jumping off point in his plan to seize Russia's essential Caucasus oil fields. Without control of the Crimean Peninsula on their flank, the Germans could only advance so far into Ukraine. When the German forces assigned to take the peninsula encountered difficulties, a large component of the German force waiting to advance further eastward into Ukraine had to be diverted to help. But before the reinforced German battle group could reach the Crimea's main defensive fortification at Sevastopol, a Russian counteroffensive from the north forced the Germans to split their forces. The Reds took advantage of this situation to heavily reinforce Sevastopol.[2]

The final German effort in Crimea was led by one of Hitler's most able field commanders, Erich von Manstein. Despite difficulties, von Manstein's soldiers advanced rapidly and by mid-November held all of Crimea but for Sevastopol and its naval port. The fortifications protecting this city were formidable—a huge fortress built into a high limestone foreland amidst difficult terrain. Inside the fortress were massive concrete bunkers sheltering naval guns that could fire far inland as well as out over the water. The inner fortress was further protected by a dense ring of forts and defensive lines extending outward for 15 to 20 kilometers. All in all, it was one of the most secure bases in the world.

The Germans blasted right through all three defensive rings, but before they could penetrate the main fortification, the Soviets brought in enough reinforcements to halt the drive. The Red Army also landed three armies on the Kerch Peninsula to the northeast, forcing von Manstein to divert some of his troops to protect his flank and keep the Russians from breaking through a critical choke point. The Red Army tried four times to dislodge the Germans and took massive casualties each time. The fourth attempt, as described in an excerpt from America's National War Museum, finally allowed the Germans to resume the drive on Sevastopol.

> The final try, in April, was especially horrible, with tanks, guns, and trucks stuck in the glutinous mud and the men having to muscle shells forward by hand. Kozlov [Russian commander] had failed, and once again it was advantage Manstein. His response was Operation Trappenjagd ("Bustard Hunt," for the flightless bird that inhabits the Crimea). The Soviet offensives had petered out.[3]

The German 11th Army and its supporting Romanian troops suffered from serious supply and manpower shortages but on July 4, 1942, finally captured Sevastopol. The bill for the operation in terms of men, arms, and fuel was staggering, but the greatest cost would prove to be the time lost in reaching other important objectives. The 11th Army was by this time supposed to be providing crucial support to the German 6th Army in the capture of Stalingrad and thereafter in the capture of the Caucasus oilfields. The failure to capture Stalingrad and the destruction of the German 6th Army marked the turning point in the war. From this time forward the Germans and their Romanian ally were largely on the defensive. Much like Leningrad, Crimea devolved into a stagnant backwater that saw little fighting until late 1943.

At the time that the men in Fidel's Nordland division were getting off trains to shore up the vulnerable Oranienbaum Pocket defensive line near Leningrad, Josef's division was taking a beating in the Caucasus region. There, the Romanian and German units faced an imminent and crushing defeat, so the German command hastened their withdrawal and sent them to help hold back the Russians in Crimea on the most southern part of the Eastern Front. During the withdrawal, the Red Army followed on the heels of Josef's force and exacted a terrible toll. Then, not long after Josef's division reached Crimea, rapid Soviet advances elsewhere cut off the land-based escape route for the German and Romanian troops on the peninsula. Despite numerous pleas from German field commanders, Hitler stubbornly refused to allow his forces to evacuate by sea, even though Crimea was no longer of any strategic importance. He'd learned nothing from Stalingrad. One Russian officer later stated:

> We were in no hurry to take the Crimea. After all, it was our biggest POW cage. The Germans were virtually prisoners on the peninsula since November 1943. They guarded themselves. They supplied themselves. They went on leave and even returned by their own account.[4]

---

1. Pat McTaggart, "The Eastern Front: Germany's Futile Battle For Crimea," *WWII History* 13, no. 1 (Fall 2021), https://warfarehistorynetwork.com/article/the-eastern-front-germanys-futile-battle-for-crimea/.
2. Robert Citino, "The Peninsula: The Crimea at War," The National WWII Museum, New Orleans, July 5, 2018, https://www.nationalww2museum.org/war/articles/peninsula-crimea-war.
3. Citino, "The Peninsula."
4. McTaggart, "The Eastern Front."

40 Josef's Diary

Unlike Fidel and Hans, Josef kept a diary during his service. His chronicle is as fascinating as it is disturbing, for it provides a glimpse into one of the more underreported and vicious theaters of the war as it recounts the long but rapid German and Romanian drive into the southern depths of the Soviet Union, the collapse of that effort, and the harrowing fallback to Crimea.

The diary booklet in which Josef made his entries was printed by the German Wehrmacht for its soldiers for the 1942 calendar year. Not surprisingly, the Nazi regime interspersed this journal's pages with propaganda quotes and 14 glossy photos that included pictures of Axis politicians and generals, a female film star, a sculpture, a worker relaxing, three boys (one Hitler Youth and two Italian Balilla Youths) examining a small-caliber rifle, the Berlin Philharmonic Orchestra, a placid nature scene, the Budapest skyline, and of course an ever-vigilant Hitler. Josef's family members don't know whether he acquired the blank booklet in the course of his quartermaster duties or bartered for it. They are simply grateful that through his words, Josef was able leave a part of himself behind so they could better remember him.

The entries begin with Josef's May 1942 callup and a list of the many places he passed through during his Romanian Army unit's advance to the Caucasus region of the Soviet Union. That journey took him through a number of Soviet republics: the Moldavian Soviet Socialist Republic (called Moldova below), the Ukrainian Soviet Socialist Republic (Ukraine), the Russian Soviet Federative Socialist Republic (Russia), and the Crimean Autonomous Soviet Socialist Republic (Crimea). His battle group employed various modes of transport but traveled mainly by train.

Apparently lacking a replacement diary booklet when 1942 ended, Josef continued his stream of entries in the unused spaces in the first half of his

1942 booklet. When he reached the May section where his 1942 entries had begun, he interspersed a few May and June 1943 notes where he found space, but there the entries stop.

Josef's journey, detailed in his translated diary entries below, is also depicted on the map below. Untangling the chronological order of some of his overlapping entries was no easy task, but deciphering the village and city names he recorded was even more challenging, particularly those in the Soviet republics since at each location Josef might jot down a transliteration of the Cyrillic name, the name he heard used locally, or the German version of that name.

In the chronologically reordered translation below, the current place name is placed in square brackets if it varies with Josef's version. A bracketed question mark indicates that the named town or village could not be located or no longer exists. The journal was made available to me by Josef's granddaughter, Ingrid Slavik, who translated much of the German commentary. Gertrude Adam assisted in the interpretation of certain diary entries. Credit for decrypting the place names, constructing the map showing Josef's journey, and repositioning the errant journal entries in their proper chronological order goes to Susan Eipert.

May 1942

28 Thu: *notice to report arrived* [Josef was in the Romanian Army Reserve at home in Orzydorf, Romania]

June 1942

14 Sun: *left home, was a bad trip*
15 Mon: *arrived in Herrmannst.* [Hermannstadt, Romania; now Sibiu], *couldn't talk to* [crossed out] *until afternoon.*
16 Tue: *still nothing certain*

[The ink, script size, and place name Josef used in the June 17 space contrast sharply with the surrounding 1942 notes indicating that he interjected this entry the following year (1943). Hence, that notation is shown below as a June 1943 entry.]

19 Fri: *R. is going home for 30 days*
20 Sat: *very boring, I'm sick already*
21 Sun: *nothing*

[Like the June 17 entry, the June 23 entry must have been written in 1943 and can be found below in the June 1943 chronology.]

24 Wed:	*still waiting*
25 Thu:	*Bernhardt Hans is going to work in Cerkanie*
26 Fri:	*I signed myself in this afternoon*
27 Sat:	*still in Herrmannstadt*
28 Sun:	*this afternoon I went to Grossau* [Cristian]
29 Mon:	*haven't signed myself in here*
30 Tue:	*still not signed in*

July 1942

[The German high command launched its Unternehmen Blau summer offensive on June 29 by sending three armies and eleven armored divisions rushing toward the Caucasus Mountains. Because the place names Josef noted as his Romanian regiment advanced correlate with the timeline of the offensive, it is clear that his regiment participated in this operation.][1]

1 Wed:	*all for naught, I have to sign in, otherwise I'll be court-martialed. I was assigned today. I got outfitted today.*
15 Wed:	*loaded up today and started out.*
16-20:	[In these spaces Josef listed towns along his train route, which began in Romania and continued through Moldova and Ukraine to Rostov-on-Don in Russia.]
	Brasov [Brașov],
	Bredeal [Predeal],
	Sinaia,
	Pleoști [Ploiești],
	Remniculsarat [Râmnicu-Sărat],
	Focșani,
	Putna,
	Marasesti [Mărășești],
	Dekutsch [Tecuci],
	Pârlad [Bârlad],
	Iași,

[At this point Josef crossed into Moldova from Romania.]

Decureni [Teșcureni],
Galoraș [Călărași],
Chișinău, nistru [With *nistru*, he specified the Chișinău on the Dniestra River rather than the one in Romania.],
Tiraspol,
Gradnița [Grădinița],

[Here Josef crossed into Ukraine.]

>*Rasdolnoia* [Rozdil'na],
>*Magijeva* [Myhajeva],
>*Sitisia* [Zatyshshya],
>*Stubovca* [Chubivka],
>*Birsula* [Podilsk],
>*Balta*,
>*Seidorovka* [?],
>*Novo Ukraia* [Novoukrainka],
>*Brut* [?],
>*Bleteni-Daschea* [Pletenyi Tashlyk],
>*Girovkrat* [Kirovohrad], [should be listed after Schestogovka]
>*Schestagovka* [Shostakivka],
>*Scharovka* [Sharivka],
>*Dolinskaia* [Dolyns'ka],
>*Grivairok* [Hurivka],
>*Nikopol* [Nikopol'],
>*Sabaroschin* [Zaporizhia],
>*über den Niper* [over the Dnieper River],
>*Novokarlovka*,
>*Pologi* [Polohy],
>*Barakonstantina* [Zarekonstantinowka—a train stop],
>*Wolnowaka* [Volnovakha, Ukraine] : *unloaded.*

[Here the train was unloaded and reloaded, apparently due to the wider-gauge track used in Russia, in order to cross the border and proceed onward.]

>*Novoscherkaia* [Novocherkassk, Russia]
>*Savot Selembai* [?].
>*Rostov*, [Rostov-on-Don, Russia] *600,000 inhabitants*

[In the remaining July spaces, Josef repeated the last portion of the trip through Ukraine and Russia, perhaps to list the cities under the proper date.]

21 Tue: *Saparoschea* [Zaporizhzhia, Ukraine], *nepostroi* [Dneprostroi Dam] *here we loaded up.*

22 Wed: *We unloaded after an 8 day ride* [8 days from the starting point in Romania], *discharged in Wolnowacha* [Volnovakha, Ukraine], *Bologhi* [Polohy]

23 Thu: *today we unloaded in Wolnowacha* [Volnovakha, Ukraine], *(Bologhi)* [Polohy]

[An entry for July 24, as well as a note in the margin at the bottom of that page, fit elsewhere geographically and hence have been placed in their proper chronological spots in August and September 1942.]

25 Sat: *Uschpenskaia* [Avilo-Uspenka, Russia]
26 Sun: *Uspenskaia* [Avilo-Uspenka]
28 Tue: *Nova Cerkaisk* [Novocherkassk], *there are very beautiful factories and industrial facilities here. I've never seen something like this. Didn't think that the Russians had something like this.*
29 Wed: *We've set up our post in a very beautiful building. It must have been a university. Buschola* [?]
30 Thu: *yet still here. Novocserkoisk* [Novocherkassk]
31 Fri: *still here*

August 1942

1 Sat: *still here. We left around 6 o'clock in the evening.*

[On July 25, 1942, German troops captured Rostov-on-Don in Russia. For the Germans, this opened the Caucasus region of southern Soviet Union to invasion. The oil fields there at Maikop, Grozny, and Baku were Hitler's ultimate goal.]

2 Sun: *Sovatsch...asch* [maybe Sovetsky, a region of the city of Rostov-on-Don]. *We sit here, at the Don* [River] *in Rostov since last night 2 o'clock. We're not allowed across the bridge. Hundreds of German cars are moving.*
3 Mon: *Rostov is a very beautiful city, buildings 8 stories tall, very big. During the night we crossed the Don. Koisuk* [?]
4 Tue: *volunteered as translator in the hospital today. Butjonovka* [?], *Bataisk* [Bataysk]
5 Wed: *today was sent to the brigade. Endres and Bieber as well. Received the first postcard from home today.*
6 Thu: *Schkulinskaia* [Schkurinskaya]
7 Fri: *Leninraskostainsk* [Leningradskaya] *or Umanskaia* [Leningradskaya]
8 Sat: *Adamanska* [Atamanskaya], *Bavlovkaia* [Pavlovskaya]. *Hoffmann Paul died the 7th of August in a German hospital. He had shrapnel in his abdomen. He is buried in Malka: grave no. 20, no. 3 right.*
9 Sun: *Raschyeschiutzkaia* [Rasshevatskaya]

11 Tue:	*Horidpotkin* [Kropotkin]
12 Wed:	*Hoffmann Paul, Ghiseladorf* [50 km east of Timișoara, Romania] *No. 76. born August 10th 1920, his wife Hoffmann Ana, born April 27th 1922.*
13 Thu:	*Grigoribolischkaia* [Grigoropolisskaya]
14 Fri:	*Novapukankoia* [Novokubansk], *Javhos* [?], *Armavir*

[The following entry, which appeared in the July 24 space, logically belongs in this part of the chronology where Josef's route took him along the Kuban River from about Aug 11 through Aug 16.]

------	*Horst Krabalkin bathed in the Guban* [Kuban] *River.*
16 Sun:	*Newinameskoia* [Nevvinomyssk]
17 Mon:	*our medics were loaded here, in a Russian train, rode for 70 km*
18 Tue:	*Kursovka* [Kursavka]
19 Wed:	*rained very hard today, am completely soaked. There is a horse lying every 100 meters, can't go any further.*
20 Thu:	*Mineral neie vodi* [Mineralnyje Wody]
21 Fri:	*Karas* [Inozemtsevo], *there are Volksdeutsche* [ethnic Germans in a German colony]
22 Sat:	*Bjadikorsk Bjadigorsk* [Pyatigorsk], *a very beautiful city. You can see only Circassians here. Malka* [Malka]. *here for the first time our troops were used in an operation.*
23 Sun:	*The first wounded have arrived today. Colonel Von Ziwili's head was smashed (dead)*
24 Mon:	*We currently have 40 dead and many wounded. Have had stomach aches and diarrhea for 3 days, to the point that I don't know what to do anymore.*
25 Tue:	*Today the first Russian airplanes arrived, 8 of them. 5 p.m., they bombed heavily. At least our officers are now supported. Here in Malka, 35 km from Piatigorsk, we have buried: Wild Hans from St. Anna and Urtineanțu Petre, corporal, from Igriș. They died on the transport to the hospital. A German comrade too. They're lying here at the war heroes' cemetery, buried nicely.*
27 Thu:	*Lance-corporal Walter Josef, born August 17th, 1909, Vienna third district, Apostelgasse, 13/3, lies in grave no. 16, right (3), Malka*
28 Fri:	*Today we've had the first dead Călăraș* [cavalryman] *Dascăr Aurel, Section I. Brancater, from Balșa Hunedoara, contig. 1933, in Malka, the 15th grave.*
30 Sun:	*deceased: Varga Florea, str. Poetului no. 63, Arad, Seica. I think he was my servant in 35.* [Josef crossed out *Knecht* and wrote

	Diener instead, probably because *servant* in German conveys more respect than *farmhand*].
31 Mon:	*So far we've had more than 800 wounded. In our hospital 21 died. We have more than enough work to do.*

September 1942

1 Tue:	*One of our medics died yesterday, a cavalryman as well. (Färber wounded)*
2 Wed:	*Today 4 medics died. There are more than 1300 wounded in our hospital. 35 have died. It's been raining for 3 days uninterrupted. We're still in Malka.*

[Josef wrote the first of the two entries for September 6 in an unused July slot.]

------	*Biatigorski. Malka, we've been here for 14 days already. Today, the 6th of September, I confessed and went to Holy Communion.*
6 Sun:	*78 dead and about 2,000 wounded*

[At this time, when German and Romanian forces encountered heavy resistance and bogged down in their Caucasus drive, Hitler sacked his German commander, Field Marshal Wilhelm List, and took charge himself.]

14 Mon:	*I'm with the reconnaissance unit now. Every Volksdeutsche is doing 5–6 hours of training every day.*
16 Wed:	*Ill again. Stomach ache and diarrhea. I'm completely exhausted already.*
29 Wed:	*I'm in the registry again, at the quartermasters. I'm better now.*

October 1942

18 Sun:	*about to go down to sleep*
19 Mon:	*Tjebo Jakob from Triebswetter [60 km NW of Timișoara] baked Krumpirenflute today, was good.* [*Krumbireflutte* is Orzydorf dialect for a dish made with potatoes and flour.]
20 Tue:	*Today he made potatoes and Knödeln* [dumplings] *and steamed apples to go with it*
21 Wed:	*The others are all outside harvesting corn (400 Joch). Had to stand guard this evening again.*
22 Thu:	*Jacketed potatoes today, I brought the butter.*
28 Wed:	*Today we left Malka for Bakssan* [Baksan], *22 km. Many wounded are coming. Among them an Eipert Rudolf from Temesvar* [Hungarian form of Temeswar/Timișoara].

29	Thu:	*The second section drove to Nalcsik [Nalchik], 25 km. Have the registry in the warehouse now. Works well.*
30	Fri:	*We went to Nalschik today too. It was a beautiful town. The aircraft have pretty much destroyed it.*
31	Sat:	*Have a nice room here with sergeant Radu. Received mail today, after 3 weeks.*

November 1942

1	Sun:	*Today is All Saint's Day and I don't even have one hour off—have to write and calculate an extract. Have no clean clothes (and have some lice). (sad.)*
2	Mon:	*The Russians are crowded in a narrow pass. The German airplanes and tanks are destroying everything. There are very many dead.*

[The German coalition forces were stopped at these positions and could advance no further into the Caucasus region.]

5–7:		*Digora. So far we've advanced quite fast, but as of tonight there is fierce resistance. The whole night long the Russian planes attacked and bombed us. The bombs fell at a 50-100-150 meter distance. One thought that no house could remain standing. It was horrible. Nobody slept, my heart was pounding in my throat. Tonight it was the same. At some point the front is merely 3–4 km away.*
8	Sun:	*Kirchweih Sunday* [important Orzydorf festive Church holiday/parish fair during which everyone dressed in their finest traditional costume]. *Digora*
9	Mon:	*Heavy artillery is shooting over us.*
11	Wed:	*We're still here in Digora, a big village. The battle here was big.*
12	Thu:	*very many dead, panzers, cars, heavy artillery, etc*
13	Fri:	<u>*Digora, Hell*</u>
15	Sun:	*Nachkirchweih* [Orzydorf holiday marking the end of the Kirchweih week festivities] *When the first lieutenant and the staff sergeant are eating the fine meals, I look out the window and tell them that 10 to 15 airplanes are again on the way. They leave everything lying on the table and run to the shelter, so I make myself comfortable and spread their marmalade and butter, because they're not going to come out of the hole for half a day.*
20	Fri:	*They are still flying attacks day and night. No chance to sleep.*
21	Sat:	*The whole house is shaking. In the morning we're full of dust and mud.*
22	Nov:	*At night you wake up when the tent shakes, then you hear it when he fires the shell, he switches off the motor in the next moment. Also*

boom, boom, etc. [Josef was likely referring to nearby German tank or assault gun crews starting an engine, lining up a target, firing, then shutting the engine off again. The booms are probably the detonation of outgoing shells exploding on Russian targets but could also be from incoming shells somewhere in the vicinity.]

24 Nov: *Here lie German and Russian tanks, the people inside are mostly charred and crushed, the people are mostly charred and smashed, glued to the tanks, here lie the dead and yet more dead so that often one cannot even pass without bodies lying in your way. The German tanks also push through like the Russians* [presumably bulldozing right over the bodies and wreckage in their haste], *the Russians have good weapons maybe even better than the German*

27 Fri: *The drum of German artillery fire began today. It's appalling that the Russian planes can habitually make our officers sit inside the shelter all day long. I haven't yet been inside.*

December 1942

2 Wed: *we are still in Digora in front of Alagir (Oschonikisi)* [Ordzhonikidze; now Vladikavkaz]. *Oschonikisi is heavily defended (fortress)*

3 Thu: *Don't think we'll be here long, the Russians are already firing with heavier artillery and incendiaries, the village of Procktille* [?], *one can hear them whistle overhead, see, see, a terrifying attack is already underway, during the day it isn't so bad since you can see, but at night.*

[Soviet offensives had by this date made it impossible for Josef's Romanian unit to retreat westward via the route of its arrival; hence it was forced to flee toward the Taman Peninsula where, along with German units it would need to cross the Kerch Strait to reach the Crimean Peninsula.

6 Sun: *We drove away from Digora today towards Argutan* [Argudan]

8 Tue: *things went well for me here. Chickens, geese, turkeys enough. Also the supply room is well stocked. Left alone we're probably fine*

24 Thu: *Christmas, am in the supply room, and help distribute everything, most for the wounded. There are very many here, they have had it bad at the front, we have here all variety* [of wounded], *it's been very cold the whole day in the supply room, and in the evening I always have much to write up.*

26 Sat: *One hears such miscellaneous things about Stalingrad, but doubt that it's all true. The Romanians are again always very wrong about the Germans*

31 Thu: *all troops to pull back, allegedly to Rostov—I can't understand this*

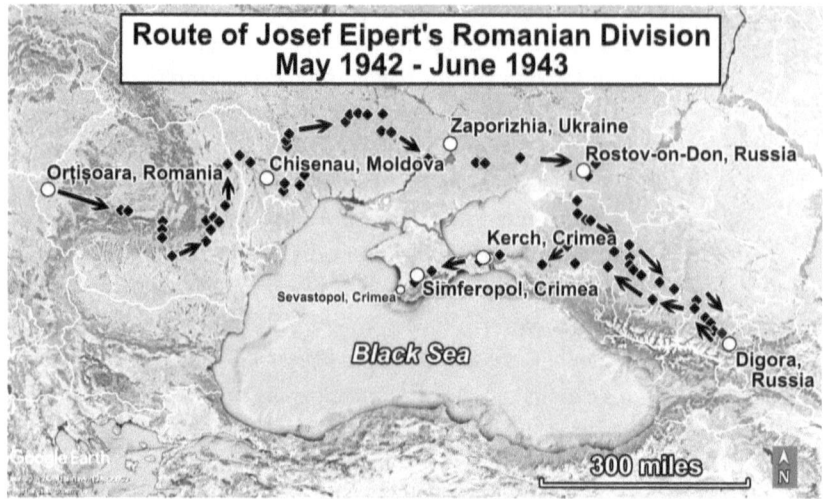

Modern map of southeastern Europe showing Josef's path as his Romanian Army unit advanced deep into the Caucasus region of the Soviet Union, then quickly retreated. The diamonds and circles indicate stops noted by Josef in his diary. Selected cities (circles) are labeled. Background map: Google Earth, Data SIO, NOAA, US Navy, NGA, GEBCO, Image Landsat / Copernicus.

January 1943

[The 1942 diary booklet ended with pages for the first few days of January 1943, and it is here that Josef recorded his earliest 1943 entries.]

1 Fri: *Today we went back from Argutan* [Argudan] *to Nalcsik* [Nalchik] *60 km*

2 Sat: *Today as far as Biatikorky* [Pyatigorsk], *again 60 km. We are in a cavalry barracks, is very pleasant*

3 Sun: *We're still in Piatikor, here it's still very cold*

4 Mon: *Got drunk from Russian vodka, soon forgot myself, was sick 2 days*

[Josef added another entry for January 1 in a blank space near the diary's beginning:]

------   *On the first we left Argutan, a horrible freezing cold set in.*

[When Josef filled the last of the diary spaces, he started using the blank spaces at the beginning of the 1942 booklet to make January 1943 entries. For January, he chose to place his entries under the correct day of the week rather than the correct numerical calendar date. In the last week of the month, he crossed off each numerical date, replacing it with the correct one for that day of the week. The chronological listing here shows the corrected date and day of the week for each entry.]

5	Tue:	*V ks Gehl (Silai)* [Vako-Zhile]
7	Thu:	*we cover 45–50 km every day*
13	Wed:	*we keep marching rearward, very cold.*
18	Mon:	*Today we've arrived in Timirhoiavskai* [Temirgoevskaya]. *I think we'll stay here for a few days. I'm completely worn out, it's been a tough tour.*
20	Wed:	*It's a beautiful area here, many factories etc.*
21	Thu:	*we keep marching backwards*
24	Sun:	*Today we crossed the Kuban* [River]. *Supposedly the front is meant to be held here.*
25	Mon:	*It's raining and is awfully cold.*

[The military situation on this front had now turned into another rout for the Germans and their Romanian ally. Their combined losses now totaled half a million dead, an even greater number wounded, and 200,000 captured.]

26	Tue:	*Went ahead by car and have lost the platoon.*
27	Wed:	*not found yet, it's very cold*
28	Thu:	*Dinskaia* [Dinskaya]
29	Fri:	*Timashovskaia* [Timashevsk]. *Today I found the ambulance* [unit]
30	Sat:	*we'll rest here for 2 days*
31	Sun:	*the car with the records archive got lost, can't do anything. Still here Sunday*

February 1943

[From here forward, Josef crossed out the printed 1942 day of the week and replaced it with the correct 1943 day so that entries corresponded with the printed numerical date.]

1	Mon:	*haven't received any mail for 6 weeks. Can't write either, it's being blocked.*
2	Tue:	*Timoshefskaia* [Timashevsk], *a train of 3–4 km length is parked here at the railway station. It's full of underwear and clothes, everyone can take as much as they want. A storeroom a kilometer long will all be blown up.*
4	Thu:	*have taken 10 sets of underwear, one pair of mountaineer Bankansch* [Pakantsch is Orzydorf dialect for boots], *very nice and one pair of yellow boots and 3 pairs of German trousers.*

5–6:		*still going backwards*
7	Sun:	*103 men have been flown out by plane, among them Nagram. Maybe they'll have better luck?*
8–9:		*still moving rearwards*
10	Wed:	*it is very cold*
12	Fri:	*we're lying on the outskirts of Slawinskaja* [Slavyansk-na-Kubani]. *The Russians are bombarding the town heavily. If only we can make it through*
17	Wed:	*we're 40 km away from the sea. This is a very poor region, only swampland, have slept outside last night, haven't received any bread in 3 weeks, it's going very badly*
19	Fri:	*it snowed again, very cold*
22	Mon:	*I'm completely bedraggled, if only I wasn't sick again*
23	Tue:	*pretty soon I won't be able to keep up anymore*

March 1943

1	Mon:	*as of today we're to get 300 grams of bread. Have negotiated a bucket of flour from a German comrade in exchange for a Russian revolver. Stadtfelter and Augustin baked bread on the fender of a car. It is very good. 2 kilos of cheese powder—fine*

[Here, Josef's unit reached the Kerch Strait, which it will cross to reach Crimea.]

3	Wed:	*today we've arrived on the headland of Ilitsch* [Il'ich, Russia], *we can't cross over, the sea is completely frozen, they blast the ice but new ice always forms.*
5	Fri:	*we're lying outside, it's dreadfully cold.*
7	Sun:	*still here in Ilitsch. Augustin, Stadtfelder (from Johannisfeld) and I have dug a hole* [foxhole] *in the ground, it is still very cold.*
9	Tue:	*today at 11 o'clock we were ferried across* [to the Crimean Peninsula]. *5 airplanes came, the flak guns chased them off. Were fortunate to get across, I'd also have liked to have a life jacket at hand.*
10	Wed:	*drove through Kertsch* [Kerch, Crimea]. *Hundreds of bombed vehicles are lying around. Mariental* [Hornostaivka], *Sulvirovka* [Chernyakovo?]
11	Thu:	*Kertsch an auto graveyard*
14	Sun:	*the Crimea has claimed a lot of victims. It is one graveyard next to the other. SS* [Waffen SS]
17	Wed:	*my birthday! 34 years old*

18 Thu:	*Simferopol, a very beautiful city, 12 km from here we'll be split up. We're waiting for the battalions (field troops), 1 kilogram of bread. 20 marks*
19 Fri:	*My patron saint's day! We've arrived in Sabli* [Partyzans'ke – near Simferopol]
20 Sat:	*A very poor village. 1 kilo of ground corn cost 15 marks*
21 Sun:	*ground barley is being cooked and eaten. Am the quartermaster for the forage, money works quite well. One can still get corn and barley.*
22–25:	*Sabli*
28 Sun:	*still in Sabli, have very much work in the registry, I'm tired of everything.*
30 Tue:	*Sabli. have received the Christmas mail today, my loved ones have written beautifully to me.*

April 1943

5–8:	*Sably*
9–11:	*Sably*

Facing pages from Josef's 1942 Wehrmacht Merkbuch (notebook). On the left, Josef corrected the printed 1942 days of the week to correspond to 1943 days. The translation of his entry of Monday (*Montag*), April 12, reads, "of 117 horses we have 37 left. (80 are gone). I'm making 3 records for each horse, 240 entries. Also Nagram helps me [unreadable]" The facing page, one of the glossy Nazi propaganda photos within the booklet, shows Reich foreign minister von Rippentrop and Italian foreign minister Count Ciano in 1939 signing what was called the Pact of Steel. This treaty obliged one ally to join in any war the other engaged in.

12 Mon:	*of 117 horses we have 37 left. (80 are gone). I'm making 3 records for each horse, 240 entries. Also Nagram helps me* [unreadable]
16–18:	*Sably*
19–22:	*Sably*
26–29:	*Sably*

May 1943

3–6:	*Sably*
10–13:	*Sably*
17–20:	*Sably*

[In 1943, after Josef reached the first entry he made in the diary (May 28, 1942), he continued to add an occasional brief 1943 entry on pages that still had unused space.]

24–27:	*Sably*

June 1943

7–10:	*Sably*
11–13:	*Sably*

[Josef wrote the entries in the June 17 and June 23 sections in a bolder script and different ink than the other entries he had made in Romania in June 1942. These two notes, one of which mentions a Crimea location, clearly relate to 1943 events. Assuming the month of the entry is correct (June), his unit had by then backtracked and left Sably (Partyzans'ke) for a location farther away from the port at Sevastopol.]

17:	*We're moving forward again. drove for 2 days and one night. Arrived in Karasubasar* [Bilohirs'k], *sleeping with Nagram and Negeli in the warehouse. Have found myself a good accommodation: a room at the Tartar Gimil Gemil Feodosia St. No. 5*
23:	*am ill again. Diarrhea, fever, stomach aches. Bad nutrition, meat, butter and jam are rotten. Have lot of work to do. It's awfully hot here.*

[It is unfortunate that the diary pages were filled before the final chaotic and catastrophic events at Sevastopol unfolded months later. I would guess that Josef did continue to make entries on paper of some sort and that these notes were lost in the fast-moving events accompanying the collapse of the Eastern Front.]

---

1. C. Peter Chen, "Caucasus Campaign," World War II Database, January 2012, https://ww2db.com/battle_spec.php?battle_id=284.

41 Josef's Fate

In March 1944 the Red Army smashed through the German defensive lines securing the northern neck of the Crimean Peninsula. A short time later the Reds also swarmed across the Kerch Strait from the east in pursuit of Josef's division and the other German and Romanian units that had withdrawn from Rostov and other positions east of Crimea. The Soviet pursuit was relentless and left the Romanian units so short of men and equipment that they could barely function. The German divisions chased south by the main body of Stalin's force didn't fare much better. As described by one writer and historian, "The German retreat was relatively sloppy, with no effort at deception... Axis morale in the Crimea was collapsing... no one wanted to be left behind—all thoughts were on getting to Sevastopol and the evacuation ships."[1]

The Russian armies swept through Crimea in just 10 days and stayed on the heels of the demoralized German and Romanian defenders all the way to the southeastern tip of the peninsula. The Sevastopol fortress became the last toehold for Hitler's retreating force. The once formidable and massive structure was now vulnerable to attack because it was no longer protected by the vast outer defensive rings the Germans had destroyed in 1942 when they'd captured the fortress from the Russians. Predictably, Hitler once again refused to permit the trapped German and Romanian combat force to evacuate. Only nonessential support personnel and wounded men could leave. For three weeks the Axis force remained under siege while the Russians assembled an overwhelming attack group. Preparation for the final assault commenced on May 9, 1944, when the Reds unleashed a massive artillery bombardment that continued incessantly for two days and pushed Josef and the other trapped soldiers ever farther back on the peninsula's tip.

Only after the senseless slaughter of thousands of his soldiers did Hitler relent and allow a full evacuation. The army commander at Sevastopol, General Karl Allmendinger, then consulted with Admiral Otto Shultz of the German Navy, and the two of them hastily devised a plan for a sea rescue. The German and Romanian troops successfully disengaged and retreated to a beach but found no German ships waiting. Schulz had arrived with his flotilla, but his boats hadn't received the final loading point locations and directions because the Russians jammed the radio channel the Germans had agreed to use. The frustrated admiral then sent out a signal on another channel, directing all boats to gather near the mouth of Kamyshevaya Bay, just off Cape Kherson. From there they were to be piloted to the embarkation points. That message too was lost in the airwaves.

The confusion was compounded by the smoke drums the Germans deployed around installations to thwart air attack. Some were deliberately ignited by the soldiers to give themselves cover while waiting to embark, but most were set off by the intense Soviet artillery barrage pounding their positions. The resulting massive smokescreen obscured both the docks and landing areas and made it next to impossible for the sailors on the German ships to see anything. Some intrepid German skippers made it to shore despite the chaos. The ferries, motor-torpedo boats, and transport ships they commanded groped their way through the dense smoke to find the soldiers of the land force and pick them up, but many units were stranded onshore and out of luck. The fate of the German 111th Infantry Division, which had the misfortune to be one of the marooned units, was noted in the following excerpt from an account of the disaster when no major ship reached

> the division's embarkation point. As dawn broke on May 12, most of the division was still on shore, an inviting target . . . the Soviets attacked the near-helpless division with tanks and infantry . . . eyewitness accounts speak of German officers and Russian auxiliaries being lined up and shot after the division had surrendered, a bitter end to Hitler's Crimean venture.[2]

Another account states that by 11 p.m. on May 11, the defenders had been pushed back into a cluster on a small piece of ground at Cape Chersonese (Mys Khersones). With their backs to the sea, the soldiers were helpless as they waited for their boats to arrive. The Soviet onslaught was so intense that

> fighters who had no boats grabbed anything they could to cross the bay, and there are even stories of the use of coffins that had been stockpiled by German supply officers . . . . According to

the memoirs of survivors, the sea was so full of the corpses of enemy soldiers, horses, cars, and military equipment that the water was barely visible for the first 100 meters from the shore. Thus ended the German occupation of Crimea.[3]

As at Stalingrad and Leningrad, the losses were appalling. Of the approximately 230,000 Axis soldiers, auxiliaries, and civilians that comprised Hitler's 17th Army on the peninsula at the start of the venture, some 100,000 were killed or captured. The remainder were evacuated by sea or air, but anywhere from 11,000 to 42,000 of the evacuees died when their vessels were sunk by the Soviets.[4] [5]

Magdalena heard nothing from her husband for nearly two months in early 1944. Greatly upset and fearing the worst, much of the meaning went out of her life. A sliver of hope returned in mid-April when she learned the Romanian Royal Navy and the German Navy had launched a Hitler-sanctioned rescue—Operation 60,000—to bring out the noncombatants and wounded. This effort preceded the final evacuation described above by about a month. But Magdalena's hopes evaporated once again when Josef wasn't among the returnees.

Another month passed before she learned that her husband was one of the lucky men who'd gotten out before the Reds overran the last Axis defensive positions at the port in Sevastopol. Josef had made it aboard a German boat and also survived the fierce shelling, bombing, and submarine attacks that the rescue vessels braved after they pulled away from the shore. He was now back in Romania somewhere.

This defeat and the chaos of other collapsing front positions provided many a Banat soldier in the Romanian Army an opportunity to desert and return home. But Josef remained with the army and before long sent word that he'd secured a supply sergeant posting at Orastie, not too far from Orzydorf. He subsequently transferred to Lipova, 65 kilometers from Orzydorf, where Fidel had done his Romanian Army training. After two or three weeks in this job Josef returned home regularly on weekends, arriving on Saturday and returning on Monday. This arrangement lasted until mid-August when the Russians overran Romania and knocked it out of the German orbit. Shortly thereafter on the night of Aug 22, 1944, the government in Bucharest changed hands and the new government abruptly announced its allegiance to the Russian side.

Elements of the Red Army arrived in the district seat of Timișoara the following day, and occupied Orzydorf at about the same time. Everyone in the village feared the Russians, for they'd all heard the horror stories of the vicious rape, shooting, and looting sprees that accompanied the Soviet "liberators" across the Baltics and East Prussia. The first time that

Magdalena encountered Red soldiers, she clambered over a fence to hide. After Josef's father, who spoke some Russian, had talked to some of the occupiers, he assured Magdalena and others that they could trust the Russians. Magdalena was surprised that he was not ill-disposed towards them, considering that following World War I he'd spent four years as a Russian POW in the Russian far east port of Vladivostok. To get home, he'd made his way across Siberia by train to Finland, traveled on to London, and then to Romania.

The family soon came to know a few Russian officers, for Magdalena's in-laws were required to billet several of them in the larger of their two houses. After her father-in-law's reassurance that she'd come to no harm, Magdalena and Josef's 7-year-old daughter Leni stopped fearing the men. Nevertheless, Magdalena said she nearly had a heart attack one day on seeing a Russian strolling down the street hand-in-hand with Leni.

The ethnic Germans of Romania were far luckier than their ethnic German brethren throughout the rest of Central Europe because in Romania the Red Army largely behaved itself. Although the Russian soldiers entered houses in Orzydorf to steal food off tables and demand wine, no one was physically harmed. The Romanians who arrived on the heels of the Red Army were more troublesome.

In Romania's capital of Bucharest, a contingent of Stalin's communist proxies who'd spent the war years in Moscow clashed with other Romanian factions, both communist and noncommunist, as they vied for control of the government. With Stalin pulling the strings in the background, his puppets triumphed. Many Romanians sensed opportunity and promptly declared themselves communists. A contingent of these newly minted communists seized the largest house in Orzydorf and turned it into their local party headquarters. The owner, Fidel and Magdalena's aunt, had to move in with her sister, Magdalena Sr.

Fidel's former hired helper, a boy who could neither read nor write, had been one of the few Romanians living in or around Orzydorf before the war. Fidel talked to him in 1970 during his first return to Orzydorf after an absence of 27 years. He'd already been told by his family that when Orzydorf's new communist leaders needed a figurehead administrator that they could control, they turned to this man. The helper, who'd learned to sign his name by then, suited their purpose and was appointed mayor. The man told Fidel that when the communists approached him with their proposal to make him the mayor, he replied that if he was to accept, he and his family needed their own house. He was told to just take one from the Germans because they couldn't do anything about it anymore. More and more Romanians poured into town and did likewise. The newcomers were largely from the poor mountainous area to the east. Fortunately, this takeover was largely nonviolent and nothing like what occurred in my mother's Sudetenland village and throughout most of Central and Eastern Europe, where rape, torture, and murder occurred on a massive scale. My mother, who was herself a rape victim, witnessed many such crimes and lived in fear for most of a year under Russian occupation.[6]

With so many husbands and sons away at war, at wheat harvest time in 1944 many farm households were short of help. Magdalena's was no exception. Josef was at the army base in Lipova, 48 kilometers distant, so a neighbor named Nicholas Holtzinger pitched in. Shortly after the harvest, the communist takeover occurred. Uncertainty about how that would affect the farmers hung in the air, but only after the corn was harvested and in the hof granaries weeks later did the devious Marxist administrators order half the crop be delivered to the state. Naturally, this action angered the hard-working and independent-minded farmers.

As distressing as this outright theft was, Magdalena couldn't dwell on it because she was preoccupied with Josef's delayed return. The war had ended for the Romanian Army, at least in its alliance with the Germans, and the other village soldiers who'd survived Romanian service had already returned. Magdalena grew more anxious each day. Then one day in mid-September 1944 when Magdalena and the family were in their hof, an ethnic Bulgarian arrived from the neighboring village of Vinga and said he brought news. When he declared that Josef was dead, the family was stunned, for there'd been no fighting anywhere in the vicinity. Magdalena had lived with the despair of believing Josef dead before, only to have him reappear. But this time hope was lost. As soon as it sank in that he wouldn't be returning, she broke down. Her world had just turned upside down again.

The news about Josef spread rapidly through the neighborhood and in short order a sizeable crowd of friends and relatives gathered. The Bulgarian, reluctant to go into detail for fear he would upset the communist authorities and bring consequences to himself, volunteered only the barest facts. However, the family's sharp questioning forced him to disclose more of what he knew.

He said that when Romania switched sides, their small army detachment lost touch with its parent unit. He, Josef, and an ethnic Hungarian from Vinga decided to call it quits and set out together on foot along roads and across fields in the direction of their homes. Along the way, just outside the village of Seceani, the trio was stopped by the despised Romanian police. With the Russians now occupying the country, these thugs no longer felt the need for constraint in dealing with ethnic Germans, so they'd resumed their old bullying ways.

The Bulgarian's story remained vague in parts, and somewhat inconsistent, so Magdalena was never quite sure whether the three soldiers had been taken to the police station for questioning or were grilled right in the field outside the village. The man eventually revealed that while all three of them wore a Romanian Army uniform, Josef's was newer and of better quality. Because standard issue Romanian uniforms were typically old and shoddy, this aroused the suspicions of the police. They certainly should have known that soldiers who could afford to do so often bought themselves more comfortable uniforms. Fidel's brother Hans had certainly done so, and Josef must have done likewise. Following his escape from the Crimean Peninsula, Josef would have needed a new one for his staff posting.

Apparently, the uniform was all the evidence the police needed to convict Josef of being a German deserter who'd donned a Romanian uniform in order to return home. They could have detained Josef while they checked with his base at Lipova. And they certainly should have recognized that Josef was fully fluent in Romanian, since he'd been speaking it daily for two years. By contrast, men who'd served in the Waffen SS spoke it awkwardly because they used it little and had long since forgotten much.

The Bulgarian eventually also revealed that the police thugs beat Josef during the questioning and after killing him hid the murder by burying his body in a field. For reasons unknown, the police also executed the ethnic Hungarian soldier. When Magdalena told me that the Hungarian was shot too, she also said the family heard a rumor that the executioner was actually a Russian soldier on horseback. That isn't hard to believe, for the police could have been under the supervision of a Russian officer.

The loss crushed Josef's parents, but these stalwart people were determined to give Josef a proper burial in his own village. The new local communist masters then exposed the extent of their vindictiveness and hostility toward ethnic Germans by denying Josef's father permission to retrieve his son's body. Yet, Josef's father persisted. He traveled to Timișoara and successfully petitioned a higher authority for an official permit that allowed him to recover his son's body. On September 21, Josef's father and Nicholas Holzinger hitched a team of horses to a farm wagon and set out to bring Josef home. Upon opening the grave, the men found both bodies, one atop the other. It is hard to imagine how difficult it must have been for Josef's father to dig up the decomposing corpse of his son in a distant farm field and cart it home in the back of a wagon. He was surely choking on his earlier words about being able to trust the Russians.

Josef's father would certainly have brought home any of his son's possession from the grave, but no diary was recovered. Given that Josef was in the habit of making frequent entries, it is hard to believe he hadn't continued to keep a diary when the pages of his original booklet were filled. The momentous events at Sevastopol and the dramatic evacuation that followed would have compelled him to record it. He probably had paper on which to write; he was, after all, a soldier who dealt with supplies and kept paper records. His journal was precious enough that he'd likely have carried it with him. This all leads me to think that to hide their crime, Josef's killers removed their victims' identification documents and stole their possessions.

Magdalena confessed that she often cried inconsolably in the weeks that followed. During this stretch her daughter, Leni, spent much of her time at her uncle Hans's family home where the company of her younger cousin Linde helped her deal with the loss. She frequently ate and slept there too. Magdalena Sr., because of her own experience of pulling through a difficult time after the loss of her husband, was a beacon of strength for her daughter. Magdalena recalled her mother saying, "You won't die from sorrow so don't let it ruin your life."

In their profound grief, Josef's parents frequently isolated themselves from Magdalena and Leni. Magdalena speculated that Josef's father, in particular, did not want her to see him weeping. She came to believe his breakdown was related to his own traumatic experiences in World War I and his subsequent years of imprisonment in Russia.

The only compassion the new government showed Magdalena and other local war widows of men who'd been Romanian soldiers was a grant that in essence allowed them to retain a Halbgrund portion of the land they already owned. It was a hollow gesture at best, for the land was actually a part of the new collective farms the authorities were assembling and only nominally belonged to the grantees. In the takeover, Magdalena not only lost her husband, she also lost her means of independent subsistence. Life suddenly looked very bleak for her and her German neighbors. The once proud and prosperous community of farmers, whose ancestors had toiled and sacrificed to secure a sustaining existence for themselves and their descendants, were reduced to paupers every bit as poor as the destitute Romanians who'd swarmed into their village. Magdalena mourned for her husband, but three months later grief became a luxury she could no longer indulge when another calamity descended and threatened her own life.

1. Mitch Williamson, "German Defeat in the Crimea, 1944 Part II," Weapons and Warfare, January 4, 2016, https://web.archive.org/web/20180219112716/https://weaponsandwarfare.com/2016/01/04/german-defeat-in-the-crimea-1944-part-ii/.
2. Pat McTaggart, "The Eastern Front: Germany's Futile Battle For Crimea," *WWII History* 13, no. 1 (Fall 2021), https://warfarehistorynetwork.com/article/the-eastern-front-germanys-futile-battle-for-crimea/.
3. Alexander Korolkov, "The Embattled Peninsula: The Struggle for Crimea during WWII," Russia Beyond, May 9, 2014, https://www.rbth.com/society/2014/05/09/the_embattled_peninsula_the_struggle_for_crimea_during_wwii_36195.html.
4. "The Evacuation of the 17th Army from the Crimea," *Axis History Forum*, 2006, https://forum.axishistory.com/viewtopic.php?t=103363.
5. Mitch Williamson, "German Defeat in the Crimea, 1944 Part II."
6. Erich Eipert, *The Secret She Carried: A Perilous Odyssey Through the Time of Hitler* (Turnbuckle Press, 2015), 222.

42 Slave Labor Roundup

Not in her wildest dreams could Magdalena have conjured up what befell her next, for it affected her family just as profoundly as Josef's murder and the loss of her family's livelihood. The new misfortune was the result of Stalin's Secret Order 7161, issued through the Soviet Union's State Defense Committee in December 1944 while the war was still raging. This directive imposed a cruel form of war reparation on the ethnic Germans of Eastern Europe—a modern version of Ottoman Turk abduction of early German Banat settlers. Below is a translation of the first article of this order:

> Resolution
> dated December 16, 1944 No. GKO-7161ss
>
> ON THE INTERNING OF EMPLOYABLE GERMANS IN THE TERRITORY OF ROMANIA, YUGOSLAVIA, HUNGARY, BULGARIA AND CZECHOSLOVAKIA
>
> The State Defense Committee decides:
>
> 1. To mobilize and intern with the assignment for work in the USSR of all able-bodied Germans aged - men from 17 to 45 years old, women - from 18 to 30 years old, who are in the territories of Romania, Yugoslavia, Hungary, Bulgaria and Czechoslovakia liberated by the Red Army.[1]

Only after the fact did Stalin ask for approval from his allies—US President Truman and British Prime Minister Churchill. Even then, approval was requested only because Stalin wished to continue receiving the enormous amount of economic aid America supplied. Both leaders consented even though this painted them as hypocrites when they later tried German Nazis for the identical war crime of making slave laborers of a conquered people. Every Romanian ethnicity had fought for Germany against the Soviets during the war, but only its ethnic Germans were punished for doing so.

Magdalena said that the Russians had originally asked that only male laborers be sent to the USSR, but the Romanian communists deliberately targeted mothers and young girls to spite the minority that they hated. The age range Romania set for females was 18 to 30, and for males, 16 to 45. The quota for Orzydorf, a village of 2,000 before several hundred of its men were put into uniform, was 360—more than a fifth of its remaining population. Magdalena believed the selection process was very deliberate, particularly targeting land holders. No German with a Romanian name appeared on the final list, and she knew one German man who was released because he had the Romanian name of Ardilon. In practice, girls as young as 15 were placed on the list despite being well under the minimum age. Nearly every working-aged man left in Orzydorf was included, even World War I veterans no longer capable of doing heavy labor. But with so many young men off to war or already dead, the manifest consisted primarily of females.

Some four decades after the roundup of the designated slave laborers, I interviewed Magdalena and others about their experiences. Their anguish was still very much alive. This pain was equally apparent to a German-speaking friend, Esther Neeser, when she reinterviewed Magdalena in 1990 in Nuremberg, Germany, at my request to flesh out some of the details.

Magdalena recalled that the nightmare began on the evening of January 14, 1945, when a brutish mob of Romanians from Vinga arrived with bats and clubs to round up Germans. These men, acting on the orders of their Russian bosses, collared the men first, even those who'd just returned from the horrors of serving their country in the Romanian Army. People already asleep were rousted out of bed and ordered to assemble at the school.

Magdalena was exiting the church next door to the school when she was grabbed by the ruffians and locked inside a school classroom. Locked up with her were about 30 other Germans. Apparently, the thugs told their captives they were being transported somewhere because Magdalena recalled asking them to allow her to go home and see young Leni, then seven years old, and pack for the trip. They refused, but before long Magdalena heard Leni calling from outside. She opened a window and shouted for Leni to hurry and let the family know what was happening and to have them pack her warmest winter clothes. But Magdalena Sr. had already learned what was happening and rushed to fill a couple of suitcases with clothes and other necessities, along with a large ham and other food. When she arrived at the school with the supplies, the hoodlums insisted there wasn't room for the suitcases in the classroom; they needed to be stashed in a separate room. This pretext allowed them to steal everything brought by relatives.

After an uncomfortable night in the classroom, the prisoners were marched several kilometers north to Vinga, the local government seat and designated assembly point for the area's detained Germans. Back when Empress Maria Theresa's Austrian administrators were trying to tame the Banat wilderness, they couldn't get Germans to settle in Vinga because the terrain was rougher and less fertile than nearby areas, so they allocated large tracts to several Bulgarians. It was said that these tracts were as large as a man could ride around in a day, but that was surely an exaggeration. The settlers subsequently induced to come there were not as skilled or persistent as the Germans around them and eventually sold off much of the land.

In Vinga, both male and female prisoners were packed together into boxcars assembled on a rail siding. These were bare freight cars without toilets or water. The prisoners had to break a hole in the side and another in the floor to relieve themselves. To maintain some dignity, they held up blankets when using the makeshift toilets. One small steel-barred window in each car provided light, but it was too high to peer out of without being lifted up.

Magdalena arrived with nothing but the clothes she wore because she didn't know that her suitcases had been stolen until she was marched away. Fortunately, her mother and grandmother learned what happened and rushed to Vinga with more clothes, bedding, and food. The prisoners were allowed only a small amount of food and drink twice per day, and even that was permitted only because Orzydorf family members brought provisions and pestered the guards until they could pass them into the boxcars.

The Orzydorfers had witnessed a group of imprisoned Germans passing through their village on a similar train a few days earlier, but hadn't fully comprehended what was happening at the time. They couldn't imagine then that the same could happen to them. The poor souls on that train had wailed mournfully because they'd been torn from their families and didn't know where they were going. Or what was to happen to them! They were from the Yugoslavian portion of the Banat where a scourge of ethnic cleansing was in full swing—one that saw ethnic Germans rounded up, robbed, beaten, raped, and massacred. They and their surviving Serbian German family members were never allowed to return to their former homes.

The train cars in Vinga remained stationary for two long days while the frightened captives fretted and worried. The guards showed only the barest humanity in allowing mothers a few minutes with their young children in the evening. On the second night, Magdalena had an opportunity to escape and hide in Timișoara, but remained because her captors had made it known to everyone that they'd take someone else in in the family if anyone fled. Her grandfather was the next most likely family member to go, and she wanted to spare him.

Magdalena heard of one man who ran off and hid before the roundup because he'd been tipped off by a relative working in the mayor's office. Another woman adamantly insisted she wouldn't go without her two children, so the Romanians set her free and took someone in her place. Another woman, Magdalena learned later, escaped and hid for 12 days before returning home. Magdalena also knew a woman who was over the age limit, but insisted on going anyway because her young daughter was on the list and couldn't bear to see the girl go alone. Others also went along to be with their children. Magdalena knew of two fathers who accompanied their girls. One had two daughters aboard the train.

Several women on the list hurriedly married Romanians in Vinga. The grooms were family employees who agreed to a sham marriage for a cash payment. The going rate was 100,000 lei, a considerable sum. Magdalena learned later that the father of one of her friends spent more than a day running about Vinga with a basket of money, in search of someone who'd marry his daughter.

Magdalena said that she could have gotten out by marrying her half-German cousin Cure Mihai, who had a Romanian name. He'd learned about the sham marriage trick days earlier when the Serbian Germans passed through Orzydorf, but hadn't told anyone at the time because he didn't expect local Germans to meet the same fate. In Vinga, Cure hung around the train and hinted to Magdalena that the situation was serious because the train's destination was Russia. Yet, he never actually came out and mentioned that country directly for fear that it would have put him in danger too. Magdalena admitted that because she was in denial, she didn't take Cure seriously enough to work out a marriage arrangement. She still believed that whatever the destination, the conditions would be tolerable.

Magdalena confessed that had she tried, she probably could also have arranged to flee with her entire family, like a few others did. This was possible because the Romanian police and their auxiliaries guarding the prisoners were corrupt scoundrels and could be bought. The same applied to the Russian officials that the police guards answered to. Magdalena believed a bribe was how one of her neighbors obtained a release at the last minute.

The detainees were organized into street-by-street groups before they were locked in the rail cars, but this order broke down during the chaos of loading, and people from different parts of the village and even people from different villages were mixed together. The prisoners were packed tightly enough that there wasn't enough floor space for everyone to lie down, so crude stacked bunks were hastily constructed to allow prisoners enough room to sleep. By the time the train pulled out, 450 people were jammed into five cars. Magdalena learned later that her train was just one of many such trains that passed through Orzydorf. Russia had set a quota of 150,000 laborers from Romania and Serbia alone.

On departure, Magdalena's train headed south. The Orzydorf exiles could sense when they reached their village, and many shrieked and cried in despair, but the train didn't stop until reaching Timişoara. There, it picked up more cars packed with terrified Germans. Magdalena didn't know it at the time, but a good friend of hers, Maria Krabel, was among the Germans taken on there.

The weather was icy cold, but the prisoners stayed reasonably warm because of the feather comforters their families had packed for them. At this point they didn't yet believe the Soviet Union, which Magdalena simply called Russia, was their destination because they hadn't been told to prepare for a Russian winter. One of the prisoners in Magdalena's car had even overheard two guards discussing the destination city, but Magdalena still refused to believe she was going to Russia. It was too frightening a thought. Only after the train reached the Soviet border and everyone was herded into the larger boxcars that ran on the wider-gauge Soviet tracks, did her denial dissolve. The crowding did not lessen with transfer to the larger cars because the guards simply jammed in more people. By then the prisoners had been on the rails for four days.

In Russia, Magdalena and her fellow prisoners caught glimpses of similar trains teeming with prisoners, but headed in the opposite direction. They had no idea who those people were or where they were going, but those prisoners were equally frightened. The doors remained locked and had not been opened during the entire transit through Romania, but now with enough distance between the train and the Soviet border, the guards opened the doors and passed in some dried mutton. At this point they could still put off eating such stomach-turning fare because of the food they'd brought along. The meat stank and was so revolting that they hung it outside through the high barred windows. The Germans were then surprised to see locals running alongside the tracks, begging for the piteous mutton. In that empire of boundless rich soil, people were starving because of the Soviet system's inefficiency, mismanagement, and farm collectivization mandate. The latter had taken the lives of millions of peasants. Had the mutton been more palatable, Magdalena was convinced the train would have been mobbed by the starving populace.

Days later, the train stopped at noon in an urban area with a concentration of heavy industry. Here, the prisoners were allowed to disembark and heat their ham. Magdalena later learned this was Stalino, in the Ukrainian province of Dnipropetrovsk. From reading Josef's war diary, she'd have recognized the area as one he'd passed through in 1942. She might also have recalled the name from letters her brother Hans had written when the Germans occupied the area. The city had been known as Yuzivka until Stalin renamed it in his own honor. In 1961 it became Donetsk. When Magdalena saw it, much of the city lay in ruins because it had been fought over twice in the war. The region was a center of coal and iron mining as well as iron and steel production.

To Germans at this time, Stalino was widely associated with the nearby town of Grischino because the Propaganda Ministry had publicized a particularly gruesome massacre of over 500 Germans by Soviet soldiers there. Had Magdalena's group been aware of what the Soviets had done to these POWs, German Red Cross nurses, and civilian workers, their fear of what lay ahead surely would have soared. The victims hadn't just been executed. Many had their noses, ears, and genitals cut off and stuffed into mouths. Nurses had been viciously raped and carved up, and one group of 120 men was machine-gunned inside a train station cellar.[2]

When the leading three cars of the train were detached from the other five as the prisoners ate their lunch, Magdalena and the other captives realized that not everyone would end up in the same place. Back in Vinga, Magdalena's family had urged her to stick with Bohn's Pat, should the group ever be split up. Banat families were often known by their house name. Bohn was the house name for Josef's family, and Pat was the word for godfather. The Pat they urged her to stick with was Josef's godfather and uncle. His 1906 birthday had left him too old for the Romanian Army, but not too old to be sent to Russia for strenuous slave labor.

The separation of the train alarmed Magdalena because the godfather and his possessions were on the other train. The guards allowed some family members to stay together, but no amount of pleading let Magdalena move to the front three cars before they pulled out. Happily, the uncle survived the brutal ordeal that killed many a younger man and eventually made it back home.

Anna Brunner, an Orzydorf woman in the cars left behind, tried to make herself sound like a communist when she shouted loudly that the first three cars held the Hitler supporters. She thought that denouncing the others would ingratiate her with the guards and buy special treatment, but even the Russian guards laughed at her charade. Brunner gained no favors; she and her daughter had to work every bit as hard as the others. The heavy pushcart the poor woman labored behind eventually killed her.

1. "On the internment of able-bodied Germans in the territory of Romania, Yugoslavia, Hungary, Bulgaria and Czechoslovakia," online translation, Resolution of the State Treasury No. GKO-7161ss, December 16, 1944, https://ru.wikisource.org/wiki/Постановление ГКО № 7161сс от 16.12.44.
2. Alfred M. De Zayas, *Wehrmacht War Crimes Bureau, 1939-1945*. (Lincoln: University of Nebraska Press, 1989), 189.

43 Classmate Josef Adam

Josef Adam, a friend and schoolmate of Fidel's, had academic ambitions as a boy. Although the two friends differed in career ambitions, Josef exhibited the same sort of survival guile as Fidel when it came to soldiering. As with Fidel, it allowed him to survive the war and left him with a story to tell. Fortunately, that story was preserved because his daughter, Gertrude Adam, collected it in parts over time and passed some of it along to me. Josef's education was to diverge from my father's after the fourth grade when Josef's parents chose to have him begin his secondary education (Gymnasium) in Timișoara. But when the poor harvest that year didn't provide enough income to pay for it, he attended Orzydorf's elementary school for his fifth year. Fortunately, he was able to attend the school in Timișoara the following year and thereafter. Upon graduation from the Gymnasium program at the age of 20 in 1941, he was required to fulfill his military obligation by training for six months before he could proceed with further studies. However, because Romania had become heavily committed to Hitler's invasion of Russia by then, he was called up periodically for further months of military service. By the time he was transferred to the Waffen SS in 1943 along with most other ethnic German soldiers in the Romanian Army, he'd already served for over a year. Like Fidel and the other Banaters, Josef ended up on the Eastern Front but took a different route because his advanced education had put him on an officer track.

Gertrude was unsure of her father's original occupational specialty in the Waffen SS, but thought that later in 1944 he'd become some sort of a motorcycle messenger near Lublin, Poland. That winter, he found himself in Andau, in the Neusiedl am See district of eastern Austria. He told his daughter that it was "an unbelievably cold winter. The population had little food so the soldiers hunted for game, rabbits, pheasants, and partridges to improve the food situation." In Gertrude's words, Josef was then transported to the vicinity of

> the Berlin-Sachsenhausen concentration camp at the beginning of 1945 together with other comrades, where they wanted to train soldiers to become parachutists. It was especially for those with language skills. These soldiers were supposed to jump behind Russian lines and attack from the rear. On examination it was found that my father could not fully extend one arm; he broke it once in school in physical education class, so he was not taken for this parachutist training.

Incredibly enough, the Berlin-Sachsenhausen concentration camp that Josef described was within walking distance of Friedenthal, Fidel's station at the time. Had the stay of the two men overlapped by a more than week or two, they'd surely have learned of each other's presence because the training for the type of mission described by Gertrude looks suspiciously like the type of operation connected to Skorzeny's Jagdverband Mitte battalion.

Josef then ended up back in Austria, most likely in his division's replacement battalion, where at the war's end he and his comrades were disarmed by the 11th US Armored Division and held as prisoners in an open field at Gallneukirchen, near Linz. Josef said that after spending a few days there, on May 14th, 1945, in "scorching heat" the Americans marched their 15,000 prisoners to Pregarten "in a seemingly endless column, and handed us over to the Red Army." Soviet soldiers and soldiers of their allies served as guards as the march continued. As they walked along, Josef became acquainted with a Moldovan guard. By conversing in Romanian and pretending to be an ethnic Romanian, Josef gained the Moldovan's sympathy. Gertrude wrote, "The two men seem to have understood each other well, and not only in terms of language. When the prisoners were allowed to drink water at the next well, my father let himself fall into the bushes . . . and the Moldovan looked away and didn't see, or want to see."

Once the column had moved on and it was safe to emerge, Josef made his way to a monastery where he received shelter, food, and new clothes. From there he began a long walk home, moving only at night, for German soldiers were actively being hunted down by the Russians. It seemed all of Europe was going somewhere on foot in those days. A good many of those on the move were ethnic Germans trying to return to homes farther east after fleeing westward to escape the Russian front in the autumn of 1944. Josef's 650-kilometer trek took two weeks.

His mother Magdalena was home alone when he arrived because Josef's father had been sent to Russia as a slave laborer the previous January. His mother became frightened when she heard a noise outside, but because the dog didn't bark and only whimpered, she realized that the visitor must be someone familiar. At this point Josef knocked softly and said quietly, "Mother, it's me." It was a painful reunion that followed because Josef had to tell his mother that he'd recently learned from another soldier that his brother Hansi had died at Narva, Estonia, with the Nordland division the year before. And in turn, Josef's mother had to tell Josef that his father was a prisoner in Russia.

Because the Romanians too were hunting down German military returnees, Josef's return had to remain secret. Gertrude said several other men found their way back later, but Josef was likely the first. To avoid arousing suspicion, Josef's mother needed to attend Mass the day following his arrival, a Catholic holiday. In her pew, she broke down and cried bitterly over the death of her younger son. The people around her thought she was still distraught over her husband's kidnapping. After the mass, a neighbor, Hagersch Besl Marie, accompanied Magdalena home. When "like a detective," she became suspicious that something was up when she noticed white smoke coming from the chimney of Josef's family home. She shouted, "Leni, there is smoke, it is white smoke!"

White smoke was a telltale sign of a corn-cob fire, and such a fire left burning earlier by Magdalena should have gone out long before because cobs burn up rapidly. Prior to leaving for church, Magdalena had told Josef to keep the cookstove going so that the soup she'd prepared for lunch would cook. Josef's mother couldn't recall just how she explained away such a fire when no one was home, but managed to throw the neighbor off the scent.

Both mother and son now realized that hiding in the house was too dangerous. Josef then hid out for a time with a family named Brück. Josef and his grief-stricken mother had been apart since 1942 and the two of them longed to spend time together, but dared only meet secretly at night. The secret meetings continued for the next several months, but eventually when even that became too risky, Josef went to Timișoara where a prelate named Nischbach hid Josef and several other men in the seminary. From there, Josef moved to Bokschan in the Banat Highlands, where a friendly mill owner named Weber hired him as his personal coachman. "After a while, the Bokschans noticed that this coachman was always reading something while waiting for his master. What kind of coachman was this?" So he moved on again. In time, when things had cooled down enough in Orzydorf that former German soldiers could again venture out in public, he and several other survivors returned. Due to the lack of opportunities in the new communist economy, in October 1947 Josef migrated illegally to Austria. He was determined to go no farther than that from his home for he'd promised his mother, "Up to the Leitha [River] and not a step further west."

44 Berlin and Hans's Destiny

Hans had once shared his brother Fidel's disdain of soldiering. But by 1943, five years of service had left him confident of his abilities and turned him into a professional soldier. Family members speculated he'd even become ambivalent about leaving the military once the war was won. During an Orzydorf home leave in 1944, his pride showed when he had a portrait taken. By then his uniform indicated that after a year of service in the Waffen SS he'd already advanced to the rank of *Rottenführer*, the equivalent of corporal in the American army. That rank would have placed him in charge of a squad or team. The field post number (43111B) on his mail indicates that he was assigned to the 1st battery of the 11th SS Flak Abteilung.

Hitler lost faith in the Wehrmacht after the July 1944 officer-led assassination attempt—and then in the Waffen SS when it failed to keep the Soviets bottled up in the east. His mental state prevented him from seeing that his own arrogance, ambition, and incompetence had destroyed the morale of his military and brought defeat and ruin on Germany by repeatedly demanding his soldiers do the impossible. Toward the end, Hitler shuffled around paper armies that no longer existed and steadfastly declared that he would fight on as long as there was any German territory left unoccupied. Most military commanders had stopped briefing him on the true situation by then, for whenever they tried, he raged to such an extent that he trembled and drooled saliva.[1]

When Oberstgeneral Raus reported to Hitler in March 1945, Raus could scarcely believe the man's deterioration. He'd first met Hitler three years earlier at the führer's Eastern Front headquarters, Führerhauptquartier Werwolf, near Vinnytsia, Ukraine. Raus was so appalled by Hitler's decrepit appearance in 1945 that he wrote, "I faced a physically broken-down, embittered, and suspicious man whom I scarcely recognized. The knowledge that Adolf Hitler—now only a human wreck—held the fate of the German people in his hands alone was a deep shock to me."[2]

When Raus tried to reason with Hitler about the army's hopeless situation along the Oder River in Pomerania, 65 km east of Berlin, Hitler rejected Raus's assessment and relieved him as commander of the 3rd Panzer Army. This sacking likely saved the general's life because Raus's understrength force was squared off against a Russian force 20 times larger—a situation similar to that which existed across all German fronts. At the Oder, the ragtag remnants of a few German divisions were supposed to stop 2.5 million Red soldiers, 6,250 tanks, 7,500 aircraft, 3,255 truck-mounted Katyusha rocket launchers, over 95,000 motor vehicles, and 41,600 artillery pieces and mortar tubes. At his post, Raus would likely have been killed in the fighting or captured by the Russians and never seen again.[3]

Hans's belt buckle, and the buckles of all Waffen SS soldiers, was inscribed with the motto, MEINE EHRE HEIßT TREUE (My honor is my loyalty). As already noted, Hitler didn't reciprocate. He consistently failed the warriors he harangued to fight ever harder for him. Conditions and morale on the Eastern Front were dismal, but most soldiers had no alternative but to fight on because survival demanded it. Entire units might have called it quits and pushed westward to surrender to the Americans except for two things—the Russian army and their own military police. Since German units often lacked sufficient transport and fuel for a motorized retreat, they were at a great disadvantage if they abandoned their defensive positions on foot. The more-mobile Russians would quickly catch up with them. Fleeing Germans also had reason to fear the Feldgendarmarie (Wehrmacht military police) and late in the war, a new super-military police force called the Feldjägerkorps. Feldjägers were selected from among highly decorated officers and noncoms who had at least three years of frontline combat experience. These soldiers answered only to the top German commanders and had the authority to deal harshly with ranks much above them. These two police forces not only prevented desertion, but toward the close of the war also acted as an armed barrier to turn back panicking troops, much like the NKVD did with Soviet soldiers.

Soldiers on the fronts could only watch in dread as their friends around them were cut down or blown apart in the war's late stages. The wounded on battlefields could no longer always count on retrieval or medical treatment because of the need for rapid flight. This was particularly true for the companies sacrificed as rearguards so larger German units could retreat. Yet despite it all, Hans pulled through and survived the ever-worsening disaster that the collapsing Eastern Front had become.

Back in 1943, when most of the Nordland division received orders to proceed south to Croatia, Hans's 11th Flak Abteilung subunit had headed north to Arys, East Prussia, for further training. Upon completion of that extensive training course in February 1944, 11th Flak's five batteries were issued weapons and vehicles, then loaded onto a train headed eastward to Narva, Estonia, to rejoin its parent division and help shore up Nordland's section of the collapsing Leningrad Front. As previously noted, that trip ended prematurely when Polish resistance partisans sabotaged the tracks and caused a train derailment that resulted in many injuries and the destruction of much of Flak's equipment.[4] As a result, Hans and the other injured men were hospitalized in Marienburg. This was when his stay coincided with Fidel's, and neither brother knew the other was there.

Hans's battalion returned to the Ayrs training area to be refitted with new equipment and made battle-worthy again. In mid-April, 11th Flak was sent out a second time and joined Nordland at Narva, where it sited its guns in strategic locations and helped secure artillery units and bridges. The unit showed its mettle in successfully shooting down aircraft, knocking out tanks, destroying enemy artillery positions, and breaking up Soviet infantry spearheads. Flak also proved instrumental in holding the important road junction between the Hermannsburg and Ivangorod Fortresses.[5]

At the end of July when enemy pressure grew severe, 11th Flak covered the pullback of the Wehrmacht's heavy guns and supplied fire support for the rearguard fighters holding off the Reds. In the process, Flak's 4th Battery was outflanked and cut off from the main force of retreating Germans. For two days its men battled their way out of the encirclement and forged a circuitous path through difficult swampy terrain and forest. During this escape, they fought as infantry troops to clear out the small Soviet units positioned between them and the retreating main German force.

At the Tannenberg Line, the dangerous bridgehead position where Fidel called it quits and shot himself, Flak battled for two straight weeks and downed more than 20 Russian planes. In this time, it absorbed heavy losses when attacked by air, armor, and infantry. The sector's depleted and exhausted German defenders, by then down to only 22,000 men, faced off against eight times that number of Russians. Although the Germans suffered an estimated 10,000 casualties, they inflicted 170,000 casualties on the Reds. However, the disproportionate losses made little difference to Stalin because harsh conscription campaigns allowed him the luxury of continuously replacing destroyed divisions with fresh ones.[6]

When 11th Flak withdrew from this position weeks later, it fought rearguard actions through a succession of villages and towns along the entire length of the pullback. Near Riga, it supplied fire support as German troops frantically scrambled to build a new defensive line across Courland (Kurland), a nub of Latvia jutting out into the Baltic Sea. These weeks of fighting took a further heavy toll on the unit.

In late September and early October 1944, the Reds broke the back of the German 3rd Panzer Army west of Riga and surged all the way to the Baltic coast. This advance severed the westward escape route of 33 divisions belonging to the German 16th and 18th Armies and trapped 200,000 men on the Courland Peninsula. Despite a desperate need for these soldiers elsewhere, Hitler once again ordered them to hold fast and refused to allow them to evacuate by ship. In his delusional state, he still expected to regain the upper hand and wanted Courland as a bridgehead for the eastern offensive that would win the war. Nordland, as one of the 33 German divisions trapped in this Courland Pocket, again found itself in the thick of fierce fighting

After days of ferocious Russian artillery bombardment, the fields and pastures surrounding the German defenders became deeply scarred with artillery-shell furrows and 12-centimeter mortar shell craters. Little remained of the villages aside from fire-blackened cellar pits filled with rubble and stubs of masonry chimneys. The defenders could do little to protect themselves from the devastating mortar shells that dropped almost vertically with enough force to make even dug-in shelters useless.[7]

Had Hans kept a diary, he'd have noted spending the fall and winter in squalid pits and cellars within the ruins while fighting off frequent Russian attacks. He'd also have mentioned how the men battled a tiny but even more persistent second enemy—fleas. The tiny creatures ate them up inside their clothing. The men devoted considerable time to trying to pick all the tiny wingless insects from their clothing. And he'd have described the terrible cold exposure that came of frequent wetness from cold rain or from lying in mud, ice, snow, or slush for hours while under fierce attack. The shelling was often so intense that nothing else could be heard through the din. The ground heaved continuously beneath the defenders and shrapnel filled the air above them. Sleep was physically impossible during such mayhem.

In the midst of ongoing tank, aircraft, artillery, and mortar attacks, flak and artillery men like Hans had to suppress their terror and ignore the shells raining down around them in order to fire their own guns. And the moment the enemy's big guns and Stalin organs stopped firing during one of these exchanges, ground troops attacked and had to be repelled. Even the ambulatory wounded had to man guns then. At times the Russian infantry penetrated so far into the German lines that only hand-to-hand combat stopped them. More than a few Germans cracked under this strain, and of course many others suffered horrible wounds and mutilations.

On January 23, 1945, the Russians mounted their fourth offensive against Nordland defenders. As the battle raged, the attackers broke through the German line several times, but Hans and his fellow Nordland soldiers counterattacked each time and took back the ground they'd lost. The vastly outnumbered Waffen SS soldiers battled the Russians fiercely for 10 days as wave after wave of infantrymen screaming the Red Army's "urrää!" battle cry charged the Nordland positions. Toward the end, so many bodies had piled up that the new Russian waves forced to rush across the killing field panicked. But whenever they turned to run, their own commissars and NKVD blocking troops cut them down mercilessly.

Like the Soviet army in the Oranienbaum Pocket, the Germans were trapped. Despite being vastly outmanned and outgunned, they managed to hold their isolated pocket by fending off six major Russian offensives. Eventually, the German divisions stabilized their line enough to maintain it until the end of the war. By holding this flanking position and diverting some of the enemy force, they slowed Stalin's westward advance. But unlike the Russians, the Germans never had the strength to break out of their pocket.[8]

Hans's badly mauled flak battery was spared from participating in the fifth and sixth Russian Courland offensives because in late January Hitler finally relented and allowed the evacuation of seven of the 33 weakened divisions trapped in the Courland Pocket. Nordland boarded ships in the port of Libau but left behind, in graves, half the number it had arrived with. After two days at sea, Hans and his fellow survivors disembarked on German soil near the mouth of the Oder River at the port city of Stettin (now the Polish city of Szczecin). Stettin had been turned into a wasteland of blackened rubble by the American and British bombers that had firebombed it with a mix of high explosive and incendiary phosphorous bombs. The latter created fires to destroy what the explosives missed. Nordland bivouacked some distance east of the Oder near a village of prosperous farmers and villagers after pushing through the remains of Stettin. While the men were enjoying a two-week reprieve from the fighting, the Russians broke through the poorly organized German defensive line along the Vistula River to the southeast and poured westward.

The loss of this natural defensive line was a disaster in itself, but the enormous cost in men and equipment compounded the troubles of the German commanders. They had no more reserves or replacement troops to throw against the surging Reds, and their supply lines barely existed anymore. American and British planes now constantly prowled the skies in support of the Red Army. The planes pounced on anything moving by road or rail. German soldiers reported that helpless streams of women, children, and old men fleeing the fighting were also often indiscriminately bombed and strafed by the planes.⁹ Columns of Allied POWs freed from German captivity, some of whom had been on a slow-moving march for months westward toward Germany from the east, were also sometimes attacked. The POWs typically refused transport by rail or truck so they wouldn't be mistaken for German soldiers by the planes. One noted strafing attack killed a large number of POWs, some of whom had been prisoners since Dunkirk at the beginning of the war.¹⁰

In the second week of February 1945, shortly after Fidel departed Friedenthal for the Bavarian Alps as part of Skorzeny's service company relocation, Hans and Nordland returned to the fighting. About 30 kilometers northeast of Stettin, near the village of Massow (now Maszewo, Poland), the division encountered heavy shelling. The soldiers could do nothing but hunker down and endure three days of ceaseless pounding. A cold rain added to their misery as the men crouched in bombed-out cellars and muck-filled pits. Hans escaped some of this wretchedness when his flak battalion was sent to lend fire support to another division fighting near Freinwalde (now Stargard, Poland). There, he and his fellow gunners destroyed 10 Soviet tanks before pulling back.

On March 1, the front in northern Germany collapsed completely and the remaining German fighters were no longer able to hold back the massive Russian assault. Hans and his companions engaged in combat almost continuously during the hectic rearward scramble that followed. The new losses now left every German division struggling to remain functional. Commanders improvised by assembling ad hoc units from whatever stragglers and survivors they could muster. The heavy Russian onslaught made it impossible for the Germans to set up static defensive lines. All they could do was engage the invaders village by village in their withdrawal.

In mid-March, after participating in a series of short and risky rearguard actions, Hans and 11th Flak were sent to the outskirts of Stettin's Altdamm suburb to support the remnants of Nordland's SS Panzergrenadier Regiment 23 Norge. The bridgehead was to be held at all costs because it was the designated escape route for the ragged German divisions trying to hold up whole Russian Armies further east. The continuous combat carved ever deeper into 11th Flak's roster. After several days of rearguard fighting, the men couldn't hold out any longer and scrambled across the Oder bridge just before combat engineers detonated the explosives planted under it. As Hans and his fellow flak gunners drew ever closer to Berlin, they fought more and more as infantrymen because most of their flak guns and support weapons had been destroyed and their remaining vehicles had little fuel.¹¹ ¹²

By then, there wasn't much territory left to defend in Hitler's Third Reich. An example of the black humor at the time has one person asking another, "Tell me, what are you going to do after the war?" The second person replies, "I'm finally going to take a vacation and see all of Germany," to which the first person responds, "And what are you going to do in the afternoon?"[13] Yet, Hitler continued to delude himself and carry on as if he still controlled an empire. On April 19 he emerged from his bunker to conduct the annual ceremonial induction of 10-year-old boys and girls into the Hitler Youth at the domed hall of the Reich Sports Ground in the western part of Berlin. The sounds of the nearby front were clearly audible in the background.[14]

Stalin, in a rush to seize as much German territory as possible before it fell into the hands of his Western Allies, ordered his Red Army commanders to advance full out and not spare their troops. This reckless use of Soviet troops as cannon fodder allowed the outgunned Germans to inflict many more casualties than they themselves took. By then, Stalin's ethnic Russian, Siberian, and Ukrainian units had long since been destroyed, so the Germans now mainly faced Mongolians, Khirghis, and other Soviet Asian nationalities.[15]

When Hans and the 11th Flak soldiers lost the Stettin bridgehead and rejoined the main body of their division, Nordland no longer had enough soldiers to remain functional as a fighting unit. To bring its numbers back up to a minimal level of combat strength, several hundred foreign Waffen SS men from other units—Frenchmen, Spaniards, and even a few Brits—reinforced Nordland.[16] [17] The refit took place at the Schwedt bridgehead, where Nordland was temporarily designated a reserve force. Schwedt was the site of Fidel's earlier aborted scouting mission and the place that Skorzeny's commandos had just pulled out of. The reserve status lasted but a few days. On April 16, Hans and the other remaining Nordland soldiers were thrown right back into the fight when the Russians opened their final offensive to take Berlin.[18]

Nordland was hurriedly dispatched southeast of Berlin to Frankfurt on the Oder but, for lack of fuel and vehicles, got no farther than Berlin's eastern outskirts before it was attacked by a large Red force. The men fought hard but found themselves pushed relentlessly westward into Berlin proper. Even with its new replacements, Nordland numbered just 1,500 men—about a 10th of its complement a year and a half earlier.

Hitler and his inner circle, safely ensconced in the Führerbunker, were oblivious to the "unending stream of wounded with mangled flesh filling every space in the makeshift hospitals" throughout the city.[19] At a conference on April 22, when Hitler learned the elaborate Berlin defense plans he'd devised the previous day couldn't be implemented, he fell into a howling rage and shouted that the war was lost because of his generals. He now declared that he'd stay in Berlin and commit suicide at the end rather than evacuate to Berchtesgaden. The following day he placed General Helmuth Weidling in charge of Berlin's defense. Other than the city's police force, Hitler Youth boys, and older Volkssturm men, Weidling had only a few skeleton Heer and Waffen SS divisions at his disposal.

The general promptly divided the city into eight defense sectors, A through H, and installed Brigadeführer Gustav Krukenberg as commander of Berlin's defense sector C. Krukenberg led the French volunteers that comprised all that was left of the SS Charlemagne Division. His paltry group was still near the Oder and like Nordland, possessed few vehicles. He was unable to take all his soldiers to Berlin, so asked for volunteers. As the story goes, too many men responded, so he had to leave some of them behind. When Krukenberg's soldiers reached Tempelhof Airport in southeast Berlin, the place where the Nordland survivors were fighting, he merged his unit into the Nordland division.

On April 24 in the vicinity of Treptow Park, Nordland once again found itself in the path of a major Russian assault. The soldiers fended off the attackers for several hours but were so heavily outnumbered and outgunned that they had to withdraw westward into Neukölln. Hans's flak unit had fought running battles most of the way from Narva to Berlin with vehicle-towed guns, but for lack of fuel the men now pushed and pulled the last of these—relatively small 20mm antiaircraft guns—by hand. After destroying several attacking Russian tanks in the vicinity of Tempelhof Airfield with their last rounds of ammunition, they spiked their guns with grenades. Out of hundreds of 11th Flak men, only 63 remained.[20]

The Reds pushed Hans and the other Nordland defenders out of Neukölln and Templehof on April 26. The division rallied about a kilometer northeast near Hermannplatz, where Krukenberg had set up a temporary command post in an opera house. During the pullback, Krukenberg's French SS soldiers and a few Hitler Youth boys knocked out 14 Soviet tanks from a strategically placed machine-gun position near the Halensee Bridge further west and helped hold up a Soviet advance for two entire days.[21]

On April 27, only Nordland and another drastically understrength unit, Panzer Division Müncheberg, were left to defend southeast Berlin. The latter was barely functional, having been formed just weeks earlier as an ad hoc division. These two skeleton units were about all that stood between the Zentrum (Central Berlin) and five advancing Soviet armies. Hans and his fellow defenders had no hope of delaying hundreds of thousands of attackers for long and soon lost their Hermannplatz toehold. The survivors edged rearward to the government district in the Zentrum, since little else remained under German control. Every man knew the center would be their last stand because the city was now surrounded. The Reich, at least in northern Germany, was now truly miniscule. In the Zentrum, Hans and his comrades joined several thousand survivors from other divisions already concentrated there in the rubble and cellars.

General Weidling renamed the Zentrum zone Sector Z and assigned Nordland to the eastern section that began at Wilhelmstraße, just a block east of Hitler's bunker and the Reichstag. Krukenberg established his new command post in a passenger subway car in the Stadtmitte U-Bahn station, less than five blocks from Hitler's Führerbunker in the garden of the Reich Chancellery. The Russians were by then approaching the city center from three directions: the southeast along the Frankfurter Allee, the south along Sonnen Allee, and the north on several routes.[22]

Hans and his fellow soldiers fought fiercely because capture meant almost certain death, and not necessarily a quick and painless one. They defended their remaining territory, house by house, sometimes in hand-to-hand combat. With a stock of *Panzerfausts*, Krukenberg's contingent of French SS fighters destroyed many Russian tanks. This shoulder-fired weapon, whose name means "tank fist," consisted of a cheap, preloaded, single-shot, recoilless launch tube that fired a small antitank warhead. Late in the war the Russians incorporated the best features of this and the American bazooka into their own design. Eventually it evolved into the infamous RPG-2—a weapon still popular with terrorists around the world today. Of the 108 Soviet tanks destroyed by the Germans in Berlin's Zentrum, Nordland's small contingent of French SS men claimed half.[23]

In the early morning hours of April 30, General Weidling informed Hitler that the 40,000 Berlin defenders he'd started with days before had dwindled to 10,000, and that these soldiers would run out of ammunition that night. Only then did Hitler grant permission for the survivors to try to break out through the Russian lines so they could surrender to American or British troops. At half past three that afternoon, Hitler and Eva Braun committed suicide and left instructions that their bodies were to be immediately cremated with gasoline. In his hastily dictated last will and testament, Hitler appointed a stalwart Nazi, Admiral Karl Dönitz, president of Germany and propaganda chief Joseph Goebbels chancellor.

As the fighting elements of the 1.5-million-man Russian force pressed relentlessly toward the city center, Hans and the other German defenders found themselves confined to an ever-dwindling space. Most fighting ceased on May 1, 1945, when the German defenders ran out of ammunition or the Soviets overran their positions. It was no coincidence that the end came on this date. International Workers' Day is a holiday the Soviet Union's communist government had hijacked long before, so a May

1 capture of Berlin was of enormous propaganda value to Stalin. Consequently, he'd demanded that the city be taken by then no matter the cost. His generals had no choice but to drop any strategic or systematic approach and mount an all-out assault. Stalin's self-serving order cost the lives of many a Soviet soldier.

During the night of May 1, most of Berlin's remaining defenders attempted to break out in various directions. Krukenberg, his Frenchmen, and a few other Nordland soldiers crossed the Spree River just before dawn. Most died fighting to the death near the Gesundbrunnen U-Bahn Station when they came under deadly fire. Only one sizeable group of Germans, proceeding west through the Tiergarten (zoo) and across the Havel River into Spandau, successfully passed through the inner Russian circle. Several small groups and individuals managed to get through elsewhere, but very few made it far enough west to surrender to the Western Allies. Most were killed or captured by the peripheral Soviet encircling forces.[24]

With the exception of a few pockets of resistance, the Zentrum fighting ceased on May Day. The Reich Chancellery and the massively fortified Zoo flak tower were two notable holdouts; all other buildings were pulverized by artillery fire. The 350-strong SS-held garrison of the flak tower eventually had to abandon its fortification. Many Waffen SS soldiers throughout the city committed suicide rather than allow themselves to be captured. Hiding was difficult for them because the Russians immediately searched house to house and room to room for anyone in a uniform. The searchers weren't particular about what sort of a uniform it was—policemen, firemen, and rail workers all fell into their net. The 80,000 men they arrested in and around the city were trucked or marched eastward as POWs.[25]

By May 1, Hans had survived countless enemy bullets, artillery bombardments, air attacks, and infantry assaults. His seven years in uniform had left him the most seasoned of seasoned veterans. Surviving that long had required the greatest luck, savvy, and will to survive, because at this point not one soldier in 20 who had been with Nordland in the summer of 1943 was still standing.

Hans and several other Banat men hid in a cellar through the night of May 1. They'd hatched an escape plan of their own and didn't join any of the breakout groups attempting to fight their way through the Russian lines during the night. Hans, likely the ranking NCO of the group, ventured up to street level in the early morning of May 2. He probably expected to find the streets empty after the night-long Russian drinking, raping, and looting spree that had ensued. Whether Hans was checking for enemy soldiers or scouting out the escape route will never be known because he met his destiny that morning. For a soldier, there is no greater irony than to survive years of combat, only to fall to a sniper's bullet as soon as the fighting has stopped.

The rest of the group, some six or seven men I was told, ditched their uniforms and donned the civilian clothes they'd hidden in their cellar. Three names Hans's family members recalled are Krisamer, Gauk, and Brunner. Some, maybe all, even dressed as women, they speculated. The entire group somehow escaped, and word of this later reached Han's family. Unfortunately, the story came to me too late to learn how these wily Banaters managed to pull it off. The principals had long since passed on, and I could no longer find anyone who possessed more details.[26] Hans apparently died in his uniform. His family members speculated that perhaps Hans was by then too proud and professional a soldier to take the uniform off and disguise himself as a civilian or woman. Or perhaps he simply thought the disguise wouldn't work. Another possibility is that Hans hadn't yet donned his disguise and momentarily let his guard down when he ventured up to the street to have a look at the situation.

---

1. Marc J. Rikmenspoel, *Waffen SS: The Encyclopedia* (Garden City, N.Y.: Military Book Club, 2002), 242.
2. Erhard Raus, *Panzer Operations: The Eastern Front Memoir of General Raus, 1941-1945*, ed. Steven H. Newton (Cambridge, MA: Da Capo Press, 2005), 334.
3. Earl F Ziemke, *The Battle for Berlin: End of the Third Reich* (London: Pan Books, 1974), 71.
4. Stiftelsen norsk Okkupasjonshistorie (Norwegian Occupation History Foundation), "The 'Nordland' SS Division Flak Units," 114764, accessed August 8, 2016, http://sno.no/files/documents/114764.pdf.
5. Stiftelsen norsk Okkupasjonshistorie (Norwegian Occupation History Foundation), "The 'Nordland' SS Division Flak Units."
6. Mart Laar, *Sinimäed 1944: II Maailmasõja Lahingud Kirde-Eestis (Sinimäed 1944: Battles of World War II in Northeast Estonia)* (Tallinn: Varrak, 2006).
7. Erik Wallin, *Twilight of the gods: a Swedish Waffen-SS volunteer's experiences with 11th SS-Panzergrenadier Division "Nordland," Eastern Front 1944-45* (Solihull: Helion, 2001).
8. Wallin, *Twilight of the gods*, 21.
9. Wallin, *Twilight of the gods*, 31.
10. John Nichol and Tony Rennell, *The Last Escape: The Untold Story of Allied Prisoners of War in Europe, 1944-45* (New York: Viking, 2003), 330.
11. Stiftelsen norsk Okkupasjonshistorie (Norwegian Occupation History Foundation), "The 'Nordland' SS Division Flak Units."
12. Wallin, *Twilight of the gods*.
13. Rudolf Herzog, *Dead Funny: Humor in Hitlers Germany* (Brooklyn, N.Y.: Melville House, 2011), 188.
14. Melita Maschmann, *Account Rendered: A Dossier on My Former Self* (London ; New York: Abelard-Schuman, 1965), 167.
15. Wallin, *Twilight of the gods*, 41
16. Stiftelsen norsk Okkupasjonshistorie (Norwegian Occupation History Foundation), "The 'Nordland' SS Division Flak Units."
17. Jewish Virtual Library. "The SS (Schutzstaffel): 11th SS Volunteer Panzergrenadier Division Nordland." Accessed August 2, 2016. https://www.jewishvirtuallibrary.org/11th-ss-volunteer-panzergrenadier-division-nordland.
18. Stiftelsen norsk Okkupasjonshistorie (Norwegian Occupation History Foundation), "The 'Nordland' SS Division Flak Units."
19. Maschmann, *Account Rendered*.

20. Wilhelm Tieke, *Tragedy of the Faithful: A History of the III. (Germanisches) SS-Panzer-Korps* (Winnipeg, Manitoba: J.J. Fedorowicz Publishing, 2001), 318.
21. Antony Beevor, *Berlin: The Downfall, 1945* (London: Viking, 2002), 303.
22. Beevor, *Berlin: The Downfall, 1945*, 257.
23. Beevor, *Berlin: The Downfall, 1945*, 353.
24. Beevor, *Berlin: The Downfall, 1945*, 257.
25. Beevor, *Berlin: The Downfall, 1945*, 388.
26. Ingrid Slavik, "Johann Eipert" (Email, 2009).

45 A Slave Labor Sentence

Four months before Hans died from the sniper bullet in Berlin and Fidel shed his Waffen SS uniform in Bavaria, their sister Magdalena found herself moving ever deeper into the frightening nightmare that was Stalin's Soviet Union. When Magdalena's train was split up in Stalino, her section of boxcars was routed to Novomoskovsk, which regained its original name of Samar in 2024. That place was then a grim Ukrainian city the ethnic German prisoners called Neu Moskau (New Moscow). When the train dropped them there on February 1, 1945, Magdalena and her companions had spent what seemed an eternity—15 days—locked inside the icy, cramped freight cars. They'd received little consideration from the guards and had largely subsisted on food brought from home. Sanitation was a nightmare, and the stench from the hole-in-the-floor toilet in each car must have been overpowering. No one had been able to wash themselves or their soiled clothes. Still, Magdalena's group was luckier than later groups who traveled even deeper into the USSR—some as far as Siberia.

At Novomoskovsk, Magdalena and the others joined earlier arrivals, including Siebenbürgen-Sachsen Germans from Romania and the Serbian Germans who'd passed through Orzydorf days before Orzydorf's own nightmare began. Despite the fierce winter conditions, no indoor accommodations awaited the new arrivals, so they sheltered under pieces of sheet-metal roofing. Eventually, Magdalena and more than a dozen other women were crowded into a dark, windowless room inside a dank stone building that had bare wood pallets for beds.

Regardless of the lack of a stove or fireplace in the crude, icy hovel, the women devoted hours to breaking a hole through a wall. Although the opening would allow in cold wind and snow, the occupants desperately needed light and fresh air. Eventually the women managed to beat out enough stones to provide circulation. On those rare occasions that they found themselves inside the hut during the short daylight hours, the hole also allowed in enough light to let them see what they were doing.

The conditions at Novomoskovsk were extreme. Magdalena couldn't believe that people would deliberately treat others so abysmally. When the last of the food from home ran out, the prisoners became dependent on the camp administrators. Not only did these officials skimp on the amount of food they fed the prisoners, the fare they served was so grossly unfit for human consumption that it was hard to swallow. The prisoners became hungry enough that whenever locals arrived at the camp to barter, the prisoners traded away much of the warm clothing they'd brought from home.

The laborers weren't even provided water, so Magdalena and her roommates dug holes in the ground to collect runoff water for drinking, bathing, and washing their clothes. Toward the end of the five months Magdalena spent at Novomoskovsk, even this source of water ran low. When only a mud hole remained for collecting drinking water, Magdalena began to fear that she wouldn't survive the USSR. She said that if she hadn't been transferred to a different camp at this point she'd surely have succumbed.

Magdalena's worksite in Novomoskovsk was a steel-rolling mill heavily damaged by the Germans in the war. Ironically, it was Germans who'd built it in the first place only a handful of years earlier. The slave laborers were not there to repair the roofless building, but rather to put the mill back into production. Doing so required them to toil at this job in the open air throughout the winter and spring.

Shifts lasted 12 hours, and there were no days off. Magdalena's first job was clearing the floor of debris and cleaning mortar off frozen-together bricks. The only tools provided were a pry bar and a pushcart. In the bitterly cold weather, snow covered everything because fierce winds blew it around relentlessly. The prisoners were issued padded jackets as well as kerchiefs with which to cover their faces, but that wasn't protection enough. Warding off frostbite required them to move continuously. Once, Magdalena's group built a small fireplace of bricks in the work yard and collected a little wood so they could warm their food, but a guard kicked the contraption over and warned them that fires and cooking were not allowed. When their work at the site ended after five months, only 450 of the original 1,000 Germans remained alive. The surrounding grounds were dotted with so many unmarked graves that Magdalena truly despaired.

The weather had become less debilitating by the time the dirty work of getting the mill up and running was finished at the end of June 1945. Still, Magdalena was fortunate that Soviet workers were brought in to replace the slave laborers, for it bought her and the other survivors a desperately needed reprieve. That relief came in the form of a transfer to another Ukrainian industrial center, to which the prisoners were once again shipped like freight, in boxcars. The new location, Makejewka, was near the industrial city of Stalino.

Upon arrival, the prisoners were distributed among several camps and work sites, but everyone was so weak from starvation and the brutal conditions at Novomoskovsk that it took two weeks of rest and a diet of marginally better food to restore enough strength for them to resume work. The work turned out to be just as hard as before, but to the surprise of the everyone, they were paid for their work. Soviet workers had a maxim "We pretend to work and they pretend to pay us." The first part certainly didn't hold for ethnic German forced laborers, for the work was again brutally hard. But the second part was on the mark. The pay was such a token amount that it didn't buy anything useful aside from a propaganda claim that the workers were being compensated.

Makejewka was the site of four labor camps. Each contained small, primitive barracks along with several other buildings. Magdalena learned of a fifth camp near the end of her confinement—this one for German POWs. From the four civilian camps, armed military guards marched workers to and from their jobs at factories each day. Occasionally, new German prisoners arrived from larger camps to replace the latest casualties. Despite slightly improved living conditions, many prisoners died here too. The death rate declined somewhat in 1946 when a new policy released some prisoners before they succumbed. Prior to then, nothing was done for those who became too sick or spent to work. Released Germans from Romania were fortunate enough to still have homes or relatives to return to. Other nationalities no longer did because many of the Soviet-occupied countries east of Germany's postwar-shrunken borders had cleansed their territories of the millions of ethnic Germans with homelands there. However, having a place to return to didn't mean that the sick were actually sent there. The Russians often found it more convenient to dump them in the American or British zones of occupied Germany to become someone else's problem.

Magdalena's Makejewka quarters were in a three-room barracks building. Unfortunately, none of the three rooms were designed for the comfort of the occupants. Two of them held eight beds that slept 24 people. The smaller room contained four beds for eight people. Each camp had a number of such buildings. Magdalena bunked in one of the large rooms with 23 other women. Half were from Orzydorf and occupied one side of the room. The other 12 women came from Romania's Siebenbürger Sachsen region and occupied the other side. Their building, like every other one, also contained a room that had a small pantry used mainly for washing soiled clothes. Some of the buildings housed both men and women, but the rooms were segregated.

Magdalena's camp was run by aged communists. In typical communist fashion, they set up five small supply buildings that each distributed a different item. One might offer shoes, another overalls, a third, jackets, etc. Each camp also had a blockhouse for gatherings such as the indoctrination sessions inmates were required to attend. At Makejewka, Magdalena was again assigned to work at a blast furnace. This one too had sustained major war damage and was roofless. As at the previous plant, the emphasis was on production rather than reconstruction, so in effect Magdalena worked outdoors, exposed to the elements once again. Far too often that meant enduring rain, snow, heat, or cold.

In this job Magdalena was paired with a local woman. The team's task was to grab each piece of glowing sheet metal with steel tongs as it came out of the blast furnace. "We dragged it over to the roller and there, with a half turn, fastened it down tight. When there was a problem or some failure, I or my partner was blamed," she said.

Heat from the blast furnace kept Magdalena's eyebrows and lashes singed off, and shooting embers gave her numerous burn scars. Conditions were worst in the winter because of frequent snow showers. The furnace heat melted the snow as it fell, soaking her overalls. As a result, her back froze and her front cooked. Then on the walk back to the barracks after her shift ended, the entire wet outfit froze. "They would stand up by themselves if taken off," she said. However, taking them off was risky because clothes left unguarded were soon stolen. And the loss of essential clothing was a threat to survival in the harsh winter conditions. Sanitation was another problem. When Magdalena and her coworkers returned from the night shift, they could seldom bathe to clean off the black coal soot that covered them.

Survival in such brutal conditions demanded both vigilance and adaptability. The pitiless conditions could quickly kill anyone who fell into decline. The smarter prisoners quickly realized that their best chance of remaining alive was to band together, for groups were better able to exploit small opportunities that appeared. Magdalena and six other women in her room bonded because their personalities meshed and they all shared the same primary objective—doing whatever it took to make it back home. Magdalena said, "We all helped each other because if someone did not remain healthy, they were not going to survive. From that time on [at Makejewka], because I had more food, I no longer doubted that I would return home. I wanted to make it back to Leni and prayed for this to happen." The same desperate longing to see their families again also drove her roommates.

The Russian guards perceived the prisoners' intense longing for home and used it to play a sadistic game. Magdalena said, "They would tell us we were to be transported home the next day. Of course, nothing came of it. They only wanted to arouse our hopes and then see our disappointment."

Desperation to get home completely overcame some people. Magdalena particularly recalled one man from a village near Orzydorf who had a work accident in which he suffered a bad cut. When Magdalena saw him pack dirt into the open wound she asked, "Why are you doing this? Do you want to die here?" He replied, "Do you think I want to stay here forever and work in a rolling mill?" He thought his injury would get him sent home. Eight days later he was dead.

Late in her internment, Magdalena herself incurred a serious cut on her leg from a piece of sheet metal roofing she was unloading from a truck. She cleaned and doctored it constantly but the wound refused to heal during her remaining time in the USSR. The overall risk for men was greater than for women because their job assignments were often more hazardous. It didn't help that some of them were so addicted to smoking that they traded away some of their meager food ration for tobacco. They rolled tobacco in any kind of paper at hand but preferred to use the Russian newspapers printed on special paper suitable for rolling smokes.

Because the living conditions were crowded and primitive, certain rules evolved in order to allow so many people to coexist without constant friction. One involved bathing. When circumstances allowed, women brought water to their room and washed in a basin. The men knew they weren't to come in at those times. If they did want to enter, they were to knock first, then ask permission. Nevertheless, one day while washing herself near the door, Magdalena heard a knock and assumed it was a female because there was no request for permission to enter. To her surprise, upon opening the door, she saw a man standing there. She reacted by flinging the whole washbasin of water at him. She had to clean up the mess afterwards, but seeing the man's shocked reaction was worth it. "He hadn't respected the rule," Magdalena chuckled after relating the story.

Toward the end of the confinement, the bathing situation improved when camp inmates were allowed an occasional shower in a separate building. Unlike their living quarters, this building was heated. Men and women went there in separate groups. When the women showered, the Russian male workers who heated the place climbed up to a vantage point that allowed them to peer into the enclosure and ogle the naked women. Because there was nothing to be done about it, the women tolerated it.

Sometimes inspectors came to the barracks and made the women strip naked and line up in front of them. But in general, women weren't molested in the camps, and she knew of few rapes. Magdalena knew of one case in which a woman had a child by a Russian, but didn't believe it was the result of a rape. Magdalena said the Russian guards in the camp didn't need to beat the prisoners; the hard work, poor food, and bone-chilling cold did it for them. She recalled one woman who became so weak from the harsh conditions that on one occasion she wasn't even able to even pull her pants back up in the latrine outbuilding and had to ask a man to do it for her. Magdalena said that this poor woman was already half dead.

The cold of winter was not the only weather extreme. June could be very hot, which made working at the blast furnace a different type of agony. But the prisoners also faced torments other than physical hardship. When the weather was agreeable, the administrators hung up canvas sheets for movie screens and showed communist films. Magdalena said that propaganda nonsense at the mandatory sessions was hard to watch. For one thing, the films were in Russian, so few comprehended the language well enough to understand what was said. During the films some of the men sneaked behind the screen, climbed atop one another to get across the high fence, and returned to their rooms. Even the Soviets had a hard time stomaching those atrocious films. From time to time live indoctrination sessions were also held. Mercifully, the administrators didn't press the inmates very hard to attend because they realized that getting the work done was more important than pushing ideology onto nonreceptive foreign slave laborers.

The prisoners picked up just enough Russian to get by; very few wanted to learn more. With a trace of sarcasm, Magdalena said, "We could stay alive but we couldn't learn Russian." Her point was that the prisoners resisted learning the language of their oppressors. With so little control over their own lives, the rejection of anything Russian was one of the few expressions of defiance open to them.

Adaptation was just as crucial to survival as food, and not everyone learned that quickly enough. "I was so innocent in the beginning, but then I got an education," Magdalena confided. Early on, when a man at the camp persuaded her to help him get a padded jacket, she agreed to let him hold the one she had while she went to the supply room to tell the worker she had none. The Russian clerk refused to give her a new one, so she went to retrieve her own and learned the man had vanished. Consequently, Magdalena had to go without a jacket for a time—something that could have proved fatal. Harsh lessons like this taught her how to take care of herself.

With a wry grin, Magdalena related an example of how resourceful she and the other women became. She and her roommates sewed up the hems of their dungarees to create small pockets inside their cuffs so they could smuggle small items out of the plant. Near the end of their shift, they stuffed these pockets with small lumps of coal or sticks of wood for a bit of heat in their barracks. The tricky part was getting past the single-file checkpoint at the plant exit. Once, when a Siebenbürgen woman was caught smuggling out such material at the checkpoint, she applied her wits by screaming, dropping to the ground, and thrashing about wildly. Her gyrations made it hard for the guards to remove the coal from her hidden pockets. Meanwhile, the distraction allowed seven or eight other women behind her to slip through the checkpoint.

Heat was precious in the fierce cold. This smuggling tactic alone didn't provide enough fuel for the women's needs, so they also scraped holes under the factory fence or broke holes in it to pass wood or coal through for later retrieval. Sometimes they simply threw the fuel over the fence. Scaling a wall or fence to get at a stash was not unheard of either. But while a little heat and lots of clothing were important, those things were not the most critical necessity in the camp. Magdalena found that what was most crucial in remaining healthy was adequate food.

The prisoners grew so used to death and suffering that they toughened mentally and came to view even the worst abuse dispassionately. Magdalena related the following story to illustrate how the conditions muted emotions. On that occasion armed soldiers forced a man to dig his own grave for a rule infraction. With the man's son in attendance, they led the prisoner to the grave's edge and shot him. After the victim fell into the hole, the son impassively jumped into the pit and in a mechanical manner laid his father out and straightened his clothes, then climbed back out. This grave joined all the other anonymous mounds. Every prisoner knew that such a hole was all that they could expect if they died in the USSR. The graves didn't even get a cross or marker. The only decency accorded the deceased, if it could even be called a decency, was a notation of the victim's name in a record.

To improve morale for the purpose of increasing production, the slave laborers were eventually allowed to write home. The communication was limited to a small postcard once every three months. Magdalena wrote in the tiniest script she could make legible in order to maximize use of the space. The outgoing cards were collected on schedule, but the prisoners learned this didn't mean they were dispatched in a timely manner. Neither did return mail always reach the laborers promptly. Often it sat somewhere for three or four months before delivery. Not once during her internment did Magdalena receive any real news of Romania. The censors allowed only personal news to pass through—information concerning births, deaths, marriages, and the like. She didn't even learn until after her release that the Moscow faction of communists had consolidated all power in Romania.

Magdalena said she was fortunate that her Russian partner at the blast furnace was a good person. It should be noted that because Novomoskovsk was in the so-called republic of Ukraine within the Soviet Union, the locals might be either ethnic Russians or ethnic Ukrainians. Magdalena didn't draw a distinction between the two and referred to both as Russians.

Magdalena's coworker was raising two children alone and had little enough herself, but still sometimes brought food for Magdalena and others. Occasionally Magdalena was able to return the favor by giving things to her friend. When Magdalena was once allowed to visit the woman's home, she was appalled at the abject poverty in which her friend lived. Her biggest surprise was finding the woman's home was a communal one inside a building identical to the prisoner barracks. She then realized that to build the slave labor camps, the authorities had simply walled off some of the communal residential buildings to form prison compounds.

When the Russians began shipping out some of the prisoners too weak to work during Magdalena's second year of slave labor, some of the more desperate Germans contemplated allowing themselves to decline so they'd be sent home. But most understood that this strategy was very risky, for the frail often died before release or incurred permanent health damage. The harsh conditions already assured that a decline in health was unavoidable. The major contributor at Makejewka was the food. There was more of it than at Novomoskovsk, but it was still shockingly bad.

Each morning, the prisoners received a loaf of bread that was small, dense, and had a revolting kerosene-like taste. Lunch consisted of watery soup. Later in the confinement a daily spoonful of millet, a nutritious grain rich in iron, phosphorus, vitamins, and amino acids, was dispensed to alleviate the colitis that ran rampant in the malnourished laborers. This was done less out of a wish to improve the prisoners' health than to increase production. Because the camp diet lacked any fat, the workers were also supposed to get a daily spoonful of oil. However, oil was valuable and scarce, so the kitchen staff stole it. The only good thing to come of the oil-dispensing idea was that each laborer was provided the spoon the oil should have been poured into. A spoon made the bowl of thin soup easier to eat.

The greater number of calories at Makejewka staved off some of the debilitating weakness they laborers had experienced at Novomoskovsk, but their hunger was still so overpowering that during the growing season most workers collected and ate grass. It often made them sick, but they kept doing it anyway to fill their stomachs. Magdalena could never tolerate grass, herself. On one occasion rotten, boiled meat served by the camp kitchen gave many workers food poisoning. Magdalena was among the ones hospitalized. She recovered, but a number of prisoners did not and died.

The food shortage was exacerbated by the particularly poor harvest of 1946. Even the Russians didn't eat well then. The monotonous fare served in the evening consisted mainly of cabbage and beets. Cabbage was the staple during the growing season, but it usually had to be eaten raw for lack of wood to cook with. Only the prisoners assigned to construction labor were allowed to build a crude stove in their work yard, but even they weren't always able to scrounge wood for a fire.

During Magdalena's first two-and-a-half years in the camps, the prisoners used ration coupons issued to them to obtain their bread. In 1947 a better harvest and the USSR's latest ruble devaluation marginally improved conditions. The government had decided to curb inflation and bring down food prices by reducing the amount of money in circulation. This also diminished the competition for consumer goods, which were always in short supply. Peasants were the main target of the government action because many had been selling food at wartime prices, which resulted in the accumulation of small hordes of cash. The new policy exchanged one new ruble for 10 old rubles, and limited redemptions to 3,000 rubles. The prisoners were now required to buy their bread with their wages, since the new rules abolished the ration coupon system they'd been living under. Fortunately, bread suddenly became affordable enough to buy with the meager pay. Toward the end of Magdalena's internment in 1949, the laborers were also able to buy a bit of other food, although they still had to eat it raw for lack of cooking fuel.

When the prisoners had first arrived at Makejewka, the working conditions were just as appalling as at Novomoskovsk. As before, they had to use crude tools to tackle the snow- and ice-covered piles of frozen rubble that were once parts of the factory roof and walls. After the plants were up and running again a year later, the bosses brought in local production workers. Magdalena was then reassigned to a rail-yard locomotive fueling station where her job was to help keep five or six engines operating by delivering coal, drums of oil, and other supplies. Every other day these machines needed to be supplied with 200-liter (52-gallon) drums of oil and piles of coal. Magdalena had no handling equipment for the heavy drums so had to roll them. She wasn't a large person, but could move them by herself when the surface was flat. What she couldn't do alone was roll the drums up a ramp to get them into the horse-drawn delivery cart. This required the help of an old Russian man assigned to be her co-worker.

Once the drums were loaded onto the horse cart, Magdalena and the old man delivered them to the locomotives, which weren't always in the rail yard. At first, Magdalena didn't have suitable clothing for the demanding, dirty work, so the old man took pity and drove her to a supply warehouse for rubber boots and a slightly better work outfit. The dirtiest part of the job involved shoveling coal aboard locomotive tenders. The coal dust this raised blackened her skin and left her clothes so filthy that they wouldn't come clean by ordinary washing. A Russian woman showed Magdalena the solution—washing them in gasoline. Magdalena said of the Russians, "They could be helpful sometimes and weren't all bad." She confided that she harbored more resentment towards the Romanian police and auxiliary police back home than toward ordinary Russians. "The Romanian police," she said, "were nasty and to be feared."

The filthy fueling job lasted for a year and a half, after which Magdalena joined a construction crew. Only then did she acquire work clothes of a somewhat decent quality. Following the construction stint, she toiled on a collective farm. Until these last two jobs came along, she'd worked long hours every day with barely any time off. Now the work hours moderated, and the slave laborers were given Sundays off. To maintain their sanity, the prisoners had always devised their own entertainment during their scant slack time. Magdalena couldn't recall a single instance of the Russian bosses providing them entertainment until the free Sundays came along. After that, on one occasion the administrators brought in a ballet troupe. The performance cost the prisoners a considerable portion of their meager savings, but it broke the monotony. With an entire day free now, Magdalena was also allowed an occasional pass to visit fellow Orzydorf prisoners in the neighboring camps. A couple of times she and some of the other women even attended a dance at the German POW camp. A single weekly day of rest didn't allow for much of a social life, but it was enough to remind Magdalena that someday the nightmare had to end and she'd experience normal life again with her daughter and family, far away from the unfeeling harshness of the Soviet Union. It was a good thing she didn't know what lay ahead in Romania.

46 Magdalena's Return

That Magdalena was a strong and determined woman, I had no doubt. But I felt compelled to ask her how many of the 1000 prisoners that arrived with her at Novomoskovsk, the first camp, were left when she was finally released. She replied that of the 450 who survived Novomoskovsk to be transported to Makejewka, just a quarter remained at the end of the five-year hell. That put her in a select group of only one in 10 to make it to the end. A few people had been shipped out of the USSR in the final years after becoming too debilitated to work, but the majority of prisoners had died.

A few of the weakest prisoners were sent back to Romania as early as 1945, but the Russians didn't release larger numbers until 1948. Then, more of the chronically ill pared the numbers down. But as Magdalena found out, being one of the strongest was a mixed blessing, for the strong were held for five long years. In 1948 the authorities had opted to release women born in 1918 or earlier. Magdalena just missed the cut-off. This was an especially bitter pill for her to swallow because it cost her many extra months of hell.

Few male prisoners ever made it home. The vast majority had been 40 to 50 years old. They were already beyond their physical prime when they arrived, so they needed to be particularly strong to survive. And lucky, because men were given the most hazardous job assignments. The majority on Magdalena's train ended up in coal or salt mines around Stalino, where conditions were so atrocious that few survived their sentence. But Magdalena conceded that the Russian hierarchy was almost as cruel to its own people.

The earliest sick workers to be released were sent directly back to Romania. Then, from the end of 1945 through 1948, the infirm were dumped in West Germany to fend for themselves. A return to their families from Germany required them to build up sufficient health to navigate their way through Soviet-occupied eastern Austria and Hungary using their own resourcefulness.

Magdalena's exodus from Ukraine finally came about near the end of 1949. Not surprisingly, the details remained sharp in her memory when she recalled it 50 years later. On November 12, 1949, a rumor of release swept the camp. After many previous disappointments, Magdalena couldn't allow herself to believe that the nightmare was truly over. But on the following day an extraordinary announcement followed the morning roll call. Everyone was to remain in the camp! This order marked the end of five years of grueling labor, most of it spent toiling long hours seven days a week.

To Magdalena's dismay, the joy of what should have been a very happy occasion was dampened when a complication prevented her leaving with her friends and Orzydorf neighbors, as she'd counted on. The delay was the result of a clerical snafu—Russians pronounced names phonetically, so the clerks had spelled hers Aipert instead of Eipert. For some reason, fixing the paperwork involved more than a few extra strokes of a typewriter key. A cynic might suspect such an error would never have held up her extraction from Romania to the Soviet Union. Her release didn't take place until the very last transport departed. By this time, she was one of only six or seven people left in her barracks.

Magdalena and several other holdovers raised such a ruckus that the camp *Lagerleiter* (German for camp administrator), an aged Russian Jew, summoned them to his office. Magdalena understood a bit of Russian by this time and was able to follow the man's chiding remarks when he said, "You lasted this long, so a day or two isn't going to make much difference. You might as well go back to your rooms and have a good time until the next train comes."

With the rubles left from her scanty pay, Magdalena bought sweets to take back home. It was rumored that such things weren't available in Romania. These confections, along with other goods and food, had just recently begun to appear in the local government shops, but few people could afford to buy them in the Soviet worker's paradise because their pay was so paltry. Even educated and skilled workers like doctors and engineers earned but a pittance.

Whatever possessions Magdalena couldn't take back with her, she gave to her Russian friend—the woman who'd shared her own meager food ration when the two of them had worked together at the blast furnace. Two days of waiting felt like an eternity, but the disappointment of the delay disappeared when Magdalena stepped from her barracks for the final assembly. Some of her new joy waned again when a military officer appeared and ominously stepped up to address the group. It wasn't the best news, but not the worst either, when he said that everyone might as well become better acquainted. No one needed to be told that this meant the train would be late.

Upon exiting the gate for the last time, Magdalena felt no compunction to look back. She'd seen enough of that prison and was focused on nothing but getting to the rail yard and climbing into her assigned boxcar. In the icy car, Magdalena had no desire to talk. All she wanted to do was bundle up and hunker down until she reached the Romanian border. "Leave me alone, I only want to sleep," she recalled saying to her fellow passengers as the train rolled out of Makejewka.

At a siding close to the Romanian border two days later, everyone was ordered to pick up their possessions and leave the train for an inspection. There, soldiers meticulously pawed through every possession and bit of baggage the laborers had brought along. Anything with writing on it was closely checked. The guards confiscated any little memento, letter, or hidden scrap of paper. They also seized the bibles, books, letters, and family photos that had sustained the laborers through their years of confinement. "We realized everything would be burnt up," Magdalena said. She recalled one woman tearing the cover off her bible so she'd at least have that.

Magdalena grew quite chilled in the winter air as she hung back in the hope the searchers would grow laxer toward the end. The tactic didn't work. When her turn came around, they still took away her precious mementos. One of the items was a photo of Fidel and me. My mother had somehow been able to send it to her from Germany. On the photograph she'd jotted down my age (two). Had I thought to ask her to describe the photo, I could have surprised her and replaced it with a copy.

Following the inspection, the returnees were fed. For the first time in five years, Magdalena sat down to a full meal. The group was then loaded into a different set of boxcars for the final leg of the journey to the border. For that segment the passengers enjoyed the luxury of straw-stuffed mattresses to sleep on. On reaching the border, the guards there combed through the straw after ordering the prisoners to dump out their mattresses. Other guards then searched the train again. Despite their intrusiveness, this batch of Russian officials and guards were almost friendly—even the army officer who delivered a goodbye speech. Respect was not something the prisoners were used to. The officer's farewell was a last-ditch attempt to soften the prisoners' attitude toward the Soviet Union. The man thanked the Germans for their labor and in an apologetic tone said that he was sorry they'd had it so rough and had been given so little, but his own people hadn't had it much better. It was a nice speech but couldn't begin to make up for all the criminality, misery, and deliberate cruelty.

Before anyone could board the narrow-gauge train that awaited on Romania's side of the border, the entire group was once again ordered to line up in the freezing cold while the train they'd just vacated was searched for a second time. Then they had to wait while the Romanian train they were about to board was searched. By then, explanations as to the purpose of it all were no longer needed or expected; it was simply the communist way! The Romanian train delivered them to the nearby ethnically Hungarian city of Sighet. One of the Russian officers who escorted them there made one last pitch to the returnees when he said, "Don't say we treated you badly, because we gave you everything we had, too." It echoed the earlier speech, but again rang hollow because it failed to justify the pitiless harshness and criminality of slave labor.

At Sighet the returnees spent eight days in a rehabilitation camp so they could be fattened up. The Russians didn't want the returnees to look quite so gaunt and starved. That might leave the wrong impression of Mother Russia on the Romanians they would soon encounter. So the ex-prisoners were allowed to eat as much as they liked, but of course their shrunken stomachs couldn't hold much at first.

Magdalena and her cohorts were surprised by how much the shops and vendor stands there offered in comparison to Russia. She even saw coffee beans for sale, something she hadn't run across in a very long time. On leaving Sighet, the Germans were issued enough money to buy whatever local train tickets they still needed to reach their homes from the mainline station in Arad. At this point, for the first time in five years, the returnees were accorded seats in a regular passenger train. These seats were in two reserved cars to minimize contact with the public. To maintain this segregation, the Russians placed a Romanian military policeman aboard to keep everyone else out. However, after the guard noticed that no Russians had come along, he jumped off at the next stop. During the journey west, the reserved cars were switched onto other trains two or three times to route them to Arad in the western part of Romania. Magdalena noticed that the farther they got from the border, the less interest in them the authorities had. At some point, she finally fell into a sound sleep.

Because Romanian was not the first language of the ethnic Germans, they'd largely forgotten how to speak it after five years of disuse and were barely able to inquire about the local trains they needed to take to get to their homes. Magdalena said that while they may have felt lost with the language, they didn't feel lost on re-encountering the much warmer air of their native climate.

In Arad, 30 kilometers north of Orzydorf, the ex-prisoners said their goodbyes and split up. On the last leg of Magdalena's journey, she and several other returnees found themselves seated among Romanians. Those people immediately became curious about the Germans. Despite the language difficulty, the ex-prisoners got across that they'd just returned from five years of slave labor in the USSR. The surprised Romanians responded sympathetically and shared their food. This is when Magdalena learned that beyond the German communities, no one knew about the slavery. When the Romanians asked Magdalena and the others just where they'd been in Russia, they were frustrated in not being able to supply precise answers. All they could do was recite the place names, for not once in their five years had they seen a map.

As Magdalena's train pulled into Orzydorf on November 25, 1949, well-wishers from all over the village rushed to the station to greet her. Tears still welled up in her eyes 50 years later as she recalled the event. "There were so many people there at the train station!" The villagers knew her approximate return date because she'd written to her family from Sighet and alerted them of her imminent arrival. Despite all the well-wishers, Magdalena quickly spotted Linde, her niece and goddaughter, in the arms of Tante [aunt] Rabong, the woman whose house the communists had seized for their headquarters. Later, it and her farmstead became a tractor-driving school, according to Fidel. Linde had been a tiny infant when Magdalena was exiled; now the girl was five years old. Magdalena recalled the occasion of the baby's baptism because it was interrupted by an air raid siren. Luckily, the target of the raid had been Timişoara, not Orzydorf.

Of course, the person Magdalena most longed to see was her daughter, Leni, now twelve years old. Family members told Magdalena that her little girl had lived every day with the hope that her mother was alive and that one day she'd see her return. All the other surviving mothers were already back. Copious and unabashed tears of joy flowed from Magdalena's eyes as soon as they caught sight of Leni.

Leni too was unable to forget the day her mother returned. While her mother was away in the Soviet Union, she'd been living with her grandmothers. On Sundays she would arrive at the home of Magdalena Sr. and stay there for three nights. She recalled that in the evenings they played a lot of cards. Then on Wednesday she'd go stay with Josef's mother for the next four nights. When Leni learned that her mother was on the way at last, she begged to skip school. Yet, waiting at the train station each day was impractical, so she made an arrangement with the little Romanian girl who now lived next door with her family in the other house within the Eipert family hof. The girl was to run to the school and alert Leni the moment her mother arrived. Several days later, Leni was in her classroom when there was a tiny knock on the door. As soon as the teacher opened the door and Leni saw her small neighbor, she bounded from her desk and darted through the door. Words couldn't relay her feelings as she tried to relay the joy of seeing her mother once again. The event still tugged at her heart and couldn't be related with dry eyes when I spoke with her in Nuremberg in 1990.

As might be expected, the harsh conditions of those years exacted a physical toll on Magdalena—particularly the year and a half in the rolling mills. Magdalena believed that the long hours on her feet had left her with the persistent leg problems and painful varicose veins that plagued her for the rest of her life. Magdalena was also emotionally damaged. Leni's own daughter, Ingrid, who over the years provided me immeasurable help with interviews and inquiries, revealed that her grandmother was unable to cry or show emotion for nearly 50 years after she returned from Russia. Ingrid noted that during the last conversation she had with Magdalena about the ordeal, her grandmother kept fingering the hem of her blouse and rolling it up, betraying a new inner emotional stirring that Ingrid hadn't seen in her grandmother before. Magdalena was only able to cry or show feelings again during the last five years of her life. Apparently, she'd finally reached some sort of internal accommodation with her traumatic experience.

Leni said her grandmother thought that because Magdalena was small, she wouldn't survive Russia. But Magdalena proved her wrong and did survive while many larger and more muscular people died. Magdalena, when asked, attributed her survival to strength and believed she was one of the strongest people in her camp. It was obvious to me that my aunt was no weakling, despite her small stature, but I understood that her claim had at least as much to do with inner mettle as with physical strength. Fortunately, she brought that strength back to Orzydorf with her, for without it she couldn't have persevered in the insane political climate she returned to. Some semblance of her fierce determination and self-confidence must have already been part of her makeup when her eastbound train left Vinga for the USSR at the beginning of 1945 as a single mother and recent widow, but it was vastly fortified by her many trials in Stalin's Soviet Union.

A variety of factors kept Magdalena going in the face of grief, sorrow, and hardship. She told me that she mourned and cried a great deal after Josef was murdered but forged on because others relied on her and there was so much work to do. At that time, she numbly went out to the fields each day and did whatever needed to be done. It helped immensely that she was supported by her family, particularly three women who served as

The Eipert family in Orzydorf in 1949. Seated and dressed in black is Magdalena Sr., Fidel's mother. To her right are her granddaughter Linde with Linde's mother, Magdalena, the widow of her son Hans. To her left is granddaughter Leni, the child of her daughter Magdalena and the late Josef. All four were either husbandless or fatherless because of war. Leni had also been motherless for five years because her mother remained a slave laborer in the Soviet Union. Fidel was not in the photo because he was in West Germany after being exiled by the new Romanian communist government for serving in the German military at the behest of the previous Romanian government.

her mentors and role models, and in return, felt obligated to support. The three were: her mother, a person always stalwart, well-tempered, and caring; her grandmother, whose piety and unfettered optimism helped carry Magdalena through many a low point in her daily life; and her mother-in-law, a woman loyal and understanding through thick and thin.

Magdalena said that never during her time in the USSR did she allow herself to succumb to depression or despair. She focused so hard on survival that despair just couldn't take root. From the first, she saw but two stark choices—forge on or give up. There was no room for the latter if she was to see Leni and the rest of her family again.

After enduring five years of communist depravity in the Soviet Union, it is unlikely that Magdalena expected the Romanian brand of communism to be blissful when she set foot in Orzydorf again. Yet, she couldn't have anticipated what she found. In her absence the Romanian government had been completely subjugated by Stalin's proxies and had adopted the same peculiar Marxist logic that equated property with crime. By owning land, her family members had in effect become "enemies of the people." The consequences of the policy had gone into effect on August 23, 1945, eight months after Magdalena's abduction. At that time the state began appropriating the farms, machinery, and livestock of ethnic German farmers for redistribution in the name of agrarian reform.

The German minority became the first target because of its alleged collaboration with the Nazis. The communists conveniently chose to forget that as a German ally the entire country had collaborated. The new government intended to form Soviet-style collective farms from the seized property, but because it needed the support of Romania's peasants, lied about its true intentions and announced the land would go to small-holder peasants and the landless. Some of the German farmland was then distributed, but the beneficiaries of the land were only offered an amount too small to improve their situation much. In addition, they had to purchase this land, although the price was favorable. Not surprisingly, crop production declined to the point that the country could no longer feed itself. To amend this situation, nearly all land was collectivized several years later.

The devious government waited until the German farmers had expended their own labor harvesting their cereal grain crops in 1946 before beginning the land seizures. During the course of the expropriation, the local governments in ethnic German areas also seized many German houses and gave them to Romanians. On her return, Magdalena learned her family had lost the house of her grandparents in her mother's hof. Fortunately, the new occupants were affable and got along with the family.

Magdalena also learned that despite the land confiscation, she still held title to a portion of land in compensation for her husband Josef's death while serving in the Romanian Army. In reality, this ownership was a sham, because in her absence the ground was incorporated into a collective farm under an arrangement that allowed the collective to dictate what was planted and to collect the bulk of the harvest.

Magdalena became convinced that land ownership was the prime reason the communist functionaries had put her name on the slave labor list in the first place. Exile got her out of their way for years, and if she perished in Russia, the ownership problem disappeared altogether. The inconvenience of her survival and return brought the problem back for them because now Magdalena was able to reclaim her land and with the help of other farmers raise an abundant crop in 1951. The local government's solution was blunt. It allowed the local collective to seize it all—even the share that was rightfully hers. Magdalena fought back by hiring a lawyer, but the legal proceedings went nowhere and consumed what little money her family had. It was Russia all over again; she'd toiled for the state and received nothing for her labor. However, five years of coping with the oppressive system there had taught her a thing or two about how to survive under communism.

During the grain threshing, she stashed some of the sacked wheat under the straw pile left by the threshing machine. She had two of those sacks subsequently ground into flour. When collective officials learned of the deception through a snitch and showed up to seize the flour, the family hurriedly flung the flour sacks out of a window and hid them at a neighbor's house. Unfortunately, the collective learned of that too, as well as about the rest of the hidden grain. Magdalena then had no choice but to turn in both the flour and grain. At this point Magdalena Sr. took on a job at the cemetery in order to keep the family in food.

Magdalena herself was assigned to work at the collective, a place where she'd be at the mercy of the hostile managers. When she told the authorities that she'd already done that in the USSR and wouldn't do it again, the bosses expelled her from the collective. In the course of her continuing legal sparring with the managers, she was in and out of the collective several more times. In retaliation for my aunt's continued resistance, the collective barred Leni from admittance to the local *Gymnasium* (high school) because she was the daughter of an "exploiter of the people," a euphemism for land owner. This escalation came as a terrible blow to Magdalena because it meant the battle had become personal.

During the course of the sparring, the administrators kept inventing new ways to harass the family. One particularly vile tactic was sending armed men to deliver orders and decisions at midnight. Early in 1953 the agrarian committee sent Magdalena an ultimatum: farm the land and plant a crop, or lose it! Her family had been without horses, implements, or seed ever since the war ended nine years earlier. Failure to comply meant the loss of the title to the land and an end to the traditional means of support the family had relied on for the previous 175 years. The officials knew Magdalena no longer had the means to conform and were confident that they had finally defeated her. Without a crop, the family would at last find it impossible to subsist outside of the communist system. The land did not provide the family much, but Magdalena hung on in the hope that someday the system would be reformed.

Despite their apparent victory, the collective's bosses continued the harassment. Out of sheer vindictiveness they initiated criminal proceedings that would result in two years of imprisonment upon conviction. Magdalena's family and five others were accused of subversive activities before the court. The accused were all of German ancestry and had a history of prosperity resulting from good farming practices and hard work. Unfortunately, on the day of Magdalena's court date in Timişoara, the train ran late. When Magdalena entered the courtroom, she learned that she'd just been sentenced to two years in prison. The never-ending persecution brought her close to despair.

However, Magdalena rallied and objected to the sentence. That appeal consumed another year but deferred her sentence. Things finally appeared to go her way when the local collective went bust and collapsed. Magdalena was then acquitted because it became obvious to the court and everyone else that the collective's directors were incompetent political hacks, not managers or farmers. The court also restored her nominal land ownership. Afterward, a close family friend who worked as a notary in the Orzydorf parish hall helped Magdalena regain admittance to the reorganized collective. Belonging to the collective was necessary because it owned all the farm machinery. Beyond that, Magdalena still needed to find the money to grease the palms of certain officials, pay her lawyer, and buy seed. The proceeds from the sale of a house still owned by her mother-in-law made it happen.

Unfortunately, the legal victory didn't end the struggle. The new collective managers were communists of the same stripe as the old and declared that landowner status made Magdalena ineligible to work at the reorganized collective for wages. A frantic job search ensued because the family could no longer get by without further income. Luckily, the work experience Magdalena had gained as a slave laborer now came in handy and helped her land a job as a day laborer. And in the perplexing logic of the prevailing brand of Marxism, now that Magdalena was a member of the working class, Leni was eligible for high school.

In 1956 Leni's excellent high school marks earned the girl acceptance to an industrial chemistry program at the university in Timișoara. However, the *unhealthy ancestry* label refused to relinquish its grip. Leni was expelled during her second semester when student demonstrators marched in support of the ultimately unsuccessful anticommunist revolution in neighboring Hungary. She was subjected to hours of interrogation by Romania's hated secret police (Departamentul Securității Statului) for nothing more than observing the protest from the sidelines. That was enough to get her banished from further studies.

The official grounds for expulsion related to her original university application form. The Securitate determined that the application was incomplete because Leni had failed to reveal that her father had owned land in the pre-communist days. Completing the application had presented Leni with a Catch 22 conundrum. Revealing prior landowner status meant automatic rejection, and not revealing it mean automatic expulsion if found out. Fortunately, through the persistence of a supportive professor, Leni was readmitted to the university six months later and allowed to study mathematics. She went on to earn a degree in mathematics, but her career advancement possibilities were permanently damaged because of her family's history of bucking the Communist Party.

47 Romania, Farewell

As the 1950s drew to a close, Romania found itself in dire straits. The war reparations Stalin imposed, the abject failure of the Communist agrarian program, and the poor performance of the centrally planned economy resulted in extreme food and consumer goods shortages. The country was by then under such a foreign debt load that it had to export almost everything it produced. A steep decline in the already poor living standards followed. By the end of 1984, flour, bread, sugar, and milk rationing was imposed everywhere in the country, except for the capital of Bucharest. Frequent power outages had been the norm for years, but eventually electricity and fuel needed to be rationed also. Many homes now went unheated in the winter, and often schools closed for the season for lack of heating. By 1989 corruption was rampant, people queued all day for food, and little work got done. Romania had become a failed country.[1]

It didn't help that during the 1980s, Romanian dictator Nicole Ceaușescu became obsessed with "building himself a palace of unprecedented proportions, along with an equally grandiose neighborhood, Centrul Civic, to accompany it." At the same time that he spent vast sums of public money on his palace, his government shamelessly promoted the widespread food rationing as "a means to reduce obesity" and "rational eating." Meanwhile, much of the rationed food being sold to Romanians was the low-quality, export-rejected leftovers.[2]

Not surprisingly, even as early as the 1950s, most ethnic Germans no longer saw a future in Romania and wanted to leave for West Germany where the combination of America's Marshall Plan investments and western capitalism began to work an economic miracle. The Romanian government was only too willing to rid itself of this minority just as the Czech, Polish, and Hungarian communist governments had done. But because Stalin didn't approve, the German outflow from Romania remained a trickle.

The dynamics of the situation changed in 1962 when the Romanian communists were so desperate for cash that they became willing to monetize any resource. In a secret agreement with newly prosperous West Germany, they agreed to ransom the ethnic Germans who wanted out. The arrangement placed a price on the head of each working-aged ethnic German. The charge was based on the skill and education level of the worker. Romania was paid in hard currency, trade credits, and technology transfers.[3]

Romania had mucked about in this moral swamp before, so it knew how human trafficking worked. Gheorghiu-Dej, the first Communist leader of Romania, had in the 1950s dealt with a London-based Jewish Hungarian middleman named Henry Jacober, who paid hard cash for the release of Romanian Jews. He eventually ransomed hundreds of Jews for four to six thousand dollars apiece. Other Zionist organizations soon became involved, and in time approximately 300,000 Jews were sold to Israel. But Gheorghiu-Dej couldn't rightly claim credit for inventing this scheme. It had already been played by the pro-German Romanian government during World War II. Instead of sending all of its Jews to its Romanian-occupied Soviet territory for execution, the leadership found that these people could just as easily be sent to Zionist organizations abroad for cash and goods.[4] [5]

Gheorghiu-Dej's scheme was taken over by Nicolae Ceaușescu in 1965 when he became Romanian Communist Party general secretary and assumed leadership of Romania. By the time the communist system collapsed in 1989, Romania had ransomed nearly a quarter million ethnic Germans.[6] The centrally planned economy was such a disaster that the sale of Germans became the country's largest source of foreign exchange. During this period, Leni married and gave birth to two children. She and her husband wanted to leave Romania like everyone else, but they had a special problem—both were teachers. Under the ransom scheme cost schedule, their level of education made them the priciest Germans in the village at 25,000 marks each. Because West Germany's priority was to buy out the greatest number of people it could for its budget, Leni and her husband were among the last to go. Magdalena and my grandmother, Magdalena Sr., were free to leave Romania without recompense. As far as Romania was concerned, their age simply made them two extra mouths to feed and provide medical care for.

My grandmother, whose age had already made her eligible to leave 20 years earlier, had in fact taken advantage of that status in 1966 when she came to stay with Fidel and Maria in America. But she'd returned after a few months and was unwilling to leave again unless the rest of her family did so as well. Her earlier exodus came about when Fidel and his cousin

Hans invited her and her sister, Hans's mother, to come stay with them in the United States. Both men had become established there by then. The women accepted the offer and the appropriate arrangements followed. Their arrival in Iowa marked the first time these women had seen or spoken to their sons in 23 years. And it was the first time they'd laid eyes on their American grandchildren. However, two weeks on the farm left my grandmother homesick enough that she asked to return to Orzydorf, despite the poverty and the despised communist administrators there. Adjusting to America without the rest of her family around her had proven too difficult, for she spoke no English, found American farm life too isolated, and missed her friends.

In the early 1980s, when Leni and her husband learned they'd at last been ransomed by West Germany, there was much to be done for they had to be ready to leave as soon as their exit papers arrived. In preparation, they sold almost everything of value—the piano, the clunky Eastern-bloc car, the furniture, and even the dishes and kitchen utensils. The family still needed to eat, so several of Leni's Romanian colleagues helped out through the loan of pots, pans, and other kitchen essentials. The whole family then exited together when the clearance papers finally arrived, including Magdalena Sr. Despite having called Orzydorf her home for 87 years, the destructive effects of Marxism left her more than willing to leave her memories, house, and cherished possessions behind. Magdalena said her mother had told the family, "I'm coming along to start a new life with you in Germany. We are after all a *Großfamilie* (extended family)."

Sixteen years after her return to Orzydorf from the United States my grandmother moved to the urban setting of Nuremberg, Germany with the rest of her family. Although she hadn't adapted well to America, she did take to Germany, where she could speak the language and had the satisfaction of seeing her family live in hope, security, and prosperity once again. The old ways of life in Romania were gone forever, she knew. Magdalena Sr. died a peaceful death at the age of 91, four years after arriving in Nuremberg. She'd outlived her husband by 64 years. In recalling my grandmother today, what I find most remarkable about her is that despite all the tragedy and hardship in her life, she never allowed herself to become bitter.

My aunt Magdalena also adapted well. She could breathe easier after jobs and aid from the West German government allowed the family to buy a home of its own and weave itself into the new country and community. Because the family chose to locate in a city where many other Orzydorf Germans had recently settled, a support structure already existed upon arrival. The family's new residence was in a pleasant area of Nuremberg in which some of their former Orzydorf neighbors became their neighbors again. Once Leni and her husband secured permanent teaching jobs, Magdalena finally found some semblance of the normal home life she'd dreamed of back in the Soviet Union—one without the continual harassment of communist officials.

A home purchase was possible in part because of compensation from the West German government for property lost in Romania. To qualify, the family needed some form of ownership proof. The Romanian communists didn't allow ethnic Germans to leave the country with such records, so in 1985 Magdalena's family in Nurnberg asked Fidel, my sister Mary, and her husband, Steve, to smuggle out a document during the trio's upcoming visit to Orzydorf. That blueprint of the hectare-sized hof compound they'd formerly owned showed the layout of the surrounding wall and the two houses within. Family members in Orzydorf who'd not yet emigrated were able to help locate this record. As the visitors neared the border on leaving, Steve tucked the old blueprint into the back of his shorts and under his t-shirt.

In relaying the story, Mary and Steve noted that they were nervous about this smuggling because three years earlier on a visit to Orzydorf, they'd all been detained at the border for five hours in a waiting room while their possessions and every part of the rental car were minutely searched. The guards had even made the travelers tear out the rear seat. At the time of the blueprint smuggling in 1985, the guards were less meticulous but still scrutinized the car as well as the contents of pockets and suitcases. After being cleared to proceed, Mary discovered that two small paper Romanian currency notes she'd stuck inside a book in the glove compartment had been stolen. But the hof blueprints made it out!

Magdalena retained many fond memories of her old home in Romania, but the years of painful struggle staved off any feelings of homesickness. The Orzydorf of old was long gone. The cultural traditions had diminished or vanished altogether as the place became ever more Romanian and secular. Yet, she and other former Orzydorf residents managed to salvage some of their village's culture and bring it with them to Germany. The Orzydorf organization the former residents formed still holds a reunion every two years. My parents, my sister and her husband, and my wife and I have all attended at least one such gathering over the years. The session I attended in 2015 was no longer quite as large and festive as the those of earlier decades because the generation that best remembered Orzydorf had largely passed on. Nevertheless, the ethnic costumes, the food, the dancing, and the memories were still to be found. The former residents who once attended the gathering from as far away as Australia and North America have tapered off, but the tradition lives on.

Magdalena lived out her 20 remaining years with her family around her and with other Orzydorf families in proximity. Unfortunately, those years did not pass without health problems that sprang from the depravities of her slave labor sentence. The horrendous conditions of that time had exacted a toll on her body and she died 10 years short of the age most women in the family reached. Still, considering the terrible punishment her body had endured, she did well to reach the age of 82. She lies buried in a Nuremberg cemetery far from the grave of her husband, Josef, in Orzydorf.

Left: Josef Eipert's final resting place in Orzydorf's cemetery after his body was retrieved from the field where he was murdered. A translation of the engraving reads: RESTING PLACE OF THE SPOUSES—JOSEF AND MAGDALENA EIPERT—JOSEF BORN 1909 DIED 1944—35 YEARS OLD—MAGDALENA BORN 1919 DIED 19[space left blank]—[space left blank] YEARS OLD. REST PEACEFULLY! Because Magdalena chose to emigrate from Romania to Germany and is buried there, the blank spaces were never filled. Interestingly, the maintenance of this cemetery has been largely funded by an association of former residents and their descendants. *Right:* Front and back view of gravestone for three Magdalenas—Fidel's mother, sister, and cousin Anni Leichnam—in Nuremberg, Germany.

---

1. *Communist Romania* (inyourpocket Essential City Guides: Bucharest, 2022), https://www.inyourpocket.com/bucharest/Communist-Romania_73620f.
2. "Socialist Republic of Romania," Military Wiki, January 2015, https://military-history.fandom.com/wiki/Socialist_Republic_of_Romania.
3. Florin Abraham, *Romania since the Second World War: A Political, Social and Economic History* (Bloomsbury Publishing, 2016)
4. Gal Beckerman, "The Cold War's Strangest Bedfellows How Romania Sold Its Jews to Israel, and What It Got in Return," The Forward, February 11, 2005, https://forward.com/culture/2923/the-cold-war-e2-80-99s-strangest-bedfellows-how-romania/.
5. Radu Ioanid, *The Holocaust in Romania: The Destruction of Jews and Roma under the Antonescu Regime, 1940–1944* (Rowman & Littlefield, 2022), 483.
6. Remus Anghel and Laura Gheorghiu, "The Mass Migration of Romania's Germans. Patterns, Timeframes and Romanian-German Inter-Institutional Arrangements in the 20th Century," December 10, 2020, 25–46.

48 Orzydorf Via an Outsider's Eyes

I have seen Orzydorf only twice. Both visits were in the early 1970s when Romania was sequestered behind the Iron Curtain by border fences, guard towers, and secret police goons. That the Marxist-Leninist ideology of the Soviet Union, and corruption, had ruined Romania's economy and my father's boyhood village along with it couldn't have been more obvious. The iron grip of despotic Nicolae Ceaușescu and his predecessor had choked the life out of the Banat breadbasket that my paternal ancestors and their fellow pioneers had built up at an enormous cost in toil and lives. The only remarkable legacy of the communists was how quickly they were able to bankrupt and destroy self-sufficient, functional communities like Orzydorf. As I walked through my father's village, I saw unpaved streets waiting to turn to muck with the next rain, dilapidated buildings crying out for paint, and impoverished residents unable to buy enough food staples. It was hard to see how the situation could get much worse, but it did. The severe food shortages of the 1980s would make the conditions during my visit seem like a time of plenty.

My education in how things worked here began on day one of my first visit in 1971 as I rolled across the Banat plain on my motorcycle and passed through a small city. There I learned that a traffic cop on foot could flag down a passing car and order the driver to pursue another vehicle. Apparently, my newish British bike bearing a western license plate stood out. My imaginary traffic infraction was of course made to disappear via my wallet.

My Vietnam infantry experience was only three months behind me then and still fresh enough to allow me to recognize a decrepit country when I saw one. If the police-state nature of the country hadn't been apparent enough already by virtue of the rigid border control, razor-wire-topped fences, and watchtowers, it became obvious when my Orzydorf relatives mentioned that visitors needed to register at the police station. Whether they took care of that for me or ignored the requirement, I didn't ever learn.

Romania had no civil war in progress like Vietnam, where weapons and soldiers were visible everywhere, but it had a similar wrung-out, apathetic look to it. Even the traditionally whitewashed trunks of trees lining the highways had become dingy and neglected. These *white stockings* were nevertheless still useful at night, especially because it was the local custom for drivers to switch off their headlights when oncoming vehicles approached.

By virtue of growing up on an Iowa farm and spending many hours on tractor seats, I knew what healthy crops were supposed to look like. What grew in the fields of the state farms along the highways left much for improvement, which is to be expected when worker morale is low, management competence is trumped by party loyalty, and money for fertilizer and chemicals is in short supply. I tried to picture how differently the now-huge fields would have looked back when they'd been a patchwork of holdings tended by hardworking farmers like my father. Visualizing the agricultural past was easier within Orzydorf itself because many of the farmyard hofs, though now dilapidated, were still recognizable. It was hard to comprehend the ideological rigidity and stupidity it took to reduce a country blessed with rich soil, large oil deposits, the scenic Danube River, a long Black Sea coastline, and flourishing villages like Orzydorf to beggar status by cloning a system that had already failed spectacularly in the USSR.

At the time of my visits, Magdalena and her family members no longer tilled more than their gardens. By then they'd lost all hope of ever recovering the land stolen from them. Fortunately, they were not as wanting as most city-dwelling Romanians because their gardens provided them a considerable amount of food to supplement the paltry, spotty offerings in the state stores.

Although the communists had stolen their farms, machinery, and livestock, and then neglected the infrastructure, some of the local ethnic Germans were still attached enough to their community to feel embarrassed by its sorry state. This became evident on my second visit in 1974 when on a mud-rutted street an old man on a rickety wagon pulled by a bony horse noticed my wife and me walking by with our western clothes and Japanese camera. In his Swabian German dialect he called out, "You should have seen it in the old days." Well, it turned out that in a way, I would "see it in the old days" through the words and memories of my father and others who'd known the place in its heyday. I regret not pursuing this *seeing* earlier when more of those who had lived it daily were still around. Had I been more attuned then to their incredible experiences, the biographical aspects of this account would have been much fuller.

Upon leaving Orzydorf in 1971, I turned my motorcycle south to a slightly less impoverished place, Yugoslavia. There, it wasn't long before I encountered another legacy of World War II not long after clearing the sleepy border post at which I was detained for a time when the border guards suspected that the hard candy in the small brown bag my grandmother had given me was drugs. A few kilometers beyond the border I found myself being eyed by the pairs of armed soldiers and policemen stationed along the lightly traveled rural highway every one- or two-hundred meters. This was a little unsettling, considering that to ward off the springtime morning chill, I wore an American military field jacket scrounged at a US Air Force barracks in Germany.

The roadside armed presence continued for another hour or so as I rolled down that highway. Eventually, the guards waved all traffic to the shoulder of the road in a coordinated effort and within minutes a three-vehicle convoy of black limousines sped by. Somehow, I learned from a local that the fuss was for none other than communist dictator Josip Broz, better known as Tito. Tito had consolidated command of the several hundred thousand partisans battling the German occupiers during the war. When the "liberation" fighting was finished, like dictators everywhere he forgot to turn over power to the people for whose independence he'd fought. It had been Tito's partisans that the Germans were engaged with when Fidel's platoon was sent to Dubrovnik to retrieve munitions abandoned by the Italians. Fortunately, Fidel never came as close to Tito as I did.

Historians have treated Tito kindlier than Romania's Ceaușescu, but when it came to ethnic cleansing, Tito was no slacker. Before the war, Yugoslavia had been a monarchical kingdom cobbled together from many ethnicities and nationalities at Versailles in 1919 by the Allied victors of World War I. The bulk of the country's ethnic Germans lived in eastern Croatia and the Vojvodina region of northern Serbia. Once Tito solidified his command of the partisans during the war, the Allies recognized him as Yugoslavia's legitimate head of state. About a year after Fidel's Nordland division left Croatia, Tito and the communists he led decreed that all ethnic Germans in Yugoslavia were "enemies of the people." Many ethnic Germans sensed what was coming with a communist takeover and fled to Austria along with retreating German forces in 1944–1945. Those who stayed or couldn't get out—over 200,000—were stripped of their citizenship, relieved of all their property, and subjected to arrest, torture, and massacres. Many of those not exported to the USSR as slave laborers were starved or worked to death in slave labor camps in Yugoslavia.[1]

Of the Eastern-bloc countries with a considerable ethnic German population, Romania was the only one that didn't expel most of its Germans after the war. Even though the communist government treated the remaining ethnic Germans badly, a coexistence between Romanians and Germans developed over time as the war memories faded. Long after migrating to Germany, Magdalena's family still retained Romanian friends in Orzydorf and visited them on occasion.

Leni's daughter, Ingrid, related that during one such visit to Orzydorf, she had a cordial encounter with an older Romanian man she didn't recall ever meeting. After spotting her from a window in a bar, he rushed outside, grabbed her hand, and gleefully announced that he remembered her from the 1970s when Ingrid was still a school girl. A new Romanian law had just mandated that workers take tests to show they had an eighth-grade math and reading competency. Passing these exams was problematic for the older people who'd had little or no schooling. Leni, the teacher administering the math test, had chosen Ingrid to assist her as an exam monitor. The testing occurred over a period of days and during this time Ingrid, with Leni's approval, and perhaps the government's too, discretely helped people with answers on the exams. Everyone knew that the government simply wanted to boast about its education system and the general population's high literacy rate. The man from the bar delightedly exclaimed, "You helped me pass that exam!"

When Magdalena's extended family was finally ransomed by West Germany, Romania limited the entire family of six to a mere 70 kilograms of baggage. Possessions had to be pared down so drastically that many cherished family mementos were destroyed. Everything that couldn't be sold or given away went into a burn pile. Once the culling was complete, a match set the pile alight. With the fire roaring, Magdalena tossed in the bundle of precious postcards she'd mailed home from the USSR. They'd accumulated into a storybook-sized packet despite her having been allowed to send only one card every few months. After each new card arrived and had been passed around, it joined the collection. In the excitement of emigration to a new life in Germany, the family didn't appreciate how priceless a memento had just been tossed into the blaze.

Magdalena's postcards scattered as they left her hand. When they hit the bonfire the searing flames set them alight almost instantly. The hot updraft from the fire sucked up the still-burning ashes and spewed them about. One hot ember landed on Magdalena's exposed collarbone to cause two small burns. The burns healed after a few days, but the scars never went away. Years later in a conversation with her grandmother, Ingrid introspectively asked about the scars that her experience in Russia had left. Magdalena well knew that Ingrid meant psychological scars, but poignantly indicated the two spots near her neck and said, "They are here." For her, the scars of the burning postcards had become synonymous with the pain collected during those years. Ingrid later wrote to me and said,

> I still don't understand why they burned all of my grandmother's postcards from Russia. I would have loved to have them. I used to have them in my little hide-out on the roof of one of the houses in Orzidorf. I was about 13 years old and treasured them very much, though I had never read them, since they were all written in the same old German handwriting. But they were so small and delicate, and the writing was so small that I could guess that my grandmother would have tried to squeeze everything onto this small piece of paper that she could send every other month, as far as I know. They were kept together by a small ribbon (I think light blue, but that might just be my own memory, since I like blue).[2]

---

1. Steffen Prauser and Stanislav Sretenovic, "The 'Expulsion' of the German Speaking Minority from Yugoslavia," in *The Expulsion of the "German" Communities from Eastern Europe at the End of the Second World War*, EUI Working Paper HEC No. 2004/1 (San Domenico, Italy: Badia Fiesolana, 2004), 54–57,
https://web.archive.org/web/20090304100309/http://www.iue.it/PUB/HEC04-01.pdf.
2. Ingrid Slavik, "Anni" (Email, November 27, 2009).

49 Anni's Story

Magdalena Leichnam, a cousin to Fidel, Magdalena, and Hans, was also tragically affected by Hitler's war. In the 1980s, Anni (the name she went by) left Romania for Nurnberg, Germany, along with Magdalena and her household. I had the pleasure of seeing Anni over the years when visiting Germany. My wife Susan and I sometimes played a tile game called Rummikub with her and my cousin Ingrid while we chatted. It wasn't until Anni was in her nineties that Leni, Ingrid, and Hans's granddaughter Edda helped us to tug out Anni's story as we looked through her old photos.

Anni was born at the start of World War I after her father, Adam, had been mobilized to fight for the Austro-Hungarian Empire. Adam was unable to return until the war ended; hence he didn't meet his daughter until she'd turned four. However, Adam's misfortunes had begun long before this extended absence. Prior to the war he'd raised swine for export to Vienna, but he lost his business when a shipment of his hogs became sick during train transport. He and his wife didn't own enough land to make a living from farming, so they sold out and moved to another village where land was more affordable. There, they started a dairy business that shipped milk to Timișoara. Then the war began. The government provided no hardship deferments to men like Adam, so the family had to give up the dairy business also because Anni's mother was unable to operate it on her own. When Adam returned from the war, he supported the family by working various jobs but died from a stomach ailment when Anni was a young teen. Anni's mother, who suffered from a chronic lung disease, wasn't in the best of health either. Whenever she became too ill to care for her daughter, Anni was sent to Orzydorf to stay with her paternal grandmother. Because her grandmother was also the grandmother of Fidel, Hans, and Magdalena, the cousins came to know each other well.

The luck of Adam's two siblings wasn't much better. His sister Margaretha was the woman who couldn't conceive and wanted children badly enough to beg Magdalena Sr. to give up baby Fidel so she and her husband could adopt him. And his sister Elizabeth had the misfortune of being torn from her three children and sent to the USSR as a slave laborer. While away, her husband died.

Anni hadn't yet begun school when World War I ended; hence she was not as greatly affected by the Banat's transfer from Hungary to Romania as were older children who'd been taught in Hungarian. Anni attended Romanian schools for all eight years of her education—the first four in a secular school and the second four in a Catholic school taught by nuns. Being eight years older than her cousin Fidel gave her an older child's perspective of my father as a youngster. During one of my visits with her, she sang a song that Fidel had learned in kindergarten and brought home with him. Anni described Fidel as a boy too clever for his own good sometimes, such as the time he no longer felt like going to religious instruction and told the teacher that his mother wouldn't allow him to attend anymore. That did not go over well with his mother.

Anni worked in several Timișoara stores as a sales clerk selling linoleum and carpets when her school days were over. Later she worked in a bonbon shop, then in a furniture store. For the most part, these shops were owned by Jews. The city had a thriving Hungarian Jewish population at the time. Interestingly, many of them survived the war and secured good positions for themselves during the communist era, once they became communists. Anni said that even then (circa 2010) their descendants still spoke Hungarian and German.

In the late fall of 1944, like the other Germans in Timișoara 26-year-old Anni heard rumors of a mass deportation to Russia. "But I didn't believe it," she said. Then, one afternoon during the Christmas holidays a policeman came to her home and delivered a document. In the awkwardness of the moment, Anni and her mother offered him cake and wine. He ate and drank, then left. On Sunday, January 14, the police returned to tell Anni that she needed to prepare because they would collect her in a couple of hours. She hid in the flour chest beneath the attic staircase when they knocked at the door, but didn't remain there long, for her mother knocked on the chest to tell her that she was being taken in place of Anni. Rather than allow such a thing, Anni climbed out of the chest, grabbed her bundle of clothes and bedding, and accompanied the officers to the Paap Movie Theater where the Germans in her district were being assembled. She and the others spent an uncomfortable night in the theater. That evening Ella Dienstl, an acquaintance also on the list but not present in the theater, shot herself.

After family members delivered food to the prisoners the next day, guards with guns marched their charges through snow-covered fields to the town of Freidorf and locked them up in a large dance hall. Thereafter, relatives and friends of the prisoners shuttled back and forth frantically with supplies of food and other necessities for whatever might lay ahead. On Wednesday night, after two days inside the building, the guards herded the prisoners into huge trucks and drove them to a rail yard. There, the trucks backed up to freight cars and disgorged their human cargo directly into the cars like cattle. Only two adaptations had been made for human transport. One was a hole in the floor for a toilet. The other was a freestanding stove to ward off the winter cold. Unfortunately, the stove was useless because there was no firewood. Escape was impossible. Families milled around outside the cars helplessly while the prisoners poked a finger through any small opening so their loved ones could locate and touch them. "I'm here where my finger is!" was a common cry until the train pulled away.

When the train reached Soviet Moldova at the border town of Ungheni, the prisoners were transferred to similar cars parked on the wider Russian tracks. The interned Germans spent the next two weeks traveling on those wider tracks. Anni recalled only one stop, where the prisoners were allowed to relieve themselves in a snow-covered field. On February 2nd, the human cargo was delivered to a three-story building in Dubowaia-Balka (Dubova Balka near Kryvyi Rih) in Soviet Ukraine. In that building, the authorities bunked the men on the first and third floors. The women were crammed into the second floor, which contained a kitchen and dining hall. The camp went by the name Bolschewik, or camp number 1403. Because it was situated in an iron-ore mining district, many of the men had the misfortune of being assigned to work in the mines. The war damage throughout the area was so great that everything needed to be rebuilt.

Anni said the guards didn't wish to bother with names at roll call, so "they simply shouted out only our numbers." Initially the camp held 2,000 Germans from Timişoara, Sackelhausen, Jahrmarkt and several other Romanian communities. The prisoners here were fortunate to have good officers who encouraged them by saying *skoro domoi* (home soon). Upon arrival, Anni was assigned to be an ice chopper. She worked the night shift and recalled how sparks flew in the dark when one steel tool struck another. Her second job was construction. There was a great need for replacement housing because so much of it had been destroyed in the war. Anni's work crew built temporary housing for Soviet workers at a furious pace, but unfortunately, many of these "temporary" structures became permanent residences. Anni counted herself lucky to get this job because so many others were worse. She was particularly happy to have avoided the dangerous sand pits where workers risked being buried alive from pit-wall collapses.

Hazardous job or not, everyone faced risks from the terrible food or from physical and mental illness. Anni said that everyone confronted death because there seemed little hope of surviving on just bread, tea, and turnip-top soup. But hardest to bear was the loss of all connection to home. Considering the terrible conditions, Anni thought her immediate group handled their ordeal quite well, saying:

> Uncertainty drained our strength . . . but we proved that we´d prevail. Except for six persons who I´m very sorry for—the young Szaboliev from 12th street number 11, who was still a student and didn´t survive the cold; Mr. Fleck from 5th street; and Mrs. Pohlen from 3rd street, who left 2 twin daughters behind. As well as Hermine Brandl, a young girl from 14th street, who we moaned for and whose parents were heartbroken. Then Michael Wildau and Ujváry Alladar. I know of two other victims who died at home of the consequences of the mine work. An armor of stone built itself around their lungs, something that was called 'stone lung.' Those were the teacher Franz Weissgerber and Mr. Zapfl. We others managed to survive.

Anni's interaction with Russia, and with Russians, was not as extreme as Magdalena's. She said, "Our relationship with the Russians was good; we were allowed to visit other camps. The inmates from Jahrmarkt were

Left: Anni Leichnam, sometime after her return from five years of slave labor in Russia. *Right:* Anni Leichnam in late middle age.

even allowed to have a *Kirchweih* (festival) with a brass band from a different camp. Occasionally somebody cried from hunger or other hardship, but that passed. We bore our fate with patience until our homecoming."

Homecoming for Anni arrived five years after she'd said goodbye to her mother. Like Magdalena, she was one of the last to leave her camp. In Timișoara she became a store-clerk once again, then later worked as a storage and inventory manager. But no matter the job, the quality of life in the communist era was a far cry from prewar days. As ever more Romanians poured into the city, the cohesiveness that once existed in the German neighborhoods disappeared. The need to house these newcomers pushed Germans out of their homes. Anni lost her house and moved in with her mother.

Only after relating her stint in Russia did Anni mention the personal tragedy that preceded her ordeal—the death of her fiancé late in the war. Like Fidel, Hans, and tens of thousands of other ethnic German men, her intended ended up in a Waffen SS uniform. Although Anni didn't directly say so, he'd likely already spent several years in a Romanian uniform prior to this, since his age was presumably close to Anni's. Anni went on to say that the war kept the two of them apart and unable to marry for five years. By the time the war ended, he was dead and she was 30 years old. The Soviet internment then cost her another five years and left her beyond marriageable age in her culture.

Such a history would have embittered most people, but despite her travails Anni had an unusually gentle and sweet disposition. She accepted with grace and dignity that which could not be changed. This doesn't mean she didn't have a sharp wit. In 2010, as we played Rummikub, my cousin Ingrid asked Anni if she was able to say "thank you" in Russian. Ingrid already knew she could say it in Hungarian, Serbian, German, Romanian, and French. Anni replied, "No, we didn't need it there!"

50 Fidel's Haven

On May 9, 1945, the day after the war ended in Europe, Fidel and his friend Richard moved cautiously along Bavarian back roads and paths to evade the American MPs that patrolled the roads in their jeeps. Fidel had a particular destination in mind as he and Richard picked their way along. The last part of their journey, which took them to the east edge of Teisendorf, was along train tracks. Fidel was familiar with the locale because of the three days he'd spent repairing the holzgas truck when his supply company first arrived at his posting in Teisendorf in February.

The two men left the tracks where the rails passed over a road on a viaduct Fidel watched for. After scrambling down the embankment, they made a beeline to the second farmhouse just down the road—the one where Fidel had bartered for food twice using the same set of clothes. He knew that the girl who lived there would likely help him again. The girl's father fed the men but was unable to offer them a place to stay because he was already accommodating eight or nine other German soldiers. So the two men backtracked to the first farmhouse they'd passed and knocked on the door to beg the farmer's permission to sleep in his barn's hayloft.

The woman who answered the door was kind and told them her house was already full up with civilians who'd fled the mass destruction in Munich, but they could sleep in her barn. She then fetched a couple of blankets, which unlike the ones from the Austrian police station, were free of fleas. Because the people inside the house were all news-starved and curious about the newcomers, she invited Fidel and Richard inside to sit and chat for a bit. The civilians wanted to know what was taking place around them, but were also very interested in the soldiers' stories. In the course of the conversation that followed, the men revealed their background and mentioned that because they were cut off from their homes presently and liked the Teisendorf area, they hoped to stay for a time if they could find work. The hostess, another Anni, replied that she'd help by asking a nearby farmer friend if he knew of anyone who needed a worker.

By the time the men rolled out of their makeshift beds at seven the next morning, she'd already walked the three kilometers to the neighboring village of Wimmern where the farmer friend lived and brought him back with her. According to local custom, last names were stated first, so the man introduced himself as Brunner, Stempi. Having already learned of Fidel's farming experience, he pointed to Fidel and said, "I want you." My father started work that very day.

Fidel was to replace a Yugoslavian POW working on Brunner's farm. The POW was still there because he couldn't report to the repatriation collection camp that was being set up until the following week. Fidel came to know the man, and as with the other POWs he'd interacted with during the war, got on well with him. Richard stayed on at the farm where he and Fidel had spent the night and worked there for a month or two, after which Fidel found him a job with another farmer in Wimmern.

Wimmern was, and still is, a tiny but picturesque village. In 1945 it had about a dozen houses, an historic old church with an onion-dome steeple, and a view of the Alps even superior to Teisendorf's. The villagers had already been required to make rooms available to displaced Germans from bombed-out cities. Still to be distributed here and throughout Germany were millions of ethnic Germans expelled by the new puppet communist governments of Central and Eastern Europe. Millions more refugees would arrive from territory stripped from Germany as war compensation. These newcomers would consist largely of women, children, and the aged, since most working-aged men were either dead or interned in POW camps. In Wimmern, Richard roomed in the house that my mother would be assigned to the following year after the Czechs violently expelled her and three million other Sudeten Germans from their ancestral homeland, and stole their property in the bargain.

To Fidel's surprise, a barbed wire POW facility sprang up right outside of Wimmern. Quite literally, Fidel now hid in plain sight. This camp, and others like it, held German soldiers who'd surrendered to the Allies when the war ended, as well as soldiers captured earlier during the war. Technically, all were now Disarmed Enemy Forces (DEF), a classification invented two years earlier. It allowed the Allies to get by with feeding the prisoners less and housing them in primitive conditions without technically skirting Geneva Convention rules.

The majority of America's prisoners at this time slept on open ground behind barbed wire in crowded conditions, rain or shine, and subsisted on 1,000 to 1,500 calories per day. Between two and three million prisoners were kept for months this way in the Rheinwiesenlager, a series of 19 camps constructed along the Rhein River. The pens resembled enormous cattle feedlots. Not surprisingly, many prisoners died in the unsanitary conditions. Charges of unduly punishing Germans were leveled, but the Allied commanders insisted they simply weren't able to adequately feed so many prisoners. The issue is still controversial today.

During one of my Wimmern visits, I learned that a number of village women baked bread to help feed the prisoners in the nearby camp. But that camp existed only for a few weeks. The prisoners were then consolidated closer to Munich in Rosenheim, where they were pointlessly detained another four or five months in similar primitive and wretched conditions before being processed and released.

Eventually, the American occupation authority required all former German soldiers to report to an American MP station in order to secure identity papers. Fidel and Richard already possessed Romanian passports as identification papers, but a return to Romania meant prison-camp internment or execution. Their only realistic option was to remain in Germany and acquire German residence papers. So, along with five or six area ex-soldiers who'd survived the war, they went to apply. About a dozen other men who'd gone off to war from the tiny village were not able to apply for their names now resided only in the memories of their loved ones and on the large plaque in the foyer of Wimmern's small church. Wimmern was far from unique in this respect. In 1953 the Pittsburg Press reported that "In all of Germany only one hamlet of 89 persons, a farm village called Predoehl near the Soviet-occupied border, could offer thankful prayers that all its menfolk had come back."[1]

The Allies preferred to punish all Waffen SS soldiers for war crimes committed by several overzealous units who'd done so mainly early in the war. As a result, many innocent men suffered along with the guilty. Most Waffen SS soldiers could be identified by a small square black ink tattoo on the underside of their left arm near the armpit. This tattoo identified the soldier's blood group to aid in an emergency when a blood transfusion was needed. Not all SS men received this tattoo because late in the war expediency sometimes precluded the inscription. On the other hand, such a tattoo didn't necessarily mean that a man had been in the Waffen SS. Wounded men from other German military services treated in SS hospitals also received the tattoo. The marking doomed many a POW who'd committed no war crimes, or hadn't even been in the Waffen SS, when the Soviets executed prisoners having the tattoo.

Predictably, many soldiers removed the tattoo by one means or another, even though this left a telltale scar. Fidel and Richard feared that their tattoos might land them in a POW camp or complicate their lives in the future, so they sliced them off with a razor blade. At their MP summons, the tattoo, or at least the scarred spot where it had been, proved a nonissue. Fidel and Richard were cleared because their Romanian documents were accepted as proof they'd been involuntarily inducted. Each was issued an Erlassenschein—a document that acquitted them of war crimes and Nazi Party membership.

Word that two of their own resided in Wimmern spread among imprisoned Banat ex-soldiers, and upon release many found their way to Fidel and Richard. One, another Hans, was from Orzydorf. As a child, Hans had lived in America for several years and attended school there. Because he spoke reasonably good English, Fidel suggested that he'd do well going to Munich to work for the Americans. Hans did so and prospered. When the young man later returned for a visit, he stood out because he was attired in new clothes and shoes. New clothing on Germans was uncommon at that time. Hans told Fidel, "You just tell the Americans what you want and they get it!" Two other military friends of Fidel's found jobs near Stuttgart and settled there. Several Orzydorf schoolmates, veterans who'd survived the Eastern Front, settled in Saarbrücken. Even amidst the chaos and poverty, the Banat veterans found each other and became a fraternity that helped one another out.

Some of the Banat men, particularly the older married ones with families, were willing to risk sneaking back to Romania. One such man, whom Fidel helped by finding him temporary work in Wimmern, packed up after a couple of months and made it back home. He was one of the lucky ones because Romania only locked him up for a month. Fidel knew several young men who'd gone back only to be executed by the Romanians at the border. As much as Fidel loved his family and former life in the Banat, he knew the old existence was gone. Things would not be the same there for some time. Going back was not just risky for himself; his presence could also cause serious problems for his family with the local authorities.

At the train station in Teisendorf, Fidel once encountered three ethnic Romanian veterans who'd told him, "You can't go home. They don't want us." They'd already tried to return and had been turned away. When even the Romanians who'd been required to fight for the Germans by their government weren't wanted in Romania, what chance would an ethnic German have, he asked himself. Just getting to the border could be difficult. The Soviets occupied the eastern half of Austria, which made it necessary to sneak through by stealthily hopping freight trains. And after that, returnees still needed to cross Soviet-occupied Hungary before they reached the guarded Romanian border.

Banaters were still trying to return home years later. In 1948 the 60-year-old father-in-law of Fidel's brother and an unrelated Banat woman turned up in Wimmern. Like Fidel's sister and Anni, they were among the hundreds of thousands of ethnic Germans who'd been taken to the Soviet Union as slave laborers. When the extreme toil and brutal conditions weakened the pair to the point that they were no longer of use, the Russians dropped them in the American-occupied zone of Germany rather than return them home to Romania. Hans's father-in-law had somehow learned Fidel was in Bavaria and located him after having been turned back by border guards while trying to cross into Austria over a railroad bridge.

Fidel accompanied the two back to the border and talked to the Austrian guard at the gate. The guard insisted he couldn't allow them to pass, but Fidel could be very persuasive. He explained that these people had no intention of staying in Austria; they simply wanted to rejoin their families in Romania after being dumped in Bavaria by the Russians. Fidel also told the guard that the man spoke Hungarian, which would get him into and through Hungary. But undoubtedly, the half kilogram of hard-to-get coffee that Fidel pressed into the guard's hands was the most persuasive argument. The guard looked the other way while the two refugees slipped past. Fidel later learned later that both made it home, although Hans's father-in-law had to spend some weeks in jail.

In those days many rural Bavarian village residents were known by the historical name attached to their house rather than by their surname. *Brunner* was the house name of the farmer that Fidel went to work for in Wimmern; hence, the man was called *Brunner*, and his wife *die Brunnerin*. During a Wimmern visit I once asked this woman about my father's arrival. Her memory differed slightly from Fidel's. She said that the woman in whose barn Fidel and Richard spent their second night of freedom, a relative of hers, brought Fidel to Wimmern as opposed to Brunner going there to see him. Whichever way it was, Fidel was hired. Experienced farm labor was in short supply because many farmers and their sons either hadn't survived the war or were POWs somewhere. Fidel helped several other village farmers in addition to Brunner over the months that followed and picked up what odd jobs he could during the agricultural slack season. His farm work resumed in the spring of 1946, but his life changed after a Sudetenland expellee named Maria arrived in the village that spring. This woman was my mother, and Fidel's story merged into hers not long after her arrival.

Maria had not had an easy time of it when the war ended. Her Sudetenland homeland was Austrian in culture and had for centuries been inhabited by a mix of ethnic Germans and Czechs. But after the Austrian Empire was dissolved after losing World War I, the war's victors cobbled together a discordant nation with a Czech majority: Czechoslovakia. The Czechs had never had much love for their ethnic German neighbors and things only got worse after Hitler took control of the Sudetenland in 1938. When Maria arrived in Wimmern in mid-1946, she had just been expelled from her Soviet-occupied homeland, The story of this young woman who'd endured a nightmarish year of lawlessness and terror under the rule of communist Czech partisans and the Soviet Army has already been told in *The Secret She Carried*, so only a summary of what is most pertinent to Fidel's narrative will be revisited here.

Left: **Fidel in Wimmern, Bavaria, as a single man after the war.** ***Right:*** **Maria after her arrival in Wimmern in 1946. This picture is likely an identification document photo.**

Maria left no doubt that she felt profound relief on arrival in Wimmern. For nearly a year she'd lived in constant fear—a fear that began the moment Soviet occupation troops and freshly self-proclaimed Czech partisans swarmed into her village on the day the war ended (May 8, 1945). There was no rule of law; the occupiers were free to terrorize the ethnic German population and steal anything they desired, including houses and farms. During the occupation, Maria and the entire German populace of her village had been forced to watch the public execution of a neighbor for a trivial offense. She herself experienced another type of violence and carried the legacy of that crime—her two-month-old baby, Renate—in her arms when she arrived in Bavaria. This baby, my sister, resulted from the captivity and gang rape of a number of young ethnic German women and girls by a group of Czech partisans early in the occupation. Thereafter, Maria slept in her clothes so that she that she had a chance to escape into nearby fields should the nightly hunt for women by the drunken partisans and Russians target her home. She'd also been arrested after a false accusation and served a stint in a prison camp.

Her new life in West Germany would remain a struggle for her because she arrived penniless, with few clothes or possessions. Nearly everything she'd owned had been stolen, and the shortage of goods in Germany assured that she'd continue to do without for years. Although she was happy to be assigned a room of her own in a farmhouse, that space did not come rent-free. Like all other refugees physically able to work, she had rent to pay. In her case, she paid it in the form of farm labor for the landlord.

Fidel continued to live in the Brunner house for several months after Maria's arrival. Then, upon marrying my mother, he moved into her room in the house of the farmer she worked for. Sadly, baby Renate had died of an infection by then, so it was only the two of them at that point. That single upstairs bedroom, which had neither running water nor a kitchenette, would remain their home for the next five years. More spacious housing simply wasn't available. My parents had to make the best of that situation even after I, and then my sister Ingrid, came along. Maria somehow managed to feed her family by cooking on a small electric hotplate. That she was able to cope in this tiny living space with such limited facilities until I was nearly five remains a heroic feat in my mind.

Left: Fidel and Maria's wedding portrait. *Right:* Maria in a summer dress and Fidel in Lederhosen, outdoors in Wimmern with their new baby (the author).

---

1. David M. Nichol, "The Pittsburgh Press," January 2, 1953,
   https://news.google.com/newspapers?nid=1144&dat=19530102&id=mXwbAAAAIBAJ&sjid=l00EAAAAIBAJ&pg=4985,188567.

51 Postwar Hell Primer

The moment the Western Allies saw the horrific Nazi concentration camps, they lost what little sympathy they had for the German populace. Neither they nor the people back home could believe that ordinary Germans hadn't known of, and condoned, the extermination of Jews and other so-called undesirables. Retribution was called for, and the occupation authority delivered by making life hard for Germans in postwar Germany. With the infrastructure already bombed to smithereens, erecting roadblocks to economic recovery and preventing the building of additional housing was all the victors needed to do to punish the Germans. The bombed-out city dwellers who'd been squeezed into whatever housing that remained were subsequently further squeezed to make room for the continuing flood of refugees that kept arriving in Germany.

However, the Allied military governors administering the British, French, and American zones of Germany were soon forced to recognize that the footloose humanity surging about everywhere in their sectors of Germany was not just one homogenous group of Germans. What they had on their hands was a jumble of groups, most of whom happened to speak German. The reasoning went that since they bore different degrees of Nazi-guilt, they merited different degrees of punishment. Thereafter, Germany's postwar population became stratified in terms of treatment. The complexity of applying varying degrees of punishment had the side effect of necessitating a specialized vocabulary. Here is partial list of terms and definitions derived from one historical report:

> Ausländer—foreigner
>
> Aussiedler—ethnic German migrating to the Federal Republic after 1950, literally: resettler
>
> Deutschtum—Germaness

Eingliederungsgeld—integration benefit

Flüchtlinge—refugees

Grundgesetz—Basic Law

Heimat—native land, place of origin

Landsmannschaft—regional-cultural organisation (of ethnic German expellees)

Lastenausgleich—burden sharing

Ostgebiete—collective term for those territories of the German Reich ceded to Poland and the Soviet Union after 1945 (i.e., East Prussia and the territories east of the Oder-Neisse line)

Reichsdeutsche—German citizens as of 1937

Staatsangehörigkeit—citizenship

Übersiedler—collective term for refugees from East Germany

Umsiedler—collective term used in East Germany for all ethnic German expellees and refugees resettled there after 1945

Vertriebene—expellees

Volksdeutsche—ethnic Germans, primarily in Central and Eastern Europe, but not German citizens

Volkszugehörigkeit—nationality, ethnic group membership[1]

As had happened after World War I when Germany lost, the World War II victors stripped the loser of territory. Millions of Germans and ethnic Germans who were expelled from the newly reallocated territory or ejected from other Central European countries had nowhere to go but downsized, bomb-gutted Germany. They had to compete with forced laborers, war refugees who'd fled the fighting fronts, and newly liberated German ally POWs already milling around inside Germany. This left the Germany of 1945 woefully short of resources, food, and housing.

The situation continued to worsen as Stalin and his menagerie of freshly installed East European communist puppet regimes enthusiastically purged their lands of those ethnic Germans who hadn't yet fled. Estimates of the prewar ethnic German population of Eastern Europe vary considerably, but by 1950 the communists had rid themselves of 12 to 18 million ethnic Germans. In the years that followed, the Soviet Bloc states continued to shove out the relatively few ethnic Germans that remained.[2]

Germany was in a desperate housing bind even before the influx. Not only was much of their water, electrical, telephone, sewage, and transportation infrastructure in ruins, they were also short of food, medicine, clothing, and basic necessities because most factories had been bombed out of existence. Fuel for cooking, heating, and transportation was next to impossible to obtain. Then, along came what some would call another punishment—the Allied denazification process.

Under Nazi control, everyone had needed to prove they weren't a Jew. Under American administration, they needed to prove they hadn't been a Nazi. The denazification required all Germans to fill out a lengthy form. This procedure also punished the authorities because they had to process the mountain of paperwork this created and to investigate suspect answers.

As for the guilty, the western powers hung several of the highest-ranking Nazis after procuring verdicts in the Nuremberg public trials. Mid-level Nazis received a prison sentence and administrative punishment through the issuance of identity documents that restricted their future prospects. The Soviets participated in the Nuremberg trials, but in their own occupation zone, dealt with lesser Nazis and those accused of being Nazis in a much harsher manner. High-level party members met a swift end. Mid-level Nazis, at least the ones the communist leaders didn't find useful in a new role, acquired berths in recently liberated Nazi concentration camps and faced a slow death through work and starvation. Ordinary Germans endured endless communist re-education.

To say that the Germans in western Germany were unloved by the Allied military governments is an understatement. A particularly perceptive view of the situation is to be found in an intriguing biography by István Kálmán, a Hungarian expat who later anglicized his name to Steve Colman. Colman arrived in postwar Germany as a refugee and was not favorably disposed toward Germans. He'd been a Hungarian soldier, and much like Fidel and his brother, was given no choice but to fight for the German cause. Colman discarded his uniform as soon as practical at the war's end and despite his hatred of Germans, made his way to Germany. Parts of his story are worth recounting here because they fill in some of the gaps that Fidel's experience in rural Germany did not cover.[3]

The pertinent part of Colman's account begins with the "liberation" of Budapest by the Red Army, and mirrors what occurred in Berlin and other German cities taken by the Soviets. After the worst of the fighting ceased, the Russians prioritized the liberation of alcohol warehouses and wine cellars. The liquored-up soldiers then went from "flat to flat searching for [German] women and raping them wherever they were found. Young or old, as long as they were women, were thrown to the ground, held by one and raped by the other one or two or dozens" for half of the night. The victims stopped screaming when they realized that no one was coming to help them and they did not have any Hungarian's sympathy.

"Lets make no mistakes, we despised and hated the Germans at this stage of our lives, for what they have done to us and the rest of the World . . . they were all guilty." However, Colman's view softened after a few weeks in Germany when he came to believe that "some were innocent." Then, after several months in Germany he could say, "We realised that some were actually disapproving what Hitler and the nazis stood for but had as little chance to influence events as we had in Hungary."

It took the occupation authorities considerably longer to develop any sympathy for Germans. The main emphasis remained punishment rather than re-education or economic relief. All Germans were assumed to have a Nazi past until they proved otherwise, so a great many remained locked up in camps awaiting exoneration by denazification courts. Meanwhile, more refugees were being made. Colman wrote, "With the eastern areas of Germany being taken over by the Poles and Czechs and some areas becoming part of the USSR, millions of Germans were given just a few hours to take to the road towards Germany." If they didn't depart quickly, they were locked inside cattle and freight cars to be sent there. Upon arrival, most were "penniless and started work almost the day of their arrival. Their will to succeed and their successful absorption into post-war Germany was one of the reasons for the so-called Economic Miracle which commenced in 1948."

To cope, the military governors imposed price controls as well as rationing. Like Hitler before them, they printed large amounts of money to finance the government. As too much money chased a limited amount of goods, reichsmarks lost value. The Soviets exacerbated the problem by using captured offset printing plates to print even more reichsmarks to pay their occupation soldiers because their own economic system was a catastrophe. The huge amount of money in circulation provided the average postwar worker enough of a wage to buy their ration booklet allotment of food, but the problem was the whole quota was seldom available to buy. And even if it were available, it was far short of what was needed to fight off hunger. The starving population turned to barter and the black market.

In post-war Germany, barter was not just for the individual; businesses too had to demand payment in kind when government-set prices had no basis in economic reality. To stay in business, they often acquired supplies on the black market, which in turn left them paying their workers in kind. Coal industry operation illustrates the concept.

> Coal miners were partially paid in coal . . . an arrangement known as *deputatkohle*, the coal allowance. Coal . . . was one of

the favored substitutes to paper money. Miners even received their pensions in coal. They exchanged this coal for other goods, as would the mining firms themselves. If they sold their coal for cash at the official price, they would suffer a loss. Since the product was undervalued at its official price, train engineers felt even more justified in slowing their coal trains when passing cities and towns so locals could climb onto the wagons and take coal for themselves. Coal was often stolen from unguarded railroad sidings with impunity.[4]

The cigarette became the most common money substitute. Cigarettes had been provided to starving German soldiers during the war and were made accessible to civilians after the war because smoking was a means of fighting hunger. A note the state council of the American Zone sent to the military government acknowledged this by stating, "In present-day Germany, tobacco is not only a luxury foodstuff but first and foremost a pacifier and a means of distraction from hunger and worry."[5]

The cigarette as money was convenient because it "came in standardized cartons off packages each containing twenty cigarettes. Besides being easily divisible, cigarettes are tolerably durable, nonperishable, light, and . . . also varied less in value across regions as compared to other goods." The greatest source of this currency was the American soldier, who was issued 200 free cigarettes per week and could buy many more packs cheaply from post exchanges or have them sent by mail from the United States. Until the practice was banned, up to half of the millions of military mail parcels arriving in Germany each month were cigarette shipments that went to buy goods and services of far greater value. With cigarettes so valuable, it was only natural that other sources of supply would also pop up. One source was local entrepreneurs who opened "small factories to manufacture cigarettes from the butt-ends collected at cinemas, messes, and soldiers clubs."[6]

Colman wrote that in practice, because American soldiers received 10 packs per week free and could buy more for 7 cents in the PX (post exchange store), they were rich enough to buy almost anything. "Equate the cost of 7 cents . . . to the German average monthly wage . . . equivalent to 30–35 cigarettes," and it is easy to understand why women were lined up outside US Army barracks or offices. Many of these women were middle-class wives or widows urged to find themselves an "Ami friend" by their families so they could all get by.[7]

In the following example, Colman illustrated how incongruous the substitute currency system was:

> A pair of non-black-market shoes might cost only RM [Reichsmarks] 15.00, - provided one had the necessary permits from the authorities to buy one, while the black market price of a cigarette was RM 5.00, thus three cigarettes bought a pair of shoes. The same crazy values applied to restaurants and generally service industries. During our stay in Germany we could afford to eat in the best restaurants, albeit we had to have the required ration cards, which were presented to the waiter, who cut off little coupons for 50 grams of meat, 50 grams of bread, 5 grams of butter or fat etc. The menu showed exactly how many grams of what coupons were to be presented for the meal. The price was also shown, but was of no real importance, provided you had ways and means to obtain cigarettes.[8]

The Germany of 1945–1948 was not a happy place for anyone other than the occupiers at the top of the heap, but Colman made it clear that some segments had it worse than others.

> If you had to be in Germany it was advisable, not be a German. Our situation, with or without official Displaced Person status was much better than if we would have been Germans, but it was still pretty difficult . . . . The pecking order in Germany was very clearly defined: there was the American Officer, then the G.I., then came the British, then nothing and then the US negro soldier. Following them were those Allied soldiers, who had their country occupied during World War II, such as the French, the Dutch, etc. Next the Military Government and UNRRA Officers followed by a huge gap after which came, 2nd Class Officers, D.P.'s and miles later the Germans, who were being humiliated, insulted and broken by the conscious effort of the Occupying Powers.[9]

Change did not begin until after 1947. The previous winter (1946–1947) was the worst of the 20th century across Northern Europe. Many people died from the cold and shortage of food. Germans came to know it as *Hungerwinter*. Children were constantly hungry. People lived meal to meal and subsisted on as little as one-third the calories consumed in normal times. Many schools, restaurants, and businesses could not operate and shut down for the season. Desperate people scrounged for wood to burn in the ruins of buildings and throughout the countryside. Gas and electricity, which were already rationed, were often shut off quite suddenly. It wasn't until more than a year after the Hungerwinter that change finally came about. In part, this was due to a growing empathy for the long-suffering Germans and the fading of wartime bitterness. But the greatest driver of change was a political event in 1948—the blockade of road, rail, and canal access to West Berlin by Stalin. The former capital of Germany was situated entirely within the Soviet zone of Germany, but had been divided so that the western part of the city was administered by the western Allies and the eastern part by the Russians.

Stalin decided to block all access to West Berlin through Soviet-occupied eastern Germany until the Allies met his demand to cancel the currency reform they were about to implement. The Allies had a couple of reasons for replacing the reichsmark with a new Deutsche Mark. Germany needed a stable currency if it was ever going to become self-supporting and financially stable again. Stalin needed to stop the reform because it would render the old reichsmark currency valueless. This would be disastrous for him because he was largely covering the Soviet occupation costs by printing vast quantities of reichsmarks with the printing plates America had allowed to fall into his hands.

The United States and its western allies had finally awakened to the fact that preventing further Soviet westward expansion required cutting off the free money and allowing western Germany to rebuild and prosper. They had no desire to confront the Soviets militarily and start another war, so they decided to save West Berlin and draw the world's scorn upon the Russians by undertaking a massive and expensive airlift. For over a year, with some 250,000 flights, they delivered food, fuel, and even coal. In the end, embarrassment in the eyes of the world forced Stalin to relent and reopen the land corridors. Colman described what happened next.

> In the Western Zones, as soon as the currency reform occurred, everything became available once again and not against barter, but for money, which was a very scarce commodity.... Cigarettes became what they once were and were used for the purpose of being lit and inhaled by those addicted to the habit. They became almost as useless as the old Reichs Mark. Manufacture of consumer goods commenced and efficient output of all products was aided by the fact that most if not all capital equipment having been destroyed in the war, the factories had new technologies and higher productivity. Additionally, German thoroughness and quality was now joined by the limitless energy and the will to work of the German worker, aided by American capital flowing into the country.[10]

The rural Germany of Fidel and Maria became increasingly crowded as the Eastern European Soviet puppet governments dumped off ever more freshly expelled refugees. Few American GIs were stationed there, so the area didn't enjoy the same access to the American consumer goods that American cigarettes made possible around cities like Munich, but living in a nonurban area did have one advantage—local farmers could grow food crops and people had room to plant gardens. Hence, the food situation never became as dire as in the cities. Rural areas also had forests to provide wood for heating and cooking.

---

1. David Rock and Stefan Wolff, eds., *Coming Home to Germany? The Integration of Ethnic Germans from Central and Eastern Europe in the Federal Republic* (New York: Berghahn, 2002).
2. Steffen Prauser and Arfon Rees, "Introduction," in *The Expulsion of the "German" Communities from Eastern Europe at the End of the Second World War*, EUI Working Paper HEC No. 2004/1 (San Domenico, Italy: Badia Fiesolana, 2004), 54–57, https://web.archive.org/web/20090304100309/http://www.iue.it/PUB/HEC04-01.pdf.
3. Steve Colman, "The Explanation," 2013, https://nenadcuic.com/steve%20coleman%20memoirs/The-Explanation-2013-Original.pdf.
4. Daniel DeMatos, "Barter and Money in Post-War Germany," The Tontine Coffee-House: A History of Finance, January 3, 2022, https://tontinecoffeehouse.com/2022/01/03/barter-and-money-in-post-war-germany/.
5. "A Relic from Germany's Post-War Era: A Hoard of Cigarette Boxes," CoinsWeekly, October 14, 2009, https://coinsweekly.com/a-relic-from-germanys-post-war-era-a-hoard-of-cigarette-boxes/.
6. DeMatos, "Barter and Money in Post-War Germany."
7. DeMatos, "Barter and Money in Post-War Germany."
8. Colman, "The Explanation," 130.
9. Colman, "The Explanation," 130.
10. Colman, "The Explanation," 132.

52 The New Family

Following expulsion from Czechoslovakia and a brief confinement in a displaced persons (DP) camp in the spring of 1946, Maria had an assigned room waiting for her and Renate in Wimmern because the Allied Control Council, a joint military administrative board drawn from all four occupying powers, had recently issued Act Number 18. The Act was better known as the Wohnungsgesetz (Housing Law), and required local governments to set up housing departments to shelter homeless DPs by confiscating living space in existing dwellings. The law came down particularly hard on Nazis and war criminal landlords, but appropriated space in virtually every dwelling in Germany. Wimmern was no exception.

The enormous influx of refugees, along with the housing law, raised resentment throughout Germany. Expellees were often treated poorly as a result, especially since many arrived in decrepit condition because of the hell they'd just experienced. Not surprisingly, landlords viewed them as primitive. The truth was that most DPs had enjoyed the same standard of living and education as native Germans. Maria said most Wimmern residents were friendly and accepting when she arrived, but not all. A few treated her and the other newcomers unkindly, not just because of their arrival condition, but also because they were outsiders and not real Germans. Fortunately, in Wimmern these people eventually realized they'd overreacted.

The villagers had fathomable reasons for resenting the DPs. In *The Secret She Carried*, I noted that refugees like her

> came from a different culture, spoke an unfamiliar dialect, and posed a threat to the static little village. The threat was change . . . not only would the new arrivals substantially boost the local population, they would also sit at the family table and voice their views—no small thing in an insulated, conservative

community. But it wasn't just the villagers who had concerns. The newcomers were just as reluctant to move into the house of strangers as the strangers were to accept them.[1]

One thing that lessened the landlords' rancor for having to tolerate strangers in their homes was the rental income they brought in. Few had no use for the extra money. The boarders paid for their keep either by working for the owner or holding an outside job. Only boarders too physically impaired to work were assisted by relief agencies. Maria had a tiny infant to care for, but this did not exempt her from labor.

In 2010, 64 years after the fact, a lifelong Wimmern resident I'd fondly chatted with during visits over the years still vividly recalled Maria's arrival. She was Maria's next-door neighbor, Anna Mösenlechner, whose family operated a small dairy farm. When Anna and her brother took over the family farm from her parents, by custom she became known as *die Bachter Nanni* because Bachter was her house name and Nanni was the name she

Left: Bachter Nanni's 16-year-old siter, Maria Mösenlechner, minding the Eipert children, circa 1950. Maria went on to become a nun and nurse. *Right:* Bachter Nanni and the author six decades later in Wimmern, Bavaria.

went by. Nanni told me that as young teens, she and her sister often helped my mother by babysitting my younger sister and me. As noted in *The Secret She Carried*, Nanni could still vividly remember

> the day of Maria's arrival because the newcomers were more than an idle curiosity. Nanni even remembered that these women, dropped off on the main road passing through the village, had begun their journey at a camp in Landkreis Znaim [in the Sudetenland]. Besides Maria and [baby] Renate, the group consisted of two unrelated young women and their mothers. Maria and one of the young women, Nessi, quickly became good friends.[2]

Nanni fondly recalled the child and described her as a *fichts Kind* (a happy, likeable child) with round eyes, blond hair, and a beaming broad face that smiled a lot. She was a pleasant baby to mind. Nanni said she and her teen sister fought over which of them got to babysit Renate when she needed looking after.[3]

The following year, my birth formed my own connection to my mother's friend Nessi when in her capacity as a midwife, she delivered me. Although I wasn't Maria's first child, I came into the world as her only child because of the tragedy my mother experienced several months after arriving in Wimmern. Renate had contracted a staphylococcus infection from the daughter of the landlord and died of a rapidly spreading sepsis. Villagers who knew Maria said she'd been devoted to her baby and was deeply affected by the child's death.

Maria never wanted her children to learn of their deceased sister because it meant exposure of the rape. She was a victim and bore no blame, but like many women in her situation, revealing the circumstances of the degrading crime was too shameful for her. If Fidel hadn't told me, my wife, and one of my sisters about Renate decades later during a visit to Wimmern and then shown us her grave site in Teisendorf, my mother would have carried the secret to her grave.

In 1946 the quaint farming village of Wimmern consisted of only 10 or 11 families and three bachelors—some 75 residents in all. To maintain the viability of the surrounding small farms, they could be inherited by only one child. And because the land holdings were minimal, farmers couldn't afford to retire early and turn over their land to a young heir as soon he or she married, as had been the custom in Fidel's homeland. This meant that the eventual heir often couldn't afford to marry until later in life when the farmer retired or died.

Wimmern had no real stores, so villagers needed to shop in the market town of Teisendorf, three kilometers away. The only retail businesses in the village itself were a drinking establishment and a tiny grocery—both operated in homes. During one stay, the tavern proprietor proudly showed my visiting family the plaque she'd recently received from a local brewery for having served their beer for the past 50 years. Frau Reiter operated the establishment in her living room. She and her husband were good friends of my parents, and I stayed in that house a number of times over the years. I always marveled when local men joined us in the living room. They entered with a bottle of beer they'd just plucked from the cases stacked in the hallway, found a seat, and took part in the conversation. Of course, in a village so tiny, everyone who entered was already well known by the family.

My lifelong friend Lenz, the Reiters' son, explained how that little business worked. "Regarding . . . paying for the beer . . . most of the time you paid in cash. But there was also a booklet in which the debts of the respective customer were noted and paid off the next day or week." Lenz went on to explain that considerable card playing went on as well. For such sessions his parents recorded the number of drinks consumed on a slate similar to what children used in school at the time. These debts went into the booklet if not paid off when the customer left.

Wimmern's compact, six-centuries-old, onion-dome church (St. Laurentius), its traditional Bavarian farmhouses, and the picturesque narrow, winding farm roads leading from the village are striking, but the village's prime feature is its panoramic view. *Picturesque* probably understates the spectacular setting. From the village's perch at the crest of a hill, every house enjoys a breathtaking view of the Bavarian Alps and the highest section of the Austrian Alps across the valley to the south. A mere 20 kilometers to the east lie the Austrian border and the historic city of Salzburg.

Maria had been assigned a room in one of the traditional older farmhouses. She was lucky in that her corner room on the second floor was off a hallway with direct access to a stairway that led to the front door and allowed her to enter and exit without passing through the owner's living area. Two small, east-facing windows in her room provided a partial view of the Alps. If Maria needed any reminder of who'd set in motion the catastrophic events that led to her presence here, she merely had to gaze toward the southeast from those windows. There, on a clear day, she could see Obersalzberg, the mountain valley where Hitler, Göring, Goebbels, Bormann, Speer, and other top Nazis had built their grand vacation homes.

Hitler had first discovered the Obersalzberg mountain retreat area of the Bavarian Alps above the town of Berchtesgaden in 1923. He returned to Berchtesgaden several years later after a short stint in a comfortable prison and there put the finishing touches on his book, *Mein Kampf*. The book not only popularized his ideology, it turned him into a wealthy man after he acquired part ownership of the publisher, Standarte GmbH & Herold Press. This new wealth allowed Hitler to afford his own retreat in Obersalzberg.[4]

In a village as tiny as Wimmern, it was unavoidable that my parents would meet. According to Maria, their first encounter came at the Schmidt house where she lived. Their paths subsequently crossed more than once while working in the fields. She could see Fidel was a hard worker, but her impression of him wasn't entirely favorable at first. More than once, she'd noticed him coming home in a tipsy state after a card playing bout. She'd also seen him in white knee socks and lederhosen sauntering back from Teisendorf with his arm around a woman.

In his defense, such behavior wasn't unusual for a single man who'd missed out on the company of women for years because of the war. The men who survived readily found female companionship because young women greatly outnumbered men of their age after the war—women who too had gone without the company of the opposite sex. The carousing was a necessary part of Fidel's transition back to normal life. Combat-affected soldiers needed to decompress, drive out the demons, and make up for lost time. A whole generation had missed out on the carefree days of young adulthood and independence because of Nazi regimentation and combat. Fidel had much to block out—his traumatic experiences in Croatia and Russia, being unable to return to his home and fiancée, the slave-labor imprisonment of his sister, and the death of his brother and a great many friends.

That Fidel and Maria should come together was understandable. They came from similar backgrounds and were both attractive, lonely, young people deeply affected by the war and the loss of their family and homeland. And their respective Schwäbish and Austrian-flavored German dialects fit together comfortably in a place where the local German Bavarian dialect differed so greatly from standard German that it sounded like a foreign language.

By arriving right at the war's end, Fidel beat the rush for housing that followed in the wake of the expellee resettlement process. After settling in, he worked for Brunner and other farmers for the next three years but also juggled a variety of parttime jobs. Then, in 1948 when the allied currency reform took effect and revalued 10 of the old inflated reichsmarks to one new deutsche mark, farmers could no longer afford to pay Fidel and other agricultural workers a living wage. So Fidel found a job replacing railroad ties. By working extra hard he was able "to replace six or eight ties in four hours in the morning and get paid for a full day," which allowed him to take on a second job as a bricklayer's helper in the afternoon. After that stint, he turned out wooden shoes in a small Teisendorf factory owned by a Jewish businessman. That facility then converted to producing wood packing crates for canned fish. When the business eventually went bankrupt, Fidel somehow managed to get himself laid off first in order to collect the skimpy unemployment benefit available and to have a better chance of finding another job, for he had a growing family to support by this time. Fidel's next venture involved an old car he acquired. By cutting off the rear of the body and mounting a cargo box in the open space, he fashioned a makeshift pickup truck that he and a partner began using in 1951 to sell wool throughout the local area. Later, he switched to peddling what he called kitchen stuff. Lacking a license to sell within towns or across the border in Austria, he had to sell his dishware door to door at farm houses within Germany. Meanwhile, he also continued to help out Wimmern farmers.

Times were hard and called for flexibility, but Fidel still considered himself lucky to wind up in this beautiful, out-of-the-way place where adequate food and heat were available. Although Fidel never mentioned it, he was also lucky in never being picked up by American MPs and confined in a camp. Until Bachter Nanni explained that the nearby POW camp field kitchen was located right at the edge of the Schmidt farm, I hadn't realized just how close the American MPs were.

The picturesque village of Wimmern in Bavaria, where Fidel found not only a grand view of the Alps but also a postwar refuge and a lifelong spouse.

Nanni told me that her mother had been one of the women who baked bread to feed the hungry German soldiers in the camp. It was an interesting period for a girl of 12, she said. The summer school break had just begun when the war ended and American soldiers and their equipment suddenly filled the roads. She particularly remembered her mother scolding her for asking each GI she encountered for chocolate. My friend Lenz Reiter, being four years older than me, could also recall this time. He asked soldiers on every passing tank or jeep not just for chocolate, but cigarettes too. They gave him little cakes and chocolate, but never cigarettes. How long the GIs kept handing out goodies is unclear, but the American army remained in Teisendorf until 1949. Nanni said she was reminded of their former presence several decades later when from her window she saw a black GI wandering around. When she went out to talk to him, he told her that he was touring the places his father had been stationed after the war.

Maria, and just about everyone else in the village, disliked the slovenly farmer in whose house she lived. Schmidt was a control freak who gave his spouse little leeway. "His poor wife, Mari, had to put up with him." But luckily, "She was a slob too," Maria said.

Maria had no kitchen utensils or place to cook when she arrived, so she was forced to eat at the Schmidt table. She never forgot how disgusting their eating habits were, particularly the way they ate soup out of the pot together and reused the same vinegar every day when preparing cucumber salad. It turned Maria's stomach. For a time, two ex-soldiers also boarded there. One was from Prussia, the other from Maria's homeland. One day the Prussian, Rudolf, had had enough. Maria laughed when she recalled Rudolf quietly standing up, picking up the salad bowl, and dumping the vinegar down the sink.

The Schmidts were so stingy that they even cooked and ate a sick hen when it died. At hog-butchering time, they preserved some of the meat in brine, but the rest, "they would eat and eat, even after it started to stink. But they never seemed to get sick from it," Maria said. She herself once got so sick from eating at their table that she had to be taken to a doctor in Traunstein to have her stomach pumped.

Schmidt had been adopted as a child and was still a young man when his father died and his mother deeded the farm and house to him. Maria said that instead of showing gratitude, Schmidt treated his mother so shabbily that he wouldn't even let her take an apple from a tree. Only after all the fruit had been picked was she allowed to have an apple from the ground. If she needed anything, she had to ask her son for it. The poor woman was relegated to an upstairs room down the hall from Maria. She was such a kindly soul that after I came along, she allowed Maria to store much of our family's food in her room. Our tiny 3- x 5-meter room that served as our kitchen, bedroom, and living room, had no space to spare.

Before marrying Fidel, Maria had more contact with the Schmidts than she liked. Besides working in their fields, she needed to help in the house because Frau Schmidt held an outside job as a maid. One of Maria's duties was to care for Schmidt's little boy and infant daughter. Lenz said his grandmother told him that Schmidt's baby girl had been adopted around the same time that Maria arrived with Renate, and that while Schmidt tolerated Renate at first, he soon came to resent the baby because she took too much attention away from his daughter. Thereafter, he wanted Maria and Renate gone—an attitude the other villagers thought despicable. Schmidt didn't really want the other boarders in his house either, yet was glad to have his farm work done by them because he was extremely lazy.

Maria and Fidel's wedding took place in the small village church. Following a midday meal of meatloaf at the Brunner house, Fidel moved his few possessions into Maria's room. The couple had no money for something as frivolous as a honeymoon. Life in Germany was a struggle, and like most Germans then, had to get by as best they could since there was almost nothing available in shops until 1948. Maria said that fortunately, rebuilding was something that Fidel was good at. I would have to say that Maria was not bad at it herself after having lost her homeland, home, possessions, two brothers, and her baby.

Refugees like my mother were in the same situation as bombed-out city dwellers when it came to making do with very little. Most of the former had had to leave even basic necessities behind when they fled the fighting or were expelled. Fortunately for Maria, some villagers were kind and helped her young family out. When she needed something like a dress, Fidel would barter for it. Only in the last year or two before the family left for America did goods begin to reappear in the Teisendorf shops. The severe shortage meant that when my sister and I came along, my mother had trouble finding clothes for us. Things were so bad that at the time I was born, she hadn't yet been able to procure any diapers for me. And what little clothing was available to buy was often of poor quality. Maria related

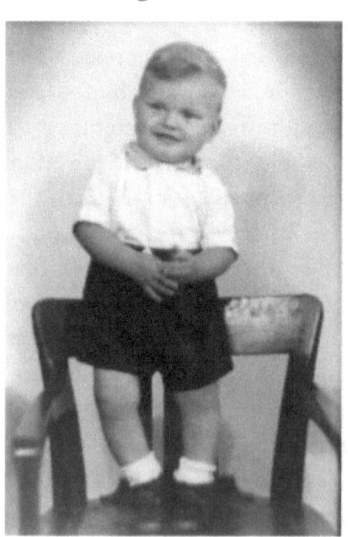 

Left: The author posing on a chair in a photography studio at the time of the wetting accident that caused the blue dye in his poor-quality shorts to run. *Right:* Fidel in Wimmern with his friend Richard on his right and an unidentified man, likely another former German soldier, on his left.

a vivid example. When I was two, she and Fidel decided to have a family portrait taken. I had nothing appropriate to wear, so for the occasion she bought me a pair of blue shorts she came across. During the shooting session I had a wetting accident that caused everything in contact with the shorts to turn blue because of the poorly dyed fabric

At times, the Eiperts' table was bare and they had to rely on a kindly neighbor. Despite having little themselves, my parents often assisted the many Banat soldiers who found their way to Wimmern after their release from Allied POW camps. Maria said she cooked for these poor men because they had nothing. Some stayed and worked in Wimmern for a time before they found a more permanent job elsewhere.

One of the few things those hard times were good for was forging friendships. My parents made many friends among the ethnic German DPs in the surrounding area. Maria particularly recalled three couples who originated from Hungary, Yugoslavia, and the German state of Prussia. She said the Prussians had the hardest time of it in Bavaria because the locals harbored a traditional dislike of Prussians. The Yugoslavians were their closest friends of the three. But their most enduring friendships were with Lenz's parents and a couple other Wimmern farmer families.

Maria had to keep working until late in her pregnancy with me even though she often felt nauseous. She went into labor late one morning near the end of spring. Few doctors were available in those days and none in tiny Wimmern. The nearest was away from his office on house calls and unavailable at the time. When no transportation to a hospital could be found, my mother's friend, Nessi, stepped in and tended Maria during her three hours of labor. And Nessi continued to look after Maria during the week that followed when she was largely confined to bed. Many years later I had the pleasure of visiting Nessi in Germany with my mother. She no longer lived in Wimmern by then and was unfortunately herself confined to a hospital sickbed at the time.

My mother owned so little at the time of my birth that the attending women couldn't even find something suitable in her kitchen to serve as a basin for washing me. Eventually Nessi was able to borrow an oval pan with a handle from someone, but it was dirty and needed a good scrubbing. Because Maria hadn't yet found any diapers, she was at a loss for what to put on me until someone in the village dug some old diapers out of a closet and came to the rescue. During my mother's labor, someone set out to find Fidel, who was away working at a job somewhere. Eventually he arrived on the scene, but I don't know if he made it back by the time of my birth.

The birth of my sister Ingrid, nearly two years later, was less chaotic. This time Maria was able to get to the small hospital in Teisendorf, and everything was more orderly. However, winters were very real during

February in that mountainous part of Bavaria. At the baptism in the small unheated church, the shockingly cold holy water poured on the infant's scalp induced a screaming fit in my baby sister. Maria remembered Nessi asking the priest, "Why in this weather?"

Maria's life wasn't an easy one, for in addition to taking care of my sister and me, she also needed to help Schmidt with the farm work to pay for the room. Fidel was busy working for several farmers at once as well as holding down one or more part-time jobs outside the village. Maria said that because he had farming in his blood, it wasn't uncommon for him to help village farmers even when he didn't have to. "He worked hard, and a lot," she said, "sometimes for 24 hours straight." Even Schmidt, a man whose concept of work was "toil done by others," sometimes had his help. Various neighbors had Fidel's assistance out of friendship, but Schmidt wasn't one of them.

Some of Fidel's later jobs took him far and wide. He particularly remembered selling dishes around Berchtesgaden out of the converted pickup. But even before then, he'd needed a means of motorized transportation because of a job that required him to work well into the night in Teisendorf. So in 1948 he acquired a loud little contraption of a motorbike that gave a couple of neighbors cause to complain when he putt-putted it up the hill to the village late at night. They called his motorbike the *Schnaufer*, or puffer. Maria urged him to shut it off and push it up the final part of the hill, but of course he never did.

One night while riding home from Teisendorf at three in the morning following his shift, Fidel had an accident. His little Schnaufer was lugging his leather briefcase at the time—a carrier that served as a saddlebag because it was spacious enough to hold more than just papers and lunch. Earlier that day he'd stuffed it with the groceries that Maria had tasked him with bringing home. He was arriving so late because he and his coworkers had played cards in his employer's office after their shift, and that required beer. This was Bavaria, after all! Not far outside of Wimmern, either the beer or sleepiness got to Fidel and he veered off the road into a shallow ditch bordered by a barbed-wire fence. Fidel was shaken but not seriously injured, so he picked himself and the motorbike back up and continued on his way. Maria recalled that he arrived home with a jacket full of holes and a torn earlobe, yet the groceries were all accounted for and intact. But groceries weren't the only thing in the briefcase. She discovered that it also contained the office books. Fidel had no clue as to how they'd come to be there.

Maria noted that just like farming, Fidel had cards in his blood and was always out playing when not working. She didn't like it but couldn't change him. In Wimmern he usually played with three or four other DPs.

Sometimes on a Sunday when there was no Mass in Wimmern, Fidel took me to church with him in Teisendorf. After Mass, the two of us walked across the street to where there was always a card game in progress. There, he'd buy me sausage from a vender to keep me content. Maria added that the other card players fed me sausages as well, along with "all kinds of other stuff." She recalled that on one such occasion I came home with a little Bavarian hat with a feather in it that Fidel had bought me.

Left: The author and his sister astride Fidel's loud Schnaufer motorcycle in Wimmern, Bavaria, circa 1951. *Right:* The author with Fidel and his pig, circa 1950

When Fidel worked the factory late shift, he needed to sleep during the day. That was something particularly hard for him to do in our cramped one-room quarters because my lack of toys caused me to play with my mother's pots and pans. Apparently, I loved to bang on them or make other noise with them. In suitable weather, Maria took me and my sister outside as much as possible to give Fidel some peace. Often, she took us to a grassy area near the church because it had a bench under a linden tree where she could sit. We usually had it to ourselves because there were only one or two other toddlers in the village at the time. Once I was able to run around on my own, my older and mischievous friend Lenz and I were often to be found at the Bachter house, where Nanni and her sister enjoyed our antics.

Two other spots Maria often took my sister and me to were our family garden plot and our pig stall. In the latter, I became familiar with the pigs eventually destined to wind up on our dinner plates and the nest boxes of two laying hens that provided our eggs. Maria recalled those hens fondly and noted what an exceptional layer one of them was. She said this chicken was so dedicated to its work that it even died on the job in the nest. When a little older, I ventured out into the fields along with Fidel. I particularly recall one harvesttime occasion when for a snack he and other workers roasted some potatoes in the ground under a fire.

Maria said my sister and I were good babies and that I generally looked out for my sister. However, I lapsed on one occasion when my mother left the room for a few minutes. Apparently, I climbed up on a chair to work the knobs on the hotplate like I saw my mother do. When my sister clambered up too, I helped her take a seat on the burner. Her howl brought my mother on the run, but it was too late to avoid a circular heating-coil burn pattern on her bottom.

When Maria went shopping or took me or my sister to the dentist or doctor in Teisendorf, she had to walk three kilometers (two miles) each way while pushing a baby carriage. The return trip was the most strenuous, for it was largely uphill. But the biggest challenge in both directions was a ravine with a small creek at its bottom just outside of Wimmern. In those days there was no bridge along that route, so a descent down a steep slope, then a climb back up on the other bank, was required. Maria never forgot one especially trying passage when I was four and was to have my teeth checked by a dentist. I balked at the creek, so she had to drag me up the slope step by step. Then in the dentist's chair, I refused to open my mouth. The dentist tried to bribe me with candy, but I still refused. Finally, Fidel was summoned and he pried my mouth open. Doctor visits were an entirely different story. The doctor's wife loved children and couldn't have any herself, so she came into the office to play with my sister and me whenever we came in. Apparently, we liked her too.

---

1. Erich Eipert, *The Secret She Carried: A Perilous Odyssey Through the Time of Hitler* (Turnbuckle Press, 2015), 299.
2. Eipert, *The Secret She Carried*, 299.
3. Eipert, *The Secret She Carried*, 309.
4. Eipert, *The Secret She Carried*, 300.

53 Farewell, Alps

Fidel and Maria could never agree on who first suggested leaving Germany. However, there was no disagreement over why they left. Their one-room living situation had become intolerable. But more pressing for Fidel was a desire to farm on his own again. He'd been working a variety of jobs, often more than one at a time, and didn't care to do that forever. Although the Wimmern farmers were collectively willing to help build Fidel and Maria a house, finding affordable land nearby was problematic. As in most of West Germany, the local farms were small, passed down in families, and seldom came up for sale. A second impediment for Fidel was the tight government regulation of agriculture in Germany. Farming attracted him for the independence it offered. He'd experienced it in Romania, where already as an enterprising teen Fidel had been an innovator who cultivated the equivalent of several Wimmern farms. That type of operation was unlikely to ever come his way in Germany, where despite the many hours he worked, he'd accumulated little in savings. Both he and Maria felt that they were going nowhere.

The couple's first flirtation with emigration came along in 1950 when Fidel's cousin Hans Rabong, who'd deserted the Romanian Army in 1943 and settled near Fidel in the Bavarian town of Rupolding after the war, became convinced that the adverse situation in Romania was mellowing. Hans's wife even confided to my mother that Hans told her the two of them would live in his family's large house and she'd get a diamond ring upon their return to Orzydorf. Apparently, after the resumption of mail service between West Germany and Romania in 1948, Hans expected that Romania's political system would soon have to revert to some semblance of its old self in order for the country to become economically viable again. Hans's optimism turned out to be misplaced. Fidel, on the other hand, had never bought into the idea that the communists would relinquish control, but he and my mother had identity photos taken and prepared travel documents just in case Fidel ever did get an opportunity to reclaim his portion of the family's land.

When the situation in Romania failed to improve, my parents considered South America as a place to start over after Fidel was contacted by a second cousin who'd settled in Argentina. This man almost certainly lauded the opportunities available there. A friend of this cousin subsequently helped my parents procure identification documents that were supposed to clear the way for the family's entry into the country. Fidel chuckled when he told me the papers listed his birthplace as Banat, France, to make things easier. When the scheme began to look too sketchy, my parents backed out. America didn't come up as a potential destination until 1951, six years after Fidel arrived in Wimmern. The thought of the USA as a home was not totally alien to him because he'd known several former Orzydorf residents who'd prospered in America before the war and then returned to Romania to live well in retirement.

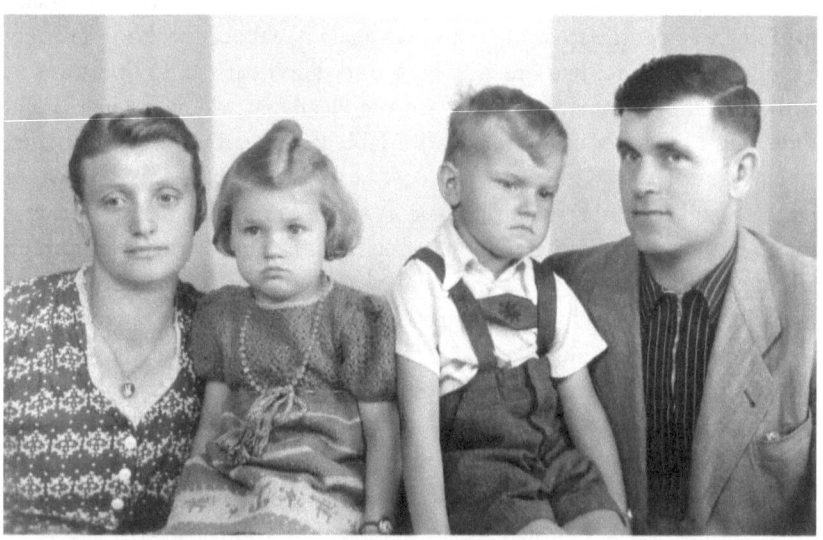

Family portrait, circa 1951, prior to the Eipert family's emigration from Bavaria to America. What the author is pouting about has been lost to time.

The Displaced Persons Relocation Program (US Public Law 774) of June 1948 provided for the US resettlement of European displaced persons, expellees, and orphans. Applicants approved for resettlement were matched with sponsors and provided free transportation to the US. The 132,800 applicants resettled by June 1950 were mostly non-German East European DPs and included only 10,090 ethnic German expellees. In June 1950 Congress amended the act, extending the program to December 31, 1951. The amendment also initiated three special programs for ethnic

German expellees, Greek orphans, and war orphans that would run through June 20, 1952. This amendment upped the number of visa slots for ethnic Germans expelled from their homeland in Central or Eastern Europe to a total of 54,744, which made more room for people like my parents.[1]

The end of the main program was reported on January 2, 1952, by the New York Times, when it noted that a family from Soviet-ruled Estonia had become "the last of 312,554 persons to qualify for entry under the three-year American displaced persons program."[2]

On January 3rd, 1952, the New York Times ran a follow-up story that touted the selectivity of the displaced persons resettlement program and boasted of the anticommunist benefits of the program with a paragraph headed "Only Three D. P.'s Deported."

> On the closed-out portion of the program Mr. Gibson [DP Commission director] reported: Only three displaced persons had to be deported, one of them a mental case. Visas were refused to about 9,000 abroad for security reasons. Those who came escaped communism and other dictatorships and were eager to fight for freedom. Their combined letters home, estimated at 5,000,000 annually, constitute "one of the greatest counter-actions against communism."[3]

At some point Hans alerted Fidel that new slots for expellees had become available. With many young American men once again in uniform and fighting in the Korean War, America faced a farm worker shortage. The skilled farmers among the DPs were now a more valuable commodity. Both Fidel and Hans applied and were matched with sponsors.

Fidel and Maria recalled submitting their application in June or July of 1951. In October they were summoned to the city of Rosenheim for a US Immigration Service interview and background check. They'd already passed a US-mandated vetting process five years earlier to procure German identity papers, but America's emigration procedure required yet a second screening.[4]

Unfortunately, the new expellee program got off to a slow start because of organizational problems. An additional bottleneck resulted from new 1950 restrictions that prohibited members of Communist organizations from being accepted by the resettlement programs. This stipulation stemmed from a political firestorm that erupted when the anticommunist fervor of the McCarthy era pushed US politicians to introduce a stringent new applicant investigation to weed out communists along with Nazis.[5]

Fidel and Maria grew concerned as week after week slipped by without word about the application. At last, in January of 1952, they received instructions to proceed to Munich for exit processing. So after Fidel built two sturdy wooden chests—most likely at the fish crate plant where he sometimes worked—Maria packed the essentials the family needed to set up a new household in America. In went most of the pots and pans, dishes, flatware, clothes, mementos, and bedding she'd accumulated. I particularly recall the puffy feather comforters and pillows that subsequently remained with us for years. Whatever didn't fit in the crates was sold or given away. Those dovetail-joined, rodent-proof brown crates went on to serve our family for two subsequent moves before they took up residence in a machine shed on what became our family farm.

The Munich facility to which my family was summoned, Funk Kaserne, had housed the German Wehrmacht's radio and radar operations in the latter part of the war. Postwar, the Emigration and Repatriation division of the United Nations Relief and Rehabilitation Administration (UNRRA) repurposed the facility as a camp that accommodated up to 10,000 East European DPs as they underwent resettlement processing. This UN subagency was established to reduce Western Europe's gargantuan DP problem. The following excerpt from a report detailing the process describes the enormity of its mission:

> By 1947, UNRRA was running nearly 800 resettlement camps, housing seven million people. Through herculean efforts, by 1951 only 177,000 displaced persons remained in the camps. Millions had been resettled; even more were repatriated; and significant numbers emigrated .... By 1951, a new legal and institutional framework existed in order to respond to the phenomenon of refugees, with the creation of the UN High Commissioner for Refugees (UNHCR) to succeed UNRRA.[6]

The new UN agency continued to employ some of the same camps used by its predecessor. The Funk Kaserne no longer exists, but back in the 1950s was on the outskirts of Munich. Today, the site is on the Frankfurter Ring and well within the city. The compound was built for the Luftwaffe in 1936 and somehow survived the wartime bombing. Its emigration processing role began in 1948 after the US 84th Congress passed Public Law 774 and set up the Displaced Persons Commission to oversee the admission of more than 400,000 DPs to the United States.

After being selected for processing under the act, applicants like my parents had to pass a thorough "character, history, and eligibility" vetting by the Department of the Army investigators. Questionable visa applications came with attached documents describing any evidence of participation in a movement that "is or has been hostile to the U.S. or the form of government of the U.S." The US Immigration and Naturalization

Service determined whether the applicant met current immigration laws and issued the actual visas.⁷

The United States, like Canada and other countries that accepted refugees, wanted healthy workers able to support themselves, so exit camps like Funk Kaserne also conducted medical exams. English-speaking medical personnel administered the physical exams, but relied on interpreters to set up appointments, answer questions, and move the applicants through.

My mother found this camp chaotic. "It was a mess," she exclaimed. The DPs there spoke many languages, and no one ever fully understood what was going on. Our family shared one small room with another family. Decades later, Maria still shuddered when she recalled the straw mattresses and the tiny amount of living space allocated to us. One reason she found the place exceptionally uncomfortable was that she was five months pregnant. Beyond that, there was no privacy in that accommodation, for only ceiling-hung blankets separated us and the other family. After three weeks of this discomfort, my parents were confounded to learn that the program's transportation component had failed to materialize and that we needed to return to Wimmern. I remember none of it.

In that era Congress tried to protect the taxpayers by requiring immigrants to have a sponsor who assumed financial support should the new immigrant family encounter difficulties. Our sponsors were a California farm couple—the Hartleys—desperate for farm labor. Mr. Hartley, after learning of the long transportation delay, fired off a letter to my father in Wimmern. My parents couldn't read English, so they had to scramble to find someone who could. Hartley simply wanted to know what he could do to speed up arrival. Despite his unhappiness about the delay, the political problem was too intractable for either him or my parents to do anything about.

Our family was called back to Munich again five or six weeks after returning to Wimmern. Fidel's cousin Hans Rabong and his family had better luck and were long gone by then. He reported that they'd encountered rough seas during their transatlantic passage on a spartan ocean liner, but had arrived safely at their destination in Iowa. Upon our recall to Munich, my mother was nearly eight months pregnant. In deference to the limited medical care available on the passenger ships and the rough conditions, families with a late term expectant mother or a newborn infant were sent by air. Unfortunately, no planes were immediately available upon our arrival in the camp, and the program subsequently ran out of money. My parents despaired that they'd have to return to Wimmern a second time and need to wait until the baby was born. But another organization, the Red Cross, came through with emergency funds that picked up the cost of chartering more planes. By the time everything was sorted out, we'd spent another three weeks in the camp.

The second stay in the Funk Kaserne resettlement camp, was harder on my mother than the first. The food in particular gave her difficulty. There was always "fish, fish, fish" on our plates—canned herring and sardines, something that made her stomach turn. My sister didn't tolerate the fare any better and ate very little. Maria lamented that Fidel wasn't much help with my sister and me because he played cards all the time. "It was just like in Wimmern," she exclaimed, where he worked lots of hours in his various jobs, then wanted to play cards during his scant time off. Maria said she maintained her sanity by taking outdoor walks.

My sole memory of the camp is being with my father at an outdoor card game. I would guess that Fidel was anxious about how his growing family would get along in the new country. His only preparation for the new culture had been two weeks of spotty English night school somewhere. Playing cards was probably one way to avoid thinking about the difficult road ahead.

The American camp authorities wanted to make sure the DPs were free of lice, fleas, and infectious diseases, so the stay also served as a quarantine period. Maria said she herself wasn't worried about fleas because after the various unsanitary camps in Czechoslovakia and Germany she'd transited, she knew fleas didn't find her tasty. But colds and other infectious ailments were a concern because in the crowded conditions they had considerable opportunity to establish themselves. My sister was the only one of us to become sick during our stay. The severe cold she caught shortly before our departure sent Maria into a frenzy of doctoring because she couldn't stomach the thought of having to spend even one extra day in the camp.

---

1. U.S. Displaced Persons Commission, *The DP Story: The Final Report of the United States Displaced Persons Commission*. (Washington: United States Government Printing Office, 1952), v, 37-40, 77 https://babel.hathitrust.org/cgi/pt?id=uc1.31822016341265&view=1up&seq=1.
2. The United Press, "Estonian Family Is Last under U.S. Refugee Act," *New York Times*, January 2, 1952.
3. Special to The New York Times, "D. P. Group Reports on Its 3-Year Task: All 336,000 Visas Assigned," *New York Times*, January 3, 1952.
4. U.S. Displaced Persons Commission, *The DP Story*, 167-182.
5. U.S. Displaced Persons Commission, *The DP Story*, 70-71, 84-86.
6. Colin Bundy, "Migrants, Refugees, History and Precedents," *Forced Migration Review*, no. 51 (January 2016), http://www.fmreview.org/destination-europe/bundy.html.
7. U.S. Displaced Persons Commission, *The DP Story*, 53, 172-176.

54 Troubled Journey

Some of my parents' anxiety and fears eased when our names moved up high enough on the departure list to assure us seats on the second of two flights to New York City in the coming week. That flight was to leave on Saturday, April 5, 1952. Then, after several names were apparently scratched off the earlier flight leaving on April 2, our names were added to that flight roster. At the time, Maria considered herself lucky to cut out three tedious days in the camp. Had she known what lay in store, I'm sure she'd have gladly have exchanged places with a Jewish couple she had a conversation with. They were booked on the later Saturday flight and faced a conundrum because their beliefs forbade them to travel on their Sabbath. How this played out for them, she never learned.

Following breakfast on the morning of April 2, 1952, Fidel and Maria were undoubtedly nervous as they packed the last of their belongings in their suitcases and herded my sister and me to the appointed assembly area. They were only too happy to leave the converted Luftwaffe radar and radio facility behind, but would miss the company of the family they'd shared their room with for the previous two weeks. The two couples had bonded and would remain in contact for decades. The same applied to a pair of other families they met in the camp. I recall a reunion with one of them when our family visited them several years later in their home near Madison, Wisconsin.

From the camp assembly point, we air passengers would have been herded aboard spartan buses and driven to nearby Munich-Riem Airport. Because our papers had already been processed, the buses likely dropped us off right at the wheeled boarding ramp lodged against our plane. That aircraft was a chartered DC-4 airliner with El Al Airlines markings. El Al was at the time a young Israeli airline formed only four years earlier. The airline operated only leased planes until 1949, when it bought its first two

DC-4 aircraft. A few more purchases followed, and our plane, which the company designated with the code 4X-ADC, followed. The El Al name was a biblical reference meaning *to the above*. Later in the journey Maria and Fidel must have desperately prayed our particular El Al plane would stay in the *above* and not descend to the *below* before the pilots directed it to.

It turns out that plane 4X-ADC has quite an interesting history. A query sent to the airline's historian, along with a copy of our 1952 flight manifest, netted the following reply:

> EL AL operated six DC-4 aircraft during 1949–1952. 4X-ADC was EL AL's last operating DC-4 . . . . Its special flight… arrived at New York-Idlewild on 5 April 1952 [actually, April 7 because of delays] was its last passenger flight . . . . It is interesting to note that the 4X-ADC aircraft operated on the 1950–51 airlift of Iraqi Jews to Israel while being registered temporarily to a Cuban airline with a Cuban registration number.
>
> I also note that the crew manifest list is signed by Captain Sam Lewis of EL AL. He was Chief Pilot of EL AL in its early years and was famous as the head pilot of the foreign volunteers ('Mahal') air transport division during Israel's War of Independence.[1]

Coach seating room in the 1950s was more generous than today, but for El Al in that era, expediency over comfort was sometimes called for. Such was the case when Israel decided to evacuate threatened Jews from Middle East trouble spots. Yemen was one such spot in 1949.

> A DC-4 normally seated about 50 passengers. However, the Yemenites were thin, and five persons usually could fit into seats designed for four. So the normal seats were removed, and wooden benches installed with seat belts across them, to hold more passengers. As Capt. Sam Lewis related, "When a 'plane was loaded, a crew member would stand at the top of the stairway sizing up the passengers and, when necessary to crowd more on a bench, would yell 'give me a thin one.' " . . . . Thus, each DC-4 took off with about 120 people packed inside.
>
> The Yemenites had never seen a plane before, so one can imagine their numb astonishment on encountering this great bird and wondering how it flew. Once inside the aircraft they usually sat stoically and in awe… Once a pilot passed back to the cabin a request for some water. Soon a Yemenite youngster brought to the cockpit a cup of freshly boiled tea. This jolted the crew because they knew there were no facilities for boiling

water on the plane. Hastening back to the passenger cabin, they were astonished to see the Yemenites firing a makeshift stove on the floor, heating a kettle of water for tea!

At the peak of Operation Magic Carpet, aircraft flew constantly to Israel.... They had to fly a narrow corridor along the middle of the Red Sea and Gulf of Eilat to skirt Arab countries, with instruments of dubious accuracy and deprived of radio guidance. Engines suffered from desert sand and dust, and a forced landing anywhere would have meant disaster, but remarkably no mishaps occurred.[2]

Given that "engines suffered from desert sand and dust," it is no wonder then that these planes might be prone to mechanical problems, such as what the Eiperts were to experience. Other airlifts followed, including an even larger one that flew Iraqi Jews to Israel. The 4X-ADC participated in this rescue while temporarily registered to a Cuban airline.[3]

El Al DC-4 (number 4X-ADC) airliner, within which the Eipert family endured the 7-leg flight that carried them from Munich to New York.

The DC-4 was a four-engine propeller-driven craft built by the Douglas Aircraft Company. The wartime model first rolled off the assembly line in 1942 and was dedicated to the war effort. It had a range of 2,500 miles, a cruising speed of 280 miles per hour, and a 14,000-foot ceiling. The US Army Air Force named their version the C-54 Skymaster, while the US Navy called theirs the R5D. Both used this reliable workhorse of a plane, which had a 10-ton payload, to move both cargo and passengers.

After the war, some 500 were sold as surplus by the US Defense Department. Douglas converted the craft for civilian use and called it the DC-4. Airlines scooped them up to build a burgeoning postwar commercial passenger service. The military continued to operate its planes and eventually employed nearly half in the remarkable Berlin Airlift of 1948–1949 to break the Russian stranglehold blockade of West Berlin. These planes delivered everything the city depended on, even coal.

One shortcoming of the DC-4 was its unpressurized cabin. During development, the military learned that pressurization would make production costly, so like in most other warplanes of the era, that feature was omitted. This restricted the plane's flight ceiling and limited it to flying through rough weather instead of above it like modern airliners. Despite its often-bumpy flight, the DC-4 became the mainstay of many a new airline. It allowed El Al to launch a charter business to the United States from Israel, with stops in Rome (Italy), Shannon (Ireland), Gander (Newfoundland), and Idlewild (New York).

By the end of the 1940s, the world's major airlines had upgraded to pressurized planes that could fly above the turbulent air produced by weather. El Al couldn't afford such planes, so it picked up castoff DC-4s. Our particular plane and a sister craft retained their United Air Lines' dark blue and silver colors because the El Al executives liked the look and could save the cost of repainting. The airline subsequently painted their other DC-4s to match.[4]

Maria and Fidel had never flown before, so understandably they'd have boarded the plane with some trepidation. But because they'd faced much more physically daunting situations than flying, I expect cutting ties to their culture, friends, and Europe concerned them more. Perhaps most worrisome was the palpable uncertainty of how they and their children would be received in a country that not long before had conducted a fierce war and propaganda hate campaign against Germans.

That country also came with a language neither of them spoke nor understood, leaving them unable to express themselves or make their needs known. After arrival, they'd have no interpreter during the daunting journey across the continent to their sponsor's farm in a remote area on California's northern border, so the language problem would surface immediately. There was also the matter of two small children to feed and clothe with no savings to rely on. And within two or three weeks the new baby would come along. Maria confessed she was tempted to back out and return to Wimmern from the camp more than once.

According to Maria, our flight departed Munich at 11 a.m. When the passengers had been briefed about what to expect back at Funk Kaserne, they were told that because the plane was not pressurized, the less they ate, the better off they'd be when the flight got rough. But El Al didn't take the *limited eating* caution seriously. "We were fed a lot," Maria remarked. An attendant passed out bananas, apples, and oranges after takeoff. Upon arrival in Amsterdam at 1 p.m., lunch in an airport cafeteria awaited. At 3 p.m. the plane took off once again for a short hop to London, where another meal awaited. Fidel recalled only cookies and coffee there, but Maria insisted that we sat down to heartier fare that included meat. She was probably in a better position to recall, for meat would have been a most welcome relief from the fish diet.

At 7 p.m., our plane departed on its third leg. By the time it touched down in Iceland at Keflavik Airport four or five hours later, my parents were surely exhausted. Because of the time zone change, the evening was not yet far advanced—so we passengers were served another evening meal while the plane refueled. Food service aboard airliners was still evolving then, and not all passenger planes were equipped to serve meals. The standard DC-4 conversion that the airlines favored seated 44 passengers and included a galley. To allow for extra seats, our charter plane had no galley; hence it served only apples, oranges, and sandwiches. My parents recalled that the plane had about 60 seats, but the flight manifest listed 70 passengers.

Thirty-two of the passengers were Polish nationals—many of them Jews. The ethnic Germans from various countries totaled 22. As for the rest: stateless (2), Estonian (3), Hungarian (2), Russian (6), and Ukrainian (2). During the course of the trip my parents bonded with an ethnic German couple named Hanecker. Frau Hanecker, like most of the women aboard, was also expecting, which gave her and Maria much to talk about. The two women were apparently a steadying comfort to each other during the frequent bouts of turbulence.

Our Newfoundland-bound plane left Iceland around 11 p.m. and all appeared to be going well for about an hour. But then, well out over the North Atlantic, the plane experienced engine trouble and two engines either stopped or had to be shut down. My parents didn't recall, or perhaps were never told, the specific problem that required the plane to turn around and limp back on its two remaining engines. Fortunately, the pilots managed to keep the aircraft in the air long enough to return to Iceland, but my parents and the other adult passengers surely completed the flight with white knuckles.

I never learned whether it was the airline or local administrators who had to scramble to find accommodations for us at the airport, but eventually each family received a room key with a number tag. These accommodations might have been hotel rooms, but could also have been in-transit military facilities from the war years. We lodged there the rest of that night and two more while the plane awaited replacement parts and maintenance. I wonder now if the engine problem had anything to do with the "desert sand and dust" of past Israeli rescue missions.

On the morning of our first day in Iceland, a priest sought out our group after hearing that a plane with children aboard had an unexpected layover. He'd come to deliver a parcel of games for them and their parents. What games my sister and I scored, I don't recall, but both my parents remembered that Fidel got a checkerboard set.

When an American reading a newspaper saw my father walk by with his checkerboard, he approached Fidel and asked if he knew how to play. My father didn't understand the question until the man pointed at the board. At that point Fidel nodded and said "Ja!" He'd learned the fundamentals somewhere, so the two men sat and played. Fidel had picked up just enough English at the night school in Munich to allow some small interchange. When my sister and I came over to watch, the man excused himself briefly, then returned with candy bars for us. Of course, Fidel also played cards with other men from the plane during the stay. Maria said she hardly saw him the entire time because he was always playing cards. Early on Saturday morning, we passengers clambered back into the presumably repaired plane to continue the journey.

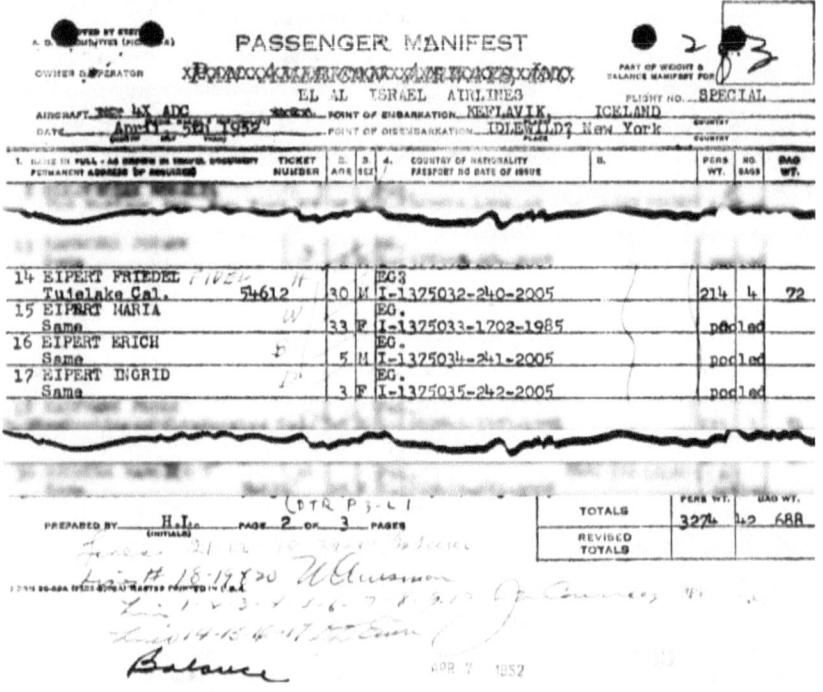

Cutouts from the passenger manifest for the Saturday, April 5, 1952, flight from Keflavik, Iceland, to Idlewild, New York. Shown is the Eipert family's spot in the roster for this, the 5th leg of the problem-laden air journey from West Germany to the United States.

I have no memory of the nighttime flight that experienced engine trouble, but then I was not quite five years of age and almost certainly sleeping soundly. However, I do have a couple of memories from what must have been our second Iceland departure. I recall peering out the window and marveling at the many white icebergs below. Another memory is being offered chewing gum to relieve the pain of the air pressure changes in my ears. Not having been around American GIs, I didn't know what to do with it. Something I didn't recall was being frightened the first time our plane took off. Maria said that unlike my relatively calm 3-year-old sister, I wouldn't release my firm grip on the seat rests and refused to look out the window.

Our flights were quite turbulent at times and my mother said that she could never forget the misery of a nearby couple who seemed to vomit constantly. Fortunately, their two children were fine. Maria also told me that the violent shaking frightened a Polish woman so severely that she became hysterical, stripped off her clothing, and writhed around naked on the floor of the aisle. Despite her own advanced pregnancy, Maria experienced no nausea the entire trip.[5][6]

The second flight from Iceland—our fifth of the journey—successfully cleared the North Atlantic and this time deposited us in Gander, Newfoundland, late in the morning. We deplaned for a quick meal in a cafeteria while the plane refueled, then began what was supposed to be the last segment of the journey. Flight number six was uneventful until around 4 p.m. on Saturday afternoon as we approached our destination. Under beautifully clear skies, my parents recalled gazing out the window at dazzling New York City. Then came the bad news. Immigration, or perhaps our program's agents, were unable to process us over the weekend. The plane's crew was no doubt cursing their abysmal string of bad luck, or someone's failure to check ahead, for now they had to retrace the 1155 air miles back to Newfoundland.

After disembarking for the night in the same place we'd left earlier that day, each family was assigned a room, just as in Iceland. My mother didn't say whether she again lost Fidel to cards the next day, but it would have been unusual for him not to have played a few games between the calls for breakfast, lunch, and supper that Sunday. Fidel only recalled having a conversation with a Romanian-speaking pilot sometime during the day.

With departure for New York set for very early Monday morning, we passengers were awakened at 1 a.m. and summoned to breakfast. Then, inside a large hangar, we reboarded the 4X-ADC and waited for dense ground fog to lift. While in the hanger, we passengers learned that the Saturday plane that left Munich three days later than ours had caught up and was also waiting to depart. Its passengers had enjoyed an uneventful journey.

Around 6 a.m., after two or three hours in our seats, we were allowed to leave the plane and return to the terminal to stretch our legs and have a second breakfast. We then reboarded, but the stubborn gray fog lingered for several more hours. Fidel recalled that many of the men subsequently took breaks and left the plane. Maria said some of the women did also. Only late in the morning did the fog clear enough for the tower to give our pilots clearance. Around 5 p.m. on Monday, April 7, 1952—five-and-a-half days and seven flights into the journey—the Eiperts finally set foot in the United States.

Immigration flights such as ours were met by the sponsoring agency's port liaison officers, who then took charge. My parents didn't mention how we got from New York International Airport (Idlewild) in Queens to our hotel for the night, but it was almost certainly by charter bus. After receiving $7 in the hotel lobby for an evening meal, our travel-weary family rode up the elevator to an assigned room. My parents had never been in a high-rise building, and between them recalled that we rode up either to the 11th or 14th floor. Once we'd settled in, Fidel returned to the street to find us some food. He ventured a block in one direction, then a block in the other, but he could neither read the signs nor get anyone to understand what he wanted. At one point in his excursion, he ran into some Italian speakers, but they couldn't understand him either. He laughed when he recalled it and said, "I couldn't even say 'I want a hamburger.'" Maria said he eventually returned with a few bread rolls. But it was not the lack of satisfying food that she remembered most about that layover—it was the inhabitants we shared our room with. "There were mice running around," she exclaimed. "I couldn't sleep because I was afraid a mouse would jump on me."

The next morning a program agent who spoke German met our family in the lobby and informed my parents that he'd been forwarded $300 by our sponsor in California. The money, which would later come out of Fidel's wages, was to pay for our train tickets to Klamath Falls, Oregon, the nearest train station to our new home outside of Tulelake, California. The agent already had the tickets in hand, which came as good news to my parents. But I can guarantee his next revelation, that the trip would take about four days, during which time we'd be sleeping in our seats, was not well received by Maria. It was not something a woman over eight months pregnant wanted to hear. The tickets cost $219, my father recollected. Calculating that my sister and I each traveled half fare, the price of the adult cross-continental fare works out to about $70, meals included. This left our family with $81 to cover contingency expenses. Later, the same agent escorted a group of us to our train in Pennsylvania Station and alerted my parents to expect a four-hour layover and a change of trains in Chicago.

Fidel and Maria's new friends from the plane, the Haneckers, were on the same train but in a different car. They had a far shorter journey that ended in Columbus, Ohio. At Union Station in Chicago, early on Wednesday afternoon, someone guided us to a small waiting room. Our luggage eventually followed. While there, Fidel phoned Karl Nachbrunn, a relative in Chicago. Karl was a first cousin of Fidel's mother and had emigrated to the United States four years earlier. The two men had met and become friends in Bavaria after the war. Karl too had been a stranded Banat soldier. He now offered to help Fidel and Maria stay in Chicago, a place where we'd have a support system and German-speaking neighbors. My parents readily agreed, so Karl phoned Fidel's sponsors in California and offered to reimburse the $300 forwarded for the train journey. The Hartleys remained adamant that Fidel needed to come and work on the farm, but reluctantly agreed to let our family remain in Chicago for a few days.

Somehow, my parents found their way to the Nachbrunn apartment. We happened to arrive during Easter week, so Karl was free for three of the four days we stayed with his family. This gave the adults time to catch up on all that had happened since they'd last met and allowed my parents the chance to meet some of the Nachbrunn family's German acquaintances. The stopover also educated my parents a bit about how things worked in America. Maria said that her impression of her new country was not overly favorable at this point.

On Monday afternoon my family returned to Union Station to board the train. What my parents didn't appreciate at first was that this train, the *California Zephyr*, followed what was arguably the most picturesque route in the country. The 3:30 p.m. daily departure allowed passengers to marvel at the most spectacular sections of the scenery-packed trip in daylight on the second day. The highlights appeared when the train reached the Colorado Front Range. The beauty continued to roll by the next day when the train passed through scenic Glenwood Canyon, worked its way along California's rugged Feather River Canyon, and finally wound through the rolling green hills of Altamont Pass before the trip terminated in Oakland.[7] Before the days of Amtrak, the *California Zephyr* was operated jointly by three independent companies—the Chicago, Burlington & Quincy (CB&Q), Denver & Rio Grande Western (D&RGW), and Western Pacific (WP) railroads. The Zephyr's route was assembled as the *Exposition Flyer* in 1939 to carry visitors from the Midwest to the Golden Gate International Exposition on Treasure Island in San Francisco Bay. The natural wonders made this route so popular that the three railroads continued its operation after the special event closed. In the 1940s, the Flyer upgraded to diesel locomotives and lighter cars. The Burlington Line further streamlined their train several years after World War II, and the other railroads followed its lead.

The Burlington Line's name came from the small city of Burlington, Iowa, which according to the train schedule of the day, the *Zephyr* reached at 6:35 p.m. daily.[8] Somehow, the Burlington part of the name survived a number of mergers and today remains the lead name of the huge Burlington Northern Santa Fe Railway. Quite coincidentally, Fidel's cousin Hans was then living only 10 miles outside of Burlington, where he was sponsored by a local farmer. Hans's family had left Germany for America by ship a month earlier. Our families wouldn't yet have been able to re-establish contact, and the stop at Burlington, just across the Mississippi River from Illinois, was a short one that would have made anything but the briefest of meetings all but impossible at this time. My parents could not have suspected that in the not-too-distant future they'd see that Burlington station again,

One contributor to the success of the *California Zephyr* was a newly designed railway car it adopted in 1949—the Zephyr. These cars offered a unique option: a topside glass viewing dome that the company promoted as the Vista Dome. The California Zephyr used at least five of these dome cars on each train. The spectacular scenery as viewed from a dome sold many a ticket for this train.[9] I don't know how much time our family spent on the observation deck, but it was probably a considerable amount. Without doubt, the vast scale of the countryside rolling by outside the windows proved far greater than my parents could have imagined. Central Europe had no precedent.

Adding to the popularity of the route was the exceptional service provided by the female attendants called Zephyrettes. Aside from the Burlington Line, no operator offered the equivalent of what were called airline stewardesses in that day. These Zephyrettes were said to hold "a combination of jobs from social director to tour guide and train nurse; essentially, they performed nearly any task requested by the train crew or passengers and always did so with a friendly smile."[10]

I don't specifically remember the women in the pale-blue uniforms, but my parents surely interacted with them a number of times, since they didn't speak or read English. I seem to recall having a little constipation problem on this trip and wouldn't be surprised to learn that a Zephyrette helped my mother deal with it.

Although the Zephyr route terminated in Oakland, we exited four stops earlier in Sacramento during the early afternoon to catch a connecting train north to Klamath Falls, Oregon. My parents didn't note which train we boarded then, but the schedule makes it likely that we reached Klamath Falls, Oregon, at 2:25 a.m. on the Southern Pacific Streamliner Cascade.

From 1937 until 1951, the Cascade was an all-Pullman train, but by the time we rode it in 1952, the sleeper cars had been steadily replaced with seat carriages to reduce costs. The 252-mile trip to Klamath Falls from Sacramento took seven hours, so once again my parents found themselves trying to sleep in reclining seats. At some point we'd have visited the train's distinctive triple-unit dining car assemblage, which was painted in two distinctive shades of gray. Afterwards, Maria and Fidel were probably too anxious about what they'd find at the end of the journey to do more than catnap. For starters, they had to trust that there'd been no miscommunication and their sponsor would be at the station to pick us up. That part of our trip must have gone smoothly because they never mentioned a problem in reaching our new accommodations.

---

1. Marvin Goldman, "Response to El Al Company Historical Questions" (Email, October 26, 2019).
2. Marvin G. Goldman, "Chapter 2 – EL AL to the Skies: The DC-4 Era (1948-1950)," in *EL AL: Israel's Flying Star* (Israel Airline Museum, 2021), http://www.israelairlinemuseum.org/el-al-israels-flying-star/chapter-2-el-al-to-the-skies-the-dc-4-era/.
3. Goldman, "Response to El Al Company Historical Questions."
4. Goldman, "Chapter 2 – EL AL to the Skies: The DC-4 Era (1948-1950)."
5. "New York, New York, Passenger and Crew Lists, 1909, 1925-1957: 8128 - Vol 17783-17784: Image 289 of 1325," database with images, Family Search (Citing NARA microfilm publication T715 (Washington, D.C.: National Archives and Records Administration), April 7, 1952), https://familysearch.org/ark:/61903/3:1:3QS7-L94K-JDNY?cc=1923888&wc=MFKZ-QZS%3A1030234201.
6. "New York, New York, Passenger and Crew Lists, 1909, 1925-1957: 8128 - Vol 17783-17784: Image 286 of 1325," database with images, Family Search (Citing NARA microfilm publication T715 (Washington, D.C.: National Archives and Records Administration), April 7, 1952), https://familysearch.org/ark:/61903/3:1:3QS7-L94K-JDJ9?cc=1923888&wc=MFKZ-QZS%3A1030234201.
7. Adam Burns, "The California Zephyr," American Rails.com, December 25, 2022, https://www.american-rails.com/cz.html.
8. National Railway Publication Company, "The California Zephyr: Official Guide," Streamliner Schedules, August 1950, http://www.streamlinerschedules.com/concourse/track5/calzephyr195008.html.
9. Burns, "The California Zephyr."
10. Burns, "The California Zephyr."

55 The Tule Lake Basin

Had my mother known how primitive her new accommodations would be and how isolated she'd be on a farm miles from any town, I probably wouldn't be an American today. This is not to say the Tule Lake area where our family found itself is a dreadful place, for in several visits as an adult I found the locale both likeable and interesting. The Klamath Reclamation Project that drained most of a large, shallow lake created a marvelously fertile valley of lakebed soil. And the millions of migrating waterfowl that passed through the Tule Lake National Wildlife Refuge twice yearly are certainly a wonderous sight, as are the lava tubes at the Lava Beds National Monument and the vistas of the Medicine Lake Highlands Recreation Area to the south. But the reality for my mother was something different. These attractions had little bearing on the life of a struggling immigrant mother with three young children.

The poor accommodations that so disheartened Maria upon arrival in Tule Lake had roots in a dark thread of World War II. Even though she was unaware of the history of the house we lived in, that accommodation surely reminded her of the insufferable camp housing she thought she'd left behind by coming to America. What neither she nor my father knew upon arrival was that the town of Tulelake was infamously associated with an enormous internment camp constructed when a wave of war hysteria followed the Japanese Empire's sneak attack on Pearl Harbor in December 1941. The president, the military, and many American citizens feared a mainland invasion because the Japanese had already aggressively seized a considerable amount of Asian territory. America, in its panic, feared that Japanese Americans, 80 percent of whom lived along the West Coast, would become a center of espionage and sabotage. Under the doctrine of military necessity, President Roosevelt on February 19, 1942, signed Executive Order 9066 to counter that threat and ease the public's fear. The order gave the secretary of war the power to designate military areas from which "any or all persons may be excluded." Furthermore, it authorized military commanders to initiate orders they deemed advisable to enforce such action.[1]

Unfortunately, the US military command responded by incarcerating all West Coast Japanese Americans—many of them US citizens—in remote internment camps for the duration of World War II. The Canadian government soon followed suit and interned its Japanese-Canadian residents of British Columbia. The Tule Lake basin was one of 10 American sites chosen for the construction of large camps of barracks buildings. The Tule Lake Unit of the WWII Valor in the Pacific National Monument has this to say about the Tule Lake camp:

> Isolated in northern California, the Tule Lake area is remote and self-sustained by farming, which made the area fit the War Relocation Authority's (WRA) ideal model for a relocation camp. Set on over 7,400 acres, the Tule Lake complex included the typical infrastructure of a normal American town with a post office, high school, hospital, cemetery, several factory and warehouse buildings, two sewage treatment plants, and over 3,500 acres of irrigated farmland made available by the efforts of the CCC. During the Tule Lake Segregation Center's tenure, roughly four years, nearly 1,500 babies were born and over 300 people died. At its peak capacity, Tule Lake was the temporary home to more than 18,000 internees and 1,200 soldiers. To accommodate these individuals the camp had 1,036 barrack dorms, 518 latrines, and 144 administrative and support buildings.[2]

The construction and support needs of the camp saw a small town, Newell, rise on the periphery. Today, the internment barracks are all gone from near Newell, but over 50 administration and service buildings, as well as a considerable section of barbwire-topped, chain-link fence outside the prisoner enclosure survive and serve various purposes.[3]

In 1943 the Tule Lake War Relocation Center's name changed to Tule Lake Segregation Center when a portion of the facility became the primary detention center for those Japanese Americans that the government believed were disloyal or posed a security risk. Eventually, soldiers were stationed there to provide security. The National Park Service noted that with these changes,

> The population at Tule Lake rose from 15,276 to 18,789 within just a few months. Though additional barracks were built and the camp was expanded, the camp housed almost 4,000 over its

intended capacity. This ... created discontent, which grew as security increased and additional soldiers were assigned to Tule Lake. Soon a lighted seven foot high chain link fence topped with barbed wire was added, Army tanks arrived on site, and the number of guard towers around the center was increased from six to 19. The farm areas were also surrounded by a warning fence, a security fence, and 16 new guard towers.

Row of Tule Lake War Relocation Center (later renamed Tule Lake Segregation Center) barracks buildings during the spring thaw of 1942. Its tarpaper-covered buildings were offered to local farmers at an affordable price when the camp closed after the war. Purchasers could buy either a whole structure or a half produced by sawing a building in two. One such half became the Eipert family's home upon their arrival in Tule Lake, California.

As a segregation center, Tule Lake was a mix of 'loyals' with no intention of leaving the United States, pro-Japan Japanese Americans who wished to repatriate or expatriate as soon as possible, and many whose feelings fell somewhere between these extremes. Internal friction between groups as well as with the US Army resulted in harassment, beatings, riots, mass demonstrations, military intervention and occupation.... As discontent grew within the Segregation Center, the Army took control of the camp in late 1943, declaring martial law on November 13, which lasted until January 15, 1944.[4]

The Tule Lake camp remained open several months longer than the other nine WRA camps and closed on March 20, 1946. Today, this site differs from the other sites in that the entire footprint is still visible. Because of this, the descendants of the internees want much more of it to become part of the Tule Lake National Monument. The difficulty is that most of the land came under private ownership after the war, and the flying service that operates on it now is one of the largest local employers. The site also serves as Tulelake's municipal airport. As it stands, the national monument includes only the Segregation Center portion of the camp and a smaller Isolation Center at a site called Camp Tulelake, 10 miles away. This smaller camp served as a secure holding facility for the Japanese American men who actively resisted the camp authorities at the main camp and internees arrested after protesting their incarceration by refusing to answer two poorly phrased questions on a loyalty questionnaire.

The Isolation Center later also came to house a number of Japanese American inmates brought in from other concentration camps at significantly higher wages as strikebreakers to undermine the hundreds of Tule Lake prisoners who in 1943 refused to help harvest district crops until their demands for safer working conditions and related grievances were met. The strikebreakers had to be housed away from the main camp for their own safety. When the national head of the WRA came to Tule Lake to assess the unrest and was greeted by a mob of more than 5,000 protestors, he declared the camp out of control and sent in armed forces with tanks and tear gas.[5]

During the worker strike when Camp Tulelake isolated the Segregation Center's "troublemakers" and protected the strikebreakers, the government decided to further ease the harvest labor shortage hitting local farmers by building a POW camp with labor supplied by 150 Italian POWs from Camp White in Oregon. The new fences, guard towers, latrines, and water lines they constructed would then house the German POWs brought in for the farm labor. According to a display in the Tule Lake National Monument visitor center, the German POW labors proved so popular with area farmers that by March 1945 nearly a thousand German prisoners were tending the onion and potato crops for a wage of 80 cents per day. Some of those POWs remained in the Tule Lake area until the camp closed in 1946.[6]

No barracks buildings remained in the internment camp itself when the Eiperts arrived six years later, but those buildings hadn't just disappeared. As described in an article looking back at Tule Lake's history, they contributed greatly to the final phase of homesteading and economic growth of the area when they

> were dismantled and many hundreds of buildings were moved and repurposed nearby as houses and farm outbuildings, strongly influencing the Tule Lake basin's aesthetic character to this day.... A post-war phase of homesteading for returning Anglo veterans occurred from 1946–49, and the camp's existence to a large extent made this feasible. The areas opened to homesteaders were ... within six miles due north and south. Homesteaders were each allowed one barracks building, which, for $150, was cut in half and moved to farmsteads that were approximately a quarter mile square. Other barracks buildings were available for purchase from the Bureau of Reclamation ... and the camp's farm and other equipment and materials were also sold to new farmers ... most of the moved buildings remained relatively close, because transporting them over the rough, unpaved secondary roads of the 1940s was difficult.[7]

The camp touched the lives of Maria and Fidel because the Hartleys acquired one of these barracks buildings. Half of that tarpapered building became a storage shed on the Hartley farmstead. The other half was placed in the corner of a field separated from the farmstead by two parallel irrigation ditches, fitted with exterior siding, and modified as necessary to repurpose it as a farmhand residence. This small house, bordered by the canals, lonely County Road 100, and a dusty field, served as our new home.

Left: Photo of the Eipert family's barracks-building home near Tulelake, as it looked from across the adjoining weedy irrigation canals. The picture was taken 25 years after the Eiperts lived there. *Right:* The author on the county road that ran past the Eiperts' home. The house and barn, no longer there in 2012, once hugged the bank of the canal on the right. Although the irrigation canal is full of water in this growing season photo, during much of the year that channel was an empty, weedy ditch.

In a situation much like Maria's arrival in Wimmern, extensive reporting and photos of the ragged DPs in post-war Europe caused many Americans to assume people like my parents had come from poverty-stricken backgrounds and would be grateful to live in practically any building with a roof. The truth was, like the bulk of the millions of their fellow ethnic German DPs from Eastern and Central Europe, my parents had grown up in homes on a par with that of most Americans. And even in postwar Germany where living conditions were tight and cramped, houses were built solidly enough to keep out the weather. Had my parents been aware of the origin of their leaky new home, they'd have certainly recognized the irony of leaving the squalid German Funk Kaserne camp housing only to end up in American camp housing.

The barracks house might have been more satisfactory had it received more than a perfunctory remodeling. Although it had at some point acquired interior sheetrock, the building lacked insulation and had many leaky cracks. Most local residents who converted such buildings for their own use improved them enough that a great number survive to this day. As one local observer wrote,

> The landscape is peppered with these buildings in various states of modification and structural integrity. Their layouts were modified into T or L footprints, with improvements to enhance appearance and structural integrity, and to mask their origin. In fact, the Bureau of Reclamation offered remodeling plans to homesteaders to help make the idea of living in them more attractive to their wives.[8]

The Hartleys apparently had no idea how disappointing the poor housing was to the new residents and were probably unaware that in Europe farmers lived in town. Except for Fidel's military stint, both he and Maria had resided in villages, surrounded by friends and family. Their new setting was an alien environment that isolated them on a table-flat lakebed in a high desert landscape. Even a glimpse of the miles-away lake, or rather the irrigation sump that the lake had now become, would have helped.

Tule Lake was once a natural wetland of 96,000 acres with a water surface area that varied seasonally. Maps suggest that a good snow melt brought it up to 19 miles in length and 12 miles in breadth. The drainage project reduced that surface to two odd-shaped, but connected, remnants. On May 29, 1952, not long after my family's arrival, a story on page five of The Tulelake Reporter noted that Tule Lake, once known as Rhett Lake, was down to 13,200 acres in size and that in 1928 the remains of the lake and some additional surrounding land had been designated Tule Lake National Wildlife Refuge. The 39,116-acre refuge preserved an important rest stop for the massive biannual migration of waterfowl along the Pacific Flyway.

Bare dirt and patches of the previous year's dead weeds surrounded our new dwelling when we arrived. The weather was wintery and cold in comparison to what Maria was used to, and she would find that spring arrived much later here, given the 4,000-foot (1,200-meter) elevation. Learning that she was miles from Tulelake, the closest town with a store, was also disheartening. Even worse, she had no close neighbors other than the Hartleys, whose farmstead was separated from our house by the irrigation canals. Loneliness set in quickly. The house didn't even have a telephone. Later, Maria did acquire a radio for company but confessed she'd "sit in front of it and not understand a word." When I asked my mother for her reaction on arrival, she said, "I sat on the bed with my coat on and just wanted to go back to Germany."

On a clear day, glaciated Mt. Shasta was visible far to the west, but a single distant peak was a far cry from the sight of the beautiful Alps and the lush, green Alpine valley Maria had left behind. Aside from Mt. Shasta, her view now consisted of an unpainted small barn, the county road, vast potato fields, brownish hills in the middle distance, and the two weedy irrigation canals. These big ditches, one of which brought water to the fields and the other that drained away the runoff during the growing season, were particularly repugnant to Maria because they often were nearly empty and a haven for muskrats. Recalling them decades later, she shook her head, grimaced in abhorrence, and said "Ugh!"

The canals were part of the vast irrigation system that made local agriculture possible, and sustained Fidel's job. At the time of our arrival in 1952, the multi-decade drainage project was nearly complete after having excavated some 600 miles of canal. Once reclaimed and stabilized, the land had been allocated to homesteaders through a series of lotteries. The most recent giveaway had been the last homestead offering in the lower 48 states. The earliest allotments had gone to World War I veterans. Later, World War II soldiers became the beneficiaries via a process described by the Oregon Historical Society.

The Bureau of Reclamation lottery process drawings that distributed the first 86 post-World War II homestead allocations of about 160 acres each attracted national headlines when announced on August 1, 1946. A screening process reduced the initial 2,150 applicants to 1,305. Each of the finalists was assigned a number that was then sealed inside a gelatin capsule and placed in a 3-gallon pickle jar. When the December 18, 1946, drawing took place over national radio, the Klamath Union High School band played patriotic songs while the capsules were drawn, smashed open with a mallet, and the numbers inside matched with the winning entrants' names on a blackboard.

An additional 130 homestead units opened in the following two years, but these were on less desirable land. The last tract was refused by 20 alternates because of its alkali content. Other units were "littered with lava rock that had to be removed. Some sections needed leveling." The Bureau of Reclamation aided the new homesteaders by selling them surplus farm equipment and buildings from the Japanese internment camp at Newell. Each homesteader was "eligible to receive a 20x100 foot barracks for a $50 clean site deposit."[9] For an extra $150, that building would be cut into halves.

Maria wasn't the only new resident who didn't take to life in the basin. A significant number of the land-lottery winners came to feel likewise and left in the 1950s and 1960s when their dreams of an instant windfall proved illusory. "The hardships of the lifestyle, isolation of the area and lack of management skills" exacted a toll.[10]

Yet, there were other newcomers who came to love the environment. In the course of researching the lottery, I learned that a number of wartime German POWs who'd worked for local farmers grew fond of the area and asked to stay upon their release. The US government denied their requests and repatriated them all back to Europe, but six managed to return and at least two of them even attempted to apply for a homestead, perhaps because the wording of the 1946 homestead lottery eligibility requirements was loose in one aspect. Posted on a display panel in the Tulelake-Butte Valley Fairgrounds Museum were the following stipulations:

1. $2,000 minimum in assets or capital

2. At least two years of farming experience

3. A medical certificate declaring the applicant's ability to operate a farm

4. Letters of character reference

5. Proof of World War II military service

6. Male or female veterans would receive equal consideration

7. To avoid speculation, the homesteader was required to farm his/her unit for 5 consecutive years before he/she was given free ownership

8. Persons applying had to currently own less than 160 acres of land

The fifth requirement caught my eye because the "proof of World War II military service," didn't specifically stipulate US service. That made me wonder whether the German POWs who wanted to stay in America hoped they'd found a loophole that would allow them to be considered.[11]

Had our family been housed in the small town of Tulelake, Maria would have been much happier. Out on the farm, the Hartleys might as well have lived in the next county. They weren't particularly amiable toward our family, so no camaraderie ever developed. Perhaps what happened when my sister was born two weeks after our arrival doomed any possible friendship between Maria and Mrs. Hartley. When Maria went into labor, Fidel had to rely on Mr. Hartley to drive them to the hospital, 35 miles away in Klamath Falls, Oregon. Fidel had no idea how to get there and couldn't have adequately communicated with the staff upon arrival. Fortunately, Maria ended up in the care of a Jewish doctor who spoke some German.

Meanwhile, my sister and I were left under the care of Mrs. Hartley. It was upon my mother's return home that things soured between the two women. To Maria's horror, she found that Mrs. Hartley had taken it upon herself to give my sister a severe haircut. "She had practically no hair left," Maria exclaimed in recounting the affair. Mrs. Hartley's brazenness left Maria fuming, but unable to adequately relay her feelings. Thereafter, she never let the Hartleys mind my sister and me unless she was desperate.

Left: The author and his sister Ingrid playing in a sand pile next to the barn and irrigation canal outside their Tulelake home. *Right:* The author and his sister perched on the fenders of the Ford farm pickup parked at the landowner's farmstead on the other side of the canals from the Eipert home. The other half of the Eiperts sawn-in-two barracks home, with its original tarpaper siding, is visible in the background.

My parents' dependence on the Hartleys decreased when Fidel was given use of their white F-series Ford pickup truck. Somehow, we squeezed five people onto the bench seat of that vehicle when we went anywhere. On these ventures we encountered little animosity because the German POWs who'd worked for many of the basin farmers had left a favorable impression. The new freedom of movement led to my parents meeting a farmer's wife who'd grown up speaking German during her childhood. She was able to help my parents in some matters, and because she and her husband were fellow parishioners at Holy Cross Catholic Church in Tulelake, agreed to become my baby sister's godparents.

Until our family's two crates of belongings found their way to Tulelake, we made do with the clothes in our luggage and whatever pots, pans, dishes, tableware, and bedding were donated to us. Cooking with her own kitchenware, eating with familiar plates and utensils, and sleeping under featherbed covers again gave Maria some comfort, but little else in that house ever did so. The house never did come to have adequate furniture. I suspect a lack of space was the main reason. Maria said we didn't have enough comfortable chairs, so we mainly sat on our beds. Maria also revealed that a lack of privacy was another problem. Only a curtain divided my parents' bedroom from that of my sister and me.

Another hardship was the lack of a washing machine. With two active young children, a new baby in constant need of clean diapers, and a husband working long days in dusty or muddy fields, the laundering demand was never ending. Maria's hands were perpetually raw and painful from washing and wringing out our clothes by hand. A consumer version of the modern washing machine had come into existence in the 1930s, but because of the poverty and unavailability of consumer goods in Germany, Maria was unaware that such a machine existed. After she learned of them in California, acquiring one became a priority, and she eventually saved up enough money to buy a used machine.

Maria quickly discovered that the Tule Lake basin was a windy place. When the wind blew, fine dust poured through every crack of her house and deposited a layer of grit on the furniture, floors, counters, beds, and particularly wet laundry on the clothesline. I recall once playing in a bare patch of dirt between the canal and small barn with my sister when a storm blew in suddenly. The dust entered my mouth, nose, and ears, and filled my eyes with grit. The air became so thick with soil that I lost sight of the house, but my mother rushed out to rescue us. I suspect the area was dustier in those days because the farming methods and crops of that period left more bare earth exposed in the spring and fall.

The dusty and cold conditions were also the bane of the Japanese Americans formerly interned at the Japanese Segregation Center, as was graphically described in a remembrance written by an internee.

> No nook or crevice is immune to the ubiquitous dust. I came home from work and found the room gritty and filthy with grime. Powdery white dust had sifted through the edges of

windows and settled on the bed, the shelves, the books, and all the clothings hung on nails. The dust disgusts and sickens me inside. One sleeps and eats with dust. No one acts human in a duststorm. Like animals, all evacuees seek shelter and all activities come to a standstill. Human rationalization is blotted out and all minds are assailed with rancor and hatred.[12]

In September, I began kindergarten at the public school in tiny Newell, three miles down the county road. Until my first return to the basin a quarter century later, I had no idea that my school had any connection to the former Japanese Segregation Center. To my astonishment, I discovered the school building was located in what had been the camp's administrative area, directly across the street from the camp's main entrance gate.

The school didn't provide bus transportation for kindergarten children, so Fidel and a neighbor with a child in my class alternated with the driving duty. I'm told I was extremely shy in school, which was understandable because I'd had very little contact with American children yet and spoke almost no English. Maria told me that the school shared some of the same deficiencies as our house—it was leaky as well as prone to drafts and blowing dust. The draftiness made for chilly classrooms during the lengthy winters.

Left: The Eipert family in their repurposed Tule Lake Japanese Segregation Center barracks home during the family's year-long stay at the Tule Lake farm. *Right:* Maria, sitting on a bed holding the family's newest addition, baby Mary. For lack of space and furniture, the bed doubled as the family's couch.

A story in a 1952 edition of The Tulelake Reporter, as archived in the museum at the Tule Lake National Monument, also noted the school's draftiness when it reported that the condition would soon be a thing of the past because plans for a new building had been submitted for approval to the state. This information emerged as I rummaged through archived copies of the weekly paper to learn if my family's arrival had been noted.

It hadn't. Local newspapers like this one relied on self-submitted news, a typical example of which appeared just below the school news story. "Margaret Ann _____, daughter of Mr. and Mrs. John _____, and her brother Mervin, have been branding cattle at the J. F. Ranch in Dorris recently. Margaret also attended a rodeo in Lakeview Sunday with Dorris friends."

Fidel was not as profoundly affected as Maria by the rural isolation because his job allowed him to interact with others and gave him exposure to more spoken English. The job also proved agriculturally educational because it schooled him in how mechanized farming was conducted in America. Fidel also found that growing potatoes in what was essentially a desert required considerable labor, not the least of which involved periodically flooding the furrows.

Maria said that Fidel's arrival allowed Hartley to semi-retire and forgo much of the farm work, for as soon as the weather turned hot, the Hartleys traveled north to Canada and spent six weeks there. Later, when the weather turned cold, they escaped to the southwest. Fidel and Hartley's son, who had his own farm in the basin, were left to do the bulk of the farming, so the pair of them often worked together. Fidel also took care of the regular chores on the farmstead when the older Hartleys were away. Use of the farm truck allowed our family an occasional drive to the wildlife preserve or elsewhere around the lake on warm Sunday afternoons following church. Maria recalled strolling there a time or two with my infant sister in a baby buggy. But Fidel and Maria didn't have a lot of free time.

Once the potatoes were harvested, there was little work on the farm. Hartley then reduced Fidel's pay to little more than his social security contribution and a bit of gas money. My parents hadn't been aware that Fidel's job was seasonal. To make up for the lost income, Fidel took on a second job, which Hartley helped him find. That off-season job—shoveling potatoes into railroad cars at a potato storage warehouse—was even more grueling than farming. It was exhausting, but the pay was good. "Two dollars an hour," Fidel said.

The potato that provided much of the income for the basin farmers was the Russet Burbank, a baking potato that had earlier replaced the Burbank Seedling potato in national popularity. Even though that variety was already waning in popularity with consumers also, Tule Lake basin farmers continued to cultivate it because their sandy soil, high altitude, warm days, and cool nights were so similar to the Andean conditions where the potato originated that it grew to an enormous size.[13]

Maria was astounded by how abundantly the potatoes grew and how large they were. She said that a potato could weigh up to five pounds and that Fidel once brought home an enormous potato that wouldn't even fit in her pot. Even though she didn't particularly like these spuds because their taste and texture didn't fit her Austrian style of cooking, potatoes were fundamental to her table and they were free. So, she learned to live with them. I recall feeding small bits of boiled potatoes to my infant sister with my fingers as she wiggled with pleasure in her highchair. It was the first solid food she'd tasted. What I don't recall is whether I'd had my mother's permission. Milk was also abundant for us, and free, thanks to a neighbor who told Fidel he should come collect it every other day because his cow provided more than his family needed.

One memory I have is playing on the machinery in the Hartley farmyard. I particularly liked to work levers and turn knobs on the little field bulldozer. On one occasion, I turned on the headlights and couldn't figure out how to turn them off again. Fearing I would get into trouble, I left without telling anyone what I'd done. Another lingering memory is witnessing a car caravan of what the locals called gypsies passing along the county road past our house. This event was notable because at least one of their old cars rode on rims without tires.

My mother's disappointments—the loneliness, blowing dust, and poor housing—assured that we wouldn't remain any longer than obliged to. In the spring of 1953, when Maria and Fidel mentioned their intent to leave, Hartley tried to induce Fidel to stay by offering him the proceeds from 10 rows of potatoes. Fidel said that in a good year this was worth a tidy sum— six to eight hundred dollars. But my parents had already made up their minds. Mrs. Hartley unfairly tried to force them to stay by contacting the immigration authorities, Maria said, but Fidel had fulfilled the program's requirements and was free to leave after a year. So the brown wooden freight crates were repacked with the family possessions and shipped off. Their destination, and ours, came about through Fidel's cousin Hans who'd taken advantage of the same agricultural worker program that had brought us to America. He and his family had been placed with a farmer in southeast Iowa, where the climate and farming conditions were closer to those found in Central Europe. Hans had learned that a nearby farmer would happily hire Fidel and provide the family a house in town. The news that the area was home to several other immigrant German families was a welcome bonus for my parents because it allowed them to express themselves more fully through their first language.

1. Russell E. Bearden, "Japanese American Relocation Camps," in *Encyclopedia of Arkansas* (Little Rock, Arkansas: Central Arkansas Library System (CALS), December 2022), https://encyclopediaofarkansas.net/entries/japanese-american-relocation-camps-2273/.
2. "California: Tule Lake Unit, Part of WWII Valor in the Pacific National Monument," U.S. National Park Service, August 23, 2017, https://www.nps.gov/articles/tulelake.htm.
3. "California: Tule Lake Unit."
4. "Tule Lake Segregation Center," in *WWII Valor in the Pacific National Monument: Tule Lake Unit*, accessed December 24, 2018, https://www.nps.gov/tule/planyourvisit/upload/Segregation_Center_6-10.pdf .
5. Stephen Most, "War Relocation Authority Camp at Tule Lake," in *Nature and History in the Klamath Basin* (Oregon History Project: Oregon Historical Society, 2014), https://www.oregonhistoryproject.org/narratives/nature-and-history-in-the-klamath-basin/the-great-depression-and-world-war-ii/war-relocation-authority-camp-at-tule-lake/#.Y7cEv9XMKUk.
6. "California: Tule Lake Unit."
7. Shelley Cannady, "Tule Lake Today: Internment and Its Legacies," *Boom* 3, no. 1 (May 1, 2013): 17–33, https://doi.org/10.1525/boom.2013.3.1.17 .
8. Robert Wilson, "Landscapes of Promise and Betrayal: Reclamation, Homesteading, and Japanese American Incarceration," *Annals - Association of American Geographers* 101, no. 2 (2011): 435.
9. *The Tulelake Homesteaders* (Klamath Basin in Crisis), accessed June 26, 2020, http://www.klamathbasincrisis.org/tulelakehomesteaders.htm.
10. *The Tulelake Homesteaders*.
11. Anne Hiller Clark, "Tule Lake World War II Era History," interview by Erich Eipert, February 7, 2014, Shaw Historical Library, Oregon Institute of Techology, Klamath Falls College, Klamath Falls, OR.
12. Tulean Dispatch, "Aug. 25, 1942 Duststorm," in *A Tule Lake Interlude: 1st Anniversary, May 27, 1942-43*, ed. George R. Nakamura (Newell, CA, 1943), 103–4, https://oac.cdlib.org/ark:/13030/kt4779n6vr/?order=110&brand=oac4.
13. Lawrence Davis-Hollander, "The Origin and Evolution of the Burbank Potato," Mother Earth Gardener, September 22, 2016, https://www.motherearthgardener.com/plant-profiles/origin-evolution-burbank-potato-zmaz15saeva.

56 Where the Tall Corn Grows

We Eiperts left the Tule Lake basin in May 1953 and retraced two thousand miles of the transcontinental journey that had brought us west the previous year. The Southern Pacific's overnight Streamliner Cascade left Klamath Falls daily at 11:30 p.m. in that era and arrived in Sacramento at 6:30 a.m. Six hours later, aboard the California Zephyr on its eastward passage from Sacramento, Fidel and Maria would have been eagerly anticipating getting off the train in Burlington, Iowa. All I remember of the two-day trip as I looked out from coach windows and the glass-dome viewing area is the vastness of the western rangeland and the numerous cattle and pronghorns that inhabited it.

Fidel's new employer, a farmer named Theodore Berning, collected us at the station and drove us 15 miles north to our new home in Mediapolis, Iowa, via US Highway 61—a two-laned ribbon of concrete that stretches 1,714 miles between New Orleans and the Canadian border. Our destination was a rural town of 1,600 that Maria was pleased to find came with green lawns, trees, and a real house for her on a paved street. And she happily learned that a grocery store and other shops were but a few blocks away. Neither she nor Fidel had any notion yet of the broader world of friends and socialization the move would open them to.

The square, hip-roofed, two-story structure that the Bernings delivered us to had been a recent purchase of theirs. From the sidewalk that ran along the street, a concrete walkway and three wooden steps led to a balustrade that enclosed the porch extending across the front of the house. At the side of the house toward the rear, a second door through a protruding entrance led to a laundry room and then the kitchen. At the rear of lot sat a utility shed, and behind that ran an alley.

The address—Middle Street—couldn't have been more fitting for a Midwest town whose name was cobbled together from two Greek words meaning *middle* and *city*. The name was appropriate for a town that at the time of its founding lay halfway between the small cities of Wapello and Burlington via the Burlington, Cedar Rapids and Minnesota Railway.

The Bernings were supportive in helping us settle into the new community and seeing to our needs. Mr. Berning soon helped Fidel acquire an Iowa driver's license and buy a used car. A vehicle was necessary for Fidel in order to commute to his job on the Berning farm, as well as for family transportation. That car, a blue 1940s Plymouth 4-door sedan with suicide rear doors that opened forward, was definitely an improvement over the pickup truck with the cramped bench seat our family of five had squeezed into in California. And it certainly simplified my mother's next trip to the hospital when she went into labor with my baby brother during the summer of 1954.

I began first grade that fall and have a vague memory of a classmate's parents transporting me to school on the opposite side of town. Fidel must have sometimes done so as well, but by second grade, I usually walked on my own. I recall sometimes varying my route near the school because of a bully who lived nearby. Another memory that stands out is the first mass polio vaccination, which took place at the school. The paralysis caused by the polio virus so terrified the parents of young children during that era that they readily gave consent for the new killed-virus immunization. No parent wanted to see their child tucked into an iron lung—a mechanical, negative-pressure respirator that enclosed the victim's body from the neck down. Some large hospitals of that era had entire wards filled with these machines, so it is understandable that mass immunization events were held throughout the country. A few years later, live-virus oral vaccine took much of the drama out of the process when it replaced the injected vaccine.

What most pleased my parents in Mediapolis, aside from accommodations in a comfortable and roomier house, was something they'd lacked the past year—companionship. They quickly made new friends among other local German immigrant families. One couple's youngest child, I later learned, was a girl they'd taken in as an infant somewhere in the chaos of the postwar period. Having friends with whom they could hold a real conversation was liberating for Maria and Fidel during this time when they were still learning English. Maria soon acquired a close friend in a farmer's wife of her own age. Trudy had come to America with her new husband, whom she'd met while he served as an occupation force GI. Trudy's children closely matched the ages of my younger siblings, which made it convenient for the two women to babysit for each other.

The isolation that had held Fidel and Maria back in picking up English and adapting to American ways and customs was now over. The new friendships and daily exchanges that came from having neighbors saw to that and greatly sped up their conversion into Americans. My enrollment in school, with all that entailed, further broadened their horizon. Having enough space and furniture in their new living situation to entertain visitors was also a help. The larger house even made it possible to put up overnight guests. The first of these were an older couple whom Fidel had been introduced to in Chicago on our trip west. The husband was a distant cousin who decades earlier had worked for my father's family in Orzydorf before emigrating to America. After their visit, my sister and I hoped for many return visits because they'd brought us a whole carton of candy bars. That was but one of the treats the new environment exposed me to. Others were soda pop and the staples of American picnics—hot dogs, hamburgers, and marshmallows. The latter indulgences made it hard for me to accept missing the school picnic at the end of my second-grade school year when I contracted chicken pox.

One particularly fond memory pertains to the bicycle Fidel bought for me when I turned eight. It was blue, used, and way too tall for me. But somehow, I learned to ride it standing up while straddling the bar. At some point I also acquired a best friend with whom I could run through the neighborhood. Jimmy lived nearby on Main Street in a newish, single-story, masonry ranch house. When he told me that his mother was a radio star. I had no idea what that meant and should have asked what a star did, but was too embarrassed to reveal my ignorance. On one of our neighborhood forays, Jimmy and I tried to climb over a tall chain-link fence to explore a derelict, empty swimming pool. Jimmy slipped while his arm hung over the top, and the raw end of a thick wire link punched a neat hole into his upper arm. I could see yellow fatty tissue in the hole before it started to bleed. On another occasion while playing in the alley behind my house, a construction worker grasping his bloody, mangled hand walked over from a building site across the street. He'd just caught it in a portable cement mixer and was surely in shock when he calmly asked me, a young kid, where he could find a doctor. I had no idea and couldn't take my eyes off his injury. When there was no school, I sometimes accompanied my father out to the Berning farm and hung out with the Bernings' youngest son. He was two or three years older, but tolerated me.

Mediapolis was a Protestant town without a Catholic church, so each Sunday my parents had to go elsewhere to attend Mass. The service alternated weekly between two small churches in two tiny hamlets called Sperry and Kingston. Church attendance put my parents in touch with yet more families in the area.

Given the more tolerant growing conditions of the Midwest, Maria was able to plant flowers and grow a greater variety of garden vegetables than in Tulelake. For his part in supplementing the fare on the family table, Fidel built several wire-mesh cages between the shed and alley at the back of our yard and raised a few domestic rabbits. However, he and my mother quickly learned that Iowa was hog and cattle country. Our table began to reflect that when they learned that it was possible to buy a hog and then have it butchered, cut up to their specifications, packaged, and frozen. The same could be done with a side or quarter of beef. The processing occurred at a meat-locker shop where the consumer rented appropriately sized storage drawers within a large walk-in freezer. The packaged meat could then be withdrawn as needed.

My parents got on well with the Bernings, and the couples might even have even become good friends had Maria and Fidel spoken English more fluently. Fortunately, Mr. Berning's father lived with the family and spoke just enough German to sometimes clarify things.

Fidel owed his job to the absence of another member of the Berning family. The Korean War was still raging when we arrived in Mediapolis, and the oldest son, who planned to farm with his father, was currently in the military and fighting in Korea. Thankfully, that war ended within months of our arrival, but the son still had two years of service remaining. I was unaware that America was fighting a war then but do recall once watching a long train of olive-green tanks on flatcars pass by.

Maria and Fidel managed to set aside some savings that first year, so when Fidel's cousin Hans presented a plan to buy a rental duplex in Burlington as an investment, they were able to put up half the down-payment. Hans and his family continued to live and work on the farm of his employer for another year or two before he found a job in Burlington and moved his family into one unit of the duplex. I can recall Fidel and Hans once cutting down a large, problematic maple tree on the property with a chainsaw. The upper part of the tree unavoidably fell in the street, an arterial. While talking about it decades later, Fidel laughed and said, "We didn't have a permit or anything."

Fidel knew from the start that his job would last only two years, so he lined up another job as the end point neared. However, that job of driving a delivery truck for the local Farm Service store never materialized because when he returned home from work one day in early summer, he found a Cadillac parked in front of the house and a middle-aged couple waiting for him on the family's porch swing. The strangers, who'd already talked to Maria, introduced themselves and said they wanted to rent him a farm. They explained that they'd hoped to sponsor a displaced family from Germany but learned the bureaucratic process would take up a year. They wanted a tenant right away. Maria said she had no idea why the owners wanted to rent to Germans or how they'd even found our family.

The following Sunday the whole family piled into the Plymouth and drove 40 miles to have a look at the farm. It was the longest car ride we children had ever been on. The farm was 3 miles outside of West Point, Iowa.

The first mile out of West Point was paved highway. Then came a mile and a half of county-maintained gravel road. The final half mile was a gravel lane. Mr. Berning and Trudy's husband met us at the farm to help evaluate the offer. The city-people owners had tried the country life for two years after purchasing the 148-acre farm from a neighbor. The acreage wasn't particularly large, and about half of it was wooded pasture, but because they also operated an appliance store 10 miles away in the city of Fort Madison, working the soil too had proved too much.

My youngest sister, Mary, recalled that after the long ride in the back seat of the car, she was convinced that "we'd arrived at the end of the world." Her 3-year-old mind thought the sky surely came down to meet the ground nearby and we couldn't possibly go much farther. Ingrid, my other sister, was six at the time and greatly disappointed on arrival. "I liked to roller skate and there were no sidewalks," she recalled. However, some of that unhappiness melted away when she found a litter of kittens to play with.

As for myself, I was thrilled. The farm's nine outbuildings provided an exploration wonderland. One chicken house particularly sticks in my mind for it was surrounded by a jungle of tall horseweed. And just a hundred yards beyond was a newish pond. The owner liked to fish, so he'd had it constructed and stocked with bass and bluegill. I was also excited that day by my first glimpse of television. A silly kid's show of vaudeville antics, puppets, and skits—The Pinky Lee Show—was playing on the small black-and-white set in the farmhouse living room. I knew then that we'd have to acquire one too.

A rental agreement soon came about, and my family moved onto the farm in August 1955, shortly before I began third grade. Not until 50 years later did I learn how geographically and historically fitting the new setting was for people of my parents' situation and background. This reasoning was explained in *The Secret She Carried*.

> The farm where my parents deposited me and their other possessions lay southeast of West Point, Iowa, a town situated near the middle of Lee County. Lee is the most irregularly shaped of the 99 counties that make up Iowa in part because it benefited from the addition of a piece of ground that in 1824 had become an historical oddity known as a Half-Breed Tract. Through a treaty with the Sac and Fox tribes, Congress

declared what is now the southern part of Lee County a reservation...

Congress designated this particular 119,000 acres and several other Half-Breed Tracts elsewhere as homes for Indian and European mixed-race people, who in those days did not fit in well with either the natives or the European settlers.

My parents never appreciated the appropriateness of their own settlement near the Half-Breed Tract, that triangular tip of land jutting down into northeast Missouri like a boat rudder steering the ship of Iowa westward. Although they arrived a century late, and the farm was a tad north of the Tract boundary, I like to think the placement was close enough to qualify as a partial fulfillment of the Tract's original purpose: a home for people caught between two cultures.[1]

The farm came with a small Ford 8N-series tractor and a line of basic machinery. It was this equipment that helped convince my father that he could make the farm viable. However, he recognized that he'd also have to take on an outside job because there'd be many bills to pay before any farm income was realized. He had no crops to harvest, children to support, and livestock to buy. So my hope for a TV set couldn't materialize until several years later. However, that was due to more than just a shortage of money. A single-bedroom home housing a family with four children simply didn't offer enough space for a TV viewing area.

My parents were always grateful to the Bernings for helping them get a start in farming. They'd given Fidel a pay raise in his final months, allowed him to board two newly purchased milk cows and two bred sows until it was time to move to the farm, and loaned him their pickup truck for the actual moving. By the time Fidel had delivered our well-traveled brown packing crates, the livestock, and the rest of the family's possessions to the farm, we'd become a family of six by the birth of my baby brother Gerhard.

From that time forward, Fidel was truly back in his element. The plunge into farming took nerve, discipline, and hard work because by then he was 34 years old, had four young children to provide for, lacked any appreciable savings, and still struggled to fully express himself in English. Although Maria never said so directly, I don't think she'd been quite as enthused about moving to the farm as Fidel. She'd become used to the convenience of living in town, where she had other people around her and none of the countless chores that come with an active farm. Yet, after her grueling post-war experiences—a year of terror under cruel Czech partisan and Red Army occupiers, a rape pregnancy, a stint of prison and forced labor stemming from a false accusation, and the death of her baby—she could handle hardship. The new venture was risky, but it was also an opportunity to lock in long-term security.

My parents' social life in Iowa differed vastly from that in Tulelake, for they now had a car and a network of friends they saw regularly. Once their communication skills improved, they made many American friends as well, particularly in the Conrad and Reuter families just down the road. The integration process in the town of West Point also proceeded more smoothly than it might have in many other places because the entire community revolved around the local Catholic church and school. In addition, many of the residents were the descendants of German-Catholic immigrants who'd settled the area in the second half of the 1800s. This made the local telephone directory read much like that of a German village. This is not to say that some residual anti-German sentiment from the war years didn't exist, but it largely simmered beneath the surface. I don't recall any taunting myself, but my brother said he was targeted on occasion.

Without doubt, we four children were the greatest driver of our parent's integration into the community via our school attendance and activities. West Point was Catholic to such a degree that nearly all children attended the St. Mary of the Assumption parochial school from first grade through high school. The school district did operate a public school in town for the primary grades but had so few students that all eight grades filled only one classroom. All local children did attend West Point's public kindergarten, however.

West Point's Catholic church had been established by Father John Alleman in 1842 as a mission church for nearby Fort Madison, Iowa. A week of collecting money for the building netted Fr. Alleman a sum of 85 cents. Apparently, that was enough to start erecting a frame structure just south of the present church.[2] At the time of my family's arrival the parochial school was supervised by the parish's progressive pastor, Father J. A. Wagner, and taught by nuns of the Franciscan order. In the early years, Fr. Wagner helped my parents out a time or two when they encountered a communication problem.

Times were lean on our farm in the beginning, particularly the first year. Supporting four children on a small rented farm was demanding in the best of times, but with no crops to harvest for another year, Fidel looked for work in town. For her part, Maria raised chickens so that she could sell eggs and dressed pullets. After the two cows Fidel brought to the farm bore calves, Maria could also sell the cream she separated from the cows' excess milk. This cream was delivered regularly to the local creamery in stainless-steel milk cans.

Our compact farmhouse was in some ways even more primitive than our converted-barracks house in California had been. It was built atop the basement foundation of a house that burned down during the prohibition era. The farm's owners then, a pair of bachelor brothers named Hoenig, distilled and sold moonshine liquor out of the building's cellar until their illegal still exploded and burned down the house. When I'd earlier mentioned the farm's nine outbuildings, I hadn't included the two-seat outhouse that was our only toilet. For reasons known only to the bachelor brothers, an indoor bathroom in the replacement house they built didn't seem necessary.[3]

Maria in the mid-1950s washing dishes in her small kitchen on the farm near West Point, Iowa.

Our new home's single bedroom was obviously inadequate for a family of six, so Fidel turned the living room into two additional bedrooms almost immediately. Apparently, he and the owners had reached an understanding about that modification before we ever moved in. This sacrifice of the living room left Maria's small kitchen doubling as our living room. In the warm months the adjacent summer-kitchen building with its wood-burning cookstove helped ease the constraint. That building also housed the cream separator—a machine that removed the cream from whole milk by centrifugation. I can remember listening to daily news reports on the radio out there while my mother cooked breakfast. At the time, I was 11 and had developed an interest in the ongoing Cuban Revolution, perhaps because it was led by another Fidel, Fidel Castro.

The following year, revolution arrived at our house too. First, Fidel carved out an indoor bathroom from the bedroom space shared by my sisters. This eliminated the arresting experience of visiting the outdoor privy in the depths of a Midwest winter. That same year, 1959, also saw additional space added to the house when Fidel constructed a room that spanned the area between the house and summer kitchen. My brother could pinpoint when this expansion took place because he recalled looking up at the sky through bare rafters as a 3-year-old riding his tricycle on the subfloor of the addition. The expansion allowed the enlargement of Maria's cramped kitchen and furnished the family with a spacious new living room. The latter finally provided the television viewing space I'd coveted since my first visit to the farm.

The ability to function for long periods of time without repair was not a standard feature of TV sets in that era. At least it wasn't for our Admiral console. Consequently, we came to know Jim, our TV repairman, quite well for he came out to the farm to replace failed vacuum tubes regularly. My sister Mary recalled that whenever he had to take the set back to the shop with him, he left its spindly legged base behind, which gave her a chance to pretend the stand was a horse and ride it. Despite being limited to only three often-fuzzy stations because of our rural location, that cathode-ray black-and-white TV earned its keep for it delivered the popular culture of America to the whole family. Maria had by then taught herself to read English through the textbooks that we children brought home from school, and Fidel had acquired his more modest reading ability here and there out of practical necessity. But it was that TV set that most broadened their comprehension and communication skills.

It took Maria some time to readjust to the remoteness of living in the country. The dead-end county road that connected us to civilization served only four farms. Two of the farms were a mile distant and run by bachelor farmers who still depended on horses or mules, although one did have an old tractor for some jobs. He lived with his two unmarried sisters—women who sometimes helped Maria by babysitting my younger siblings. My parents got on well with these stalwart people, and they became friends. I saw them most during the summer when I helped Fidel bale their hay or biked over to ride a horse.

Several years after our arrival, a younger generation of the Conrad family took over the operation of the farm nearest us. Their small children often came to our house to play with my brother and youngest sister. At age 14, I began to drive my siblings, and often the Conrad children, to school and back. This was legal by virtue of the special driving permit issued by the state of Iowa for situations in which rural schools offered no bus transportation. It was also at the age of 14 that I received a driving citation from the state patrol. I'd been driving outside of school hours because Fidel had instructed me to pick him up from the field where he was harvesting soybeans with his combine.

Until she learned to drive three or four years after moving to the country, Maria was largely confined to the farm during the work week when Fidel was away at his outside jobs. Relief came via Saturday shopping and Sunday morning Mass. On Sunday afternoons, the family often visited, or was visited by, families from among the area's community of German immigrants. One of those was a German-speaking Polish family in West Point.

Because some farm operations require help, farm wives commonly stepped into this role. Maria had worked hard on farms in Czechoslovakia and Germany, and still helped with some tasks, but with a baby and a preschooler to attend to, Maria hadn't been able to leave her domain long enough to learn to operate a tractor. She never really needed to because I was only too eager to do that. I began on the little Ford almost immediately after our move to the farm, then moved up to larger tractors when they came along. My mother also hadn't had much exposure to cars, so hadn't learned to drive a car, either. But because mobility was such a necessity out on a farm, she eventually needed to, despite the fact that this skill didn't come naturally to her. And being taught by a spouse whose PTSD sometimes left him short of patience was not ideal.

One driving lesson we children all remember well commenced as the family was coming home from town. Maria was behind the wheel for the gravel road segment of the trip, and as she approached the turnoff for our lane from the county road, something went wrong either in communication or execution. Instead of completing a 90-degree right turn, the car made just a 60-degree turn and lurched through our neighbor's barbed wire gate at the entrance to a field. I don't recall whose foot hit the brake pedal, but stop we did. Fortunately, the car suffered only a few scratches. We were all able to laugh about it years later, but not at the time.

Maria did eventually come to value the independence of living on the farm after the exhausting demands of the first years. But in the beginning, these demands were never ending. Besides cooking, laundering, and cleaning up after her children and husband, she milked several cows twice daily, maintained a flock of chickens and other fowl, and tended a large vegetable garden and flower beds in the yard. That garden and yard became ever more laced with flowers and fruit trees as the years went by.

Neither of my parents ever completely abandoned the skills and traditions they'd picked up from their village childhood. Given Maria's exposure to American popular culture and what was available in supermarkets, she couldn't avoid incorporating American recipes and foods into her cooking. But she continued to bake bread, churn butter, and prepare the Austrian-style dishes of her childhood for many years. The recipes for the latter were in her head and included such things as spaetzle, bean soup, creamed spinach, potato salads, and a variety of dumplings. Particularly well received by her children were strudels, cream puffs, fried doughnuts, and baked rice pudding with fruit.

Meat was a staple in the Austrian and German cultures Maria and Fidel came from, and in this too my parents kept their traditions alive. We children particularly enjoyed Maria's roasts, goulash, meat loaf, pork chops, and wiener schnitzel. For years my parents self-butchered a hog as needed on the farm, from which they prepared bacon, sausages, and various meat cuts. They left the farm-grown beef processing to a butcher in town, who had instructions to grind a generous portion into hamburger. I consumed a fair amount of this as a growing teen when I commonly fried up two burgers after school before helping Fidel with farm work. Despite an abundance of fresh milk from our cows, we children never cared for the taste of raw milk and pressured our parents into buying processed milk from the store.

While a great fondness for their land and the independence of country life grew on both Fidel and Maria, I believe they'd still have preferred the village setting of their youths, where they lived amidst family and friends. In America the distances and the complexities of modern farming made living in town impractical, if not impossible. Maria in particular never forgot the intimate village atmosphere of mutual cooperation and social interaction she'd grown up in. Even in her emotional lows when she felt isolated and longed for the old life that no longer existed, she tried to keep those feelings to herself. Still, her longing for the bygone world occasionally seeped through, and the reflections that followed were prefaced with: "Where I come from." Occasionally she did express contempt for the Czech nationalists and communists who treated their Sudeten German neighbors so horribly, but never went into any specifics.

We children heard very little about our parents' old communities or the horror of the war and its cruel aftermath. Hence, we didn't connect with that past and weren't primed to ask questions relating to that time. I was aware only that Maria's family members had been expelled to West Germany and that Fidel's family continued to suffer in Romania. My parents exchanged letters with their European relatives, but little of that filtered down to us children. Suffused with the self-centeredness of youth, I never thought to ask questions; hence, much family history eluded me.

One opportunity to learn more about my family's extraordinary history came and went when Fidel and his cousin Hans arranged for their mothers to emigrate to America and escape the poverty of Romania. When the two sisters arrived together in 1966 and went to live with their sons, both women would have had much to tell, had I asked. The few weekends I returned to the farm from college during that period weren't enough to get to know my grandmother well. I attribute this failure to engage her more fully to a degree of self-absorption and my diminished ability to converse in German. The opportunity to ask questions soon passed because neither sister adapted well to the America they encountered. The isolation, language barrier, and alien culture allowed homesickness to set in, and within three months my grandmother asked Fidel to make the necessary arrangements for her return. Her sister pleaded the same, but Hans wasn't as accommodating and the woman's mental health deteriorated. She died a year or two after my grandmother returned to Romania.

By the time Fidel moved to the farm in Iowa, he no longer had any expectation that the situation in Romania would return to normal in the near future. It had been five years since his sister Magdalena had returned from slave labor in the Soviet Union, and yet she was still being persecuted by local communist administrators for trying to hold on to a piece of farm ground that was legally hers. In that "class-free" Marxist system where those in control lived a little more comfortably than everyone else, slave-labor-hardened Magdalena knew how to hang on, but not how to prosper. Fidel believed the hope of retaining, much less reclaiming, more of the family's land was futile. Still, in 1955 he couldn't have anticipated that the regressive Romanian system would continue to wear Magdalena down for another 27 years.

Despite Fidel and Maria's own poverty in the early years on the farm, they helped Magdalena and her family by mailing money and packages of items difficult or impossible to buy in Romania. One such parcel contained several yards of a special white fabric my mother bought by request. This remained memorable for Maria because Magdalena subsequently sent a photo of Leni wearing the wedding gown sewn from that fabric.

Nine years after moving to the farm, Fidel and Maria were finally financially secure enough to sign a purchase agreement with the owners. Knowing that they'd at last have the security of owning their home and land was the culmination of a long struggle. It had taken Fidel three decades to work himself back to the family farm status he'd already enjoyed as a teen in Romania. But by the time this came about, he no longer harbored the same sort of youthful ambitions about growing his operation to join the ranks of the largest local farmers. His family farm was compact by Midwest standards, but by raising livestock, renting two other small farms, custom-baling hay, and harvesting corn and soybeans for other farmers with his combine, the operation was large enough to provide for the family. Only when I was in high school could Fidel finally free himself from the necessity of holding a second job in town. Over the years he'd maintained city streets, wielded a carpenter hammer, butchered cattle and hogs at a small slaughterhouse, assembled farm machinery for an implement dealership, and unloaded lumber, roofing, and coal from boxcars for a lumber yard.

With only farming to think about, Fidel now often found time for a morning coffee or afternoon card game in town. He and Maria also could also spend more time socializing with friends and attending area festivals and German-themed dances. Coinciding with this extra free time and the more secure financial footing came a loosening of restrictions in Eastern Europe that finally made it possible for long-separated family members to meet once again. Toward the end of the 1960s, a quarter century after Fidel last set foot in Orzydorf, he and Maria obtained tourist visas and visited Fidel's boyhood home. I'd liked to have been there for the emotional reunions that his long absence brought about. Embracing his sister after all she'd been through must have been the highlight. Besides catching up with his own family members, Fidel also visited the families of his childhood friends and exchanged information. But none of his boyhood friends lived there anymore. Like Fidel, they'd all had to serve, and the few who survived had been forced to establish lives elsewhere after being prohibited from returning when Romania became a Soviet puppet state.

Fidel with his arms around his mother and sister during a 1974 visit to his boyhood home in Romania, the village of Orzydorf.

On that trip, Maria had no desire to visit her homeland in Czechoslovakia. The brutality that the Czech partisans and Soviet occupation army had inflicted on her and her community was still too painful. She wished to remember her village as the place it once was, not as the dilapidated eyesore her relatives told her it had become under Czech communist rule. She and Fidel revisited Fidel's family in Orzydorf once again later. Thereafter, they made a number of trips to various destinations in Germany where they visited the members of Fidel's resettled family, acquaintances from Wimmern, and Maria's resettled relatives, But Maria's former home in the Sudetenland was never on their itinerary because that would have been too painful for her.

Fidel dancing with his sister Magdalena in Nuremberg, Germany, at the 1985 annual celebratory gathering of former residents of Orzydorf, Romania.

A decade into the 21st century, not long before her death, Maria did finally see her village again, but only through my photos and stories after I visited it for her. That trip to Europe was highly memorable for me because it allowed me to meet and spend time with two close friends of Maria's brother Eduard who'd died late in the war. These men, who now resided in Germany and Austria, filled in much about Eduard's life and my mother's family. And at my request, each also shared their own personal harrowing experiences in the war—stories that appear in *The Secret She Carried*. Both men had been involuntarily consigned to the German Army at age 18 and sent to the Eastern Front where each managed to survive a serious wound that should have killed them.

When Fidel found himself with more free time after outside jobs were no longer necessary, he acquired an interest in farm auctions. These sales were a ready source of affordable farm equipment and tools, and the auction atmosphere was stimulating. Before long, auctions also became social events where he made many new friends and acquaintances among the regular attendees and auctioneers.

The time Fidel could devote to auctions, traveling, playing cards, and dancing expanded greatly in 1982 when in keeping with the tradition of his village in Romania, he retired at age 60 and relinquished the farm to my younger brother. Gerhard, by then a building contractor, was open to returning to the farm and operating his business from there. As part of the farm purchase agreement, he built Maria and Fidel a new house on a site some distance up the farm lane. This siting too was in keeping with a tradition Fidel had grown up with, for within his ethnic German community it had been customary for the retiring farmer to build or move into a second house within the family farmstead as one of his offspring took over the land. My parents' new situation relieved them of daily farm chores but still left them comfortably near the land they'd come to love. Fidel helped on the farm occasionally when needed, but assumed a near-daily routine of morning coffee in town and cards with friends in the afternoon. This routine was usually only interrupted when grandchildren visited or when he was off to auctions.

Auction attendance became an avid hobby that sent Fidel throughout the southeast corner of Iowa and the proximal parts of Illinois and Missouri. He quickly learned what sort of items were in demand and had enough value to be resold at a profit, which led him to specialize in antiques and collectables. His stock found shelter in two of the farm's machine sheds. Fidel's knack for buying was fortunately matched by a flair for selling, which took place by word of mouth or through ads in a local sale publication. In place of the homemade pickup truck he'd relied on when he sold dishware by knocking on doors in Germany after the war, he now used a large white utility van. The hobby provided him a small source of income, but I believe he'd have engaged in it even had it earned him nothing. For a time, an antique dealer from Texas dropped by occasionally with a truck and bought a considerable part of Fidel's cache. Exploring his collection certainly made my own visits to the farm more exciting, particularly since some items were of local historical interest. And they were free for the taking, since he refused payment from family members.

1. Erich Eipert, *The Secret She Carried: A Perilous Odyssey Through the Time of Hitler* (Turnbuckle Press, 2015), 17.
2. "Learn More about Us," St. Mary of the Assumption, accessed October 8, 2021, http://www.westpointstmary.org/parish-history.html.
3. Gerhard Eipert, "Moonshine Still" (Email, October 1, 2021).

57 Their Passing

As Fidel aged, the decades of hard labor manifested itself in joint problems. Then congestive heart failure and the weakening effects of prostate cancer drugs further robbed him of strength and vigor. By the time he approached his upper seventies, I suspect that his infirmities were telling him that the end was fast approaching because he seemed to be tidying up his affairs and disposing of his personal effects. The calm with which he proceeded told me he was unafraid of death. The fatalism seared into him long before by what he'd seen and participated in on the Eastern Front surely played a part in that. I thought myself equally prepared for his end. But when the dreaded phone call came on the eve of his 80th birthday, his passing stunned me, for I'd expected to be talking to him by phone the next day instead of rushing to hop on a plane.

On his last day, Fidel followed his normal routine and drove to town after lunch to play cards with his friends at the Corner Tap tavern. Upon his return home that hot July afternoon, he parked the car and sat down in a lawn chair under the shade of a tree in the front yard. And there, his heart gave out. He died in a hospital bed several hours later. If there is a more appropriate way for a farmer to fade than in sight of land he'd spent much of his life and energy nurturing, I don't know of it. He outlived his sister Magdalena by just seven months. The party scheduled for his 80th birthday never happened, and the funeral home open-casket visitation just a day after the planned celebration was a bitter substitute.

As I cast eyes on my father for the last time, I tucked a deck of cards under his arm in a symbolic gesture. Earlier, I'd stopped at the Corner Tap where Fidel played most afternoons, to ask for a deck. The bartender, who knew Fidel well, gave me the very pack he and his friends used. When Fidel's former neighbor and longtime friend Don Conrad saw me put the cards in the casket, he placed 30 cents alongside them, explaining that he'd lost the money to Fidel in a card game days earlier and hadn't yet had a chance to pay up. Fidel would have appreciated the symbolism.

Maria was able to carry on alone out in the country after Fidel's death because she was a strong woman like Fidel's mother and sister. Surviving an avaricious stepmother, hellacious events during the war and its aftermath, and cancer fostered resolute strength. She remained there for three years after Fidel's death, tending her garden, fruit trees, and flowers. But toughness ultimately has no chance in defeating the aging process. After it became obvious to my siblings and me that interaction with her neighbors and friends had become too difficult for her, Maria agreed to the convenience of town living where groceries, friends, church, and health care were just a short distance away. She stayed in her small house in West Point for another three years, but toward the end of that time, dementia had begun to cloud her mind and her days of independent living came to an end.

Shortly after my sisters moved Maria to a group home near their own neighborhood in Burlington, Iowa, I stayed in her house for several days to settle her affairs and help take care of her personal effects. A few of her most familiar and prized keepsakes went to Maria's new accommodation, but the bulk of her belongings had to go. The stashes of old letters, keepsakes, and photos that I sorted through reeked with sentiment, but over the course of a long day, sentiment gave way to practicality, and the job got done.

A broken hip less than a year after Maria's arrival at the group home necessitated a move to assisted living, which eventually turned to full nursing care. Maria was fortunate that her body shut down before her dementia progressed to the stage where she no longer recognized her offspring. She was ready to let go of life by then, and her survivors were prepared to let her go. She outlived Fidel by nine years and passed away quietly at age 91.

For many years out on the farm, Maria had joked about wanting to be buried without fuss under the hickory tree along the fence line of the 63-acre wooded pasture west of the old farm house. And for years we'd played along with this and teased her about it, knowing it was all in fun. Yet in the end, the jesting became a reality that she'd have appreciated. She shares a gravestone with Fidel in the church cemetery in West Point, but her family members and close neighbors know most of her ashes rest beneath the battered old hickory tree, by then just barely alive. Burying her ashes there seemed like the best way to preserve her memory. So it was under this tree that we gathered after the funeral formalities. In my mind, her spirit still reposes peacefully there, not far from where she tended her garden and flowers for the bulk of her life.

Fidel's sudden death hadn't allowed for the same gradual letting go. Still begging for resolution were questions left unasked—questions for which the things he left behind provided no answers. Upon cleaning out his desk, I was able to sort through his life in just a couple of hours. Things like old medical records, insurance statements, farm receipts, and utility bills were relegated to the trash can. More personal records and his remaining few meaningful mementos went into a cardboard box for later attention. All in all, considering the eventful life he'd lived and the experiences he'd accrued, the box seemed to contain far too little to adequately remember him by. But I soon learned that my remembrance of him didn't depend on the contents of that box. Many years have now gone by since his passing, but I still have no trouble picturing him out on the farm in the life he loved, and his memory never fails to spark a touch of nostalgia when I recall how engaged he was in life.

I recognize that Fidel never attained great fame, fortune, or influence, but then, he had no interest in this type of success. He was satisfied to have escaped the war with his life and a capacity to live in the present—something that eluded many a fellow veteran. The town marshal described in my childhood tale-of-two-men memory that opened this narrative was one. He couldn't stop the past from undercutting the present, and things ended badly for him when he shot himself to die. By contrast, Fidel shot himself to live and never lost sight of why. For me, this was true success because it gave me a father to recall fondly—a hardworking farmer who sat down to my mother's cooking when he came in from fieldwork, laughed along with his children at black-and-white TV sitcom antics, danced with my mother at festivals, indulged in his auction hobby, and played cards around a table with friends.

This series

If you enjoyed *By Accident of Geography*, consider posting an online review. And check out the companion volume in this two-book series, *The Secret She Carried: A Perilous Odyssey Through the Time of Hitler*. This chronicle relates the World War II era experiences of the author's mother as she and other members of her tiny Sudetenland German community grapple with survival in the tumultuous period encompassing the world wars and in the ruinous apocalyptic peace that followed. More at https://ericheipert.com.

Works of fiction by the author

Books for young or not-so-young adults who relish adventure, youthful heroes, wry humor, a real plot, and a pinch of romance. Learn more about where to buy an ebook or paperback copy of *Butterfly Powder and The Mountains of Iowa* and *Guy Going Under* at https://ericheipert.com.

Guy Going Under

Guy just wanted to win a girl a little beyond his reach. He didn't plan to get himself, and a too-smart girl he couldn't stand, trapped in a cave that concealed a gruesome historical secret.

Butterfly Powder and the Mountains of Iowa

In 1960s rural Iowa, meet underachiever and improbable hero Gilbert Perles, the train he comes to call his own, an alluring girl named Alice, and the rival he would later re-encounter in a new and unexpected setting—war-torn Vietnam.

About the author

Erich lived the postwar part of his father's experiences but with only a child's level of awareness of the hardships of postwar Germany, the social isolation of living in a converted Japanese-American internment camp barracks building in remote California, and the monumental struggle of making an Iowa rental property a viable family farm. Not until Erich's own encounter with war, which came with a Vietnam combat infantry badge and a purple heart, was the need for a deeper understanding of his parents' saga piqued. This decades-long quest eventually made him feel qualified to write *The Secret She Carried*, his mother's traumatic story, and now his father's eventful companion volume, *By Accident of Geography*. Erich, who lives with his wife in Seattle, is also the author of two novels.

Image Attributions

Note: Unattributed images used in this book are the property of Erich Eipert or members of his family and may not be used without permission.

Chapter 1
Map showing Romanian territorial losses of 1940; adapted from:
Rowanwindwhistler Romania_1940_1941_es.svg
[https://commons.wikimedia.org/wiki/File:
PérdidasTerritorialesRumanas1940.svg]—licensed under CC BY-SA 3.0
[http://creativecommons.org/licenses/by-sa/3.0/] by Anton Gutsunaev.
The adaptation is licensed under CC BY-SA 4.0
[https://creativecommons.org/licenses/by-sa/4.0/] by Susan Eipert.

Chapter 3
The distribution of German ethnic groups within the Austrian Empire; adapted from: Austria Hungary ethnic.svg—released into the public domain by its author, Andrein
[https://commons.wikimedia.org/wiki/File:Austria_Hungary_ethnic.svg].
The adaptation is licensed under CC BY-SA 4.0
[https://creativecommons.org/licenses/by-sa/4.0/] by Susan Eipert.

Chapter 4
Regional map of modern Germany and a segment of France; adapted from:
Blank Map Germany States.png
[https://en.wikipedia.org/wiki/File:Blank_Map_Germany_States.png]—
licensed under the CC BY-SA 3.0
[http://creativecommons.org/licenses/by-sa/3.0/] by
Ahoerstemeier/Postmann Michael. The adaptation is licensed under CC BY-SA 4.0 [https://creativecommons.org/licenses/by-sa/4.0/] by Susan Eipert.

The course of the Danube River on a map with modern Europe's borders; adapted from: Danube basin.png
[https://commons.wikimedia.org/wiki/File:Danube_basin.png]—licensed under the GNU Free Documentation License and CC BY-SA 4.0

470   By Accident of Geography

International [https://creativecommons.org/licenses/by-sa/4.0/]. The adaptation is licensed under CC BY-SA 4.0 by Susan Eipert.

The Danube River flowing through a strategically important narrows; Werfenstein Vischer big.jpg [https://commons.wikimedia.org/wiki/File:Werfenstein_Vischer_big.jpg]—public domain.

Chapter 21

Map showing the relative position of Leningrad and the Oranienbaum Pocket; adapted from Siege of Leningrad, 1941-09-21.svg [https://commons.wikimedia.org/wiki/File:Siege_of_Leningrad,_1941-09-21.svg]—licensed under CC BY-SA 3.0 [http://creativecommons.org/licenses/by-sa/3.0/] by Hellerick. The adaptation is licensed under CC BY-SA 4.0 [https://creativecommons.org/licenses/by-sa/4.0/] by Susan Eipert.

Chapter 22

German horses struggling through the deep mud; cropped from: Bundesarchiv Bild 101I-289-1091-26, Russland, Pferdegespann im Schlamm.jpg [https://commons.wikimedia.org/wiki/File:Bundesarchiv_Bild_101I-289-1091-26,_Russland,_Pferdegespann_im_Schlamm.jpg]—licensed under CC BY-SA 3.0 Germany [http://creativecommons.org/licenses/by-sa/3.0/de] by Bundesarchiv, Bild 101I-289-1091-26 / Dinstühle. The adaptation is licensed under CC BY-SA 4.0 [https://creativecommons.org/licenses/by-sa/4.0/] by Susan Eipert.

Chapter 23

Workers assembling Organization Todt (OT) designed military field ovens; CH11.579.jpg—provided by Manfred Grieger from Volkswagen Corporate Archives and used with permission.

Exhibit showing a field oven; CH11.606.jpg—provided by Manfred Grieger from Volkswagen Corporate Archives and used with permission.

Map showing the situation at the Oranienbaum Pocket shortly before the Red Army breakout; adapted from: The retreat and the battle of the Luga River | The Battle of Narva 1944 — Ep. 2—provided by and used with permission of The AceDestroyer. The adaptation is licensed under CC BY-SA 4.0 [https://creativecommons.org/licenses/by-sa/4.0/] by Susan Eipert. Chapter 24

Chapter 30

Map of Buchenwald Concentration Camp complex; Buchenwald concentration camp, spring 1945 [https://encyclopedia.ushmm.org/content/en/map/buchenwald-concentration-camp-spring-1945]—courtesy of United States Holocaust Memorial Museum.

Chapter 34

Map showing the location of Skorzeny's Friedenthal Schloss headquarters; adapted from Sachsenhausen Environs, 1944 [https://encyclopedia.ushmm.org/content/en/map/sachsenhausen-environs-1944]—courtesy of United States Holocaust Memorial Museum.

Schloss Friedenthal as it looked in 1939; Gunter Buse_Bild 10.jpg—provided by Christian Becker of Stadt Oranienburg Archive and used with permission.

Waffen SS soldiers lined up for inspection at Friedenthal; Friedenthal inspection.png—provided by Christian Becker of Stadt Oranienburg Archive and used with permission

1930s photo showing a business district along linden-tree-lined Breite Straße; Oranienburg_Buildings Breite Straße_western side_Photo_about 1930_without text.jpg—provided by Christian Becker of Stadt Oranienburg Archive and used with permission.

Chapter 35

The Order of Battle (organization chart) of Otto Skorzeny's Jagdverbände; Order of Battle of SS Jagdverbände [https://www.cia.gov/readingroom/docs/GERMAN%20INTELLIGENCE%20SERVICE%20%28WWII%29%2C%20%20VOL.%202_0003.pdf]—public domain, courtesy of CIA Freedom of Information Act Electronic Reading Room. Area encompassing the Nazi Alpine Fortress (Alpenfestung); created by Susan Eipert from background image by Google Earth, Image Landsat / Copernicus—used under license according to terms defined by Google. The adaptation is licensed under CC BY-SA 4.0 [https://creativecommons.org/licenses/by-sa/4.0/] by Susan Eipert.

Chapter 36

Photo (taken Apr 15, 1945) showing a portion of the vast hoard of precious metals, art works, foreign currency, and other loot; 28-1239a.gif—public domain, courtesy of the US National Archives from the American Commission For the Protection and Salvage of Artistic and Historic Monuments in War Areas [https://catalog.archives.gov/id/540135]

Map of the Nazi Alpine Fortress; created by Susan Eipert from background image by Google Earth, Image Landsat / Copernicus—used under license according to terms defined by Google. The adaptation is licensed under CC BY-SA 4.0 [https://creativecommons.org/licenses/by-sa/4.0/] by Susan Eipert.

Chapter 37

"Hitler Dead" headline; Stars_&_Stripes_&_Hitler_Dead2.jpg [https://en.wikipedia.org/wiki/Death_of_Adolf_Hitler#/media/File:Stars_&_Stripes_&_Hitler_Dead2.jpg]—public domain, Stars and Stripes

Chapter 40

Map of southeastern Europe (with modern borders) showing Josef's path; created by Susan Eipert from background image by Google Earth, Data SIO, NOAA, US Navy, NGA, GEBCO, Image Landsat / Copernicus—used under license according to terms defined by Google. The adaptation is licensed under CC BY-SA 4.0 [https://creativecommons.org/licenses/by-sa/4.0/] by Susan Eipert.

Chapter 54

El Al DC-4 (number 4X-ADC) airliner; 4X-ADC 1951 about, at Zurich, EL AL Archive, Alex Jzbicki photo, MGGoldman Imagae Coll'n.tif.jpg—used by permission, courtesy of El Al Archives. El Al flight evacuating threatened Jews from Yemen in 1949; Op_Magic_Carpet_(Yemenites).jpg [https://commons.wikimedia.org/wiki/File:Op_Magic_Carpet_(Yemenites).jpg]—public domain

Cutouts from passenger manifest and crew list—public domain from US National Archives and Records Administration.

Chapter 55

Panoramic view of the vast Tule Lake Japanese internment camp; Tule_Lake_War_Relocation_Center.jpg [https://commons.wikimedia.org/wiki/File:Tule_Lake_War_Relocation_Center.jpg]—public domain as a work of the US federal government.

Row of Tule Lake Internment Camp barracks buildings during the spring thaw; 3f03bf93-b7b1-4bf4-8dc2-a762a0948e05 [https://www.nps.gov/npgallery/AssetDetail/3f03bf93-b7b1-4bf4-8dc2-a762a0948e05]—public domain as a work of the US federal government (Department of the Interior. War Relocation Authority).

www.ingramcontent.com/pod-product-compliance
Lightning Source LLC
Chambersburg PA
CBHW031400290426
44110CB00011B/219